T0076317

Get the eBook FREE!

(PDF, ePub, Kindle, and liveBook all included)

We believe that once you buy a book from us, you should be able to read it in any format we have available. To get electronic versions of this book at no additional cost to you, purchase and then register this book at the Manning website.

Go to https://www.manning.com/freebook and follow the instructions to complete your pBook registration.

That's it!
Thanks from Manning!

Math and Architectures of Deep Learning

KRISHNENDU CHAUDHURY
WITH
ANANYA H. ASHOK
SUJAY NARUMANCHI
DEVASHISH SHANKAR

FOREWORD BY PRITH BANERJEE

MANNING
SHELTER ISLAND

For online information and ordering of this and other Manning books, please visit www.manning.com. The publisher offers discounts on this book when ordered in quantity. For more information, please contact

Special Sales Department
Manning Publications Co.
20 Baldwin Road
PO Box 761
Shelter Island, NY 11964
Email: orders@manning.com

Manning Publications Co.
20 Baldwin Road
PO Box 761
Shelter Island, NY 11964

Development editor: Christina Taylor
Technical development editor: Mike Shepard
Review editor: Aleksandar Dragosavljević
Production editor: Andy Marinkovich
Copy editor: Tiffany Taylor
Proofreader: Keri Hales
Technical proofreader: Lucian Mircea Sasu
Typesetter: Westchester Publishing Services
Cover designer: Marija Tudor

ISBN: 9781617296482
Printed in the United States of America

brief contents

contents

foreword

As a lifelong student of the business of technological innovation, I have often wondered: what sets apart an expert from regular practitioners in any area of technology? An expert tends to have many micro-insights into the subject that often elude the ordinary practitioner. This enables them to come up with solutions that are not visible to others. The primary appeal of this book is to generate that kind of micro-intuitions into the complex subject of machine learning. For all their ubiquitousness, episodic internet recipes do not build such intuitions in a systematic, connected way. This book does.

I also agree with the author's position that such intuitions are impossible to build without a firm grasp of the mathematical understanding of the core principles of machine learning. Of course, all this has to be combined with programming knowledge, without which it becomes idle theory. I like the way this book attends to both theory and practice of machine learning by presenting the mathematics alongside PyTorch code snippets.

At present, deep learning is indeed shaping human history. Machine learning and data science jobs are consistently rated as the best. If you are looking for a rewarding career in technology, this may be the area for you. And if you are looking for a book that gives you expert-level understanding but only assumes fairly basic knowledge of mathematics and programming, this is your book. With its joint, side-by-side treatment of math and PyTorch programming, it is perfect for professionals who want to become serious practitioners of the art and science of machine learning. Machine learning lies at the confluence of linear algebra, multivariate statistics, and Python programming, and this book combines them into a single coherent narrative—starting from the basics but rapidly moving into advanced topics.

A particularly delightful aspect of the book is how it creates geometric intuitions behind complex mathematical concepts. Symbols may be forgotten, but the picture remains in the head.

—PRITH BANERJEE, Chief Technology Officer ANSYS, Inc., ex Senior Vice President of Research and Director, HP Labs, formerly Professor and Director of Computational Science and Engineering, University of Illinois at Urbana-Champaign

preface

Artificial intelligence (*machine learning* or *deep learning* to insiders) is quite the rage at this point of time. Media is full of eager and/or paranoid predictions about a world governed by this new technology and quite justifiably so. It's a knowledge revolution happening in front of our very eyes.

Working on computer vision and image processing problems for decades for my PhD, then at Adobe Systems, then at Google, and then at Drishti Technologies (the Silicon Valley start-up that I co-founded), I have been at the bleeding edge of this revolution for a long time. I've seen not only what works, but also—perhaps more importantly—what does *not* work and what *almost* works. This gives me a unique perspective. Often when trying to solve practical problems, none of the textbook theories will work directly. We must mix various ideas to create a winning concoction. This requires a *feel* for what works and why and what doesn't work and why. It is this *feel*, this understanding of the inner workings of the machine/deep learning theory, along with the insights and intuitions that I hope to transmit to my readers.

This brings me to another point. Because of the popularity of the subject, a large volume of "deep-learning-made-easy"-type material exists in print and/or online. These articles don't do justice to the subject. My reaction to them is "everything should be made as simple as possible, but not simpler." Deep learning can't be learned by going through a small fragmented set of simplified recipes from which all math has been scrubbed out. This is a mathematical topic and mastery requires understanding the math along with the programming. What is needed is a resource which presents this topic with the requisite amount of math—no more and no less—with the connection between the deep learning and math explicitly spelled out. This is exactly what this book strives to provide with its dual presentation of the math and corresponding PyTorch code snippets.

acknowledgments

The authors would collectively like to thank all their colleagues at Drishti Technologies, especially Etienne Dejoie and Soumya Dipta Biswas, who actively engaged in many lively discussions of the topics covered in the book; Pinakpani Mukherjee, who created some of the early diagrams; and all the MEAP reviewers whose anonymous contributions made the book possible. They would also like to thank the Manning team for their professionalism and competence, in particular Tiffany Taylor for her sharp and deep reviews.

To all the reviewers: Al Krinker, Atul Saurav, Bobby Filar, Chris Giblin, Ekkehard Schnoor, Erik Hansson, Gaurav Bhardwaj, Grigory Sapunov, Ian Graves, James J. Byleckie, Jeff Neumann, Jehad Nasser, Juan Jose Rubio Guillamon, Julien Pohie, Kevin Cheung, Krzysztof Kamyczek, Lucian Mircea Sasu, Matthias Busch, Mike Wall, Mortaza Doulaty, Morteza Kiadi, Nelson González, Nicole Königstein, Ninoslav Čerkez, Obiamaka Agbaneje, Pejvak Moghimi, Peter Morgan, Rauhsan Jha, Sean T. Booker, Sebastián Palma Mardones, Stefano Ongarello, Tony Holdroyd, Vishwesh Ravi Shrimali, and Wiebe de Jong, your suggestions helped make this a better book.

From Krish Chaudhury: First and foremost, I would like to thank my family:

- Devyani (my wife), for covering my back for all these years despite an abundance of reasons not to, and for teaching me the value of pursuing excellence in whatever I do.
- Anwesa (my daughter), who fills my life with indescribable joy with her love, positive attitude, and empathy.
- Gouri (my mother), for her unquestioning faith in me.

- (Late) Dr. Sujit Chaudhury (my father), for teaching me the value of insights, sincerity, and a life of letters as a goal in itself.
- I would also like to thank Dr. Vineet Gupta (my former colleague from Google) and Dr. Srayanta Mukherjee (my former colleague from Flipkart), for their valuable comments and encouragement.

From Ananya Honnedevasthana Ashok: Writing this book has been much harder than I initially expected. It has been a massive learning experience that wouldn't have been possible without the unwavering support of my family. In particular, I'd like to thank:

- Dr. Ashok (my father), for being a perennial role model and always being there for me.
- Jayanthi (my mother), for her unequivocal belief in me.
- Susheela (my grandmother), for her unconditional love despite chiding me for spending long hours on the book during weekends.
- I would also like to thank all my teachers, especially Dr. Viraj Kumar and Prof. N.S. Kumar, for inspiring and indoctrinating a love of learning within me.

From Sujay Narumanchi: This book has been a labor of love, requiring more effort than I anticipated but giving me a truly fulfilling learning experience that I will forever cherish. My family and friends have been my pillars of strength throughout this journey. I'd like to thank:

- Sivakumar (my father), for always believing in me and encouraging me to pursue my dreams.
- Vinitha (my mother), for being my rock and providing unwavering support throughout my life.
- Prabhu (my brother), for being a constant source of fun and wisdom.
- (Late) Ramachandran (my grandfather), for instilling in me a love of mathematics and teaching me the value of learning from first principles.
- My friends Ambika, Anoop, Bharat, Neel, Pranav, and Sanjana, for providing a listening ear and a shoulder to lean on.

From Devashish Shankar: I would like to begin by thanking my parents, Dr. Shiv Shanker and Dr. Sadhana Shanker, for their unwavering support, love, and guidance. Additionally, I would like to honor the memory of my late grandfather, Dr. Ajai Shanker, who instilled in me a deep sense of curiosity and a passion for scientific thinking that has guided me throughout my life. I am also deeply grateful to my mentors and colleagues for their guidance and support.

about this book

Are you the type of person who wants to know *why* and *how* things work? Instead of feeling satisfied, even grateful, that a tool solves the problem at hand, do you try to understand what the tool is really doing, why it behaves a certain way, and whether it will work under different circumstances? If yes, you have our sympathy—life won't be peaceful for you. You also have our best wishes—these pages are dedicated to you.

The internet abounds with prebuilt deep learning models and training systems that hardly require you to understand the underlying principles. But practical problems often do not fit any of the publicly available models. These situations call for the development of a custom model architecture. Developing such an architecture requires understanding the mathematical underpinnings of optimization and machine learning.

Deep learning and computer vision are very practical subjects, so these questions are relevant: "Is the math necessary? Shouldn't we spend the time learning, say, the Python nuances of deep learning?" Well, yes and no. Programming skills (in particular, Python) are mandatory. But without an intuitive understanding of the mathematics, the *how* and *why* and the answer to "Can I repurpose this model?" will not be visible to you. Mathematics allows you to see the abstractions behind the implementation.

In many ways, the ability to form abstractions is the essence of higher intelligence. Abstraction enabled early humans to divine a digging and defending tool from what was merely a sharply pointed stone to other animals. The abstraction of the description of where something is with respect to another thing fixed in the environment (aka coordinate systems and vectors) has done wonders for human civilization. Mathematics is the language for abstractions: the most precise, succinct, and unambiguous known to humankind. Hence, mathematics is absolutely necessary as a tool to study deep learning. But we must remember that it is a tool—no more and no less. The ultimate purpose of all the math in the book is to bring out the intuitions and insights that are necessary to gain expertise in the complex world of machine learning.

Another equally important tool is the programming language—we have chosen PyTorch—without which all the wisdom cannot be put to practical use. This book connects the two pillars of machine learning—mathematics and programming—via numerous code snippets typically presented together with the math. The book is accompanied by fully functional code in the GitHub repository. We expect readers to work out the math with paper and pencil and then run the code on a computer to understand the results. This book is not bedtime reading.

Having (hopefully) made a case for studying the underlying mathematical principles of deep learning and computer vision, we hasten to add that mathematical rigor is *not* the goal of this book. Rather, the goal is to provide mathematical (in particular, geometrical) insights that make the subject more intuitive and less like black magic. At the same time, we provide Python coding exercises and visualization aids throughout. Thus, reading this book can be regarded as learning the mathematical foundations of deep learning via geometrical examples and Python exercises.

Mastery over the material presented in this book will enable you to

- Understand state-of-the-art deep learning research papers. The book provides in-depth, intuitive explanations of some of today's seminal papers.
- Study and understand a deep learning code base.
- Use code snippets from the book in your tasks.
- Prepare for an interview for a role as a machine learning engineer/scientist.
- Determine whether a real-life problem is amenable to machine/deep learning.
- Troubleshoot neural network quality issues.
- Identify the right neural network architecture to solve a real-life problem.
- Quickly implement a prototype architecture and train a deep learning model for a real-life problem.

A word of caution: we often start with the basics but quickly go deeper. It's important to read individual chapters from beginning to end, even if you're familiar with the material presented at the start.

Finally, the ultimate justification for an intellectual endeavor is to have fun pursuing it. So, the authors will consider themselves successful if you enjoy reading this book.

Who should read this book?

This book is aimed toward the reader with a basic understanding of engineering mathematics and Python programming, with a serious intent to learn deep learning. For maximum benefit, the math should be worked out with paper and pencil and the PyTorch programs executed on a computer. Here are some possible reader profiles:

- A person with a degree in engineering, science, or math, possibly acquired a while ago, who is considering a career switch to deep learning. No prior knowledge of machine learning or deep learning is required.

- An entry- or mid-level machine learning practitioner who wants to gain deeper insights into the workings of various techniques and graduate from downloading models from the internet and trying them out to developing custom deep learning solutions for real problems, and/or develop the ability to read and understand research publications on the topic.
- A college student embarking on a career of deep learning.

How this book is organized: A road map

This book consists of 14 chapters and an appendix. In general, all mathematical concepts are examined from a machine learning point of view. Geometric insights are brought out and PyTorch code is provided wherever appropriate.

- Chapter 1 is an overview of machine learning and deep learning. Its purpose is to establish the big picture context in the reader's mind and familiarize the reader with some machine learning concepts like input space, feature space, model training, architecture, loss, and so on.
- Chapter 2 covers the core concepts of vectors and matrices which form the building blocks for machine learning. It introduces the notions of dot product, vector length, orthogonality, linear systems, eigenvalues and eigenvectors, Moore-Penrose pseudo inverse, matrix diagonalization, spectral decomposition, and so on.
- Chapter 3 provides an overview of vector calculus concepts needed for understanding deep learning. We introduce gradients, local approximation of multidimensional functions via Taylor expansion in arbitrary dimensional spaces, Hessian matrices, gradient descent, convexity, and the connection of all these with the idea of loss minimization in machine learning. This chapter provides the first taste of PyTorch model building.
- Chapter 4 introduces principal component analysis (PCA) and singular value decomposition (SVD)—key linear algebraic tools for machine learning. We provide end-to-end PyTorch implementation of a SVD-based document retrieval system.
- Chapter 5 explains the basic concepts of probability distributions from a deep learning point of view. We look at the important properties of distributions like expected value, variance and covariance, and we also cover some of the most popular probability distributions like Gaussian, Bernoulli, binomial, multinomial, categorical, and so on. We also introduce the PyTorch distributions package.
- Chapter 6 explores Bayesian tools for machine learning. We study the Bayes theorem, understand model parameter estimation techniques like maximum likelihood estimation (MLE) and maximum a posteriori (MAP) estimation. We also look at latent variables, regularization, MLE for Gaussian distributions, entropy, cross entropy, conditional entropy, and KL divergence. We finally look at Gaussian mixture models (GMMs) and how to model and estimate the parameters of a GMM.
- Chapter 7 deep dives into neural networks. We study perceptrons, the basic building block of neural networks and how multilayered perceptrons can model

arbitrary polygonal decision boundaries as well as common logic gate operations. This enables them to perform classification. We discuss Cybenko's universal approximation theorem.

- Chapter 8 covers activation functions for neural networks, the importance and intuition behind layers. We look at forward propagation and backpropagation (with mathematical proofs) and implement a simple neural network with PyTorch. We study how to train a neural network end to end.
- Chapter 9 provides an in-depth look into various loss functions which are crucial for effective learning of neural networks. We study the math and the intuitions behind popular loss functions like cross entropy loss, regression loss, focal loss, and so on, implementing them via PyTorch. We look at geometrical insights underlying various optimization techniques like SGD, Nesterov, Adagrad, Adam, and others. Additionally, we understand why regularization is important and its relationship with MLE and MAP.
- Chapter 10 introduces convolutions, a core operator for computer vision models. We study 1D, 2D, and 3D convolution, as well as transposed convolutions and their intuitive interpretations. We also implement a simple convolutional neural network via PyTorch.
- Chapter 11 introduces various neural network architectures for image classification and object detection in images. We look at several image classification architectures in detail like LeNet, VGG, Inception, and Resnet. We also provide an in-depth study of Faster R-CNN for object detection.
- Chapter 12 explores the manifolds, the properties of manifolds like homeomorphism, Haussdorf property, and second countable property, and also how manifolds tie in with neural networks.
- Chapter 13 provides an introduction to Bayesian parameter estimation. We look at injection of prior belief into parameter estimation and how it can be used in unsupervised/semi-supervised settings. Additionally, we understand conjugate priors and the estimation of Gaussian likelihood parameters under conditions of known/unknown mean and variances.
- Chapter 14 explores latent spaces and generative modeling. We understand the geometric view of latent spaces and the benefits of latent space modeling. We take another look at PCA with this new lens, along with studying autoencoders and variational autoencoders. We study how variational autoencoders regularize the latent space and hence exhibit superior properties to autoencoders.
- The appendix covers mathematical proofs and derivations for some of the mathematical properties introduced in the chapters.

About the code

This book contains many examples of source code both in numbered listings and in line with normal text. In both cases, source code is formatted in a `fixed-width font` `like this` to separate it from ordinary text. Sometimes code is also **in bold** to highlight code that has changed from previous steps in the chapter, such as when a new feature adds to an existing line of code.

In many cases, the original source code has been reformatted; we've added line breaks and reworked indentation to accommodate the available page space in the book. In rare cases, even this was not enough, and listings include line-continuation markers (➥). Additionally, comments in the source code have often been removed from the listings when the code is described in the text. Code annotations accompany many of the listings, highlighting important concepts.

You can get executable snippets of code from the liveBook (online) version of this book at https://livebook.manning.com/book/math-and-architectures-of-deep-learning. Fully functional code backing the theory discussed in the book can be found on GitHub at https://github.com/krishnonwork/mathematical-methods-in-deep-learning-ipython and from the Manning website at www.manning.com. The code is presented in the form of Jupyter notebooks (organized by chapter) that can be executed independently. The code is written in Python and uses the popular PyTorch library. Important code snippets are presented as code listings throughout the book, and key concepts are highlighted using code annotations. To get started with the code, clone the repository and follow the steps described in the README.

liveBook discussion forum

Purchase of *Math and Architectures of Deep Learning* includes free access to liveBook, Manning's online reading platform. Using liveBook's exclusive discussion features, you can attach comments to the book globally or to specific sections or paragraphs. It's a snap to make notes for yourself, ask and answer technical questions, and receive help from the author and other users. To access the forum, go to https://livebook.manning.com/book/math-and-architectures-of-deep-learning/discussion. You can also learn more about Manning's forums and the rules of conduct at https://livebook.manning.com/discussion.

Manning's commitment to our readers is to provide a venue where a meaningful dialogue between individual readers and between readers and the author can take place. It is not a commitment to any specific amount of participation on the part of the author, whose contribution to the forum remains voluntary (and unpaid). We suggest you try asking the authors some challenging questions lest their interest stray! The forum and the archives of previous discussions will be accessible from the publisher's website for as long as the book is in print.

about the authors

KRISHNENDU CHAUDHURY is the CTO and a co-founder of Drishti Technologies in Palo Alto, California, which applies AI to manufacturing. He has been a technology leader and inventor in the field of deep learning and computer vision for decades. Before starting Drishti, Krishnendu spent over 20 years at premier organizations, including Google (2004–2015) and Adobe Systems (1996–2004). He was with Flipkart as head of image sciences from 2015 to 2017. In 2017, he left Flipkart to start Drishti. Krishnendu earned his PhD in computer science from the University of Kentucky in Lexington. He has several dozen patents and publications in leading journals and global conferences to his credit.

ANANYA HONNEDEVASTHANA ASHOK, SUJAY NARUMANCHI, and **DEVASHISH SHANKAR** are practicing machine learning engineers with multiple patents in the deep learning and computer vision area. They are all members of the founding engineering team at Drishti.

about the cover illustration

The figure on the cover of *Math and Architectures of Deep Learning* is "Femme Wotyak," or "Wotyak Woman," taken from a collection by Jacques Grasset de Saint-Sauveur, published in 1797. Each illustration is finely drawn and colored by hand.

In those days, it was easy to identify where people lived and what their trade or station in life was just by their dress. Manning celebrates the inventiveness and initiative of the computer business with book covers based on the rich diversity of regional culture centuries ago, brought back to life by pictures from collections such as this one.

1 An overview of machine learning and deep learning

This chapter covers

- A first look at machine learning and deep learning
- A simple machine learning model: The cat brain
- Understanding deep neural networks

Deep learning has transformed computer vision, natural language and speech processing in particular, and artificial intelligence in general. From a bag of semi-discordant tricks, none of which worked satisfactorily on real-life problems, artificial intelligence has become a formidable tool to solve real problems faced by industry, at scale. This is nothing short of a revolution going on under our very noses. To lead the curve of this revolution, it is imperative to understand the underlying principles and abstractions rather than simply memorizing the "how-to" steps of some hands-on guide. This is where mathematics comes in.

In this first chapter, we present an overview of deep learning. This will require us to use some concepts explained in subsequent chapters. Don't worry if there are some open questions at the end of this chapter: it is aimed at orienting your mind toward this difficult subject. As individual concepts become clearer in subsequent chapters, you should consider coming back and re-reading this chapter.

1.1 A first look at machine/deep learning: A paradigm shift in computation

Making decisions and/or predictions is a central requirement of life. Doing so essentially involves taking in a set of sensory or knowledge inputs and processing them to generate decisions or estimates.

For instance, a cat's brain is often trying to choose between the following options: *run away* from the object in front of it vs. *ignore* the object in front of it vs. *approach* the object in front of it and purr. The cat's brain makes that decision by processing sensory inputs like the perceived *hardness* of the object in front of it, the perceived *sharpness* of the object in front of it, and so on. This is an instance of a *classification* problem, where the output is one of a set of possible classes.

Some other examples of classification problems in life are as follows:

- *Buy* vs. *hold* vs. *sell* a certain stock, from inputs like the *price history of this stock* and the *change in price of the stock in recent times*
- Object recognition (from an image):
  - Is this a car or a giraffe?
  - Is this a human or a non-human?
  - Is this an inanimate object or a living object?
  - Face recognition—is this Tom or Dick or Mary or Einstein or Messi?
- Action recognition from a video:
  - Is this person running or not running?
  - Is this person picking something up or not?
  - Is this person doing something violent or not?
- Natural language processing (NLP) from digital documents:
  - Does this news article belong to the realm of politics or sports?
  - Does this query phrase match a particular article in the archive?

Sometimes life requires a *quantitative* estimation instead of a classification. A lion's brain needs to estimate how far to jump so as to land on top of its prey, by processing inputs like speed of the prey and distance to the prey. Another instance of quantitative estimation is estimating a house's price based on inputs like current income of the house's owner, crime statistics for the neighborhood, and so on. Machines that make such quantitative estimators are called *regressors*.

Here are some other examples of quantitative estimations required in daily life:

- Object localization from an image: identifying the rectangle bounding the location of an object
- Stock price prediction from historical stock prices and other world events
- Similarity score between a pair of documents

Sometimes a classification output can be generated from a quantitative estimate. For instance, the cat brain described earlier can combine the inputs (hardness, sharpness, and so on) to generate a quantitative threat score. If that threat score is high, the cat runs away. If the threat score is near zero, the cat ignores the object in front of it. If the threat score is negative, the cat approaches the object and purrs.

Many of these examples are shown in figure 1.1. In each instance, a machine—that is, a brain—transforms sensory or knowledge inputs into decisions or quantitative estimates. The goal of machine learning is to emulate that machine.

Note that machine learning has a long way to go before it can catch up with the human brain. The human brain can single-handedly deal with thousands, if not millions, of such problems. On the other hand, at its present state of development, machine learning can hardly create a single general-purpose machine that makes a wide variety of decisions and estimates. We are mostly trying to make separate machines to solve individual tasks (such as a stock picker or a car recognizer). At this point, you may ask, "Wait: converting inputs to outputs—isn't that exactly what computers have been doing for the last 30 or more years? What is this paradigm shift I am hearing about?" The answer is that it *is* a paradigm shift because we do not provide a step-by-step instruction

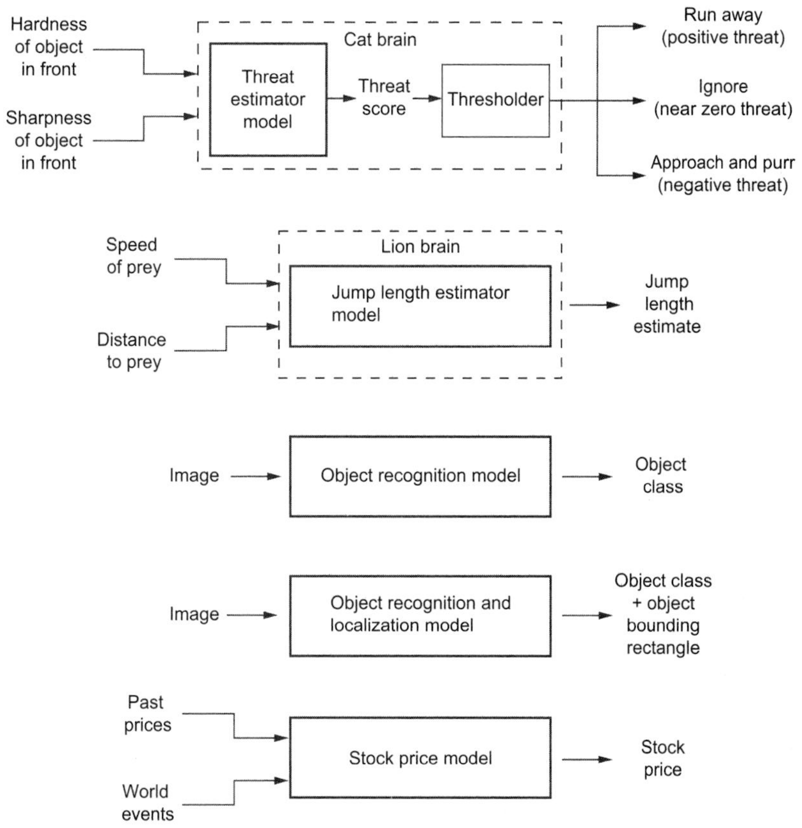

Figure 1.1 Examples of decision making and quantitative estimations in life

set—that is, a program—to the machine to convert the input to output. Instead, we develop a mathematical model for the problem.

Let's illustrate the idea with an example. For the sake of simplicity and concreteness, we will consider a hypothetical cat brain that needs to make only one decision in life: whether to *run away from the object in front of it* or *ignore the object* or *approach and purr.* This decision, then, is the output of the model we will discuss. And in this toy example, the decision is made based on only two quantitative inputs (aka features): the perceived hardness and sharpness of the object (as depicted in figure 1.1). We do *not* provide any step-by-step instructions such as "if sharpness greater than some threshold, then run away." Instead, we try to identify a *parameterized* function that takes the input and converts it to the desired decision or estimate. The simplest such function is a *weighted sum of inputs*:

$$y\left(hardness,\ sharpness\right) = w_0 \times hardness + w_1 \times sharpness + b$$

The weights w_0, w_1 and the bias b are the parameters of the function. The output y can be interpreted as a threat score. If the threat score exceeds a threshold, the cat runs away. If it is close to 0, the cat ignores the object. If the threat score is negative, the cat approaches and purrs. For more complex tasks, we will use more sophisticated functions.

Note that the weights are not known at first; we need to estimate them. This is done through a process called *model training.*

Overall, solving a problem via machine learning has the following stages:

- We design a parameterized model function (e.g., weighted sum) with unknown parameters (weights). This constitutes the *model architecture.* Choosing the right model architecture is where the expertise of the machine learning engineer comes into play.
- Then we estimate the weights via model training.
- Once the weights are estimated, we have a complete *model.* This model can take arbitrary inputs not necessarily seen before and generate outputs. The process in which a trained model processes an arbitrary real-life input and emits an output is called *inferencing.*

In the most popular variety of machine learning, called *supervised learning,* we prepare the training data before we commence training. Training data comprises *example input items, each with its corresponding desired output.*[1] Training data is often created manually: a human goes over every single input item and produces the desired output (aka target output). This is usually the most arduous part of doing machine learning.

For instance, in our hypothetical cat brain example, some possible training data items are as follows

[1] If you have some experience with machine learning, you will realize that we are talking about "supervised" learning here. There are also machines that do not need known outputs to learn—so-called "unsupervised" machines—and we will talk about them later.

input: $(hardness = 0.01,\ sharpness = 0.02) \rightarrow$ threat = −0.90 → *decision:* "approach and purr"

input: $(hardness = 0.50,\ sharpness = 0.60) \rightarrow$ threat = 0.01 → *decision:* "ignore"

input: $(hardness = 0.99,\ sharpness = 0.97) \rightarrow$ threat = 0.90 → *decision:* "run away"

where the input values of hardness and sharpness are assumed to lie between 0 and 1.

What exactly happens during training? Answer: we iteratively process the input training data items. For each input item, we know the desired (aka target) output. On each iteration, we adjust the model weight values in a way that the output of the model function on that specific input item gets at least a little closer to the corresponding target output. For instance, suppose at a given iteration, the weight values are $w_0 = 20$ and $w_1 = 10$, and $b = 50$. On the input $(hardness = 0.01,\ sharpness = 0.02)$, we get an output threat score $y = 50.3$, which is quite different from the desired $y = -0.9$. We will adjust the weights: for instance, reducing the bias so $w_0 = 20$, $w_1 = 10$, and $b = 40$. The corresponding threat score $y = 40.3$ is still nowhere near the desired value, but it has moved closer. After we do this on many training data items, the weights will start approaching their ideal values. Note that how to identify the adjustments to the weight values is not discussed here; it requires somewhat deeper math and will be discussed later.

As stated earlier, this process of iteratively tuning weights is called *training* or *learning*. At the beginning of learning, the weights have random values, so the machine outputs often do not match desired outputs. But with time, more training iterations happen, and the machine "learns" to generate the correct output. That is when the model is ready for deployment in the real world. Given arbitrary input, the model will (hopefully) emit something close to the desired output during inferencing.

Come to think of it, that is probably how living brains work. They contain equivalents of mathematical models for various tasks. Here, the weights are the strengths of the connections (aka synapses) between the different neurons in the brain. In the beginning, the parameters are untuned; the brain repeatedly makes mistakes. For example, a baby's brain often makes mistakes in identifying edible objects—anybody who has had a child will know what we are talking about. But each example tunes the parameters (eating green and white rectangular things with a $ sign on them invites much scolding—should not eat them in the future, etc.). Eventually, this machine tunes its parameters to yield better results.

One subtle point should be noted here. During training, the machine is tuning its parameters so that it produces the desired outcome—*on the training data input only*. Of course, it sees only a small fraction of all possible inputs during training—we are *not* building a lookup table from known inputs to known outputs. Hence, when this machine is released in the world, it mostly runs on input data it has never seen before. What guarantee do we have that it will generate the right outcome on never-before-seen data? Frankly, there is no guarantee. Only, in most real-life problems, the inputs are not really random. They have a pattern. Hopefully, the machine will see enough during training to capture that pattern. Then its output on unseen input will be close to the desired value. The closer the distribution of the training data is to real life, the more likely that becomes.

1.2 A function approximation view of machine learning: Models and their training

As stated in section 1.1, to create a brain-like machine that makes classifications or estimations, we have to find a mathematical function (model) that transforms inputs into corresponding desired outputs. Sadly, however, in typical real-life situations, we do not know that transformation function. For instance, we do not know the function that takes in past prices, world events, and so on and estimates the future price of a stock—something that stops us from building a stock price estimator and getting rich. All we have is the training data—a set of inputs on which the output is known. How do we proceed, then? Answer: we will try to model the unknown function. This means we will create a function that will be a proxy or surrogate to the unknown function. Viewed this way, machine learning is nothing but function approximation—we are simply trying to approximate the unknown classification or estimation function.

Let's briefly recap the main ideas from the previous section. In machine learning, we try to solve problems that can be abstractly viewed as transforming a set of inputs to an output. The output is either a class or an estimated value. Since we do not know the true transformation function, we try to come up with a model function. We start by designing—using our physical understanding of the problem—a model function with tunable parameter values that can serve as a proxy for the true function. This is the *model architecture*, and the tunable parameters are also known as *weights*. The simplest model architecture is one where the output is a weighted sum of the input values. Determining the model architecture does not fully determine the model—we still need to determine the actual parameter values (weights). That is where *training* comes in. During training, we find an optimal set of weights that transform the training inputs to outputs that match the corresponding training outputs as closely as possible. Then we deploy this machine in the world: its weights are estimated and the function is fully determined, so on any input, it simply applies the function and generates an output. This is called *inferencing*. Of course, training inputs are only a fraction of all possible inputs, so there is no guarantee that inferencing will yield a desired result on all real inputs. The success of the model depends on the appropriateness of the chosen model architecture and the quality and quantity of training data.

Obtaining training data

After mastering machine learning, the biggest struggle turns out to be the procurement of training data. When practitioners can afford it, it is common practice to use humans to hand-generate the outputs corresponding to the training data inputs (these target outputs are sometimes referred to as *ground truth*). This process, known as *human labeling* or *human curation*, involves an army of human beings looking at a substantial number of training data inputs and producing the corresponding ground truth outputs. For some well-researched problems, we may be lucky enough to get training data on the internet; otherwise it becomes a daunting challenge. More on this later.

Now, let's study the process of model building with a concrete example: the cat brain machine shown in figure 1.1.

1.3 A simple machine learning model: The cat brain

For the sake of simplicity and concreteness, we will deal with a hypothetical cat that needs to make only one decision in life: whether to run away from the object in front of it, ignore it, or approach and purr. And it makes this decision based on only two quantitative inputs pertaining to the object in front of it (shown in figure 1.1).

> **NOTE** This chapter is a lightweight overview of machine/deep learning. As such, it relies some on mathematical concepts that we will introduce later. You are encouraged to read this chapter now, nonetheless, and perhaps re-read it after digesting the chapters on vectors and matrices.

1.3.1 Input features

The input features are x_0, signifying *hardness*, and x_1, signifying *sharpness*. Without loss of generality, we can *normalize* the inputs. This is a pretty popular trick whereby the input values ranging between a minimum possible value v_{min} and a maximum possible value v_{max} are transformed to values between 0 and 1. To transform an arbitrary input value v to a normalized value v_{norm}, we use the formula

$$v_{norm} = \frac{(v - v_{min})}{(v_{max} - v_{min})} \tag{1.1}$$

In mathematical parlance, transformation via equation 1.1, $v \in [v_{min}, v_{max}] \rightarrow v_{norm} \in [0, 1]$ maps the values v from the input domain $[v_{min}, v_{max}]$ to the output values v_{norm} in the range $[0, 1]$.

A two-element vector $\vec{x} = \begin{bmatrix} x_0 \\ x_1 \end{bmatrix} \in [0, 1]^2$ represents a single input instance succinctly.

1.3.2 Output decisions

The final output is multiclass and can take one of three possible values: *0*, implying running away from the object in front of the cat; *1*, implying ignoring the object; and *2*, implying approaching the object and purring. It is possible in machine learning to compute the class directly. However, in this example, we will have our model estimate a *threat score*. It is interpreted as follows: threat high positive = run away, threat near zero = ignore, and threat high negative = approach and purr (negative threat is attractive).

We can make a final multiclass run/ignore/approach decision based on threat score by comparing the threat score y against a threshold δ, as follows:

$$y \begin{cases} > \delta \rightarrow & \text{high threat, run away} \\ >= -\delta \text{ and } <= \delta \rightarrow & \text{threat close to zero, ignore} \\ < -\delta \rightarrow & \text{negative threat, approach and purr} \end{cases} \tag{1.2}$$

1.3.3 *Model estimation*

Now for the all-important step: we need to estimate the function that transforms the input vector to the output. With slight abuse of terms, we will denote this function as well as the output by y. In mathematical notation, we want to estimate $y(\vec{x})$.

Of course, we do not know the ideal function. We will try to estimate this unknown function from the training data. This is accomplished in two steps:

1. *Model architecture selection*—Designing a parameterized function that we expect is a good proxy or surrogate for the unknown ideal function
2. *Training*—Estimating the parameters of that chosen function such that the outputs on training inputs match corresponding outputs as closely as possible

1.3.4 *Model architecture selection*

This is the step where various machine learning approaches differ from one another. In this toy cat brain example, we will use the simplest possible model. Our model has three parameters, w_0, w_1, b. They can be represented compactly with a single two-element vector $\vec{w} = \begin{bmatrix} w_0 \\ w_1 \end{bmatrix} \in \mathbb{R}^2$ and a constant bias $b \in \mathbb{R}$ (here, $\mathbb{R}$ denotes the set of all real numbers, $\mathbb{R}^2$ denotes the set of 2D vectors with both elements real, and so on). It emits the threat score, y, which is computed as

$$y(x_0, x_1) = w_0 x_0 + w_1 x_1 + b = \begin{bmatrix} w_0 & w_1 \end{bmatrix} \begin{bmatrix} x_0 \\ x_1 \end{bmatrix} + b = \vec{w}^T \vec{x} + b \qquad (1.3)$$

Note that b is a slightly special parameter. It is a constant that does not get multiplied by any of the inputs. It is common practice in machine learning to refer to it as *bias*; the other parameters are multiplied by inputs as weights.

1.3.5 *Model training*

Once the model architecture is chosen, we know the exact parametric function we are going to use to model the unknown function $y(\vec{x})$ that transforms inputs to outputs. We still need to estimate the function's parameters. Thus, we have a function with unknown parameters, and the parameters are to be estimated from a set of inputs with known outputs (training data). We will choose the parameters so that the outputs on the training data inputs match the corresponding outputs as closely as possible.

Iterative training

This problem has been studied by mathematicians and is known as a *function-fitting* problem in mathematics. What changed with the advent of machine learning, however, is the sheer scale. In machine learning, we deal with training data comprising millions and millions of items. This altered the philosophy of the solution. Mathematicians use a *closed-form solution*, where the parameters are estimated by directly solving equations involving *all* the training data items together. In machine learning, we go for iterative solutions, dealing with a *few* training data items (or perhaps only one) at a time. In the iterative solution, there is no need to hold all the training data in the computer's memory. We simply load small portions of it at a time and deal with only that portion. We will exemplify this with our cat brain example.

Concretely, the goal of the training process is to estimate the parameters w_0, w_1, b or, equivalently, the vector $\vec{w}$ along with constant b from equation 1.3 in such a way that the output $y\left(x_0, x_1\right)$ on the training data input $\left(x_0, x_1\right)$ matches the corresponding known training data outputs (aka ground truth [GT]) as much as possible.

Let the training data consist of $N+1$ inputs $\vec{x}^{(0)}, \vec{x}^{(1)}, \cdots \vec{x}^{(N)}$. Here, each $\vec{x}^{(i)}$ is a 2×1 vector denoting a single training data input instance. The corresponding desired threat values (outputs) are $y_{gt}^{(0)}, y_{gt}^{(1)}, \cdots y_{gt}^{(N)}$, say (here, the subscript *gt* denotes ground truth). Equivalently, we can say that the training data consists of $N+1$ (input, output) pairs:

$$\left(\vec{x}^{(0)}, y_{gt}^{(0)}\right), \left(\vec{x}^{(1)}, y_{gt}^{(1)}\right) \cdots \left(\vec{x}^{(N)}, y_{gt}^{(N)}\right)$$

Suppose $\vec{w}$ denotes the (as-yet-unknown) optimal parameters for the model. Then, given an arbitrary input $\vec{x}$, the machine will estimate a threat value of $y_{predicted} = \vec{w}^T \vec{x} + b$. On the ith training data pair, $\left(\vec{x}^{(i)}, y_{gt}^{(i)}\right)$ the machine will estimate

$$y_{predicted}^{(i)} = \vec{w}^T \vec{x}^{(i)} + b$$

while the desired output is $y_{gt}^{(i)}$. Thus the squared error (aka loss) made by the machine on the ith training data instance is[2]

$$e_i^2 = \left(y_{predicted}^{(i)} - y_{gt}^{(i)}\right)^2$$

The overall loss on the entire training data set is obtained by adding the loss from each individual training data instance:

$$E^2 = \sum_{i=0}^{i=N} e_i^2 = \sum_{i=0}^{i=N} \left(y_{predicted}^{(i)} - y_{gt}^{(i)}\right)^2 = \sum_{i=0}^{i=N} \left(\vec{w}^T \vec{x}_i + b - y_{gt}^{(i)}\right)^2$$

The goal of training is to find the set of model parameters (aka weights), $\vec{w}$, that minimizes the total error E. Exactly how we do this will be described later.

In most cases, it is not possible to come up with a closed-form solution for the optimal $\vec{w}, b$. Instead, we take an iterative approach depicted in algorithm 1.1.

---

2 In this context, note that it is a common practice to square the error/loss to make it sign independent. If we desire an output of, say, 10, we are equally happy/unhappy if the output is 9.5 or 10.5. Thus, an error of +5 or −5 is effectively the same; hence we make the error sign independent.

Algorithm 1.1 Training a supervised model

Initialize parameters $\vec{w}, b$ with random values
▷ iterate while error not small enough
while $\left(E^2 = \sum_{i=0}^{i=N} \left(\vec{w}^T \vec{x}_i + b - y_{gt}^{(i)}\right)^2 > threshold\right)$ **do**
  ▷ iterate over all training data instances
  for $\forall i \in [0, N]$ **do**
    ▷ details provided in section 3.3 after gradients are introduced
    Adjust $\vec{w}, b$ so that E^2 is reduced
  end for
end while
▷ remember the final parameter values as optimal
$\vec{w}_* \leftarrow \vec{w}$, $b_* \leftarrow b$

In this algorithm, we start with random parameter values and keep tuning the parameters so the total error goes down at least a little. We keep doing this until the error becomes sufficiently small.

In a purely mathematical sense, we continue the iterations until the error is minimal. But in practice, we often stop when the results are accurate enough for the problem being solved. It is worth re-emphasizing that *error* here refers only to error on training data.

1.3.6 Inferencing

Finally, a trained machine (with optimal parameters $\vec{w}_*$, b_* is deployed in the world. It will receive new inputs $\vec{x}$ and will infer $y_{predicted}(\vec{x}) = \vec{w}_*^T \vec{x} + b_*$. Classification will happen by thresholding $y_{predicted}$, as shown in equation 1.2.

1.4 Geometrical view of machine learning

Each input to the cat brain model is an array of two numbers: x_0 (signifying hardness of the object), x_1 (signifying sharpness of the object) or, equivalently, a 2×1 vector $\vec{x}$. A good mental picture is to think of the input as a point in a high-dimensional space. The input space is often called the *feature space*—a space where all the characteristic features to be examined by the model are represented. The feature space dimension is two in this case, but in real-life problems it will be in the hundreds or thousands or more. The exact dimensionality of the input changes from problem to problem, but the intuition that it is a point remains.

The output y should also be viewed as a point in another high-dimensional space. In this toy problem, the dimensionality of the output space is one, but in real problems, it will be higher. Typically, however, the number of output dimensions is much smaller than the number of input dimensions.

Geometrically speaking, a machine learning model essentially maps a point in the feature space to a point in the output space. It is expected that the classification or estimation job to be performed by the model is easier in the output space than in the feature space. In particular, *for a classification job, input points belonging to separate classes are expected to map to separate clusters in output space.*

Let's continue with our example cat brain model to illustrate the idea. As stated earlier, our feature space is 2D, with two coordinate axes X_0 signifying hardness and X_1 signifying sharpness.[3] Individual points in this 2D space are denoted by coordinate values (x_0, x_1) in lowercase (see figure 1.2). As shown in the diagram, a good way to model the threat score is to measure the distance from line $x_0 + x_1 = 1$.

From coordinate geometry, in a 2D space with coordinate axes X_0 and X_1, the signed distance of a point (a, b) from the line $x_0 + x_1 = 1$ is $y = \frac{a+b-1}{\sqrt{2}}$. Examining the sign of y, we can determine which side of the separator line the input point belongs to. In the simple situation depicted in figure 1.2, observation tells us that the threat score can be proxied by the signed distance, y, from the diagonal line $x_0 + x_1 - 1 = 0$. We can make the run/ignore/approach decision by thresholding y. Values close to zero imply ignore, positive values imply run away, and negative values imply approach and purr. From

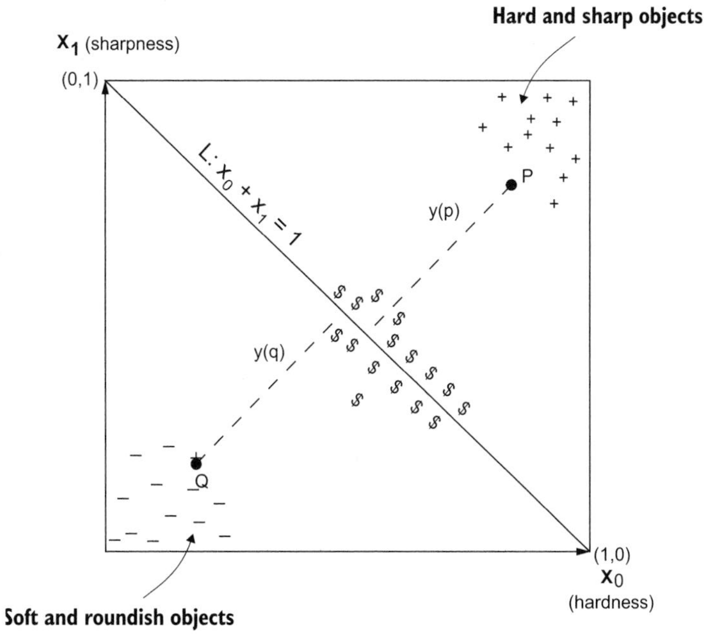

Figure 1.2 2D input point space for the cat brain model. The bottom-left corner shows objects with low hardness and low sharpness objects (–), while the top-right corner shows objects with high hardness and high sharpness (+). Intermediate values are near the diagonal ($).

3 We use X_0, X_1 as coordinate symbols instead of the more familiar X, Y so as not to run out of symbols when going to higher-dimensional spaces.

high school geometry, the distance of an arbitrary input point ($x_0 = a, x_1 = b$) from line $x_0 + x_1 - 1 = 0$ is $\frac{a+b-1}{\sqrt{2}}$. Thus, the function $y(x_0, x_1) = \frac{x_0+x_1-1}{\sqrt{2}}$ is a possible model for the cat brain threat estimator function. Training should converge to $w_0 = \frac{1}{\sqrt{2}}$, $w_1 = \frac{1}{\sqrt{2}}$ and $b = -\frac{1}{\sqrt{2}}$.

Thus, our simplified cat brain threat score model is

$$y(x_0, x_1) = \frac{1}{\sqrt{2}}x_0 + \frac{1}{\sqrt{2}}x_1 - \frac{1}{\sqrt{2}} \tag{1.4}$$

It maps the 2D input points, signifying the hardness and sharpness of the object in front of the cat, to a 1D value corresponding to the signed distance from a separator line. This distance, physically interpretable as a threat score, makes it possible to separate the classes (negative threat, neutral, positive threat) via thresholding, as shown in equation 1.2. The separate classes form distinct clusters in the output space, depicted by +, –, and $ signs in the output space. Low values of inputs produce negative threats (the cat will approach and purr): for example, $y(0, 0) = -\frac{1}{\sqrt{2}}$. High values of inputs produce high threats (the cat will run away): for example, $y(1, 1) = \frac{1}{\sqrt{2}}$. Medium values of inputs produce near-zero threats (the cat will ignore the object): for example, $y(0.5, 0.5) = 0$. Of course, because the problem is so simple, we could come up with the model parameters via simple observation. In real-life situations, this will need training.

The geometric view holds in higher dimensions, too. In general, an n-dimensional input vector $\vec{x}$ is mapped to an m-dimensional output vector (usually $m < n$) in such a way that the problem becomes much simpler in the output space. An example with 3D feature space is shown in figure 1.3.

1.5 Regression vs. classification in machine learning

As briefly outlined in section 1.1, there are two types of machine learning models: *regressors* and *classifiers.*

In a *regressor,* the model tries to emit a desired value given a specific input. For instance, the first stage (threat-score estimator) of the cat brain model in section 1.3 is a regressor model.

Classifiers, on the other hand, have a set of prespecified classes. Given a specific input, they try to emit the *class* to which the input belongs. For instance, the full cat brain model has three classes: (1) run away, (2) ignore, and (3) approach and purr. Thus, it takes an input (hardness and sharpness values) and emits an output decision (aka class).

In this example, we convert a regressor into a classifier by thresholding the output of the regressor (see equation 1.2). It is also possible to create models that directly output the class without having an intervening regressor.

1.6 Linear vs. nonlinear models

In figure 1.2 we faced a rather simple situation where the classes could be separated by a line (a hyperplane in higher-dimensional surfaces). This does not happen often in real

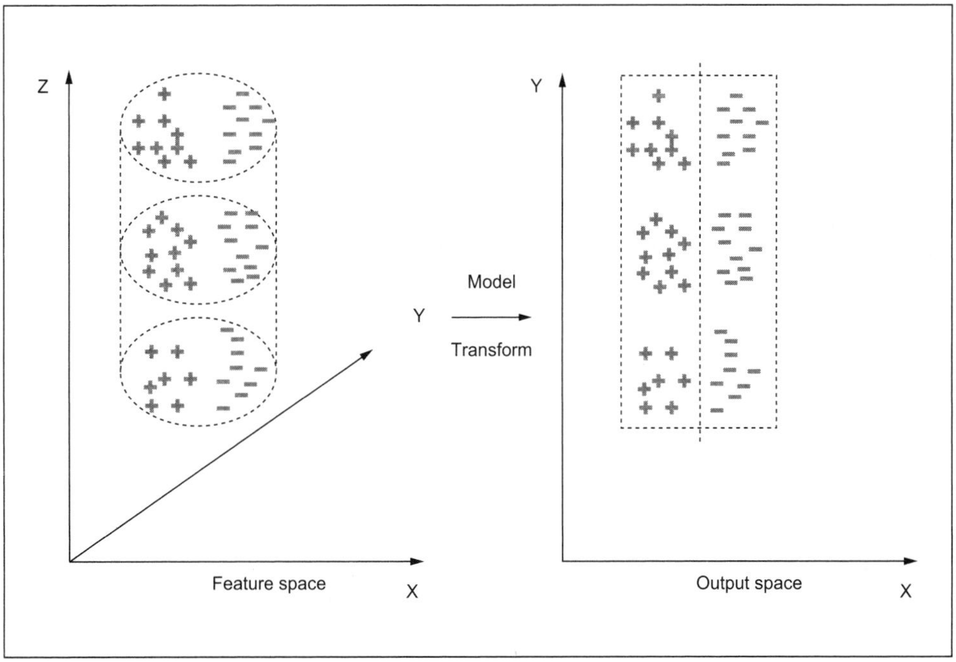

Figure 1.3 A model maps the points from input (feature) space to an output space where it is easier to separate the classes. For instance, in this figure, input feature points belonging to two classes, red (+) and green (–) are distributed over the volume of a cylinder in a 3D feature space. The model unfurls the cylinder into a rectangle. The feature points are mapped onto a 2D planar output space where the two classes can be discriminated with a simple linear separator.

life. What if the points belonging to different classes are as shown in figure 1.4? In such cases, our model architecture should no longer be a simple weighted combination. It is a nonlinear function. For instance, check the curved separator in figure 1.4. Nonlinear models make sense from the function approximation point of view as well. Ultimately, our goal is to approximate very complex and highly nonlinear functions that model the classification or estimation processes demanded by life. Intuitively, it seems better to use *nonlinear functions* to model them.

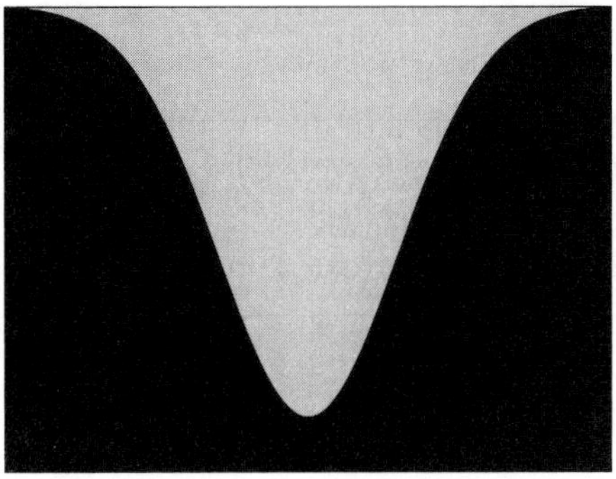

Figure 1.4 The two classes (indicated by light and dark shades) cannot be separated by a line. A curved separator is needed. In 3D, this is equivalent to saying that no plane can separate the surfaces; a curved surface is necessary. In still higher-dimensional spaces, this is equivalent to saying that no hyperplane can separate the classes; a curved hypersurface is needed.

A very popular nonlinear function in machine learning is the *sigmoid* function, so named because it looks like the letter *S*. The sigmoid function is typically symbolized by the Greek letter σ. It is defined as

$$\sigma(x) = \frac{1}{1 + e^{-x}} \tag{1.5}$$

The graph of the sigmoid function is shown in figure 1.5. Thus we can use the following popular model architecture (still kind of simple) that takes the sigmoid (without parameters) of the weighted sum of the inputs:

$$y = \sigma\left(\vec{w}^T \vec{x} + b\right) \tag{1.6}$$

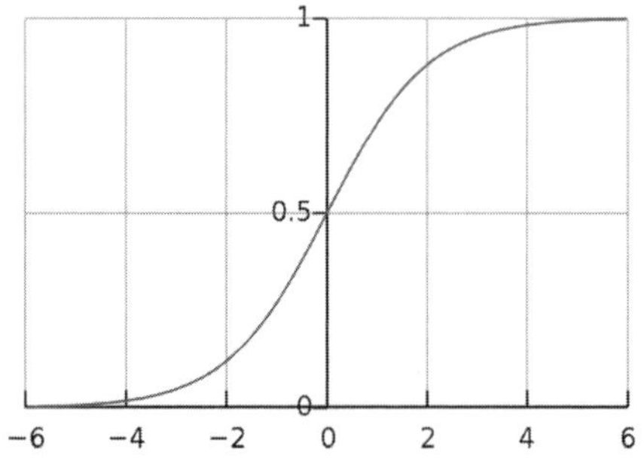

Figure 1.5 The sigmoid graph

The sigmoid imparts the nonlinearity. This architecture can handle relatively more complex classification tasks than the weighted sum alone. In fact, equation 1.6 depicts the basic building block of a neural network.

1.7 Higher expressive power through multiple nonlinear layers: Deep neural networks

In section 1.6 we stated that adding nonlinearity to the basic weighted sum yielded a model architecture that is able to handle more complex tasks. In machine learning parlance, the nonlinear model has more *expressive power.*

Now consider a real-life problem: say, building a dog recognizer. The input space comprises pixel locations and pixel colors (x, y, r, g, b, where r, g, b denote the red, green, and blue components of a pixel color). The input dimensionality is large (proportional to the number of pixels in the image). Figure 1.6 gives a small glimpse of the possible variations in background and foreground that a typical deep learning system (such as a dog image recognizer) has to deal with. We need a machine with really high expressive power here. How do we create such a machine in a principled way?

Instead of generating the output from input in a single step, how about taking a cascaded approach? We will generate a set of intermediate or hidden outputs from the

Figure 1.6 A glimpse into background and foreground variations that a typical deep learning system (here, a dog image recognizer) has to deal with

inputs, where each hidden output is essentially a single logistic regression unit. Then we add another layer that takes the output of the previous layer as input, and so on. Finally, we combine the outermost hidden layer outputs into the grand output.

We describe the system in the following equations. Note that we have added a superscript to the weights to identify the layer (layer 0 is closest to the input; layer L is the last layer, furthest from the input). We have also made the subscripts two-dimensional (so the weights for a given layer become a matrix). The first subscript identifies the destination node, and the second subscript identifies the source node (see figure 1.7).

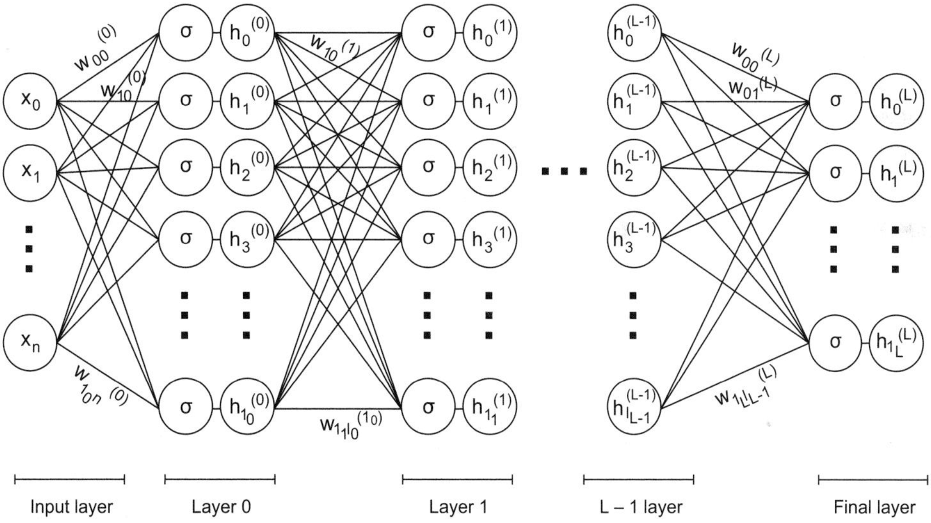

Figure 1.7 Multilayered neural network

The astute reader may notice that the following equations do *not* have an explicit bias term. That is because, for simplicity of notation, we have rolled it into the set of weights and assumed that one of the inputs (say, $x_0 = 1$) and the corresponding weight (such as w_0) is the bias.

Layer 0: generates n_0 hidden outputs from $n+1$ inputs

$$\begin{aligned}
h_0^{(0)} &= \sigma\left(w_{00}^{(0)} x_0 + w_{01}^{(0)} x_1 + \cdots w_{0n}^{(0)} x_n\right)\\
h_1^{(0)} &= \sigma\left(w_{10}^{(0)} x_0 + w_{11}^{(0)} x_1 + \cdots w_{1n}^{(0)} x_n\right)\\
&\vdots\\
h_{n_0}^{(0)} &= \sigma\left(w_{n_0 0}^{(0)} x_0 + w_{n_0 1}^{(0)} x_1 + \cdots w_{n_0 n}^{(0)} x_n\right)
\end{aligned} \tag{1.7}$$

Layer 1: generates n_1 hidden outputs from n_0 hidden outputs from layer 0

$$\begin{aligned}
h_0^{(1)} &= \sigma\left(w_{00}^{(1)} h_0^{(0)} + w_{01}^{(1)} h_1^{(0)} + \cdots w_{0n_0}^{(1)} h_{n_0}^{(0)}\right)\\
h_1^{(1)} &= \sigma\left(w_{10}^{(1)} h_0^{(0)} + w_{11}^{(1)} h_1^{(0)} + \cdots w_{1n_0}^{(1)} h_{n_0}^{(0)}\right)\\
&\vdots\\
h_{n_1}^{(1)} &= \sigma\left(w_{n_1 0}^{(1)} h_0^{(0)} + w_{n_1 1}^{(1)} h_1^{(0)} + \cdots w_{n_1 n_0}^{(1)} h_{n_0}^{(0)}\right)
\end{aligned} \tag{1.8}$$

$$\cdots$$

Final layer (L): generates $m+1$ visible outputs from n_{L-1} previous layer hidden outputs

$$\begin{aligned}
h_0^{(L)} &= \sigma\left(w_{00}^{(L)} h_0^{(L-1)} + w_{01}^{(L)} h_1^{(L-1)} + \cdots w_{0n_{L-1}}^{(L)} h_{n_{L-1}}^{(L-1)}\right)\\
h_1^{(L)} &= \sigma\left(w_{10}^{(L)} h_0^{(L-1)} + w_{11}^{(L)} h_1^{(L-1)} + \cdots w_{1n_{L-1}}^{(L)} h_{n_{L-1}}^{(L-1)}\right)\\
&\vdots\\
h_m^{(L)} &= \sigma\left(w_{m0}^{(L)} h_0^{(L-1)} + w_{m1}^{(L)} h_1^{(L-1)} + \cdots w_{mn_{L-1}}^{(L)} h_{n_{L-1}}^{(L-1)}\right)
\end{aligned} \tag{1.9}$$

These equations are shown in figure 1.7. The machine depicted in figure 1.7 can be incredibly powerful, with huge expressive power. We can adjust its expressive power systematically to fit the problem at hand. It then is a neural network. We will devote the rest of the book to studying this.

Summary

In this chapter, we gave an overview of machine learning, leading all the way up to deep learning. The ideas were illustrated with a toy cat brain example. Some mathematical notions (e.g., vectors) were used in this chapter without proper introduction, and you are encouraged to revisit this chapter after vectors and matrices have been introduced.

We would like to leave you with the following mental pictures from this chapter:

- Machine learning is a fundamentally different paradigm of computing. In traditional computing, we provide a step-by-step instruction sequence to the computer, telling it what to do. In machine learning, we build a mathematical model that tries to approximate the unknown function that generates a classification or estimation from inputs.

- The mathematical nature of the model function is stipulated from the physical nature and complexity of the classification or estimation task. Models have parameters. Parameter values are estimated from training data—inputs with known outputs. The parameter values are optimized so that the model output is as close as possible to training outputs on training inputs.
- An alternative geometric view of a machine is a transformation that maps points in the multidimensional input space to a point in the output space.
- The more complex the classification/estimation task, the more complex the approximating function. In machine learning parlance, complex tasks need machines with greater expressive power. Higher expressive power comes from nonlinearity (e.g., the sigmoid function; see equation 1.5) and a layered combination of simpler machines. This takes us to deep learning, which is nothing but a multilayered nonlinear machine.
- Complex model functions are often built by combining simpler basis functions.

Tighten your seat belts: the fun is about to get more intense.

Vectors, matrices, and tensors in machine learning

2

This chapter covers

- Vectors and matrices and their role in data science
- Working with eigenvalues and eigenvectors
- Finding the axes of a hyper-ellipse

At its core, machine learning, and indeed all computer software, is about number crunching. We input a set of numbers into the machine and get back a different set of numbers as output. However, this cannot be done randomly. It is important to organize these numbers appropriately and group them into meaningful objects that go into and come out of the machine. This is where vectors and matrices come in. These are concepts that mathematicians have been using for centuries—we are simply reusing them in machine learning.

In this chapter, we will study vectors and matrices, primarily from a machine learning point of view. Starting from the basics, we will quickly graduate to advanced concepts, restricting ourselves to topics relevant to machine learning.

We provide Jupyter Notebook-based Python implementations for most of the concepts discussed in this and other chapters. Complete, fully functional code that can be downloaded and executed (after installing Python and Jupyter Notebook) can be found at http://mng.bz/KMQ4. The code relevant to this chapter can be found at http://mng.bz/d4nz.

2.1 Vectors and their role in machine learning

Let's revisit the machine learning model for a cat brain introduced in section 1.3. It takes two numbers as input, representing the hardness and sharpness of the object in front of the cat. The cat brain processes the input and generates an output threat score that leads to a decision to *run away* or *ignore* or *approach and purr*. The two input numbers usually appear together, and it will be handy to group them into a single object. This object will be an ordered sequence of two numbers, the first representing hardness and the second representing sharpness. Such an object is a perfect example of a vector.

Thus, a *vector* can be thought of as an ordered sequence of two or more numbers, also known as an *array* of numbers.[1] Vectors constitute a compact way of denoting a set of numbers that together represent some entity. In this book, vectors are represented by lowercase letters with an overhead arrow and arrays by square brackets. For instance, the input to the cat brain model in section 1.3 was a vector $\vec{x} = \begin{bmatrix} x_0 \\ x_1 \end{bmatrix}$, where x_0 represented hardness and x_1 represented sharpness.

Outputs to machine learning models are also often represented as vectors. For instance, consider an object recognition model that takes an image as input and emits a set of numbers indicating the probabilities that the image contains a dog, human, or cat, respectively. The output of such a model is a three element vector $\vec{y} = \begin{bmatrix} y_0 \\ y_1 \\ y_2 \end{bmatrix}$, where the number y_0 denotes the probability that the image contains a dog, y_1 denotes the probability that the image contains a human, and y_2 denotes the probability that the image contains a cat. Figure 2.1 shows some possible input images and corresponding output vectors.

In multilayered machines like neural networks, the input and output to a layer can be vectors. We also typically represent the parameters of the model function (see section 1.3) as vectors. This is illustrated in section 2.3.

One particularly significant notion in machine learning and data science is the idea of a *feature vector*. This is essentially a vector that describes various properties of the object being dealt with in a particular machine learning problem. We will illustrate the idea with an example from the world of natural language processing (NLP). Suppose we have a set of documents. We want to create a document retrieval system where, given a new document, we have to retrieve similar documents in the system. This essentially boils down to estimating the similarity between documents in a quantitative fashion. We

---

[1] In mathematics, vectors can have an infinite number of elements. Such vectors cannot be expressed as arrays—but we will mostly ignore them in this book.

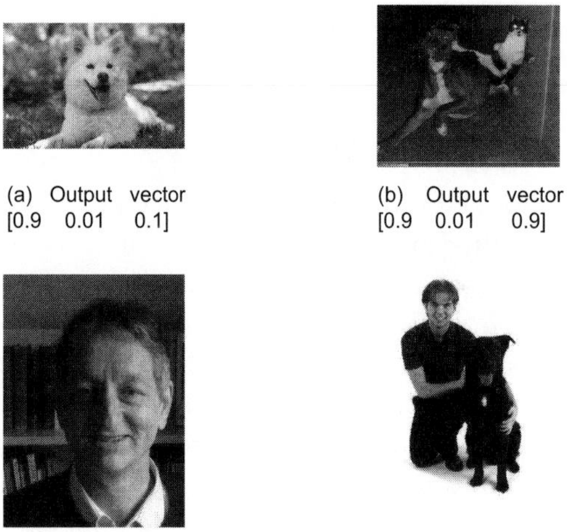

(a) Output vector [0.9 0.01 0.1]

(b) Output vector [0.9 0.01 0.9]

(c) Output vector [0.01 0.99 0.01]

(d) Output vector [0.88 0.9. 0.001]

Figure 2.1 Input images and corresponding output vectors denoting probabilities that the image contains a dog and/or human and/or cat, respectively. Example output vectors are shown.

will study this problem in detail later, but for now, we want to note that the most natural way to approach this is to create feature vectors for each document that quantitatively describe the document. In section 2.5.6, we will see how to measure the similarity between these vectors; here, let's focus on simply creating descriptor vectors for the documents. A popular way to do this is to choose a set of interesting words (we typically exclude words like "and," "if," and "to" that are present in all documents from this list), count the number of occurrences of those interesting words in each document, and make a vector of those values. Table 2.1 shows a toy example with six documents

Table 2.1 Toy documents and corresponding feature vectors describing them. Words eligible for the feature vector are bold. The first element of the feature vector indicates the number of occurrences of the word *gun* and the second *violence*.

docid	Document	Feature vector
d_0	Roses are lovely. Nobody hates roses.	$\begin{bmatrix} 0 & 0 \end{bmatrix}$
d_1	**Gun violence** has reached an epidemic proportion in America.	$\begin{bmatrix} 1 & 1 \end{bmatrix}$
d_2	The issue of **gun violence** is really over-hyped. One can find many instances of **violence**, where no **guns** were involved.	$\begin{bmatrix} 2 & 2 \end{bmatrix}$
d_3	**Guns** are for **violence** prone people. **Violence** begets **guns**. **Guns** beget **violence**.	$\begin{bmatrix} 3 & 3 \end{bmatrix}$
d_4	I like **guns** but I hate **violence**. I have never been involved in **violence**. But I own many **guns**. **Gun violence** is incomprehensible to me. I do believe **gun** owners are the most anti **violence** people on the planet. He who never uses a **gun** will be prone to senseless **violence**.	$\begin{bmatrix} 5 & 5 \end{bmatrix}$
d_5	**Guns** were used in a armed robbery in San Francisco last night.	$\begin{bmatrix} 1 & 0 \end{bmatrix}$
d_6	Acts of **violence** usually involves a weapon.	$\begin{bmatrix} 0 & 1 \end{bmatrix}$

and corresponding feature vectors. For simplicity, we have considered only two of the possible set of words: *gun* and *violence*, plural or singular, uppercase or lowercase.

As a different example, the sequence of pixels in an image can also be viewed as a feature vector. Neural networks in computer vision tasks usually expect this feature vector.

2.1.1 The geometric view of vectors and its significance in machine learning

Vectors can also be viewed geometrically. The simplest example is a two-element vector $\vec{x} = \begin{bmatrix} x_0 \\ x_1 \end{bmatrix}$. Its two elements can be taken to be x and y, Cartesian coordinates in a two-dimensional space, in which case the vector corresponds to a point in that space. *Vectors with n elements represent points in an n-dimensional space.* The ability to see inputs and outputs of a machine learning model as points allows us to view the model itself as a geometric transformation that maps input points to output points in some high-dimensional space. We have already seen this in section 1.4. It is an enormously powerful concept we will use throughout the book.

A vector represents a point in space. Also, an array of coordinate values like $\begin{bmatrix} x \\ y \end{bmatrix}$ describes the position of one point *in a given coordinate system.* Hence, an array (of coordinate values) can be viewed as the quantitative representation of a vector. See figure 2.2 to get an intuitive understanding of this.

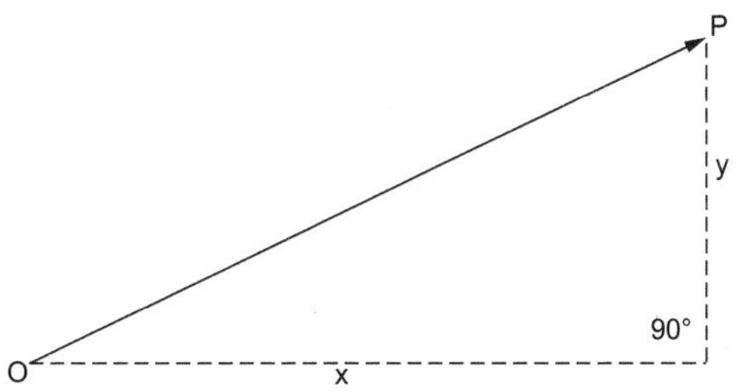

Figure 2.2 A vector describing the position of point P with respect to point O. The basic mental picture is an arrowed line. This agrees with the definition of a vector that you may have learned in high school: a vector has a magnitude (length of the arrowed line) and direction (indicated by the arrow). On a plane, this is equivalent to the ordered pair of numbers x, y, where the geometric interpretations of x and y are as shown in the figure. In this context, it is worthwhile to note that only the relative positions of the points O and P matter. If both the points are moved, keeping their relationship intact, the vector does not change.

For a real life example, consider the plane of a page of this book. Suppose we want to reach the top-right corner point of the page from the bottom-left corner. Let's call the bottom-left corner O and the top-right corner P. We can travel the width (8.5 inches) to the right to reach the bottom-left corner and then travel the height (11 inches) upward to reach the top-right corner. Thus, if we choose a coordinate system with the bottom-left corner as the origin and the X-axis along the width, and the Y-axis along the height, point P corresponds to the array representation $\begin{bmatrix} 8.5 \\ 11 \end{bmatrix}$. But we could also travel along the diagonal from the bottom-left to the top-right corner to reach P from O. Either way, we end up at the same point P.

This leads to a conundrum. The vector $\vec{OP}$ represents the abstract geometric notion "position of P with respect to O" independent of our choice of coordinate axes. On the other hand, the array representation depends on the choice of a coordinate system. For example, the array $\begin{bmatrix} 8.5 \\ 11 \end{bmatrix}$ represents the top-right corner point P only under a specific choice of coordinate axes (parallel to the sides of the page) and a reference point (bottom-left corner). Ideally, to be unambiguous, we should specify the coordinate system along with the array representation. Why don't we ever do this in machine learning? Because in machine learning, it doesn't exactly matter what the coordinate system is as long as we stick to any fixed coordinate system. Machine learning is about minimizing loss functions (which we will study later). As such, absolute positions of point are immaterial, only relative positions matter.

There are explicit rules (which we will study later) that state how the vector transforms when the coordinate system changes. We will invoke them when necessary. All vectors used in a machine learning computation must consistently use the same coordinate system or be transformed appropriately.

One other point: planar spaces, such as the plane of the paper on which this book is written, are two-dimensional (2D). The mechanical world we live in is three-dimensional (3D). Human imagination usually fails to see higher dimensions. In machine learning and data science, we often talk of spaces with thousands of dimensions. You may not be able to see those spaces in your mind, but that is not a crippling limitation. You can use 3D analogues in your head. They work in a surprisingly large variety of cases. However, it is important to bear in mind that this is not always true. Some examples where the lower-dimensional intuitions fail at higher dimensions will be shown later.

2.2 PyTorch code for vector manipulations

PyTorch is an open source machine learning library developed by Facebook's artificial intelligence group. It is one of the most elegant practical tools for developing deep learning applications at present. In this book, we aim to familiarize you with PyTorch and similar programming paradigms alongside the relevant mathematics. Knowledge of Python basics will be assumed. You are strongly encouraged to try out all the code snippets in this book (after installing the appropriate packages like PyTorch, that is).

All the Python code in this book is produced via Jupyter Notebook. A summary of the theoretical material presented in the code is provided before the code snippet.

2.2.1 PyTorch code for the introduction to vectors

Listing 2.1 shows how to create and access vectors and subvectors and slice and dice vectors using PyTorch.

NOTE Fully functional code demonstrating how to create a vector and access its elements, executable via Jupyter Notebook, can be found at http://mng.bz/xm8q.

Listing 2.1 Introduction to vectors via PyTorch

```
v = torch.tensor([0.11, 0.01, 0.98, 0.12, 0.98,
                  ,0.85, 0.03, 0.55, 0.49, 0.99,
                  0.02, 0.31, 0.55, 0.87, 0.63],
                  dtype=torch.float64)

first_element = v[0]
third_element = v[2]

last_element = v[-1]
second_last_element = v[-2]

second_to_fifth_elements = v[1:4]

first_to_third_elements = v[:2]
last_two_elements = v[-2:]

num_elements_in_v = len(v)

u = np.array([0.11, 0.01, 0.98, 0.12, 0.98, 0.85, 0.03,
              0.55, 0.49, 0.99, 0.02, 0.31, 0.55, 0.87,
              0.63])

u = torch.from_numpy(u)

diff = v.sub(u)

u1 = u.numpy()
```

- torch.tensor represents a multidimensional array. The vector is a 1D tensor that can be initialized by directly specifying values.
- Tensor elements are floats by default. We can force tensors to be other types such as float64 (double).
- The square bracket operator lets us access individual vector elements.
- Negative indices count from the end of the array. -1 denotes the last element. -2 denotes the second-to-last element.
- The colon operator slices off a range of elements from the vector.
- Nothing before a colon denotes the beginning of the array. Nothing after a colon denotes the end of the array.
- Torch tensors can be initialized from NumPy arrays.
- The difference between the Torch tensor and its NumPy version is zero.
- Torch tensors can be converted to NumPy arrays.

2.3 Matrices and their role in machine learning

Sometimes it is not sufficient to group a set of numbers into a vector. We have to collect several vectors into another group. For instance, consider the input to training a machine learning model. Here we have several input instances, each consisting of a sequence of numbers. As seen in section 2.1, the sequence of numbers belonging to a single input instance can be grouped into a vector. How do we represent the entire collection of input instances? This is where the concept of matrices comes in handy from the world of mathematics. A *matrix* can be viewed as a rectangular array of numbers arranged in a fixed count of rows and columns. Each row of a matrix is a vector, and so is each column. Thus a matrix can be thought of as a collection of row vectors. It can also be viewed as a collection of column vectors. We can represent the entire set of numbers that constitute the training input to a machine learning model as a matrix, with each row vector corresponding to a single training instance.

Consider our familiar cat-brain problem again. As stated earlier, a single input instance to the machine is a vector $\vec{x} = \begin{bmatrix} x_0 \\ x_1 \end{bmatrix}$, where x_0 describes the hardness of the object in front of the cat. Now consider a training dataset with many such input instances, each with a known output threat score. You might recall from section 1.1 that the goal in machine learning is to create a function that maps these inputs to their respective outputs with as little overall error as possible. Our training data may look as shown in table 2.2 (note that in real-life problems, the training dataset is usually large—often millions of input-output pairs—but in this toy problem, we will have 8 training data instances).

Table 2.2 Example training dataset for our toy machine learning–based cat brain

	Input value: Hardness	Input value: Sharpness	Output: Threat score
0	0.11	0.09	−0.8
1	0.01	0.02	−0.97
2	0.98	0.91	0.89
3	0.12	0.21	−0.68
4	0.98	0.99	0.95
5	0.85	0.87	0.74
6	0.03	0.14	−0.88
7	0.55	0.45	0.00

From table 2.2, we can collect the columns corresponding to hardness and sharpness into a matrix, as shown in equation 2.1—this is a compact representation of the training dataset for this problem.[2]

$$\text{Example cat-brain dataset matrix } X = \begin{bmatrix} 0.11 & 0.09 \\ 0.01 & 0.02 \\ 0.98 & 0.91 \\ 0.12 & 0.21 \\ 0.98 & 0.99 \\ 0.85 & 0.87 \\ 0.03 & 0.14 \\ 0.55 & 0.45 \end{bmatrix} \tag{2.1}$$

Each row of matrix X is a particular input instance. Different rows represent different input instances. On the other hand, different columns represent different feature elements. For example, the 0th row of matrix X is the vector $\begin{bmatrix} x_{00} & x_{01} \end{bmatrix}$ representing

[2] We usually use uppercase letters to symbolize matrices.

the 0th input instance. Its elements, x_{00} and x_{01} represent different feature elements, hardness and sharpness respectively of the 0th training input instance.

2.3.1 Matrix representation of digital images

Digital images are also often represented as matrices. Here, each element represents the brightness at a specific pixel position (x, y coordinate) of the image. Typically, the brightness value is normalized to an integer in the range 0 to 255. 0 is black, 255 is white, and 128 is gray.[3] Following is an example of a tiny image, 9 pixels wide and 4 pixels high:

$$I_{4,9} = \begin{bmatrix} 0 & 8 & 16 & 24 & 32 & 40 & 48 & 56 & 64 \\ 64 & 72 & 80 & 88 & 96 & 104 & 112 & 120 & 128 \\ 128 & 136 & 144 & 152 & 160 & 168 & 176 & 184 & 192 \\ 192 & 200 & 208 & 216 & 224 & 232 & 240 & 248 & 255 \end{bmatrix} \tag{2.2}$$

The brightness increases gradually from left to right and also from top to bottom. I_{00} represents the top-left pixel, which is black. $I_{3,8}$ represents the bottom-right pixel, which is white. The intermediate pixels are various shades of gray between black and white. The actual image is shown in figure 2.3.

Figure 2.3 Image corresponding to matrix $I_{4,9}$ in equation 2.2

2.4 Python code: Introducing matrices, tensors, and images via PyTorch

For programming purposes, you can think of tensors as multidimensional arrays. Scalars are zero-dimensional tensors. Vectors are one-dimensional tensors. Matrices are two-dimensional tensors. RGB images are three-dimensional tensors ($colorchannels \times height \times width$). A batch of 64 images is a four-dimensional tensor ($64 \times colorchannels \times height \times width$).

Listing 2.2 Introducing matrices via PyTorch

A matrix is a 2D array of numbers: i.e., a 2D tensor.
The entire training data input set for a machine-learning model can be viewed as a matrix.
Each input instance is one row.
Row count ≡ number of training examples, column count ≡ training instance size

```
X = torch.tensor(
```

[3] In digital computers, numbers in the range 0..255 can be represented with a single byte of storage; hence this choice.

```
    [
        [0.11, 0.09], [0.01, 0.02], [0.98, 0.91],
        [0.12, 0.21], [0.98, 0.99], [0.85, 0.87],
        [0.03, 0.14], [0.55, 0.45]
    ]
)
```

Cat-brain training data input: 8 examples, each with two values (hardness, sharpness). An 8 × 2 tensor is created by directly specifying values.

```
print("Shape of the matrix is: ".format(X.shape))
```

The shape of a tensor is a list. For a matrix, the first list element is num rows; the second list element is num columns.

```
first_element = X[0, 0]
```

Square brackets extract individual matrix elements.

```
row_0 = X[0, :]
row_1 = X[1, 0:2]
```

A standalone colon operator denotes all possible indices.
The colon operator denotes the range of indices.

```
column_0 = X[:, 0]
column_1 = X[:, 1]
```

0th column
1st column

Listing 2.3 Slicing and dicing matrices

Ranges of rows and columns can be specified via the colon operator to slice off (extract) submatrices.

```
first_3_training_examples = X[:3, ]
```

Extracts the first three training examples (rows)

```
print("Sharpness of 5-7 training examples is: "

      .format(X[5:8, 1]))
```

Extracts the sharpness feature for the 5th to 7th training examples

Listing 2.4 Tensors and images in PyTorch

PyTorch tensors can be used to represent tensors.
A vector is a 1-tensor, a matrix is a 2-tensor, and a scalar is a 0-tensor.

```
tensor = torch.rand((5, 5, 3))
```

Creates a random tensor of specified dimensions

All images are tensors. An RGB image of height H, width W is a 3-tensor of shape [3, H, W].

```
I49 = torch.tensor([[0, 8, 16, 24, 32, 40, 48,  56,  64],
                  [64,  72,  80,  88,  96, 104, 112, 120, 128],
                   [128, 136, 144, 152, 160, 168, 176, 184, 192],
                   [192, 200, 208, 216, 224, 232, 240, 248, 255]],
                  )
```

4×9 single-channel image shown in figure 2.3

```
img = torch.tensor(cv2.imread('../../Figures/dog3.jpg'))
```

Reads a $199 \times 256 \times 3$ image from disk

```
img_b = img[:, :, 0]
img_g = img[:, :, 1]
img_r = img[:, :, 2]
img_cropped = img[0:100, 0:100, :]
```

Usual slicing dicing operators work. Extracts the red, green, and blue channels of the image as shown in figure 2.4.

Crops out a 100×100 subimage as shown in figure 2.5

2.5 Basic vector and matrix operations in machine learning

In this section, we introduce several basic vector and matrix operations along with examples to demonstrate their significance in image processing, computer vision, and

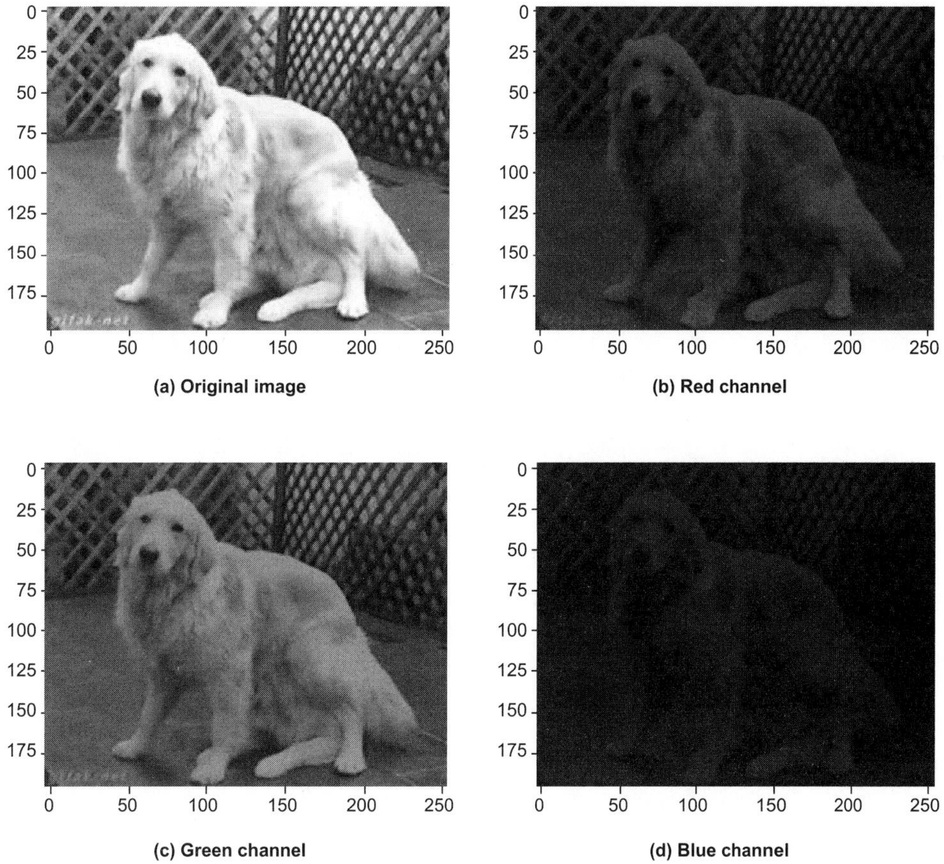

Figure 2.4 Tensors and images in PyTorch

Figure 2.5 Cropped image of dog

machine learning. It is meant to be an application-centric introduction to linear algebra. But it is *not* meant to be a comprehensive review of matrix and vector operations, for which you are referred to a textbook on linear algebra.

2.5.1 Matrix and vector transpose

In equation 2.2, we encountered the matrix $I_{4,9}$ depicting a tiny image. Suppose we want to rotate the image by 90° so it looks like figure 2.6. The original matrix $I_{4,9}$ and its transpose $I^T_{4,9} = I_{9,4}$ are shown here:

$$I_{4,9} = \begin{bmatrix} 0 & 8 & 16 & 24 & 32 & 40 & 48 & 56 & 64 \\ 64 & 72 & 80 & 88 & 96 & 104 & 112 & 120 & 128 \\ 128 & 136 & 144 & 152 & 160 & 168 & 176 & 184 & 192 \\ 192 & 200 & 208 & 216 & 224 & 232 & 240 & 248 & 255 \end{bmatrix}$$

$$I^T_{4,9} = I_{9,4} = \begin{bmatrix} 0 & 64 & 128 & 192 \\ 8 & 72 & 136 & 200 \\ 16 & 80 & 144 & 208 \\ 24 & 88 & 152 & 216 \\ 32 & 96 & 160 & 224 \\ 40 & 104 & 168 & 232 \\ 48 & 112 & 176 & 240 \\ 56 & 120 & 184 & 248 \\ 64 & 128 & 192 & 255 \end{bmatrix} \tag{2.3}$$

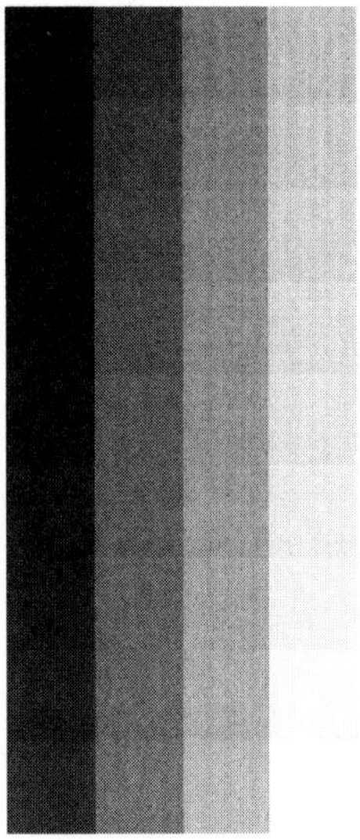

Figure 2.6 Image corresponding to the transpose of matrix $I_{4,9}$ shown in equation 2.3. This is equivalent to rotating the image by 90°.

By comparing equation 2.2 and equation 2.3, you can easily see that one can be obtained from the other by interchanging the row and column indices. This operation is generally known as *matrix transposition.*

Formally, the transpose of a matrix $A_{m,n}$ with m rows and n columns is another matrix with n rows and m columns. This transposed matrix, denoted $A^T_{n,m}$, is such that $A^T\ [i, j] = A\ [j, i]$. For instance, the value at row 0 column 6 in matrix $I_{4,9}$ is 48; in the transposed matrix, the same value appears in row 6 and column 0. In matrix parlance, $I_{4,9}[0, 6] = I^T_{9,4}[6, 0] = 48$.

Vector transposition is a special case of matrix transposition (since all vectors are matrices—a column vector with n elements is an $n \times 1$ matrix). For instance, an arbitrary vector and its transpose are shown next:

$$\vec{v} = \begin{bmatrix} 1 \\ 2 \\ 3 \end{bmatrix} \tag{2.4}$$

$$\vec{v}^T = \begin{bmatrix} 1 & 2 & 3 \end{bmatrix} \tag{2.5}$$

2.5.2 Dot product of two vectors and its role in machine learning

In section 1.3, we saw the simplest of machine learning models where the output is generated by taking a weighted sum of the inputs (and then adding a constant bias value). This model/machine is characterized by the weights w_0, w_1, and bias b. Take the rows of table 2.2. For example, for row 0, the input values are the hardness of the approaching object = 0.11 and softness = 0.09. The corresponding model output will be $y = w_0 \times 0.11 + w_1 \times 0.09 + b$. In fact, the goal of training is to choose w_0, w_1, and b such that model outputs are as close as possible to the known outputs; that is, $y = w_0 \times 0.11 + w_1 \times 0.09 + b$ should be as close to −0.8 as possible, $y = w_0 \times 0.01 + w_1 \times 0.02 + b$ should be as close to −0.97 as possible, that is In general, given an input instance $\vec{x} = \begin{bmatrix} x_0 \\ x_1 \end{bmatrix}$, the model output is $y = x_0 w_0 + x_1 w_1 + b$.

We will keep returning to this model throughout the chapter. But first, let's consider a different question. In this toy example, we have only three model parameters: two weights, w_0, w_1, and one bias b. Hence it is not very messy to write the model output flat out as $y = x_0 w_0 + x_1 w_1 + b$. But, with longer feature vectors (that is, more weights) it will become unwieldy. Is there a compact way to represent the model output for a specific input instance, irrespective of the size of the input?

Turns out the answer is yes—we can use an operation called *dot product* from the world of mathematics. We have already seen in section 2.1 that an individual instance of model input can be compactly represented by a vector, say $\vec{x}$ (it can have any number of input values). We can also represent the set of weights as vector $\vec{w}$—it will have the same number of items as the input vector. The dot product is simply the element-wise multiplication of the two vectors $\vec{x}$ and $\vec{w}$. Formally, given two vectors $\vec{x} = \begin{bmatrix} x_0 \\ x_1 \\ \vdots \\ x_n \end{bmatrix}$ and $\vec{w} = \begin{bmatrix} w_0 \\ w_1 \\ \vdots \\ w_n \end{bmatrix}$, the dot product of the two vectors is defined as

$$\vec{x} \cdot \vec{w} = x_0 w_0 + x_1 w_1 + \cdots x_n w_n \tag{2.6}$$

In other words, the sum of the products of corresponding elements of the two vectors is the dot product of the two vectors, denoted $\vec{a} \cdot \vec{b}$.

NOTE The dot product notation can compactly represent the model output as $y = \vec{w} \cdot \vec{x} + b$. The representation does not increase in size even when the number of inputs and weights is large.

Consider our (by now familiar) cat-brain example again. Suppose the weight vector is $\vec{w} = \begin{bmatrix} 3 \\ 2 \end{bmatrix}$ and the bias value $b = 5$. Then the model output for the 0th input instance from table 2.2 will be $\begin{bmatrix} 0.11 \\ 0.09 \end{bmatrix} \cdot \begin{bmatrix} 3 \\ 2 \end{bmatrix} = 0.11 \times 3 + 0.09 \times 2 + 5 = 5.51$. It is another matter that these are bad choices for weight and bias parameters, since the model output 5.51 is a far cry from the desired output −0.89. We will soon see how to obtain better parameter values. For now, we just need to note that the dot product offers a neat way to represent the simple weighted sum model output.

NOTE The dot product is defined only if the vectors have the same dimensions.

Sometimes the dot product is also referred to as *inner product*, denoted $\left\langle \vec{a}, \vec{b} \right\rangle$. Strictly speaking, the phrase *inner product* is a bit more general; it applies to infinite-dimensional vectors as well. In this book, we will often use the terms interchangeably, sacrificing mathematical rigor for enhanced understanding.

2.5.3 Matrix multiplication and machine learning

Vectors are special cases of matrices. Hence, matrix-vector multiplication is a special case of matrix-matrix multiplication. We will start with that.

MATRIX-VECTOR MULTIPLICATION

In section 2.5.2, we saw that given a weight vector, say $\vec{w} = \begin{bmatrix} 3 \\ 2 \end{bmatrix}$, and the bias value $b = 5$, the weighted sum model output upon a single input instance, say $\begin{bmatrix} 0.11 \\ 0.09 \end{bmatrix}$, can be represented using a vector-vector dot product $\vec{w} \cdot \vec{x} + b = \begin{bmatrix} 0.11 \\ 0.09 \end{bmatrix} \cdot \begin{bmatrix} 3 \\ 2 \end{bmatrix} + 5$. As depicted in equation 2.1, during training, we are dealing with many training data instances at the same time. In real life, we typically deal with hundreds of thousands of input instances, each having hundreds of values. Is there a way to represent the model output for the entire training dataset compactly, such that it is independent of the count of input instances and their sizes?

The answer turns out to be yes. We can use the idea of matrix-vector multiplication from the world of mathematics. The product of a matrix X and column vector $\vec{w}$ is another vector, denoted $X\vec{w}$. Its elements are the dot products between the row vectors of X and the column vector $\vec{w}$. For example, given the model weight vector $\vec{w} = \begin{bmatrix} 3 \\ 2 \end{bmatrix}$ and the bias value $b = 5$, the outputs on the toy training dataset of our familiar cat-brain model (equation 2.1) can be obtained via the following steps:

$$\begin{bmatrix} 0.11 & 0.09 \\ 0.01 & 0.02 \\ 0.98 & 0.91 \\ 0.12 & 0.21 \\ 0.98 & 0.99 \\ 0.85 & 0.87 \\ 0.03 & 0.14 \\ 0.55 & 0.45 \end{bmatrix} \begin{bmatrix} 3 \\ 2 \end{bmatrix} = \begin{bmatrix} 0.11 \times 3 + 0.09 \times 2 = 0.51 \\ 0.01 \times 3 + 0.02 \times 2 = 0.07 \\ 0.98 \times 3 + 0.91 \times 2 = 4.76 \\ 0.12 \times 3 + 0.21 \times 2 = 0.78 \\ 0.98 \times 3 + 0.99 \times 2 = 4.92 \\ 0.85 \times 3 + 0.87 \times 2 = 4.29 \\ 0.03 \times 3 + 0.14 \times 2 = 0.37 \\ 0.55 \times 3 + 0.45 \times 2 = 2.55 \end{bmatrix} \tag{2.7}$$

Adding the bias value of 5, the model output on the toy training dataset is

$$\begin{bmatrix} 5 + 0.51 = 5.51 \\ 5 + 0.07 = 5.07 \\ 5 + 4.76 = 9.76 \\ 5 + 0.78 = 5.78 \\ 5 + 4.92 = 9.92 \\ 5 + 4.29 = 9.29 \\ 5 + 0.37 = 5.37 \\ 5 + 2.55 = 7.55 \end{bmatrix} \tag{2.8}$$

In general, the output of our simple model (biased weighted sum of input elements) can be expressed compactly as $\vec{y} = X\vec{w} + \vec{b}$.

MATRIX-MATRIX MULTIPLICATION

Generalizing the notion of matrix times vector, we can define matrix times matrix. A matrix with m rows and p columns, say $A_{m,p}$, can be multiplied with another matrix with p rows and n columns, say $B_{p,n}$, to generate a matrix with m rows and n columns, say $C_{m,n}$: for example, $C_{m,n} = A_{m,p}\, B_{p,n}$. Note that the number of columns in the left matrix must match the number of rows in the right matrix. Element i, j of the result matrix, $C_{i,j}$, is obtained by point-wise multiplication of the elements of the ith row vector of A and the jth column vector of B. The following example illustrates the idea:

$$A_{3,2} = \begin{bmatrix} a_{11} & a_{12} \\ a_{21} & a_{22} \\ a_{31} & a_{32} \end{bmatrix}$$

$$B_{2,2} = \begin{bmatrix} b_{11} & b_{12} \\ b_{21} & b_{22} \end{bmatrix}$$

$$C_{3,2} = \begin{bmatrix} a_{11} & a_{12} \\ \mathbf{a_{21}} & \mathbf{a_{22}} \\ a_{31} & a_{32} \end{bmatrix} \begin{bmatrix} \mathbf{b_{11}} & b_{12} \\ \mathbf{b_{21}} & b_{22} \end{bmatrix}$$

$$= \begin{bmatrix} c_{11} = a_{11}b_{11} + a_{12}b_{21} & c_{12} = a_{11}b_{12} + a_{12}b_{22} \\ \mathbf{c_{21} = a_{21}b_{11} + a_{22}b_{21}} & c_{22} = a_{21}b_{12} + a_{22}b_{22} \\ c_{31} = a_{31}b_{11} + a_{32}b_{21} & c_{32} = a_{31}b_{12} + a_{32}b_{22} \end{bmatrix}$$

The computation for $C_{2,1}$ is shown via bolding by way of example.

NOTE Matrix multiplication is not commutative. In general, $AB \neq BA$.

At this point, the astute reader may already have noted that the dot product is a special case of matrix multiplication. For instance, the dot product between two vectors $\vec{w} = \begin{bmatrix} w_0 \\ w_1 \end{bmatrix}$ and $\vec{x} = \begin{bmatrix} x_0 \\ x_1 \end{bmatrix}$ is equivalent to transposing either of the two vectors and then doing a matrix multiplication with the other. In other words,

$$\vec{w} \cdot \vec{x} = \vec{w}^T \vec{x} = \begin{bmatrix} w_0 \\ w_1 \end{bmatrix}^T \begin{bmatrix} x_0 \\ x_1 \end{bmatrix} = \begin{bmatrix} w_0 & w_1 \end{bmatrix} \begin{bmatrix} x_0 \\ x_1 \end{bmatrix} = \vec{x}^T \vec{w} = w_0 x_0 + w_1 x_1$$

The idea works in higher dimensions, too. In general, given two vectors $\vec{x} = \begin{bmatrix} x_0 \\ x_1 \\ \vdots \\ x_n \end{bmatrix}$ and $\vec{w} = \begin{bmatrix} w_0 \\ w_1 \\ \vdots \\ w_n \end{bmatrix}$, the dot product of the two vectors is defined as

$$\vec{x} \cdot \vec{w} = \vec{w}^T \vec{x} = \begin{bmatrix} w_0 & w_1 & \cdots & w_n \end{bmatrix} \begin{bmatrix} x_0 \\ x_1 \\ \vdots \\ x_n \end{bmatrix}$$

$$= \vec{x}^T \vec{w} = \begin{bmatrix} x_0 & x_1 & \cdots & x_n \end{bmatrix} \begin{bmatrix} w_0 \\ w_1 \\ \vdots \\ w_n \end{bmatrix}$$

$$= x_0 w_0 + x_1 w_1 + \cdots x_n w_n \tag{2.9}$$

Another special case of matrix multiplication is row-vector matrix multiplication. For example, $\vec{b}^T A = \vec{c}$ or

$$\begin{bmatrix} b_1 & b_2 & b_3 \end{bmatrix} \begin{bmatrix} a_{11} & a_{12} \\ a_{21} & a_{22} \\ a_{31} & a_{32} \end{bmatrix} = \begin{bmatrix} c_1 = a_{11}b_1 + a_{21}b_2 + a_{31}b_3 & c_2 = a_{12}b_1 + a_{22}b_2 + a_{32}b_3 \end{bmatrix}$$

TRANSPOSE OF MATRIX PRODUCTS

Given two matrices A and B, where the number of columns in A matches the number of rows in B (that is, it is possible to multiply them), the transpose of the product is the product of the individual transposes, in reversed order. The rule also applies to matrix-vector multiplication. The following equations capture this rule:

$$\begin{aligned} (AB)^T &= B^T A^T \\ (A\vec{x})^T &= \vec{x}^T A^T \\ \left(\vec{x}^T A\right)^T &= A^T \vec{x} \end{aligned} \tag{2.10}$$

2.5.4 Length of a vector (L2 norm): Model error

Imagine that a machine learning model is supposed to output a target value $\bar{y}$, but it outputs y instead. We are interested in the *error* made by the model. The error is the difference between the target and the actual outputs.

> **Squared error**
>
> When a computing error occurs, we are only interested in how far the computed value is from ideal. We do not care whether the computed value is bigger or smaller than ideal. For instance, if the target (ideal) value is 2, the computed values 1.5 and 2.5 are equally in error—we are equally happy or unhappy with either of them. Hence, it is common practice to *square* error values. Thus for instance, if the target value is 2 and the computed value is 1.5, the error is $(1.5 - 2)^2 = 0.25$. If the target value is 2.5, the error is $(2.5 - 2)^2 = 0.25$. The squaring operation essentially eliminates the sign of the error value. We can then follow it up with a square root, but it is OK not to.
>
> You might ask, "But wait: squaring alters the value of the quantity. Don't we care about the exact value of the error?" The answer is, we usually don't; we only care about *relative* values of errors. If the target is 2, we want the error for an output value of, say, 2.1 to be less than the error for an output value of 2.5; the exact values of the errors do not matter.

Let's apply this idea of squaring to machine learning model error. As seen earlier in section 2.5.3, given a model weight vector, say $\vec{w} = \begin{bmatrix} 3 \\ 2 \end{bmatrix}$, and the bias value $b = 5$, the weighted sum model output upon a single input instance, say $\begin{bmatrix} 0.11 \\ 0.09 \end{bmatrix}$, is $\begin{bmatrix} 0.11 \\ 0.09 \end{bmatrix} \cdot \begin{bmatrix} 3 \\ 2 \end{bmatrix} + 5 =$ 5.51. The corresponding target (ideal) output, from table 2.2, is −0.8. The squared error $e^2 = (-0.8 - 5.51)^2 = 39.82$ gives us an idea of how good or bad the model parameters 3, 2, 5 are. For instance, if we instead use a weight vector $\vec{w} = \begin{bmatrix} 1 \\ 1 \end{bmatrix}$ and bias value −1, we get model output $\vec{w} \cdot \vec{x} + b = \begin{bmatrix} 0.11 \\ 0.09 \end{bmatrix} \cdot \begin{bmatrix} 1 \\ 1 \end{bmatrix} - 1 = -0.8$. The output is exactly the same as the target. The corresponding squared error $e^2 = (-0.8 - (-0.8))^2 = 0$. This (zero error) immediately tells us that 1, 1, −1 are much better choices of model parameters than 3, 2, 5.

In general, the error made by a biased weighted sum model can be expressed as follows. If $\vec{w}$ denotes the weight vector and $\vec{b}$ denotes the bias, the output corresponding to an input instance $\vec{x}$ can be expressed as $y = \vec{w} \cdot \vec{x} + b$. Let $\bar{y}$ denote the corresponding target (ground truth). Then the error is defined as $e = (y - \bar{y})^2$.

Thus we see that we can compute the error on a single training instance by taking the difference between the model output and the ground truth and squaring it. How do we extend this concept over the entire training dataset? The set of outputs corresponding to the entire set of training inputs can be expressed as the output vector $\vec{y} = X\vec{w} + \vec{b}$. The corresponding target output vector, consisting of the entire set of ground truths can be expressed as $\bar{\vec{y}}$. The differences between the target and model output over the entire training set can be expressed as another vector $\bar{\vec{y}} - \vec{y}$. In our particular example:

$$\vec{y} = \begin{bmatrix} 5.51 \\ 5.07 \\ 9.76 \\ 5.78 \\ 9.92 \\ 9.29 \\ 5.37 \\ 7.55 \end{bmatrix} \quad \bar{\vec{y}} = \begin{bmatrix} -0.8 \\ -0.97 \\ 0.89 \\ -0.67 \\ 0.97 \\ 0.72 \\ -0.83 \\ 0.00 \end{bmatrix} \text{ and } \bar{\vec{y}} - \vec{y} = \begin{bmatrix} 5.51 \\ 5.07 \\ 9.76 \\ 5.78 \\ 9.92 \\ 9.29 \\ 5.37 \\ 7.55 \end{bmatrix} - \begin{bmatrix} -0.8 \\ -0.97 \\ 0.89 \\ -0.67 \\ 0.97 \\ 0.72 \\ -0.83 \\ 0.00 \end{bmatrix} = \begin{bmatrix} 6.31 \\ 6.04 \\ 8.87 \\ 6.45 \\ 8.95 \\ 8.57 \\ 6.2 \\ 7.55 \end{bmatrix}$$

Thus the total error over the entire training dataset is obtained by taking the difference between the output and the ground truth vector, squaring its elements and adding them up. Recalling equation 2.9, this is exactly what will happen if we take the *dot product of the difference vector with itself*. That happens to be the definition of the *squared magnitude* or *length* or *L2 norm* of a vector: the dot product of the vector with itself. In the previous example, the overall training (squared) error is:

$$E^2 = \left(\bar{\vec{y}} - \vec{y}\right) \cdot \left(\bar{\vec{y}} - \vec{y}\right) = \left(\bar{\vec{y}} - \vec{y}\right)^T \left(\bar{\vec{y}} - \vec{y}\right) = \begin{bmatrix} 6.31 \\ 6.04 \\ 8.87 \\ 6.45 \\ 8.95 \\ 8.57 \\ 6.2 \\ 7.55 \end{bmatrix} \cdot \begin{bmatrix} 6.31 \\ 6.04 \\ 8.87 \\ 6.45 \\ 8.95 \\ 8.57 \\ 6.2 \\ 7.55 \end{bmatrix}$$

$$= (6.31)^2 + (6.04)^2 + (8.87)^2 + (6.45)^2 + (8.95)^2 + (8.57)^2 + (6.2)^2 + (7.55)^2$$

Formally, the length of a vector $\vec{v} = \begin{bmatrix} v_1 \\ v_2 \\ \vdots \\ v_n \end{bmatrix}$, denoted $||\vec{v}||$, is defined as $||\vec{v}|| = \sqrt{\vec{v}^T\vec{v}}$ $= \sqrt{v_1^2 + v_2^2 + \cdots v_n^2}$. This quantity is sometimes called the L2 norm of the vector.

In particular, given a machine learning model with output vector $\vec{y}$ and a target vector $\bar{\vec{y}}$, the error is the same as the magnitude or L2 norm of the difference vector

$$e = ||\bar{\vec{y}} - \vec{y}|| = \sqrt{\left(\bar{\vec{y}} - \vec{y}\right) \cdot \left(\bar{\vec{y}} - \vec{y}\right)} = \sqrt{\left(\bar{\vec{y}} - \vec{y}\right)^T \left(\bar{\vec{y}} - \vec{y}\right)}$$

2.5.5 Geometric intuitions for vector length

For a 2D vector $\vec{v} = \begin{bmatrix} x \\ y \end{bmatrix}$, as seen in figure 2.2, the L2 norm $||\vec{v}|| = \sqrt{x^2 + y^2}$ is nothing but the hypotenuse of the right-angled triangle whose sides are elements of the vector. The same intuition holds in higher dimensions.

A *unit vector* is a vector whose length is 1. Given any vector $\vec{v}$, the corresponding unit vector can be obtained by dividing every element by the length of that vector. For example, given $\vec{v} = \begin{bmatrix} 1 \\ 1 \end{bmatrix}$, length $||\vec{v}|| = \sqrt{1^2 + 1^2} = \sqrt{2}$ and the corresponding unit vector $\hat{v} = \begin{bmatrix} \frac{1}{\sqrt{2}} \\ \frac{1}{\sqrt{2}} \end{bmatrix}$. Unit vectors typically represent a direction.

NOTE Unit vectors are conventionally depicted with the hat symbol as opposed to the little overhead arrow, as in $\hat{u}^T \hat{u} = 1$.

In machine learning, the goal of training is often to minimize the length of the error vector (the difference between the model output vector and the target ground truth vector).

2.5.6 Geometric intuitions for the dot product: Feature similarity

Consider the document retrieval problem depicted in table 2.1 one more time. We have a set of documents, each described by its own feature vector. Given a pair of such documents, we must find their similarity. This essentially boils down to estimating the similarity between two feature vectors. In this section, we will see that the dot product between a pair of vectors can be used as a measure of similarity between them.

For instance, consider the feature vectors corresponding to d_5 and d_6 in table 2.1. They are $\begin{bmatrix} 1 \\ 0 \end{bmatrix}$ and $\begin{bmatrix} 0 \\ 1 \end{bmatrix}$. The dot product between them is $1 \times 0 + 0 \times 1 = 0$. This is low and agrees with our intuition that there is no common word of interest between them, so the documents are very dissimilar. On the other hand, the dot product between feature vectors of d_3 and d_4 is $\begin{bmatrix} 3 \\ 3 \end{bmatrix} \cdot \begin{bmatrix} 5 \\ 5 \end{bmatrix} = 3 \times 5 + 3 \times 5 = 30$. This is high and agrees with our intuition that they have many commonalities in words of interest and are similar documents. Thus, we get the first glimpse of an important concept. Loosely speaking, *similar vectors have larger dot products, and dissimilar vectors have near-zero dot products.*

We will keep revisiting this problem of estimating similarity between feature vectors and solve it with more and more finesse. As a first attempt, we will now study in greater detail how dot products measure similarities between vectors. First we will show that the component of a vector along another is yielded by the dot product. Using this, we will show that the "similarity/agreement" between a pair of vectors can be estimated using the dot product between them. In particular, we will see that if the vectors point in more or less the same direction, their dot products are higher than when the vectors are perpendicular to each other. If the vectors point in opposite directions, their dot product is negative.

DOT PRODUCT MEASURES THE COMPONENT OF ONE VECTOR ALONG ANOTHER

Let's examine a special case first: the component of a vector along a coordinate axis. This can be obtained by multiplying the length of the vector with the cosine of the angle between the vector and the relevant coordinate axis. As shown for 2D in figure 2.7a, a vector $\vec{v}$ can be broken into two components along the X and Y axes as

$$\vec{v} = \begin{bmatrix} \|v\| \cos\theta \\ \|v\| \cos(90^\circ - \theta) \end{bmatrix} = \begin{bmatrix} \|v\| \cos\theta \\ \|v\| \sin\theta \end{bmatrix}$$

Note how the length of the vector is preserved:

$$\left\| \begin{bmatrix} \|v\| \cos\theta \\ \|v\| \sin\theta \end{bmatrix} \right\| = \|v\| \left(\cos^2\theta + \sin^2\theta\right) = \|v\|$$

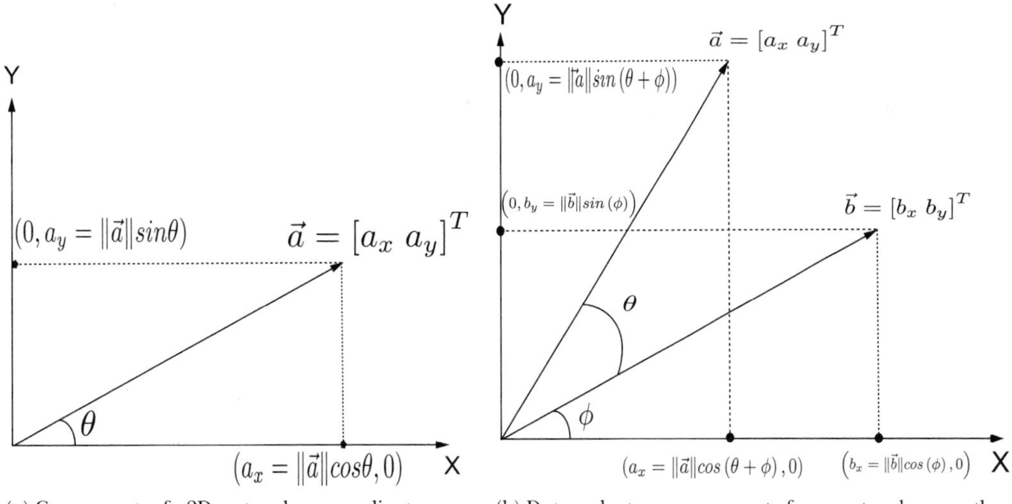

(a) Components of a 2D vector along coordinate axes. Note that $\|\vec{a}\|$ is the length of hypotenuse.

(b) Dot product as a component of one vector along another $\vec{a} \cdot \vec{b} = \vec{a}^T \vec{b} = a_x b_x + a_y b_y = \|\vec{a}\| \|\vec{b}\| cos(\theta)$.

Figure 2.7 Vector components and dot product

Now let's study the more general case of the component of one vector in the direction of another arbitrary vector (figure 2.7b). The component of a vector $\vec{a}$ along another vector $\vec{b}$ is $\vec{a} \cdot \vec{b} = \vec{a}^T \vec{b}$. This is equivalent to $\|\vec{a}\| \|\vec{b}\| cos(\theta)$, where θ is the angle between the vectors $\vec{a}$ and $\vec{b}$. (This has been proven for the two-dimension case discussed in section A.1 of the appendix. You can read it if you would like deeper intuition.)

DOT PRODUCT MEASURES THE AGREEMENT BETWEEN TWO VECTORS

The dot product can be expressed using the cosine of the angle between the vectors. Given two vectors $\vec{a}$ and $\vec{b}$, if θ is the angle between them, we have (see figure 2.7b)

$$\vec{a} \cdot \vec{b} = a_x b_x + a_y b_y \quad \text{for two dimensions}$$
$$\vec{a} \cdot \vec{b} = \vec{a}^T \vec{b} = \|\vec{a}\| \|\vec{b}\| cos\left(\theta\right) \quad \text{for all dimensions} \tag{2.11}$$

Expressing the dot product using cosines makes it easier to see that it measures the *agreement* (aka *correlation*) between two vectors. If the vectors have the same direction, the angle between them is 0 and the cosine is 1, implying maximum agreement. The cosine becomes progressively smaller as the angle between the vectors increases, until the two vectors become perpendicular to each other and the cosine is zero, implying no correlation—the vectors are independent of each other. If the angle between them is 180°, the cosine is −1, implying that the vectors are anti-correlated. Thus, the dot product of two vectors is proportional to their directional agreement.

What role do the vector lengths play in all this? The dot product between two vectors is also proportional to the lengths of the vectors. This means agreement scores between bigger vectors are higher (an agreement between the US president and the German chancellor counts more than an agreement between you and me).

If you want the agreement score to be neutral to the vector length, you can use a normalized dot product between unit-length vectors along the same directions:

$$cosine\_similarity\left(\vec{a}, \vec{b}\right) = \frac{\vec{a}^T \vec{b}}{\|\vec{a}\| \|\vec{b}\|} = cos\left(\theta\right)$$

The normalized dot product (aka cosine similarity measure) indicates pure directional agreement. It is often used in document processing. Suppose we have some query text that we want to match against various archive documents and retrieve them rank-ordered by their similarity to the query text. A descriptor vector corresponds to the query text as well as to each archived document. We can use the dot product between descriptor vectors as a measure of similarity, but we do *not* want longer documents to automatically score higher in similarity. Hence, we use cosine similarity to make the similarity score independent of the length of the document. Document retrieval and cosine similarity are discussed in detail in section 4.6.1.

DOT PRODUCT AND THE DIFFERENCE BETWEEN TWO UNIT VECTORS

To obtain further insight into how the dot product indicates agreement or correlation between two directions, consider the two unit vectors $\hat{u} = \begin{bmatrix} u_x \\ u_y \\ u_z \end{bmatrix}$ and $\hat{v} = \begin{bmatrix} v_x \\ v_y \\ v_z \end{bmatrix}$. The difference between them is $\hat{u} - \hat{v} = \begin{bmatrix} u_x - v_x \\ u_y - v_y \\ u_z - v_z \end{bmatrix}$.

Note that since they are unit vectors, $||\hat{u}|| = \sqrt{u_x^2 + u_y^2 + u_z^2} = ||\hat{v}|| = \sqrt{v_x^2 + v_y^2 + v_z^2} = 1$. The length of the difference vector

$$\begin{aligned}
||\hat{u} - \hat{v}|| &= \sqrt{(u_x - v_x)^2 + (u_y - v_y)^2 + (u_z - v_z)^2} \\
&= \sqrt{u_x^2 + u_y^2 + u_z^2 + v_x^2 + v_y^2 + v_z^2 - 2\left(u_x v_x + u_y v_y + u_z v_z\right)} \\
&= \sqrt{2 - 2\hat{u}^T\hat{v}} = \sqrt{2\left(1 - \hat{u} \cdot \hat{v}\right)}
\end{aligned}$$

From the last equality, it is evident that a larger dot product implies a smaller difference: that is, more agreement between the vectors.

2.6 Orthogonality of vectors and its physical significance

Try moving an object at right angles to the direction in which you are pushing it. You will find it impossible. The larger the angle, the less effective your force vector becomes (finally becoming totally ineffective at a 90° angle). This is why it is easy to walk on a horizontal surface (you are moving at right angles to the direction of gravitational pull, so the gravity vector is ineffective) but harder on an upward incline (the gravity vector is having some effect against you).

These physical notions are captured mathematically in the notion of a dot product. The dot product between two vectors $\vec{a}$ (say, the push vector) and $\vec{b}$ (say, the displacement of the pushed object vector) is $||\vec{a}||\,||\vec{b}||cos\theta$, where θ is the angle between the two vectors. When θ is 0 (the two vectors are aligned), $cos\theta = 1$, the maximum possible value of $cos\theta$, so push is maximally effective. As θ increases, $cos\theta$ decreases, and push becomes less and less effective. Finally, at $\theta = 90°$, $cos\theta = 0$, and push becomes completely ineffective.

Two vectors are orthogonal if their dot product is zero. Geometrically, this means the vectors are perpendicular to each other. Physically, this means the two vectors are independent: one cannot influence the other. You can say there is nothing in common between orthogonal vectors. For instance, the feature vector for d_5 is $\begin{bmatrix} 1 \\ 0 \end{bmatrix}$ and that for d_6 is $\begin{bmatrix} 0 \\ 1 \end{bmatrix}$ in table 2.1. These are orthogonal (dot product is zero), and you can easily see that none of the feature words (*gun*, *violence*) are common to both documents.

2.7 Python code: Basic vector and matrix operations via PyTorch

In this section, we use Python PyTorch code to illustrate many of the concepts discussed earlier.

> **NOTE** Fully functional code for this section, executable via Jupyter Notebook, can be found at http://mng.bz/ryzE.

2.7.1 PyTorch code for a matrix transpose

The following listing shows the PyTorch code for a matrix transpose.

Listing 2.5 Transpose

The torch.arange function creates a vector whose elements go from *start* to *stop* in increments of step. Here we create a 4×9 image corresponding to $I_{4,9}$ in equation 2.2, shown in figure 2.3.

```
I49 = torch.stack([torch.arange(0, 72, 8), torch.arange(64, 136, 8),
                   torch.arange(128, 200, 8), torch.arange(192, 264, 8)])
```

The transpose operator interchanges rows and columns. The 4×9 image becomes a 9×4 image (see figure 2.6). The element at position (i, j) is interchanged with the element at position (j, i).

```
I49_t = torch.transpose(I49, 0, 1)

for i in range(0, I49.shape[0]):
    for j in range(0, I49.shape[1]):
        assert I49[i][j] == I49_t[j][i]
```

Interchanged elements of the original and transposed matrix are equal.

```
assert torch.allclose(I49_t, I49.T, 1e-5)
```

The .T operator retrieves the transpose of an array.

2.7.2 PyTorch code for a dot product

The dot product of two vectors $\vec{a}$ and $\vec{b}$ represents the components of one vector along the other. Consider two vectors $\vec{a} = [a_1 \ a_2 \ a_3]$ and $\vec{b} = [b_1 \ b_2 \ b_3]$. Then $\vec{a}.\vec{b} = a_1b_1 + a_2b_2 + a_3b_3$.

Listing 2.6 Dot product

```
a = torch.tensor([1, 2, 3])
b = torch.tensor([4, 5, 6])
a_dot_b = torch.dot(a, b)
print("Dot product of these two vectors is: "
             "".format(a_dot_b))
```

Outputs 32: $1 * 4 + 2 * 5 + 3 * 6$

```
# Dot product of perpendicular vectors is zero
vx = torch.tensor([1, 0]) # a vector along X-axis
vy = torch.tensor([0, 1]) # a vector along Y-axis
print("Example dot product of orthogonal vectors:"
             " ".format(torch.dot(vx, vy)))
```

Outputs 0: $1 * 0 + 0 * 1$

2.7.3 PyTorch code for matrix vector multiplication

Consider a matrix $A_{m,n}$ with m rows and n columns that is multiplied with a vector $\vec{b_n}$ with n elements. The result is a m element column vector $\vec{c_m}$. In the following example, $m = 3$ and $n = 2$.

$$\begin{bmatrix} a_{11} & a_{12} \\ a_{21} & a_{22} \\ a_{31} & a_{32} \end{bmatrix} \begin{bmatrix} b_1 \\ b_2 \end{bmatrix} = \begin{bmatrix} c_1 = a_{11}b_1 + a_{12}b_2 \\ c_2 = a_{21}b_2 + a_{22}b_2 \\ c_3 = a_{31}b_2 + a_{32}b_2 \end{bmatrix}$$

In general,

$$c_i = a_{i1}b_1 + a_{i2}b_2 + \cdots + a_{in}b_n$$

Listing 2.7 Matrix vector multiplication

A linear model comprises a weight vector $\vec{w}$ and bias b.
For each training data instance $\vec{x}_i$, the model outputs $y_i = \vec{x}_i^T \vec{w} + b$.
For the training data matrix X (whose rows are training data instances), the model outputs $X\vec{w} + \vec{b} = \vec{y}$.

```
X = torch.tensor([[0.11, 0.09], [0.01, 0.02], [0.98, 0.91], [0.12, 0.21],
                  [0.98, 0.99], [0.85, 0.87], [0.03, 0.14], [0.55, 0.45],
                  [0.49, 0.51], [0.99, 0.01], [0.02, 0.89], [0.31, 0.47],
                  [0.55, 0.29], [0.87, 0.76], [0.63, 0.24]])
```

Cat-brain 15×2 training data matrix (equation 2.7)

```
w = torch.rand((2, 1))
b = 5.0
```

Random initialization of weight vector

Model training output: $\vec{y} = X\vec{w} + b$.
The scalar b is automatically replicated to create a vector.

```
y = torch.matmul(X, w) + b
```

2.7.4 PyTorch code for matrix-matrix multiplication

Consider a matrix $A_{m,p}$ with m rows and p columns. Let's multiply it with another matrix $B_{p,n}$ with p rows and n columns. The resultant matrix $C_{m,n}$ contains m rows and n columns. Note that the number of columns in the left matrix A should match the number of rows in the right matrix B:

$$\begin{bmatrix} c_{11} & c_{12} \\ c_{21} & c_{22} \\ c_{31} & c_{32} \end{bmatrix} = \begin{bmatrix} a_{11} & a_{12} \\ a_{21} & a_{22} \\ a_{31} & a_{32} \end{bmatrix} \begin{bmatrix} b_{11} & b_{12} \\ b_{21} & b_{22} \end{bmatrix}$$

$$c_{11} = a_{11}b_{11} + a_{12}b_{21}$$
$$c_{12} = a_{11}b_{12} + a_{12}b_{22}$$
$$c_{21} = a_{21}b_{11} + a_{22}b_{21}$$
$$c_{22} = a_{21}b_{12} + a_{22}b_{22}$$
$$c_{31} = a_{31}b_{11} + a_{32}b_{21}$$
$$c_{32} = a_{31}b_{12} + a_{32}b_{22}$$

In general,

$$c_{ij} = \sum_{i=1}^{p} a_{ip}b_{pj}$$

Listing 2.8 Matrix-matrix multiplication

```
A = torch.tensor([[1, 2], [3, 4], [5, 6]])
B = torch.tensor([[7, 8], [9, 10]])
```

$C = AB \implies C[i, j]$ is the dot product of the ith row of A and jth column of B.

```
C = torch.matmul(A, B)
```

$$\begin{bmatrix} 1 & 2 \\ 3 & 4 \\ 5 & 6 \end{bmatrix} \begin{bmatrix} 7 & 8 \\ 9 & 10 \end{bmatrix} = \begin{bmatrix} 25 & 28 \\ 57 & 64 \\ 89 & 100 \end{bmatrix}$$

```
w = torch.tensor([1, 2, 3])
x = torch.tensor([4, 5, 6])
assert torch.dot(w, x) == torch.matmul(w.T, x)
```

The dot product can be viewed as a row matrix multiplied by a column matrix.

2.7.5 PyTorch code for the transpose of a matrix product

Given two matrices A and B, where the number of columns in A matches the number of rows in B, the transpose of their product is the product of the individual transposes *in reversed order*: $(AB)^T = B^T A^T$.

Listing 2.9 Transpose of a matrix product

Asserts equality between $(AB)^T$ and $B^T A^T$

```
assert torch.all(torch.matmul(A, B).T == torch.matmul(B.T, A.T))
```

Applies to matrix-vector multiplication, too: $(A^T \vec{x})^T = \vec{x}^T A$

```
assert torch.all(torch.matmul(A.T, x).T == torch.matmul(x.T, A))
```

2.8 Multidimensional line and plane equations and machine learning

Geometrically speaking, what does a machine learning classifier really do? We provided the outline of an answer in section 1.4. You are invited to review that and especially figures 1.2 and 1.3. We will briefly summarize here.

Inputs to a classifier are feature vectors. These vectors can be viewed as points in some multidimensional feature space. The task of classification then boils down to separating the points belonging to different classes. The points may be all jumbled up in the input space. It is the model's job to transform them into a different (output) space where it is easier to separate the classes. A visual example of this was provided in figure 1.3.

What is the geometrical nature of the separator? In a very simple situation, such as the one depicted in figure 1.2, the separator is a line in 2D space. In real-life situations, the separator is often a line or a plane in a high-dimensional space. In more complicated situations, the separator is a curved surface, as depicted in figure 1.4.

In this section, we will study the mathematics and geometry behind two types of separators, lines, and planes in high-dimensional spaces, aka hyperlines and hyperplanes.

2.8.1 Multidimensional line equation

In high school geometry, we learned $y = mx + c$ as the equation of a line. But this does not lend itself readily to higher dimensions. Here we will study a better representation of a straight line that works equally well for any finite-dimensional space.

As shown in figure 2.8, a line joining vectors $\vec{a}$ and $\vec{b}$ can be viewed as the set of points we will encounter if we

- Start at point $\vec{a}$
- Travel along the direction $\vec{b} - \vec{a}$

Different points on the line are obtained by traveling different distances. Denoting this arbitrary distance by α, the equation of the line joining vectors $\vec{a}$ and $\vec{b}$ can be

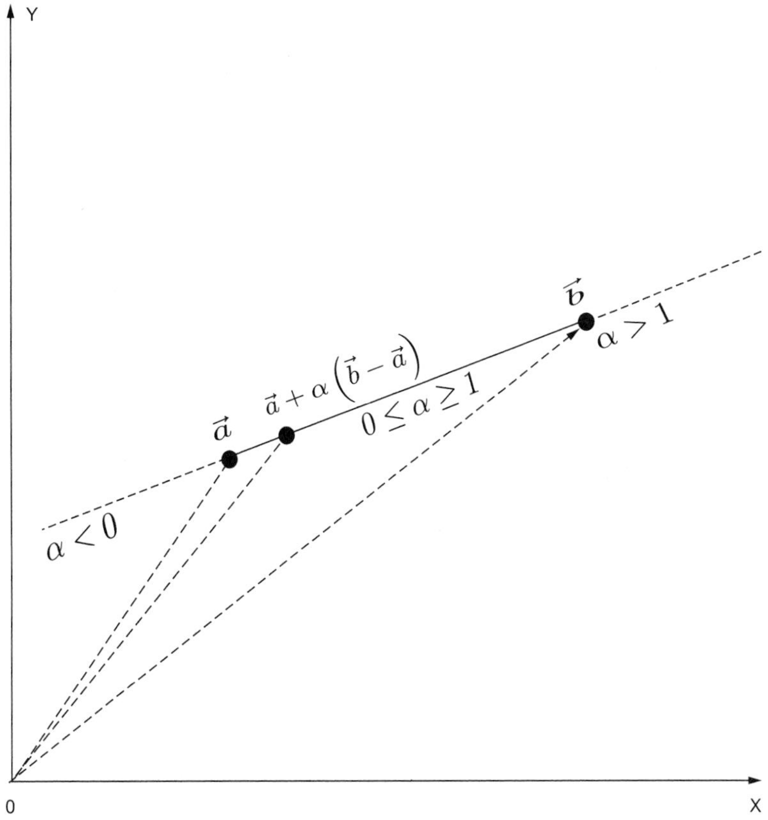

Figure 2.8 Any point $\vec{x}$ on the line joining two vectors $\vec{a}, \vec{b}$ is given by $\vec{x} = \vec{a} + \alpha\left(\vec{b} - \vec{a}\right)$.

expressed as

$$\vec{x} = \vec{a} + \alpha\left(\vec{b} - \vec{a}\right) = (1 - \alpha)\,\vec{a} + \alpha\vec{b}$$
$$\text{or }\ (1 - \alpha)\,\vec{a} + \alpha\vec{b} - \vec{x} = 0 \tag{2.12}$$

Equation 2.12 says that any point on the line joining $\vec{a}$ and $\vec{b}$ can be obtained as a weighted combination of $\vec{a}$ and $\vec{b}$, the weights being α and $1 - \alpha$. By varying α, we obtain different points on the line. Also, different ranges of α values yield different segments on the line. As shown in figure 2.8, values of α between 0 and 1 yield points between $\vec{a}$ and $\vec{b}$. Negative values of α yield points to the left of $\vec{a}$. Values of α greater than 1 yield points to the right of $\vec{b}$. This equation for a line works for any dimensions, not just two.

2.8.2 *Multidimensional planes and their role in machine learning*

In section 1.5, we encountered classifiers. Let's take another look at them. Suppose we want to create a classifier that helps us make *buy* or *no-buy* decisions on stocks based on only three input variables: (1) *momentum*, or the rate at which the stock price is changing (positive momentum means the stock price is increasing and vice versa);

(2) the *dividend* paid last quarter; and (3) *volatility*, or how much the price has fluctuated in the last quarter. Let's plot all training points in the feature space with coordinate axes corresponding to the variables *momentum, dividend, volatility*. Figure 2.9 shows that the classes can be separated by a plane in the three-dimensional feature space.

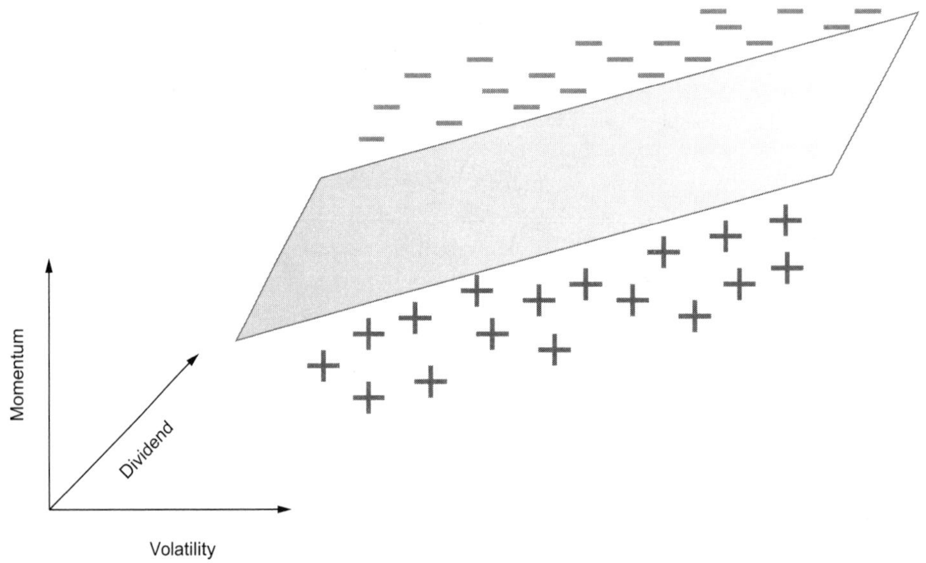

Figure 2.9 A toy machine learning classifier for stock buy vs. no-buy decision-making. A plus (+) indicates no-buy, and a dash (-) indicates buy. The decision is made based on three input variables: momentum, dividend, and volatility.

Geometrically speaking, our model simply corresponds to this plane. Input points above the plane indicate buy decisions (dashes [-]), and input points indicate no-buy decisions (pluses [+]). In general, you want to buy high-positive-momentum stocks, so points at the higher end of the momentum axis are likelier to be *buy*. However, this is not the only indicator. For more volatile stocks, we demand higher *momentum* to switch from *no-buy* to *buy*. This is why the plane slopes upward (higher *momentum*) as we move rightward (higher *volatility*). Also, we demand less *momentum* for stocks with higher *dividends*. This is why the plane slopes downward (lower *momentum*) as we go toward higher *dividends*.

Real problems have more dimensions, of course (since many more inputs are involved in the decision), and the separator becomes a hyperplane. Also, in real-life problems, the points are often too intertwined in the input space for any separator to work. We first have to apply a transformation that maps the point to an output space where it is easier to separate. Given their significance as class separators in machine learning, we will study hyperplanes in this section.

In high school 3D geometry, we learned $ax + by + cz + d = 0$ as the equation of a plane. Now we will study a version of it that works in higher dimensions.

Geometrically speaking, given a plane (in any dimension), we can find a direction called the *normal direction*, denoted $\hat{n}$, such that

- If we take any pair of points on the plane, say $\vec{x}_0$ and $\vec{x}$, ...
- The line joining $\vec{x}$ and $\vec{x}_0$—i.e., the vector $\vec{x} - \vec{x}_0$—is orthogonal to $\hat{n}$.

Thus, if we know a fixed point on the plane, say $\vec{x}_0$, then all points on the plane will satisfy

$$\hat{n} \cdot (\vec{x} - \vec{x}_0) = 0 \quad \text{or}$$
$$\hat{n}^T (\vec{x} - \vec{x}_0) = 0$$

Thus we can express the equation of a plane as

$$\hat{n}^T \vec{x} - \hat{n}^T \vec{x}_0 = 0 \tag{2.13}$$

Equation 2.13 is depicted pictorially in figure 2.10.

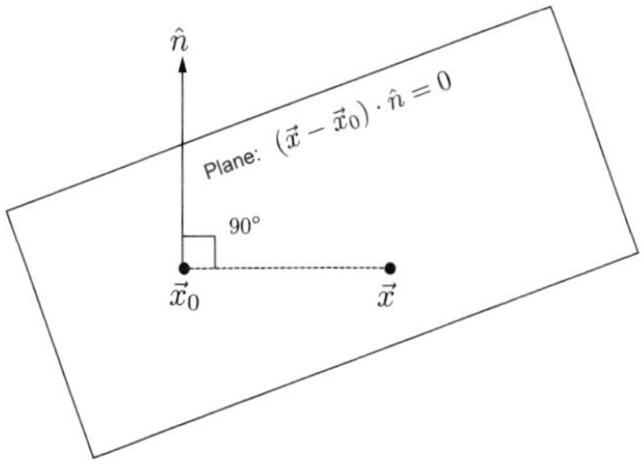

Figure 2.10 The normal to the plane is the same at all points on the plane. This is the fundamental property of a plane. $\hat{n}$ depicts that normal direction. Let $\vec{x}_0$ be a point on the plane. All other points on the plane, depicted as $\vec{x}$, will satisfy the equation $(\vec{x} - \vec{x}_0) \cdot \hat{n} = 0$. This physically says that the line joining a known point $\vec{x}_0$ on the plane and any other arbitrary point $\vec{x}$ on the plane is at right angles to the normal $\hat{n}$. This formulation works for any dimension.

In section 1.3, equation 1.3, we encountered the simplest machine learning model: a weighted sum of inputs along with a bias. Denoting the inputs as $\vec{x}$, the weights as $\vec{w}$, and the bias as b, this model was depicted as

$$\vec{w}^T \vec{x} + b = 0 \tag{2.14}$$

Comparing equations 2.13 and 2.14 , we get the geometric significance: the simple model of equation 1.3 is nothing but a planar separator. Its weight vector $\vec{w}$ corresponds to the plane's orientation (normal). The bias b corresponds to the plane's location (a fixed point on the plane). During training, we are learning the weights and biases—this is essentially learning the orientation and position of the optimal plane that will separate the training inputs. To be consistent with the machine learning paradigm, henceforth we will write the equation of a hyperplane as equation 2.14 for some constant $\vec{w}$ and b.

Note that $\vec{w}$ need not be a unit-length vector. Since the right-hand side is zero, if necessary, we can divide both sides by $||\vec{w}||$ to convert to a form like equation 2.13.

The sign of the expression $\vec{w}^T \vec{x} + b$ has special significance. All points $\vec{x}$ for which $\vec{w}^T \vec{x} + b < 0$ lie on the same side of the hyperplane. All points $\vec{x}$ for which $\vec{w}^T \vec{x} + b > 0$ lie on the other side of the hyperplane. And of course, all points $\vec{x}$ for which $\vec{w}^T \vec{x} + b = 0$ lie on the hyperplane.

It should be noted that the 3D equation $ax+by+cz+d=0$ is a special case of equation 2.14 because $ax+by+cz+d=0$ can be rewritten as

$$\begin{bmatrix} a & b & c \end{bmatrix} \begin{bmatrix} x \\ y \\ z \end{bmatrix} + d = 0$$

which is same as $\vec{w}^T\vec{x}+b=0$ with $\vec{w}=\begin{bmatrix} a \\ b \\ c \end{bmatrix}$ and $\vec{x}=\begin{bmatrix} x \\ y \\ z \end{bmatrix}$. Incidentally, this tells us that in 3D, the normal to the plane $ax+by+cz+d=0$ is $\hat{n}=\frac{1}{\sqrt{a^2+b^2+c^2}}\begin{bmatrix} a \\ b \\ c \end{bmatrix}$.

2.9 Linear combinations, vector spans, basis vectors, and collinearity preservation

By now, it should be clear that machine learning and data science are all about points in high-dimensional spaces. Consequently, it behooves us to have a decent understanding of these spaces. For instance, given a space, we may need to ask, "Would it be possible to express all points in the space in terms of a set of a few vectors? What is the smallest set of vectors we really need for that purpose?" This section is devoted to the study of these questions.

2.9.1 Linear dependence

Consider the vectors (points) shown in figure 2.11. The corresponding vectors in 2D are

$$\vec{v}_0=\begin{bmatrix} 1 \\ 1 \end{bmatrix} \qquad \vec{v}_1=\begin{bmatrix} 2 \\ 2 \end{bmatrix}$$

$$\vec{v}_2=\begin{bmatrix} 3 \\ 3 \end{bmatrix} \qquad \vec{v}_3=\begin{bmatrix} 4 \\ 4 \end{bmatrix}$$

We can find four scalars $\alpha_0=2$, $\alpha_1=2$, $\alpha_2=2$, and $\alpha_3=-3$ such that

$$\alpha_0\vec{v}_0+\alpha_1\vec{v}_1+\alpha_2\vec{v}_2+\alpha_3\vec{v}_3=\begin{bmatrix} 0 \\ 0 \end{bmatrix}$$

If we can find such scalars, not all zero, we say the vectors $\vec{v}_0$, $\vec{v}_1$, $\vec{v}_2$, and $\vec{v}_3$ are *linearly dependent*. The geometric picture to keep in mind is that points corresponding to linearly dependent vectors lie on a single straight line in the space containing them.

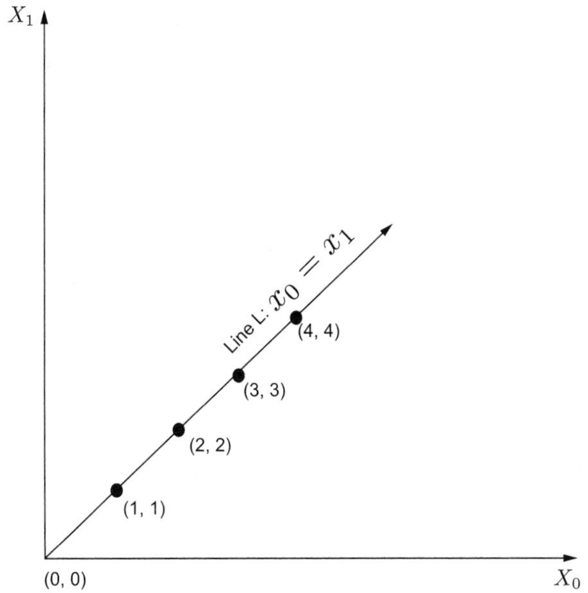

Figure 2.11 Linearly dependent points in a 2D plane

COLLINEARITY IMPLIES LINEAR DEPENDENCE

Proof: Let $\vec{a}$, $\vec{b}$ and $\vec{c}$ be three collinear vectors. From equation 2.12, there exists some $\alpha \in \mathbb{R}$ such that

$$\vec{c} = (1 - \alpha)\,\vec{a} + \alpha\vec{b}$$

This equation can be rewritten as

$$\alpha_1\vec{a} + \alpha_2\vec{b} + \alpha_3\vec{c} = 0$$

where $\alpha_1 = (1 - \alpha)$, $\alpha_2 = \alpha$ and $\alpha_3 = -1$. Thus we have proven that three collinear vectors $\vec{a}$, $\vec{b}$, and $\vec{c}$ must also be linearly dependent.

LINEAR COMBINATION

Given a set of vectors $\vec{v_1}$, $\vec{v_2}$, ... $\vec{v_n}$ and a set of scalar weights α_1,α_2, ...α_n, the weighted sum $\alpha_1\vec{v_1} + \alpha_2\vec{v_2} + + \cdots \alpha_n\vec{v_n}$ is called a *linear combination.*

GENERIC MULTIDIMENSIONAL DEFINITION OF LINEAR DEPENDENCE

A set of vectors $\vec{v_1}$, $\vec{v_2}$, ... $\vec{v_n}$ are *linearly dependent* if there exists a set of weights α_1,α_2, ...α_n, not all zeros, such that $\alpha_1\vec{v_1} + \alpha_2\vec{v_2} + + \cdots \alpha_n\vec{v_n} = 0$. For example, the row vectors $\begin{bmatrix} 1 & 1 \end{bmatrix}$ and $\begin{bmatrix} 2 & 2 \end{bmatrix}$ are linearly dependent, since $-2\begin{bmatrix} 1 & 1 \end{bmatrix} + \begin{bmatrix} 2 & 2 \end{bmatrix} = 0$.

2.9.2 *Span of a set of vectors*

Given a set of vectors $\vec{v_1}$, $\vec{v_2}$, ... $\vec{v_n}$, their *span* is defined as the set of all vectors that are linear combinations of the original set . This includes the original vectors.

For example, consider the two vectors $\vec{v}_{x\perp} = \begin{bmatrix} 1 \\ 0 \end{bmatrix}$ and $\vec{v}_{y\perp} = \begin{bmatrix} 0 \\ 1 \end{bmatrix}$. The span of these two vectors is the entire plane containing the two vectors. Any vector, for instance, the vector $\begin{bmatrix} 18 \\ 97 \end{bmatrix}$ can be expressed as a weighted sum $18\vec{v}_{x\perp} + 97\vec{v}_{y\perp}$. You can probably recognize that $\begin{bmatrix} 1 \\ 0 \end{bmatrix}$ and $\begin{bmatrix} 0 \\ 1 \end{bmatrix}$ are the familiar Cartesian coordinate axes (X-axis and Y-axis, respectively) in the 2D plane.

2.9.3 Vector spaces, basis vectors, and closure

We have been talking informally about vector spaces. It is time to define them more precisely.

VECTOR SPACES

A set of vectors (points) in n dimensions form a *vector space* if and only if the operations of *addition* and *scalar multiplication* are defined on the set. In particular, this implies that it is possible to take linear combinations of members of a vector space.

BASIS VECTORS

Given a vector space, a set of vectors that span the space is called a *basis* for the space. For instance, for the space $\mathbb{R}^2$, the two vectors $\begin{bmatrix} 1 \\ 0 \end{bmatrix}$ and $\begin{bmatrix} 0 \\ 1 \end{bmatrix}$ are basis vectors. This essentially means any vector in $\mathbb{R}^2$ can be expressed as a linear combination of these two. The notion can be extended to higher dimensions. For $\mathbb{R}^n$, the vectors $\begin{bmatrix} 1 \\ 0 \\ \vdots \\ 0 \end{bmatrix}, \begin{bmatrix} 0 \\ 1 \\ \vdots \\ 0 \end{bmatrix}, \cdots, \begin{bmatrix} 0 \\ 0 \\ \vdots \\ 1 \end{bmatrix}$ form a basis.

The alert reader has probably guessed by now that the basis vectors are related to coordinate axes. In fact, the basis vectors just described constitute the Cartesian coordinate axes.

So far, we have only seen examples of basis vectors that are mutually orthogonal, such as the dot product of the two basis vectors in $\mathbb{R}^2$ shown earlier: $\begin{bmatrix} 0 \\ 1 \end{bmatrix} \cdot \begin{bmatrix} 1 \\ 0 \end{bmatrix} = \begin{bmatrix} 0 & 1 \end{bmatrix} \begin{bmatrix} 1 \\ 0 \end{bmatrix} = 0$. However, basis vectors do not have to be orthogonal. Any pair of linearly independent vectors forms a basis in $\mathbb{R}^2$. Basis vectors, then, are by no means unique. That said, orthogonal vectors are most convenient, as we shall see later.

MINIMAL AND COMPLETE BASIS

Exactly n vectors are needed to span a space with dimensionality n. This means the basis set for a space will have at least as many elements as the dimensionality of the space.

That many basis vectors are also sufficient to form a basis. For instance, exactly n vectors are needed to form a basis in (that is, span) $\mathbb{R}^n$.

A related fact is that in $\mathbb{R}^n$, any set of m vectors with $m > n$ will be linearly dependent. In other words, the largest size of a set of linearly independent vectors in an n-dimensional space is n.

CLOSURE

A set of vectors is said to be *closed* under linear combination if and only if the linear combination of any pair of vectors in the set also belongs to the same set. Consider the set of points $\mathbb{R}^2$. Recall that this is the set of vectors with two real elements. Take any pair of vectors $\vec{a}$ and $\vec{b}$ in $\mathbb{R}^2$: for instance, $\vec{a} = \begin{bmatrix} 11.2 \\ 31.766 \end{bmatrix}$ and $\vec{b} = \begin{bmatrix} 177.01 \\ 1031.99 \end{bmatrix}$. Any linear combination of these two vectors will also comprise two real numbers—that is, will belong to $\mathbb{R}^2$. We say $\mathbb{R}^2$ is a *vector space* since it is *closed* under linear combination.

Consider the space $\mathbb{R}^2$. Geometrically speaking, this represents a two dimensional plane. Let's take two points on this plane, $\vec{a}$ and $\vec{b}$. Linear combinations of $\vec{a}, \vec{b}$ geometrically correspond to points on the line joining them. We know that if two points lie on a plane, the entire line will also lie on the plane. Thus, in two dimensions, a plane is closed under linear combinations. This is the geometrical intuition behind the notion of closure on vector spaces. It can be extended to arbitrary dimensions.

On the other hand, the set of points on the surface of a sphere is *not* closed under linear combination because the line joining an arbitrary pair of points on this set will not wholly lie on the surface of that sphere.

2.10 Linear transforms: Geometric and algebraic interpretations

Inputs to a machine learning or data science system are typically feature vectors (introduced in section 2.1) in high-dimensional spaces. Each individual dimension of the feature vector corresponds to a particular property of the input. Thus, the feature vector is a descriptor for the particular input instance. It can be viewed as a point in the feature space. We usually transform the points to a friendlier space where it is easier to perform the analysis we are trying to do. For instance, if we are building a classifier, we try to transform the input into a space where the points belonging to different classes are more segregated (see section 1.3 in general and figure 1.3 in particular for simple examples). Sometimes we transform to simplify the data, eliminating axes along which there is scant variation in the data. Given their significance in machine learning, in this section we will study the basics of transforms.

Informally, a transform is an operation that maps a set of points (vectors) to another. Given a set S of $n \times 1$ vectors, any $m \times n$ matrix T can be viewed as a transform. If $\vec{v}$ belongs to the set S, multiplication with the matrix T will map (transform) $\vec{v}$ to a vector $T\vec{v}$. We will later see that matrix multiplication is a subclass of transforms that preserve collinearity—points that lie on a straight line before the transformation will continue to lie on a (possibly different) straight line post the transformation. For instance, consider the matrix

$$R = \begin{bmatrix} \frac{1}{\sqrt{2}} & \frac{1}{\sqrt{2}} \\ -\frac{1}{\sqrt{2}} & \frac{1}{\sqrt{2}} \end{bmatrix}$$

In section 2.14, we will see that this is a special kind of matrix called a rotation matrix; for now, simply consider it an example of a matrix. R is a transformation operator that maps a point in a 2D plane to another point in the same plane. In mathematical notation, $R : \mathbb{R}^2 \rightarrow \mathbb{R}^2$. In fact, as depicted in figure 2.14, this transformation (multiplication by matrix R) rotates the position vector of a point in the 2D plane by an angle of $45°$.

The output and input points may belong to different spaces in such transforms. For instance, consider the matrix

$$P = \begin{bmatrix} 1 & 0 & 0 \\ 0 & 1 & 0 \end{bmatrix}$$

It is not hard to see that this matrix projects 3D points to the 2D X-Y plane:

$$P \begin{bmatrix} x \\ y \\ z \end{bmatrix} = \begin{bmatrix} x \\ y \end{bmatrix}$$

Hence, this transformation (multiplication by matrix P) projects points from three to two dimensions. In mathematical parlance, $P : \mathbb{R}^3 \rightarrow \mathbb{R}^2$.

The transforms R and P share a common property: *they preserve collinearity*. This means a set of vectors (points) $\vec{a}, \vec{b}, \vec{c}, \cdots$ that originally lay on a straight line remain so after the transformation.

Let's check this out for the rotation transformation in the example from section 2.9. There we saw four vectors:

$$\vec{o} = \begin{bmatrix} 0 \\ 0 \end{bmatrix} \qquad \vec{a} = \begin{bmatrix} 1 \\ 1 \end{bmatrix}$$

$$\vec{b} = \begin{bmatrix} 2 \\ 2 \end{bmatrix} \qquad \vec{c} = \begin{bmatrix} 3 \\ 3 \end{bmatrix}$$

These vectors all lie on a straight $L : x = y$. The rotation transformed versions of these vectors are

$$\vec{o}' = R\vec{o} = \begin{bmatrix} 0 \\ 0 \end{bmatrix} \qquad \vec{a}' = R\vec{a} = \begin{bmatrix} \sqrt{2} \\ 0 \end{bmatrix}$$

$$\vec{b}' = R\vec{b} = \begin{bmatrix} 2\sqrt{2} \\ 0 \end{bmatrix} \qquad \vec{c}' = R\vec{c} = \begin{bmatrix} 3\sqrt{2} \\ 0 \end{bmatrix}$$

It is trivial to see that the transformed vectors also lie on a (different) straight line. In fact, $\vec{o}'$, $\vec{a}'$, $\vec{b}'$, $\vec{c}'$ lie on the Y-axis, which is the 45° rotated version of the original line $y = x$.

The projection transform represented by matrix P also preserves collinearity. Consider four collinear vectors in 3D:

$$\vec{o} = \begin{bmatrix} 0 \\ 0 \\ 0 \end{bmatrix} \qquad \vec{a} = \begin{bmatrix} 1 \\ 1 \\ 1 \end{bmatrix}$$

$$\vec{b} = \begin{bmatrix} 2 \\ 2 \\ 2 \end{bmatrix} \qquad \vec{c} = \begin{bmatrix} 3 \\ 3 \\ 3 \end{bmatrix}$$

The corresponding transformed vectors

$$\vec{o}' = P\vec{o} = \begin{bmatrix} 0 \\ 0 \end{bmatrix} \qquad \vec{a}' = P\vec{a} = \begin{bmatrix} 1 \\ 1 \end{bmatrix}$$

$$\vec{b}' = P\vec{b} = \begin{bmatrix} 2 \\ 2 \end{bmatrix} \qquad \vec{c}' = P\vec{c} = \begin{bmatrix} 3 \\ 3 \end{bmatrix}$$

also lie on a straight line in 2D.

The class of transforms that preserves collinearity are known as *linear transforms.* They can always be represented as a matrix multiplication. Conversely, all matrix multiplications represent a linear transformation. A more formal definition is provided later.

2.10.1 Generic multidimensional definition of linear transforms

A function ϕ is a linear transform if and only if it satisfies

$$\phi\left(\alpha\vec{a} + \beta\vec{b}\right) = \alpha\phi\left(\vec{a}\right) + \beta\phi\left(\vec{b}\right) \quad \forall \alpha, \beta \in \mathbb{R} \tag{2.15}$$

In other words, *a transform is linear if and only if the transform of the linear combination of two vectors is the same as the linear combination (with the same weights) of the transforms of individual vectors.* (This can be remembered as: *Linear transform means transforms of linear combinations are same as linear combinations of transforms.*) Multiplication with a rotation or projection matrix (shown earlier) is a linear transform.

2.10.2 All matrix-vector multiplications are linear transforms

Let's verify that matrix multiplication satisfies the definition of linear mapping (equation 2.15). Let $\vec{a}, \vec{b} \in \mathbb{R}^n$ be two arbitrary n-dimensional vectors and $A_{m,n}$ be an arbitrary matrix with n columns. Then following the standard rules of matrix-vector multiplication,

$$A\left(\alpha\vec{a} + \beta\vec{b}\right) = \alpha\left(A\vec{a}\right) + \beta\left(A\vec{b}\right)$$

which mimics equation 2.15 with ϕ replaced with matrix A. Thus we have proven that all matrix multiplications are linear transforms. The reverse is not true. In particular, linear transforms that operate on infinite-dimensional vectors are not matrices. But all linear transforms that operate on finite-dimensional vectors can be expressed as matrices. (The proof is a bit more complicated and will be skipped.)

Thus, in finite dimensions, multiplication with a matrix and linear transformation are one and the same thing. In section 2.3, we saw the array view of matrices. The corresponding geometric view, that all matrices represent linear transformation, was presented in this section.

Let's finish this section by studying an example of a transform that is *not* linear. Consider the function

$$\phi\left(\vec{x}\right) = ||\vec{x}||$$

for $\vec{x} \in \mathbb{R}^n$. This function ϕ maps n-dimensional vectors to a scalar that is the length of the vector, $\phi : \mathbb{R}^n \to \mathbb{R}$. We will examine if it satisfies equation 2.15 with $\alpha_1 = \alpha_2 = 1$. For two specific vectors $\vec{a}, \vec{b} \in \mathbb{R}^n$,

$$\phi\left(\vec{a}\right) = \phi\left(\begin{bmatrix} a_1 \\ a_2 \\ \cdots \\ a_n \end{bmatrix}\right) = \sqrt{a_1^2 + a_2^2 + \cdots a_n^2}$$

$$\phi\left(\vec{b}\right) = \phi\left(\begin{bmatrix} b_1 \\ b_2 \\ \cdots \\ b_n \end{bmatrix}\right) = \sqrt{b_1^2 + b_2^2 + \cdots b_n^2}$$

Now

$$\phi\left(\vec{a}\right) + \phi\left(\vec{b}\right) = \sqrt{a_1^2 + a_2^2 + \cdots a_n^2} + \sqrt{b_1^2 + b_2^2 + \cdots b_n^2}$$

and

$$\phi\left(\vec{a} + \vec{b}\right) = \phi\left(\begin{bmatrix} a_1 + b_1 \\ a_2 + b_2 \\ \vdots \\ a_n + b_n \end{bmatrix}\right) = \sqrt{(a_1 + b_1)^2 + (a_2 + b_2)^2 + \cdots (a_n + b_n)^2}$$

Clearly, these two are not equal; hence, we have violated equation 2.15: ϕ is a nonlinear mapping.

2.11 Multidimensional arrays, multilinear transforms, and tensors

We often hear the term *tensor* in connection with machine learning. Google's famous machine learning platform is named *TensorFlow*. In this section, we will introduce you to the concept of a tensor.

2.11.1 Array view: Multidimensional arrays of numbers

A tensor may be viewed as a generalized n-dimensional array—although, strictly speaking, not all multidimensional arrays are tensors. We will learn more about the distinction between multidimensional arrays and tensors when we study multilinear transforms. For now, we will not worry too much about the distinction. A vector can be viewed as a 1 tensor, a matrix is a 2 tensor, and a scalar is a 0 tensor.

In section 2.3, we saw that digital images are represented as 2D arrays (matrices). A color image—where each pixel is represented by three colors, R, G, and B (red, green, and blue)—is an example of a multidimensional array or tensor. This is because it can be viewed as a combination of three images: the R, G, and B images, respectively.

The inputs and outputs to each layer in a neural network are also tensors.

2.12 Linear systems and matrix inverse

Machine learning today is usually an iterative process. Given a set of training data, you want to estimate a set of machine parameters that will yield target values (or close approximations to them) on training inputs. The number of training inputs and the size of the parameter set are often very large. This makes it impossible to have a closed-form solution where we solve for the unknown parameters in a single step. Solutions are usually iterative. We start with a guessed set of values for the parameters and iteratively improve the guess by processing training data.

Having said that, we often encounter smaller problems in real life. We are better off using more traditional closed-form techniques here since they are much faster and more accurate. This section is devoted to gaining some insights into these techniques.

Let's go back to our familiar cat-brain problem and refer to its training data in table 2.2. As before, we are still talking about a weighted sum model with three parameters: weights w_0, w_1 and bias b. Let's focus on the top three rows from the table, repeated here in table 2.3 for convenience.

Table 2.3 Example training dataset for our toy machine learning–based cat brain

	Input value: Hardness	Input value: Sharpness	Output: Threat score
0	0.11	0.09	−0.8
1	0.01	0.02	−0.97
2	0.98	0.91	0.89

The training data says that with a hardness value 0.11 and a sharpness value 0.09, we expect the system's output to match (or closely approximate) the target value −0.8, and so on. In other words, our estimated values for parameters w_0, w_1, b should ideally satisfy

$$0.11w_0 + 0.09w_1 + b = -0.8$$
$$0.01w_0 + 0.02w_1 + b = -0.97$$
$$0.98w_0 + 0.91w_1 + b = 0.89$$

We can express this via matrix multiplication as the following equation:

$$\begin{bmatrix} 0.11 & 0.09 & 1 \\ 0.01 & 0.02 & 1 \\ 0.98 & 0.91 & 1 \end{bmatrix} \begin{bmatrix} w_0 \\ w_1 \\ b \end{bmatrix} = \begin{bmatrix} -0.08 \\ -0.97 \\ 0.89 \end{bmatrix}$$

How do we obtain the values of w_0, w_1, b that make this equation true? That is, how do we solve this equation? There are formal methods (discussed later) to directly solve such equations for w_0, w_1, and b (in this very simple example, you might just "see" that $w_0 = 1$, $w_1 = 1$, $b = -1$ solves the equation, but we need a general method).

This equation is an example of a class of equations called a *linear system.* A linear system in n unknowns $x_1, x_2, x_3, \cdots, x_n$,

$$a_{11}x_1 + a_{12}x_2 + a_{13}x_3 + \cdots + a_{1n}x_n = b_1$$
$$a_{21}x_1 + a_{22}x_2 + a_{23}x_3 + \cdots + a_{2n}x_n = b_2$$
$$\vdots$$
$$a_{n1}x_1 + a_{n2}x_2 + a_{n3}x_3 + \cdots + a_{nn}x_n = b_n$$

can be expressed via matrix and vectors as

$$A\vec{x} = \vec{b}$$

where

$$A = \begin{bmatrix} a_{11} & a_{12} & a_{13} & \cdots & a_{1n} \\ a_{21} & a_{22} & a_{23} & \cdots & a_{2n} \\ \vdots & \vdots & \vdots & \vdots & \vdots \\ a_{n1} & a_{n2} & a_{n3} & \cdots & a_{nn} \end{bmatrix} \text{ and } \quad \vec{x} = \begin{bmatrix} x_1 \\ x_2 \\ \cdots x_n \end{bmatrix} \text{ and } \vec{b} = \begin{bmatrix} b_1 \\ b_2 \\ \cdots \\ b_n \end{bmatrix}$$

Although equivalent, the matrix depiction is more compact and dimension-independent. In machine learning, we usually have many variables (thousands), so this compactness makes a significant difference. Also, $A\vec{x} = \vec{b}$ looks similar to the one-variable equation we know so well: $ax = b$. In fact, many intuitions can be transferred from 1D to higher dimensions.

What is the solution to the 1D equation? You may have learned it in fifth grade: The solution of $ax = b$ is $x = a^{-1}b$ where $a^{-1} = \frac{1}{a}$, $a \neq 0$.

We can use the same notation in all dimensions. The solution of $A\vec{x} = \vec{b}$ is $\vec{x} = A^{-1}\vec{b}$, where A^{-1} is the matrix inverse. The inverse matrix A^{-1} has the determinant of the matrix, $\frac{1}{det(A)}$, as a factor. We will not discuss determinant and inverse matrix computation here—you can obtain that in any standard linear algebra textbook—but will state some facts that lend insights into determinants and inverse matrices:

- The inverse matrix A^{-1} is related to matrix A in the same way the scalar a^{-1} is related to the scalar a. a^{-1} exists if and only if $a \neq 0$. Analogously, A^{-1} exists if $det(A) \neq 0$, where $det(A)$ refers to the determinant of a matrix.
- The product of a scalar a and its inverse a^{-1} is 1. Analogously, $AA^{-1} = A^{-1}A = \mathbf{I}$, where $\mathbf{I}$ denotes the identity matrix that is the higher-dimension analog for 1 in scalar arithmetic. It is a matrix in which the diagonal terms are 1 and all other terms are 0. The n-dimensional identity matrix is as follows:

$$\mathbf{I}_{n,n} = \begin{bmatrix} 1 & 0 & 0 & \cdots & 0 \\ 0 & 1 & 0 & \cdots & 0 \\ 0 & 0 & 1 & \cdots & 0 \\ \vdots & & & & \\ 0 & 0 & 0 & \cdots & 1 \end{bmatrix}$$

  When there is no subscript, the dimensionality can be inferred from the context. For any matrix A, $\mathbf{I}A = A\mathbf{I} = A$. For any vector $\vec{a}$, $\mathbf{I}\vec{a} = \vec{a}^T\mathbf{I} = \vec{a}$. These can be easily verified using the rules of matrix multiplication.

There are completely precise but tedious rules for computing determinants and matrix inverses. Despite the importance of the concept, we rarely need to compute them in life as all linear algebra software packages provide routines to do this. Furthermore, computing matrix inverses is not good programming practice because it is numerically unstable. We will not discuss the direct computation of determinant or matrix inverse here (except that in section A.2 of the appendix, we show how to compute the determinant of a 2×2 matrix). We will discuss pseudo-inverses, which have more significance in machine learning.

2.12.1 Linear systems with zero or near-zero determinants, and ill-conditioned systems

We saw earlier that a linear system $A\vec{x} = \vec{b}$ has the solution $\vec{x} = A^{-1}\vec{b}$. But A^{-1} has $\frac{1}{det(A)}$ as a factor. What if the determinant is zero?

The short answer: when the determinant is zero, the linear system cannot be exactly solved. We may still attempt to come up with an approximate answer (see section 2.12.3), but an exact solution is not possible.

Let's examine the situation a bit more closely with the aid of an example. Consider the following system of equations:

$$\begin{aligned} x_1 + x_2 &= 2 \\ 2x_1 + 2x_2 &= 4 \end{aligned}$$

It can be rewritten as a linear system with a square matrix:

$$\begin{bmatrix} 1 & 1 \\ 2 & 2 \end{bmatrix} \begin{bmatrix} x_1 \\ x_2 \end{bmatrix} = \begin{bmatrix} 2 \\ 4 \end{bmatrix}$$

But you can quickly see that the system of equations cannot be solved. The second equation is really the same as the first. In fact, we can obtain the second by multiplying the first by a scalar, 2. Hence, we don't really have two equations: we have only one, so the system cannot be solved. Now examine the row vectors of matrix A. They are $\begin{bmatrix} 1 & 1 \end{bmatrix}$ and $\begin{bmatrix} 2 & 2 \end{bmatrix}$. They are linearly dependent because $-2\begin{bmatrix} 1 & 1 \end{bmatrix} + \begin{bmatrix} 2 & 2 \end{bmatrix} = 0$. Now examine the determinant of matrix A (section A.2 of the appendix shows how to compute the determinant of a 2×2 matrix). It is $2 \times 1 - 1 \times 2 = 0$. These results are not coincidences. Any one of them implies the other. In fact, the following statements about the linear system $A\vec{x} = \vec{b}$ (with a square matrix) are equivalent:

- Matrix A has a row/column that can be expressed as a weighted sum of the others.
- Matrix A has linearly dependent rows or columns.
- Matrix A has zero determinant (such matrices are called *singular* matrices).
- The inverse of matrix A (i.e., A^{-1}) does not exist. A is called *singular*.
- The linear system cannot be solved.

The system is trying to tell you that you have fewer equations than you think you have, and you cannot solve the system of equations.

Sometimes the determinant is not exactly zero but close to zero. Although solvable in theory, such systems are *numerically unstable*. Small changes in input cause the result to change drastically. For instance, consider this nearly singular matrix:

$$A = \begin{bmatrix} 2 & 1 \\ 4 & 2.001 \end{bmatrix} \tag{2.16}$$

Its determinant is 0.002, close to zero. Let $\vec{b} = \begin{bmatrix} 3 \\ 6 \end{bmatrix}$ be a vector.

$$A^{-1} = \begin{bmatrix} 1000.5 & -500.0 \\ -2000. & 1000.0 \end{bmatrix} \tag{2.17}$$

(Note how large the elements of A^{-1} are. This is due to division by an extremely small determinant and, in turn, causes the instability illustrated next.) The solution to the equation $A\vec{x} = \vec{b}$ is $\vec{x} = A^{-1}\vec{b} = \begin{bmatrix} 1.5 \\ 0 \end{bmatrix}$. But if we change $\vec{b}$ just a little and make $\vec{b} = \begin{bmatrix} 3 \\ 6.01 \end{bmatrix}$, the solution changes to a drastically different $\vec{x} = A^{-1}\vec{b} = \begin{bmatrix} -3.5 \\ 10.0 \end{bmatrix}$. This is inherently unstable and arises from the near singularity of the matrix A. Such linear systems are called *ill-conditioned.*

2.12.2 PyTorch code for inverse, determinant, and singularity testing of matrices

Inverting a matrix and computing its determinant can be done with a single function call from the linear algebra package linalg.

Listing 2.10 Matrix inverse for an invertible matrix (nonzero determinant)

```
def determinant(A):
    return torch.linalg.det(A)

def inverse(A):
    return torch.linalg.inv(A)

A = torch.tensor([[2, 3], [2, 2]], dtype=torch.float)

A_inv = inverse(A)

I = torch.eye(2)

assert torch.all(torch.matmul(A, A_inv) == I)
assert torch.all(torch.matmul(A_inv, A) == I)

assert torch.all(torch.matmul(I, A) ==  A)
assert torch.all(A == torch.matmul(A,I))
```

Annotations:
- `A = torch.tensor(...)`: $A = \begin{bmatrix} 2 & 3 \\ 3 & 2 \end{bmatrix}$
- `A_inv = inverse(A)`: $A = \begin{bmatrix} -1 & 1.5 \\ 1 & -1 \end{bmatrix}$
- `I = torch.eye(2)`: **The PyTorch function $torch.eye(n)$ generates an identity matrix I of size n.**
- **Verify** $\begin{bmatrix} 2 & 3 \\ 3 & 2 \end{bmatrix}\begin{bmatrix} -1 & 1.5 \\ 1 & -1 \end{bmatrix} = \begin{bmatrix} 1 & 0 \\ 0 & 1 \end{bmatrix}$
- **I is like 1. Verify $AI = IA = A$.**

A singular matrix is a matrix whose determinant is zero. Such matrices are non-invertible. Linear systems of equations with singular matrices cannot be solved.

Listing 2.11 Singular matrix

```
B = torch.tensor([[1, 1], [2, 2]], dtype=torch.float)
try:

    B_inv = inverse(B)

except RuntimeError as e:
    print("B cannot be inverted: ".format(B, e))
```

Annotations:
- `B = torch.tensor(...)`: $B = \begin{bmatrix} 1 & 1 \\ 2 & 2 \end{bmatrix}$
- `B_inv = inverse(B)`: **Determinant = $1 \times 2 - 2 \times 1 = 0$. Singular matrix; attempting to compute the inverse causes a runtime error.**

2.12.3 Over- and under-determined linear systems in machine learning

What if the matrix A is *not* square? This implies that the number of equations does not match the number of unknowns. Does such a system even make sense? Surprisingly, it does. As a rule, machine learning systems fall in this category: the number of equations corresponds to the number of training data instances collected, while the number of unknowns is a function of the number of weights in the model which is a function of the particular model family chosen to represent the system. These are independent of each other. As stated earlier, we often solve these systems iteratively. Nonetheless, it is important to understand linear systems with nonsquare matrices A, to gain insight.

There are two possible cases, assuming that the matrix A is $m \times n$ (m rows and n columns):

- Case 1: $m > n$ (more equations than unknowns; overdetermined system)
- Case 2: $m < n$ (fewer equations than unknown; underdetermined system)

For instance, table 2.2 leads to an overdetermined linear system. Let's write the system of equations:

$$
\begin{aligned}
0.11w_0 + 0.09w_1 + b &= -0.8\\
0.01w_0 + 0.02w_1 + b &= -0.97\\
0.98w_0 + 0.91w_1 + b &= 0.89\\
0.12w_0 + 0.21w_1 + b &= -0.68\\
0.98w_0 + 0.99w_1 + b &= 0.95\\
0.85w_0 + 0.87w_1 + b &= 0.74\\
0.03w_0 + 0.14w_1 + b &= -0.88\\
0.55w_0 + 0.45w_1 + b &= 0.00
\end{aligned}
$$

These yield the following overdetermined linear system:

$$
\begin{bmatrix}
0.11 & 0.09 & 1\\
0.01 & 0.02 & 1\\
0.98 & 0.91 & 1\\
0.12 & 0.21 & 1\\
0.98 & 0.99 & 1\\
0.85 & 0.87 & 1\\
0.03 & 0.14 & 1\\
0.55 & 0.45 & 1
\end{bmatrix}
\begin{bmatrix}
w_0\\
w_1\\
b
\end{bmatrix}
=
\begin{bmatrix}
-0.8\\
-0.97\\
0.89\\
-0.68\\
0.95\\
0.74\\
-0.88\\
0.00
\end{bmatrix}
\tag{2.18}
$$

This is a nonsquare 15×3 linear system. There are only 3 unknowns to solve for (w_0, w_1, b), and there are 15 equations. This is highly redundant: we needed only three equations and could have solved it via linear system solution techniques (section 2.12). But the important thing to note is this: *the equations are not fully consistent.* There is no single set of values for the unknown that will satisfy all of them. In other words, the training data is noisy—an almost universal occurrence in real-life machine learning systems. Consequently, we have to find a solution that is optimal (causes as little error as possible) over all the equations.

We want to solve it such that the overall error $||A\vec{x} - \vec{b}||$ is minimized. In other words, we are looking for $\vec{x}$ such that $A\vec{x}$ is as close to $\vec{b}$ as possible. This closed-form (that is, non-iterative) method is an extremely important precursor to machine learning and data science. We will revisit this multiple times, most notably in sections 2.12.4 and 4.5.

2.12.4 Moore Penrose pseudo-inverse of a matrix

The pseudo-inverse is a handy technique to solve over- or under-determined linear systems. Suppose we have an overdetermined system with the not-necessarily square $m \times n$ matrix A:

$$A\vec{x} = \vec{b}$$

Since A is not guaranteed to be square, we can take neither the determinant nor the inverse in general. So the usual $A^{-1}\vec{b}$ does not work. At this point, we observe that although the inverse cannot be taken, transposing the matrix is always possible. Let's multiply both sides of the equation with A^T:

$$A\vec{x} = \vec{b} \Leftrightarrow A^T A\vec{x} = A^T\vec{b}$$

Notice that $A^T A$ is a square matrix: its dimensions are $(m \times n) \times (n \times m) = m \times m$. Let's assume, without proof for the moment, that it is invertible. Then

$$A\vec{x} = \vec{b} \Leftrightarrow A^T A\vec{x} = A^T\vec{b} \Leftrightarrow \vec{x} = \left(A^T A\right)^{-1} A^T\vec{b}$$

Hmmm, not bad; we seem to be onto something. In fact, we just derived the *pseudo-inverse* of matrix A, denoted $A^+ = \left(A^T A\right)^{-1} A^T$. Unlike the inverse, the pseudo-inverse does not need the matrix to be square with linearly independent rows. Much like the regular linear system, we get the solution of the (possibly nonsquare) system of equations as $A\vec{x} = \vec{b} \Leftrightarrow \vec{x} = A^+\vec{b}$.

The pseudo-inverse-based solution actually minimizes the error $||A\vec{x} - \vec{b}||$. We will provide an intuitive proof of that in section 2.12.5. Meanwhile, you are encouraged to write the Python code to evaluate $\left(A^T A\right)^{-1} A^T\vec{b}$ and verify that it approximately yields the expected answer $\begin{bmatrix} 1 \\ 1 \\ -1 \end{bmatrix}$ for equation 2.18.

2.12.5 Pseudo-inverse of a matrix: A beautiful geometric intuition

A matrix $A_{m \times n}$ can be rewritten in terms of its column vectors as $\left[\vec{a}_1, \vec{a}_2, \ldots \vec{a}_n\right]$, where $\vec{a}_1 \ldots \vec{a}_n$ are all m-dimensional vectors. Then if $\vec{x} = \begin{bmatrix} x_1 \\ x_2 \\ \ldots \\ x_n \end{bmatrix}$, we get $A\vec{x} = x_1\vec{a}_1 + x_2\vec{a}_2 + \cdots x_n\vec{a}_n$. In other words, $A\vec{x}$ is just a linear combination of the column vectors of A with the elements of $\vec{x}$ as the weights (you are encouraged to write out a small 3×3 system and verify this). The space of all vectors of the form $A\vec{x}$ (that is, the linear span of the column vectors of A) is known as the *column space* of A.

The solution to the linear system of equations $A\vec{x} = \vec{b}$ can be viewed as finding the $\vec{x}$ that minimizes the difference of $A\vec{x}$ and $\vec{b}$: that is, minimizes $||A\vec{x} - \vec{b}||$. This means we are trying to find a point in the column space of A that is closest to the point $\vec{b}$. Note that this interpretation does not assume a square matrix A. Nor does it assume a nonzero determinant. In the friendly case where the matrix A is square and invertible, we can find a vector $\vec{x}$ such that $A\vec{x}$ becomes exactly equal to $\vec{b}$, which makes $||A\vec{x} - \vec{b}|| = 0$. If A is not square, we will try to find $\vec{x}$ such that $A\vec{x}$ is closer to $\vec{b}$ than any other vector in the column space of A. Mathematically speaking,[4]

$$||A\vec{x} - \vec{b}|| \leq ||A\vec{y} - \vec{b}|| \quad \forall \vec{y} \in \Re^n \tag{2.19}$$

From geometry, we intuitively know that the closest point to $\vec{b}$ in the column space of A is obtained by dropping a perpendicular from $\vec{b}$ to the column space of A (see figure 2.12). The point where this perpendicular meets the column space is called the *projection* of $\vec{b}$ on the column space of A. The solution vector $\vec{x}$ to equation 2.19 that we are looking for should correspond to the projection of $\vec{b}$ on the column space of A. This in turn means $\vec{b} - A\vec{x}$ is orthogonal (perpendicular) to all vectors in the column space of A (see figure 2.12). We represent arbitrary vectors in the column space of A as $A\vec{y}$ for arbitrary $\vec{y}$. Hence, for all such $\vec{y}$,

$$\begin{aligned}(A\vec{y}) \perp \left(\vec{b} - A\vec{x}\right) &\Leftrightarrow (A\vec{y})^T \left(\vec{b} - A\vec{x}\right) = 0 \\ &\Leftrightarrow y^T A^T \left(\vec{b} - A\vec{x}\right) = 0\end{aligned}$$

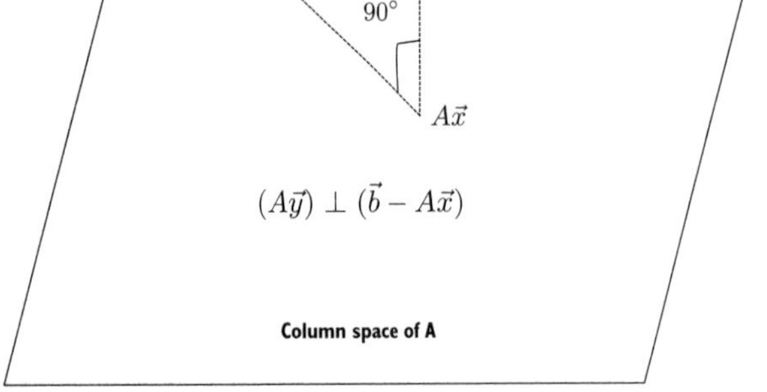

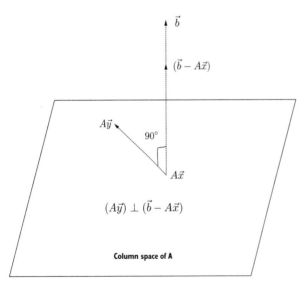

Figure 2.12 Solving a linear system $A\vec{x} = \vec{b}$ is equivalent to finding the point on the column space of A that is closest to $\vec{b}$. This means we have to drop a perpendicular from $\vec{b}$ to column space of A. If $A\vec{x}$ represents the point where that perpendicular meets the column space (aka projection), the difference vector $\vec{b} - A\vec{x}$ corresponds to the line joining $\vec{b}$ and its projection $A\vec{x}$. This line will be perpendicular to all vectors in the column space of A. Equivalently, it is perpendicular to $A\vec{y}$ for any arbitrary $\vec{y}$.

[4] The mathematical symbol $\forall$ stands for "for all." Thus, $\forall \vec{y} \in \Re^n$ means "all vectors y in the n-dimensional space."

For the previous equation to be true for all vectors $\vec{y}$, we must have $A^T\left(\vec{b}-A\vec{x}\right)=0$. Thus, we have

$$\begin{aligned}&A^T\left(\vec{b}-A\vec{x}\right)=0\\ \Leftrightarrow\ &A^TA\vec{x}=A^T\vec{b}\\ \Leftrightarrow\ &\vec{x}=\left(A^TA\right)^{-1}A^T\vec{b}\end{aligned}$$

which is exactly the Moore-Penrose pseudo-inverse.

For a machine learning-centric example, consider the overdetermined system corresponding to the cat brain earlier in the chapter. There are 15 training examples, each with input and desired outputs specified.

Our goal is to determine three unknowns w_0, w_1, and b such that for each training input $\vec{x}_i=\begin{bmatrix}x_{i,0}\\ x_{i,1}\end{bmatrix}$, the model output

$$y_i=x_{i,0}w_0+x_{i,1}w_1+b=\begin{bmatrix}x_{i,0} & x_{i,1}\end{bmatrix}\begin{bmatrix}w_0\\ w_1\end{bmatrix}+b=\begin{bmatrix}x_{i,0} & x_{i,1} & 1\end{bmatrix}\begin{bmatrix}w_0\\ w_1\\ b\end{bmatrix} \tag{2.20}$$

matches the desired output (aka ground truth) $\bar{y}_i$ as closely as possible.

NOTE We employed a neat trick here: we added a 1 to the right of the input, which allows us to depict the entire system (including the bias) in a single compact matrix-vector multiplication. We call this *augmentation*—we augment the input row vector with an extra 1 on the right.

Collating all the training examples together, we get

$$\begin{bmatrix}x_{0,0} & x_{0,1} & 1\\ x_{1,0} & x_{1,1} & 1\\ \vdots & \vdots & \vdots\\ x_{N,0} & x_{N,1} & 1\end{bmatrix}\begin{bmatrix}w_0\\ w_1\\ b\end{bmatrix}=\begin{bmatrix}y_0\\ y_1\\ \cdots\\ y_N\end{bmatrix} \tag{2.21}$$

which can be expressed compactly as

$$X\vec{w}=\vec{y}$$

where X is the augmented input matrix with a rightmost column of all 1s. The goal is to minimize $\|\vec{y}-\bar{\vec{y}}\|$. To this end, we formulate the over-determined linear system

$$X\vec{w}=\bar{\vec{y}}$$

Note that *this is not a classic system of equations—it has more equations than unknowns.* We cannot solve this via matrix inversion. We *can*, however, use the pseudo-inverse mechanism to solve it. The resulting solution yields the "best fit" or "best effort" solution, which minimizes the total error over all the training examples.

The exact numerical system (repeated here for ease of reference) is

$$X = \begin{bmatrix} 0.11 & 0.09 & 1.00 \\ 0.01 & 0.02 & 1.00 \\ 0.98 & 0.91 & 1.00 \\ 0.12 & 0.21 & 1.00 \\ 0.98 & 0.99 & 1.00 \\ 0.85 & 0.87 & 1.00 \\ 0.03 & 0.14 & 1.00 \\ 0.55 & 0.45 & 1.00 \end{bmatrix} \quad \vec{y} = \begin{bmatrix} -0.8 \\ -0.97 \\ 0.89 \\ -0.67 \\ 0.97 \\ 0.72 \\ -0.83 \\ 0.00 \end{bmatrix} \quad \vec{w} = \begin{bmatrix} w_0 \\ w_1 \\ b \end{bmatrix} \tag{2.22}$$

We solve for $\vec{w}$ using the pseudo-inverse formula $\vec{w} = (X^T X)^{-1} X^T \vec{y}$

2.12.6 PyTorch code to solve overdetermined systems

NOTE Fully functional code for this section, executable via Jupyter Notebook, can be found at http://mng.bz/PPJ2.

Listing 2.12 Solving an overdetermined system using the pseudo-inverse

```
def pseudo_inverse(A):
    return torch.matmul(torch.linalg.inv(torch.matmul(A.T, A)), A.T)

X = torch.column_stack((X, torch.ones(15)))

w = torch.matmul(pseudo_inverse(X), y)

print("The solution is ".format(w))
```

- X is the augmented data matrix from equation 2.22. (annotates `X = torch.column_stack(...)`)
- The Pytorch column stack operator adds a column to a matrix. Here, the added column is all 1s.
- It is easy to verify that the solution to equation 2.22 is roughly $w_0 = 1, w_1 = 1, b = -1$. But the equations are not consistent: no one solution perfectly fits all of them. The pseudo-inverse finds the "best fit" solution: it minimizes total error for all the equations. (annotates `w = torch.matmul(...)`)
- Expect the solution to be close to [1, 1, -1]
- The solution is [1.08, 0.90, -0.96] (annotates `print(...)`)

2.13 Eigenvalues and eigenvectors: Swiss Army knives of machine learning

Machine learning and data science are all about finding patterns in large volumes of high-dimensional data. The inputs are feature vectors (introduced in section 2.1) in high-dimensional spaces. Each feature vector can be viewed as a point in the feature space descriptor for an input instance. Sometimes we transform these feature vectors—map the feature points to a friendlier space—to simplify the data by reducing dimensionality. This is done by eliminating axes along which there is scant variation in the data. Eigenvalues and eigenvectors are invaluable tools in the arsenal of a machine learning engineer or a data scientist for this purpose. In chapter 4, we will study how to use these tools to simplify and find broad patterns in a large volume of multidimensional data.

Let's take an informal look at eigenvectors first. They are properties of square matrices. As seen earlier, matrices can be viewed as linear transforms which map vectors (points) in one space to different vectors (points) in the same or a different space. But a typical linear transform leaves a few points in the space (almost) unaffected. These points are called *eigenvectors*. They are important physical aspects of the transform. Let's look at a simple example. Suppose we are *rotating* points in 3D space about the Z-axis (see figure 2.13). The points on the Z-axis will stay where they were despite the rotation. In general, points on the axis of rotation (Z in this case) do not go anywhere after rotation. The axis of rotation is an eigenvector of the rotation transformation.

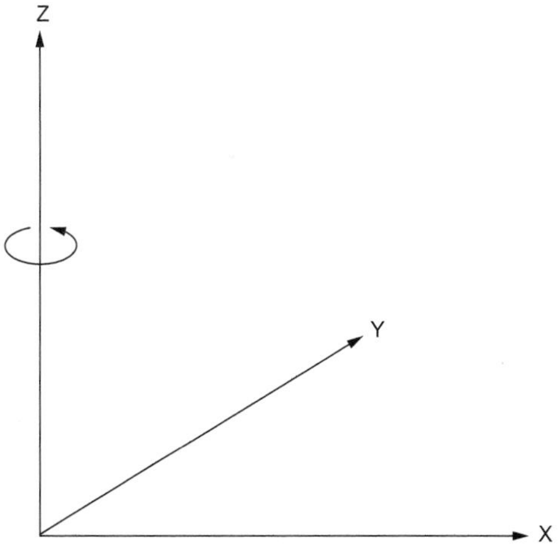

Figure 2.13 During rotation, points on the axis of rotation do not change position.

Extending this idea, when *transforming* vectors $\vec{x}$ with a matrix A, are there vectors that do not change, at least in direction? Turns out the answer is yes. These are the so-called *eigenvectors*—they do not change direction when undergoing linear transformation by a matrix A. To be precise, if $\vec{e}$ is an eigenvector of the square matrix A,[5] then

$$A\vec{e} = \lambda \vec{e}$$

Thus the linear transformation (that is, multiplication by matrix A) has changed the length but not the direction of $\vec{e}$ because $\lambda \vec{e}$ is parallel to $\vec{e}$.

How do we obtain λ and $\vec{e}$? Well,

$$\begin{aligned} & A\vec{e} = \lambda \vec{e} \\ \Leftrightarrow & A\vec{e} - \lambda \vec{e} = \vec{0} \\ \Leftrightarrow & (A - \lambda \mathbf{I})\, \vec{e} = \vec{0} \end{aligned}$$

where **I** denotes the identity matrix.

[5] You can compute eigenvectors and eigenvalues only of square matrices.

Of course, we are only interested in nontrivial solutions, where $\vec{e} \neq \vec{0}$. In that case, $A - \lambda\mathbf{I}$ cannot be invertible, because if it were, we could obtain the contradictory solution $\vec{e} = (A - \lambda\mathbf{I})^{-1}\vec{0} = \vec{0}$. Thus, $(A - \lambda\mathbf{I})$ is non-invertible, implying the determinant

$$det\,(A - \lambda\mathbf{I}) = 0$$

For an $n \times n$ matrix A, this yields an nth-degree polynomial equation with n solutions for the unknown λ. *Thus, an $n \times n$ matrix has n eigenvalues, not necessarily all distinct.*

Let's compute eigenvalues and eigenvectors of a 3×3 matrix, just for kicks. The matrix we use is carefully chosen, as will be evident soon. But for now, think of it as an arbitrary matrix:

$$A = \begin{bmatrix} \frac{1}{\sqrt{2}} & \frac{1}{\sqrt{2}} & 0 \\ -\frac{1}{\sqrt{2}} & \frac{1}{\sqrt{2}} & 0 \\ 0 & 0 & 1 \end{bmatrix} \tag{2.23}$$

We will compute the eigenvalues and eigenvectors of A:

$$(A - \lambda\mathbf{I}) = \begin{bmatrix} \frac{1}{\sqrt{2}} & \frac{1}{\sqrt{2}} & 0 \\ -\frac{1}{\sqrt{2}} & \frac{1}{\sqrt{2}} & 0 \\ 0 & 0 & 1 \end{bmatrix} - \begin{bmatrix} \lambda & 0 & 0 \\ 0 & \lambda & 0 \\ 0 & 0 & \lambda \end{bmatrix}$$

$$= \begin{bmatrix} \frac{1}{\sqrt{2}} - \lambda & \frac{1}{\sqrt{2}} & 0 \\ -\frac{1}{\sqrt{2}} & \frac{1}{\sqrt{2}} - \lambda & 0 \\ 0 & 0 & 1 - \lambda \end{bmatrix}$$

Thus,

$$\begin{aligned}
& det\,(A - \lambda\mathbf{I}) && = 0 \\
\Leftrightarrow\; & (1 - \lambda)\left(\left(\frac{1}{\sqrt{2}} - \lambda\right)\left(\frac{1}{\sqrt{2}} - \lambda\right) + \frac{1}{\sqrt{2}}\frac{1}{\sqrt{2}}\right) && = 0 \\
\Leftrightarrow\; & (1 - \lambda)\left(\lambda^2 - 2\frac{1}{\sqrt{2}}\lambda + \frac{1}{2} + \frac{1}{2}\right) && = 0 \\
\Leftrightarrow\; & (1 - \lambda)\left(\lambda^2 - \sqrt{2}\lambda + 1\right) && = 0 \\
\Leftrightarrow\; & \lambda = 1 \text{ or } \lambda = \left(\frac{1}{\sqrt{2}} + i\frac{1}{\sqrt{2}}\right) \text{ or } \lambda = \left(\frac{1}{\sqrt{2}} - i\frac{1}{\sqrt{2}}\right) \\
\Leftrightarrow\; & \lambda = 1 \text{ or } \lambda = e^{i\frac{\pi}{4}} \text{ or } \lambda = e^{-i\frac{\pi}{4}} \text{ using De Moivre's rule}
\end{aligned}$$

Here, $i = \sqrt{-1}$. If necessary, you are encouraged to refresh your memory of imaginary and complex numbers from high school algebra.

Thus, we have found (as expected) three eigenvalues: 1, $e^{i\frac{\pi}{4}}$, and $e^{-i\frac{\pi}{4}}$. Each of them will yield one eigenvector. Let's compute the eigenvector corresponding to the eigenvalue of 1 by way of example:

$$A\vec{e_1} = 1 \cdot \vec{e_1}$$

$$\Leftrightarrow \begin{bmatrix} \frac{1}{\sqrt{2}} & \frac{1}{\sqrt{2}} & 0 \\ -\frac{1}{\sqrt{2}} & \frac{1}{\sqrt{2}} & 0 \\ 0 & 0 & 1 \end{bmatrix} \vec{e_1} = \vec{e_1}$$

$$\Leftrightarrow \begin{bmatrix} \frac{1}{\sqrt{2}} & \frac{1}{\sqrt{2}} \\ -\frac{1}{\sqrt{2}} & \frac{1}{\sqrt{2}} \end{bmatrix} \begin{bmatrix} e_{11} \\ e_{12} \end{bmatrix} = \begin{bmatrix} e_{11} \\ e_{12} \end{bmatrix}$$

$$\Leftrightarrow e_{11} = e_{12} = 0 \Leftrightarrow \vec{e_1} = \begin{bmatrix} 0 \\ 0 \\ 1 \end{bmatrix}$$

Thus, $\begin{bmatrix} 0 \\ 0 \\ 1 \end{bmatrix}$ is an eigenvector for the eigenvalue 1 for matrix A. So is $\begin{bmatrix} 0 \\ 0 \\ k \end{bmatrix}$ for any real k. In fact, if $\lambda, \vec{e}$ is an eigenvalue, eigenvector pair for matrix A, then

$$A\vec{e} = \lambda \vec{e} \Leftrightarrow A\left(k\vec{e}\right) = \lambda\left(k\vec{e}\right)$$

That is, λ, $\left(k\vec{e}\right)$ is also an eigenvalue, eigenvector pair of A. In other words, we can only determine the eigenvector up to a fixed scale factor. We take the eigenvector to be of unit length ($\vec{e}^T\vec{e} = 1$) without loss of generality.

The eigenvector for our example matrix turns out to be the Z-axis. This is not an accident. Our matrix A was, in fact, a rotation about the Z-axis. *A rotation matrix will always have* 1 *as an eigenvalue. The corresponding eigenvector will be the axis of rotation. In 3D, the other two eigenvalues will be complex numbers yielding the angle of rotation.* This is detailed in section 2.14.

2.13.1 Eigenvectors and linear independence

Two eigenvectors of a matrix corresponding to unequal eigenvalues are linearly independent. Let's prove this to get some insights. Let $\lambda_1, \vec{e_1}$ and $\lambda_2, \vec{e_2}$ be eigenvalue, eigenvector pairs for a matrix A with $\lambda_1 \neq \lambda_2$. Then

$$A\vec{e_1} = \lambda_1\vec{e_1}$$

$$A\vec{e_2} = \lambda_2\vec{e_2}$$

If possible, let there be two constants α_1 and α_2 such that

$$\alpha_1\vec{e_1} + \alpha_2\vec{e_2} = 0 \tag{2.24}$$

In other words, suppose the two eigenvectors are linearly dependent. We will show that this assumption leads to an impossibility.

Multiplying equation 2.24 by A, we get

$$\begin{aligned} \alpha_1 A\vec{e_1} + \alpha_2 A\vec{e_2} &= 0 \\ \Leftrightarrow \alpha_1 \lambda_1 \vec{e_1} + \alpha_2 \lambda_2 \vec{e_2} &= 0 \end{aligned}$$

Also, we can multiply equation 2.24 by λ_2. Thus we get

$$\begin{aligned} \alpha_1 \lambda_1 \vec{e_1} + \alpha_2 \lambda_2 \vec{e_2} &= 0 \\ \alpha_1 \lambda_2 \vec{e_1} + \alpha_2 \lambda_2 \vec{e_2} &= 0 \end{aligned}$$

Subtracting, we get

$$\alpha_1 (\lambda_1 - \lambda_2) \vec{e_1} = 0$$

By assumption, $\alpha_1 \neq 0$, $\lambda_1 \neq \lambda_2$ and $\vec{e_1}$ is not all zeros. Thus it is impossible for their product to be zero. Our original assumption (the two eigenvectors are linearly dependent) must have been wrong.

2.13.2 Symmetric matrices and orthogonal eigenvectors

Two eigenvectors of a symmetric matrix that correspond to different eigenvalues are mutually orthogonal. Let's prove this to get additional insight. A matrix A is symmetric if $A^T = A$. If $\lambda_1, \vec{e_1}$ and $\lambda_2, \vec{e_2}$ are eigenvalue, eigenvector pairs for a symmetric matrix A, then

$$A\vec{e_1} = \lambda_1 \vec{e_1} \tag{2.25}$$

$$A\vec{e_2} = \lambda_2 \vec{e_2} \tag{2.26}$$

Transposing equation 2.25,

$$\vec{e_1}^T A^T = \lambda_1 \vec{e_1}^T$$

Right-multiplying by $\vec{e_2}$, we get

$$\begin{aligned} \vec{e_1}^T A^T \vec{e_2} &= \lambda_1 \vec{e_1}^T \vec{e_2} \\ \Leftrightarrow \vec{e_1}^T A \vec{e_2} &= \lambda_1 \vec{e_1}^T \vec{e_2} \end{aligned}$$

where the last equation follows from the matrix symmetry. Also, left-multiplying equation 2.26 by $\vec{e_1}^T$, we get

$$\vec{e_1}^T A \vec{e_2} = \lambda_2 \vec{e_1}^T \vec{e_2}$$

Thus

$$\begin{aligned} \vec{e_1}^T A \vec{e_2} &= \lambda_1 \vec{e_1}^T \vec{e_2} \\ \vec{e_1}^T A \vec{e_2} &= \lambda_2 \vec{e_1}^T \vec{e_2} \end{aligned}$$

Subtracting the equations, we get

$$0 = (\lambda_1 - \lambda_2) \vec{e_1}^T \vec{e_2}$$

Since $\lambda_1 \neq \lambda_2$, we must have $\vec{e_1}^T \vec{e_2} = 0$, which means the two eigenvectors are orthogonal. Thus, if A is an $n \times n$ symmetric matrix with eigenvectors $\vec{e_1}, \vec{e_2}, \cdots \vec{e_n}$, then $\vec{e_i}^T \vec{e_j} = 0$ for all i, j satisfying $\lambda_i \neq \lambda_j$.

2.13.3 PyTorch code to compute eigenvectors and eigenvalues

NOTE Fully functional code for this section, executable via Jupyter Notebook, can be found at http://mng.bz/1rEZ.

Listing 2.13 Eigenvalues and vectors

```
from torch import linalg as LA

A = torch.tensor([[0.707, 0.707, 0],
      [-0.707, 0.707, 0], [0, 0, 1]])

l, e = LA.eig(A)

print("Eigen values are ".format(l))
print("Eigen vectors are ".format(e.T))
```

$A = \begin{bmatrix} cos(45°) & sin(45°) & 0 \\ -sin(45°) & cos(45°) & 0 \\ 0 & 0 & 1 \end{bmatrix}$ **Rotates points in 3D space around the Z-axis. The axis of rotation is the Z-axis: $\begin{bmatrix} 0 & 0 & 1 \end{bmatrix}^T$**

Function eig() in the torch linalg package computes eigenvalues and vectors.

Eigenvalues or vectors can contain complex numbers involving $j = \sqrt{-1}$.

2.14 Orthogonal (rotation) matrices and their eigenvalues and eigenvectors

Of all the transforms, rotation transforms have a special intuitive appeal because of their highly observable behavior in the mechanical world. Furthermore, they play a significant role in developing and analyzing several machine learning tools. In this section, we overview rotation (aka orthogonal) matrices. (Fully functional code for the Jupyter notebook for this section can be found at http://mng.bz/2eNN.)

2.14.1 Rotation matrices

Figure 2.14 shows a point (x, y) rotated about the origin by an angle θ. The original point's position vector made an angle α with the X-axis. Post-rotation, the point's new coordinates are (x', y'). Note that by definition, rotation does not change the distance from the center of rotation; that is what the circle indicates.

Some well-known rotation matrices are as follows:

- **Planar rotation by angle θ about the origin** (see figure 2.14):

$$R_{2d} = \begin{bmatrix} \cos\theta & -\sin\theta \\ \sin\theta & \cos\theta \end{bmatrix} \tag{2.27}$$

- **Rotation by angle θ in 3D space about the Z-axis:**

$$R_{3dz} = \begin{bmatrix} \cos\theta & -\sin\theta & 0 \\ \sin\theta & \cos\theta & 0 \\ 0 & 0 & 1 \end{bmatrix} \tag{2.28}$$

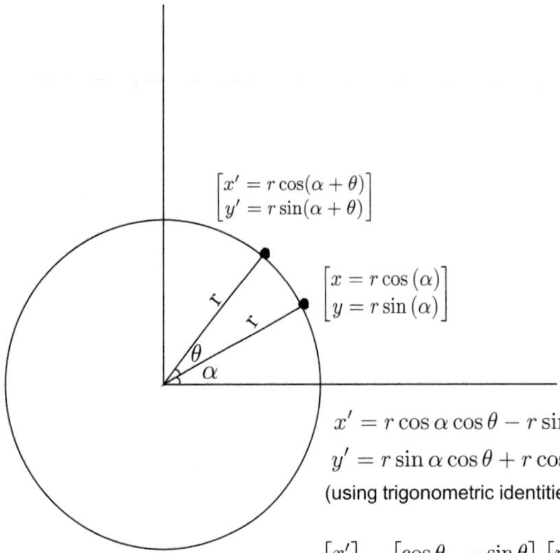

$$x' = r\cos\alpha\cos\theta - r\sin\alpha\sin\theta$$
$$y' = r\sin\alpha\cos\theta + r\cos\alpha\sin\theta$$

(using trigonometric identities)

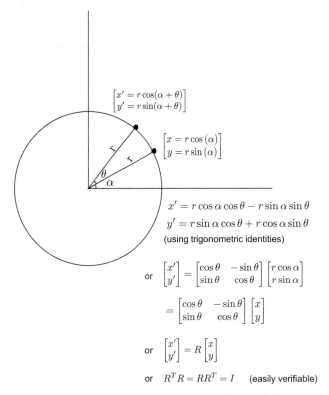

or $$\begin{bmatrix} x' \\ y' \end{bmatrix} = \begin{bmatrix} \cos\theta & -\sin\theta \\ \sin\theta & \cos\theta \end{bmatrix} \begin{bmatrix} r\cos\alpha \\ r\sin\alpha \end{bmatrix}$$

$$= \begin{bmatrix} \cos\theta & -\sin\theta \\ \sin\theta & \cos\theta \end{bmatrix} \begin{bmatrix} x \\ y \end{bmatrix}$$

or $$\begin{bmatrix} x' \\ y' \end{bmatrix} = R \begin{bmatrix} x \\ y \end{bmatrix}$$

or $R^T R = RR^T = I$ (easily verifiable)

Figure 2.14 Rotation in a plane about the origin. By definition, rotation does not change the distance from the center of rotation (indicated by the circle).

Note that the z coordinate remains unaffected by this rotation:

$$\begin{bmatrix} \cos\theta & -\sin\theta & 0 \\ \sin\theta & \cos\theta & 0 \\ 0 & 0 & 1 \end{bmatrix} \begin{bmatrix} x \\ y \\ z \end{bmatrix} = \begin{bmatrix} \cdot \\ \cdot \\ z \end{bmatrix}$$

This rotation matrix has an eigenvalue of 1, and the corresponding eigenvector is the Z-axis—you should verify this. This implies that a point on the Z-axis maps to itself when transformed (rotated) by the previous matrix, which is in keeping with the property that the z coordinate remains unchanged by this rotation.

- **Rotation by angle θ in 3D space about the *X*-axis**:

$$R_{3dx} = \begin{bmatrix} 1 & 0 & 0 \\ 0 & \cos\theta & -\sin\theta \\ 0 & \sin\theta & \cos\theta \end{bmatrix} \tag{2.29}$$

Note that the X coordinate remains unaffected by this rotation and the X-axis is an eigenvector of this matrix:

$$\begin{bmatrix} 1 & 0 & 0 \\ 0 & \cos\theta & -\sin\theta \\ 0 & \sin\theta & \cos\theta \end{bmatrix} \begin{bmatrix} x \\ y \\ z \end{bmatrix} = \begin{bmatrix} x \\ \cdot \\ \cdot \end{bmatrix}$$

- **Rotation by angle θ in 3D space about the *Y*-axis:**

$$R_{3dy} = \begin{bmatrix} \cos\theta & 0 & -\sin\theta \\ 0 & 1 & 0 \\ \sin\theta & 0 & \cos\theta \end{bmatrix} \quad (2.30)$$

Note that the Y coordinate remains unaffected by this rotation and the Y-axis is an eigenvector of this matrix:

$$\begin{bmatrix} \cos\theta & 0 & -\sin\theta \\ 0 & 1 & 0 \\ \sin\theta & 0 & \cos\theta \end{bmatrix} \begin{bmatrix} x \\ y \\ z \end{bmatrix} = \begin{bmatrix} \cdot \\ y \\ \cdot \end{bmatrix}$$

Listing 2.14 Rotation matrices

Returns the matrix that performs in-plane 2D rotation by angle theta about the origin. Thus, multiplication with this matrix moves a point to a new location. The angle between the position vectors of the original and new points is theta (figure 2.14).

```
def rotation_matrix_2d(theta):
    return torch.tensor([[cos(radians(theta)), -sin(radians(theta))],
                         [sin(radians(theta)), cos(radians(theta))]])
```

Returns the matrix that rotates a point in 3D space about the chosen axis by angle theta degrees. The axis of rotation can be 0, 1, or 2, corresponding to the X-, Y-, or Z-axis, respectively.

```
def rotation_matrix_3d(theta, axis):
    if axis == 0:    <-- R_3dx from equation 2.29
      return torch.tensor([[1, 0, 0],
                           [0, cos(radians(theta)),-sin(radians(theta))],
                           [0, sin(radians(theta)),cos(radians(theta))]])
    elif axis == 1:    <-- R_3dy from equation 2.30
      return torch.tensor([[cos(radians(theta)),0,-sin(radians(theta))],
                           [0, 1, 0],
                           [sin(radians(theta)),0,cos(radians(theta))]])
    elif axis == 2:    <-- R_3dz from equation 2.28
      return torch.tensor([[cos(radians(theta)),-sin(radians(theta)),0],
                           [sin(radians(theta)),cos(radians(theta)),0],
                           [0, 0, 1]])
```

Listing 2.15 Applying rotation matrices

```
u = torch.tensor.array([1, 1, 1], dtype=torch.float)    ← Creates vector ū (see figure 2.15)

R3dz = rotation_matrix_3d(45, 2)    ← R_3dz from equation 2.28, 45° about Z-axis
v = torch.matmul(R3dz, u_row)    ← v̄ (see figure 2.15) is ū rotated by R_3dz.

R3dx = rotation_matrix_3d(45, 0)    ← R_3dx from equation 2.28, 45° about X-axis
w = torch.matmul(R3dx, u_row)    ← w̄ (see figure 2.15) is v̄ rotated by R_3dx.
```

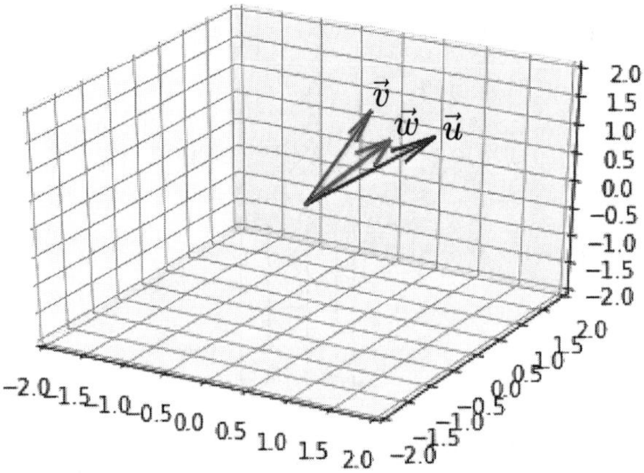

Figure 2.15 Rotation visualized. Here the original vector u is first rotated by 45 degrees around the Z-axis to get vector v, which is subsequently rotated again by 45 degrees around the X-axis to get vector w.

2.14.2 Orthogonality of rotation matrices

A matrix R is *orthogonal* if and only if it its transpose is also its inverse: that is, $R^T R = RR^T = \mathbf{I}$. *All rotations matrices are orthogonal matrices. All orthogonal matrices represent some rotation.* For instance:

$$\begin{bmatrix} \cos\theta & -\sin\theta \\ \sin\theta & \cos\theta \end{bmatrix}^T \begin{bmatrix} \cos\theta & -\sin\theta \\ \sin\theta & \cos\theta \end{bmatrix} = \begin{bmatrix} \cos\theta & \sin\theta \\ -\sin\theta & \cos\theta \end{bmatrix} \begin{bmatrix} \cos\theta & -\sin\theta \\ \sin\theta & \cos\theta \end{bmatrix}$$

$$= \begin{bmatrix} \cos^2\theta + \sin^2\theta & 0 \\ 0 & \cos^2\theta + \sin^2\theta \end{bmatrix} = \begin{bmatrix} 1 & 0 \\ 0 & 1 \end{bmatrix} = \mathbf{I}$$

You are encouraged to verify, likewise, that all the rotation matrices shown here are orthogonal.

ORTHOGONALITY AND LENGTH-PRESERVATION

Orthogonality implies that rotation is length-preserving. Given any vector $\vec{x}$ and rotation matrix R, let $\vec{y} = R\vec{x}$ be the rotated vector. The lengths (magnitudes) of the two vectors $\vec{x}, \vec{y}$ are equal since it is easy to see that

$$||\vec{y}|| = \vec{y}^T\vec{y} = (R\vec{x})^T\ (R\vec{x}) = \vec{x}^T R^T R\vec{x} = \vec{x}^T \mathbf{I}\vec{x} = \vec{x}^T\vec{x} = ||\vec{x}||$$

From elementary matrix theory, we know that

$$(AB)^T = B^T A^T$$

NEGATING THE ANGLE OF ROTATION

Negating the angle of rotation is equivalent to inverting the rotation matrix, which is equivalent to transposing the rotation matrix. For instance, consider in-plane rotation. Say a point $\vec{x}$ is rotated about the origin to vector $\vec{y}$ via matrix R. Thus

$$R = \begin{bmatrix} \cos\theta & -\sin\theta \\ \sin\theta & \cos\theta \end{bmatrix}$$

$$\vec{y} = R\vec{x}$$

Now we can go back from $\vec{y}$ to $\vec{x}$ by rotating by $-\theta$. The corresponding rotation matrix is

$$\begin{bmatrix} \cos(-\theta) & -\sin(-\theta) \\ \sin(-\theta) & \cos(-\theta) \end{bmatrix} = \begin{bmatrix} \cos\theta & \sin\theta \\ -\sin\theta & \cos\theta \end{bmatrix} = R^T$$

In other words, R^T inverts the rotation: that is, rotates by the negative angle.

2.14.3 PyTorch code for orthogonality of rotation matrices

Let's verify the orthogonality of the rotation matrix by creating one in PyTorch, imparting a transpose to it, and verifying that the product of the original matrix and the transpose is the identity matrix.

Listing 2.16 Orthogonality of rotation matrices

```
R_30 = rotation_matrix_2d(30)

assert torch.allclose(
    torch.linalg.inv(R_30),
    R_30.T
    )

assert torch.allclose(
    torch.matmul(R_30, R_30.T),
    torch.eye(2)
    )

u = torch.tensor([[4],[0]], dtype=torch.float)

v = torch.matmul(R_30, u)

assert torch.linalg.norm(u)==torch.linalg.norm(v)
```

- **Creates a rotation matrix, R_{30}**
- **The inverse of a rotation matrix is the same as its transpose.**
- **Multiplying a rotation matrix and its inverse yields the identity matrix.**
- **A vector $\vec{u}$ rotated by matrix R_{30} to yield vector $\vec{v}$, $R_{30}\vec{u} = \vec{v}$.**
- **The norm of a vector is the same as its length. Rotation preserves the length of a vector $||R\vec{u}|| = ||\vec{u}||$.**

```
R_neg30 = rotation_matrix_2d(-30)
w = torch.matmul(R_neg30, v)
assert torch.all(w == u)

assert torch.allclose(R_30, R_neg30.T)
assert torch.allclose(
    torch.matmul(R_30, R_neg30),
    torch.eye(2))
```

Rotation by an angle followed by rotation by the negative of that angle takes the vector back to its original position. Rotation by a negative angle is equivalent to inverse rotation.

A matrix that rotates by an angle is the inverse of the matrix that rotates by the negative of the same angle.

2.14.4 Eigenvalues and eigenvectors of a rotation matrix: Finding the axis of rotation

Let $\lambda, \vec{e}$ be an eigenvalue, eigenvector pair of a rotation matrix R. Then

$$R\vec{e} = \lambda\vec{e}$$

Transposing both sides,

$$\vec{e}^T R^T = \lambda\vec{e}^T$$

Multiplying the left and right sides, respectively, with the equivalent entities $R\vec{e}$ and $\lambda\vec{e}$, we get

$$\vec{e}^T R^T \left(R\vec{e}\right) = \lambda\vec{e}^T \left(\lambda\vec{e}\right) \Leftrightarrow \vec{e}^T \left(R^T R\right)\vec{e} = \lambda^2\vec{e}^T\vec{e} \Leftrightarrow \vec{e}^T \left(\mathbf{I}\right)\vec{e} = \lambda^2\vec{e}^T\vec{e}$$
$$\Leftrightarrow \vec{e}^T\vec{e} = \lambda^2\vec{e}^T\vec{e} \Leftrightarrow \lambda^2 = 1 \Leftrightarrow \lambda = 1$$

(The negative solution $\lambda = -1$ corresponds to reflection.) Thus, all rotation matrices have 1 as one of their eigenvalues. The corresponding eigenvector $\vec{e}$ satisfies $R\vec{e} = \vec{e}$. This is the axis of rotation: the set of points that stay where they were post-rotation.

2.14.5 PyTorch code for eigenvalues and vectors of rotation matrices

The following listing shows the code for the axis of rotation.

Listing 2.17 Axis of rotation

```
R = torch.tensor([[0.7071, 0.7071, 0],
                  [-0.7071, 0.7071, 0],
                  [0, 0, 1]])

l, e = LA.eig(R)

axis_of_rotation = e[:, torch.where(l == 1.0)]

axis_of_rotation = torch.squeeze(axis_of_rotation)

assert torch.allclose(
    axis_of_rotation.real,
    torch.tensor([0, 0, 1], dtype=torch.float)
```

Matrix $R = \begin{bmatrix} cos(45°) & sin(45°) & 0 \\ -sin(45°) & cos(45°) & 0 \\ 0 & 0 & 1 \end{bmatrix}$ rotates 45° about the Z-axis. All rotation matrices will have an eigenvalue 1. The corresponding eigenvector is the axis of rotation (here, the Z-axis).

The PyTorch function eig() computes eigenvalues and eigenvectors.

The PyTorch function where() returns the indices at which the specified condition is true.

Obtains the eigenvector for eigenvalue 1

The axis of rotation is the Z-axis.

```
)

p = torch.randint(0, 10, (1,)) * axis_of_rotation
assert torch.allclose(torch.matmul(R, p.real), p.real)
```

Takes a random point on this axis and applies the rotation to this point; its position does not change.

2.15 Matrix diagonalization

In section 2.12, we studied linear systems and their importance in machine learning. We also remarked that the standard mathematical process of solving linear systems via matrix inversion is not very desirable from a machine learning point of view. In this section, we will see one method of solving linear systems without matrix inversion. In addition, this section will help us develop the insights necessary to understand quadratic forms and, eventually, principal component analysis (PCA), one of the most important tools in data science.

Consider an $n \times n$ matrix A with n linearly independent eigenvectors. Let S be a matrix with these eigenvectors as its columns. That is,

$$\begin{aligned} A\vec{e_1} &= \lambda_1 \vec{e_1} \\ A\vec{e_2} &= \lambda_2 \vec{e_2} \\ &\vdots \\ A\vec{e_n} &= \lambda_n \vec{e_n} \end{aligned}$$

and

$$S = \begin{bmatrix} \vec{e_1} & \vec{e_2} & \cdots \vec{e_n} \end{bmatrix}$$

Then

$$AS = A\begin{bmatrix} \vec{e_1} & \vec{e_2} & \cdots \vec{e_n} \end{bmatrix} = \begin{bmatrix} A\vec{e_1} & A\vec{e_2} & \cdots A\vec{e_n} \end{bmatrix} = \begin{bmatrix} \lambda_1\vec{e_1} & \lambda_2\vec{e_2} & \cdots \lambda_n\vec{e_n} \end{bmatrix}$$

$$= \begin{bmatrix} \vec{e_1} & \vec{e_2} & \cdots \vec{e_n} \end{bmatrix} \begin{bmatrix} \lambda_1 & 0 & \cdots & 0 \\ 0 & \lambda_2 & \cdots & 0 \\ \vdots & \vdots & \vdots & \vdots \\ 0 & 0 & \cdots & \lambda_n \end{bmatrix} = S\Lambda$$

where

$$\Lambda = \begin{bmatrix} \lambda_1 & 0 & \cdots & 0 \\ 0 & \lambda_2 & \cdots & 0 \\ \vdots & \vdots & \vdots & \vdots \\ 0 & 0 & \cdots & \lambda_n \end{bmatrix}$$

is a diagonal matrix with the eigenvalues of A on the diagonal and 0 everywhere else.

Thus, we have

$$AS = S\Lambda$$

which leads to

$$A = S\Lambda S^{-1}$$

and

$$\Lambda = S^{-1}AS$$

If A is symmetric, then its eigenvectors are orthogonal. Then $S^T S = SS^T = \mathbf{I} \Leftrightarrow S^{-1} = S^T$, and we get the diagonalization of A:

$$A = S\Lambda S^T$$

Note that diagonalization is not unique: a given matrix may be diagonalized in multiple ways.

2.15.1 PyTorch code for matrix diagonalization

Now we will study the PyTorch implementation of the math we learned in section 2.15. As usual, we will only show the directly relevant bit of code here.

NOTE Fully functional code for this section, executable via Jupyter Notebook, can be found at http://mng.bz/RXJn.

Listing 2.18 Diagonalization of a matrix

```
def diagonalize(matrix):       # Diagonalization is factorizing a matrix A = SΣS^-1.
                               # S is a matrix with eigenvectors of A as columns.
                               # Σ is a diagonal matrix with eigenvalues of A in the diagonal.
    try:
        l, e = torch.linalg.eig(matrix)    # The PyTorch function eig() returns
                                           # eigenvalues and vectors.

        sigma = torch.diag(l)    # The PyTorch function diag() creates a diagonal
                                 # matrix of given values.

        return e, torch.diag(l), torch.linalg.inv(e)    # Returns the three factors

    except np.linalg.LinAlgError:
        print("Cannot diagonalize matrix!")

A = torch.tensor([[0.7071, 0.7071, 0],
                  [-0.7071, 0.7071, 0],    # Creates a matrix A
                  [0, 0, 1]])

S, sigma, S_inv = diagonalize(A)

A1 = torch.matmul(S, torch.matmul(sigma, S_inv))    # Reconstructs A from its factors

assert torch.allclose(A, A1.real)    # Verifies that the reconstructed
                                     # matrix is the same as the original
```

2.15.2 Solving linear systems without inversion via diagonalization

Diagonalization has many practical applications. Let's study one now. In general, matrix inversion (that is, computing A^{-1}) is a very complex process that is numerically unstable. Hence, solving $A\vec{x} = \vec{b}$ via $\vec{x} = A^{-1}\vec{b}$ is to be avoided when possible. In the case of a square symmetric matrix with n distinct eigenvalues, diagonalization can come to the rescue. We can solve this in multiple steps. We first diagonalize A:

$$A = S\Lambda S^T$$

Then

$$A\vec{x} = \vec{b}$$

can be written as: $S\Lambda S^T \vec{x} = \vec{b}$

where S is the matrix with eigenvectors of A as its columns:

$$S = \begin{bmatrix} \vec{e_1} & \vec{e_2} & \cdots \vec{e_n} \end{bmatrix}$$

(Since A is symmetric, these eigenvectors are orthogonal. Hence $S^T S = SS^T = \mathbf{I}$.) The solution can be obtained in a series of very simple steps:

$$\underbrace{S\,\Lambda\,\underbrace{S^T\vec{x}}_{y_2}}_{y_1} = \vec{b}$$

First solve

$$S\vec{y_1} = \vec{b}$$

as

$$\vec{y_1} = S^T\vec{b}$$

Notice that both the transpose and matrix-vector multiplications are simple and numerically stable operations, unlike matrix inversion. Then we get

$$\Lambda\left(S^T\vec{x}\right) = \vec{y_1}$$

Now solve

$$\Lambda\vec{y_2} = \vec{y_1}$$

as

$$\vec{y_2} = \Lambda^{-1}\vec{y_1}$$

Note that since Λ is a diagonal matrix, inverting it is trivial:

$$\begin{bmatrix} \lambda_1 & 0 & \cdots & 0 \\ 0 & \lambda_2 & \cdots & 0 \\ \vdots & \vdots & \vdots & \vdots \\ 0 & 0 & \cdots & \lambda_n \end{bmatrix}^{-1} = \begin{bmatrix} \frac{1}{\lambda_1} & 0 & \cdots & 0 \\ 0 & \frac{1}{\lambda_2} & \cdots & 0 \\ \vdots & \vdots & \vdots & \vdots \\ 0 & 0 & \cdots & \frac{1}{\lambda_n} \end{bmatrix} \tag{2.31}$$

As a final step, solve

$$S^T\vec{x} = \vec{y_2}$$

as

$$\vec{x} = S\vec{y_2}$$

Thus we have obtained $\vec{x}$ without a single complex or unstable step.

2.15.3 PyTorch code for solving linear systems via diagonalization

Let's try solving the following set of equations:

$$\begin{aligned} x+y+z&=8 \\ 2x+2y+3z&=15 \\ x+3y+3z&=16 \end{aligned}$$

This can be written using matrices and vectors as

$$A\vec{x}=\vec{b}$$

$$\text{where } A=\begin{bmatrix}1 & 2 & 1\\ 2 & 2 & 3\\ 1 & 3 & 3\end{bmatrix} \quad \vec{x}=\begin{bmatrix}x\\ y\\ z\end{bmatrix} \quad \vec{b}=\begin{bmatrix}8\\ 15\\ 16\end{bmatrix}$$

Note that A is a symmetric matrix. It has orthogonal eigenvectors. The matrix with eigenvectors of A in columns is orthogonal. Its transpose and inverse are the same.

Listing 2.19 Solving linear systems using diagonalization

```
A = torch.tensor([[1, 2, 1], [2, 2, 3], [1, 3, 3]],
                 dtype=torch.float)                  # Creates a symmetric matrix A

assert torch.all(A == A.T)                           # Asserts that A may be symmetric

b = torch.tensor([8, 15, 16], dtype=torch.cfloat)    # Creates a vector b

x_0 = torch.matmul(torch.linalg.inv(A),
                   b.real)
# Solves Ax = b using matrix inversion, x = A^-1 b.
# Note: matrix inversion is numerically unstable.

w, S = torch.linalg.eig(A)
# Solves Ax = b via diagonalization. A = S Σ S^T.
# S Λ S^T x = b, where y2 = S^T x and y1 = Λ S^T x

y1 = torch.matmul(S.T, b)            # 1. Solve: S y1 = b as y1 = S^T b (no matrix inversion)

y2 = torch.matmul(torch.diag(1/ w), y1)
# 2. Solve: Λ y2 = y1 as y2 = Λ^-1 y1
# (inverting a diagonal matrix is easy; see equation 2.31.)

x_1 = torch.matmul(S, y2)            # 3. Solve: S^T x = y2 as x = S y2 (no matrix inversion)

assert torch.allclose(x_0, x_1.real) # Verifies that the two solutions are the same
```

Annotations:

- Creates a symmetric matrix A
- Asserts that A may be symmetric
- Creates a vector $\vec{b}$
- Solves $A\vec{x}=\vec{b}$ using matrix inversion, $\vec{x}=A^{-1}\vec{b}$. Note: matrix inversion is numerically unstable.
- Solves $A\vec{x}=\vec{b}$ via diagonalization. $A=S\Sigma S^T$. $\underbrace{S\,\Lambda\,\underbrace{S^T\vec{x}}_{y_2}}_{y_1}=\vec{b}$.
- 1. Solve: $S\vec{y_1}=\vec{b}$ as $\vec{y_1}=S^T\vec{b}$ (no matrix inversion)
- 2. Solve: $\Lambda\vec{y_2}=\vec{y_1}$ as $\vec{y_2}=\Lambda^{-1}\vec{y_1}$ (inverting a diagonal matrix is easy; see equation 2.31.)
- 3. Solve: $S^T\vec{x}=\vec{y_2}$ as $\vec{x}=S\vec{y_2}$ (no matrix inversion)
- Verifies that the two solutions are the same

2.15.4 Matrix powers using diagonalization

If matrix A can be diagonalized, then

$$\begin{aligned} &A=S\Lambda S^{-1} \\ &A^2=S\Lambda S^{-1}S\Lambda S^{-1}=S\Lambda\mathbf{I}\Lambda S^{-1}=S\Lambda^2S^{-1} \\ &\vdots \\ &A^n=\cdots=\cdots=S\Lambda^nS^{-1} \end{aligned}$$

For a diagonal matrix

$$\Lambda = \begin{bmatrix} \lambda_1 & 0 & \cdots & 0 \\ 0 & \lambda_2 & \cdots & 0 \\ \vdots & \vdots & \vdots & \vdots \\ 0 & 0 & \cdots & \lambda_n \end{bmatrix}$$

the nth power is simply

$$\Lambda^n = \begin{bmatrix} \lambda_1^n & 0 & \cdots & 0 \\ 0 & \lambda_2^n & \cdots & 0 \\ \vdots & \vdots & \vdots & \vdots \\ 0 & 0 & \cdots & \lambda_n^n \end{bmatrix}$$

If we need to compute various powers of an $m \times m$ matrix A at different times, we should precompute the matrix S and compute any power with only $O\left(m\right)$ operations—compared to the $\left(nm^3\right)$ operations necessary for naive computations.

2.16 Spectral decomposition of a symmetric matrix

We have seen in section 2.15 that a square symmetric matrix with distinct eigenvalues can be decomposed as

$$A = S\Lambda S^T$$

where

$$S = \begin{bmatrix} \vec{e_1} & \vec{e_2} & \cdots & \vec{e_n} \end{bmatrix}$$

Thus,

$$A = \begin{bmatrix} \vec{e_1} & \vec{e_2} & \cdots & \vec{e_n} \end{bmatrix} \begin{bmatrix} \lambda_1 & 0 & \cdots & 0 \\ 0 & \lambda_2 & \cdots & 0 \\ \vdots & \vdots & \vdots & \vdots \\ 0 & 0 & \cdots & \lambda_n \end{bmatrix} \begin{bmatrix} \vec{e_1}^T \\ \vec{e_2}^T \\ \vdots \\ \vec{e_n}^T \end{bmatrix}$$

This equation can be rewritten as

$$A = \lambda_1 \vec{e_1}\vec{e_1}^T + \lambda_2 \vec{e_2}\vec{e_2}^T + \cdots + \lambda_n \vec{e_n}\vec{e_n}^T \qquad (2.32)$$

Thus a square symmetric matrix can be written in terms of its eigenvalues and eigenvectors. This is the spectral resolution theorem.

2.16.1 PyTorch code for the spectral decomposition of a matrix

The following listing shows the relevant code for this section.

Listing 2.20 Spectral decomposition of a matrix

```
def spectral_decomposition(A):
  assert len(A.shape) == 2     ←  Asserts that A is a 2D tensor (i.e., matrix)
```

```
        and A.shape[0] == A.shape[1]          # A is square: i.e., A.shape[0] (num rows) ≜ A.shape[1] (num columns)

        and torch.all(A == A.T)               # Asserts that A is symmetric: i.e., A == A^T

    l, e = torch.linalg.eig(A)                # The PyTorch function eig() returns eigenvectors and values.

    assert len(torch.unique(l.real)) == A.shape[0],
           "Eigen values are not distinct!"

    C = torch.zeros((A.shape[0],
                     A.shape[0],
                     A.shape[0]))             # Defines a 3D tensor C of shape n x n x n
                                              # to hold the n components from equation 2.32.
                                              # Each term λ_i e_i e_i^T is an n x n matrix. There are n
                                              # such terms, all compactly held in tensor C.

    for i, lambda_i in enumerate(l):
        e_i = e[:, i]
        e_i = e_i.reshape((3, 1))
        C[i, :, :] = (lambda_i * torch.matmul(e_i, e_i.T)).real   # Computes C[i] = λ_i e_i e_i^T
    return C

A = torch.tensor([[1, 2, 1], [2, 2, 3], [1, 3, 3]]).float()
C = spectral_decomposition(A)

A1 = C.sum(axis=0)              # Reconstructs A by adding its components stored in C

assert torch.allclose(A, A1)    # Verifies that the matrix reconstructed from
                                # spectral components matches the original
```

2.17 An application relevant to machine learning: Finding the axes of a hyperellipse

The notion of an ellipse in high-dimensional space (aka hyperellipse) keeps coming back in various forms in machine learning. Here we will make a preliminary review of them. We will revisit these concepts later.

Recall the equation of an ellipse from high school math:

$$\frac{x^2}{a^2} + \frac{y^2}{b^2} = 1$$

This is a rather simple ellipse: it is two-dimensional and centered at the origin, and its major and minor axes are aligned with the coordinate axes. Denoting $\vec{x} = \begin{bmatrix} x \\ y \end{bmatrix}$ as the position vector, the same equation can be written as

$$\vec{x}^T \Lambda \vec{x} = 1$$

where $\Lambda = \begin{bmatrix} \frac{1}{a^2} & 0 \\ 0 & \frac{1}{b^2} \end{bmatrix}$ is a diagonal matrix. Written in this form, the equation can be extended beyond 2D to an n-dimensional axis-aligned ellipse centered at the origin. Now let's apply a rotation R to the axis. Then every vector $\vec{x}$ transforms to $R\vec{x}$. The equation of the ellipse in the new (rotated) coordinate system is

$$
\begin{aligned}
(R\vec{x})^T \Lambda (R\vec{x}) &= 1 \\
\Leftrightarrow \vec{x}^T \left(R^T \Lambda R\right) \vec{x} &= 1
\end{aligned}
$$

where $A = (R^T \Lambda R)$.
The generalized equation of the ellipse is

$$\vec{x}^T A \vec{x} = 1$$

Note the following:

- The ellipse is no longer axis aligned.
- The matrix A is no longer diagonal.
- A is symmetric. We can easily verify that $A^T = \left(R^T \Lambda R\right)^T = R^T \Lambda^T R = R^T \Lambda R$ (remember, the transpose of a diagonal matrix is itself).

If, in addition, we want to get rid of the "centered at the origin" assumption, we get

$$(\vec{x} - \mu)^T A (\vec{x} - \mu) = 1 \tag{2.33}$$

Now let's flip the problem around. Suppose we have a generic n-dimensional ellipse. How do we compute its axes' directions?

Clearly, if we can rotate the coordinate system so that the matrix in the middle is diagonal, we are done. Diagonalization (see section 2.15) is the answer. Specifically, we find the matrix S with eigenvectors of A in its columns. This is a rotation matrix (being orthogonal, since A is symmetric). We transform (rotate) the coordinate system by applying this matrix. In this new coordinate system, the ellipse is axis aligned. Stated another way, the new coordinate axes—these are the eigenvectors of A—yield the axes of the ellipse.

2.17.1 PyTorch code for hyperellipses

Let's try finding the axes of the hyperellipse described by the equation $5x^2 + 6xy + 5y^2 = 20$. Note that the actual ellipse we use as an example is 2D (to facilitate visualization), but the code we develop will be general and extensible to multiple dimensions.

The ellipse equation can be written using matrices and vectors as $\vec{x}^T A \vec{x} = 1$, where

$$A = \begin{bmatrix} 5 & 3 \\ 3 & 5 \end{bmatrix} \quad \vec{x} = \begin{bmatrix} x \\ y \end{bmatrix}$$

To find the axes of the hyperellipse, we need to transform the coordinate system so that the matrix in the middle becomes diagonal. Here is how this can be done: if we diagonalize A into $S\Sigma S^{-1}$, then the ellipse equation becomes $\vec{x}^T S\Sigma S^{-1} \vec{x} = 1$, where Σ is a diagonal matrix. Since A is symmetric, its eigenvectors are orthogonal. Hence, the matrix containing these eigenvectors as columns is orthogonal: i.e., $S^{-1} = S^T$. In other words, S is a rotation matrix. So the ellipse equation becomes $\vec{x}^T S\Sigma S^T \vec{x} = 1$ or

$(\vec{x}^T S)\,\Sigma\,(S^T \vec{x}) = 1$ or $\vec{y}^T \Sigma \vec{y} = 1$ where $\vec{y} = S^T \vec{x}$. This is of the desired form since Σ is a diagonal matrix. Remember, S is a rotation matrix. Thus, rotating the coordinate system by S aligns the coordinate axes with the ellipse axes.

Listing 2.21 Axes of a hyperellipse

```
ellipse_eq = sy.Eq(5*x**2 + 5*y**2 +
                   6*x*y, 20)

A = torch.tensor([[5, 3], [3, 5]]).float()

l, S = torch.linalg.eig(A)

x_axis_vec = torch.zeros((A.shape[0]))

first_eigen_vec = S[:, 0]

dot_prod = torch.dot(x_axis_vec, first_eigen_vec)

theta = math.acos(dot_prod)
theta = math.degrees(theta)
```

Equation of the ellipse: $5x^2 + 6xy + 5y^2 = 20$ or $\vec{x}^T A \vec{x} = 20$, where $A = \begin{bmatrix} 5 & 3 \\ 3 & 5 \end{bmatrix}, \vec{x} = \begin{bmatrix} x \\ y \end{bmatrix}$

X-axis vector

Major axis of the ellipse

The dot product between two vectors is the cosine of the angle between them.

The angle between the ellipse's major axis and the X-axis: 45° (see figure 2.16)

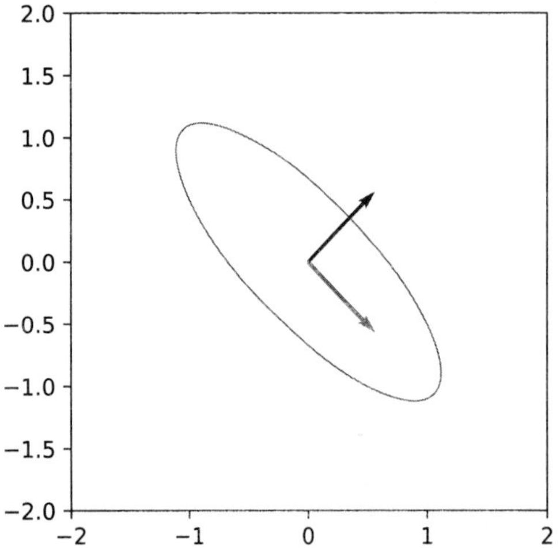

Figure 2.16 Note that the ellipse's major axis forms an angle of 45 degrees with the X-axis. Rotating the coordinate system by this angle will align the ellipse axes with the coordinate axes. Subsequently, the first principal vector will also lie along this direction.

Summary

- In machine learning, a vector is a one-dimensional array of numbers and a matrix is a two-dimensional array of numbers. Inputs and outputs of machine learning models are typically represented as vectors or matrices. In multilayered models, inputs and outputs of each individual layer are also represented as vectors or matrices. Images are two-dimensional arrays of numbers corresponding to pixel color values. As such, they are represented as matrices.

- An n-dimensional vector can be viewed as point in $\mathbb{R}^n$ space. All models can be viewed as functions that map points from input to output space. The model is designed so that it is easier to solve the problem of interest in the output space.
- A dot product between a pair of vectors $\vec{x} = \begin{bmatrix} x_1 & x_2 & \cdots & x_n \end{bmatrix}$ and $\vec{y} = \begin{bmatrix} y_1 & y_2 & \cdots & y_n \end{bmatrix}$ is the scalar quantity $\vec{x} \cdot \vec{y} = x_1 y_1 + x_2 y_2 + \cdots + x_n y_n$. It is a measure of how similar the vectors are. Dot products are widely used in machine learning. For instance, in supervised machine learning, we train the model so that its output is as similar as possible to the known output for a sample set of input points known as training data. Here, some variant of the dot product is often used to measure the similarity of the model output and the known output.

  Two vectors are orthogonal if their dot product is zero. This means the vectors have no similarity and are independent of each other.

  A vector's dot product with itself is the square of the magnitude or length of the vector $\vec{x} \cdot \vec{x} = ||\vec{x}||^2 = x_1 x_1 + x_2 x_2 + \cdots + x_n x_n$.
- Given a set of vectors $\vec{x}_1, \vec{x}_2, \cdots, \vec{x}_n$, the weighted sum $a_1 \vec{x}_1 + a_2 \vec{x}_2 + \cdots + a_n \vec{x}_n$ (where $a_1, a_2, \cdots, a_n$ are arbitrary scalars) is known as a linear combination. In particular, if the coefficients $a_1, a_2, \cdots, a_n$ are non-negative and they sum to 1, the linear combination is called a *convex* combination.

  If it is possible to find a set of coefficients $a_1, a_2, \cdots, a_n$, not all zero, such that the linear combination is a null vector (meaning all its elements are zeros), then the vectors $\vec{x}_1, \vec{x}_2, \cdots, \vec{x}_n$ are said to *linearly dependent*. On the other hand, if the only way to obtain a linear combination that is a null vector is to make every coefficient zero, the vectors are said to be *linearly independent*.
- One important application of matrices and vectors is to solve a system of linear equations. Such a system can be expressed in matrix vector terms as $A\vec{x} = \vec{b}$, where we solve for an unknown vector $\vec{x}$ satisfying the equation. This system has an exact solution if and only if A is invertible. This means A is a square matrix (the number of rows equals the number of columns) and the row vectors are linearly independent. If the row vectors are linearly independent, so are the column vectors, and vice versa. If the rows and columns are linearly independent, the determinant of A is guaranteed to be nonzero. Hence, linear independence of rows/columns and nonzero determinant are equivalent conditions. If any one of them is satisfied, the linear system has an exact and unique solution.

  In practice, this requirement is often not met, and we have an over- or under-determined system. In such situations, the Moore-Penrose inverse leads to a form of best approximation. Geometrically, the Moore-Penrose method yields the point that is closest to $\vec{b}$ in the space of vectors spanned by columns of A. Equivalently, the Moore-Penrose solution $\vec{x}_*$ yields the point closest to $\vec{b}$ on the space of vectors spanned by the columns of A.
- For a square matrix A, if and only if $A\hat{e} = \lambda \hat{e}$, we say λ is an eigenvalue (a scalar) and $\hat{e}$ is an eigenvector (a unit vector) of A. Physically, the eigenvector $\hat{e}$ is a unit vector

whose direction does not change when transformed by the matrix A. The transform can magnify its length by the scalar scale factor λ, which is the eigenvalue.

An $n \times n$ matrix A has n eigenvalue/eigenvector pairs. The eigenvalues need not all be unique. The eigenvectors corresponding to different eigenvalues are linearly independent. If the matrix A is symmetric, satisfying $A^T = A$, the eigenvectors corresponding to different eigenvalues are orthogonal.

A rotation matrix is a matrix in which the rows are orthogonal to each other and so are the columns. Such a matrix is also known as an orthogonal matrix. An orthogonal matrix R satisfies the equation $R^T R = \mathbf{I}$, where $\mathbf{I}$ is the identity matrix. In the special case when the matrix A is a rotation matrix R, one of the eigenvalues is always 1. The corresponding eigenvector is the axis of rotation.

A matrix A with n linearly independent eigenvectors can be decomposed as $A = S \Lambda S^{-1}$, where $S = \begin{bmatrix} \vec{e}_1 & \vec{e}_2 & \cdots & \vec{e}_n \end{bmatrix}$ is the matrix with eigenvectors of A as its columns and Λ is a diagonal matrix with the eigenvalues of A as its diagonal. This decomposition is called matrix diagonalization and leads to a numerically stable way to solve linear systems.

- A square symmetric matrix A can be expressed in terms of its eigenvectors and eigenvalues as $A = \lambda_1 \vec{e}_1 \vec{e}_1^{\,T} + \lambda_2 \vec{e}_2 \vec{e}_2^{\,T} + \cdots + \lambda_n \vec{e}_n \vec{e}_n^{\,T}$. This is known as the spectral decomposition of the matrix A.

3 Classifiers and vector calculus

We took a first look at the core concept of machine learning in section 1.3. Then, in section 2.8.2, we examined classifiers as a special case. But so far, we have skipped the topic of error minimization: given one or more training examples, how do we adjust the weights and biases to make the machine closer to the desired ideal? We will study this topic in this chapter by discussing the concept of gradients.

NOTE The complete PyTorch code for this chapter is available at http://mng.bz/4Zya in the form of fully functional and executable Jupyter notebooks.

3.1 Geometrical view of image classification

To fix our ideas, consider a machine that classifies whether an image contains a car or a giraffe. Such classifiers, with only two classes, are known as *binary classifiers*. The first question is how to represent the input.

3.1.1 Input representation

The car-versus-giraffe scenario belongs to a special class of problems where we are analyzing a visual scene. Here, the inputs are the brightness levels of various points in the 3D scene projected onto a 2D image plane. Each element of the image represents a point in the actual scene and is referred to as a *pixel*. The image is a two-dimensional array representing the collection of pixel values at a given instant in time. It is usually scaled to a fixed size, say 224×224. As such, the image can be viewed as a matrix:

$$X = \begin{bmatrix} X_{0,0} & X_{0,1} & \cdots & X_{0,223} \\ X_{1,0} & X_{1,1} & \cdots & X_{1,223} \\ \vdots & \vdots & \vdots & \vdots \\ X_{223,0} & X_{223,1} & \cdots & X_{223,223} \end{bmatrix}$$

Each element of the matrix, $X_{i,j}$, is a pixel color value in the range $[0, 255]$.

IMAGE RASTERIZATION

In the previous chapters, we have always seen a *vector* as the input to a machine learning system. The vector representation of the input allowed us to view it as a point in a high-dimensional space. This led to many geometric insights about classification. But here, our input is an image, which is akin to a *matrix* rather than a vector. Can we represent an image (matrix) as a vector?

The answer is yes. A matrix can always be converted into a vector by a process called *rasterization*. During rasterization, we iterate over the elements of the matrix from left to right and top to bottom, storing successive encountered elements into a vector. The result is the rasterized vector. It has the same elements as the original matrix, but they are organized differently. The length of the rasterized vector is equal to the product of the row count and column count of the matrix. The rasterized vector for the earlier matrix X has $224 \times 224 = 50176$ elements $\vec{x} = \begin{bmatrix} x_0 = X_{0,0} \\ x_1 = X_{0,1} \\ \vdots \\ x_{223} = X_{0,223} \\ x_{224} = X_{1,0} \\ x_{225} = X_{1,1} \\ \vdots \\ x_{50175} = X_{223,223} \end{bmatrix}$ where $x_i \in [0, 255]$ are values of the image pixels. Thus, a 224×224 input image can be viewed as a vector (equivalently, a point) in a $50,176$-dimensional space.

3.1.2 Classifiers as decision boundaries

We see that input images can be converted to vectors via rasterization. Each vector can be viewed as a point in a high-dimensional space. But the points corresponding to any given object or class, say *giraffe* or *car*, are not distributed randomly all over the space. Rather, they occupy a small portion (subspace) in the vast high-dimensional space of inputs. This is because there is always inherent commonality in members of a class. For instance, all giraffes are predominantly yellow with a bit of black, and cars have a somewhat fixed shape. This causes the pixel values in images containing the same object to have somewhat similar values. Overall, this means points belonging to a class loosely form a *cluster*.

NOTE Geometrically speaking, a classifier is a hypersurface that separates the point clusters for the classes we want to recognize. This surface forms a *decision boundary*—the decision about which class a specific input point belongs to is made by looking at which side of the surface the point belongs to.

Figure 3.1a shows an example of a rasterized space for the giraffe and car classification problem. The points corresponding to a giraffe are marked *g*, and those corresponding to a car are marked *c*. This is a simple case. Here, the classifier surface (aka decision boundary) that separates the cluster of points corresponding to *car* from those corresponding to *giraffe* is a hyperplane, depicted in figure 3.1a.

NOTE We often call surfaces *hypersurfaces* and planes *hyperplanes* in greater than three dimensions.

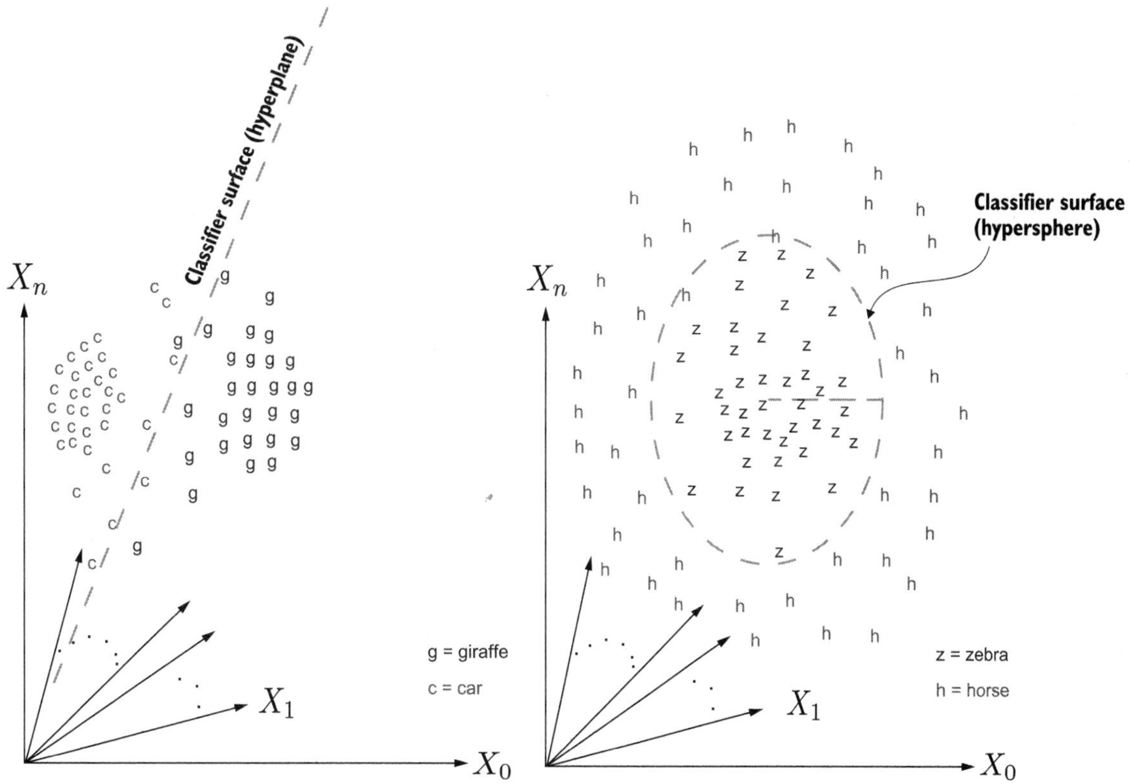

(a) Car vs. giraffe classifier (b) Horse vs. zebra classifier

Figure 3.1 Geometric depiction of a classification problem. In the multidimensional input space, each data instance corresponds to a point. In figure 3.1a, the points marked c denote cars, and points marked g denote giraffes. This is a simple case: the points form reasonably distinct clusters, so the classification can be done with a relatively simple surface, a hyperplane. The exact parameters of the hyperplane—orientation and position—are determined via training. In figure 3.1b, the points marked *h* denote horses, and those marked *z* denote zebras. This case is a bit more difficult: the classification has to be done with a curved (nonplanar) surface, a hypersphere. The parameters of the hypersphere—radius and center—are determined via training.

Figure 3.1b shows a more difficult example: horse and zebra classification in images. Here the points corresponding to horses are marked h and those corresponding to zebras are marked z. In this example, we need a nonlinear (curved) surface (such as a hypersphere) to separate the two classes.

3.1.3 *Modeling in a nutshell*

Unfortunately, in the typical scenario, we do not know the separating surface. In fact, we do not even know all the points belonging to a class of interest. All we know is a *sampled* set of inputs $\vec{x}_i$ (training inputs) and corresponding classes $\bar{\vec{y}}_i$ (the ground truth). The complete set of training inputs plus ground truth—$\left\{\vec{x}_i, \bar{\vec{y}}_i\right\}$ for a large set of i values—is called the *training data*. When we want to teach a baby to recognize a car, we show the baby several example cars and say "This is a car." The training data plays the same role for a neural network.

From only this training dataset $\left\{\vec{x}_i, \bar{\vec{y}}_i\right\} \forall i \in [1, n]$, we have to identify a good enough approximation of the general classifying surface that when presented with a random scene, we can map it to an input point $\vec{x}$, check which side of the surface that point lies on, and identify the class (car or giraffe). This process of developing a best guess for a surface that forms a decision boundary between various classes of interest is called *modeling the classifier*.

> **NOTE** The ground truth labels ($\bar{\vec{y}}_i$) for the training images $\vec{x}_i$ are often created manually. This process of manually generating labels for the training images is one of the most painful aspects of machine learning, and significant research effort is going on at the moment to mitigate it.

As indicated in section 1.3, modeling has two steps:

1. *Model architecture selection*: Choose the parametric model function $\phi\left(\vec{x}; \vec{w}, b\right)$. This function takes an input vector $\vec{x}$ and emits the class y. It has a set of parameters $\vec{w}$, b, which are unknown at first. This function is typically chosen from a bank of well-known functions that are tried and tested; for simple problems, we may choose a linear model, and for more complex problems, we choose nonlinear models. The model designer makes the choice based on their understanding of the problem. Remember, at this point the parameters are still unknown—we have only decided on the *function family* for the model.
2. *Model training*: Estimate the parameters $\vec{w}$, b such that ϕ emits the known correct output (as closely as possible) on the training data inputs. This is typically done via an iterative process. For each training data instance $\vec{x}_i$, we evaluate $y_i = \phi\left(\vec{x}_i; \vec{w}, b\right)$. This emitted output is compared with the corresponding known outputs $\bar{y}_i$. Their difference, $e_i = ||y_i - \bar{y}_i||$, is called the *training error*. The sum of training errors over all training data is the aggregate training error. We iteratively adjust the parameters $\vec{w}$, b such that the aggregate training error keeps going down. This means at each iteration, we adjust the parameters so the model output y_i moves a little closer to the target output $\bar{y}_i$ for all i. Exactly how to adjust the parameters to reduce the error forms the bulk of this chapter and will be introduced in section 3.3.

The function $\phi(\vec{x};\vec{w},b)$ represents the decision boundary hypersurface. For example, in the binary classification problem depicted in figure 3.1, $\phi(\vec{x};\vec{w},b)$ may represent a plane (shown by the dashed line). Points on one side of the plane are classified as cars, while points on the other side are classified as giraffes. Here,

$$\phi(\vec{x};\vec{w},b) = \vec{w}^T\vec{x} + b$$

From equation 2.14 we know this equation represents a plane.

In figure 3.1b, a good planar separation does not exist—we need a nonlinear separator, such as the spherical separator shown with dashed lines. Here,

$$\phi(\vec{x};\vec{w},b) = \vec{x}^T \begin{bmatrix} w_0 & 0 & \cdots & 0 \\ 0 & w_1 & \cdots & 0 \\ \vdots & \vdots & \vdots & \vdots \\ 0 & 0 & \cdots & w_n \end{bmatrix} \vec{x} + b = 0$$

This equation represents a sphere.

It should be noted that in typical real-life cases, the separating surface does not correspond to any known geometric surface (see figure 3.2). But in this chapter, we will continue to use simple examples to bring out the underlying concepts.

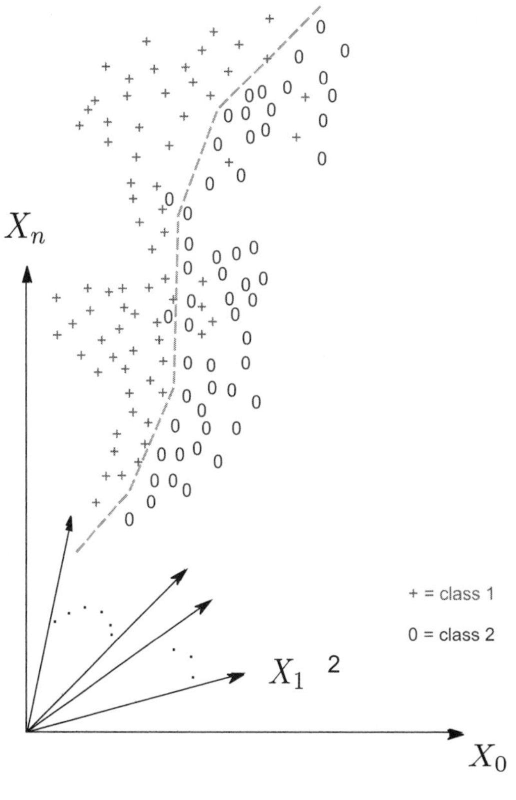

Figure 3.2 In real-life problems, the separating surface is often not a well-known surface like a plane or sphere. And often, the classification is not perfect—some points fall on the wrong side of the separator.

3.1.4 Sign of the surface function in binary classification

In the special case of binary classifiers, the *sign* of the expression $\phi\left(\vec{x};\vec{w},b\right)$ representing the decision boundary has a special significance. To see this, consider a line in a 2D plane corresponding to the equation

$$y + 2x + 1 = 0$$

All points *on* the line have x, y coordinate values satisfying this equation. The line divides the 2D plane into two half planes. All points on one half plane have x, y values such that $y + 2x + 1$ is negative. All points in the other half plane have x, y values such that $y + 2x + 1$ is positive. This is shown in figure 3.3. This idea can be extended to other surfaces and higher dimensions. Thus, in binary classification, once we have estimated an optimal decision surface $\phi\left(\vec{x};\vec{w},b\right)$, given any input vector $\vec{x}$, we can compute the sign of $\phi\left(\vec{x};\vec{w},b\right)$ to predict the class.

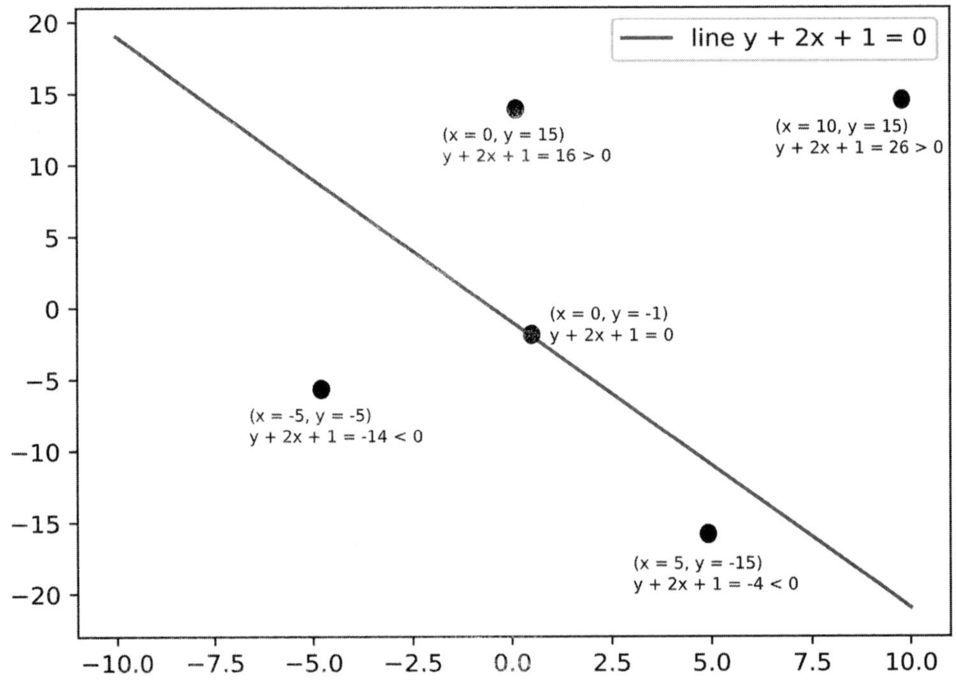

Figure 3.3 Given a point (x_0, y_0) and a separator $y + 2x + 1 = 0$, we can tell which side of the separator the point lies on from the sign of $y_0 + 2x_0 + 1$.

3.2 Error, aka loss function

As stated earlier, during training, we adjust the parameters $\vec{w}, b$ so that the error keeps going down. Let's derive a quantitative expression for this error (aka loss function). Later, we will see how to minimize it.

Overall, training data consists of a set of labeled inputs (training data instances paired with known ground truths):

$$\begin{matrix} (\vec{x}^{(0)}, & \bar{y}^{(0)}) \\ (\vec{x}^{(1)}, & \bar{y}^{(1)}) \\ \vdots & \vdots \\ (\vec{x}^{(N)}, & \bar{y}^{(N)}) \end{matrix}$$

Now we define a *loss function*. On a specific training data instance, the loss function effectively measures the error made by the machine on that particular training data—input-target pair $\left(\vec{x}^{(i)}, y^{(i)}\right)$. Although there are many sophisticated error functions more suitable for this problem, for now, let's use a squared error function for the sake of simplicity (introduced in section 2.5.4). The squared error on the ith training data element is the squared difference between the output yielded by the model and the expected or target output:

$$\left(e^{(i)}\right)^2 = \left(\phi\left(\vec{x}^{(i)}; \vec{w}, b\right) - y^{(i)}\right)^2 \tag{3.1}$$

The total loss (aka squared error) during training is

$$L\left(\vec{w}, b\right) = E^2\left(\vec{w}, b\right) = \sum_{i=0}^{i=N} \left(e^{(i)}\right)^2 \tag{3.2}$$

Note that this total error is not a function of any specific training data instance. Rather, it is the *overall error over the entire training data set.* This is what we minimize by adjusting $\vec{w}$ and b. To be precise, we estimate the $\vec{w}$ and b that will minimize $L\left(\vec{w}, b\right)$.

3.3 Minimizing loss functions: Gradient vectors

The goal of training is to estimate the weights and bias parameter $\vec{w}$, b that will minimize L. This is usually done by an iterative process. We start with random values of $\vec{w}$, b and adjust these values so that the loss $L\left(\vec{w}, b\right) = E^2\left(\vec{w}, b\right)$ declines rapidly. Doing this many times is likely to take us close to the optimal values for $\vec{w}$, b. This is the essential idea behind the process of training a model. It is important to note that we are minimizing the total error: this prevents us from over-indexing on any particular training instance. If the training data is a well-sampled set, the parameters $\vec{w}$, b that minimize loss over the training dataset will also work well during inferencing.

How do we "adjust" $\vec{w}$, b so that the value of loss $L = E^2$ declines? This is where gradients come in. For any function $L\left(\vec{w}, b\right)$, the gradient with respect to $\vec{w}$, b—that is, $\nabla_{\vec{w},b} L\left(\vec{w}, b\right)$—indicates the direction along which the maximum change in L occurs. The gradient is the analog of a derivative in 1D calculus. Intuitively, going down along the direction of the gradient of a function seems like the best strategy for minimizing the function value.

Geometrically speaking, if we start at an arbitrary point on the surface corresponding to $L\left(\vec{w}, b\right)$ and move along the direction of the gradient $\nabla_{\vec{w},b} L\left(\vec{w}, b\right)$, we will go toward the minimum at the fastest rate (this is discussed in detail throughout the rest of this section). Hence, during training, we iteratively move toward the minimum by taking steps along $\nabla_{\vec{w},b} L\left(\vec{w}, b\right)$. Note that *the gradient is with respect to weights, not the input.* The overall algorithm is shown in algorithm 3.1.

Algorithm 3.1 Training a supervised model (overall idea)

Initialize $\vec{w}, b$ with random values
while $L\left(\vec{w}, b\right) > threshold$ **do**

$$\begin{bmatrix} \vec{w} \\ b \end{bmatrix} = \begin{bmatrix} \vec{w} \\ b \end{bmatrix} - \mu \nabla_{\vec{w},b} L\left(\vec{w}, b\right)$$

Recompute L on new $\vec{w}, b$.
end while
$\vec{w}_* \leftarrow \vec{w}$, $b_* \leftarrow b$

Note the following points:

- In each iteration, we are adjusting $\vec{w}, b$ along the gradient of the error function. We will see in section 3.3 that this is the direction of maximum change for L. Thus, L is reduced at a maximal rate.
- μ is the learning rate: larger values imply longer steps, and smaller values imply shorter steps. The simplest approach, outlined in algorithm 3.1, takes equal-sized steps everywhere. In later chapters, we will study more sophisticated approaches where we try to sense how close to the minimum we are and vary the step size accordingly:
  - We take longer steps when far from the minimum, to progress quickly.
  - We take shorter steps when near the minimum, to avoid overshooting it.
- Mathematically, we should keep iterating until the loss becomes minimal (that is, the gradient of the loss is zero). But in practice, we simply iterate until the accuracy is good enough for the purpose at hand.

3.3.1 Gradients: A machine learning-centric introduction

In machine learning, we model the output as a parametric function of the inputs. We define a loss function that quantifies the difference between the model output and the known ideal output on the set of training inputs. Then we try to obtain the parameter values that will minimize this loss. This effectively identifies the parameters that will result in the model function emitting outputs as close as possible to the ideal on the set of training inputs.

The loss function depends on $\vec{x}$ (the model inputs), $\vec{y}$ (the known ideal outputs on the training data—aka ground truth), and $\vec{w}$ (the parameters). Here only the behavior of the loss function with respect to the parameters is of interest to us, so we are ignoring everything else and denoting the loss function as a function of the parameters as $L\left(\vec{w}\right)$.

NOTE For the sake of brevity, here we use the symbol w to denote all parameters—weight as well as bias.

The core question we are trying to answer is this: given a loss $L(\vec{w})$ and current parameter values $\vec{w}$, what is the optimal change in the parameters $\vec{\delta w}$ that maximally reduces the loss? Equivalently, we want to determine $\vec{\delta w}$ that will make $\delta L = L\left(\vec{w} + \vec{\delta w}\right) - L(\vec{w})$ as negative as possible. Toward that goal, we will study the relationship between the loss function $L(w)$ and change in parameter values $\vec{\delta w}$ in several scenarios of increasing complexity.[1]

ONE-DIMENSIONAL LOSS FUNCTIONS

For simplicity, we begin by examining this topic in one dimension—meaning there is a single parameter w. The first example we will study is the simplest possible case: a linear one-dimensional loss function, shown in figure 3.4a. A linear loss function in one dimension can be written as $L(w) = mw + c$. If we change the parameter w by a small amount δw, what is the corresponding change in loss δL? We have $\delta L = L(w + \delta w) - L(w) = (m(w + \delta w) + c) - (m(w) + c) = m\,\delta w$ which gives us $\frac{\delta L}{\delta w} = m$, a constant. By definition, the derivative $\frac{dL}{dw} = \lim_{\delta w \to 0} \frac{\delta L}{\delta w}$, which leads to $\frac{dL}{dw} = m$. Thus, for the straight line $L(w) = mw + c$, the rate of change of L with respect to w is constant everywhere and equals the slope m. Putting all this together, we get $\delta L = m\delta w = \frac{dL}{dw}\delta w$.

Let's now study a slightly more complex, non-linear but still one dimensional case—a parabolic loss function illustrated in figure 3.4b. This parabola can be written as $L(w) = w^2$. If we change the parameter w by a small amount δw, what is the corresponding change in in loss δL? We have $\delta L = L(w + \delta w) - L(w) = (w + \delta w)^2 - w^2 = \left(2w\delta w + \delta w^2\right)$. For infinitesimally small δw, δw^2 becomes negligibly small and we get $\lim_{\delta w \to 0} \delta L = \lim_{\delta w \to 0} \left(2w\delta w + \delta w^2\right) = 2w\delta w$ and $\frac{dL}{dw} = \lim_{\delta w \to 0} \frac{\delta L}{\delta w} = 2w$. Combining all these we get the same equation as the linear case $\delta L = \frac{dL}{dw}\delta w$. Of course, in case of the straight line this expression holds for all δw while in the non-linear curves the expression holds only for small δw.

> **δL and δw**
>
> In general, for all one-dimensional loss functions $L(w)$, the change δL caused by a change δw in parameters can be expressed as follows:
>
> $$\delta L = \frac{dL}{dw}\delta w \tag{3.3}$$
>
> To decrease L, δL must be negative. From equation 3.3, we can see that this requires δw (change in w) and $\frac{dL}{dw}$ (derivative) to have opposite signs.

Geometrically speaking, the loss function represents a curve with the loss $L(w)$ plotted along the Y axis against the parameter w plotted along the X axis (see figure 3.4 for examples). The tangent at any point can be viewed as the local approximation to the curve itself for an infinitesimally small neighborhood around the point. The derivative at any point represents the slope of the tangent to the curve at that point.

---

[1] If the change in a quantity such as w is infinitesimally small, we use the symbol dw to denote the change. If the change is small but not infinitesimally so, we use the symbol δw.

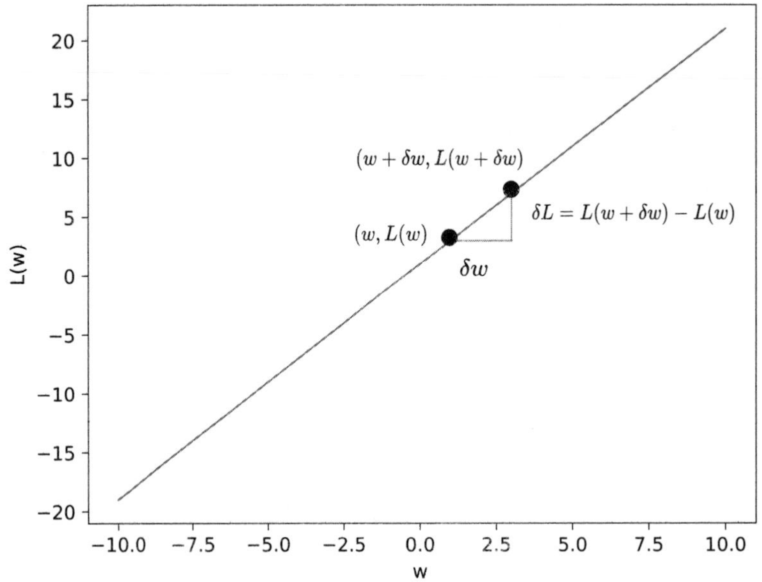

(a) Line: $L(w) = 2w + 1,\ \frac{dL}{dw} = m$

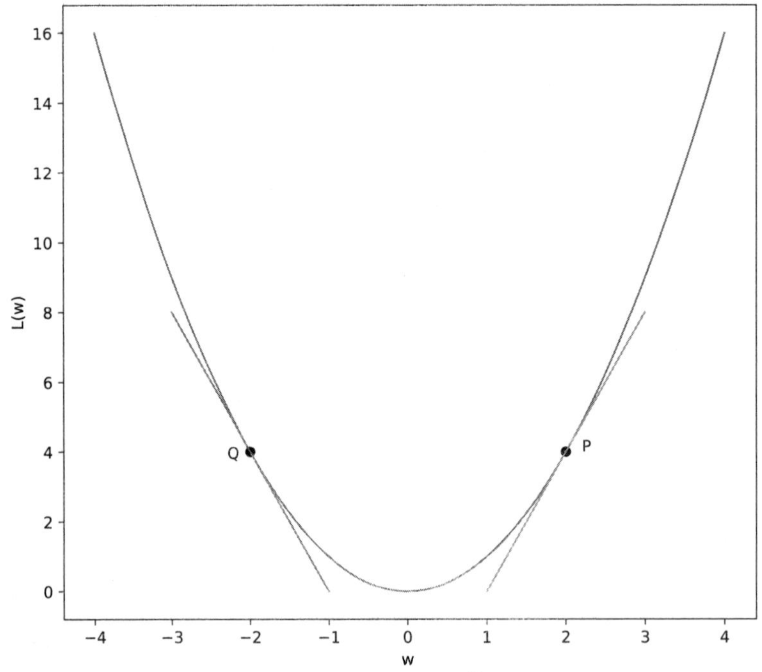

(b) Parabola: $L(w) = w^2,\ \frac{dL}{dw} = 2w$

Figure 3.4 **δL in terms of δw in one dimension, illustrated with two example curves: a straight line and a parabola. In general, $\delta L = \frac{dL}{dw}\delta w$. To decrease loss, δw must have the opposite sign of the derivative $\frac{dL}{dw}$. In (a), this implies we always have to move left (decrease w) to decrease L. In (b), if we are in the left half (e.g., point Q), the derivative is negative, and we have to move to the right to decrease L. But if we are in the right half, the derivative is positive, and we have to move to the left to decrease L. Geometrically, this is equivalent to following the tangent "downward."**

NOTE Equation 3.3 basically tells us that to reduce the loss value, we have to follow the tangent, moving to the right (i.e., positive δw) if the derivative is negative and moving to the left (i.e., negative δw) if the derivative is positive.

MULTIDIMENSIONAL LOSS FUNCTIONS

If there are many tunable parameters, our loss function will be a function of many variables, which implies that we have a high-dimensional vector $\vec{w}$ and a loss function $L(\vec{w})$. Our goal is to compute the change δL in $L(\vec{w})$ caused by a small vector displacement $\vec{\delta w}$.

We immediately note a fundamental difference from the one-dimensional case: the parameter change is a vector, $\vec{\delta w}$, which has not only a magnitude denoted $\|\vec{\delta w}\|$ but also a direction denoted by the unit vector $\hat{\delta w}$. We can take a step of the same size in the w space, and the change in $L(\vec{w})$ will be different for different directions. The situation is illustrated in figure 3.5, which shows an example loss function $L(\vec{w}) \equiv L(w_0, w_1) = 2w_0^2 + 3w_1^2$ for two independent variables w_0 and w_1. Let's examine how this loss function changes with a few concrete examples.

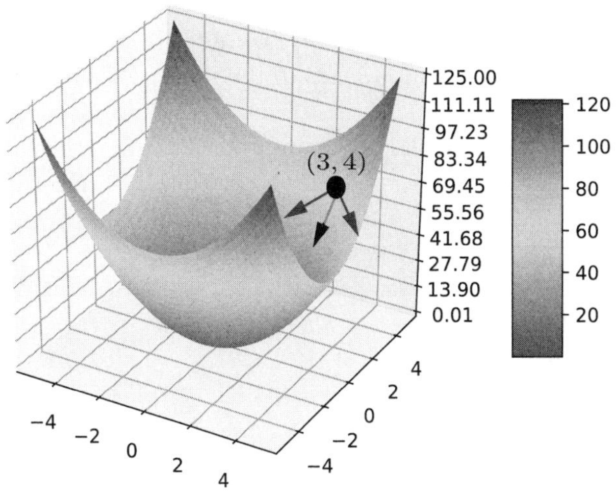

Figure 3.5 Plot for surface $L(\vec{w}) \equiv L(w_0, w_1) = 2w_0^2 + 3w_1^2$ against $\vec{w} \equiv (w_0, w_1)$. From an example point $P \equiv (w_0 = 3, w_1 = 4, L = 66)$ on the surface, we can travel in many directions to reduce L. Some of these are shown by arrows. The maximum reduction occurs when we travel along the dark arrow: this happens when $\vec{w}$ is changed along $\vec{\delta w} = [-12, -24]^T$, which is the negative of the gradient of $L(\vec{w})$ at P.

Suppose we are at $\vec{w} = \begin{bmatrix} w_0 = 3 \\ w_1 = 4 \end{bmatrix}$. The corresponding value of $L(\vec{w})$ is $2 * 3^2 + 3 * 4^2 = 66$.

Now, suppose we undergo a small displacement from this point: $\vec{\delta w} = \begin{bmatrix} 0.0003 \\ 0.0004 \end{bmatrix}$. The new value is $L\left(\vec{w} + \vec{\delta w}\right) = L(3.0003, 4.0004) = 2 * 3.0003^2 + 3 * 4.0004^2 \approx 66.0132066$. Thus this displacement vector $\vec{\delta w} = \begin{bmatrix} 0.0003 \\ 0.0004 \end{bmatrix}$ causes a change $\delta L = 66.01320066 - 66 = 0.01320066$ in L.

On the other hand, if the displacement vector is $\vec{\delta w} = \begin{bmatrix} 0.0004 \\ 0.0003 \end{bmatrix}$, we get $L\left(\vec{w} + \vec{\delta w}\right) = L(3.0004, 4.0003) = 2 * 3.0004^2 + 3 * 4.0003^2 \approx 66.0120006$. Thus, this displacement vector causes a change $\delta L = 66.0120006 - 66 = 0.0120006$ in L. The displacement vectors $\vec{\delta w} = \begin{bmatrix} 0.0003 \\ 0.0004 \end{bmatrix}$ and $\vec{\delta w} = \begin{bmatrix} 0.0004 \\ 0.0003 \end{bmatrix}$ have the same length $\sqrt{0.0003^2 + 0.0004^2} = \sqrt{0.0004^2 + 0.0003^2} = 0.0005$ but different directions. The change they cause to the function value is different. This exemplifies our thesis that in multivariable loss function, the change in the loss function depends not only on the magnitude but also on the direction of the displacement in the parameter space.

What is the general relationship between the displacement vector $\vec{\delta w}$ in the parameter space and the overall change in loss $L(\vec{w})$? To examine this question, we need to know what a partial derivative is.

PARTIAL DERIVATIVES

The derivative $\frac{dL}{dw}$ of a function $L(w)$ indicates the rate of change of the function with respect to w. But if L is a function of many variables, how does it change if only one of those variables is changed? This question leads to the notion of partial derivatives.

The *partial derivative* of a function of many variables is a derivative taken with respect to exactly one variable, treating all other variables as constants. For instance, given $L(\vec{w}) \equiv L(w_0, w_1) = 2w_0^2 + 3w_1^2$, the partial derivatives with respect to w_0 , w_1 are

$$\frac{\partial L}{\partial w_0} = 4w_0$$

$$\frac{\partial L}{\partial w_1} = 6w_1$$

TOTAL CHANGE IN A MULTIDIMENSIONAL FUNCTION

Partial derivatives estimate the change in a function if a single variable changes and the others stay constant. How do we estimate the change in a function's value if all the variables change together?

The total change can be estimated by taking a weighted combination of the partial derivatives. Let $\vec{w}$ and $\vec{\delta w}$ denote the point and the displacement vector, respectively:

$$\vec{w} = \begin{bmatrix} w_0 \\ w_1 \\ \vdots \\ w_n \end{bmatrix}$$

$$\vec{\delta w} = \begin{bmatrix} \delta w_0 \\ \delta w_1 \\ \vdots \\ \delta w_n \end{bmatrix}$$

Then

$$\begin{aligned} \delta L(\vec{w}) &= L\left(\vec{w} + \vec{\delta w}\right) - L(\vec{w}) \\ &= \frac{\partial L}{\partial w_0}\delta w_0 + \frac{\partial L}{\partial w_1}\delta w_1 + \cdots + \frac{\partial L}{\partial w_n}\delta w_n \end{aligned} \tag{3.4}$$

Equation 3.4 essentially says that the total change in L is obtained by adding up the changes caused by displacements in individual variables. The rate of change of L with respect to the change in w_i only is $\frac{\partial L}{\partial w_i}$. The displacement along the variable w_i is δw_i. Hence, the change caused by the ith element of the displacement is $\frac{\partial L}{\partial w_i}\delta w_i$— this follows from equation 3.3. The total change is obtained by adding the changes caused by individual elements of the displacement vector: that is, summing over all i from 0 to n. This leads to equation 3.4. Thus equation 3.4 is simply the multidimensional version of equation 3.3.

GRADIENTS

It would be nice to be able to represent equation 3.4 compactly. To do this, we define a quantity called a *gradient*: the vector of all the partial derivatives.

Given an n-dimensional function $L(\vec{w})$, its gradient is defined as

$$\nabla L(\vec{w}) = \begin{bmatrix} \frac{\partial L}{\partial w_0} \\ \frac{\partial L}{\partial w_1} \\ \vdots \\ \frac{\partial L}{\partial w_n} \end{bmatrix} \tag{3.5}$$

Using gradients, we can rewrite equation 3.4 as

$$\begin{aligned} \delta L(\vec{w}) &= L\left(\vec{w} + \vec{\delta w}\right) - L(\vec{w}) \\ &= \frac{\partial L}{\partial w_0}\delta w_0 + \frac{\partial L}{\partial w_1}\delta w_1 + \cdots + \frac{\partial L}{\partial w_n}\delta w_n \\ &= \left(\nabla L(\vec{w})\right)^T \vec{\delta w} = \nabla L(\vec{w}) \cdot \vec{\delta w} \end{aligned} \tag{3.6}$$

Equation 3.6 tells us that the total change, δL in $L(\vec{w})$, caused by displacement $\vec{\delta w}$ from $\vec{w}$ in parameter space is the dot product between the gradient vector $\nabla L(\vec{w})$ and the displacement vector $\vec{\delta w}$. This is the exact multidimensional analog of equation 3.3.

Recall from section 2.5.6 that the dot product of two vectors (of fixed magnitude) attains a maximum value when the vectors are aligned in direction. This yields a physical interpretation of the gradient vector: its direction is the direction in parameter space *along which the multidimensional function is changing fastest.* It is the multidimensional counterpart of the derivative. This is why, in machine learning, when we want to minimize the loss function, we change the parameter values along the direction of the gradient vector of the loss function.

THE GRADIENT IS ZERO AT THE MINIMUM

Any *optimum* (that is, maximum or minimum) of a function is a point of inflection. This means the function turns around at the optimum point. In other words, the gradient direction on one side of the optimum is the opposite of that on the other side. If we try to travel smoothly from positive values to negative values, we must cross zero somewhere in between. Thus, the gradient is zero at the exact point of inflection (maximum or minimum). This is easiest to see in 2D and is depicted in figure 3.6. However, the idea is general: it works in higher dimensions, too. The fact that the gradient becomes zero at the optimum is often used to algebraically compute the optimum. The following example illustrates this.

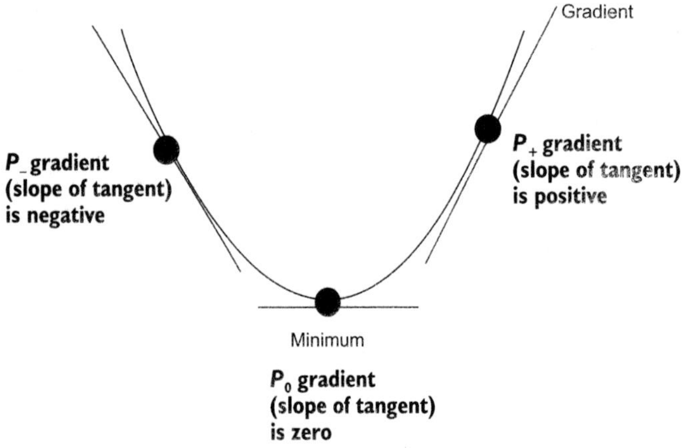

Figure 3.6 The minimum is always a point of inflection, meaning the function turns around at that point. If we consider any two points P_- and P_+ on both sides of the minimum, the gradient is positive on one side and negative on the other. Assuming the gradient changes smoothly, it must be zero in between, at the minimum.

Consider the simple example function $L(w_0, w_1) = \sqrt{w_0^2 + w_1^2}$. Its optimum occurs when its gradient is zero:

$$\nabla_{\vec{w}} L = \begin{bmatrix} \frac{\partial L}{\partial w_0} \\ \frac{\partial L}{\partial w_1} \end{bmatrix} = \frac{1}{2\sqrt{w_0^2 + w_1^2}} \begin{bmatrix} 2w_0 \\ 2w_1 \end{bmatrix} = \begin{bmatrix} 0 \\ 0 \end{bmatrix}$$

The solution is

$$w_0 = 0, \quad w_1 = 0$$

The function attains its minimum value at the origin, which agrees with our intuition.

3.3.2 Level surface representation and loss minimization

In figure 3.5, we plotted the loss function $L(\vec{w})$ against the parameter values $\vec{w}$. In this section, we study a different way of visualizing loss surfaces. This will lend further insight into gradients and minimization.

We will continue with our simple example function from the last subsection. Consider a field $L(w_0, w_1) = \sqrt{w_0^2 + w_1^2}$. Its domain is the infinite 2D plane defined by the axes W_0 and W_1. Note that the function has constant values along concentric circles centered on the origin. For instance, at all points on the circumference of the circle $w_0^2 + w_1^2 = 1$, the function has a constant function value of 1. At all points on the circumference of the circle $w_0^2 + w_1^2 = 25$, the function has a constant function value of 5. Such constant function value curves on the domain are called *level contours* in 2D. This is shown as a heat map in figure 3.7. The idea of level contours can be generalized to higher dimensions where we have level surfaces or level hypersurfaces. Note that while the $\vec{w}$, $L(\vec{w})$ in figure 3.5 was on an $(n+1)$-dimensional space (where n is the dimensionality of $\vec{w}$), the level surface/contour representation is in n-dimensional space. At any point on the domain, what is the direction along which the biggest *change* in the function value occurs? The answer is *along the direction of the gradient.* The magnitude of the change corresponds to the magnitude of the gradient. In the current example, say we are at a point (w_0, w_1). There exists a level contour through this point: the circle with origin at the center passing through (w_0, w_1). If we move along the circumference of this circle—that is, along the tangent to this circle—the function value does not change. In other words, at any point, the tangent to the level contour through that point is the direction of *minimal* change. On the other hand, *if we move perpendicular to the tangent, maximum change in the function value occurs.* The perpendicular to the tangent is known as a *normal.* This is the direction of the gradient. *The gradient at any point on the domain is always normal to the level contour through that point, indicating the direction of maximum change in the function value.* In figure 3.7, the gradients are all parallel to the radii of the concentric circles.

Recall that while training a machine learning model, we essentially define a loss function in terms of a tunable set of parameters and try to minimize the loss by adjusting (tuning) the parameters. We start at a random point and iteratively progress toward the minimum. Geometrically, this can be viewed as starting at an arbitrary point on the domain and continuing to move in a direction that minimizes the function value. Of course, we would like to progress to the minimum of the function value in as few iterations as possible. In figure 3.7, the minimum is at the origin, which is also the center of all the concentric circles. Wherever we start, we will have to always travel radially inward to reach the minimum $(0, 0)$ of the function $\sqrt{w_0^2 + w_1^2}$.

In higher dimensions, level contours become level surfaces. Given any function $L(\vec{w})$ with $\vec{w}] \in \mathbb{R}^n$, we define level surfaces as $L(\vec{w}) = constant$. If we move along the level surface, the change in $L(\vec{w})$ is minimal (0). The gradient of a function at any point is normal to the level surface through that point. This is the direction along which the function value is changing fastest. Moving along the gradient, we pass from one level surface to another, as shown in figure 3.8. Here the function is

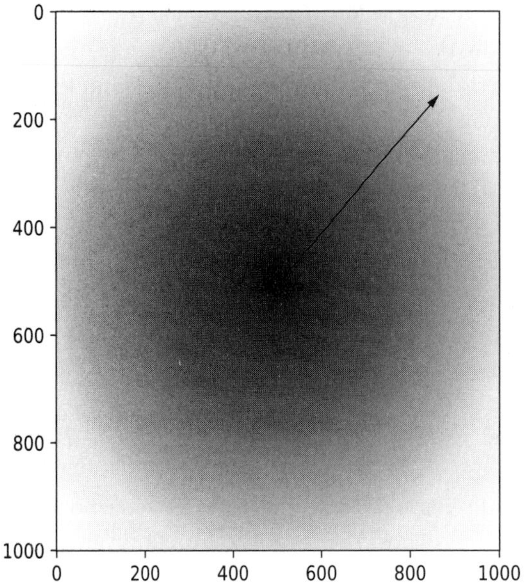

Figure 3.7 The domain of $L(w_0, w_1) = \sqrt{w_0^2 + w_1^2}$ shown as a heat map of function values. Gradients point radially outward, as shown by the arrowed line. The intensity of the heat map changes fastest along the gradient (that is, radii). This is the direction to follow to rapidly reach lower values of the function represented by the heat map.

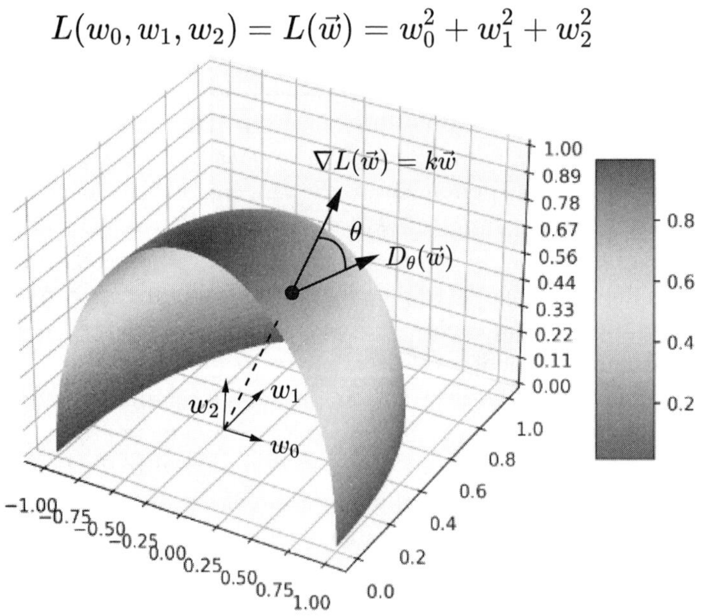

Figure 3.8 Gradient example in 3D: the function $L(w_0, w_1, w_2) = L(\vec{w}) = w_0^2 + w_1^2 + w_2^2$. The level surfaces $L(\vec{w}) = constant$ are concentric spheres with the origin as their center. One such surface is partially shown in the diagram. $\nabla L(\vec{w}) = k\,[w_0 \;\; w_1 \;\; w_2]^T$—the gradient points radially outward. Moving along the gradient, we go from one level surface to another, corresponding to maximum change in $L(\vec{w})$. Moving along any direction orthogonal to the gradient, we stay on the same level surface (sphere), which corresponds to zero change in the function value. $D_\theta(\vec{w})$ denotes the directional derivative along the displacement direction making angle θ with the gradient. If $\hat{l}$ denotes this displacement direction, $D_\theta(\vec{w}) = \nabla L(\vec{w}) \cdot \hat{l}$.

3D: $L(\vec{w}) = L(w_0, w_1, w_2) = w_0^2 + w_1^2 + w_2^2$. The level surfaces $w_0^2 + w_1^2 + w_2^2 = constant$ for various values of the constant are concentric spheres, with the origin as their center. The gradient vector at any point is along the outward-pointing radius of the sphere through that point.

Another example is shown in figure 3.9. Here the function is 3D: $L(\vec{w}) = f(w_0, w_1, w_2) = w_0^2 + w_1^2$. The level surfaces $w_0^2 + w_1^2 = constant$ for various values of the constant are coaxial cylinders, with w_2 as the axis. The gradient vector at any point is along the outward-pointing radius of the planar circle belonging to the cylinder through that point.

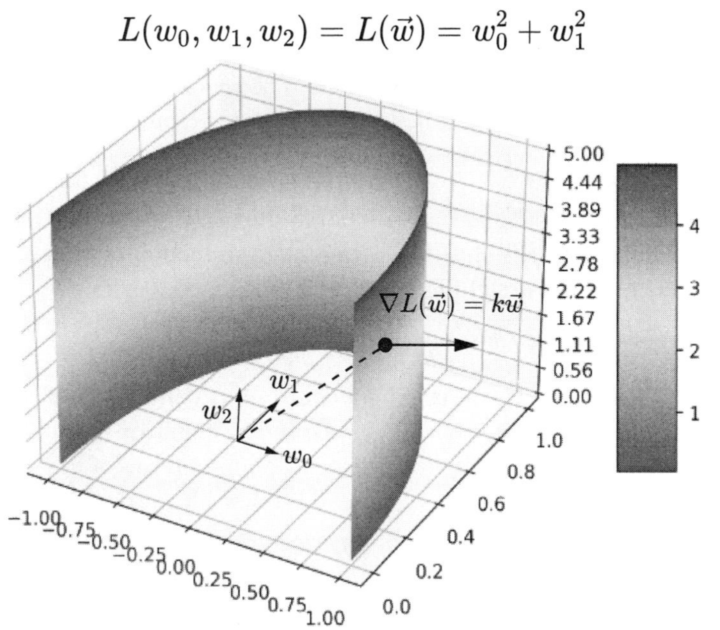

Figure 3.9 Gradient example in 3D: the function $L(w_0, w_1, w_2) = L(\vec{w}) = w_0^2 + w_1^2$. The level surfaces $f(\vec{w}) = constant$ are coaxial cylinders. One such surface is partially shown in the diagram: $\nabla L(\vec{w}) = k[w_0 \ w_1 \ 0]^T$. The gradient is normal to the curved surface of the cylinder along the outward radius of the circle. Moving along the gradient, we go from one level surface to another, corresponding to the maximum change in $L(\vec{w})$. Moving along any direction orthogonal to the gradient, we stay on the same level surface (cylinder), which corresponds to zero change in the function value.

So far, we have studied the change in loss value resulting from infinitesimally small displacements in the parameter space. In practice, the programmatic displacements undergone during parameter updates while training are small, but not infinitesimally so. Is there any way to improve the approximation in these cases? This is discussed in the following section.

3.4 Local approximation for the loss function

Equation 3.6 expresses the change δL in the loss value corresponding to displacement $\delta\vec{w}$ in the parameter space. The equation is exactly true if and only if the loss function is linear or the magnitude of the displacement is infinitesimally small. In practice, we adjust parameter values by small—but not infinitesimally small—amounts. Under these circumstances, equation 3.6 is only approximately true: the larger the magnitude of $||\vec{\delta w}||$, the worse the approximation.

A Taylor series offers a way to approximate a multidimensional function in the local neighborhood of any point by expressing it in terms of the displacements in the parameter space. It is an infinite series, meaning the equation is exactly true (zero approximation) only when we have summed an infinite number of terms. Of course, we cannot add an infinite number of terms with a computer program. But we can improve the accuracy of the approximation as much as we like by including more and more terms. In practice, we include at most up to the second term. Anything beyond that is redundant because the improvement is too small to be realized by the floating point system of current computers. First we will study a Taylor series in one dimension.

3.4.1 1D Taylor series recap

Suppose we are trying to describe the curve $L(w)$ in the neighborhood of a particular point w. If we stay infinitesimally close to w, then, as described in section 3.3, we can approximate the curve with a straight line:

$$L(w + \delta w) = L(w) + \frac{dL}{dw}\delta w$$

But in the general case, if we are describing a continuous (smooth) function in the neighborhood of a specific point, we use a Taylor series. A Taylor series allows us to describe a function in the neighborhood of a specific point in terms of the value of the function and its derivatives at that point. Doing so is relatively simple in 1D:

$$L(w + \delta w) = L(w) + \frac{(\delta w)}{1!}\frac{dL}{dw} + \frac{(\delta w)^2}{2!}\frac{d^2L}{dw^2} + \cdots \tag{3.7}$$

Note that the terms become progressively smaller (since they involve higher and higher powers of a small number δw). Hence, although the series goes on to infinity, in practice we entail a negligible loss in accuracy by dropping higher-order terms. We often use the first-order approximation (or, at most, second-order). Equation 3.7 can be rewritten as

$$\delta L = L(w + \delta w) - L(w) = \frac{(\delta w)}{1!}\frac{dL}{dw} + \frac{(\delta w)^2}{2!}\frac{d^2L}{dw^2} + \cdots$$

Note that the second term has $(\delta w)^2$ as a factor, which is nearly zero at small values of the displacement δw. So, for really small δw, we include only the first term. Then we get $\delta L = \frac{(\delta w)}{1!}\frac{dL}{dw}$, which is the same as equation 3.3. If δw is a bit larger and we want greater accuracy, we can include the second-order term. In practice, as mentioned earlier, that is hardly ever done.

A handy example of a Taylor series is the expansion of the exponential function e^x near $x = 0$

$$e^t = e^{0+t} = 1 + t + \frac{t^2}{2!} + \frac{t^3}{3!}\cdots$$

where we use the fact that $\frac{d^n}{dx^n}(e^x)|_{x=0} = e^x|_{x=0} = 1$ for all n.

3.4.2 Multidimensional Taylor series and the Hessian matrix

In equation 3.7, we express a function of one variable in a small neighborhood around a point in terms of the derivatives. Can we do a similar thing in higher dimensions? Yes. We simply need to replace the first derivative with the gradient. We replace the second derivative with its multidimensional counterpart: the Hessian matrix. The multidimensional Taylor series is as follows

$$L\left(\vec{w}+\vec{\delta w}\right)=L\left(\vec{w}\right)+\frac{1}{1!}\left(\vec{\delta w}\right)^{T}\nabla L\left(\vec{w}\right)+\frac{1}{2!}\left(\vec{\delta w}\right)^{T}H\left(L\left(\vec{w}\right)\right)\left(\vec{\delta w}\right)+\cdots \tag{3.8}$$

where $H\left(L\left(\vec{w}\right)\right)$, called the *Hessian matrix*, is defined as

$$H\left(L\left(\vec{w}\right)\right)=\begin{bmatrix}\frac{\partial^2 L}{\partial w_1^2} & \frac{\partial^2 L}{\partial w_1 \partial w_2} & \cdots & \frac{\partial^2 L}{\partial w_1 \partial w_n}\\ \frac{\partial^2 L}{\partial w_2 \partial w_1} & \frac{\partial^2 L}{\partial w_2^2} & \cdots & \frac{\partial^2 L}{\partial w_1 \partial w_n}\\ \vdots & \vdots & \vdots & \\ \frac{\partial^2 L}{\partial w_n \partial w_1} & \frac{\partial^2 L}{\partial w_n \partial w_2} & \cdots & \frac{\partial^2 L}{\partial w_n^2}\end{bmatrix} \tag{3.9}$$

The Hessian matrix is symmetric since $\frac{\partial^2 L}{\partial w_i \partial w_j}=\frac{\partial^2 L}{\partial w_j \partial w_i}$. Also, note that the Taylor expansion assumes that the function is continuous in the neighborhood.

Equation 3.8 allows us to compute the value of L in a small neighborhood around point $\vec{w}$ in the parameter space. If we displace from $\vec{w}$ by the vector $\vec{\delta w}$, we arrive at $\vec{w}+\vec{\delta w}$. The loss there is $L\left(\vec{w}+\vec{\delta w}\right)$, which is expressed by equation 3.8 in terms of the loss $L\left(\vec{w}\right)$ at the original point and the displacement $\vec{\delta w}$. This leads to

$$\delta L=L\left(\vec{w}+\vec{\delta w}\right)-L\left(\vec{w}\right)=\frac{1}{1!}\left(\vec{\delta w}\right)^{T}\nabla L\left(\vec{w}\right)+\frac{1}{2!}\left(\vec{\delta w}\right)^{T}H\left(L\left(\vec{w}\right)\right)\left(\vec{\delta w}\right)+\cdots \tag{3.10}$$

Note that the first term is same as equation 3.6 and the second term has squares of the displacement. Since the square of a small quantity is even smaller, for very small displacements, the second term disappears, and we essentially get back equation 3.6. This is called *first-order approximation.* For slightly larger displacements, we can include the second term, involving Hessians to improve the approximation. As stated earlier, this is hardly ever done in practice.

3.5 PyTorch code for gradient descent, error minimization, and model training

In this section, we study PyTorch examples in which models are trained by minimizing errors via gradient descent. Before we present the code, we briefly recap the main ideas from a practical point of view. (Complete code for this section can be found at http://mng.bz/4Zya.)

3.5.1 PyTorch code for linear models

If the true underlying function we are trying to predict is very simple, linear models suffice. Otherwise, we require nonlinear models. Here we will look at the linear model.

In machine learning, we identify the input and output variables pertaining to the problem at hand and cast the problem as generating outputs from input variables. All the inputs are represented together by the vector $\vec{x}$. Sometimes there are multiple outputs, and sometimes there is a single output. Accordingly, we have an output vector $\vec{y}$ or an output scalar y. Let's denote the function that generates the output from the input vector as f: that is, $y = f\left(\vec{x}\right)$.

In real-life problems, we do not know f. The crux of machine learning is to estimate f from a set of observed inputs $\vec{x}_i$ and their corresponding outputs y_i. Each observation can be depicted as a pair $\langle \vec{x}_i, y_i \rangle$. We model the unknown function f with a known function ϕ. ϕ is a parameterized function. Although the nature of ϕ is known, its parameter values are unknown. These parameter values are "learned" via training. This means we estimate the parameter values such that the overall error on the observations is minimized.

If $\vec{w}, b$ denotes the current set of parameters (weights, bias), then the model will output $\phi\left(\vec{x}_i, \vec{w}, b\right)$ on the observed input $\vec{x}_i$. Thus the error on this ith observation is $e_i^2 = \left(\phi\left(\vec{x}_i, \vec{w}, b\right) - y_i\right)^2$. We can batch several observations and add up the errors into a batch error $L = \sum_{i=0}^{i=N} \left(e^{(i)}\right)^2$.

The error is a function of the parameter set $\vec{w}$. The question is, how do we adjust $\vec{w}$ so that the error e_i^2 decreases? We know a function's value changes most when we move along the direction of the gradient of the parameters. Hence, we adjust the parameters $\vec{w}, b$ as follows:

$$\begin{bmatrix} \vec{w} \\ b \end{bmatrix} = \begin{bmatrix} \vec{w} \\ b \end{bmatrix} - \mu \nabla_{\vec{w},b} L\left(\vec{w}, b\right)$$

Each adjustment reduces the error. Starting from a random set of parameter values and doing this a sufficiently large number of times yields the desired model.

A simple and popular model ϕ is the linear function (the predicted value is the dot product between the input vector and parameters vector plus bias): $\tilde{y}_i = \phi\left(\vec{x}_i, \vec{w}, b\right) = \vec{w}^T \vec{x} + b = \sum_j w_j x_j + b$. Our initial implementation (listing 3.1) simply mimics this formula. For more complicated models ϕ (with millions of parameters and nonlinearities), we cannot obtain closed-form gradients like this. In such cases, we use a technique called autograd (automatic gradient computation), which does not required closed form gradients. This is discussed in the next section.

NOTE In real-world problems, we will not know the true underlying function mapping inputs to outputs. But here, for the sake of gaining insight, we will assume known output functions and perturb them with noise to make them slightly more realistic.

Listing 3.1 PyTorch linear model (closed-form gradient formula needed)

```
x = 10 * torch.randn(N)     ◄── Generates random input values
```

```
y = 1.5 * x + 2.73
y_obs = y + (0.5 * torch.randn(N))
```

Generates output values by applying a simple known function to the input and then adds noise. Let's see if our learned function matches the known underlying function.

```
for step in range(num_steps):
    y_pred = w*x + b
```

Our model, initialized with arbitrary parameter values

```
    mean_squared_error = torch.mean(
            (y_pred - y_obs) ** 2)
```

Model error is the (squared) difference between the observed and predicted values.

```
    w_grad = torch.mean(2 * ((y_pred - y_obs)* x))
    b_grad = torch.mean(2 * (y_pred - y_obs))
```

Calculates the gradient of the error using calculus. Possible only with such simple models.

```
    w = w - learning_rate * w_grad
    b = b - learning_rate * b_grad
```

Adjusts the weight, bias along the gradient of error

```
print("True function: y = 1.5*x + 2.73")
print("Learned function: y_pred = *x + ".format(w[0], b[0]))
```

The output is as follows:

```
True function: y = 1.5*x + 2.73
Learned function: y_pred = 1.50059*x + 2.746823
```

3.5.2 Autograd: PyTorch automatic gradient computation

In the PyTorch code in listing 3.1, for this specific model architecture, we computed the gradient using calculus. This approach does not scale to more complex models with millions of weights and perhaps nonlinear complex functions. For scalability, we use an *automatic differentiation* software library like PyTorch Autograd. Users of the library need not worry about how to compute the gradients—they just construct the model function. Once the function is specified, PyTorch figures out how to compute its gradient through the Autograd technology.

To use Autograd, we explicitly tell PyTorch to track gradients for a variable by setting `requires_grad = True` when creating the variable. PyTorch remembers a computation graph that is updated every time we create an expression using tracked variables. Figure 3.10 shows an example of a computation graph.

The following listing, which implements a linear model in PyTorch, relies on PyTorch's Autograd for gradient computation. Note that this method does not require the closed-form gradient.

Listing 3.2 Linear modeling with PyTorch

```
def update_parameters(params, learning_rate):
```

Updates parameters: adjusts the weight, bias along the gradient of error

```
  with torch.no_grad():
```

Doesn't track gradients during parameter updates

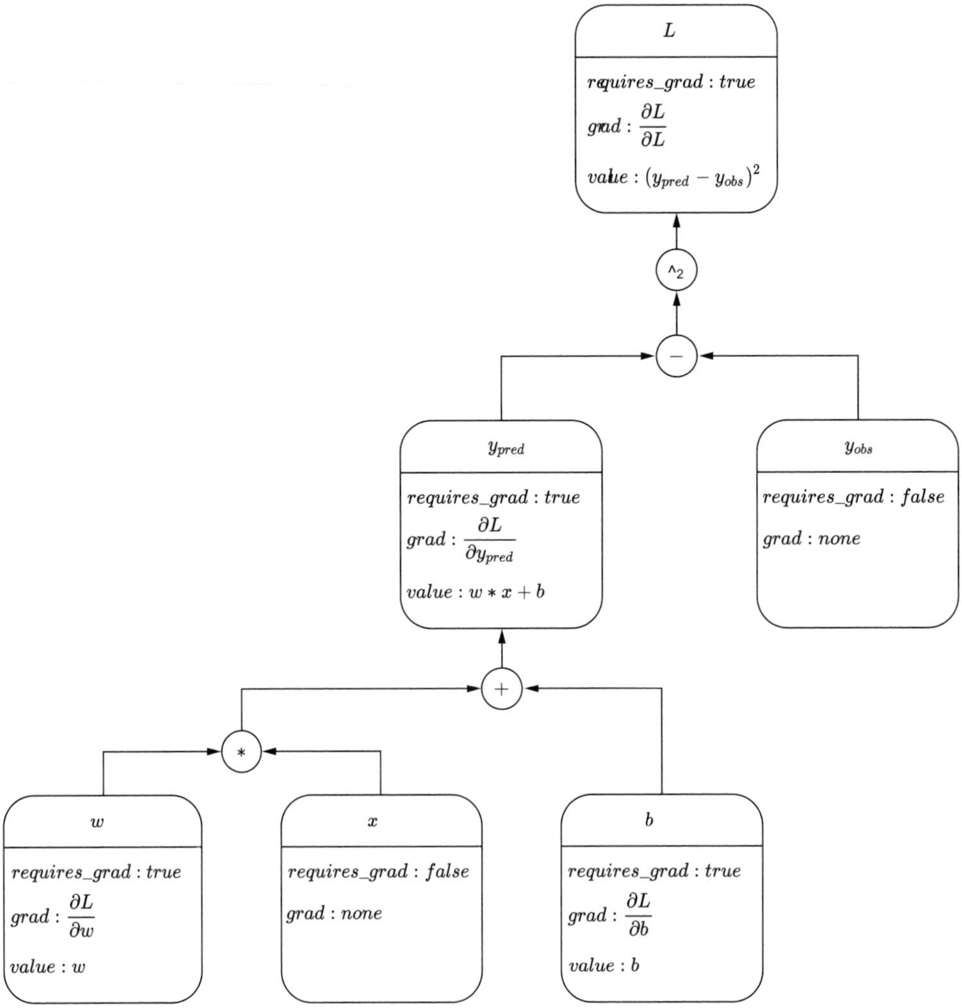

Figure 3.10 Autograd analysis

```
    for i, p in enumerate(params):
      params[i] = p - learning_rate * p.grad

    for i in range(len(params)):
      params[i].requires_grad = True      ← Restores gradient tracking

x = 10 * torch.randn(N)      ← Generates random training input

y = 1.5 * x + 2.73

y_obs = y + (0.5 * torch.randn(N))      ← Generates training output: applies a simple known function to the input and then adds noise. Let's see if our learned function matches the known underlying function.

w = torch.randn(1, requires_grad=True)
b = torch.randn(1, requires_grad=True)
params = [b, w]      ← Our model, initialized with arbitrary parameter values
```

```
for step in range(num_steps):
  y_pred = params[0] + params[1] * x

  mean_squared_error = torch.mean((y_pred - y_obs) ** 2)

  mean_squared_error.backward()

  update_parameters(params, learning_rate)

print("True function: y = 1.5*x + 2.73")
print("Learned function: y_pred = *x + "\
      .format(params[1].data[0], params[0].data.[0]))
```

The model error is the (squared) difference between the observed and predicted values.

Backpropagates: computes the partial derivatives of the error with respect to each variable and stores them in the "grad" field within the variable

Updates parameters using those partial derivatives

The output is as follows:

```
True function: y = 1.5*x + 2.73
Learned function: y_pred = 1.50059*x + 2.74783
```

3.5.3 *Nonlinear Models in PyTorch*

In listings 3.1 and 3.2, we fit a linear model to a data distribution that we know to be linear. From the output, we can see that those models converged to a pretty good approximation of the underlying output function. This is also shown graphically in figure 3.11. But what happens if the underlying output function is nonlinear?

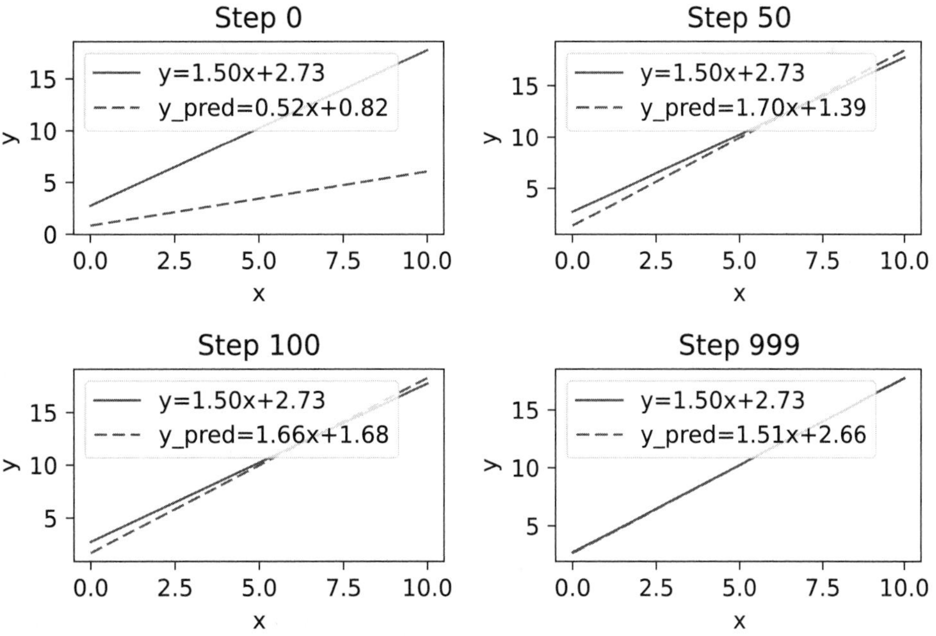

Figure 3.11 Linear approximation of linear data. By step 1,000, the model has more or less converged to the true underlying function.

First, listing 3.3 tries to use a linear model on a nonlinear data distribution. As expected (and demonstrated via the output as well as figure 3.12), this model does not do well, because we are using an inadequate model architecture. Further training will not help.

Listing 3.3 Linear approximation of nonlinear data

```
x = 10 * torch.rand(N, 1)    ← Generates random input training data

y = x**2 - x + 2.0
y_obs = y + (0.5 * torch.rand(N, 1) - 0.25)
    Generates training output: applies a known nonlinear function to the input
    and then perturbs it with noise

w = torch.rand(1, requires_grad=True)
b = torch.rand(1, requires_grad=True)
params = [b, w]
for step in range(num_steps):
  y_pred = params[0] + params[1] * x    ← Trains a linear model as in listing 3.2
  mean_squared_error = torch.mean((y_pred - y_obs) ** 2)
  mean_squared_error.backward()
  update_parameters(params, learning_rate)

print("True function: y = 1.5*x + 2.73")
print("Learned function: y_pred = *x + "\
      .format(params[1].data[0], params[0].data[0]))
```

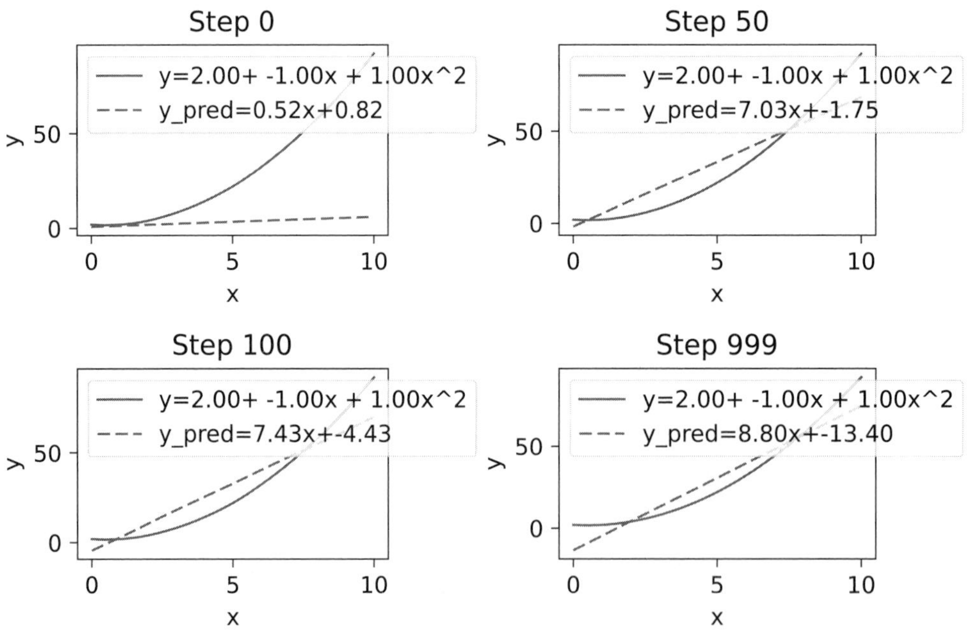

Figure 3.12 Linear approximation of nonlinear data. Clearly the model is not converging to anything close to the desired/true function. Our model architecture is inadequate.

Here is the output:

```
True function: y=x^2 -x + 2
Learned function: y_pred = 8.79633331299*x + -13.4027605057
```

Next, listing 3.4 tries a nonlinear model. As expected (and demonstrated via the output as well as figure 3.13), the nonlinear model does well. In real-life problems, we usually assume nonlinearity and choose a model architecture accordingly.

Listing 3.4 Nonlinear modeling with PyTorch

```
params = [w0, w1, w2]
for step in range(num_steps):
    y_pred = params[0] + params[1] * x + params[2] * (x**2)
    mean_squared_error = torch.mean((y_pred -y_obs) ** 2)
    mean_squared_error.backward()
    update_parameters(params, learning_rate)

print("True function: y= 2 - x + x^2")
print("Learned function: y_pred =  + *x + *x^2"\
      .format(params[0].data[0],
              params[1].data[0],
              params[2].data[0]))
```

Here is the output:

```
True function: y= 2 - x + x^2
Learned function: y_pred = 1.87116754055+-0.953767299652*x+0.996278882027*x^2
```

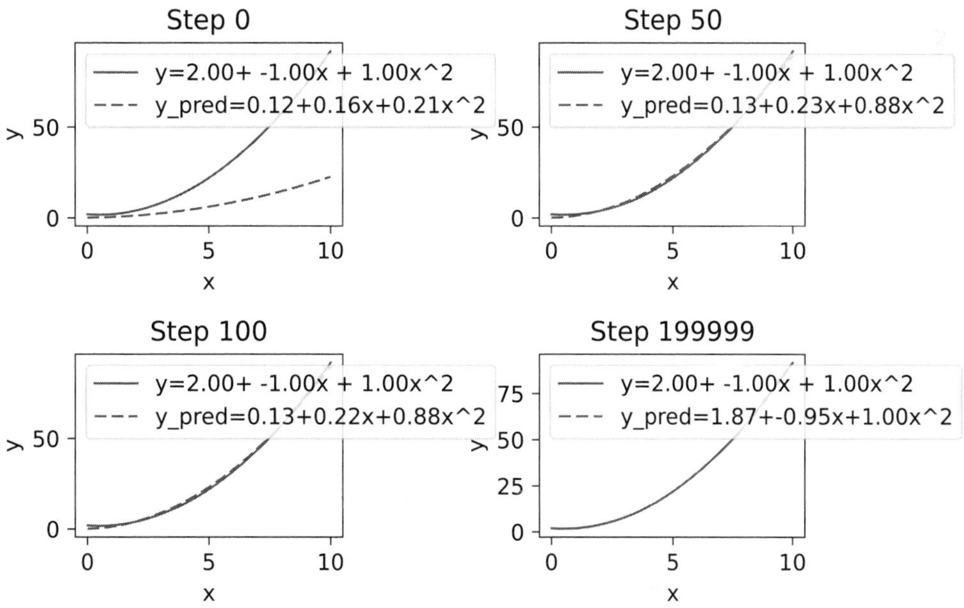

Figure 3.13 If we use a nonlinear model, it more or less converges to the true underlying function.

3.5.4 A linear model for the cat brain in PyTorch

In section 2.12.6, we solved the cat-brain problem directly via pseudo-inverse. Now, let's train a PyTorch model over the same dataset. As expected, the model parameters will converge to a solution close to that obtained by the pseudo-inverse technique (this being a simple training dataset); but in the following listing, we demonstrate our first somewhat sophisticated PyTorch model.

Listing 3.5 Our first realistic PyTorch model (solves the cat-brain problem)

```
X = torch.tensor([[0.11, 0.09], ... [0.63, 0.24]])

X = torch.column_stack((X, torch.ones(15)))

y = torch.tensor([-0.8, ... 0.37])

class LinearModel(torch.nn.Module):
    def __init__(self, num_features):
        super(LinearModel, self).__init__()

        self.w = torch.nn.Parameter(
            torch.randn(num_features, 1))

    def forward(self, X):
        y_pred  = torch.mm(X, self.w)
        return y_pred

model =  LinearModel(num_features=num_unknowns)

loss_fn = torch.nn.MSELoss(reduction='sum')

optimizer = torch.optim.SGD(model.parameters(), lr=1e-2)

for step in range(num_steps):
    y_pred = model(X)
    loss = loss_fn(y_pred, y)
    optimizer.zero_grad()

    loss.backward()

    optimizer.step()

solution_gd = torch.squeeze(model.w.data)
print("The solution via gradient descent is ".format(solution_gd))
```

Annotations:

- $X, \vec{y}$ created (see section 2.12.3) as per equation 2.22
- It is easy to verify that the solution to equation 2.22 is roughly $w_0 = 1$, $w_1 = 1$, $b = -1$. But the equations are not consistent: no one solution perfectly fits all of them. We expect the learned model to be close to $y = x_0 + x_1 - 1$.
- Adds a column of all 1s to augment the data matrix X
- Parameter is a type (subclass) of Torch Tensor suitable for model parameters (weights+bias).
- Linear model: $\vec{y} = X\vec{w}$ (X is augmented, and $\vec{w}$ includes bias)
- Ready-made class for computing squared error loss
- Ready-made class for updating weights using the gradient of error
- Zeros out all partial derivatives
- Computes partial derivatives via autograd
- Updates the parameters using gradients computed in the backward() step

The output is as follows:

```
The solution via gradient descent is [ 1.0766  0.8976 -0.9581]
```

3.6 Convex and nonconvex functions, and global and local minima

A convex surface (see figure 3.14) has a single optimum (maximum/minimum): the global one.[2] Wherever we are on such a surface, if we keep moving along the gradient in parameter space, we will eventually reach the global minimum. On the other hand, on a nonconvex surface, we might get stuck in a local minimum. For instance, in figure 3.14b, if we start at the point marked with the arrowed line indicating a gradient and move downward following the gradient, we will arrive at a local minimum. At the minimum, the gradient is zero, and we will never move out of that point.

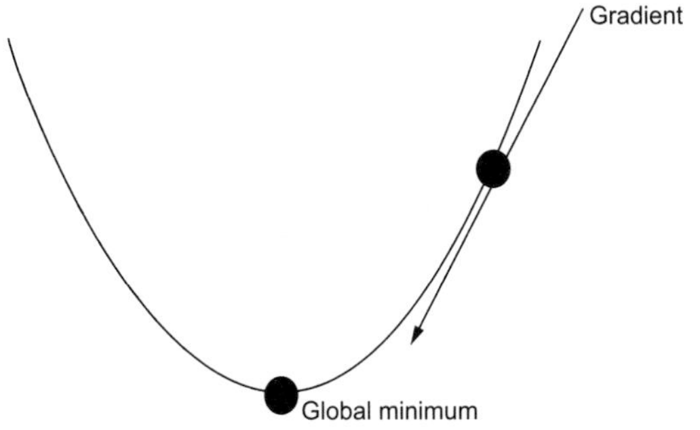

(a) A convex function

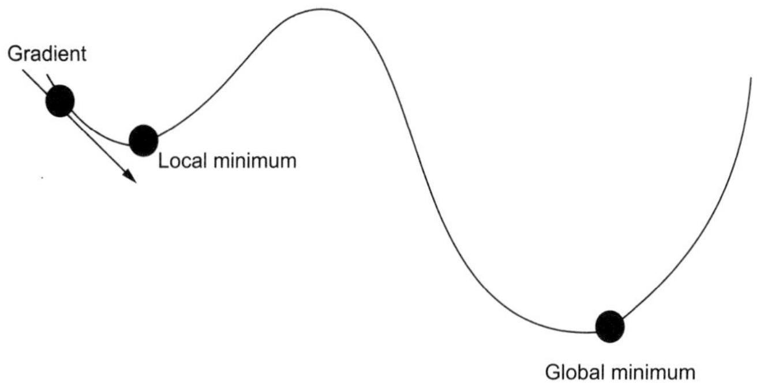

(b) A nonconvex function

Figure 3.14 Convex vs. nonconvex functions. Convex functions have only a global optimum (minimum or maximum), no local optimum. Following the gradient downward is guaranteed to reach the global minimum. Friendly error functions are convex. A nonconvex function has one or more local optima. Following the gradient may reach a local minimum and never discover the global minimum. Unfriendly error functions are nonconvex.

There was a time when researchers put a lot of effort into trying to avoid local minima. Special techniques (such as simulated annealing) were developed to avoid them. However, neural networks typically do not do anything special to deal with local minima and nonconvex functions. Often, the local minimum is good enough. Or we can retrain by starting from a different random point, which may help us escape the local minimum.

3.7 Convex sets and functions

In section 3.6, we briefly encountered convex functions and how convexity tells us whether a function has local minima. In this section, we look at convex functions in

[2] Although the theory applies to either optimum, maximum or minimum, for brevity's sake, here we will only talk in terms of the minimum

more detail. In particular, we learn how to tell whether a given function is convex. We also discuss some important properties of convex functions that will come in handy later—for instance, when we study Jensen's inequality in probability and statistics, in the appendix. We will mostly illustrate the ideas in 2D space, but they can be easily extended to higher dimensions.

3.7.1 Convex sets

Informally speaking, a set of points is said to be convex if and only if the straight line joining any pair of points in the set lies entirely within the set. For example, if we join any pair of points in the shaded region on the left-hand side of figure 3.15 with a straight line, all points on that line will also be in the shaded region. This is illustrated by points A and B in the figure. The complete set of points in any such region constitutes a convex set.

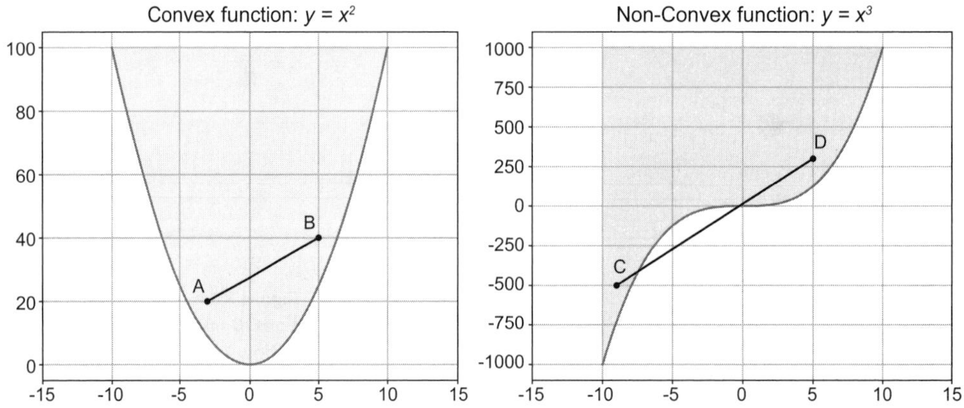

Figure 3.15 Convex and nonconvex sets. The points in the left-hand shaded region form a convex set. The line joining any pair of points in that shaded region lies entirely in the shaded region: for example, AB. The points in the right-hand shaded region form a nonconvex set. For instance, the line joining points C and D passes through a nonshaded region even though both end points belong to a shaded region.

Conversely, a set of points is nonconvex if it contains at least one pair of points whose joining line contains a point not belonging to the set. For instance, the shaded region on the right-hand side of figure 3.15 contains a pair of points C and D whose joining line passes through points not belonging to the shaded region.

The boundary of a convex set is always a convex curve.

3.7.2 Convex curves and surfaces

Consider a function $g(x)$. Let's pick any two points on the curve $y = g(x)$: $A \equiv (x_1, y_1 = g(x_1))$ and $B \equiv (x_2, y_2 = g(x_2))$. Now consider the line segment L joining A and B. From section 2.8.1 (equation 2.12 and figure 2.8), we know that all points C on L can be expressed as a weighted average of the coordinates of A and B, with the sum of weights being 1. Thus, $C \equiv (\alpha_1 x_1 + \alpha_2 x_2,\ \alpha_1 y_1 + \alpha_2 y_2)$, where $\alpha_1 + \alpha_2 = 1$. Compare

C with its corresponding point D on the curve, which has the same X coordinate: $D \equiv (\alpha_1 x_1 + \alpha_2 x_2, g(\alpha_1 x_1 + \alpha_2 x_2))$.

If and only if $g(x)$ is a convex function, C will always be above D, or

$$\alpha_1 y_1 + \alpha_2 y_2 = \alpha_1 g(x_1) + \alpha_2 g(x_2) \geq g(\alpha_1 x_1 + \alpha_2 x_2)$$

Viewed another way, if we drop a perpendicular to the X-axis from any point on the secant line joining a pair of points on the curve, that perpendicular will cut the curve at a lower point (that is, smaller in its Y-coordinate).

This is illustrated on the left-hand side of figure 3.16 with the function $g(x) = x^2$ (known to be convex) and $A \equiv (-3, 9)$ and $B \equiv (5, 25)$, $\alpha_1 = 0.3$, $\alpha_2 = 0.7$. It can be seen that the weighted average point C on the line lies above the corresponding point on the curve D. The right-hand side illustrates the nonconvex function $g(x) = x^3$, with $A \equiv (-8, -512)$ and $B \equiv (5, 125)$, $\alpha_1 = 0.3$, $\alpha_2 = 0.7$. The figure shows one weighted average point (C) on the line joining points A and B on the curve: C lies below point D on the curve, which has the same X-coordinate.

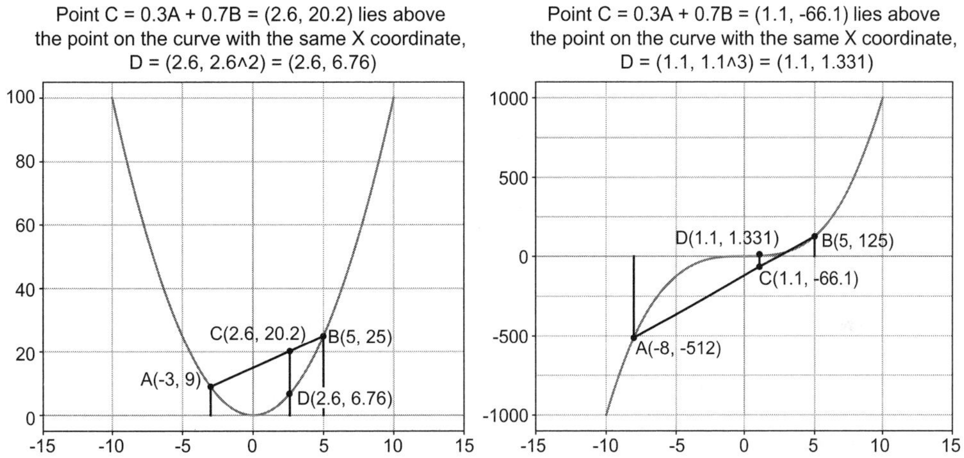

Figure 3.16 Convex and nonconvex curves. A and B are a pair of points on the curve. $C = 0.3A + 0.7B$ is a weighted average of the coordinates of A and B, with weights summing to 1. C lies on the line joining A and B. The left-hand curve is convex: C lies above the corresponding curve point D. The right-hand curve is nonconvex: C lies below the corresponding curve point D.

We need not restrict ourselves to two points. We can take the weighted average of an arbitrary number of points on the curve, with the weights summing to one. The point corresponding to the weighted average will lie above the curve (that is, above the point on the curve with the same X-coordinate). The idea also extends to higher dimensions, as discussed next.

DEFINITION 1

In general, a multidimensional function $g(\vec{x})$ is convex if and only if

- Given an arbitrary set of points on the function surface (curve, if the function is 1D), $\left(\vec{x}_1, g\left(\vec{x}_1\right)\right), \left(\vec{x}_2, g\left(\vec{x}_2\right)\right), \cdots, \left(\vec{x}_n, g\left(\vec{x}_n\right)\right)$,
- And given an arbitrary set of n weights $\alpha_1, \alpha_2, \cdots, \alpha_n$ that sum to 1 (that is, $\sum_{i=1}^{n} \alpha_i = 1$),
- *The weighted sum of the function outputs exceeds or equals the function output on the weighted sums:*

$$\sum_{i=1}^{n} \alpha_i g\left(\vec{x}_i\right) \geq g\left(\sum_{i=1}^{n} \alpha_i \vec{x}_i\right) \tag{3.11}$$

A little thought will reveal that definition 1 implies that convex curves always curl upward and/or rightward everywhere. This leads to another equivalent definition of convexity.

DEFINITION 2

In general, a multidimensional function $g\left(\vec{x}\right)$ is convex if and only if

- A 1D function $g\left(x\right)$ is convex if and only if its curvature is positive everywhere:

$$\frac{d^2 g}{dx^2} \geq 0 \quad \forall x \tag{3.12}$$

- A multidimensional function $g\left(\vec{x}\right)$ is convex if and only if its Hessian matrix (see section 3.4.2, equation 3.9) is positive semi-definite (that is, all the eigenvalues of the Hessian matrix are greater than or equal to zero). This is just the multidimensional analog of equation 3.12.

One subtle point to note is that if the second derivative is negative everywhere or the Hessian is negative semi-definite, the curve or surface is said to be *concave*. This is different from nonconvex curves, where the second derivative is positive in some places and negative in others. The negative of a concave function is a convex function. But the negative of a nonconvex function is again nonconvex.

A function that curves upward everywhere always lies above its tangent. This leads to another equivalent definition of a convex function.

DEFINITION 3

In general, a multidimensional function $g\left(\vec{x}\right)$ is convex if and only if

- A function $g\left(x\right)$ is convex if and only if all the points on the curve $S \equiv \left(x, g\left(x\right)\right)$ lie above the tangent line T at any point A on S, with S touching T only at A.
- A function $g\left(\vec{x}\right)$ is convex if and only if all the points on the surface $S \equiv \left(\vec{x}, g\left(\vec{x}\right)\right)$ lie above the tangent plane T at any point A on S, with S touching T only at A.

This is illustrated in figure 3.17.

3.7.3 *Convexity and the Taylor series*

In section 3.4.1, equation 3.7, we saw the one-dimensional Taylor expansion for a function in the neighborhood of a point x. If we retain the terms in the Taylor expansion only up to the first derivative and ignore all subsequent terms, that is equivalent to approximating the function at x with its tangent at x (see figure 3.17). This is the linear

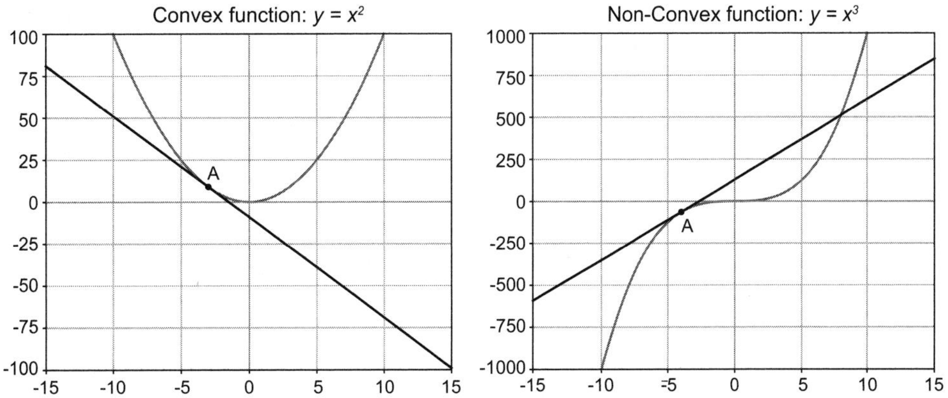

Figure 3.17 The left-hand curve is convex. If we draw a tangent line at any point A on the curve, the entire curve is above the tangent line, touching it only at A. The right-hand cuve is nonconvex: part of the curve lies above the tangent and part of it below.

approximation to the curve. If we retain one more term (that is, up to the second derivative), we get the quadratic approximation to the curve. If the second derivative of the function is always positive (as in convex functions), the quadratic approximation to the function will always be greater than or equal to the linear approximation. In other words, locally, the curve will curve so that it lies above the tangent. This connects the second derivative definition (definition 2) with the tangent definition (definition 3) of convexity.

3.7.4 Examples of convex functions

The function $g(x) = x^2$ is convex. The easiest way to verify this is to compute $\frac{d^2g}{dx^2} = \frac{d(2x)}{dx} = 2$, which is always positive. In fact, any even power of x, $g(x) = x^{2n}$ for an integer n, such as x^4 or x^6, is convex. $g(x) = e^x$ is also convex. This can be easily verified by taking its second derivative. $g(x) = logx$ is concave. Hence, $g(x) = -logx$ is convex.

Multiplication by a positive scalar preserves convexity. The sum of convex functions is also a convex function.

Summary

We would like to leave you with the following mental pictures from this chapter:

- Inputs for a machine learning problem can be viewed as vectors or, equivalently, points in a high-dimensional feature space. Classification is nothing but separating clusters of points belonging to individual classes in this space.
- A classifier is can be viewed geometrically as the hypersurface (aka decision boundary) in the high-dimensional feature space, separating the point clusters corresponding to individual classes. During training, we collect sample inputs with known classes and identify the surface that best separates the corresponding points. During inferencing, given an unknown input, we determine which side of the decision boundary this point lies in—this tells us the class.

- For two-class classifiers (aka binary classifiers), if we plug in the point in the function for the classifier hypersurface, the sign of the corresponding output yields the class.
- To compute the hypersurface decision boundary that best separates the training data, we first choose a parametric function family to model this surface (for example, a hyperplane for simple problems). Then we estimate the optimal parameter values that best separate the training data, usually in an iterative fashion.
- To estimate the parameter values that optimally separates the training data, we define a loss function that measures the difference between the model output and the known desired output over the entire training dataset. Then, starting from random initial values, we iteratively adjust the parameter values so that the loss value decreases progressively.
- At every iteration, the adjustment to the parameter values that optimally reduces the loss is estimated by computing the gradient of the loss function.
- The gradient of a multidimensional function identifies the direction in the parameter space corresponding to the maximum change in the function. Thus, the gradient of the loss function identifies the direction in which we can adjust the parameters to maximally decrease the loss.
- The gradient is zero at the maximum or minimum point of a function, which is always a point of inflection. This can be used to recognize when we have reached the minimum. However, in practice, in machine learning we often do an early stop: terminate training iterations when the loss is sufficiently low.
- A multidimensional Taylor series can be used to create local approximations to a smooth function in the neighborhood of a point. The function is expressed in terms of the displacement from the point, the first-order derivatives (gradient), second-order derivatives (Hessian matrix), and so on. This can be used to make higher-accuracy approximations to the change in loss value resulting from a displacement in the parameter space.
- Loss functions can be*convex* or *nonconvex*. In a convex function, there is no local minimum, only a single global minimum. Hence, gradient descent is guaranteed to converge to the global minimum. A nonconvex function can have both a local and a global minimum. So, gradient-based descent may get stuck in a local minimum.

4 Linear algebraic tools in machine learning

This chapter covers

- Quadratic forms
- Applying principal component analysis (PCA) in data science
- Retrieving documents with a machine learning application

Finding patterns in large volumes of high-dimensional data is the name of the game in machine learning and data science. Data often appears in the form of large matrices (a toy example of this is shown in section 2.3 and also in equation 2.1). The rows of the data matrix represent feature vectors for individual input instances. Hence, the number of rows matches the count of observed input instances, and the number of columns matches the size of the feature vector—that is, the number of dimensions in the feature space. Geometrically speaking, each feature vector (that is, row of the data matrix) represents a point in feature space. These points are not distributed uniformly over the space. Rather, the set of points belonging to a specific class occupies a small subregion of that space. This leads to certain structures in the data matrices. Linear algebra provides us the tools needed to study matrix structures.

In this chapter, we study linear algebraic tools to analyze matrix structures. The chapter presents some intricate mathematics, and we encourage you to persevere through it, including the theorem proofs. An intuitive understanding the proofs will give you significantly better insights into the rest of the chapter.

NOTE The complete PyTorch code for this chapter is available at http://mng.bz/aoYz in the form of fully functional and executable Jupyter notebooks.

4.1 Distribution of feature data points and true dimensionality

For instance, consider the problem of determining the similarity between documents. This is an important problem for document search companies like Google. Given a query document, the system needs to retrieve from an archive—in ranked order of similarity—documents that match the query document. To do this, we typically create a vector representation of each document. Then the dot product of the vectors representing a pair of documents can be used as a quantitative estimate of the similarity between the documents. Thus, each document is represented by a document descriptor vector in which every word in the vocabulary is associated with a fixed index in the vector. The value stored in that index position is the frequency (number of occurrences) of that word in the document.

NOTE Prepositions and conjunctions are typically excluded and singular; plural and other variants of words originating from the same stem are usually collapsed into one word.

Every word in the vocabulary gets its own dimension in the document space. If a word does not occur in a document, we put a zero at that word's index location in the descriptor vector for that document. We store one descriptor vector for every document in the archive. In theory, the document descriptor is an extremely long vector: its length matches the size of the vocabulary of the documents in the system. But this vector only exists notionally. In practice, we do not explicitly store descriptor vectors in their entirety. We store a <word, frequency> pair for every unique word that occurs in a document—*but we do not explicitly store words that do not occur.* This is a *sparse representation* of a document vector. The corresponding *full representation* can be constructed from the sparse one whenever necessary. In documents, certain words often occur together (for example, *Michael* and *Jackson*, or *gun* and *violence*). For example, in a given set of documents, the number of occurrences of *gun* will more or less match the number of occurrences of *violence*: if one appears, the other also appears most of the time. For a descriptor vector or, equivalently, a point in a feature space representing a document, the value at the index position corresponding to the word *gun* will be more or less equal to that for the word *violence*. If we project those points on the hyperplane formed by the axes for these correlated words, all the points fall around a 45-degree straight line (whose equation is $x = y$), as shown in figure 4.1. In figure 4.1, all the points representing documents are concentrated near the 45-degree line, and the rest of the plane is unpopulated. Can we collapse the two axes defining that plane and replace them with the single line

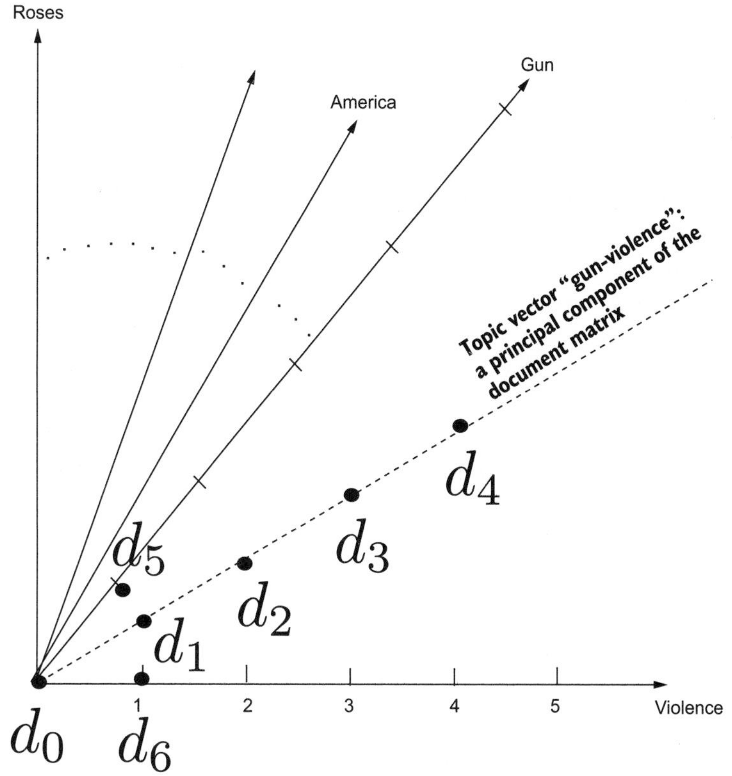

Figure 4.1 Document descriptor space. Each word in the vocabulary corresponds to a separate dimension. Dots show projections of document feature vectors on the plane formed by the axes corresponding to the terms gun and violence.

around which most data is concentrated? It turns out that yes, we can do this. Doing so reduces the number of dimensions in the data representation—we are replacing a pair of correlated dimensions with a single one—thereby simplifying the representation. This leads to lower storage costs and, more importantly, provides additional insights. We have effectively discovered a new topic called *gun-violence* from the documents.

As another example, consider a set of points in 3D, represented by coordinates X, Y, Z. If the Z coordinate is near zero for all the points, the data is concentrated around the X, Y plane. We can (and should) represent these points in two dimensions by projecting them onto the $Z = 0$ plane. Doing so approximates the positions of the points only slightly (they are projected onto a plane that they were close to in the first place). In a more realistic example, the data points may be clustered around an arbitrary plane in the 3D space (as opposed to the $Z = 0$ plane). We can still reduce the dimensionality of these data points to 2D by projecting on the plane they are close to.

In general, if a set of data points is distributed in a space so that the points are clustered around a lower-dimensional subspace within that space (such as a plane or line), we can project the points onto the subspace and perform a *dimensionality reduction* on the data. We effectively approximate the distances from the subspace with zero: since these distances are small by definition, the approximation is not too bad. Viewed another way, we eliminate smaller *from-subspace* variations and retain the larger *in-subspace* variations. The resulting representation is more compressed and also lends itself more easily to better analysis and insights as we have eliminated unimportant perturbations and are focusing on the main pattern.

These ideas form the basis of the technique called *principal component analysis* (PCA). It is one of the most important tools in the repertoire of a data scientist and machine learning practitioner. These ideas also underlie the *latent semantic analysis* (LSA) technique for document retrieval—a fundamental approach for solving natural language processing (NLP) problems in machine learning. This chapter is dedicated to studying a set of methods leading to PCA and LSA. We examine a basic document retrieval system along with Python code.

4.2 Quadratic forms and their minimization

Given a square symmetric matrix A, the scalar quantity $Q = \vec{x}^T A \vec{x}$ is called a *quadratic form*. These are seen in various situations in machine learning.

For instance, recall the equation for a circle that we learned in high school

$$(x_0 - \alpha_0)^2 + (x_1 - \alpha_1)^2 = r^2$$

where the center of the circle is (α_0, α_1) and the radius is r. This equation can be rewritten as

$$\begin{bmatrix}(x_0 - \alpha_0) & (x_1 - \alpha_1)\end{bmatrix} \begin{bmatrix}1 & 0 \\ 0 & 1\end{bmatrix} \begin{bmatrix}(x_0 - \alpha_0) \\ (x_1 - \alpha_1)\end{bmatrix} = r^2$$

If we denote the position vector $\begin{bmatrix}x_0 \\ x_1\end{bmatrix}$ as $\vec{x}$ and the center of the circle as $\begin{bmatrix}\alpha_0 \\ \alpha_1\end{bmatrix}$ as $\vec{\alpha}$, the previous equation can be written compactly as

$$(\vec{x} - \vec{\alpha})^T \mathbf{I} (\vec{x} - \vec{\alpha}) = r^2$$

Note that left hand side of this equation is a quadratic form. The original x_0, x_1-based equation only works for two dimensions. The matrix based equation is dimension agnostic: it represents a hypersphere in an arbitrary-dimensional space. For a two-dimensional space, the two equations become identical.

Now, consider the equation for an ellipse:

$$\frac{(x_0 - \alpha_0)^2}{\beta_0^2} + \frac{(x_1 - \alpha_1)^2}{\beta_1^2} = 1$$

You can verify that this can be written compactly in matrix form as

$$\begin{bmatrix}(x_0 - \alpha_0) & (x_1 - \alpha_1)\end{bmatrix} \begin{bmatrix}\frac{1}{\beta_0^2} & 0 \\ 0 & \frac{1}{\beta_1^2}\end{bmatrix} \begin{bmatrix}(x_0 - \alpha_0) \\ (x_1 - \alpha_1)\end{bmatrix} = 1$$

or, equivalently,

$$(\vec{x} - \vec{\alpha})^T A (\vec{x} - \vec{\alpha}) = 1 \tag{4.1}$$

where $A = \begin{bmatrix} \frac{1}{\beta_0^2} & 0 \\ 0 & \frac{1}{\beta_1^2} \end{bmatrix}$. Once again, the matrix representation is dimension independent. In other words, equation 4.1 represents a hyperellipsoid. Note that if the ellipse axes are aligned with the coordinate axes, matrix A is diagonal. If we rotate the coordinate system, each position vector is rotated by an orthogonal matrix R. Equation 4.1 is transformed as follows (we have used the rules for transposing the products of matrices from equation 2.10):

$$(R (\vec{x} - \vec{\alpha}))^T A (R (\vec{x} - \vec{\alpha})) = 1$$
$$(\vec{x} - \vec{\alpha})^T \left(R^T A R\right) (\vec{x} - \vec{\alpha}) = 1$$

Replacing $R^T AR$ with A, we get the same equation as equation 4.1, but A is no longer a diagonal matrix.

For a generic ellipsoid with arbitrary axes, A has nonzero off-diagonal terms but is still symmetric. Thus, the multidimensional hyperellipsoid is represented by a quadratic form. The hypersphere is a special case of this.

Quadratic forms are also found in the second term of the multidimensional Taylor expansion shown in equation 3.8: $\frac{1}{2!} \left(\vec{\delta x}\right)^T H (\vec{x}) \left(\vec{\delta x}\right)$ is a quadratic form in the Hessian matrix. Another huge application of quadratic forms is PCA, which is so important that we devote a whole section to it (section 4.4).

4.2.1 Minimizing quadratic forms

An important question is, what choice of $\vec{x}$ maximizes or minimizes the quadratic form? For instance, because the quadratic form is part of the multidimensional Taylor series, we need to minimize quadratic forms when we want to determine the best direction to move in to minimize the loss $L(\vec{x})$. Later, we will see that this question also lies at the heart of PCA computation.

If $\vec{x}$ is a vector with arbitrary length, we can make Q arbitrarily big or small by simply changing the length of $\vec{x}$. Consequently, optimizing Q with arbitrary length $\vec{x}$ is not a very interesting problem: rather, we want to know which *direction* of $\vec{x}$ optimizes Q. For the rest of this section, we discuss quadratic forms with unit vectors $Q = \hat{x}^T A \hat{x}$ (recall that $\hat{x}$ denotes a unit-length vector satisfying $\hat{x}^T \hat{x} = ||\hat{x}||^2 = 1$). Equivalently, we could use a different flavor, $Q = \frac{\vec{x}^T A \vec{x}}{\vec{x}^T \vec{x}}$, but we will use the former expression here. We are essentially searching over all possible directions $\hat{x}$, examining which direction minimizes $Q = \hat{x}^T A \hat{x}$.

Using matrix diagonalization (section 2.15),

$$Q = \hat{x}^T A \hat{x} = \hat{x}^T S \Lambda S^T \hat{x}$$

where $S = \begin{bmatrix} \vec{e_1} & \vec{e_2} & \cdots & \vec{e_n} \end{bmatrix}$ is the matrix with eigenvectors of A as its columns and Λ is a diagonal matrix with the eigenvalues of A on the diagonal and 0 everywhere else.

Substituting

$$\hat{y} = S^T \hat{x}$$

we get

$$\begin{aligned} Q &= \hat{x}^T A \hat{x} = \hat{x}^T S \Lambda S^T \hat{x} \\ &= \hat{y}^T \Lambda \hat{y} \end{aligned} \tag{4.2}$$

Note that since A is symmetric, its eigenvectors are orthogonal. This implies that S is an orthogonal matrix: that is, $S^T S = SS^T = \mathbf{I}$. Recall from section 2.14.2 that for an orthogonal matrix S, the transformation $S^T \hat{x}$ is length preserving. Consequently, $\hat{y} = S^T \hat{x}$ is a unit-length vector. To be precise,

$$\|\hat{y}\|^2 = \|S^T \hat{x}\|^2 = \left(S^T \hat{x}\right)^T \left(S^T \hat{x}\right) = \hat{x}^T S S^T \hat{x} = \hat{x}^T \hat{x} = 1 \text{ since } SS^T = \mathbf{I}$$

So, expanding the right-hand side of equation 4.2, we get

$$\begin{aligned} Q &= \begin{bmatrix} y_1 & y_2 & \cdots & y_n \end{bmatrix} \begin{bmatrix} \lambda_1 & 0 & \cdots & 0 \\ 0 & \lambda_2 & \cdots & 0 \\ \vdots & \vdots & \vdots & \vdots \\ 0 & 0 & \cdots & \lambda_n \end{bmatrix} \begin{bmatrix} y_1 \\ y_2 \\ \vdots \\ y_n \end{bmatrix} \\ &= \sum_{i=1}^{n} \lambda_i y_i^2 \end{aligned} \tag{4.3}$$

We can assume that the eigenvalues are sorted in decreasing order of magnitude (if not, we can always renumber them).

Consider this *lemma* (small proof): The quantity $\sum_{i=1}^{n} \lambda_i y_i^2$, where $\sum_{i=1}^{n} y_i^2 = 1$ and $\lambda_1 \geq \lambda_2 \geq \cdots \lambda_n$, attains its maximum value when $y_1 = 1, y_2 = \cdots y_n = 0$.

An *intuitive proof* follows. If possible, let that the maximum value occur at some other value of $\hat{y}$. We are constrained by the fact that $\hat{y}$ is an unit vector, so we must maintain $\sum_{i=1}^{n} y_i^2 = 1$.

In particular, none of the elements of $\hat{y}$ can exceed 1. If we reduce the first term from 1 to a smaller value, say $\sqrt{1-\epsilon}$, some other element(s) must go up by an equivalent amount to compensate (i.e., maintain the unit length property). Accordingly, suppose the hypothesized $\hat{y}$ maximizing Q is given by

$$\hat{y} = \begin{bmatrix} \sqrt{1-\epsilon} \\ \vdots \\ \sqrt{\delta} \\ \vdots \end{bmatrix}$$

where $\delta > 0$.

What happens if we transfer the entire mass from the later term to the first term so that

$$\hat{y} = \begin{bmatrix} \sqrt{1 - \epsilon + \delta} \\ \vdots \\ 0 \\ \vdots \end{bmatrix}$$

Doing this does not alter the length of $\hat{y}$ as the sum of the squares of the first and the other term remains $1 - \epsilon + \delta$. But the value of $Q = \sum_{i=1}^{n} \lambda_i y_i^2$ is higher in the second case (where y_1 has been beefed up at the expense of another term), since $\lambda_1 (1 - \epsilon + \delta) > \lambda_1 (1 - \epsilon) + \lambda_j \delta$ for any $j > 1$ (since, $\lambda_1 > \lambda_2 \cdots$ by assumption). Thus, whenever we have less than 1 in the first term and greater than zero in some other term, we can increase Q without losing the unit length property of $\hat{y}$ by transferring the entire mass to the first term.

This means to maximize the right hand side of equation 4.3, we must have 1 as the first element (corresponding to the largest eigenvalue) of the unit vector $\hat{y}$ and zeros everywhere else. Anything else violates the condition that the corresponding quadratic form $Q = \sum_{i=1}^{n} \lambda_i y_i^2$ is a maximum.

Thus we have established that the maximum of Q occurs at $\hat{y} = \begin{bmatrix} 1 \\ 0 \\ \vdots \\ 0 \end{bmatrix}$. The corresponding $\hat{x} = S\hat{y} = \vec{e_1}$ - the eigenvector corresponding to the largest eigenvalue of A.

Thus, the quadratic form $Q = \hat{x}^T A \hat{x}$ attains its maximum when $\hat{x}$ is along the eigenvector corresponding to the largest eigenvalue of A. The corresponding maximum Q is equal to the largest eigenvalue of A. Similarly, the minimum of the quadratic form occurs when $\hat{x}$ is along the eigenvector corresponding to the smallest eigenvalue.

As stated above, many machine learning problems boil down to minimizing a quadratic form. We will study a few of them in later sections.

4.2.2 Symmetric positive (semi)definite matrices

A square symmetric $n \times n$ matrix A is positive semidefinite if and only if

$$\vec{x}^T A \vec{x} \geq 0 \;\; \forall \vec{x} \in \mathbb{R}^n$$

In other words, a positive semidefinite matrix yields a non-negative quadratic form with all $n \times 1$ vectors $\vec{x}$. If we disallow the equality, we get symmetric positive definite matrices. Thus a square symmetric $n \times n$ matrix A is positive definite if and only if

$$\vec{x}^T A \vec{x} > 0 \;\; \forall \vec{x} \in \mathbb{R}^n$$

From equations 4.2 and 4.3, Q is positive or zero if all λ_is are positive or zero (since the y_i^2s are non-negative). Hence, symmetric positive (semi)definiteness is equivalent to the condition that all eigenvalues of the matrix are greater than (or equal to) zero.

4.3 Spectral and Frobenius norms of a matrix

A vector is an entity with a magnitude and direction. The norm $\|\vec{x}\|$ of a vector $\vec{x}$ represents its magnitude. Is there an equivalent notion for matrices? The answer is yes, and we will study two such ideas.

4.3.1 Spectral norms

In section 2.5.4, we saw that the length (aka magnitude) of a vector $\vec{x}$ is $\|\vec{x}\| = \vec{x}^T\vec{x}$. Is there an equivalent notion of magnitude for a matrix A?

Well, a matrix can be viewed as an amplifier of a vector. The matrix A amplifies the vector $\vec{x}$ to $\vec{b} = A\vec{x}$. So we can take the maximum possible value of $\|A\vec{x}\|$ over all possible $\vec{x}$; that is a measure for the magnitude of A. Of course, if we consider arbitrary-length vectors, we can make $\vec{b}$ arbitrarily large by simply scaling $\vec{x}$ for any A. That is uninteresting. Rather, we want to examine which direction of $\vec{x}$ is amplified most and by how much.

We examine this question with unit vectors $\hat{x}$: what is the maximum (or minimum) value of $\|A\hat{x}\|$, and what direction $\hat{x}$ materializes it? The quantity

$$\|A\|_2 = \max_{\hat{x}} \|A\hat{x}\|_2$$

is known as the *spectral norm* of the matrix A. Note that $A\vec{x}$ is a vector and $\|A\vec{x}\|_2$ is its length. (We will sometimes drop the subscript 2 and denote the spectral norm as $\|A\|$.)

Now consider the vector $A\hat{x}$. Its magnitude is

$$\|A\hat{x}\| = (A\hat{x})^T (A\hat{x}) = \hat{x}^T A^T A\hat{x}$$

This is a quadratic form. From section 4.2, we know it will be maximized (minimized) when $\hat{x}$ s aligned with the largest (smallest) eigenvalue of A^TA. Thus the spectral norm is given by the largest eigenvalue of A^TA

$$\|A\|_2 = \max_{\hat{x}} \|A\hat{x}\| = \sigma_1 \tag{4.4}$$

where σ_1 is the largest eigenvalue of A^TA. It is also (the square of) the largest singular value of A. We will see σ_1 again in section 4.5, when we study singular value decomposition (SVD).

4.3.2 Frobenius norms

An alternative measure for the magnitude of a matrix is the Frobenius norm, defined as

$$\|A\|_F = \sqrt{\sum_{i=1}^{m}\sum_{j=1}^{n} \|a_{ij}\|^2} \tag{4.5}$$

In other words, it is the root mean square of all the matrix elements.

It can be proved that the Frobenius norm is equal to the root mean square of the sum of all the singular values (eigenvalues of $A^T A$) of the matrix

$$\|A\|_F = \sqrt{\sum_{i=1}^{min(m,n)} \sigma_i^2} \tag{4.6}$$

4.4 Principal component analysis

Suppose we have a set of numbers, $X = \{x^{(0)}, x^{(1)}, \cdots, x^{(n)}\}$. We want to get a sense of how tightly packed these points are. In other words, we want to measure the *spread* of these numbers. Figure 4.2 shows such a distribution.

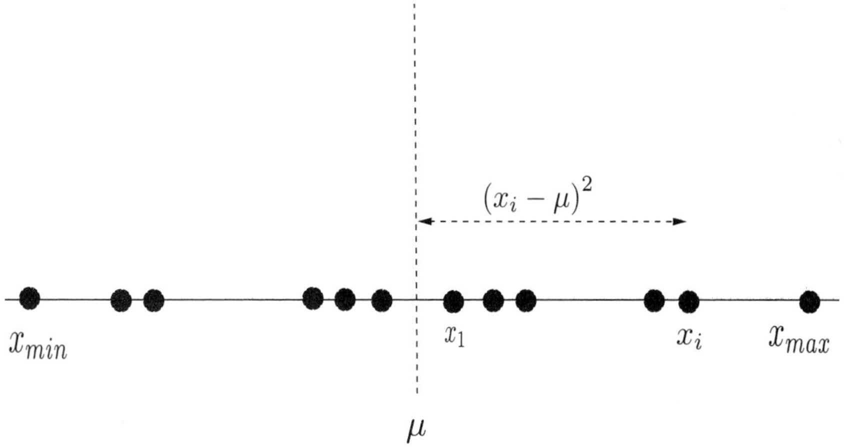

Figure 4.2 A 1D distribution of points. The distance between extreme points is *not* a fair representation of the spread of points: the distribution is not uniform, and the extreme points are far from the others. Most points are within a more tightly packed region.

Note that the points need not be uniformly distributed. In particular, the extreme points (x_{max}, x_{min}) may be far from most other points (as in figure 4.2). Thus, $\frac{x_{max}-x_{min}}{n+1}$ is not a fair representation of the average spread of points here. Most points are within a more tightly packed region. The statistically sensible way to obtain the spread is to first obtain the mean:

$$\mu = \frac{1}{n} \sum_{i=0}^{n} x^{(i)}$$

Then obtain the average distance of the numbers from the mean:

$$\sigma^2 = \frac{1}{n} \sum_{i=0}^{n} \left(x^{(i)} - \mu\right)^2$$

(If we want to, we can take the square root and use σ, but it is often not necessary to incur that extra computational burden). This scalar quantity, σ, is a good measure of the mean packing density or spread of the points in 1D. You may recognize that the previous equation is nothing but the famous variance formula from statistics. Can we extend the notion to higher-dimensional data?

Let's first examine the idea in two dimensions. As usual, we name our coordinate axes X_0, X_1, and so on, instead of X, Y, to facilitate the extension to multiple dimensions. An individual 2D data point is denoted $\vec{x}^{(i)} = \begin{bmatrix} x_0^{(i)} \\ x_1^{(i)} \end{bmatrix}$. The dataset is $\{\vec{x}^{(0)}, \vec{x}^{(1)}, \cdots, \vec{x}^{(n)}\}$.

The mean is straightforward. Instead of one means, we have two:

$$\mu_0 = \frac{1}{n} \sum_{i=0}^{n} x_0^{(i)}$$

$$\mu_1 = \frac{1}{n} \sum_{i=0}^{n} x_1^{(i)}$$

Thus we now have a mean *vector*:

$$\vec{\mu} = \begin{bmatrix} \mu_0 \\ \mu_1 \end{bmatrix} = \frac{1}{n} \sum_{i=0}^{n} \vec{x}^{(i)}$$

Now let's do the variance. The immediate problem we face is that there are infinite possible directions in the 2D plane. We can measure variance along any of them, and it will be different for each choice. We can, of course, find the variance along the X_0 and X_1 axes:

$$\sigma_{00}^2 = \frac{1}{n} \sum_{i=0}^{n} \left(x_0^{(i)} - \mu_0\right)^2$$

$$\sigma_{11}^2 = \frac{1}{n} \sum_{i=0}^{n} \left(x_1^{(i)} - \mu_1\right)^2$$

σ_{00} and σ_{11} tells us the variance along *only one* of the axes X_0 and X_1, respectively. But in general, there will be joint variation along both axes. To deal with joint variation, let's introduce a cross term:

$$\sigma_{01}^2 = \sigma_{10}^2 = \frac{1}{n} \sum_{i=0}^{n} \left(x_0^{(i)} - \mu_0\right)\left(x_1^{(i)} - \mu_1\right)$$

These equations can be written compactly in matrix vector notation:

$$\vec{\mu} = \frac{1}{n} \sum_{i=0}^{n} \vec{x}^{(i)}$$

$$C = \begin{bmatrix} \sigma_{00} & \sigma_{01} \\ \sigma_{10} & \sigma_{11} \end{bmatrix} = \frac{1}{n} \sum_{i=0}^{n} \left(\vec{x}^{(i)} - \vec{\mu}\right)\left(\vec{x}^{(i)} - \vec{\mu}\right)^T$$

NOTE In the expression for C, we are *not* taking the dot product of the vectors $\left(\vec{x}^{(i)} - \vec{\mu}\right)$ and $\left(\vec{x}^{(i)} - \vec{\mu}\right)$. The dot product would be $\left(\vec{x}^{(i)} - \vec{\mu}\right)^T \left(\vec{x}^{(i)} - \vec{\mu}\right)$. Here, the second element of the product is transposed, not the first. Consequently, the result is a matrix. The dot product would yield a scalar.)

The previous equations are general, meaning they can be extended to any dimension. To be precise, given a set of n multidimensional data points $X = \{\vec{x}^{(0)}, \vec{x}^{(1)}, \cdots, \vec{x}^{(n)}\}$, we can define

$$\vec{\mu} = \frac{1}{n} \sum_{i=0}^{n} \vec{x}^{(i)} \tag{4.7}$$

$$C = \frac{1}{n} \sum_{i=0}^{n} \left(\vec{x}^{(i)} - \vec{\mu}\right) \left(\vec{x}^{(i)} - \vec{\mu}\right)^T \tag{4.8}$$

Note how the mean has become a vector (it was a scalar for 1D data) and the scalar variance of 1D, σ, has become a matrix C. This matrix is called the *covariance matrix*. The $(n+1)$-dimensional mean and covariance matrix can also be defined as

$$\vec{\mu} = \begin{bmatrix} \mu_0 \\ \mu_1 \\ \cdots \\ \mu_n \end{bmatrix}$$

$$C = \begin{bmatrix} \sigma_{00} & \sigma_{01} & \cdots & \sigma_{0n} \\ \sigma_{10} & \sigma_{11} & \cdots & \sigma_{1n} \\ \vdots & \vdots & \vdots & \vdots \\ \sigma_{n0} & \sigma_{n1} & \cdots & \sigma_{nn} \end{bmatrix} \tag{4.9}$$

where

$$\sigma_{ij} = \sum_{k=0}^{n} \left(x_i^{(k)} - \mu_i\right) \left(x_j^{(k)} - \mu_j\right) \tag{4.10}$$

For $i = j$, σ_{ii} is essentially the variance of the data along the ith dimension. Thus the diagonal elements of matrix C contain the variance along the coordinate axes. Off-diagonal elements correspond to cross-covariances.

NOTE Equations 4.8 and 4.9 are equivalent.

4.4.1 *Direction of maximum spread*

What is the direction of maximum spread/variance? Let's first consider an arbitrary direction specified by the unit vector $\hat{l}$. Recalling that the component of any vector along a direction is yielded by the dot product of the vector with the unit direction vector, the components of the data points along $\hat{l}$ are given by

$$X' = \left\{\hat{l}^T \vec{x}^{(0)}, \hat{l}^T \vec{x}^{(1)}, \cdots, \hat{l}^T \vec{x}^{(n)}\right\}$$

NOTE Remember figure 2.8b, which showed that the component of one vector along another is given by the dot product between them? $\hat{l}^T \vec{x}^{(i)}$ are dot products and hence scalar values.

The spread along direction $\hat{l}$ is given by the variance of the scalar values in X'. The mean of the values in X' is given by

$$\begin{aligned}\mu' &= \frac{1}{n}\sum_{i=0}^{n} \hat{l}^T \vec{x}^{(i)} \\ &= \hat{l}^T \left(\frac{1}{n}\sum_{i=0}^{n} \vec{x}^{(i)} \right) \\ &= \hat{l}^T \vec{\mu}\end{aligned}$$

and the variance is

$$\begin{aligned}C' &= \frac{1}{n}\sum_{i=0}^{n} \left(\hat{l}^T \vec{x}^{(i)} - \hat{l}^T \vec{\mu} \right) \left(\hat{l}^T \vec{x}^{(i)} - \hat{l}^T \vec{\mu} \right)^T \\ &= \frac{1}{n}\sum_{i=0}^{n} \hat{l}^T \left(\vec{x}^{(i)} - \vec{\mu} \right) \left(\hat{l}^T \left(\vec{x}^{(i)} - \vec{\mu} \right) \right)^T \\ &= \frac{1}{n}\sum_{i=0}^{n} \hat{l}^T \left(\vec{x}^{(i)} - \vec{\mu} \right) \left(\vec{x}^{(i)} - \vec{\mu} \right)^T \hat{l} \\ &= \hat{l}^T \left(\frac{1}{n}\sum_{i=0}^{n} \left(\vec{x}^{(i)} - \vec{\mu} \right) \left(\vec{x}^{(i)} - \vec{\mu} \right)^T \right) \hat{l} \\ &= \hat{l}^T C \hat{l}\end{aligned}$$

Note that $C' = \hat{l}^T C \hat{l}$ is the variance of the data components along the direction $\hat{l}$. As such, it represents the spread of the data along that direction. What is the direction $\hat{l}$ along which this spread $\hat{l}^T C \hat{l}$ is maximal? It is the direction $\hat{l}$ that maximizes $C' = \hat{l}^T C \hat{l}$. This maximizing direction can be identified using the quadratic form optimization technique we discussed in 4.2. Applying that, we have the following results:

- Variance is maximal when $\hat{l}$ is along the eigenvector corresponding to the largest eigenvalue of the covariance matrix C. This direction is called the *first principal axis* of the multidimensional data.
- The components of the data vectors along the principal axis are known as *first principal components.*
- The value of the variance along the first principal axis, given by the corresponding eigenvalue of the covariance matrix, is called the *first principal value.*
- The second principal axis is the eigenvector of the covariance matrix corresponding to the second largest eigenvalue of the covariance matrix. Second principal components and values are defined likewise.
- The principal axes are orthogonal to each other because they are eigenvectors of the symmetric covariance matrix.

What is the practical significance of PCA? Why would we like to know the direction along which the spread is maximum for a point distribution? Sections 4.4.2 through 4.4.5 are devoted to answering this question.

4.4.2 PCA and dimensionality reduction

In section 4.1, we saw that when data points are clustered around a lower-dimensional subspace, it is beneficial to project them onto the subspace and reduce the dimensionality of the data representation. The dimensionally reduced data is more compactly representable and more amenable to deriving insights and analysis. In the particular case where the data points are clustered around a straight line or hyperplane, PCA can be used to generate a lower-dimensional data representation by getting rid of the principal components corresponding to relatively small principal values. The technique is agnostic to the dimensionality of the data. The line or hyperplane can be anywhere in the space, with arbitrary orientation.

For instance, consider the 2D distribution shown in figure 4.3a. Here, the data is 2D and plotted on a plane, but the main spread of the data is along a 1D line (shown by the thick two-arrowed line in the figure). There is very little spread in the direction orthogonal to that line (indicated by the little perpendiculars from the data points to the line in the figure). PCA reveals this internal structure. There are two principal values (because the data is 2D), but one of them is much smaller than the other: this reveals that dimensionality reduction is possible. The principal axis corresponding to the larger principal value is along the line of maximum spread. The small perturbations along the other principal axis can be eliminated with little loss of information. Replacing each data point with its projection on the first principal axis converts the 2D dataset into a 1D dataset, brings out the true underlying pattern in the data (straight line), eliminates noise (little perpendiculars), and reduces storage costs.

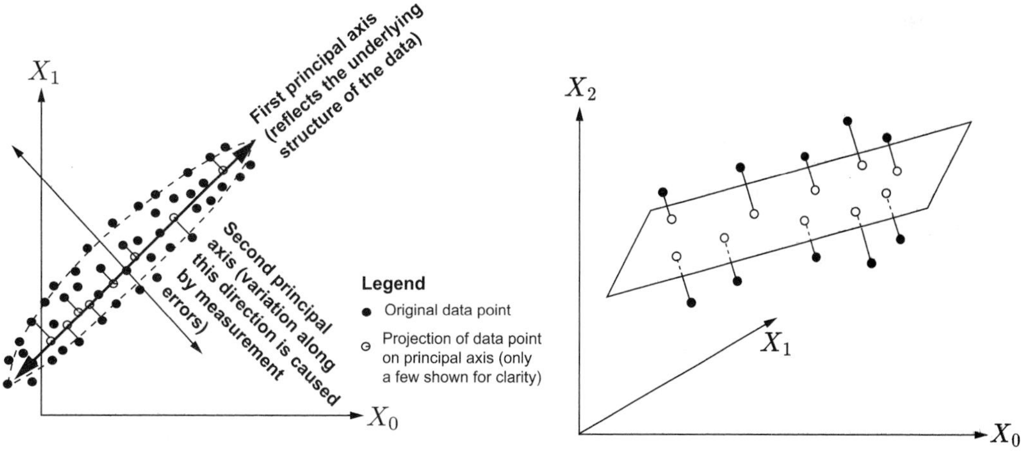

(a) Dimensionality reduction from 2D to 1D (b) Dimensionality reduction from 3D to 2D

Figure 4.3 Dimensionality reduction via PCA. Original data points are shown with filled little circles, and hollow circles represent lower-dimensional representations.

In figure 4.3b, the data is 3D, but the data points are clustered around a plane in 3D space (shown as the rectangle in the figure). The main spread of the data is *along* the plane, while the spread in the direction normal to that plane (shown with little perpendiculars from data points to the plane) is small. PCA reveals this: there are three principal values (because the data is 3D), but one of them is much smaller than the other two, revealing that dimensionality reduction is possible. The principal axis corresponding to the small principal value is normal to the plane. We can ignore these perturbations (perpendiculars in figure 4.3b) with little loss of information. This is equivalent to projecting the data onto the plane formed by the first two principal axes. Doing so brings out the underlying data pattern (plane), eliminates noise (little perpendiculars), and reduces storage costs.

4.4.3 PyTorch code: PCA and dimensionality reduction

In this section, we provide a PyTorch code sample for PCA computation in listing 4.1. Then we provide PyTorch code for applying PCA on a correlated dataset and an uncorrelated dataset in listings 4.2 and 4.3, respectively. The results are plotted in figure 4.4.

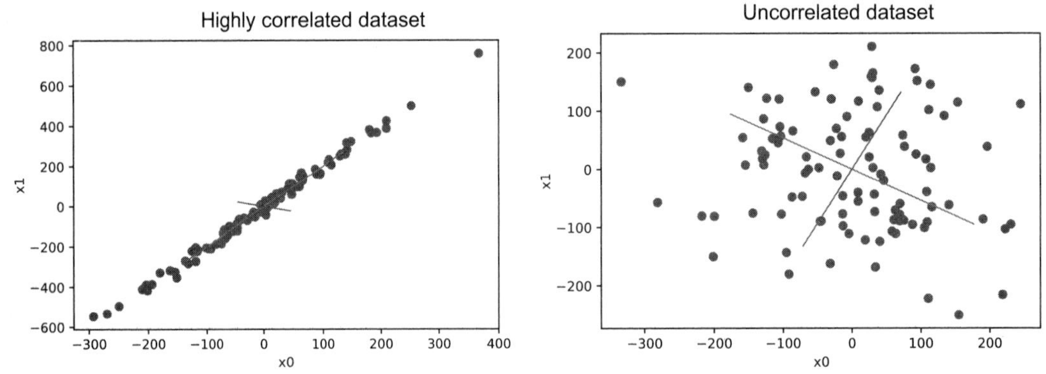

(a) PCA on correlated data

(b) PCA on uncorrelated data

Figure 4.4 PCA results. In (a), the data points are around the straight line $y = 2x$. Consequently, one principal value is much larger than the other, indicating that dimensionality reduction will work. In (b), both principal values are large. Dimensionality reduction will not work.

NOTE The complete PyTorch code for this section is available at http://mng.bz/aoYz in the form of fully functional and executable Jupyter notebooks.

Listing 4.1 PCA computation

```
def pca(X):                  ← Returns principal values and vectors

    covariance_matrix = torch.cov(X.T)
    l, e = torch.linalg.eig(covariance_matrix)
    return l, e
```

NOTE Fully functional code for the PCA computation in listing 4.1 is available at http://mng.bz/DRYR.

Listing 4.2 PCA on synthetic correlated data

```
x_0 = torch.normal(0, 100, (N,))    <-- Random feature vector

x_1 = 2 * x_0 + torch.normal(0, 20, (N,))    <-- Correlated feature
                                                  vector + minor noise
X = torch.column_stack((x_0, x_1))

^ Data matrix spread mostly along y = 2x

principal_values, principal_vectors = pca(X)

^ One large principal value       ^ First principal vector
  and one small                     along y = 2x

X_proj = torch.matmul(X, first_princpal_vec)    <-- Dimensionality reduction
                                                    by projecting on the
                                                    first principal vector
```

The output is as follows:

```
Principal values are: [62.6133, 48991.0469]
First Principal Vector is: [-0.44, -0.89]
```

NOTE Fully functional code for the PCA computation in listing 4.2 is available at http://mng.bz/gojl.

Listing 4.3 PCA on synthetic uncorrelated data

```
x_0 = torch.normal(0, 100, (N,))    | Random uncorrelated
x_1 = torch.normal(0, 100, (N,))    | feature-vector pair
X = torch.column_stack((x_0, x_1))

principal_values, principal_vectors = pca(X)

    ^ Principal values close to each other. The spread of
      the data points is comparable in both directions.
```

Here is the output:

```
Principal values are [ 9736.4033, 7876.6592]
```

NOTE Fully functional code for the PCA computation in listing 4.3 is available at http://mng.bz/e5Kz.

4.4.4 Limitations of PCA

PCA assumes that the underlying pattern is linear in nature. Where this is not true, PCA will not capture the correct underlying pattern. This is illustrated schematically in figure 4.5a and via experimental results from listing 4.3. Figure 4.5b shows the results of running listing 4.4, where we synthetically generate non-linearly correlated data and perform PCA. The straight line at the base shows the first principal axis. Projecting data

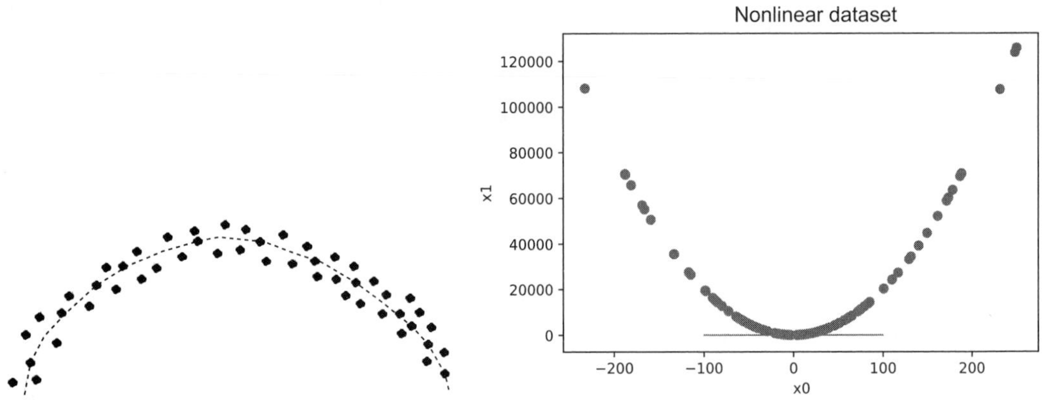

(a) Schematic 2D data distribution with a curved underlying pattern

(b) PCA results on synthetic (computer generated) non-linearly correlated data. The line at the base shows the first principal axis.

Figure 4.5 Non-linearly correlated data. The points are distributed around a curve as opposed to a straight line. It is impossible to find a straight line such that all points are near it.

on this axis results in a large error in the data positions (loss of information). Linear PCA will not do well.

Listing 4.4 PCA on synthetic nonlinearly correlated data

```
x_0 = torch.normal(0, 100, (N,))
x_1 = 2 * (x_0 ** 2) + torch.normal(0, 5, (N,))
X = torch.column_stack((x_0, x_1))

principal_values, principal_vectors = pca(X)
```

Principal vectors fail to capture the underlying distribution.

The output is as follows:

```
Principal values are [9.3440e+03, 5.3373e+08]
Mean loss in information: 68.0108526887  - high
```

4.4.5 PCA and data compression

If we want to represent a large multidimensional dataset within a fixed byte budget, what information can we can get rid of with the least loss of accuracy? Clearly, the answer is the principal components along the smaller principal values—getting rid of them actually helps, as described in section 4.4.2. To compress data, we often perform PCA and then replace the data points with their projections on first few principal axes; doing so reduces the number of data components to store. This is the underlying principle in JPEG 98 image compression techniques.

4.5 Singular value decomposition

Singular value decomposition (SVD) may be the most important linear algebraic tool in machine learning. Among other things, PCA and LSA implementations are built based on SVD. We illustrate the basic idea in this section.

NOTE There are several slightly different forms of SVD. We have chosen the one that seems intuitively simplest.

The SVD theorem states that any matrix A, singular or nonsingular, rectangular or square, can be decomposed as the product of three matrices

$$A = U\Sigma V^T \tag{4.11}$$

where (assuming that the matrix A is $m \times n$)

- Σ is an $m \times n$ diagonal matrix. Its diagonal elements contain the square roots of the eigenvalues of $A^T A$. These are also known as the singular values of A. The singular values appear in decreasing order in the diagonal of Σ.
- V is an $n \times n$ orthogonal matrix containing eigenvectors of $A^T A$ in its columns.
- U is an $m \times m$ orthogonal matrix containing eigenvectors of AA^T in its columns.

4.5.1 Informal proof of the SVD theorem

We will provide an informal proof of the SVD theorem through a series of lemmas. Going through these will provide additional insights.

LEMMA 1
$A^T A$ is symmetric positive semidefinite. Its eigenvalues—aka singular values—are non-negative. Its eigenvectors—aka singular vectors—are orthogonal.

PROOF OF LEMMA 1
Let's say A has m rows and n columns. Then $A^T A$ is an $n \times n$ square matrix

$$\left(A^T A\right)^T = A^T \left(A^T\right)^T = A^T A$$

which proves that $A^T A$ is symmetric. Also, for any $\vec{x}$,

$$\vec{x}^T A^T A \vec{x} = \left(A\vec{x}\right)^T \left(A\vec{x}\right) = \|A\vec{x}\|^2 > 0$$

which, as per section 4.2.2, proves that the matrix $A^T A$ is symmetric and positive semidefinite. Hence, its eigenvalues are all positive or zero.

We proved in section 2.13 that symmetric matrices have orthogonal eigenvectors. That proves that singular vectors are orthogonal.

Let $(\lambda_i, \hat{v}_i)$, for $i \in [1, n]$ be the set of eigenvalue, eigenvector pairs of $A^T A$—aka the singular value, singular vector pair of A. Note that without loss of generality, we can assume $\lambda_1 \geq \lambda_2 \geq \cdots \lambda_n$ (because if not, we can always renumber the eigenvalues and eigenvectors).

Now, by definition,

$$A^T A \hat{v}_i = \lambda_i \hat{v}_i \quad \forall i \in [1, n]$$

From lemma 1, singular vectors are orthogonal, and hence

$$\hat{v}_i^T \hat{v}_j = \begin{cases} 0 & i \neq j \\ 1 & i = j \end{cases} \tag{4.12}$$

Note that $\hat{v}_i$s are unit vectors (that is why we are using the hat sign as opposed to the overhead arrow). As described in section 2.13, eigenvectors remain eigenvectors if we change their length. We are free to choose any length for eigenvectors as long as we choose it consistently. We are choosing unit-length eigenvectors here.

LEMMA 2
AA^T is symmetric positive semidefinite. Its eigenvalues are non-negative and eigenvectors are orthogonal.

PROOF OF LEMMA 2

$$\left(AA^T\right)^T = \left(A^T\right)^T A^T = AA^T$$

Also,

$$\vec{x}^T AA^T \vec{x} = \left(A^T \vec{x}\right)^T \left(A^T \vec{x}\right) = \| \left(A^T \vec{x}\right) \| \geq 0$$

and so on.

LEMMA 3
$\frac{1}{\sqrt{\lambda_i}} A\hat{v}_i, \forall i \in [1, n]$ is a set of orthogonal unit vectors.

PROOF OF LEMMA 3
Let's take the dot product of a pair of these vectors:

$$\left(\frac{1}{\sqrt{\lambda_i}} A\hat{v}_i\right)^T \left(\frac{1}{\sqrt{\lambda_j}} A\hat{v}_j\right) = \frac{1}{\sqrt{\lambda_i \lambda_j}} \hat{v}_i^T A^T A\hat{v}_j$$
$$= \frac{1}{\sqrt{\lambda_i \lambda_j}} \hat{v}_i^T \left(A^T A\hat{v}_j\right)$$

Since $\lambda_j, \hat{v}_j$ are eigenvalue, eigenvector pairs of $A^T A$, the previous equation can be rewritten as

$$\frac{1}{\sqrt{\lambda_i \lambda_j}} \hat{v}_i^T \lambda_j \hat{v}_j$$

which, using equation 4.12, can be rewritten as

$$\sqrt{\frac{\lambda_j}{\lambda_i}} \hat{v}_i^T \hat{v}_j = \begin{cases} 0 & i \neq j \\ 1 & i = j \end{cases}$$

LEMMA 4
If $(\lambda_i, \hat{v}_i)$ is an eigenvalue, eigenvector pair of $A^T A$, then $\left(\lambda_i, \hat{u}_i = \frac{1}{\sqrt{\lambda_i}} A\hat{v}_i\right)$ is an eigenvalue, eigenvector pair of AA^T.

PROOF OF LEMMA 4
Given

$$A^T A\hat{v}_i = \lambda_i \hat{v}_i$$

left-multiplying both sides of the equation by A, we get

$$AA^T A\hat{v}_i = \lambda_i A\hat{v}_i$$
$$AA^T \left(A\hat{v}_i\right) = \lambda_i \left(A\hat{v}_i\right)$$

Substituting $\vec{f_i} = A\hat{v}_i$ in the last equation, we get

$$AA^T \vec{f_i} = \lambda_i \vec{f_i}$$

which proves that $\vec{f_i} = A\hat{v}_i$ is an eigenvector of AA^T with λ_i as a corresponding eigenvalue. Multiplying by $\frac{1}{\sqrt{\lambda_i}}$ converts it into a unit vector as per lemma 3. This completes the proof of the lemma.

4.5.2 Proof of the SVD theorem

Now we are ready to examine the proof of the SVD theorem.

CASE 1: MORE ROWS THAN COLUMNS IN A

If m, the number of rows in A, is greater than or equal to n, the number of columns in A, we define

$$U = \begin{bmatrix} \hat{u}_1 & \hat{u}_2 & \cdots & \hat{u}_n & \hat{u}_{n+1} & \cdots \hat{u}_m \end{bmatrix}$$

$$\Sigma = \begin{bmatrix} \sqrt{\lambda_1} & 0 & \cdots & 0 \\ 0 & \sqrt{\lambda_2} & \cdots & 0 \\ & \vdots & & \\ 0 & 0 & \cdots & \sqrt{\lambda_n} \\ 0 & 0 & \cdots & 0 \\ & \vdots & & \\ 0 & 0 & \cdots & 0 \end{bmatrix}$$

$$V = \begin{bmatrix} \hat{v}_1 & \hat{v}_2 & \cdots & \hat{v}_n \end{bmatrix}$$

Note the following:

- From lemma 1, we know that the eigenvalues of A^TA are positive. This makes the square roots, $\sqrt{\lambda_i}$s, real.
- U is an $m \times m$ orthogonal matrix whose columns are the eigenvectors of AA^T. Since, AA^T is $m \times m$, it has m eigenvalues and eigenvectors. The first n of them are $\hat{u}_1 = \frac{1}{\sqrt{\lambda_1}} A\hat{v}_1$, $\hat{u}_2 = \frac{1}{\sqrt{\lambda_2}} A\hat{v}_2, \cdots, \hat{u}_n = \frac{1}{\sqrt{\lambda_i}} A\hat{v}_n$ (from lemma 4, we know these are eigenvectors of AA^T). In this case, by our initial assumption, $n < m$. Thus AA^T has $(m-n)$ more eigenvectors, $\hat{u}_{n+1}, \cdots \hat{u}_m$.
- V is an $n \times n$ orthogonal matrix with the eigenvectors of A^TA (that is, $\hat{v}_1, \hat{v}_2, \cdots, \hat{v}_n$) as its columns.

Consider the matrix product $U\Sigma$. From basic matrix multiplication rules (section 2.5, we can see that

$$U\Sigma = \begin{bmatrix} \hat{u}_1 & \hat{u}_2 & \cdots & \hat{u}_n & \hat{u}_{n+1} & \cdots \hat{u}_m \end{bmatrix} \begin{bmatrix} \sqrt{\lambda_1} & 0 & \cdots & 0 \\ 0 & \sqrt{\lambda_2} & \cdots & 0 \\ & \vdots & & \\ 0 & 0 & \cdots & \sqrt{\lambda_n} \\ 0 & 0 & \cdots & 0 \\ & \vdots & & \\ 0 & 0 & \cdots & 0 \end{bmatrix}$$

$$= \begin{bmatrix} \sqrt{\lambda_1}\hat{u}_1 & \sqrt{\lambda_2}\hat{u}_2 & \cdots & \sqrt{\lambda_n}\hat{u}_n \end{bmatrix}$$

Note that the last columns of U, $\hat{u}_{n+1}, \cdots, \hat{u}_m$, are multiplied by all zeros in Σ and vanishing. Thus,

$$\begin{aligned} U\Sigma &= \begin{bmatrix} \sqrt{\lambda_1}\hat{u}_1 & \sqrt{\lambda_2}\hat{u}_2 & \cdots & \sqrt{\lambda_n}\hat{u}_n \end{bmatrix} \\ &= \begin{bmatrix} A\hat{v}_1 & A\hat{v}_2 & \cdots & A\hat{v}_n \end{bmatrix} \\ &= A \begin{bmatrix} \hat{v}_1 & \hat{v}_2 & \cdots & \hat{v}_n \end{bmatrix} \\ &= AV \end{aligned}$$

The later columns of U—those named with *u*s—fail to survive because they are multiplied by the zeros at the bottom of Σ.

Thus we have proved that

$$AV = U\Sigma$$

Then

$$AVV^T = U\Sigma V^T$$

Since V is orthogonal, $VV^T = \mathbf{I}$. Hence

$$A = U\Sigma V^T$$

which completes the proof of the singular value theorem.

CASE 2: FEWER ROWS THAN COLUMNS IN A

If m, the number of rows in A, is less than or equal to n, the number of columns in A, we have

$$U = \begin{bmatrix} \hat{u}_1 & \hat{u}_2 & \cdots & \cdots \hat{u}_m \end{bmatrix}$$

$$\Sigma = \begin{bmatrix} \sqrt{\lambda_1} & 0 & \cdots & 0 & \cdots & 0 \\ 0 & \sqrt{\lambda_2} & \cdots & 0 & \cdots & 0 \\ & \vdots & & & & \\ 0 & 0 & \cdots & \sqrt{\lambda_n} & \cdots & 0 \end{bmatrix}$$

$$V = \begin{bmatrix} \hat{v}_1 & \hat{v}_2 & \cdots & \hat{v}_n \end{bmatrix}$$

The proof follows along similar lines.

4.5.3 Applying SVD: PCA computation

We will illustrate the idea first with a toy dataset. Consider a 3D dataset with five points. We use a superscript to denote the index of the data instance and a subscript to denote the component. Thus the ith data instance vector is denoted as $\begin{bmatrix} x_0^{(i)} & x_1^{(i)} & x_2^{(i)} \end{bmatrix}$. We denote the entire data set with a matrix in which each feature instance appears as a row vector. The data matrix is

$$X = \begin{bmatrix} x_0^{(0)} & x_1^{(0)} & x_2^{(0)} \\ x_0^{(1)} & x_1^{(1)} & x_2^{(1)} \\ x_0^{(2)} & x_1^{(2)} & x_2^{(2)} \\ x_0^{(3)} & x_1^{(3)} & x_2^{(3)} \\ x_0^{(4)} & x_1^{(4)} & x_2^{(4)} \end{bmatrix}$$

We will assume that the data is already mean-subtracted. Now examine the matrix product $X^T X$, using ordinary rules of matrix multiplication:

$$X^T X = \begin{bmatrix} \sum_{i=0}^{4} \left(x_0^{(i)}\right)^2 & \sum_{i=0}^{4} x_0^{(i)} x_1^{(i)} & \sum_{i=0}^{4} x_0^{(i)} x_2^{(i)} \\ \sum_{i=0}^{4} x_1^{(i)} x_0^{(i)} & \sum_{i=0}^{4} \left(x_1^{(i)}\right)^2 & \sum_{i=0}^{4} x_1^{(i)} x_2^{(i)} \\ \sum_{i=0}^{4} x_2^{(i)} x_0^{(i)} & \sum_{i=0}^{4} x_2^{(i)} x_1^{(i)} & \sum_{i=0}^{4} \left(x_2^{(i)}\right)^2 \end{bmatrix}$$

From equations 4.10 and 4.9,

$$X^T X = \begin{bmatrix} \sigma_{00} & \sigma_{01} & \sigma_{02} \\ \sigma_{10} & \sigma_{11} & \sigma_{12} \\ \sigma_{20} & \sigma_{21} & \sigma_{22} \end{bmatrix} = C$$

Thus $X^T X$ is the covariance matrix of the dataset X. This holds for arbitrary dimensions and arbitrary feature instance counts.

If we create a data matrix X with each data instance forming a row, $X^T X$ yields the covariance matrix of the dataset. The eigenvalues and eigenvectors of this matrix are the principal components. Hence, performing SVD on X yields PCA of the data (assuming prior mean subtraction).

4.5.4 Applying SVD: Solving arbitrary linear systems

A linear system is a system of simultaneous linear equations

$$A\vec{x} = \vec{b}$$

We first encountered a linear system in section 2.12. It is possible to use matrix inversion to solve such a system:

$$\vec{x} = A^{-1}\vec{b}$$

However, solving a linear system with matrix inversion is undesirable for many reasons. To begin with, it is numerically unstable. The matrix inverse contains the determinant of the matrix in its denominator. If the determinant is near zero, the inverse will contain very large numbers. Minor noise in $\vec{b}$ will be multiplied by these large numbers and cause large errors in the computed solution $\vec{x}$. In this case, the inverse-based solution can be very inaccurate. Furthermore, the determinant can be zero: this can happen when one row of the matrix is a linear combination of others, indicating that we have fewer equations than we think. And what if the matrix is not square to begin with? This can happen when we have more equations than unknowns (overdetermined system) or fewer equations than unknowns (underdetermined system). In these cases, the inverse is not computable, and the system cannot be solved fully.

Even in these cases, we would like to obtain a solution that is the best approximation in some sense; and in the case of a square matrix, we would like to get the exact solution. How do we do this? Answer: we use SVD. The steps are as follows:

1. $A\vec{x} = \vec{b}$ can be rewritten as $U\left(\Sigma V^T\vec{x}\right) = \vec{b}$. We then solve $U\vec{y}_1 = \vec{b}$. This can be easily done using orthogonality of U, as $\vec{y}_1 = U^T\vec{b}$.
2. Now we have $\Sigma\left(V^T\vec{x}\right) = \vec{y}_1$ Solve $\Sigma\vec{y}_2 = \vec{y}_1$. This can be easily done because for any diagonal matrix $\Sigma = \begin{bmatrix} d_1 & 0 & \cdots & 0 \\ 0 & d_2 & \cdots & 0 \\ \vdots & \vdots & \vdots & \vdots \\ 0 & \cdots & \cdots & d_n \end{bmatrix}$ we can easily compute $\Sigma^{-1} = \begin{bmatrix} \frac{1}{d_1} & 0 & \cdots & 0 \\ 0 & \frac{1}{d_2} & \cdots & 0 \\ \vdots & \vdots & \vdots & \vdots \\ 0 & \cdots & \cdots & \frac{1}{d_n} \end{bmatrix}$

   Hence, $\vec{y}_2 = \Sigma^{-1}\vec{y}_1$.
3. Now we have $V^T\vec{x} = \vec{y}_2$. This too can be solved easily using the orthogonality of V: $\vec{x} = V\vec{y}_2$

Thus we have solved for $\vec{x}$ without inverting the matrix A:

- For invertible square matrices A, this method yields the same solution as the matrix-inverse-based method.
- For nonsquare matrices, this boils down to the Moore-Penrose inverse and yields the best-effort solution.

4.5.5 Rank of a matrix

In section 2.12, we studied linear systems of equations. Such a system can be represented in matrix-vector form:

$$A\vec{x} = \vec{b}$$

Each row of A and $\vec{b}$ contributes one equation. If we have as many independent equations as unknowns, the system is solvable. This is the simplest case; matrix A is square and invertible. $det(A)$ is nonzero, and A^{-1} exists.

Sometimes the situation is misleading. Consider the following system:

$$\begin{bmatrix} 1 & 0 & 0 \\ 0 & 1 & 0 \\ 1 & 1 & 0 \end{bmatrix} \begin{bmatrix} x_0 \\ x_1 \\ x_2 \end{bmatrix} = \begin{bmatrix} 5 \\ 7 \\ 12 \end{bmatrix}$$

Although there are three rows and apparently three equations, the equations are not independent. For instance, the third equation can be obtained by adding the first two. We really have only two equations, not three. We say this linear system is *degenerate*. All of the following statements are true for such a system $A\vec{x} = \vec{b}$:

- The linear system is degenerate.
- $det(A) = 0$.
- A^{-1} cannot be computed, and A is not invertible.
- Rows of A are linearly dependent. There exists a linear combination of the rows that sum to zero. For example, in the previous example, $\vec{r}_0 + \vec{r}_1 - \vec{r}_2 = 0$.
- At least one of the singular values of A (eigenvalues of $A^T A$) is zero. The number of linearly independent rows is equal to the number of nonzero eigenvalues.

The number of linearly independent rows in a matrix is called its *rank*. It can be proved that a matrix has as many nonzero singular values as its rank. It can also be proved that the number of linearly independent columns in a matrix matches the number of linearly independent rows. Hence, rank can also be defined as the number of linearly independent columns in a matrix.

A nonsquare rectangular matrix with m rows and n columns has a rank $r = min(m, n)$. Such matrices are never invertible. We usually resort to SVD to solve them.

A square matrix with n rows and n columns is invertible (nonzero determinant) if and only if it has rank n. Such a matrix is said to have *full rank*. Full-rank matrices are invertible. They can be solved via matrix inverse computation, but inverse computation is not always numerically stable. SVD can be applied here as well, with good numerical properties.

Non-full-rank matrices are degenerate. So, rank is a measure of the non-degeneracy of the matrix.

4.5.6 PyTorch code for solving linear systems with SVD

The listings in this section show a PyTorch-based implementation of SVD and demonstrate an application that solves a linear system via SVD.

Listing 4.5 Solving an invertible linear system with matrix inversion and SVD

```
A = torch.tensor([[1, 2, 1], [2, 2, 3], [1, 3, 3]]).float()
b = torch.tensor([8, 15, 16]).float()

x_0 = torch.matmul(torch.linalg.inv(A), b)
```

Simple test linear system of equations

Matrix inversion is numerically unstable; SVD is better.

```
U, S, V_t = torch.linalg.svd(A)
```

$\uparrow A = USV^T \implies A\vec{x} = \vec{b} \triangleq USV^T\vec{x} = \vec{b}$

```
y1 = torch.matmul(U.T, b)
```

Solves $U\vec{y}_1 = \vec{b}$. Remember $U^{-1} = U^T$ as U is orthogonal.

```
S_inv = torch.diag(1 / S)

y2 = torch.matmul(S_inv, y1)
```

Solves $S\vec{y}_2 = \vec{y}_1$. Remember S^{-1} is easy as S is diagonal.

```
x_1 = torch.matmul(V_t.T, y2)
```

Solves $V^T\vec{x} = \vec{y}_2$. Remember $V^{-T} = V$ as V is orthogonal.

```
assert torch.allclose(x_0, x_1)
```

The two solutions are the same.

Here is the output:

```
Solution via inverse: [1.0, 2.0, 3.0]
Solution via SVD: [1.0, 2.0, 3.0]
```

Listing 4.6 Solving an overdetermined linear system by pseudo-inverse and SVD

```
A = torch.tensor([[0.11, 0.09], [0.01, 0.02],
                  [0.98, 0.91], [0.12, 0.21],
                  [0.98, 0.99], [0.85, 0.87],
                  [0.03, 0.14], [0.55, 0.45],
                  [0.49, 0.51], [0.99, 0.01],
                  [0.02, 0.89], [0.31, 0.47],
                  [0.55, 0.29], [0.87, 0.76],
                  [0.63, 0.24]])
```

Cat-brain dataset: nonsquare matrix

```
A = torch.column_stack((A, torch.ones(15)))
b = torch.tensor([-0.8, -0.97, 0.89, -0.67,
                  0.97, 0.72, -0.83, 0.00,
                  0.00, 0.00, -0.09, -0.22,
                  -0.16, 0.63, 0.37])

x_0 = torch.matmul(torch.linalg.pinv(A), b)
```

Solution via pseudo-inverse

```
U, S, V_t = torch.linalg.svd(A, full_matrices=False)
```

Solution via SVD

```
y1 = torch.matmul(U.T, b)
S_inv = torch.diag(1 / S)
y2 = torch.matmul(S_inv, y1)
x_1 = torch.matmul(V_t.T, y2)

assert torch.allclose(x_0, x_1)
```

The two solutions are the same.

The output is as follows:

```
Solution via pseudo-inverse: [ 1.0766,  0.8976, -0.9582]
Solution via SVD: [ 1.0766,  0.8976, -0.9582]
```

Fully functional code for solving the SVD-based linear system can be found at http://mng.bz/OERn.

4.5.7 PyTorch code for PCA computation via SVD

The following listing demonstrates PCA computations using SVD.

Listing 4.7 Computing PCA directly and using SVD

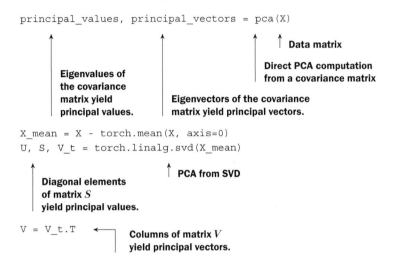

```
principal_values, principal_vectors = pca(X)
```

- Data matrix
- Direct PCA computation from a covariance matrix
- Eigenvalues of the covariance matrix yield principal values.
- Eigenvectors of the covariance matrix yield principal vectors.

```
X_mean = X - torch.mean(X, axis=0)
U, S, V_t = torch.linalg.svd(X_mean)
```

- PCA from SVD
- Diagonal elements of matrix *S* yield principal values.

```
V = V_t.T
```

- Columns of matrix *V* yield principal vectors.

The output is as follows:

```
Principal components obtained via PCA:
[[-0.44588404 -0.89509073]
 [-0.89509073  0.44588404]]
Principal components obtained via SVD:
[[-0.44588404  0.89509073]
 [-0.89509073 -0.44588404]]
```

4.5.8 Applying SVD: Best low-rank approximation of a matrix

Given a matrix A of some rank p, we sometimes want to approximate it with a matrix of lower rank r, where $r < p$. How do we obtain the best rank r approximation of A?

MOTIVATION

Why would we want to do this? Well, consider a data matrix X as shown in section 4.5.3. As explained in section 4.4.2, we often want to eliminate small variances in the data (likely due to noise) and get the pattern underlying large variations. Replacing the data matrix with a lower-rank matrix often achieves this. However, we must bear in mind that this does not work when the underlying pattern is nonlinear (such as in figure 4.5a).

APPROXIMATION ERROR

What do we mean by *best approximation*? The Frobenius norm can be taken as the magnitude of the matrix. Accordingly, given a matrix A and its rank r approximation A_r, the approximation error is $e = \|A - A_r\|_F$.

METHOD

To solidify our ideas, let's consider an $m \times n$ matrix A. From section 4.5, we know it will have $min(m, n)$ singular values. Let its rank be $p \leq min(m, n)$. We want to approximate this matrix with a rank $r(< p)$ matrix.

Let's rewrite the SVD expression. We will assume $m > n$. Also, as usual, we have the singular values sorted in decreasing order: $\lambda_1 \geq \lambda_2 \geq \lambda_n$. We will partition U, Σ, V:

$$A = U \Sigma V^T$$

$$= \begin{bmatrix} \hat{u}_1 & \cdots & \hat{u}_r & \hat{u}_{r+1} & \cdots \hat{u}_m \end{bmatrix} \begin{bmatrix} \sqrt{\lambda_1} & 0 & \cdots & \cdots & 0 & \cdots & 0 \\ 0 & \sqrt{\lambda_2} & \cdots & \cdots & 0 & \cdots & 0 \\ \vdots & \vdots & \vdots & \vdots & \vdots & \vdots & \vdots \\ 0 & 0 & \cdots & \sqrt{\lambda_r} & 0 & \cdots & 0 \\ 0 & 0 & \cdots & 0 & \sqrt{\lambda_{r+1}} & \cdots & 0 \\ \vdots & \vdots & \cdots & \vdots & \vdots & \vdots & \vdots \\ 0 & 0 & \cdots & 0 & 0 & \cdots & \sqrt{\lambda_n} \\ 0 & 0 & \cdots & 0 & 0 & \cdots & 0 \\ \vdots & \vdots & \vdots & \vdots & \vdots & \vdots & \vdots \\ 0 & 0 & \cdots & 0 & 0 & \cdots & 0 \end{bmatrix} \begin{bmatrix} \hat{v}_1^T \\ \cdots \\ \hat{v}_r^T \\ \hat{v}_{r+1}^T \\ \cdots \\ \hat{v}_n^T \end{bmatrix}$$

$$= \begin{bmatrix} U_1 & U_2 \end{bmatrix} \begin{bmatrix} \Sigma_1 & 0 \\ 0 & \Sigma_2 \end{bmatrix} \begin{bmatrix} V_1^T \\ V_2^T \end{bmatrix}$$

$$= U_1 \Sigma_1 V_1^T + U_2 \Sigma_2 V_2^T$$

It can be proved that $U_1 \Sigma_1 V_1^T$ is a rank r matrix. Furthermore, it is the best rank r approximation of A.

4.6 Machine learning application: Document retrieval

We will now bring together several of the concepts we have discussed in this chapter with an illustrative toy example: the document retrieval problem we first encountered in section 2.1. Briefly recapping, we have a set of documents $\{d_0, \cdots, d_6\}$. Given an incoming query phrase, we have to retrieve documents that match the query phrase. We will use the *bag of words* model: that is, our matching approach does not pay attention to *where* a word appears in a document; it simply pays attention to *how many times* the word appears in the document. Although this technique is not the most sophisticated, it is popular because of its conceptual simplicity.

Our documents are as follows:

- d_0: Roses are lovely. Nobody hates roses.
- d_1: *Gun violence* has reached epidemic proportions in America.

- d_2: The issue of *gun violence* is really over-hyped. One can find many instances of *violence* where no *guns* were involved.
- d_3: *Guns* are for *violence* prone people. *Violence* begets *guns*. *Guns* beget *violence*.
- d_4: I like *guns* but I hate *violence*. I have never been involved in *violence*. But I own many *guns*. *Gun violence* is incomprehensible to me. I do believe *gun* owners are the most anti *violence* people on the planet. He who never uses a *gun* will be prone to senseless *violence*.
- d_5: *Guns* were used in an armed robbery in San Francisco last night.
- d_6: Acts of *violence* usually involve a weapon.

4.6.1 Using TF-IDF and cosine similarity

Before discussing PCA, let's look at some more elementary techniques for document retrieval. These are based on term frequency-inverse document frequency (TF-IDF) and cosine similarity.

TERM FREQUENCY

Term frequency (TF) is defined as the number of occurrences of a particular term in a document. (In this context, note that in this book, we use *term* and *word* somewhat interchangeably.) In a slightly looser definition, any quantity proportional to the number of occurrences of the term is also known as term frequency. For example, the TF of the word *gun* in d_0, d_6 is 0, in d_1 is 1, in d_3 is 3, and so on. Note that we are being case independent. Also, singular/plural (*gun* and *guns*) and various flavors of the words originating from the same stem (such as *violence* and *violent*) are typically mapped to the same term.

INVERSE DOCUMENT FREQUENCY

Certain terms, such as *the*, appear in pretty much all documents. These should be ignored during document retrieval. How do we down-weight them?

The IDF is obtained by inverting and then taking the absolute value of the logarithm of the fraction of all documents in which the term occurs. For terms that occur in most documents, the IDF weight is very low. It is high for relatively esoteric terms.

DOCUMENT FEATURE VECTORS

Each document is represented by a document feature vector. It has as many elements as the size of the vocabulary (that is, the number of distinct words over all the documents). Every word has a fixed index position in the vector. Given a specific document, the value at the index position corresponding to a specific word contains the TF of the corresponding word multiplied by that word's IDF. Thus, every document is a point in a space that has as many dimensions as the vocabulary size. The coordinate value along a specific dimension is proportional to the number of times the word is repeated in the document, with a weigh-down factor for common words.

For real-life document retrieval systems like Google, this vector is extremely long. But not to worry: this vector is notional—it is never explicitly stored in the computer's memory. We store a sparse version of the document feature vector: a list of unique words along with their TF×IDF scores.

COSINE SIMILARITY

In section 2.5.6, we saw that the dot product between two vectors measures the agreement between them. Given two vectors $\vec{a}$ and $\vec{b}$, we know $\vec{a} \cdot \vec{b} = ||\vec{a}|| ||\vec{b}|| cos\,(\theta)$, where the operator $|| \cdot ||$ implies the length of a vector and θ is the angle between the two vectors (see figure 2.7b). The cosine is at its maximum possible value, 1, when the vectors are pointing in the same direction and the angle between them is zero. It becomes progressively smaller as the angle between the vectors increases until the two vectors are perpendicular to each other and the cosine is zero, implying no correlation: the vectors are independent of each other.

The magnitude of the dot product is also proportional to the length of the two vectors. We do not want to use the full dot product as a measure of similarity between the vectors because two long vectors would have a high similarity score even if they were not aligned in direction. Rather, we want to use the cosine, defined as

$$cosine\_similarity\left(\vec{a}, \vec{b}\right) = \frac{\vec{a}^T \vec{b}}{||\vec{a}|| ||\vec{b}||} \tag{4.13}$$

The cosine similarity between document vectors is a principled way of measuring the degree of term sharing between the documents. It is higher if many repeated words are shared between the two documents.

4.6.2 *Latent semantic analysis*

Cosine similarity and similar techniques suffer from a significant drawback. To see this, examine the cosine similarity between d_5 and d_6. It is zero. But it is obvious to a human that the documents are similar.

What went wrong? Answer: we are measuring only the direct overlap between terms in documents. The words *gun* and *violence* occur together in many of the other documents, indicating some degree of similarity between them. Hence, documents containing only *gun* have some similarity with documents containing only *violence*—but cosine similarity between document vectors does not look at such secondary evidence. This is the blind spot that LSA tries to overcome.

Words are known by the company they keep. That is, if terms appear together in many documents (like *gun* and *violence* in the previous examples), they are likely to share some semantic similarity. Such terms should be grouped together into a common pool of semantically similar terms. Such a pool is called a *topic*. Document similarity should be measured in terms of common topics rather than explicit common terms. We are particularly interested in topics that discriminate the documents in our corpus: that is, there should be a high variation in the degree to which different documents subscribe to the topic.

Geometrically, a topic is a subspace in the document feature space. In classical latent semantic analysis, we only look at linear subspaces, and a topic can be visualized as a direction or linear combination of directions (hyperplane) in the document feature space. In particular, any direction line in the space is a topic: it is a subspace representing a weighted combination of the coordinate axis directions, which means it is a weighted combination of vocabulary terms. We are, of course, interested in topics with high variance. These correspond to a direction along which the document vectors are well spread, which means the document vectors are well discriminated over this topic. We typically prune the set of topics, eliminating those with insufficient variance.

From this discussion, a mathematical definition of *topic* begins to emerge. Topics are principal components of the matrix of document vectors with individual document descriptor vectors along its rows. Measuring document similarity in terms of topic has the advantage that two documents may not have many exact words in common but may still have a common topic. This happens when they share words belonging to the same topic. Essentially, they share a lot of words that occur together in other documents. So even if the number of common words is low, we can have high document similarity.

For instance, in our toy document corpus, *gun* and *violence* are very correlated (both or neither is likely to occur in a document). *Gun-violence* emerges as a topic. If we express the document vector in terms of this topic instead of the individual words, we see similarities that otherwise would have escaped us. That is, we see *latent semantic* similarities. For instance, the cosine similarity between d_5 and d_6 is nonzero. This is the core idea of latent semantic analysis and is illustrated in figure 4.6.

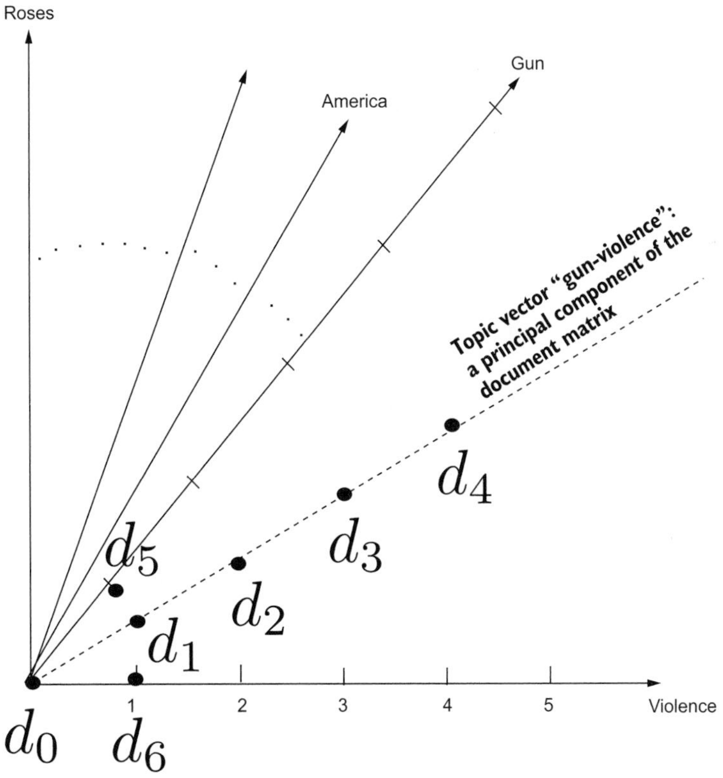

Figure 4.6 Document vectors from our toy dataset $d_0, \cdots d_6$. Each word in the vocabulary corresponds to a separate dimension. Dots show projections of document feature vectors on the plane formed by the axes corresponding to the terms gun(s) and violence.

Table 4.1 Document matrix for the toy example dataset

	Violence	Gun	America	...	Roses
d_0	0	0	0	...	2
d_1	1	1	1	...	0
d_2	2	2	0	...	0
d_3	3	3	0	...	0
d_4	5	5	0	...	0
d_5	0	1	0	...	0
d_6	1	0	0	...	0

Let's revisit our example document-retrieval problem in light of topic extraction. The document matrix (with document vectors as rows) looks like table 4.1. Rows correspond to documents, and columns correspond to terms. Each cell contains the term frequency. The terms *gun* and *violence* occur an equal number of times in most documents, indicating clear correlation. Hence *gun-violence* is a topic. The principal components (right eigenvectors) identify topics. As usual, we have omitted prepositions, conjunctions, commas, and so on. The overall steps are as follows (see listing 4.8 for the Python code):

1. Create a document term matrix X of dimension $m \times n$. Its rows correspond to documents (m documents), and its columns correspond to terms (n terms).
2. Perform SVD on the matrix. This yields U, S, and V matrices. V is an $n \times n$ orthogonal matrix, and S is a diagonal matrix.
3. The columns of matrix V yield topics. These are principal vectors for the rows of X: that is, eigenvectors of $X^T X$ or, equivalently, the covariance matrix of X.
4. The successive elements of each topic vector (column in matrix V) tell us the contribution of corresponding terms to that topic. Each column is $n \times 1$, depicting the contributions of the n terms in the system.
5. The diagonal elements of S tell us the weights (importance) of corresponding topics. These are the eigenvalues of $X^T X$: that is, principal values of the row vectors of X.
6. Inspect the weights, and choose a cutoff. All topics below that weight are discarded—the corresponding columns of V are thrown away. This yields a matrix V with fewer columns (but the same number of rows); these are the topic vectors of interest to us. We have reduced the dimensionality of the problem. If the number of retained topics is t, the reduced V is $m \times t$.
7. By projecting (multiplying) the original matrix X of document terms to this new matrix V, we get an $m \times t$ matrix of document topics (it has same number of rows as X but fewer columns). This is the projection of X to the topic space: that is, a topic-based representation of the document vectors.
8. Rows of the document topic matrix will henceforth be taken as document representations. Document similarities will be computed by taking the cosine similarity of these rows rather than the rows of the original document term matrix. This

cosine similarity, in the topic space, will capture many indirect connections that were not visible in the original input space.

4.6.3 PyTorch code to perform LSA

The following listing demonstrates how to compute the LSA for our toy dataset from table 4.1. Fully functional code for this section can be found at http://mng.bz/E2Gd.

Listing 4.8 Computing LSA

```
terms = ["violence", "gun", "america", "roses"]    # Considers only four terms for simplicity

X = torch.tensor([[0, 0, 0, 2],
                  [1, 1, 1, 0],
                  [2, 2, 0, 0],
                  [3, 3, 0, 0],
                  [5, 5, 0, 0],
                  [0, 1, 0, 0],
                  [1, 0, 0, 0]]).float()
```

Document term matrix. Each row describes a document. Each column contains TF scores for one term. IDF is ignored for simplicity.

```
U, S, V_t = torch.linalg.svd(X)
```

Performs SVD on the doc-term matrix. Columns of the resulting matrix V correspond to topics. These are eigenvectors of $X^T X$: principal vectors of the doc-term matrix. A topic corresponds to the direction of maximum variance in the doc feature space.

```
V = V_t.T

rank = 1
U = U[:, :rank]
V = V[:, :rank]
```

S indicates the diagonal matrix of principal values. These signify topic weights (importance). We choose a cut-off and discard all topics below that weight (dimensionality reduction). Only the first few columns of V are retained. Principal values (topic weights) for this dataset are shown in the output. Only one topic is retained in this example.

```
topic0_term_weights = list(zip(terms, V[:, 0]))
```

Elements of the topic vector show the contributions of corresponding terms to the topic.

```
def cosine_similarity(vec_1, vec_2):
    vec_1_norm = torch.linalg.norm(vec_1)
    vec_2_norm = torch.linalg.norm(vec_2)
    return torch.dot(vec_1, vec_2) / (vec_1_norm * vec_2_norm)

d5_d6_cosine_similarity = cosine_similarity(X[5], X[6])
```

Cosine similarity in the feature space fails to capture d, d6 similarity. LSA succeeds.

```
doc_topic_projection = torch.dot(X, V)
d5_d6_lsa_similarity = cosine_similarity(doc_topic_projection[5],
                                         doc_topic_projection[6])
```

The output is as follows:

```
Principal Values from S matrix: 8.89, 2.00, 1.00, 0.99
(Topic 0 has disproportionately high weight. We discard others)
```

```
topic0_term_weights (Topic zero is about "gun" and "violence"):
[
 ('violence', -0.706990662151775)
 ('gun', -0.7069906621517749)
 ('america', -0.018122010384881156)
 ('roses', 2.9413274625621952e-18)
]
Document 5, document 6 Cosine similarity in original space: 0.0
Document 5, document 6 Cosine similarity in topic space: 1.0
```

4.6.4 PyTorch code to compute LSA and SVD on a large dataset

Suppose we have a set of 500 documents over a vocabulary of 3 terms. This is an unrealistically short vocabulary, but it allows us to easily visualize the space of document vectors. Each document vector is a 3×1 vector, and there are 500 such vectors. Together they form a 500×3 data matrix X. In this dataset, the terms $x0$ and $x1$ are correlated: $x0$ occurs randomly between 0 and 100 times in a document, and $x1$ occurs twice as many times as $x0$ except for small random fluctuations. The third term's frequency varies between 0 and 5. From section 4.6, we know that $x0$, $x1$ together form a single topic, while $x2$ by itself forms another topic. We expect a principal component along each topic.

Listing 4.9 creates the dataset, computes the SVD, plots the dataset, and shows the first two principal components. The third singular value is small compared to the first. We can ignore that dimension—it corresponds to the small random variation within the $x0 - x1$ topic. The singular values are printed out and also shown graphically along with the data points in figure 4.7.

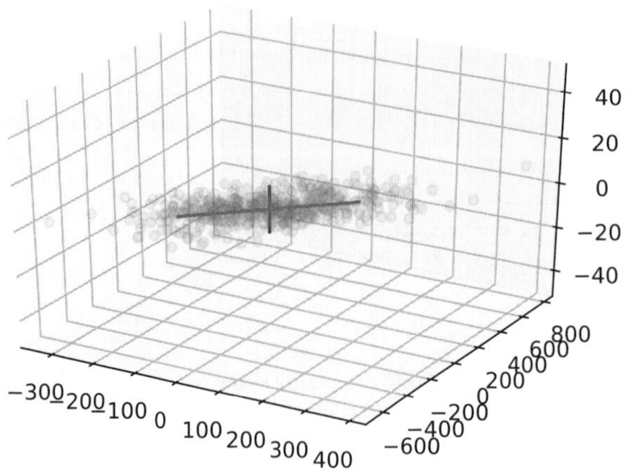

Figure 4.7 Latent semantic analysis. Note that the vertical axis line is actually much smaller than it appears to be in the diagram.

Listing 4.9 LSA using SVD

```
num_examples = 500
x0 = torch.normal(0, 100, (num_examples,)).round()
```

```
random_noise = torch.normal(0, 2, (num_examples,)).round()
x1 = 2*x0 + random_noise
x2 = torch.normal(0, 5, (num_examples,)).round()
X = torch.column_stack((x0, x1, x2))

U, S, V_t = torch.linalg.svd(X)
V = V_t.T
```

3D dataset: the first two axes are linearly correlated; the third axis has small near-zero random values.

The third singular value is relatively small; we ignore it.

The first two principal vectors represent topics. Projecting data points on them yields document descriptors in terms of the two topics.

Here is the output:

```
Singular values are: 4867.56982, 118.05858, 19.68604
```

Summary

In this chapter, we studied several linear algebraic tools used in machine learning and data science:

- The direction (unit vector) that maximizes (minimizes) the quadratic form $\hat{x}^T A \hat{x}$ is the eigenvector corresponding to the largest (smallest) eigenvalue of matrix A. The magnitude of the quadratic form when $\hat{x}$ is along those directions is the largest (smallest) eigenvalue of A.
- Given a set of points $X = \left\{\vec{x}^{(0)}, \vec{x}^{(1)}, \vec{x}^{(2)}, \cdots, \vec{x}^{(n)}\right\}$ in an $n+1$-dimensional space, we can define the mean vector and covariance matrix as

  $$\vec{\mu} = \frac{1}{n}\sum_{i=0}^{n} \vec{x}^{(i)}$$

  $$C = \frac{1}{n}\sum_{i=0}^{n} \left(\vec{x}^{(i)} - \vec{\mu}\right)\left(\vec{x}^{(i)} - \vec{\mu}\right)^T$$

  The variance along an arbitrary direction (unit vector) $\hat{l}$ is $\hat{l}^T C \hat{l}$. This is a quadratic form. Consequently, the maximum (minimum) variance of a set of data points in multidimensional space occurs along the eigenvector corresponding to the largest (smallest) eigenvalue of the covariance matrix. This direction is called the first principal axis of the data. The subsequent eigenvectors, sorted in order of decreasing eigenvalues, are mutually orthogonal (perpendicular) and yield the subsequent direction of maximum variance. This technique is known as principal component analysis (PCA).
- In many real-life cases, larger variances correspond to the true underlying pattern of the data, while smaller variances correspond to noise (such as measurement error). Projecting the data on the principal axes corresponding to the larger eigenvalues yields lower-dimensional data that is relatively noise-free. The projected data points also match the true underlying pattern more closely, yielding better insights. This is known as dimensionality reduction.
- Singular value decomposition (SVD) allows us to decompose an arbitrary $m \times n$ matrix A as a product of three matrices: $A = U\Sigma V^T$, where U, V are orthogonal

and Σ is diagonal. Matrix V has the eigenvectors of $A^T A$ as its columns. U has eigenvectors of AA^T as columns. Σ has the eigenvalues of $A^T A$ (sorted in decreasing order) in its diagonal.

- SVD provides a numerically stable way to solve the linear system of equations $A\vec{x} = \vec{b}$. In particular, for nonsquare matrices, it provides the closest approximations: that is, $\vec{x}$ that minimizes $||A\vec{x} - \vec{b}||$.
- Given a dataset X whose rows are data vectors corresponding to individual instances and columns correspond to feature values, $X^T X$ yields the covariance matrix. Thus eigenvectors of $X^T X$ yield the data's principal components. Since the SVD of X has eigenvectors of $X^T X$ as columns of the matrix V, SVD is an effective way to compute PCA.
- When using machine learning data science for document retrieval, the bag-of-words model represents documents with document vectors that contain the term frequency (number of occurrences) of each term in the document.
- TF-IDF is a cosine similarity technique for document matching and retrieval.
- Latent semantic analysis (LSA) does topic modeling: we perform PCA on the document vectors to identify topics. Projecting document vectors onto topic axes allows LSA to see latent (indirect) similarities beyond the direct overlapping of terms.

5 Probability distributions in machine learning

This chapter covers

- The role of probability distributions in machine learning
- Working with binomial, multinomial, categorical, Bernoulli, beta, and Dirichlet distributions
- The significance of entropy and cross-entropy in machine learning

Life often requires us to estimate the chances of an event occurring or make a decision in the face of uncertainty. Probability and statistics form the common toolbox to use in such circumstances. In machine learning, we take large feature vectors as inputs. As stated earlier, we can view these feature vectors as points in a high-dimensional space. For instance, gray-level images of size 224×224 can be viewed as points in a $50,176$-dimensional space, with each pixel corresponding to a specific dimension. Inputs with common characteristics, such as images of animals, will correspond to a cluster of points in that space. Probability distributions provide an effective tool for analyzing such loosely structured point distributions in arbitrarily high-dimensional spaces. Instead of simply developing a machine that emits a class given an input, we can fit a probability distribution to the clusters of input points (or a transformed version of them) satisfying some property of interest. This often lends more insight into the problem we are trying to solve.

For instance, suppose we are trying to design a recommendation system. We could design one or more classifiers that emit yes/no decisions about whether to recommend product X to person Y. On the other hand, we can fit probability distributions to specific groups of people. Doing so can lead to the discovery of significant overlap between the point clusters representing various groups—for instance, people who drink black coffee and start-up founders. We may not know the explanation or even the direction in which causality (if any) flows in the relationship. But we see the correlation and may design a better recommendation system using it.

Another situation in which probabilistic models are used in machine learning is when the problem involves a very large number of (perhaps infinitely many) classes. For instance, suppose we are creating a machine that not only recognizes cats in an image but also labels each pixel as belonging or not belonging to a cat. Effectively, the machine segments the image pixels into foreground versus background. This is called *semantic segmentation*. It is hard to cast this problem as a classification problem: we typically design a system that emits a probability of being foreground for each pixel.

Probabilistic models are also used in unsupervised and minimally supervised learning: for instance, in *variational autoencoders* (VAEs), which we discuss in chapter 14.

This chapter introduces the fundamental notion of probability and discusses probability distributions (including multivariates), with specific examples, in a machine learning-centric way. As usual, we emphasize the geometrical view of multivariate statistics. An equally important goal of this chapter is to familiarize you with PyTorch `distributions`, the PyTorch statistical package, which we use throughout the book. All the distributions discussed are accompanied by code snippets from PyTorch `distributions`.

NOTE The complete PyTorch code for this chapter is available at http://mng.bz/8NVg in the form of fully functional and executable Jupyter notebooks.

5.1 Probability: The classical frequentist view

Consider a mythical city called Statsville. Suppose we choose a random adult inhabitant of Statsville. What are the chances of this person's height being greater than 6 ft? Less than 3 ft? Between 5 ft 5 in. and 6 ft? What are the chances of this person's weight being between 50 and 70 kg (physicists would rather use the term *mass* here, but we have chosen to stick to the more common word *weight*)? Greater than 100 kg? What is the probability of the person's home being exactly 6 km from the city center? What are the chances of the person's weight being in the 50–70 kg range *and* their height being in the 5 ft 5 in. to 6 ft range? What are the chances of the person's weight being greater than 90 kg *and* their home being within 5 km of the city center?

All these questions can be answered in the frequentist paradigm by adopting the following approach:

> Count the size of the population belonging to the desired event (satisfying the criterion or criteria of interest): for instance, the number of Statsville adults taller than 6 ft. Divide that by the total size of the population (here, the number of adults in Statsville). This is the probability (chance) of that criterion/criteria being satisfied.

Formally,

$$\text{Probability of an event} = \frac{\text{Size of population belonging to that event}}{\text{Total size of population}}$$

$$= \frac{\text{Number of favorable outcomes}}{\text{Number of possible outcomes}} \tag{5.1}$$

For instance, suppose there are 100,000 adults in the city. Of them, 25,000 are 6 ft or taller. Then the size of the population satisfying the event of interest (aka the number of favorable outcomes) is 25,000. The total population size (aka the number of possible outcomes) is 100,000. So,

$$\text{Probability of a random adult Statsville resident being taller than 6 ft}$$
$$= \frac{\text{Number of adult Statsville residents taller than 6 ft}}{\text{Total number of adult Statsville residents}} = \frac{25000}{100000} = 0.25$$

Since the total population is always a superset of the population belonging to any event, the denominator is always greater than or equal to the numerator. Consequently, *probabilities are always lesser than or equal to* 1.

5.1.1 Random variables

When we talk about probability, a relevant question is, "The probability of what?" The simplest answer is, "The probability of the occurrence of an event." For example, in the previous subsection, we discussed the probability of the event that the height of an adult Statsville resident is less than 6 ft. A little thought reveals that an event always corresponds to a numerical entity of interest taking a particular value or lying in a particular range of values. This entity is called a *random variable.* For instance, the height of adult Statsville residents can be a random variable, and we can talk about the probability of it being less than 6 ft, or the weight of adult Statsville residents can be a random variable, and we can talk about the probability of it being less than 60 kg. When predicting the performance of stock markets, the Dow Jones index maybe a random variable: we can talk about the probability of this random variable crossing 19,000. And when discussing the spread of a virus, the total number of infected people may be a random variable, and we can talk about the probability of it being less than 2,000, and so on.

The defining characteristic of a random variable is that every allowed value (or range of values) is associated with a probability (of the random variable taking that value or value range). For instance, we may allow a set of only three weight ranges for adults of

Statsville: S_1, less than 60 kg; S_2, between 60 and 90 kg; and S_3, greater than 90 kg. Then we can have a corresponding random variable X representing the quantized weight. It can take one of only three values: $X = 1$ (corresponding to the weight in S_1), $X = 2$ (corresponding to the weight in S_2), or $X = 3$ (corresponding to the weight in S_3). Each value comes with a fixed probability: for example, $p(X = 1) = 0.25$, $p(X = 2) == 0.5$, and $p(X = 3) = 0.25$, respectively, in the example from section 5.1. Such random variables that take values from a countable set are known as *discrete* random variables.

Random variables can also be *continuous*. For a continuous random variable X, we associate a probability with its value being in an infinitesimally small range, $p\ (x \leq X < x + \delta x)$, with $\delta x \rightarrow 0$. This is called *probability density* and is explained in more detail in section 5.6.

> **NOTE** In this book, we always use uppercase letters to denote random variables. Usually, the same letter in lowercase refers to a specific value of the random variable: for example, $p\ (X = x)$ denotes the probability of random variable X taking the value x and $p\ (X \in \{x, x + \delta x\})$ denotes the probability of random variable X taking a value between x and $x + \delta x$. Also note that sometimes we use the letter X to denote a data set. This popular but confusing convention is rampant in the literature—generally, the usage is obvious from the context.

5.1.2 *Population histograms*

Histograms help us to visualize discrete random variables. Let's continue with our Statsville example. We are only interested in three weight ranges for Statsville adults: S_1: less than 60 kg; S_2: between 60 and 90 kg; and S_3: greater than 90 kg. Suppose the counts of Statsville adults in these weight ranges are as shown in table 5.1.

Table 5.1 Frequency table for the weights of adults in the city of Statsville

S_1: Less than 60 kg	S_2: Between 60 and 90 kg	S_3: More than 90 kg
25,000	50,000	25,000

The same information can be visualized by the histogram shown in figure 5.1. The X-axis of the histogram corresponds to possible values of the discrete random variable from section 5.1.1. The Y-axis shows the size of the population in the corresponding weight range. There are 25,000 people in range S_1, 50,000 people in range S_2, and 25,000 people in range S_3. Together, these categories account for the entire adult population of Statsville—every adult belongs to one category or another. This can be verified by adding the Y-axis values for all the categories: $25{,}000 + 50{,}000 + 25{,}000 = 100{,}000$, the adult population of Statsville.

5.2 *Probability distributions*

Figure 5.1 and its equivalent, table 5.1, can easily be converted to probabilities, as shown in table 5.2. The table shows the probabilities corresponding to allowed values of the discrete random variable X representing the quantized weight of a randomly chosen adult resident of Statsville. Table 5.2 represents what is formally known as a *probability*

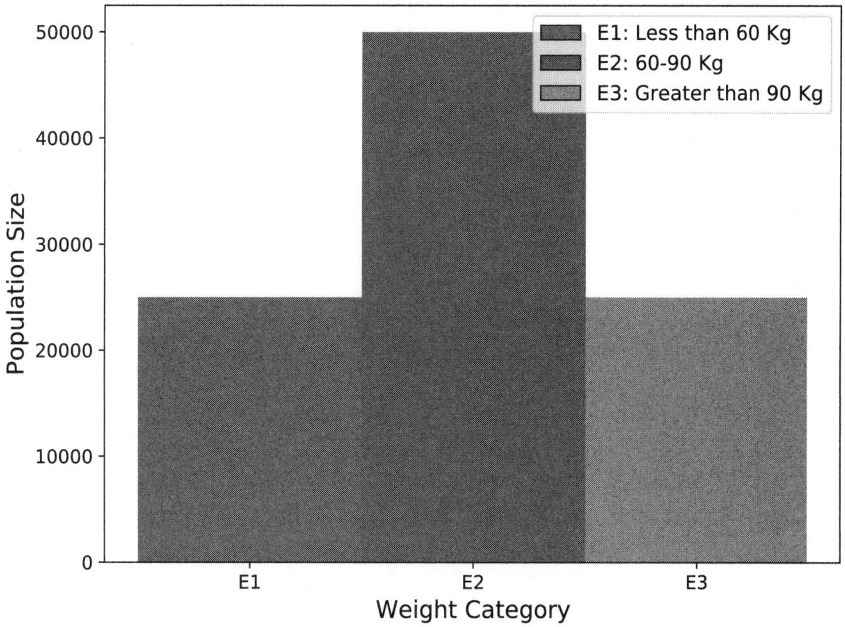

Figure 5.1 Histogram depicting the weights of adults in Statsville, corresponding to table 5.1

Table 5.2 Probability distribution for quantized weights of Statsville adults

S_1: Less than 60 kg	S_2: Between 60 and 90 kg	S_3: More than 90 kg
$p\,(X=1)=\frac{25{,}000}{100{,}000}=0.25$	$p\,(X=2)=\frac{50{,}000}{100{,}000}=0.5$	$p\,(X=3)=\frac{25{,}000}{100{,}000}=0.25$

distribution: a mathematical function that takes a random variable as input and outputs the probability of it taking any allowed value. It must be defined over all possible values of the random variable.

Note that the set of ranges $\{S_1, S_2, S_3\}$ is exhaustive in the sense that all possible values of X belong to one range or other—we cannot have a weight that does not belong to any of them. In set-theoretical terms, the union of these ranges, $S_1 \cup S_2 \cup S_3$, covers a space that contains the entire population (all possible values of X).

NOTE The set-theoretic operator $\cup$ denotes set union.

The ranges are also mutually exclusive in that any given observation of X can belong to only a single range, never more. In set-theoretic terms, the intersection of any pair of ranges is null: $S_1 \cap S_2 = S_1 \cap S_3 = S_2 \cap S_3 = \phi$.

NOTE The set-theoretic operator $\cap$ denotes set intersection.

For a set of exhaustive and mutually exclusive events, the function yielding the probabilities of these events is a probability distribution. For instance, the probability distribution in our tiny example comprises three probabilities: $P\,(X=1)=0.25$, $P\,(X=2)=0.5$, and $P\,(X=3)=0.25$. This is shown in figure 5.2, which is a three-point graph.

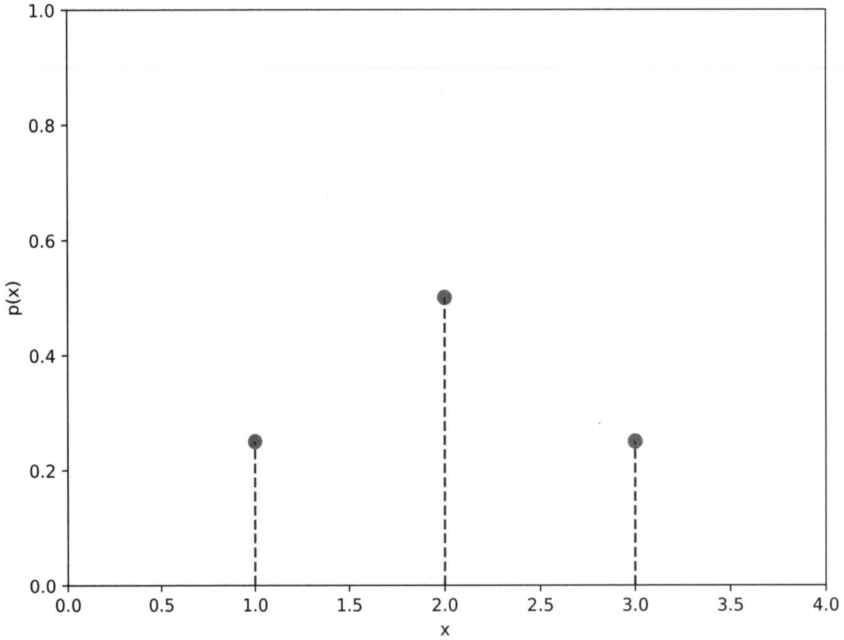

Figure 5.2 Probability distribution graph for the weights of adults in Statsville, corresponding to table 5.2. Event $E_1 \equiv X = 1 \implies$ a weight in the range S_1, Event $E_2 \equiv X = 2 \implies$ a weight in the range S_2, and Event $E_3 \equiv x = 3 \implies$ a weight in the range S_3.

5.3 Basic concepts of probability theory

In this section, we briefly touch on impossible and certain events; the sum of probabilities of exhaustive, mutually exclusive events; and independent events.

5.3.1 Probabilities of impossible and certain events

The probability of an impossible event is zero (for example, the probability that the sun will rise in the west). The probability of an event that occurs with certitude is 1 (the probability that the sun will rise in the east). Improbable events (such as this author beating Roger Federer in competitive tennis) have low but nonzero probabilities, like 0.001. Highly probable events (such as Roger Federer beating this author in competitive tennis) have probabilities close to but not exactly equal to 1, like 0.999.

5.3.2 Exhaustive and mutually exclusive events

Consider the events E_1, E_2, E_3 corresponding to the quantized weight of a Statsville adults from section 5.2 belonging to the range S_1, S_2, or S_3, respectively (equivalently, E_1 is the event corresponding to $X = 1$, E_2 is the event corresponding to $X = 2$, and E_3 is the event corresponding to $X = 3$). The events are exhaustive: their union covers the entire population space. This means all quantized weights of Statsville adults belong to one of the ranges S_1, S_2, S_3. The events are also mutually exclusive: their mutual intersections are null, meaning no member of the population can belong to more than one range. For example, if a weight belongs to S_1, it cannot belong to S_2 or S_3. For such events, the following holds true:

> The sum of the probabilities of mutually exclusive events yields the probability of one or the other of them occurring.

For instance, for events E_1, E_2, E_3,

$$p\left(E_1 \text{ or } E_2\right) = p\left(E_1\right) + p\left(E_2\right) \tag{5.2}$$

the *sum rule* says that

> The sum of the probabilities of an exhaustive, mutually exclusive set of events is always 1.

For example,

$$p\left(E_1\right) + p\left(E_2\right) + p\left(E_3\right) = p\left(E_1 \text{ or } E_2 \text{ or } E_3\right) = 1$$

This is intuitively obvious. We are merely saying that *we can say with certainty that either E_1 or E_2 or E_3 will occur.*

In general, given a set of exhaustive, mutually exclusive events $E_1, E_2, \cdots, E_n$,

$$\sum_{i=1}^{i=n} p\left(E_i\right) = 1 \tag{5.3}$$

5.3.3 Independent events

Consider the two events $E_1 \equiv$ "weight of an adult inhabitant of Statsville is less than 60 kg" and $G_1 \equiv$ "home of an adult inhabitant of Statsville is within 5 km of the city center." These events do not influence each other at all. The knowledge that a member of the population weighs less than 60 kg does not reveal anything about the distance of their home from the city center and vice versa. We say E_1 and G_1 are *independent events.* Formally,

> A set of events are independent if the occurrence of one does not affect the probability of the occurrence of another.

5.4 Joint probabilities and their distributions

Given an adult Statsville resident, let E_1 be, as before, the event that their weight is less than 60 kg. The corresponding probability is $p\left(E_1\right)$. Also, let G_1 be the event that the distance of their home from the city center is less than 5 km. The corresponding probability is $p\left(G_1\right)$. Now consider the probability that a resident weights less than 60 kg *and* their home is less than 5 km from the city center. This probability, denoted $p\left(E_1, G_1\right)$, is called a *joint probability.* Formally,

> The joint probability of a set of events is the probability of all those events occurring together.

The *product rule* says that the joint probability of independent events can be obtained by multiplying their individual probabilities. Thus, for the current example, $p\left(E_1, G_1\right) = p\left(E_1\right) p\left(G_1\right)$.

Let's continue our discussion of joint probabilities with a slightly more elaborate example. We have consolidated the weight categories, corresponding populations, and probability distributions in table 5.3 for quick reference. Similarly, we quantize the distance of residents' homes from the city center into three ranges: $D_1 \equiv$ less than 5 km, $D_2 \equiv$ between 5 and 15 km, and $D_3 \equiv$ greater than 15 km. Table 5.4 shows the corresponding population and probability distributions. The joint probability distribution of the events $\{E_1, E_2, E_3\}$ and $\{G_1, G_2, G_3\}$ is shown in table 5.5.

Table 5.3 Population probability distribution table for the weights of adult residents of Statsville. E_1, E_2, E_3 are exhaustive, mutually exclusive events, $p(E_1) + p(E_2) + p(E_3) = 1$.

Less than 60 kg (range S_1)	Between 60 and 90 kg (range S_2)	More than 90 kg (range S_3)
Event $E_1 \equiv weight \in S_1$	Event $E_2 \equiv weight \in S_2$	Event $E_3 \equiv weight \in S_3$
Population size = 25,000	Population size = 50,000	Population size = 25,000
$p(E_1) = \frac{25{,}000}{100{,}000} = 0.25$	$p(E_2) = \frac{50{,}000}{100{,}000} = 0.5$	$p(E_3) = \frac{25{,}000}{100{,}000} = 0.25$

Table 5.4 Population probability distribution table for the distance of adult Statsville residents' homes from the city center. G_1, G_2, G_3 are exhaustive, mutually exclusive events, $p(G_1) + p(G_2) + p(G_3) = 1$.

Less than 5 km (range D_1)	Between 5 and 15 km (range D_2)	Greater than 15 km (range D_3)
Event $G_1 \equiv distance \in D_1$	Event $G_2 \equiv distance \in D_2$	Event $G_3 \equiv distance \in D_3$
Population size = 20,000	Population size = 60,000	Population size = 20,000
$p(G_1) = \frac{20{,}000}{100{,}000} = 0.20$	$p(G_2) = \frac{60{,}000}{100{,}000} = 0.6$	$p(G_3) = \frac{20{,}000}{100{,}000} = 0.20$

Table 5.5 Joint probability distribution of independent events. The sum of all elements in the table is 1.

	Less than 60 kg (E_1)	Between 60 and 90 kg (E_2)	More than 90 kg (E_3)
Less than 5 km (G_1)	$p(E_1, G_1)$ $= 0.25 \times 0.2$ $= 0.05$	$p(E_2, G_1)$ $= 0.5 \times 0.2$ $= 0.1$	$p(E_3, G_1)$ $= 0.25 \times 0.2$ $= 0.05$
Between 5 and 15 km (G_2)	$p(E_1, G_2)$ $= 0.25 \times 0.6$ $= 0.15$	$p(E_2, G_2)$ $= 0.5 \times 0.6$ $= 0.3$	$p(E_3, G_2)$ $= 0.25 \times 0.6$ $= 0.15$
More than 15 km (G_3)	$p(E_1, G_3)$ $= 0.25 \times 0.2$ $= 0.05$	$p(E_2, G_3)$ $= 0.5 \times 0.2$ $= 0.1$	$p(E_3, G_3)$ $= 0.25 \times 0.2$ $= 0.05$

We can make the following statements about table 5.5:

- The sum total of all elements in table 5.5 is 1. In other words, $p(E_i, G_j)$ is a proper probability distribution indicating the probabilities of event E_i and event G_j occurring together: here, $(i, j) \in \{1, 2, 3\} \times \{1, 2, 3\}$.

- $p(E_i, G_j) = p(E_i)\,p(G_j) \quad \forall (i, j) \in \{1, 2, 3\} \times \{1, 2, 3\}$. This is because the events are independent.

NOTE The symbol $\times$ denotes the *Cartesian product.* The Cartesian product of two sets $\{1, 2, 3\} \times \{1, 2, 3\}$ is the set $\{(1, 1), (1, 2), (1, 3), (2, 1), (2, 2), (2, 3), (3, 1), (3, 2), (3, 3)\}$. And the symbol $\forall$ indicates "for all." Read $\forall (i, j) \in \{1, 2, 3\} \times \{1, 2, 3\}$ as follows: for all pairs (i, j) in the Cartesian product, $\{1, 2, 3\} \times \{1, 2, 3\}$.

In general, given a set of independent events $E_1, E_2, \cdots, E_n$, the joint probability $p(E_1, E_2, \cdots, E_n)$ of all the events occurring together is the product of their individual probabilities of occurring:

$$p(E_1, E_2, \cdots, E_n) = p(E_1)\,p(E_n) \cdots p(E_1) = \prod_{i=1}^{i=n} p(E_i) \tag{5.4}$$

NOTE The symbol $\prod$ stands for "product."

5.4.1 Marginal probabilities

Suppose we do not have the individual probabilities $p(E_i)$ and $p(G_j)$. All we have is the joint probability distribution: that is, table 5.5. Can we find the individual probabilities from them? If so, how?

To answer this question, consider a particular row or column in table 5.5—say, the top row. In this row, the E values iterate over all possibilities (the entire space of Es), but G is fixed at G_1. If G_1 is to occur, there are only three possibilities: it occurs with E_1,E_2, or E_3. The corresponding joint probabilities are $p(E_1, G_1)$, $p(E_2, G_1)$, and $p(E_3, G_1)$. If we add them, we get the probability of G_1 occurring with E_1 or E_2, or E_3: that is, event (E_1, G_1) or (E_2, G_1) or (E_3, G_1). Thus we have considered all situations under which G_1 can occur. The sum represents the probability of event G_1 occurring. Thus, $p(G_1)$ can be obtained by adding all the probabilities in the row corresponding to G_1 and writing it in the margin (this is why it is called the *marginal* probability). Similarly, by adding all the probabilities in the middle column, we obtain the probability $p(E_2)$, and so forth. Table 5.6 shows table 5.5 updated with marginal probabilities.

In general, given a set of exhaustive, mutually exclusive events $E_1, E_2, \cdots, E_n$, another event G, and joint probabilities $p(E_1, G), p(E_2, G), \cdots, p(E_n, G)$,

$$p(G) = \sum_{i=1}^{i=n} p(E_i, G) \tag{5.5}$$

By summing over all possible values of E_is, we factor out the Es. This is because the Es are mutually exclusive and exhaustive; summing over them results in a certain event that is factored out (remember, the probability of a certain event is 1).

5.4.2 Dependent events and their joint probability distribution

So far, the events we have considered jointly are "weights" and "distance of a resident's home from the city center." These are independent of each other—their joint probability is the product of their individual probabilities. Now, let's discuss a different

Table 5.6 Joint probability distribution with marginal probabilities shown

	Less than 60 kg (E_1)	Between 60 and 90 kg (E_2)	More than 90 kg (E_3)	Marginals for G's
Less than 5 km (G_1)	$p(E_1, G_1)$ $=0.25\times0.2$ $=0.05$	$p(E_2, G_1)$ $=0.5\times0.2$ $=0.1$	$p(E_3, G_1)$ $=0.25\times0.2$ $=0.05$	$p(G_1)$ $=0.05+0.1+0.05$ $=0.2$
Between 5 and 15 km (G_2)	$p(E_1, G_2)$ $=0.25\times0.6$ $=0.15$	$p(E_2, G_2)$ $=0.5\times0.6$ $=0.3$	$p(E_3, G_2)$ $=0.25\times0.6$ $=0.15$	$p(G_2)$ $0.15+0.3+0.15$ $=0.6$
More than 15 km (G_3)	$p(E_1, G_3)$ $=0.25\times0.2$ $=0.05$	$p(E_2, G_3)$ $=0.5\times0.2$ $=0.1$	$p(E_3, G_3)$ $=0.25\times0.2$ $=0.05$	$p(G_3)$ $=0.05+0.1+0.05$ $=0.2$
Marginals for Es	$p(E_1)$ $=0.05+0.15+0.05$ $0.05=0.25$	$p(E_2)$ $=0.1+0.3+0.1$ $=0.5$	$p(E_3)$ $=0.05+0.15+$ $=0.25$	

situation where the variables are connected and knowing the value of one does help us predict the other. For instance, the weights and heights of adult residents of Statsville are not independent: typically, taller people weigh more, and vice versa.

As usual, we use a toy example to understand the idea. We quantize heights into three ranges, $H_1 \equiv$ less than 5 ft 5 in., $H_2 \equiv$ between 5 ft 5 in. and 6 ft, and $H_3 \equiv$ greater than 6 ft. Let z be the random variable corresponding to height. We have three possible events with respect to height: $F_1 \equiv z \in H_1$, $F_2 \equiv z \in H_2$, and $F_3 \equiv z \in H_3$. The joint probability distribution of height and weight is shown in table 5.7.

Table 5.7 Joint probability distribution of dependent events

	Less than 60 kg (E_1)	Between 60 and 90 kg (E_2)	More than 90 kg (E_3)
Less than 5 ft 5 in. (F_1)	$p(E_1, F_1)$ $=0.25$	$p(E_2, F_1)$ $=0$	$p(E_3, F_1)$ $=0$
Between 5 ft 5 in. and 6 ft (F_2)	$p(E_1, F_2)$ $=0.$	$p(E_2, F_2)$ $=0.5$	$p(E_3, F_2)$ $=0$
More than 6 ft (F_3)	$p(E_1, F_3)$ $=0$	$p(E_2, F_3)$ $=0$	$p(E_3, F_3)$ $=0.25$

Note the following about table 5.7:

- The sum total of all elements in table 5.7 is 1. In other words, $p(E_i, F_j)$ is a proper probability distribution indicating the probabilities of event E_i and event F_j occurring together. Here $(i, j) \in \{1, 2, 3\} \times \{1, 2, 3\}$.
- $p(E_i, F_j) = 0 \; if \; i \neq j \;\; \forall (i, j) \in \{1, 2, 3\} \times \{1, 2, 3\}$. This essentially means the events are perfectly correlated: the occurrence of E_1 implies the occurrence of F_1 and

vice versa, the occurrence of E_2 implies the occurrence of F_2 and vice versa, and the occurrence of E_3 implies the occurrence of F_3 and vice versa. In other words, every adult resident of Statsville who weighs less than 60 kg is also shorter than 5 ft 5 in., and so on. (In life, such perfect correlations rarely exist; but Statsville is a mythical town.)

5.5 Geometrical view: Sample point distributions for dependent and independent variables

Let's look at a graphical view of the point distributions corresponding to tables 5.5 and 5.7. There is a fundamental difference in how the point distributions look for independent and dependent variables; it is connected to principal component analysis (PCA) and dimensionality reduction, which we discussed in section 4.4.

We use a rectangular bucket-based technique to visualize joint 2D discrete events. For instance, we have three weight-related events, E_1, E_2, E_3, and three distance-related events, G_1, G_2, G_3. Hence the joint distribution has $3 \times 3 = 9$ possible events (E_i, G_j), $\forall\,(i, j) \in \{1, 2, 3\} \times \{1, 2, 3\}$, as shown in table 5.5. Each of these nine events is represented by a small rectangle (bucket for the joint event); altogether, we have a 3×3 grid of rectangular buckets. To visualize the sample point distribution, we have drawn 1,000 samples from the joint distribution. A joint event sample is placed at a random location within its bucket (that is, all points within the bucket have an equal probability of being selected). Notice that the concentration of points is greater inside high-probability buckets and vice versa.

Graphical views of the point distribution for the independent (table 5.5) and non-independent (table 5.7) joint variable pairs are shown in figures 5.3a and 5.3b, respectively. We see that *the sample point distribution for the independent events is spread somewhat symmetrically over the domain*, while *that for the dependent events is spread narrowly around a particular line* (in this case, the diagonal). This holds true in general and for higher dimensions, too. You should have this mental picture with respect to independent versus non-independent point distributions. If we sample independent events (uncorrelated), all possible combinations of events $\{E_1, G_1\}$, $\{E_1, G_2\}$, $\{E_1, G_3\}$, $\cdots$, $\{E_3, G_3\}$ have a non-negligible probability of occurrence (see table 5.5), which is equivalent to saying that none of the events have a very high probability of occurring (remember that probabilities sum to 1, so if some events have very low probabilities [close to zero], other events must have high probabilities [near one] to compensate). This precludes the concentration of points in a small region of the space. All buckets will have many points. In other words, the joint probability samples of independent events are diffused throughout the population space (see figure 5.3a, for instance).

On the other hand, if the events are correlated, the joint probability samples are concentrated in certain high-probability regions of the joint space. For instance, in table 5.7, events (E_1, F_1), (E_2, F_2), (E_3, F_3) are far more likely than the other combinations. Hence, the sample points are concentrated along the corresponding diagonal (see figure 5.3b).

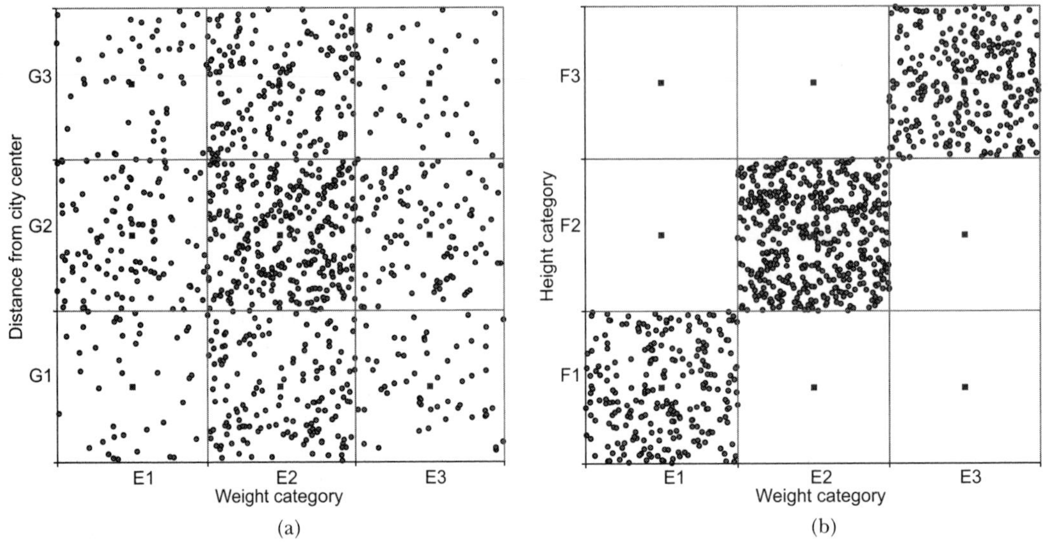

Figure 5.3 Graphical visualization of joint probability distributions. Rectangles represent buckets of different discrete events. (a) From table 5.5 (independent events). The probabilities of all nine events are non-negligible, and all nine rectangles have a relatively high concentration of sample points. Not suitable for PCA. (b) From table 5.7 (non-independent events). Events (E_1, F_1), (E_2, F_2), and (E_3, F_3) have very high probabilities, and other events have negligible probabilities. Sample points are concentrated along the rectangles on the diagonal. Suitable for PCA.

If this does not remind you of PCA (section 4.4), you should re-read that section. Dependent events such as that shown in figure 5.3a are good candidates for dimensionality reduction: the two dimensions essentially carry the same information, and if we know one, we can derive the other. We can drop one of the highly correlated dimensions without losing significant information.

5.6 Continuous random variables and probability density

So far, we have quantized our random variables and made them discrete. For instance, weight has been quantized into three buckets—less than 60 kg, between 60 and 90 kg, and greater than 90 kg—and probabilities have been assigned to each bucket. What if we want to know probabilities at a more granular level like 0 to 10 kg, 10 to 20 kg, 20 to 30 kg, and so on? Well, we have to create more buckets. Each bucket covers a narrower range of values (a smaller portion of the population space), but there are more of them. In all cases, following the frequentist approach, we count the number of adult Statsvilleans in each bucket, divide that by the total population size, and call that the probability of belonging to that bucket.

What if we want even further granularity? We create even more buckets, each covering an even smaller portion of the population space. In the limit, we have an infinite number of buckets, each covering an infinitesimally small portion of the population space. Together they still cover the population space—a very large number of very small pieces can cover arbitrary regions. At this limit, the probability distribution function is called a *probability density function.* Formally,

> The probability density function $p(x)$ for a continuous random variable X is defined as the probability that X lies between x and $x+\delta x$ with $\delta x \rightarrow 0$
>
> $$p(x) = \lim_{\delta x \rightarrow 0} probability\,(x \leq X < x+\delta x)$$

NOTE It is slightly unfortunate that the typical symbol for a random variable, X, collides with that for a dataset (collection of data vectors), also X. But the context is usually enough to tell them apart.

There is a bit of theoretical nuance here. We are saying that $p(x)$ is the probability of the random variable X lying between x and $x+\delta x$. This is not exactly the same as saying that $p(x)$ is the probability that X is *equal* to x. But because δx is infinitesimally small, they amount to the same thing.

Consider the set of events $E = \lim_{\delta x \rightarrow 0} \{x \leq X < x+\delta x\}$ for all possible values of x. All possible values of x range from negative infinity to infinity: $x \in [-\infty, \infty]$. There are infinite such events, each of which is infinitesimally narrow, but together they cover the entire domain $x \in [-\infty, \infty]$. In other words, they are exhaustive. They are also mutually exclusive because x cannot belong to more than one of them at the same time. They are continuous counterparts of the discrete events E_1, E_2, E_3 that we have seen before.

The fact that the set of events $E = \lim_{\delta x \rightarrow 0} \{x \leq X < x+\delta x\}$ in continuous space is exhaustive and mutually exclusive means we can apply equation 5.3 but the sum will be replaced by an integral as the variable is continuous.

The sum rule in a continuous domain is expressed as

$$\int_{x=-\infty}^{\infty} p(x)\, dx = 1 \tag{5.6}$$

Equation 5.6 is the continuous analog of equation 5.3. It physically means we can say with certainty that x lies somewhere in the interval $-\infty$ to ∞.

The random variable can also be multidimensional (that is, a vector). Then the probability density function is denoted as $p(\vec{x})$.

The sum rule for a continuous multidimensional probability density function is

$$\int_{\vec{x} \in D} p(\vec{x})\, d\vec{x} = 1 \tag{5.7}$$

where D is the domain of $\vec{x}$—that is, the space containing all possible values of the vector $\vec{x}$.

For instance, the 2D vector $\begin{bmatrix} x \\ y \end{bmatrix}$ has the XY plane as its domain. Note that the integral in equation 5.7 is a *multidimensional* integral (for example, for 2D $\vec{x}$, it is $\iint_{\vec{x} \in D} p(\vec{x})\, d\vec{x} = 1$).

NOTE For simplicity of notation, we usually use a single integral sign to denote multidimensional integrals. The vector sign in the domain (for example, $\vec{x} \in D$), as well the vector sign in $d\vec{x}$, indicates multiple dimensions.

You may remember from elementary integral calculus that equation 5.6 corresponds to the area under the curve for $p(x)$ (or $p(\vec{x})$). In higher dimensions, equation 5.7 corresponds to the volume under the hypersurface for $p(\vec{x})$. Thus, *the total area under a univariate probability density curve is always 1.* And in higher dimensions, *the volume under the hypersurface for a multivariate probability density function is always 1.*

5.7 Properties of distributions: Expected value, variance, and covariance

Toward the beginning of this chapter, we stated that generative machine learning models are often developed by fitting a distribution from a known family to the available training data. Thus, we postulate a parameterized distribution from a known family and estimate the exact parameters that best fit the training data. Most distribution families are parameterized in terms of intuitive properties like the mean, variance, and so on. Understanding these concepts and their geometric significance is essential for understanding the models based on them.

In this section, we explain a few properties/parameters common to all distributions. Later, when we discuss individual distributions, we connect them to the parameters of those distributions. We also show how to programmatically obtain the values of these for each individual distribution via the PyTorch `distributions` package.

5.7.1 Expected value (aka mean)

If we sample a random variable with a given distribution many times and take the average of the sampled values, what value do we expect to end up with? The average will be closer to the values with higher probabilities (as these appear more often during sampling). If we sample enough times, for a given probability distribution, this average always settles down to a fixed value for that distribution: the *expected value* of the distribution.

Formally,

> given a discrete distribution D where a discrete random variable X can take any value from the sets $\{x_1, x_2, \cdots, x_n\}$ with respective probabilities $\{p(x_1), p(x_2) \cdots, p(x_n)\}$, the expected value is given by the formula
>
> $$\mathbb{E}(X) = \lim_{N\to\infty} \frac{1}{N}\sum_{k=1}^{N} x_k \to D = \sum_{i=1}^{n} p(x_i)\, x_i \tag{5.8}$$
>
> where $x_k \to D$ denotes the kth sample drawn from the distribution D. Overall, equation 5.8 says that *the average or expected value of a very large number of samples drawn from the distribution approaches the probability-weighted sum of all possible sample values.* When we sample, the higher-probability values appear more frequently than the lower-probability values, so the average over a large number of samples is pulled closer to the higher-probability values.

For multivariate random variables:

Given a discrete distribution where a discrete multidimensional random variable X can take any value from the sets $\{\vec{x}_1, \vec{x}_2, \cdots, \vec{x}_n\}$ with respective probabilities $\{p(\vec{x}_1), p(\vec{x}_2), \cdots, p(\vec{x}_n)\}$, the expected value is given by the formula

$$\mathbb{E}(X) = \sum_{i=1}^{n} p(\vec{x}_i)\,\vec{x}_i \tag{5.9}$$

For continuous random variables (note how the sum is replaced by an integral):

The expected value of a continuous random variable X that takes values from $-\infty$ to ∞ (that is, $x \in \{-\infty, \infty\}$) is

$$\mathbb{E}(X) = \begin{cases} \int_{x=-\infty}^{\infty} x\,p(x)\,dx \Rightarrow \text{for continuous univariate distributions} \\ \int_{\vec{x}\in D} \vec{x}\,p(\vec{x})\,d\vec{x} \Rightarrow \text{for continuous multivariate distributions} \end{cases} \tag{5.10}$$

EXPECTED VALUE AND CENTER OF MASS IN PHYSICS

In physics, we have the concept of the center of mass or centroid. If we have a set of points, each with a mass, the entire point set can be replaced by a single point. This point is called the *centroid*. The position of the centroid is the weighted average of the positions of the individual points, weighted by their individual masses. If we mentally think of the probabilities of individual points as masses, the notion of expected value in statistics corresponds to the notion of centroid in physics.

EXPECTED VALUE OF AN ARBITRARY FUNCTION OF A RANDOM VARIABLE

So far, we have seen the expected value of the random variable itself. The notion can be extended to functions of the random variable.

The expected value of a function of a random variable is the probability-weighted sum of the values of that function at all possible values of the random variable. Formally,

$$\mathbb{E}(f(X)) = \sum_{i=1}^{n} f(x_i)\,p(x_i) \Rightarrow \text{for discrete univariate distributions}$$

$$\mathbb{E}(f(X)) = \sum_{i=1}^{n} f(\vec{x}_i)\,p(\vec{x}_i) \Rightarrow \text{for discrete multivariate distributions}$$

$$\mathbb{E}(f(X)) = \int_{x=-\infty}^{\infty} f(x)\;p(x)\,dx \Rightarrow \text{for continuous univariate distributions}$$

$$\mathbb{E}(f(X)) = \int_{\vec{x}\in D} f(\vec{x})\;p(\vec{x})\,d\vec{x} \Rightarrow \text{for continuous multivariate distributions} \tag{5.11}$$

EXPECTED VALUE AND DOT PRODUCT

In equation 2.6, we looked at the dot product between two vectors. Further, in section 2.5.6, we saw that the dot product between two vectors measures the agreement between the two vectors. If both point in the same direction, the dot product is larger. In this section, we show that the expected value of a function of a random variable can be viewed as a dot product between a vector representing the probability and another vector representing the function itself.

First let's consider the discrete case. Our random variable can take values $x_i, i \in \{1, n\}$.

Now, imagine a vector $\vec{f} = \begin{bmatrix} f(x_1) \\ f(x_2) \\ \cdots \\ f(x_n) \end{bmatrix}$ and a vector $\vec{p} = \begin{bmatrix} p(x_1) \\ p(x_2) \\ \cdots \\ p(x_n) \end{bmatrix}$. From equation 5.11, we see that the expected value of the function $\mathbb{E}(f(X))$ of random variable X is the same as $\vec{f}^T\vec{p} = \vec{f} \cdot \vec{p}$. This is high when $\vec{f}$ and $\vec{p}$ are aligned; thus, the expected value of the function of the random variable is high when the high function values coincide with high probabilities of the random variable and vice versa. In the continuous case, these vectors have an infinite number of components and the summation is replaced by an integral, but the idea stays the same.

EXPECTED VALUE OF LINEAR COMBINATIONS OF RANDOM VARIABLES

The expected value is a linear operator. This means the expected value of a linear combination of random variables is a linear combination (with the same weights) of the expected values of the random variables. Formally,

$$\mathbb{E}(\alpha_1 X_1 + \alpha_2 X_2 \cdots \alpha_n X_n) = \alpha_1 \mathbb{E}(X_1) + \alpha_2 \mathbb{E}(X_2) + \cdots \alpha_n \mathbb{E}(X_n) \tag{5.12}$$

5.7.2 *Variance, covariance, and standard deviation*

When we draw a very large number of samples from a given point distribution, we often like to know the spread of the point set. The spread is not merely a matter of measuring the largest distance between two points in the distribution. Rather, we want to know how densely packed the points are. If most of the points fit within a very small ball, then even if one or two points are far from the ball, we call that a *small spread* or *high packing density*.

Why is this important in machine learning? Let's start with a few informal examples. If we discover that the points are tightly packed in a small region around a single point, we may want to replace the entire distribution with that point without causing much error. Or if the points are packed tightly around a single straight line, we can replace the entire distribution with that line. Doing so gives us a simpler (lower-dimensional) representation and often leads to a view of the data that is more amenable to understanding the big picture. This is because small variations about a particular point or direction are usually caused by noise, while large variations are caused by meaningful things. By eliminating small variations and focusing on the large ones, we capture the main information content. (This could be why older people tend to be better at forming big-picture views: perhaps there are too few neurons in their heads to retain the huge amount of memory data they have accumulated over the years. Their brain performs dimensionality reduction.) This is the basic idea behind PCA and dimensionality reduction, which we saw in section 4.4.

Variance—or its square root, standard deviation—measures how densely packed around the expected value the points in the distribution are: that is, the spread of the point distribution. Formally, the variance of a probability distribution is defined as follows:

$$var\left(X\right) = \begin{cases} \sum_{i=1}^{n} \left(x_i - \mu\right)^2 p\left(x_i\right) \Rightarrow \text{for a discrete n point distribution} \\ \int_{x=-\infty}^{\infty} \left(x - \mu\right)^2 p\left(x\right) dx \Rightarrow \text{for a continuous distribution} \end{cases} \tag{5.13}$$

By comparing equation 5.13 to equations 5.10 and 5.11, we see that the variance is the expected value of the distance $(x - \mu)^2$ of sample points x from the mean μ. So if the more probable (more frequently occurring) sample points lie within a short distance of the mean, the variance is small, and vice versa. That is to say, the variance measures how tightly packed the points are around the mean.

COVARIANCE: VARIANCE IN HIGHER DIMENSIONS

Extending the notion of the expected value from the univariate case to the multivariate case was straightforward. In the univariate case, we take a probability-weighted average of a scalar quantity, x. The resulting expected value is a scalar, $\mu = \int_{x=-\infty}^{\infty} x\, p\left(x\right) dx$. In the multivariate case, we take the probability-weighted average of a vector quantity, $\vec{x}$. The resulting expected value is a vector, $\vec{\mu} = \int_{\vec{x} \in D} \vec{x}\, p\left(\vec{x}\right) d\vec{x}$.

Extending the notion of variance to the multivariate case is not as straightforward. This is because we can traverse the multidimensional random vector's domain (the space over which the vector is defined) in an infinite number of possible directions—think how many possible directions we can walk on a 2D plane—and the spread or packing density can be different for each direction. For instance, in figure 5.3b, the spread along the main diagonal is much larger than the spread in a perpendicular direction.

> The covariance of a multidimensional point distribution is a matrix that allows us to easily measure the spread or packing density in any desired direction. It also allows us to easily figure out the direction in which the maximum spread occurs and what that spread is.

Consider a multivariate random variable X that takes vector values $\vec{x}$. Let $\hat{l}$ be an arbitrary direction (as always, we use overhead hats to denote unit-length vectors signifying directions) in which we want to measure the packing density of X. We discussed in sections 2.5.2 and 2.5.6 that the dot product of $\vec{x}$ in the direction $\hat{l}$ (that is, $\vec{x}^T \hat{l}$) is the projection or component (effective value) of x along $\hat{l}$. Thus the spread or packing density of the random vector $\vec{x}$ in direction $\hat{l}$ is the same as the spread of the dot product (aka component or projection) $\hat{l}^T \vec{x}$. This projection $\hat{l}^T \vec{x}$ is a scalar quantity: we can use the univariate formula to measure its variance.

NOTE In this context, we can use $\vec{x}^T \hat{l}$ and $\hat{l}^T \vec{x}$ interchangeably. The dot product is symmetric.

The expected value of the projection is

$$\vec{\mu}_l = \int\limits_{\vec{x} \in D} \left(\hat{l}^T \vec{x}\right) p\left(\vec{x}\right) d\vec{x} = \hat{l}^T \int\limits_{\vec{x} \in D} \vec{x}\, p\left(\vec{x}\right) d\vec{x} = \hat{l}^T \vec{\mu}$$

The variance is given by

$$var\left(\hat{l}^T\vec{x}\right) = \int_{\vec{x}\in D} \left(\hat{l}^T\vec{x} - \hat{l}^T\vec{\mu}\right)^2 d\vec{x}$$

Now, since the transpose of a scalar is the same scalar, we can write the square term within the integral as the product of the scalar $\hat{l}^T\left(\vec{x}-\vec{\mu}\right)$ and its transpose:

$$var\left(\hat{l}^T\vec{x}\right) = \int_{\vec{x}\in D} \left(\hat{l}^T\vec{x} - \hat{l}^T\vec{\mu}\right)\left(\hat{l}^T\vec{x} - \hat{l}^T\vec{\mu}\right)^T d\vec{x} = \int_{\vec{x}\in D} \hat{l}^T\left(\vec{x}-\vec{\mu}\right)\left(\hat{l}^T\left(\vec{x}-\vec{\mu}\right)\right)^T d\vec{x}$$

Using equation 2.10,

$$var\left(\hat{l}^T\vec{x}\right) = \int_{\vec{x}\in D} \hat{l}^T\left(\vec{x}-\vec{\mu}\right)\left(\vec{x}-\vec{\mu}\right)^T\left(\hat{l}^T\right)^T d\vec{x} = \int_{\vec{x}\in D} \hat{l}^T\left(\vec{x}-\vec{\mu}\right)\left(\vec{x}-\vec{\mu}\right)^T\hat{l}\, d\vec{x}$$

Since $\hat{l}$ is independent of $\vec{x}$, we can take it out of the integral. Hence,

$$var\left(\hat{l}^T\vec{x}\right) = \hat{l}^T\left(\int_{\vec{x}\in D}\left(\vec{x}-\vec{\mu}\right)\left(\vec{x}-\vec{\mu}\right)^T d\vec{x}\right)\hat{l} = \hat{l}^T\mathbb{C}\left(X\right)\hat{l}$$

where

$$\mathbb{C}\left(X\right) = \begin{cases} \sum_{i=1}^{n}\left(\vec{x}-\vec{\mu}\right)\left(\vec{x}-\vec{\mu}\right)^T \Rightarrow \text{for discrete } n \text{ point distributions} \\ \int_{\vec{x}\in D}\left(\vec{x}-\vec{\mu}\right)\left(\vec{x}-\vec{\mu}\right)^T d\vec{x} \Rightarrow \text{for continuous distributions} \end{cases} \tag{5.14}$$

For simplicity, we drop the X in parentheses and simply write $\mathbb{C}\left(X\right)$ as $\mathbb{C}$. An equivalent way of looking at the covariance matrix of a d-dimensional random variable X taking vector values $\vec{x}$ is as follows:

$$\mathbb{C} = \begin{bmatrix} \sigma_{11} & \sigma_{12} & \sigma_{13}\cdots & \sigma_{1d} \\ \sigma_{21} & \sigma_{22} & \sigma_{23}\cdots & \sigma_{2d} \\ \vdots & & & \\ \sigma_{d1} & \sigma_{d2} & \sigma_{d3}\cdots & \sigma_{dd} \end{bmatrix} \tag{5.15}$$

where

$$\sigma_{i,j} = \begin{cases} \int_{x_i\in D_i}\int_{x_j\in D_j}\left(x_i-\mu_i\right)\left(x_j-\mu_j\right)dx_i dx_j \Rightarrow \text{for continuous distributions} \\ \sum_{i=1}^{n}\sum_{j=1}^{n}\left(x_i-\mu_i\right)\left(x_j-\mu_j\right) \Rightarrow \text{for discrete } n \text{ point distributions} \end{cases}$$

is the co-variance of the ith and jth dimensions of the random vector $\vec{x}$.

$\mathbb{C}\left(X\right)$ or $\mathbb{C}$ is the *covariance matrix* of the random variable X. A little thought reveals that equations 5.14 and 5.15 are equivalent.

The following things are noteworthy:

- From equation 5.14, $\mathbb{C}$ is the sum of the products of $d\times 1$ vectors $\left(\vec{x}-\vec{\mu}\right)$ and their transpose $\left(\vec{x}-\vec{\mu}\right)^T$, $1\times d$ vectors. Hence, $\mathbb{C}$ is a $d\times d$ matrix.

- This matrix is independent of the direction, $\hat{l}$, in which we are measuring the variance or spread. We can precompute $\mathbb{C}$; then, when we need to measure the variance in any direction $\hat{l}$, we can evaluate the quadratic form $\hat{l}^T \mathbb{C} \hat{l}$ to obtain the variance in that direction. Thus $\mathbb{C}$ is a generic property of the distribution, much like $\vec{\mu}$. $\mathbb{C}$ is called the *covariance* of the distribution.
- Covariance is the multivariate peer of the univariate entity variance.

That covariance is the multivariate analog of variance is evident by comparing the expressions in equations 5.13 and 5.14.

VARIANCE AND EXPECTED VALUE

As outlined previously, the variance is the expected value of the distance $(x - \mu)^2$ of sample points x from the mean μ. This can be easily seen by comparing equations 5.13, 5.10, and 5.11 and leads to the following formula (where we use the principle of the expected value of linear combinations):

$$var\,(X) = \mathbb{E}\left((X - \mu)^2\right) = \mathbb{E}\left(X^2\right) - \mathbb{E}\,(2\mu X) + \mathbb{E}\left(\mu^2\right)$$

Since μ is a constant, we can take it out of the expected value (a special case of the principal of the expected value of linear combinations). Thus we get

$$var\,(X) = \mathbb{E}\left(X^2\right) - 2\mu\mathbb{E}\,(X) + \mu^2\mathbb{E}\,(1)$$

But $\mu = \mathbb{E}\,(X)$. Also, the expected value of a constant is that constant. So, $\mathbb{E}\,(1) = 1$. Hence,

$$var\,(X) = \mathbb{E}\left(X^2\right) - 2\mu^2 + \mu^2\mathbb{E}\,(1) = \mathbb{E}\left(X^2\right) - \mu^2$$

or

$$var\,(X) = \mathbb{E}\left(X^2\right) - \mathbb{E}\,(X)^2 \tag{5.16}$$

5.8 Sampling from a distribution

Drawing a sample from the probability distribution of a random variable yields an arbitrary value from the set of possible values. If we draw many samples, the higher-probability values show up more often than lower-probability values. The sampled points form a cloud in the domain of possible values, and the region where the probabilities are higher is more densely populated than lower-probability regions. In other words, in a sample point cloud, higher-probability values are overrepresented. Thus a collection of sample points is often referred to as a *sample point cloud*. The hope, of course, is that the sample point cloud is a good representation of the entire population so that analyzing the points in the cloud will yield insights about the entire population. In univariate cases, the sample value is a scalar and represented by a point on the number line. In multivariate cases, the sample value is a vector and represented as a point in a higher-dimensional space.

It is often useful to compute aggregate statistics (such as the mean and variance) to describe the population. If we know a distribution, we can use closed-form expressions to obtain these properties. Many standard distributions and closed-form equations for obtaining their means and variance are discussed in section 5.9. But often, we don't know the underlying distribution. Under those circumstances, the sample mean and sample variance can be used. Given a set of n samples $X = \vec{x}_1, \vec{x}_2 \cdots \vec{x}_n$ from any distribution, the sample mean and variance are computed as

$$\vec{\mu}_n = \frac{1}{n} \sum_{i=1}^{n} \vec{x}_i$$

$$\sigma_n^2 = \frac{1}{n} \sum_{i=1}^{n} \left(\vec{x}_i - \vec{\mu}_n\right)^2$$

In some situations, like Gaussian distributions (which we discuss shortly), it can be theoretically proved that the sample mean and variance are optimal (the best possible guesses of the true mean and variance, given the sampled data). Also, the sample mean approaches the true mean as the number of samples increases, and with enough samples, we get a pretty good approximation of the true mean. In the next subsection, we learn more about how much is "enough."

LAW OF LARGE NUMBERS: HOW MANY SAMPLES ARE ENOUGH?

Informally speaking, the law of large numbers says that if we draw a large number of sample values from a probability distribution, their average should be close to the expected value of the distribution. In the limit, the average over an infinite number of samples will match the mean.

In practice, we cannot draw an infinite number of samples, so there is no guarantee that the sample mean will coincide with the expected value (true mean) in real-life sampling. But if the number of samples is large, they will not be too different. This is not a matter of mere theory. Casinos design games where the probability of the house winning a bet against the guest is slightly higher than the probability of the guest winning. The expected value of the outcome is that the casino wins rather than the guest. Over the very large number of bets placed in a casino, this is exactly what happens—and that is why casinos make money on the whole, even though they may lose individual bets.

How many samples is "a large number of samples?" Well, it is not defined precisely. But one thing is known: if the variance is larger, more samples need to be drawn to make the law of large numbers apply.

Let's illustrate this with an example. Consider a betting game. Suppose that the famous soccer club FC Barcelona, for unknown reasons, has agreed to play a very large number of matches against the Machine Learning Experts' Soccer Club of Silicon Valley. We can place a bet of \$100 on a team. If that team wins, we get back \$200: that is, we make \$100. If that team loses, we lose the bet: that is, we make –\$100. The betting game is happening in a country where nobody knows anything about the reputations of these clubs. A bettor bets on FC Barcelona in the first game and wins \$100. Based on this one observation, can the bettor say that by betting on Barcelona, they expect to win \$100 every time? Obviously not.

But suppose the bettor places 100 bets and wins \$100 99 times and loses \$100 once. Now the bettor can expect with some confidence that they will win \$100 (or close to it) by betting on Barcelona. Based on these observations, the sample mean winnings from a bet on FC Barcelona are $0.99 \times (100) + 0.01 \times (-100) = 98$. The sample standard deviation is $\sqrt{\left(.99 \times (98-100)^2 + 0.01 \times (98-(-100))^2\right)} = 19.8997$. Relative to the sample mean, the sample standard deviation is $\frac{19.8997}{98} = 0.203$.

Next, consider the same game, except now FC Barcelona is playing the Real Madrid football club. Since the two teams are evenly matched (the theoretical win probability of Barcelona is 0.5), the results are no longer one-sided. Suppose that after 100 games, FC Barcelona has won 60 times and Real Madrid has won 40 times. The sample mean winnings on a Barcelona bet are $0.6 \times (100) + 0.4 \times (-100) = 20$. The sample standard deviation is $\sqrt{\left(.6 \times (20-100)^2 + 0.4 \times (20-(-100))^2\right)} = 97.9795$. Relative to the sample mean, the sample standard deviation is $\frac{97.9795}{20} = 4.89897$. This is a much larger number than the previous 0.203. In this case, even after 100 trials, a bettor cannot be very confident in predicting that the expected win is the sample mean, $20.

The overall intuition is as follows:

> If we take a sufficiently large number of samples, their average is close to the expected value. The exact definition of what constitutes a "sufficiently large" number of samples is not known. However, the larger the variance (relative to the mean), the more samples are needed.

5.9 Some famous probability distributions

In this section, we introduce some probability distributions and density functions often used in deep learning. We will use PyTorch code snippets to demonstrate how to set up, sample, and compute properties like expected values, variance/covariance, and so on for each distribution. Note the following:

- In the code snippets, for every distribution, we evaluate the probability using
  - A PyTorch `distributions` function call
  - A raw evaluation from the formula (to understand the math)

  Both should yield the same result. In practice, you should use the PyTorch `distributions` function call instead of the raw formula.
- In the code snippets, for every distribution,
  - We evaluate the theoretical mean and variance using a PyTorch `distributions` function call.
  - We evaluate the sample mean and variance.

  When the sample set is large enough, the sample mean and theoretical mean should be close. Ditto for variance.

NOTE Fully functional code for these distributions, executable via Jupyter Notebook, can be found at http://mng.bz/8NVg.

Another point to remember: In machine learning, we often work with the logarithm of the probability. Since the popular distributions are exponential, this leads to simpler computations. With that, let's dive into the probability distributions.

5.9.1 Uniform random distributions

Consider a continuous random variable x that can take any value from a fixed compact range, say $[a, b]$, *with equal probability, while the probability of x taking a value outside the range is zero.* The corresponding $p(x)$ is a uniform probability distribution. Formally stated,

$$p(x) = \begin{cases} \dfrac{1}{b-a} & \text{if } x \in [a, b] \\ 0 & \text{otherwise} \end{cases} \tag{5.17}$$

Equation 5.17 means $p(x)$ is constant, $\frac{1}{b-a}$, for x between a and b and zero for other values of x. Note how the value of the constant is cleverly chosen to make the total area under the curve 1. This equation is depicted graphically in figure 5.4, and listing 5.1 shows the PyTorch code for the log probability of a univariate uniform random distribution.

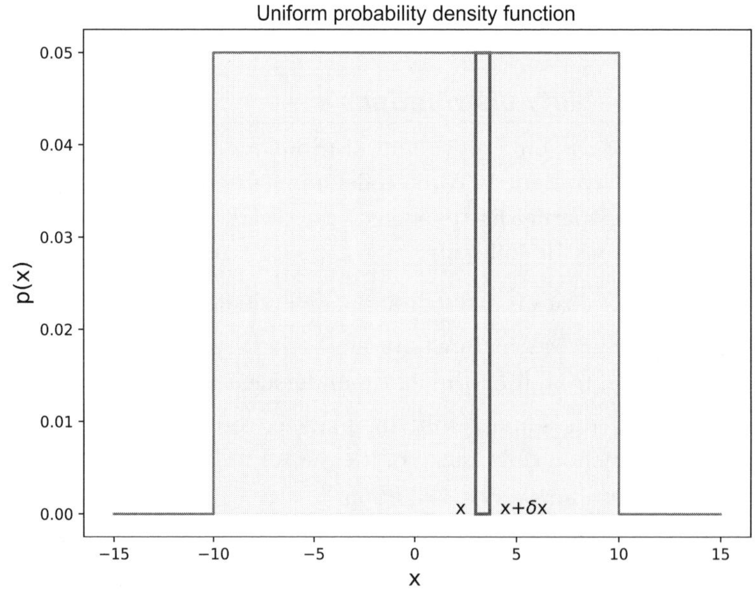

Figure 5.4 Univariate (single-variable) uniform random probability density function. Probability $p(x)$ is constant, 0.05, in the interval $[-10, 10]$ and zero everywhere outside the interval. Thus it depicts equation 5.17 with $b = 10$, $a = -10$. The area under the curve is the area of the shaded rectangle of width 20 and height 0.05, $20 \times 0.05 = 1$. The thin rectangle depicts an infinitesimally small interval corresponding to event $E = \{x \leq X < x + \delta x\}$. If we draw a random sample x from this distribution, the probability that the value of the sample is between, say, 4 and $4 + \delta x$, with $\delta x \rightarrow 0$, is $p(4) = 0.05$. The probability that the value of the sample is between, say, 15 and $15 + \delta x$, with $\delta x \rightarrow 0$, is $p(15) = 0$.

Listing 5.1 Log probability of a univariate uniform random distribution

```
from torch.distributions import Uniform          # Imports a PyTorch uniform distribution

a = torch.tensor([1.0], dtype=torch.float)        # Sets the distribution parameters
b = torch.tensor([5.0], dtype=torch.float)

ufm_dist = Uniform(a, b)                          # Instantiates a uniform distribution object

X = torch.tensor([2.0], dtype=torch.float)        # Instantiates a single-point test dataset

def raw_eval(X, a, b):
    return torch.log(1 / (b - a))

log_prob = ufm_dist.log_prob(X)                   # Evaluates the probability using PyTorch

raw_eval_log_prob = raw_eval(X, a, b)             # Evaluates the probability using the formula

assert torch.isclose(log_prob, raw_eval_log_prob, atol=1e-4)   # Asserts that the probabilities match
```

NOTE Fully functional code for the uniform distribution, executable via Jupyter Notebook, can be found at http://mng.bz/E2Jr.

EXPECTED VALUE OF A UNIFORM DISTRIBUTION

We do this for the univariate case, although the computations can be easily extended to the multivariate case. Substituting the probability density function from equation 5.17 into the expression for the expected value for a continuous variable, equation 5.10,

$$\begin{aligned}\mathbb{E}_{uniform}(X) &= \int_{-\infty}^{\infty} x\, p(x)\, dx = \int_{a}^{b} x \left(\frac{1}{b-a}\right) dx \\ &= \frac{1}{(b-a)} \int_{a}^{b} x\, dx = \frac{1}{(b-a)} \left[\frac{x^2}{2}\right]_a^b = \frac{\left(b^2 - a^2\right)}{2(b-a)} \\ &= \frac{(a+b)}{2}\end{aligned} \tag{5.18}$$

NOTE The limits of integration changed because $p(x)$ is zero outside the interval $[a, b]$.

Overall, equation 5.18 agrees with our intuition. The expected value is right in the middle of the uniform interval, as shown in figure 5.5.

VARIANCE OF A UNIFORM DISTRIBUTION

If we look at figure 5.5, it is intuitively obvious that the packing density of the samples is related to the width of the rectangle. The smaller the width, the tighter the packing and the smaller the variance, and vice versa. Let's see if the math supports that intuition:

$$var_{uniform}(x) = \int_{x=-\infty}^{\infty} (x-\mu)^2\, p(x)\, dx =$$

$$= \int_{x=-\infty}^{\infty} \left(x - \frac{a+b}{2}\right)^2 \frac{1}{(b-a)} dx =$$

$$= \frac{(b-a)^2}{12} \tag{5.19}$$

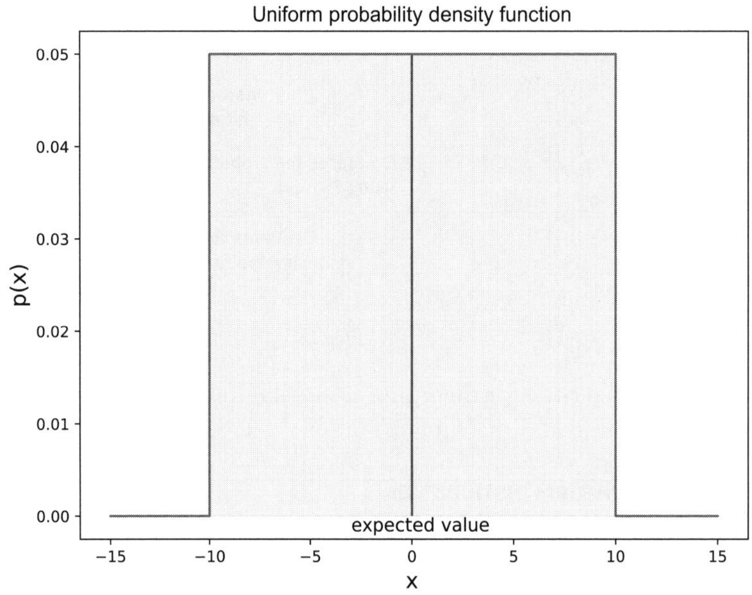

Figure 5.5 Univariate (single-variable) uniform random probability density function. The solid line in the middle indicates the expected value. Interactive visualizations (where you can change the parameters and observe how the graph changes as a result) can be found at http://mng.bz/E2Jr.

Figure 5.5 shows that the variance in equation 5.19 is proportional to the square of the width of the rectangle: that is, $(b-a)^2$.

Here is the PyTorch code for the mean and variance of a uniform random distribution.

Listing 5.2 Mean and variance of a uniform random distribution

```
num_samples = 100000                                   # Number of sample points

samples = ufm_dist.sample([num_samples])               # Obtains samples from ufm_dist
                                                       # instantiated in listing 5.1
# samples: 100000 × 1 tensor

sample_mean = samples.mean()                           # Sample mean

dist_mean = ufm_dist.mean                              # Mean via PyTorch function

assert torch.isclose(sample_mean, dist_mean, atol=0.2)

sample_var = ufm_dist.sample([num_samples]).var()      # Sample variance

dist_var = ufm_dist.variance                           # Variance via PyTorch function

assert torch.isclose(sample_var, dist_var, atol=0.2)
```

MULTIVARIATE UNIFORM DISTRIBUTION

Uniform distributions also can be multivariate. In that case, the random variable is a vector, $\vec{x}$ (not a single value, but a sequence of values). Its domain is a multidimensional volume instead of the X-axis, and the graph has more than two dimensions. For example, this is a two-variable uniform random distribution:

$$p\left(x, y\right) = \begin{cases} \frac{1}{(b_1 - a_1)(b_2 - a_2)} & \text{if } (x, y) \in [a_1, b_1] \times [a_2, b_2] \\ 0 & \text{otherwise} \end{cases} \tag{5.20}$$

Here, $(x, y) \in [a_1, b_1] \times [a_2, b_2]$ indicates a rectangular domain on the two-dimensional XY plane where x lies between a_1 and b_1 and y lies between a_2 and b_2. Equation 5.20 is shown graphically in figure 5.6. In the general multidimensional case,

$$p\left(\vec{x}\right) = \begin{cases} \frac{1}{V} & \text{if } \vec{x} \in D \\ 0 & \text{otherwise} \end{cases} \tag{5.21}$$

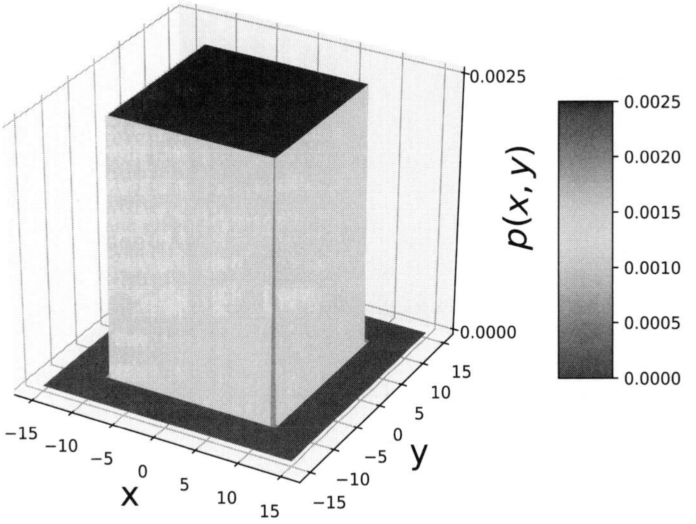

Figure 5.6 Bivariate uniform random probability density function. The probability $p\,(x, y)$ is constant, 0.0025, in the domain $(x, y) \in [-10, 10] \times [-10, 10]$ and zero everywhere outside the interval. The volume of the box of width 20×20 and height 0.0025, $20 * 20 * 0.0025 = 1$.

Here, V is the volume of the hyperdimensional box with base D. Equation 5.21 means $p\left(\vec{x}\right)$ is constant for $\vec{x}$ in the domain D and zero for other values of x. When nonzero, it has a constant value, the inverse of the volume V: this makes the total volume under the density function 1.

5.9.2 *Gaussian (normal) distribution*

This is probably the most famous distribution in the world. Let's consider, one more time, the weights of adult residents of Statsville. If Statsville is anything like a real city, the likeliest weight is around 75 kg: the largest percentage of the population will weigh this much. Weights near this value (say 70 or 80 kg) will also be quite likely, although slightly less likely than 75 kg. Weights further away from 75 kg are still less likely, and so on. The further we go from 75 kg, the lower the percentage of the population with that weight. *Outlier* values like 40 and 110 kg are unlikely. Informally speaking, a Gaussian probability density function looks like a *bell-shaped curve*. The central value has the highest probability. The probability falls gradually as we move away from the center. In theory, however, it never disappears completely (the function $p(x)$ never becomes equal to 0), although it becomes almost zero for all practical purposes. This behavior is described in mathematics as *asymptotically approaching zero*. Figure 5.7 shows a Gaussian probability density function. Formally,

$$p(x) = \frac{1}{\sqrt{2\pi}\sigma} e^{\frac{-(x-\mu)^2}{2\sigma^2}} \tag{5.22}$$

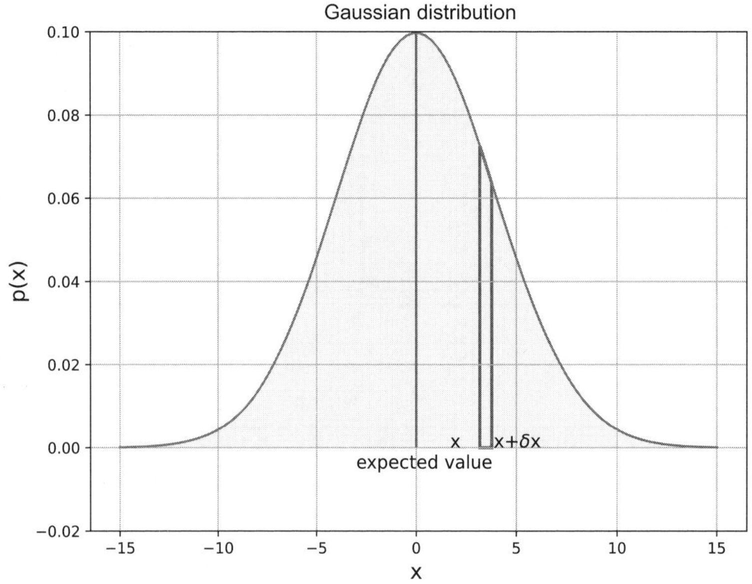

Figure 5.7 Univariate Gaussian random probability density function, $\mu = 0$ and $\sigma = 4$. The bell-shaped curve is highest at the center and decreases more and more as we move away from the center, approaching zero asymptotically. The value $x = 0$ has the highest probability, corresponding to the center of the probability density function. Note that the curve is symmetric. Thus, for instance, the probability of a random sample being in the vicinity of −5 is the same as that of 5 (0.04): that is, $p(-5) = p(5) = 0.04$. An interactive visualization (where you can change the parameters and observe how the graph changes as a result) can be found at http://mng.bz/NYJX.

Here, μ and σ are parameters; μ corresponds to the center (for example, in figure 5.7, $\mu = 0$). The parameter σ controls the width of the bell. A larger σ implies that $p(x)$ falls more slowly as we move away from the center.

The Gaussian (normal) probability density function is so popular that we have a special symbol for it: $\mathcal{N}(x, \mu, \sigma^2)$. It can be proved (but doing so is exceedingly tedious, so we will skip the proof here) that

$$\int_{x=-\infty}^{\infty} \mathcal{N}(x; \mu, \sigma^2) dx = \int_{x=-\infty}^{\infty} \frac{1}{\sqrt{2\pi}\sigma} e^{\frac{-(x-\mu)^2}{2\sigma^2}} dx = 1$$

This establishes that $\mathcal{N}(x; \mu, \sigma^2)$ is a true probability (satisfying the sum rule in equation 5.7).

Listing 5.3 Log probability of a univariate normal distribution

```
from torch.distributions import Normal                  # Imports a PyTorch univariate normal distribution

mu = torch.tensor([0.0], dtype=torch.float)             # Sets the distribution params
sigma = torch.tensor([5.0], dtype=torch.float)

uvn_dist = Normal(mu, sigma)                            # Instantiates a univariate normal distribution object

X = torch.tensor([0.0], dtype=torch.float)              # Instantiates a single-point test dataset

def raw_eval(X, mu, sigma):
    K = 1 / (math.sqrt(2 * math.pi) * sigma)
    E = math.exp( -1 * (X - mu) ** 2 * (1 / (2 * sigma ** 2)))
    return math.log(K * E)

log_prob = uvn_dist.log_prob(X)                         # Evaluates the probability using PyTorch
raw_eval_log_prob = raw_eval(X, mu, sigma)              # Evaluates the probability using the formula

assert log_prob == raw_eval_log_prob                    # Asserts that the probabilities match
```

NOTE Fully functional code for this normal distribution, executable via Jupyter Notebook, can be found at http://mng.bz/NYJX.

MULTIVARIATE GAUSSIAN

A Gaussian distribution can also be multivariate. Then the random variable x is a vector $\vec{x}$, as usual. The parameter μ also becomes a vector $\vec{\mu}$, and the parameter σ becomes a matrix $\mathbf{\Sigma}$. As in the univariate case, these parameters are related to the expected value and variance. The Gaussian multivariate probability distribution function is

$$p\left(\vec{x}\right) = \mathcal{N}\left(\vec{x};\ \vec{\mu}, \mathbf{\Sigma}\right) = \frac{1}{\left(2\pi \det \mathbf{\Sigma}\right)^{\frac{1}{2}}} e^{-\frac{1}{2}(\vec{x}-\vec{\mu})^T \mathbf{\Sigma}^{-1}(\vec{x}-\vec{\mu})} \tag{5.23}$$

Equation 5.23 describes the probability density function for the random vector $\vec{x}$ to lie within the infinitesimally small volume with dimensions $\delta\vec{x}$ around the point $\vec{x}$. (Imagine a tiny box (cuboid) whose sides are successive elements of $\delta\vec{x}$, with the top-left corner of the box at $\vec{x}$.) The vector $\vec{\mu}$ and the matrix $\mathbf{\Sigma}$ are parameters. As in the univariate case, $\vec{\mu}$ corresponds to the most likely value of the random vector. Figure 5.8 shows the Gaussian (normal) distribution with two variables in three dimensions. The shape of the base of the bell is controlled by the parameter $\mathbf{\Sigma}$.

Listing 5.4 Log probability of a multivariate normal distribution

```
from torch.distributions import MultivariateNormal     # Imports a PyTorch multivariate normal distribution

mu = torch.tensor([0.0, 0.0], dtype=torch.float)        # Sets the distribution params
```

```
C = torch.tensor([[5.0, 0.0], [0.0, 5.0]], dtype=torch.float)

mvn_dist = MultivariateNormal(mu, C)

X = torch.tensor([0.0, 0.0], dtype=torch.float)

def raw_eval(X, mu, C):
    K = (1 / (2 * math.pi * math.sqrt(C.det())))
    X_minus_mu = (X - mu).reshape(-1, 1)
    E1 = torch.matmul(X_minus_mu.T, C.inverse())
    E = math.exp(-1 / 2. * torch.matmul(E1, X_minus_mu))
    return math.log(K * E)

log_prob = mvn_dist.log_prob(X)

raw_eval_log_prob = raw_eval(X, mu, C)

assert log_prob == raw_eval_log_prob
```

Instantiates a multivariate normal distribution object (mvn_dist = MultivariateNormal(mu, C))

Instantiates a single point test dataset (X = torch.tensor(...))

Evaluates the probability using PyTorch (log_prob = mvn_dist.log_prob(X))

Evaluates the probability using the formula (raw_eval_log_prob = raw_eval(X, mu, C))

Asserts that the probabilities match (assert log_prob == raw_eval_log_prob)

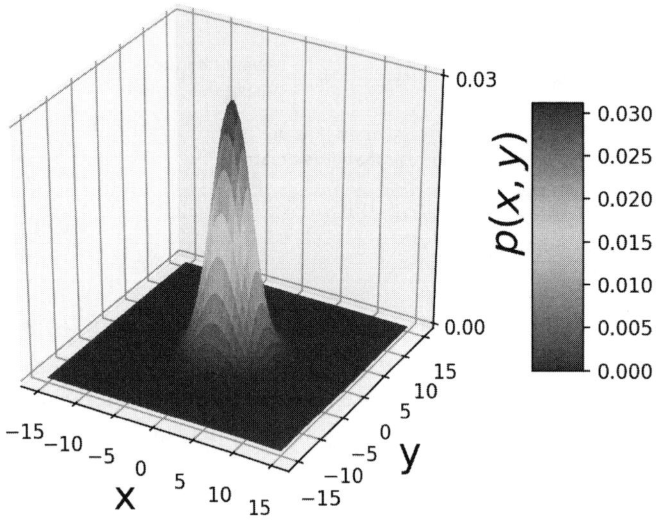

Figure 5.8 Bivariate Gaussian random probability density function. It is a bell-shaped surface: highest at the center and decreasing as we move away from the center, approaching zero asymptotically. $x = 0$, $y = 0$ has the highest probability, corresponding to the center of the probability density function. The bell has a circular base, and the Σ matrix is a scalar multiple of the identity matrix $\mathbb{I}$. An interactive visualization (where you can change the parameters and observe how the graph changes as a result) can be found at http://mng.bz/NYJX.

EXPECTED VALUE OF A GAUSSIAN DISTRIBUTION

Substituting the probability density function from equation 5.22 into the expression for the expected value of a continuous variable, equation 5.10, we get

$$\mathbb{E}_{gaussian}(X) = \int_{-\infty}^{\infty} x \frac{1}{\sqrt{2\pi}\sigma} e^{\frac{-(x-\mu)^2}{2\sigma^2}} dx$$

$$= \frac{1}{\sqrt{\pi}} \int_{-\infty}^{\infty} \frac{(x-\mu)}{\sqrt{2}\sigma} e^{\frac{-(x-\mu)^2}{2\sigma^2}} dx + \mu \int_{-\infty}^{\infty} \frac{1}{\sqrt{2\pi}\sigma} e^{\frac{-(x-\mu)^2}{2\sigma^2}} dx$$

Substituting $y = \frac{-(x-\mu)}{\sqrt{2}\sigma}$

$$\mathbb{E}_{gaussian}(X) = \frac{\sqrt{2}\sigma}{\sqrt{\pi}} \int_{-\infty}^{\infty} y e^{-y^2} dy + \mu \int_{-\infty}^{\infty} p(x)\, dx$$

Substituting $u = y^2$ and using equation 5.6

$$\mathbb{E}_{gaussian}\left(X\right) = \frac{\sqrt{2}\sigma}{2\sqrt{\pi}} \int_{\infty}^{\infty} e^{-u} du + \mu$$

Note that the limits of the integral in the first term are identical. This is because $u = y^2 \rightarrow \infty$ whether $y \rightarrow \infty$ or $y \rightarrow -\infty$. But an integral with the same lower and upper limits is zero. Thus the first term is zero. Hence,

$$\mathbb{E}_{gaussian}\left(X\right) = \mu \tag{5.24}$$

Intuitively, this makes perfect sense. The probability density $p\left(x\right) = \frac{1}{\sqrt{2\pi}\sigma} e^{\frac{-(x-\mu)^2}{2\sigma^2}}$ peaks (maximizes) at $x = \mu$. At this x, the exponent becomes zero, which makes the term $e^{\frac{-(x-\mu)^2}{2\sigma^2}}$ attain its maximum possible value of 1. This is right in the middle of the bell, as shown in figure 5.9. And, of course, the expected value coincides with the middle value if the density is symmetric and peaks in the middle. Analogously, in the multivariate case, the Gaussian multidimensional random variable X that takes vector values $\vec{x}$ in the d-dimensional domain $\mathbb{R}^d$ (that is, $\vec{x} \in \mathbb{R}^d$) has an expected value

$$\mathbb{E}_{gaussian}\left(X\right) = \vec{\mu} \tag{5.25}$$

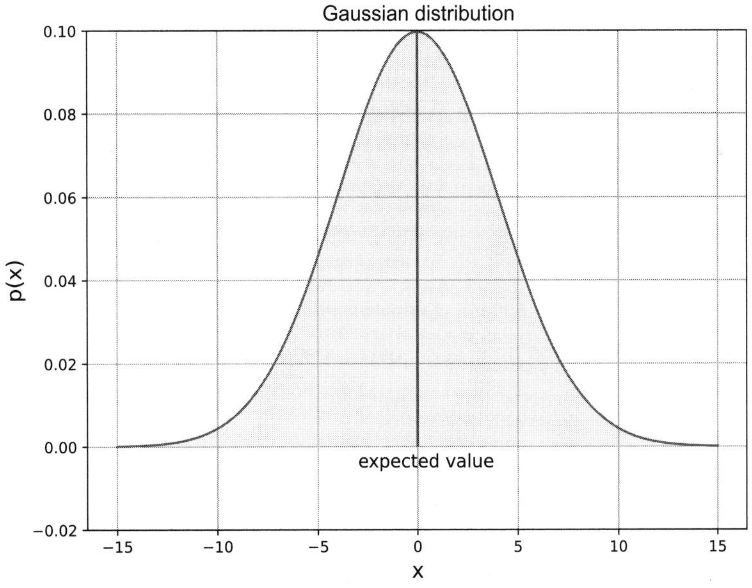

Figure 5.9 Univariate (single-variable) normal (Gaussian) random probability density function, $\mu = 0$ and $\sigma = 4$. The solid line in the middle indicates the expected value.

VARIANCE OF A GAUSSIAN DISTRIBUTION

The variance of the Gaussian distribution is obtained by substituting equation 5.22 in the integral form of equation 5.13. The mathematical derivation is shown in the book's appendix; here we only state the result.

The variance of a Gaussian distribution with probability density function $p\left(x\right) = \frac{1}{\sqrt{2\pi\sigma}} e^{\frac{-(x-\mu)^2}{2\sigma^2}}$ is σ^2, and the standard deviation is the square root of that (σ). This makes intuitive sense. σ appears in the denominator of a negative exponent in the expression for the probability density function $p\left(x\right) = \frac{1}{\sqrt{2\pi\sigma}} e^{\frac{-(x-\mu)^2}{2\sigma^2}}$. As such, $p\left(x\right)$ is an increasing function of σ: that is, for a given x and μ, a larger σ implies a larger $p\left(x\right)$. In other words, a larger σ implies that the probability decays more slowly as we move away from the center: a fatter bell curve, a bigger spread, and hence a larger variance. Figure 5.10 depicts this.

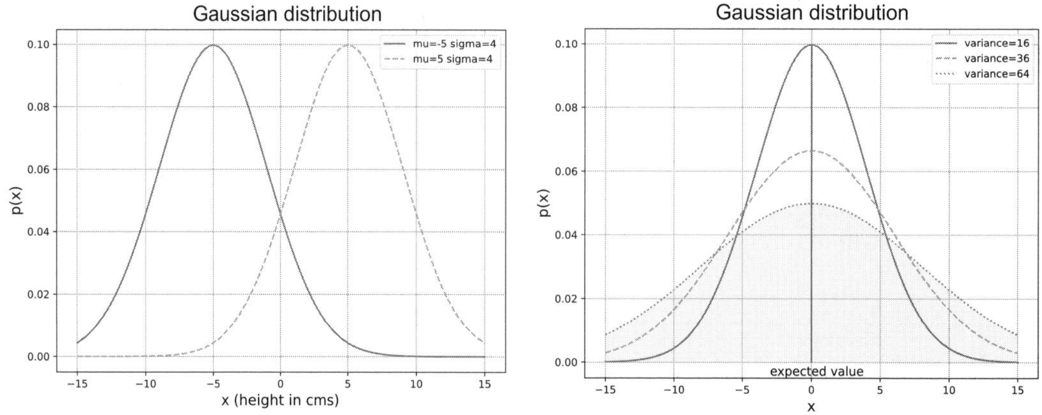

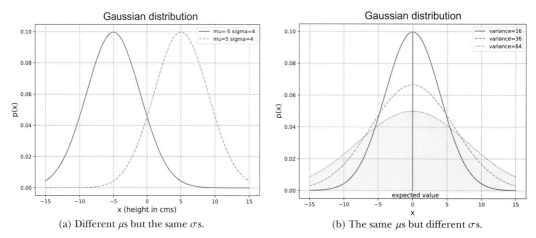

(a) Different μs but the same σs. (b) The same μs but different σs.

Figure 5.10 Gaussian densities with varying μs and σs. Changing μ shifts the center of the curve. A larger σ (variance) implies a fatter bell $\Rightarrow$ more spread. Note that fatter curves are smaller in height as the total area under the curve must be 1.

Listing 5.5 Mean and variance of a univariate Gaussian

```
num_samples = 100000
samples = uvn_dist.sample([num_samples])
sample_mean = samples.mean()
dist_mean = uvn_dist.mean
assert torch.isclose(sample_mean, dist_mean, atol=0.1)
sample_var = uvn_dist.sample([num_samples]).var()
dist_var = uvn_dist.variance
assert torch.isclose(sample_var, dist_var, atol=0.1)
```

- `num_samples = 100000` ← **Number of sample points**
- `samples` ← **100000 × 1 tensor**
- `uvn_dist.sample([num_samples])` ← **Obtains samples from uvn_dist instantiated in listing 5.3**
- `samples.mean()` ← **Sample mean**
- `uvn_dist.mean` ← **Mean via PyTorch function**
- `uvn_dist.sample([num_samples]).var()` ← **Sample variance**
- `uvn_dist.variance` ← **Variance via PyTorch function**

COVARIANCE OF A MULTIVARIATE GAUSSIAN DISTRIBUTION AND GEOMETRY OF THE BELL SURFACE

Comparing equation 5.22 for a univariate Gaussian probability density with equation 5.23 for a multivariate Gaussian probability density, we intuitively feel that the matrix $\mathbf{\Sigma}$

is the multivariate peer of the univariate variance σ^2. Indeed it is. Formally, for a multivariate Gaussian random variable with a probability distribution given in equation 5.23, the covariance matrix is given by the equation

$$\mathbb{C}_{gaussian}(X) = \Sigma \tag{5.26}$$

As shown in table 5.11, Σ regulates the shape of the base of the bell-shaped probability density function.

It is easy to see that the exponent in equation 5.23 is a quadratic form (introduced in section 4.2). As such, it defines a hyper-ellipse, as shown in figure 5.11 and section 2.17. All the properties of quadratic forms and hyper-ellipses apply here.

Listing 5.6 Mean and variance of a multivariate normal distribution

```
num_samples = 100000                                  # Number of sample points

samples = mvn_dist.sample([num_samples])              # Obtains samples from mvn_dist
                                                      # instantiated in listing 5.4
# samples: 100000 × 1 tensor

sample_mean = samples.mean()                          # Sample mean

dist_mean = mvn_dist.mean                             # Mean via PyTorch function

assert torch.allclose(sample_mean, dist_mean, atol=1e-1)

sample_var = mvn_dist.sample([num_samples]).var()     # Sample variance

dist_var = mvn_dist.variance                          # Variance via PyTorch function

assert torch.allclose(sample_var, dist_var, atol=1e-1)
```

Let's look at the geometric properties of the Gaussian covariance matrix Σ. Consider a 2D version of equation 5.23. We rewrite $\vec{x} = \begin{bmatrix} x \\ y \end{bmatrix}$ and $\vec{\mu} = \begin{bmatrix} \mu_x \\ \mu_y \end{bmatrix}$—2D vectors both. Also $\Sigma^{-1} = \begin{bmatrix} \sigma_{11} & \sigma_{12} \\ \sigma_{21} & \sigma_{22} \end{bmatrix}$—a 2×2 matrix. The probability density function from equation 5.23 becomes

$$p(x, y) = \mathcal{N}\left(x, y;\ \vec{\mu}, \Sigma\right) = \frac{1}{(2\pi \det \Sigma)^{\frac{1}{2}}} e^{-\frac{1}{2}\left(\sigma_{11}x^2 + (\sigma_{11}+\sigma_{12})xy + \sigma_{22}y^2\right)} \tag{5.27}$$

(Use what you learned in chapter 3 to satisfy yourself that equation 5.27 is a 2D analog of equation 5.23.)

If we plot the surface $p(x, y)$ against (x, y), it looks like a bell in 3D space. The shape of the bell's base, on the (x, y) plane, is governed by the 2×2 matrix Σ. In particular,

- If Σ is a diagonal matrix with equal diagonal elements, the bell is symmetric in all directions, and its base is circular.
- If Σ is a diagonal matrix with unequal diagonal elements, the base of the bell is elliptical. The axes of the ellipse are aligned with the coordinate axes.

- For a general Σ matrix, the base of the bell is elliptical. The axes of the ellipse are not necessarily aligned with the coordinate axes.
- The eigenvectors of Σ yield the axes of the elliptical base of the bell surface.

Now, if we sample the distribution from equation 5.27, we get a set of points (x, y) on the base plane of the surface shown in figure 5.8. The taller the z coordinate (depicting $p\,(x, y)$) of the surface at a point (x, y), the greater its probability of being selected in the sampling. If we draw a large number of samples, the corresponding point cloud will look more or less like the base of the bell surface.

Figure 5.11 shows various point clouds formed by sampling Gaussian distributions with different covariance matrices Σ. Compare it to figure 5.10.

GEOMETRY OF SAMPLED POINT CLOUDS: COVARIANCE AND DIRECTION OF MAXIMUM OR MINIMUM SPREAD

We have seen that if a multivariate distribution has a covariance matrix $\mathbb{C}$, its variance (spread) in any specific direction $\hat{l}$ is $\hat{l}^T \mathbb{C} \hat{l}$. What is the direction of maximum spread?

Asking this is the same as asking "What direction $\hat{l}$ maximizes the quadratic form $\hat{l}^T \mathbb{C} \hat{l}$?" In section 4.2, we saw that a quadratic form like this is maximized or minimized when the direction $\hat{l}$ is aligned with the eigenvector corresponding to the maximum or minimum eigenvalue of the matrix $\mathbb{C}$. Thus, *the maximum spread of a distribution occurs along the eigenvector of the covariance matrix corresponding to its maximum eigenvalue.* This led to the PCA technique in section 4.4.

Next, we discuss the covariance of the Gaussian distribution and geometry of the point cloud formed by sampling a multivariate Gaussian a large number of times. You may want to take a look at figure 5.11, which shows various point clouds formed by sampling Gaussian distributions with different covariance matrices Σ.

MULTIVARIATE GAUSSIAN POINT CLOUDS AND HYPER-ELLIPSES

The numerator of the exponential term in equation 5.23, $(\vec{x} - \vec{\mu})^T \Sigma^{-1} (\vec{x} - \vec{\mu})$, is a quadratic form as we discussed in section 4.2. It should also remind you of the hyper-ellipse we looked at in section 2.17, equation 2.33, and equation 4.1.

Now consider the plot of $p\,(\vec{x})$ against $\vec{x}$. This is a hypersurface in $n + 1$-dimensional space, where the random variable $\vec{x}$ is n-dimensional. For instance, if the random Gaussian variable $\vec{x}$ is 2D, the $(\vec{x}, p\,(\vec{x}))$ plot in 3D is as shown in figure 5.8. It is a bell-shaped surface. The hyper-ellipse corresponding to the quadratic form in the numerator of the probability density function in equation 5.23 governs the shape and size of the base of this bell.

If the matrix Σ is diagonal (with equal diagonal elements), the base is *circular*—this is the special case shown in figure 5.8. Otherwise, the base of the bell is elliptic. The eigenvectors of the covariance matrix Σ correspond to the directions of the axes of the elliptical base. The eigenvalues correspond to the lengths of the axes.

5.9.3 Binomial distribution

Suppose we have a database containing photos of people. Also, suppose we know that 20% of the photos contain a celebrity and the remaining 80% do not. If we randomly

(a) $\Sigma = \begin{bmatrix} 5 & 0 \\ 0 & 5 \end{bmatrix}$ (b) $\Sigma = \begin{bmatrix} 2.75 & 2.25 \\ 2.25 & 2.75 \end{bmatrix}$

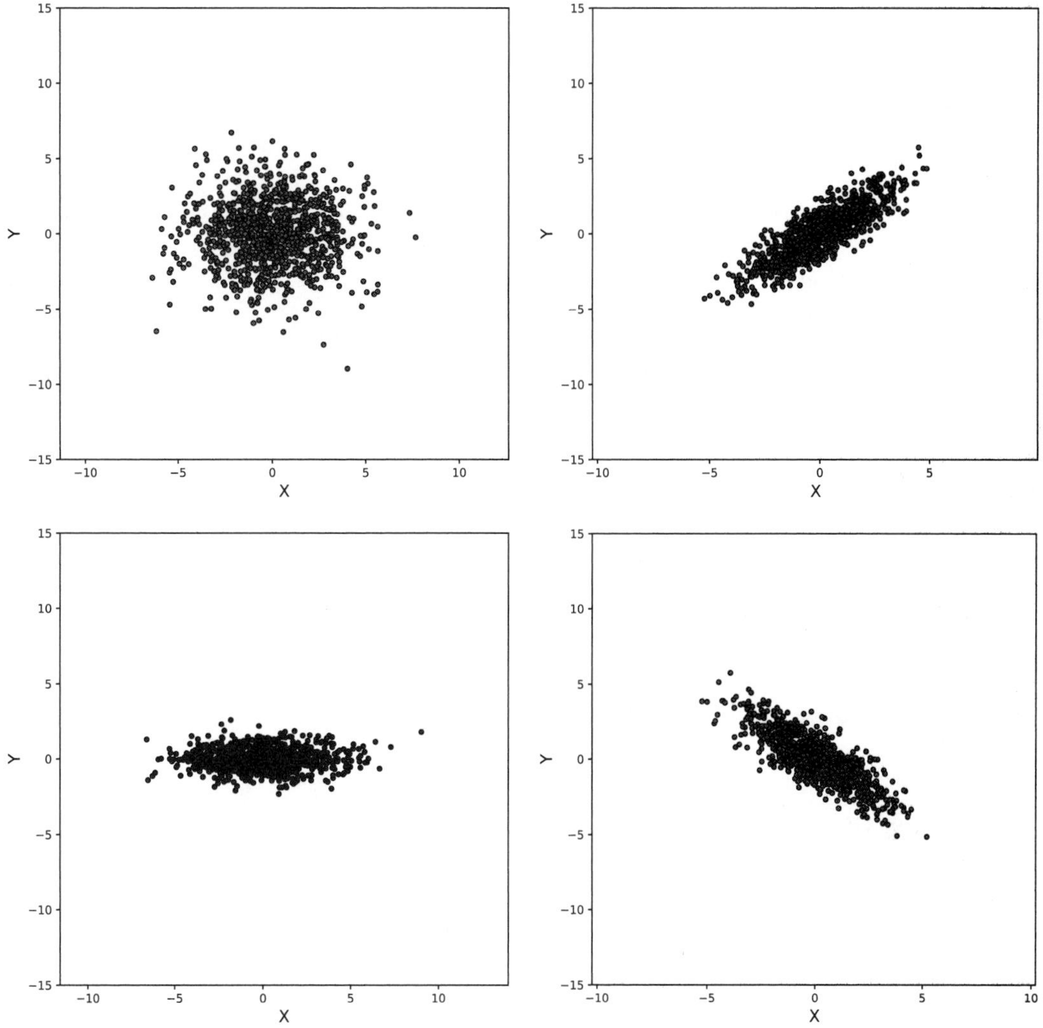

(c) $\Sigma = \begin{bmatrix} 5 & 0 \\ 0 & 0.5 \end{bmatrix}$ (d) $\Sigma = \begin{bmatrix} 2.75 & -2.25 \\ -2.25 & 2.75 \end{bmatrix}$

Figure 5.11 Point clouds formed by sampling multivariate Gaussians with the same $\vec{\mu} = [0, 0]^T$ but different Σs. These point clouds correspond to the bases of the bell curves for multivariate Gaussian probability densities. All the point clouds except (a) may be replaced by a univariate Gaussian after rotation to align the coordinate axes with the eigenvectors of Σ (dimensionality reduction). See sections 4.4, 4.5, and 4.6 for details. Interactive contour plots for the base of the bell curve can be found at http://mng.bz/NYJX.

select three photos from this database, what is the probability that two of them contain a celebrity? This is the kind of problem the binomial distribution deals with.

In a computer vision-centric machine learning setting, we would probably inspect the selected photos and try to predict whether they contained a celebrity. But for now, let's restrict ourselves to the simpler task of blindly predicting the chances from aggregate statistics.

If we select a single photo, the probability of it containing a celebrity is $\pi = 0.2$.

> **NOTE** This has nothing to do with the natural number π denoting the ratio of the circumference to the diameter of a circle. We are just reusing the symbol π following popular convention.

The probability of the photo not containing a celebrity is $1 - \pi = 0.8$. From that, we can compute the probability of, say, the first two sampled photos containing a celebrity but the last one containing a non-celebrity: that is, the event $\{S, S, F\}$ (where S denotes success in finding a celebrity and F denotes failure in finding a celebrity). Using equation 5.4, the probability of the event $\{S, S, F\}$ is $\pi \times \pi \times (1 - \pi) = 0.2 \times 0.2 \times 0.8$. However, many other combinations are also possible.

All the possible combinations that can occur in three trials are shown in table 5.8. In the table, event ids 3, 5, and 6 correspond to two successes and one failure. They occur with probabilities $0.8 \times 0.2 \times 0.2$, $0.2 \times 0.8 \times 0.2$, and $0.2 \times 0.2 \times 0.8$, respectively. If any one of them occurs, we have two celebrity photos in three trials. Thus, using equation 5.3, the overall probability of selecting two celebrity photos in three trials is the sum of these event probabilities: $0.8 \times 0.2 \times 0.2 + 0.2 \times 0.8 \times 0.2 + 0.2 \times 0.2 \times 0.8 = 0.096$.

Table 5.8 All possible combinations of three trials

Event Id	Event	Probability
0	$\{F, F, F\}$	$(1 - \pi) \times (1 - \pi) \times (1 - \pi) = 0.8 \times 0.8 \times 0.8$
1	$\{F, F, S\}$	$(1 - \pi) \times (1 - \pi) \times \pi = 0.8 \times 0.8 \times 0.2$
2	$\{F, S, F\}$	$(1 - \pi) \times \pi \times (1 - \pi) = 0.8 \times 0.2 \times 0.8$
3	$\{F, S, S\}$	$(1 - \pi) \times \pi \times \pi = 0.8 \times 0.2 \times 0.2$
4	$\{S, F, F\}$	$\pi \times (1 - \pi) \times (1 - \pi) = 0.2 \times 0.8 \times 0.8$
5	$\{S, F, S\}$	$\pi \times (1 - \pi) \times \pi = 0.2 \times 0.8 \times 0.2$
6	$\{S, S, F\}$	$\pi \times \pi \times (1 - \pi) = 0.2 \times 0.2 \times 0.8$
7	$\{S, S, S\}$	$\pi \times \pi \times \pi = 0.2 \times 0.2 \times 0.2$

In the general case, with more than three trials, it would be impossibly tedious to enumerate all the possible combinations of *success* and *failure* that can occur in a set of n trials. Fortunately, we can derive a formula. But before doing that, let's state the task of a binomial distribution in more general terms:

> Given a process that has a binary outcome (success or failure) in any given trial, and given that the probability of success in a trial is a known constant (say, π), a

binomial distribution deals with the probability of observing k successes in n trials of the process.

Imagine events with n successive items, where each individual item can be either S or F. Table 5.8 shows such events with $n = 3$. Each item has two possible values (S or F), and there are n items. Hence, altogether there can be $2 \times 2 \times \cdots 2 = 2^n$ possible events.

We are only interested in events with k occurrences of S (and therefore $(n-k)$ occurrences of F). How many of the n events are like that? Well, asking this is the same as asking how many ways we can choose k slots from a total of n possible slots. Another way to pose the same question is, "How many different orderings of n items exist, where each item is either S or F and the total count of S is k?" The answer, from combination theory, is

$$\binom{n}{k} = \frac{n!}{k!\,(n-k)!}$$

Each of these events has a probability of $\pi^k \times (1-\pi)^{n-k}$. Hence, the overall probability of k successes in n trials is $\binom{n}{k}\pi^k \times (1-\pi)^{n-k}$.

Formally, if X is a random variable denoting the number of successes in n trials, with the probability of success in any single trial being some constant value π,

$$p\,(X = k) = \binom{n}{k}\pi^k \times (1-\pi)^{n-k} \tag{5.28}$$

What values can k take? Of course, we cannot have more than n successes in n trials; therefore, the maximum possible value of k is n. All integer values between 0 and n are possible:

$$\sum_{k=0}^{k=n} p\,(X = k) = \sum_{k=0}^{k=n}\binom{n}{k}\pi^k \times (1-\pi)^{n-k}$$

The right-hand side is an expression for the generic term in the famous binomial expansion of $(a+b)^n$ with $a = \pi$ and $b = 1 - \pi$. Hence, we get

$$\sum_{k=0}^{k=n} p\,(X = k) = \sum_{k=0}^{k=n}\binom{n}{k}\pi^k \times (1-\pi)^{n-k} = (\pi + 1 - \pi)^n = 1^n = 1 \tag{5.29}$$

This agrees with intuition, since given n, k can only take values $0, 1, \cdots, n$; the sum of the probabilities on the left-hand side of equation 5.29 corresponds to a certain event with probability 1.

Also, plugging $n = 3$, $k = 2$, and $\pi = 0.2$ into equation 5.28 yields $\frac{3!}{2!\,1!}\,(0.2)^2\,(0.8)^{3-2} = 0.096$: exactly what we get from explicit enumeration.

Listing 5.7 Log probability of a binomial distribution

```
from torch.distributions import Binomial      ← Imports a PyTorch binomial distribution

num_trials = 3   ← Sets the distribution params

p = torch.tensor([0.2], dtype=torch.float)     ┐ Instantiates a binomial
                                               │ distribution object
binom_dist = Binomial(num_trials, probs=p)    ←┘
```

```
X = torch.tensor([1], dtype=torch.float)   ← Instantiates a single point test dataset

def nCk(n, k):
    f = math.factorial
    return f(n) * 1. / (f(k) * f(n-k))

def raw_eval(X, n, p):
    result = nCk(n, X) * (p ** X) * (1 - p) ** (n - X)
    return torch.log(result)

log_prob = binom_dist.log_prob(X)   ← Evaluates the probability using PyTorch

raw_eval_log_prob = raw_eval(X, num_trials, p)   ← Evaluates the probability using formula

assert torch.isclose(log_prob, raw_eval_log_prob, atol=1e-4)   ← Asserts that the probabilities match
```

NOTE Fully functional code for the binomial distribution, executable via Jupyter Notebook, can be found at http://mng.bz/DRJ0.

EXPECTED VALUE OF A BINOMIAL DISTRIBUTION

We have seen that the binomial distribution deals with a random variable X that depicts the number of successes in n trials, where the probability of success in a given trial is a constant π (again, this has nothing to do with the π denoting the ratio of the circumference to the diameter of a circle). This X can take any integer value 0 to n. Hence,

$$\mathbb{E}(X) = \sum_{k=0}^{k=n} k\, p(X=k) = \sum_{k=0}^{k=n} k \binom{n}{k} \pi^k (1-\pi)^{n-k} = \sum_{k=0}^{k=n} k \frac{n!}{k!\,(n-k)!} \pi^k \times (1-\pi)^{n-k}$$

We can drop the first term, which has the multiplier $k = 0$. Thus we get

$$\mathbb{E}(X) = \sum_{k=1}^{k=n} \frac{n!}{(k-1)!\,(n-k)!} \pi^k \times (1-\pi)^{n-k}$$

We can factor $n! = n\,(n-1)!$ and $\pi^k = \pi\,\pi^{k-1}$. Also, $n - k = (n-1) - (k-1)$. This gives us

$$\mathbb{E}(X) = \sum_{k=1}^{k=n} \frac{n\,(n-1)!}{(k-1)!\,((n-1)-(k-1))!} \pi\,\pi^{k-1} \times (1-\pi)^{n-k}$$

Substituting j for $k - 1$ and m for $n - 1$, we get

$$\mathbb{E}(X) = n\pi \sum_{j=0}^{j=m} \frac{m!}{j!\,(m-j)!} \pi^j \times (1-\pi)^{m-j} \tag{5.30}$$

The quantity within the summation is similar to that in equation 5.29 (should sum to 1). This leaves us with

$$\mathbb{E}_{binomial}(X) = n\pi \tag{5.31}$$

Equation 5.31 says that if π is the probability of success in a single trial, then the expected number of successes in n trials is $n\,\pi$. For instance, if the probability of success in a single trial is 0.2, then the expected number of successes in 100 trials is 20—which is almost intuitively obvious.

VARIANCE OF A BINOMIAL DISTRIBUTION
The variance of a binomial random variable depicting the number of successes in n trials where the probability of success in a given trial is a constant π is

$$var_{binomial} = n\pi\,(1 - \pi) \tag{5.32}$$

The proof follows the same lines as that of the expected value.

Listing 5.8 Mean and variance of a binomial distribution

```
num_samples = 100000                    # Number of sample points

samples = binom_dist.sample([num_samples])   # Obtains samples from the binom_dist
                                             # instantiated in listing 5.7
                                             # samples: 100000 × 1 tensor

sample_mean = samples.mean()            # Sample mean

dist_mean = binom_dist.mean             # Mean via PyTorch function

assert torch.isclose(sample_mean, dist_mean, atol=0.2)

sample_var = binom_dist.sample([num_samples]).var()   # Sample variance

dist_var = binom_dist.variance          # Variance via PyTorch function

assert torch.isclose(sample_var, dist_var, atol=0.2)
```

5.9.4 *Multinomial distribution*

Consider again the example problem we discussed in section 5.9.3. We have a database of photos of people. But instead of two classes, celebrity and non-celebrity, we have four classes:

- Photos of Albert Einstein (class 1): 10% of the photos
- Photos of Marie Curie (class 2): 42% of the photos
- Photos of Carl Friedrich Gauss (class 3): 4% of the photos
- Other photos (class 4): 44% of the photos

If we randomly select a photo from the database (that is, perform a random trial),

- The probability of selecting class 1 (picking an Einstein photo) is $\pi_1 = 0.1$.
- The probability of selecting class 2 (picking a Marie Curie photo) is $\pi_2 = 0.42$.
- The probability of selecting class 3 (picking a Gauss photo) is $\pi_3 = 0.04$.
- The probability of selecting class 4 (picking a photo of none of the above) is $\pi_4 = 0.44$.

Notice that $\pi_1 + \pi_2 + \pi_3 + \pi_4 = 1$. This is because the classes are mutually exclusive and exhaustive, so exactly one of these classes must occur in every trial.

Given all this, let's ask the question: "What is the probability that in a set of 10 random trials, class 1 occurs 1 time, class 2 occurs 2 times, class 3 occurs 1 time, and class 4 occurs the remaining 6 times?" This is the kind of problem multinomial distributions deal with.

Formally,

- Let $C_1, C_2, \cdots, C_m$ be a set of m classes such that in any random trial, exactly one of these classes will be selected with the respective probabilities $\pi_1, \pi_2, \cdots, \pi_m$.
- Let $X_1, X_2, \cdots, X_m$ be a set of random variables. X_i corresponds to the number of occurrences of class C_i in a set of n trials.
- Then the multinomial probability function depicting the probability that class C_1 is selected k_1 times, class C_2 is selected k_2 times, and class C_3 is selected k_m times is

$$p\left(X_1 = k_1, X_2 = k_2, \cdots, X_m = k_m\right) = \frac{n!}{k_1!\, k_2! \cdots, k_m!} \pi_1^{k_1}\, \pi_2^{k_2} \cdots \pi_m^{k_m} \tag{5.33}$$

where

$$\sum_{i=1}^{m} k_i = n$$

$$\sum_{i=1}^{m} \pi_i = 1$$

We can verify that for $m = 2$, this becomes the binomial distribution (equation 5.28). A noteworthy point is that if we look at any one of the m variables $X_1, X_2, \cdots, X_m$ individually, its distribution is binomial.

Let's work out the final probability for the example we started with: the probability that in a set of 10 random trials, class 1 occurs 1 time, class 2 occurs 2 times, class 3 occurs 1 time, and class 4 occurs the remaining 6 times. This is

$$p\left(X_1 = 1, X_2 = 2, X_3 = 1, X_4 = 6\right) = \frac{10!}{1!\,2!\,1!\,6!}\,(0.1)^1\,(0.42)^2\,(0.04)^1\,(0.44)^6 = 0.0129$$

Listing 5.9 Log probability of a multinomial distribution

```
from torch.distributions import Multinomial        # Imports a PyTorch multinomial distribution

num_trials = 10        # Sets the distribution params
P = torch.tensor([0.1, 0.42, 0.04, 0.44], dtype=torch.float)

multinom_dist = Multinomial(num_trials, probs=P)        # Instantiates a multinomial dist object

X = torch.tensor([1, 2, 1, 6], dtype=torch.float)        # Instantiates a single-point test dataset

def raw_eval(X, n, P):
    f = math.factorial
    result = f(n)
    for p, x in zip(P, X):
        result *= (p ** x) / f(x)
    return math.log(result)

log_prob = multinom_dist.log_prob(X)        # Evaluates the probability using PyTorch

raw_eval_log_prob = raw_eval(X, num_trials, P)        # Evaluates the probability using formula

assert torch.isclose(log_prob, raw_eval_log_prob, atol=1e-4)        # Asserts that the probabilities match
```

NOTE Fully functional code for the multinomial distribution, executable via Jupyter Notebook, can be found at http://mng.bz/l1gz.

EXPECTED VALUE OF A MULTINOMIAL DISTRIBUTION

Each of the random variables $X_1, X_2, \cdots, X_m$ individually subscribes to a binomial distribution. Accordingly, following the binomial distribution expected value formula from equation 5.31,

$$\mathbb{E}_{multinomial}\left(X_i\right) = n\pi_i \tag{5.34}$$

VARIANCE OF A MULTINOMIAL DISTRIBUTION

The variation of the random variables $X_1, X_2, \cdots, X_m$, following the binomial distribution variance formula from equation 5.32, is

$$var_{multinomial}\left(X_i\right) = n\pi_i\left(1 - \pi_i\right) \tag{5.35}$$

If each of the $X_1, X_2, \cdots, X_m$ is a scalar, then we can think of a random vector $X = \begin{bmatrix} X_1 \\ X_2 \\ \vdots \\ X_m \end{bmatrix}$.

The expected value of such a random variable is

$$\mathbb{E}_{multinomial}\left(X\right) = \begin{bmatrix} n\pi_1 \\ n\pi_1 \\ \vdots \\ n\pi_m \end{bmatrix}$$

and the covariance is

$$\mathbb{C}_{multinomial}\left(X\right) = \begin{bmatrix} \sigma_{11} & \sigma_{12} & \cdots \sigma_{1m} \\ \sigma_{21} & \sigma_{22} & \cdots \sigma_{2m} \\ & & \cdots \\ \sigma_{m1} & \sigma_{m2} & \cdots \sigma_{mm} \end{bmatrix} \tag{5.36}$$

where the diagonal terms are like the binomial variance $\sigma_{ii} = n\pi_i\left(1 - \pi_i\right) \forall i \in [1, m]$ and the off-diagonal terms are $\sigma_{ij} = -n\pi_i\pi_j \forall (i, j) \in [1, m] \times [1, m]$. The cross-covariance terms in the diagonal are negative because an increase in one element implies a decrease in the others.

Listing 5.10 Mean and variance of a multinomial distribution

```
num_samples = 100000                                    ◄── Number of sample points

samples = multinom_dist.sample([num_samples])           ◄── Obtains samples from the
        100000 × 1 tensor                                   multinom_dist instantiated
sample_mean = samples.mean(axis=0)   ◄── Sample mean        in listing 5.9
```

```
dist_mean = multinom_dist.mean  ◄── Mean via PyTorch function
assert torch.allclose(sample_mean, dist_mean, atol=0.2)

sample_var = multinom_dist.sample([num_samples]).var(axis=0)  ◄── Sample variance
dist_var = multinom_dist.variance  ◄── Variance via PyTorch function
assert torch.allclose(sample_var, dist_var, atol=0.2)
```

5.9.5 Bernoulli distribution

A Bernoulli distribution is a special case of a binomial distribution where $n = 1$: that is, a single success-or-failure trial is performed. The probability of success is π, and the probability of failure is $1 - \pi$.

In other words, let X be a discrete random variable that takes the value 1 (success) with probability π and the value 0 (failure) with probability $1 - \pi$. The distribution of X is the Bernoulli distribution:

$$p\,(X = 1) = \pi$$

$$p\,(X = 0) = 1 - \pi$$

Listing 5.11 Log probability of a Bernoulli distribution

```
from torch.distributions import Bernoulli  ◄── Imports a PyTorch Bernoulli distribution

p = torch.tensor([0.3], dtype=torch.float)  ◄── Sets the distribution params

bern_dist = Bernoulli(p)  ◄── Instantiates a Bernoulli distribution object

X = torch.tensor([1], dtype=torch.float)  ◄── Instantiates a single-point test dataset

def raw_eval(X, p):
    prob = p if X == 1 else 1-p
    return math.log(prob)

log_prob = bern_dist.log_prob(X)  ◄── Evaluates the probability using PyTorch
raw_eval_log_prob = raw_eval(X, p)  ◄── Evaluates the probability using the formula
assert torch.isclose(log_prob, raw_eval_log_prob, atol=1e-4)  ◄── Asserts that the probabilities match
```

NOTE Fully functional code for the Bernoulli distribution, executable via Jupyter Notebook, can be found at http://mng.bz/BRwq.

EXPECTED VALUE OF A BERNOULLI DISTRIBUTION

If there are only two classes, *success* and *failure*, we cannot speak directly of an expected value. If we run, say, 100 trials and get 30 *successes* and 70 *failures*, the average is 0.3 *success*, which is not a valid outcome. We cannot have fractional *success* or *failure* in this binary system.

We can, however, talk about the expected value of a Bernoulli distribution if we introduce an artificial construct. We assign numerical values to these binary entities:

success = 1 and *failure* = 0. Then the expected value of X is

$$\mathbb{E}(X) = \sum_{x \in \{0,1\}} xp(x) = 1 \cdot \pi + (1-\pi) \cdot 0 = \pi \tag{5.37}$$

VARIANCE OF A BERNOULLI DISTRIBUTION

Similarly, if we assign numerical values to these binary entities—*success* = 1 and *failure* = 0—the variance of the Bernoulli distribution is

$$var(X) = \sum_{x \in \{0,1\}} (x - \mathbb{E}(X))^2 p(x) = (1-\pi)^2 \pi + (0-\pi)^2 (1-\pi) = \pi(1-\pi) \tag{5.38}$$

Listing 5.12 Mean and variance of a Bernoulli distribution

```
num_samples = 100000                                 ← Number of sample points

samples = bern_dist.sample([num_samples])            ← Obtains samples from the bern_dist
                                                       instantiated in listing 5.11
        ↑ 100000 × 1 tensor

sample_mean = samples.mean()                         ← Sample mean

dist_mean = bern_dist.mean                           ← Mean via PyTorch function

assert torch.isclose(sample_mean, dist_mean, atol=0.2)

sample_var = bern_dist.sample([num_samples]).var()   ← Sample variance

dist_var = bern_dist.variance                        ← Variance via PyTorch function

assert torch.isclose(sample_var, dist_var, atol=0.2)
```

5.9.6 Categorical distribution and one-hot vectors

Consider again the example problem introduced in section 5.9.4. We have a database with four classes of photos:

- Photos of Albert Einstein (class 1): 10%
- Photos of Marie Curie (class 2): 42%
- Photos of Carl Friedrich Gauss (class 3): 4%
- Other photos (class 4): 44%

If we randomly select a photo from the database,

- The probability of selecting class 1 is $\pi_1 = 0.1$.
- The probability of selecting class 2 is $\pi_2 = 0.42$.
- The probability of selecting class 3 is $\pi_3 = 0.04$.
- The probability of selecting class 4 is $\pi_4 = 0.44$.

As before, $\pi_1 + \pi_2 + \pi_3 + \pi_4 = 1$ because the classes are mutually exclusive and exhaustive so exactly one class must occur in each trial.

In multinomial distribution, we performed n trials and asked how many times each specific class would occur. What if we perform only one trial? Then we get categorical distribution.

Categorical distribution is a special case of multinomial distribution (with the number of trials $n = 1$). It is also an extension of the Bernoulli distribution where instead of just two classes, *success* and *failure*, we can have an arbitrary number of classes.

Formally,

- Let $C_1, C_2, \cdots, C_m$ be a set of m classes such that in any random trial, exactly one of these classes will be selected, with the respective probabilities $\pi_1, \pi_2, \cdots, \pi_m$. We sometimes refer to the probabilities of all the classes together as a vector $\vec{\pi} = \begin{bmatrix} \pi_1 \\ \pi_2 \\ \vdots \\ \pi_m \end{bmatrix}$
- Let $X_1, X_2, \cdots, X_m$ be a set of random variables. X_i corresponds to the number of occurrences of class C_i in a set of n trials.
- Then the categorical probability function depicts the probability of each of the classes C_1, C_2, and so on, in a single trial.

ONE-HOT VECTOR

We can use a one-hot vector to compactly express the outcome of a single trial of categorical distribution. This is a vector with m elements. Exactly a single element is 1; all other elements are 0. The 1 indicates which of the m possible classes occurred in that specific trial. For instance, in the example with the database of photos, if a Marie Curie photo comes up in a given trial, the corresponding one-hot vector is $\vec{x} = \begin{bmatrix} 0 \\ 1 \\ 0 \\ 0 \end{bmatrix}$.

PROBABILITY OF A CATEGORICAL DISTRIBUTION

We can think of a one-hot vector X as a random variable with a categorical distribution. Note that each individual class follows a Bernoulli distribution. The probability of class C_i occurring in any given trial is

$$p\left(C_i\right) = \pi_i$$

We can express the probability distribution of all the classes together compactly

$$p\left(X = \vec{x}\right) = \pi_1^{x_1} \pi_2^{x_2} \cdots \pi_m^{x_m} = \prod_{i=1}^{i=m} \pi_i^{x_i} \tag{5.39}$$

where $\vec{x}$ is a one-hot vector. Note that all but one of the powers in equation 5.39 is 0; hence the corresponding factor evaluates to 1. The remaining power is 1. Hence the overall probability always evaluates to π_i, where i is the index of the class that occurred in the trial.

EXPECTED VALUE OF A CATEGORICAL DISTRIBUTION

Since we are talking about classes, expected value and variance do not make sense in this context. We encountered a similar situation with the Bernoulli distribution. We assigned numerical values to each class and somewhat artificially defined the expected value and variance. A similar idea can also be applied here: we can talk about the expected value and variance of the one-hot vector (which consists of numerical values 0 and 1). But it remains an artificial construct.

Given a random variable X whose instances are one-hot vectors $\vec{x}$ following a categorical distribution with m classes with respective probabilities $\pi_1, \pi_2, \cdots, \pi_m$,

$$\mathbb{E}(X) = \vec{\pi} = \begin{bmatrix} \pi_1 \\ \pi_2 \\ \vdots \\ \pi_m \end{bmatrix} \tag{5.40}$$

We skip the variance of a categorical distribution.

Summary

In this chapter, we first looked at probability and statistics from a machine learning point of view. We also introduced the PyTorch `distributions` package and illustrated each concept with PyTorch `distributions` code samples immediately following the math.

- The probability of a specific event type is defined as the fraction of the total population of all possible events occupied by events of that specific type.
- A random variable is a variable that can assume any value from a predefined range of possible values. Random variables can be discrete or continuous. A probability is associated with a discrete random variable taking a specific value. A probability is also associated with a continuous random variable taking a value in an infinitesimally small range around a specific value, called its probability density at that value.
- The sum rule of probabilities states that the sum of the probabilities of a set of mutually exclusive events is the probability of one or another of them occurring. If the set of events is exhaustive (that is, among them, they cover the entire space of possible events), then their sum is 1 because one or another of them must occur. For continuous random variables, integrating the probability density function over the domain of possible values yields 1.
- The joint probability of a set of events is the probability of all those events occurring together. If the events are independent, the joint probability is the product of their individual probabilities.
- Drawing a sample from the probability distribution of a random variable returns an arbitrary value from the set of possible values. If we draw many samples, the higher-probability values show up more often than the lower-probability values. The sampled points occupy a region (called the sample point cloud) in the domain of possible values. In a sample point cloud, the region where the probabilities are higher is more densely populated than lower-probability regions.

- The expected value of a random variable is the average of the values of points in a very large (approaching infinity) sample cloud. It is equal to the weighted sum of all possible values of the random variable, where the weight for each value is its probability of occurrence. For continuous random variables, this boils down to integration—over the domain of possible values—of the product of the random variable's value and the probability density. The physical significance of the expected value is that it is a single-point representation of the entire distribution.
- The variance of a random variable is the square root of the average squared distances of the sample point values from the mean in a very large (approaching infinity) sample cloud. It is equal to the weighted sum of the squared distances of all possible values of the random variable from the mean. The weight for each value is its probability of occurrence. For continuous random variables, this boils down to integration—over the domain of possible values—of the product of the squared distance of the random variable's value from the mean and the probability density. Physically, the variance is a measure of the spread of the points in the distribution around its mean. In the multivariate case, this spread depends on the direction. Since there are infinite possible directions in a space with two or more dimensions, we cannot speak of a single variance value. Instead, we compute a covariance matrix with which to compute the spread along any specified direction. The eigenvector corresponding to the largest eigenvalue of this covariance matrix yields the direction of maximum spread. That eigenvalue yields the maximum spread. The eigenvector corresponding to the next-largest eigenvalue yields the orthogonal direction with the next-highest spread, and so forth.
- Principal component analysis (PCA) is a technique in multivariate statistics to identify the directions of the maximum spread of data. It uses the eigenvectors and eigenvalues of the covariance matrix.
- The Gaussian distribution is the most important probability distribution. The Gaussian random variable has one value with the highest probability of occurrence. The probability decreases smoothly with increasing distance from that highest probability value. The probability density function is continuous and looks like a bell-shaped surface. The center of the bell is the highest probability value, which also happens to be the expected value of the Gaussian random variable. The covariance matrix determines the shape of the base of the bell surface. It is circular when the covariance matrix is diagonal, with equal values on the diagonal; it is elliptical in general, with the axes of the ellipse along the eigenvectors of the covariance matrix.

  The sample point cloud of a Gaussian distribution is elliptical. It corresponds to the base of the bell-shaped probability density function. The longest spread corresponds to the ellipse's major axis, which corresponds to the eigenvector corresponding to the largest eigenvalue of the covariance matrix. In the GitHub repository, we have provided an interactive visualizer for observing the shapes of Gaussian distributions in one and two dimensions as you change the parameter values. Take a look at the interactive visualization section at http://mng.bz/NYJX.

6 Bayesian tools for machine learning

This chapter covers

- Unsupervised machine learning models
- Bayes' theorem, conditional probability, entropy, cross-entropy, and conditional entropy
- Maximum likelihood estimation (MLE) and maximum a posteriori (MAP) estimation of model parameters
- Evidence maximization
- KLD
- Gaussian mixture models (GMM) and MLE estimation of GMM parameters

The Bayesian approach to statistics tries to model the world by modeling the overall uncertainties and prevailing beliefs and knowledge about the system. This is in contrast to the frequentist paradigm, where probability is strictly measured by observing a phenomenon repeatedly and measuring the fraction of time an event occurs. Machine learning, in particular *unsupervised* machine learning, is a lot closer to the Bayesian paradigm of statistics—the subject of this chapter.

In chapter 1, we primarily discussed *supervised* machine learning, where the training data is labeled: each input value is accompanied by a manually created desired output value. Labeling training inputs is a manual, labor-intensive process and often the worst pain point in building a machine learning–based system. This has led to considerable recent interest in *unsupervised* machine learning, where we build a model from *unlabeled* training data. How is this done?

The general approach is best visualized geometrically. Each input data instance is a point in a high-dimensional space. These points form an overall pattern in the space of all possible inputs. If the inputs all have a common property, the points are not distributed randomly over the input space. Rather, they occupy a region in the input space with a definite shape. If the inputs have multiple classes, each class occupies a separate cluster in the space. Sometimes we apply a transformation to the input first—the transform is chosen or learned so that the transformed points exhibit a pattern more clearly than raw input points. We then identify a probability distribution whose sample point cloud matches the shape of the (potentially transformed) training data point cloud. We can generate faux input by sampling from this distribution. We can also classify an arbitrary input by observing which cluster it falls into.

NOTE The complete PyTorch code for this chapter is available at http://mng.bz/WdZa in the form of fully functional and executable Jupyter notebooks.

6.1 Conditional probability and Bayes' theorem

As usual, the discussion is accompanied by examples. In this context, we first offer a refresher on the concepts of joint and marginal probability from section 5.4 (you may want to revisit the topic of joint probability in sections 5.4, 5.4.1, and 5.4.2).

Consider two random variables: the height and weight of adult Statsville residents. Weight (denoted W) can take three quantized values: E_1, E_2, E_3. Height (H) can also take three quantized values: F_1, F_2, F_3. Table 6.1 shows their joint probability.

6.1.1 Joint and marginal probability revisited

One glance at table 6.1 tells us that the probabilities are concentrated along the main diagonal, which indicates dependent events. This can be validated by inspecting one joint probability—say, $p\left(E_1, F_1\right)$—and the corresponding marginal probabilities $p\left(F_1\right)$ and $p\left(E_1\right)$. We can see that $p\left(E_1, F_1\right) = 0.2 \neq p\left(F_1\right) \times p\left(E_1\right) = 0.26 \times 0.26$, establishing that the random variables weight W and height H are not independent. For contrast, look at table 5.6. In that case, for any valid i, j pair, $p\left(E_i, G_j\right) = p\left(G_i\right) \times p\left(E_j\right)$: the two events (weight and distance of a resident's home from the city center) are independent. Note the following:

- *Joint probability*—This is the probability of a specific combination of values occurring *together*. Each cell in table 6.1 depicts one joint probability: for example, the probability that a resident's weight is between 60 and 90 kg *and* that their height is greater than 183 cm is $p\left(E_2, F_3\right) = 0.04$.

Table 6.1 Example population sizes and joint probability distribution for variables $W = \{E_1, E_2, E_3\}$ and $H = \{F_1, F_2, F_3\}$ (weights and heights of adult Statsville residents), showing marginal probabilities

	Less than 60 kg (E_1)	**Between 60 and 90 kg (E_2)**	**More than 90 kg (E_3)**	**Marginals for Fs**
Less than 160 cm (F_1)	pop. = 20,000 $p(E_1, F_1) = 0.2$	pop. = 4,000 $p(E_2, F_1) = 0.04$	pop. = 2,000 $p(E_3, F_1) = 0.02$	pop. = 26,000; $p(F_1) = 0.2 + 0.04 + 0.02 = 0.26$
Between 160 cm and 183 cm (F_2)	pop. = 4,000 $p(E_1, F_2) = 0.04$	pop. = 40,000 $p(E_2, F_2) = 0.4$	pop. = 4,000 $p(E_3, F_2) = 0.04$	pop. = 48,000; $p(F_2) = 0.04 + 0.4 + 0.04 = 0.48$
More than 183 cm (F_3)	pop. = 2,000 $p(E_1, F_3) = 0.02$	pop. = 4,000 $p(E_2, F_3) = 0.04$	pop. = 20,000 $p(E_3, F_3) = 0.2$	pop. = 26,000; $p(F_3) = 0.02 + 0.04 + 0.2 = 0.26$
Marginals for Es	$p(E_1) = 0.2 + 0.04 + 0.02 = 0.26$	$p(E_2) = 0.04 + 0.4 + 0.04 = 0.48$	$p(E_3) = 0.02 + 0.04 + 0.2 = 0.26$	Total pop. = 100,000; Total prob = 1

- *Sum rule*—The joint probabilities of all possible variable combinations sum to 1 (bottom right cell in table 6.1):

$$\sum_{i=1}^{3} \sum_{j=1}^{3} p(F_i, E_j) = 1$$

  The sum of probabilities is the probability of one or another of the corresponding events occurring. Here we are adding all possible event combinations—one or another of these combinations will certainly occur. Hence the sum is 1, which matches our intuition.

- *Marginal probability for a variable*—This is obtained by "summing away" the other variables (right-most column and bottom-most row in table 6.1):

$$p(E_j) = \sum_{i=1}^{3} p(F_i, E_j)$$

$$p(F_i) = \sum_{j=1}^{3} p(F_i, E_j)$$

  We have added all possible combinations of other variables, so the sum represents the probability of this one variable.

- *Marginal probabilities*—These sum to 1:

$$\sum_{j=1}^{3} p\left(E_j\right) = \sum_{i=1}^{3} p\left(F_i\right) = 1$$

The sum of the marginal probabilities is the sum of all possible joint probabilities.

- *Dependent vs. independent variables*—If and only if the variables are independent, the product of the marginal probabilities is the same as the joint probability:

$$p\left(F_i, E_j\right) \neq p\left(F_i\right) \times p\left(E_j\right) \iff \text{for dependent variables in table 5.6}$$
$$p\left(G_i, E_j\right) = p\left(G_i\right) \times p\left(E_j\right) \iff \text{for independent variables in table 6.1}$$

You should verify that this condition is *not satisfied* in table 6.1 for the weight and height variables. It *is satisfied* in table 5.6 for the weight and distance-of-home-from-city-center variables.

6.1.2 *Conditional probability*

Suppose we know that the height of a subject is between 160 and 183 cm $(H = F_2)$. What is the probability of the subject's weight being more than 90 kg $(W = E_3)$? In statistical parlance, this probability is denoted $p\left(W = E_3 | H = F_2\right)$. It is read "probability of $W = E_3$ *given* $H = F_2$," aka "probability of $W = E_3$ *subject to the condition* $H = F_2$."

This is an example of *conditional probability*. Note that if we are given that the height is between 160 and 183 cm $(H = F_2)$, our universe is restricted to the second row of table 6.1. In particular, our population size is not 100,000 (that is, the entire population of Statsville). Rather, it is 48,000: the size of the population satisfying the given condition $H = F_2$. Using the frequentist definition,

$$p\left(W = E_3 | H = F_2\right) = \frac{\text{population satisfying } W = E_3 \text{ and } H = F_2}{\text{population satisfying } H = F_2} = \frac{4K}{48K} = 0.083$$

or

$$p\left(W = E_3 | H = F_2\right) = \frac{p\left(W = E_3, H = F_2\right)}{p\left(H = F_2\right)}$$

Table 6.2 shows table 6.1 with conditional probabilities added.

6.1.3 *Bayes' theorem*

As demonstrated in table 6.2, in general,

$$p\left(W = E_j | H = F_i\right) = \frac{p\left(W = E_j, H = F_i\right)}{p\left(H = F_i\right)}$$
$$p\left(H = F_i | W = E_j\right) = \frac{p\left(W = E_j, H = F_i\right)}{p\left(W = E_j\right)}$$

This is the essence of Bayes' theorem. We can generalize and say the following: given two random variables X and Y, the conditional probability of X taking the value x given the condition that Y has value y is given by the ratio of the joint probability of the two

Table 6.2 Example population sizes and joint, marginal, and conditional probabilities for variables $W = \{E_1, E_2, E_3\}$ and $H = \{F_1, F_2, F_3\}$ (weights and heights of adult Statsville residents). (This is table 6.1 with conditional probabilities added.)

	Less than 60 kg (E_1)	**Between 60 and 90 kg (E_2)**	**More than 90 kg (E_3)**	**Marginals for Fs**
Less than 160 cm (F_1)	pop. = 20,000 $p(E_1, F_1) = 0.2$ $p(E_1 \vert F_1) = \frac{p(E_1,F_1)}{p(F_1)}$ $= 0.77$ $p(F_1 \vert E_1) = \frac{p(E_1,F_1)}{p(E_1)}$ $= 0.77$	pop. = 4,000 $p(E_2, F_1) = 0.04$ $p(E_2 \vert F_1) = \frac{p(E_2,F_1)}{p(F_1)}$ $= 0.154$ $p(F_1 \vert E_2) = \frac{p(E_2,F_1)}{p(E_2)}$ $= 0.083$	pop. = 2,000 $p(E_3, F_1) = 0.02$ $p(E_3 \vert F_1) = \frac{p(E_3,F_1)}{p(F_1)}$ $= 0.077$ $p(F_1 \vert E_3) = \frac{p(E_3,F_1)}{p(E_3)}$ $= 0.077$	pop. = 26,000; $p(F_1) = 0.2$ $+ 0.04 + 0.02$ $= 0.26$
Between 160 cm and 183 cm (F_2)	pop. = 4,000 $p(E_1, F_2) = 0.04$ $p(E_1 \vert F_2) = \frac{p(E_1,F_2)}{p(F_2)}$ $= 0.083$ $p(F_2 \vert E_1) = \frac{p(E_1,F_2)}{p(E_1)}$ $= 0.154$	pop. = 40,000 $p(E_2, F_2) = 0.4$ $p(E_2 \vert F_2) = \frac{p(E_2,F_2)}{p(F_2)}$ $= 0.83$ $p(F_2 \vert E_2) = \frac{p(E_2,F_2)}{p(E_2)}$ $= 0.83$	pop. = 4,000 $p(E_3, F_2) = 0.04$ $p(E_3 \vert F_2) = \frac{p(E_3,F_2)}{p(F_2)}$ $= 0.083$ $p(F_2 \vert E_3) = \frac{p(E_3,F_2)}{p(E_3)}$ $= 0.154$	pop. = 48,000; $p(F_2) = 0.04$ $+ 0.4 + 0.04$ $= 0.48$
More than 183 cm (F_3)	pop. = 2,000 $p(E_1, F_3) = 0.02$ $p(E_1 \vert F_3) = \frac{p(E_1,F_3)}{p(F_3)}$ $= 0.077$ $p(F_3 \vert E_1) = \frac{p(E_1,F_3)}{p(E_1)}$ $= 0.077$	pop. = 4,000 $p(E_2, F_3) = 0.04$ $p(E_2 \vert F_3) = \frac{p(E_2,F_3)}{p(F_3)}$ $= 0.154$ $p(F_3 \vert E_2) = \frac{p(E_2,F_3)}{p(E_2)}$ $= 0.083$	pop. = 20,000 $p(E_3, F_3) = 0.2$ $p(E_3 \vert F_3) = \frac{p(E_3,F_3)}{p(F_3)}$ $= 0.77$ $p(F_3 \vert E_3) = \frac{p(E_3,F_3)}{p(E_3)}$ $= 0.77$	pop. = 26,000; $p(F_3) = 0.02$ $+ 0.04 + 0.2$ $= 0.26$
Marginals for Es	$p(E_1)$ $= 0.2 + 0.04 + 0.02$ $= 0.26$	$p(E_2)$ $= 0.04 + 0.4 + 0.04$ $= 0.48$	$p(E_3)$ $= 0.02 + 0.04 + 0.2$ $= 0.26$	Total pop. = 100,000; Total prob = 1

and the marginal probability of the condition

$$p(X = x \vert Y = y) = \frac{p(X = x, Y = y)}{p(Y = y)} \tag{6.1}$$

Sometimes we drop the names of the random variable and just use the values. Using such notation, Bayes' theorem can be stated as

$$p(x \vert y) = \frac{p(x, y)}{p(y)}$$

Note that the denominator is the marginal probability, which can be obtained by summing over the joint probabilities. For instance, for continuous variables, Bayes' theorem can be written as

$$p(x \vert y) = \frac{p(x, y)}{\int_{-\infty}^{\infty} p(x, y)\, dx}$$

Bayes' theorem can be generalized further to more than two variables and multiple dimensions:

$$p\left(X_1 = \vec{x}_1 \middle| X_2 = \vec{x}_2, X_3 = \vec{x}_3, \cdots, X_n = \vec{x}_n\right) = \frac{p\left(X_1 = \vec{x}_1, X_2 = \vec{x}_2, X_3 = \vec{x}_3 \cdots, X_n = \vec{x}_n\right)}{p\left(X_2 = \vec{x}_2, \cdots, X_n = \vec{x}_n\right)} \tag{6.2}$$

$$p\left(X_1 = \vec{x}_1, X_2 = \vec{x}_2 \middle| X_3 = \vec{x}_3 \cdots, X_n = \vec{x}_n\right) = \frac{p\left(X_1 = \vec{x}_1, X_2 = \vec{x}_2, X_3 = \vec{x}_3 \cdots, X_n = \vec{x}_n\right)}{p\left(X_3 = \vec{x}_3, \cdots, X_n = \vec{x}_n\right)} \tag{6.3}$$

It is common practice to drop the name of the random variable (uppercase), retain only the value (lowercase), and state these equations informally as

$$p\left(\vec{x}_1 \middle| \vec{x}_2, \vec{x}_3, \cdots, \vec{x}_n\right) = \frac{p\left(\vec{x}_1, \vec{x}_2, \vec{x}_3 \cdots, \vec{x}_n\right)}{p\left(\vec{x}_2, \cdots, \vec{x}_n\right)}$$

$$p\left(\vec{x}_1, \vec{x}_2 \middle| \vec{x}_3 \cdots, \vec{x}_n\right) = \frac{p\left(\vec{x}_1, \vec{x}_2, \vec{x}_3 \cdots, \vec{x}_n\right)}{p\left(\vec{x}_3, \cdots, \vec{x}_n\right)}$$

What happens if the random variables are independent? Well, let's check out equation 6.1. If X and Y are independent,

$$p(x, y) = p(x)\, p(y)$$

and hence

$$p(x|y) = \frac{p(x, y)}{p(y)} = p(x)$$

This makes intuitive sense: if X and Y are independent, knowing Y does not make any difference to $p(X = x)$, so the probability of X given Y is the same as the probability of X.

6.2 Entropy

Suppose a daily meteorological bulletin informs the folks in the United States whether it rained in the Sahara desert yesterday. Is there much overall information in that bulletin? Not really—it almost always reports the obvious. The probability of "no rain" is overwhelmingly high (it is almost certain that there will be no rain), and the uncertainty associated with the outcome is very low. Even without the bulletin, if we guess the outcome "no rain," we will be right almost every time. Similarly, a daily news bulletin telling us whether it rained yesterday in Cherapunji, India—a place where it pretty much rains all the time—has little informational content because we can guess the results with high certainty even without the bulletin. Stated another way, the uncertainty associated with the probability distributions of "rain vs. no rain in the Sahara" and or "rain vs. no rain in Cherapunji" is low. This is a direct consequence of the fact that the probability of one of the events is close to 1 and the probabilities of the other events are near 0: the probability density function (PDF) has a very tall peak at one location and very low heights elsewhere.

On the other hand, a daily bulletin reporting whether it rained in San Francisco is of considerable interest because the probability of "rain" and "no rain" are comparable. Without the bulletin, we cannot guess the result with much certainty.

The concept of *entropy* attempts to quantify the uncertainty associated with a chancy event. If the probability for any one event is overwhelmingly high (meaning the probabilities of other events are very low since the sum is 1), the uncertainty is low—we pretty much know that the high-probability event will occur. On the other hand, if there are multiple events with comparable high probabilities, uncertainty is high—we cannot predict which event will occur. Entropy captures this notion of uncertainty in a system. Let's look at another example.

Suppose we have tiny images, four pixels wide by four pixels high, and each pixel is one of four possible colors: G(reen), R(ed), B(lue), or Y(ellow). Two such images are shown in figure 6.1. We want to encode such images. The simplest thing to do is to use a two-bit representation for each color:

$$
\begin{aligned}
G(reen) &= 00 \\
R(ed) &= 01 \\
B(lue) &= 10 \\
Y(ellow) &= 11
\end{aligned}
$$

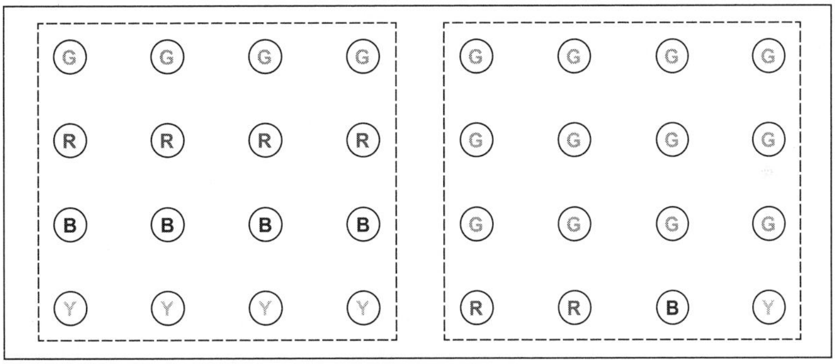

Figure 6.1 Two 4×4 images with different pixel color distributions. In the left image, the four colors R, G, B, and Y are equally probable. In the right image, one color (green) is much likelier than the others. The left image has higher entropy (uncertainty): we cannot predict any color with much certainty. In the right image, we can predict green with relative certainty.

The entire 16-pixel image on the left can be represented by the string 00 00 00 00 01 01 01 01 10 10 10 10 11 11 11 11. Here, we have iterated over the pixels in *raster scan order*, left to right and top to bottom. The total number of bits needed to store the 16-pixel image is $16 \times 2 = 32$ bits. The right image can be represented as 00 00 00 00 00 00 00 00 00 00 00 00 01 01 10 11. The total number of bits needed is $16 \times 2 = 32$ bits. Both images need the same amount of storage. But is this optimal?

Consider the right-hand image. The color G appears much more frequently than the others. We can use this fact to reduce the total number of bits required to store the image. It is not mandatory to use the same number of bits to represent each color. How about using shorter representations for the more frequently occurring (higher-probability) colors and longer representations for the infrequent (lower-probability) colors? This is the core principle behind the technique of *variable bit-rate coding*. For instance, we can use the following representation:

$$
\begin{aligned}
G(reen) &= 0 \\
R(ed) &= 10 \\
B(lue) &= 110 \\
Y(ellow) &= 111
\end{aligned}
$$

The right-hand image can thus be represented as 0 0 0 0 0 0 0 0 0 0 0 0 10 10 110 111.

NOTE This is an example of what is known as *prefix coding*: no two colors share the same prefix. It enables us to identify the color as soon as we see its code. For instance, if we see a 0 bit at the beginning, we immediately know the color is green since no other color code starts with 0. If we see 10, we immediately know the color is red since no other color code starts with 10, and so on.

With this new color code, we need $12 \times 1 = 12$ bits to store the 12 green pixels, $2 \times 2 = 4$ bits to store the 2 red pixels, $1 \times 3 = 3$ bits to store the single blue pixel, and $1 \times 3 = 3$ bits to store the single yellow pixel—a total of 22 pixels. Equivalently, we need $\frac{22}{16} = 1.375$ bits per pixel. This is less than the 32 pixels at 2 bits per pixel we needed with the simple fixed bit-rate coding.

NOTE You have just learned about Huffman encoding, an important technique in image compression.

Does the new representation result in smaller storage for the left-hand image? There, we need $4 \times 1 = 4$ bits to store the four green pixels, $4 \times 2 = 8$ pixels to store the four red pixels, $4 \times 3 = 12$ bits to store the four blue pixels, and $4 \times 3 = 12$ bits to store the single yellow pixel: a total of 36 pixels at $\frac{36}{16} = 2.25$ bits per pixel. Here, variable bit-rate coding does worse than fixed bit-rate coding.

So, the probability distribution of the various pixel colors in the image affects how much compression can be achieved. If the distribution of pixel colors is such that a few colors are much more probable than others, we can assign shorter codes to them to reduce storage for the whole image. Viewed another way, if low uncertainty is associated with the system—certain colors are more or less certain to occur—we can achieve high compression. We assign shorter codes to nearly certain colors, resulting in compression. On the other hand, if high uncertainty is associated with the system—all colors are more or less equally probable, and no color occurs with high certainty—variable bit-rate coding will not be very effective. How do we quantify this notion? In other words, can we examine the pixel color distribution in an image and estimate whether variable bit-rate coding will be effective? The answer again is entropy. Formally,

Entropy measures the overall uncertainty associated with a probability distribution.

Entropy is a measure that is *high* if everything is more or less equally probable and *low* if a few items have a much higher probability than the others. It measures the uncertainty in the system. If everything is equally probable, we cannot predict any one item with any extra certainty. Such a system has high entropy. On the other hand, if some items are much more probable than others, we can predict them with relative certainty. Such a system has low entropy.

In the discrete univariate case, for a random variable X that can take any one of the discrete values $x_1, x_2, x_3, \cdots, x_n$ with probabilities $p(x_1), p(x_2), p(x_3), \cdots, p(x_n)$, entropy is defined as

$$\mathbb{H}(X) = -\sum_{i=1}^{n} p(x_i) \log p(x_i) \tag{6.4}$$

The logarithm is taken with respect to the natural base e.

Let's apply equation 6.4 to the images in figure 6.1 to see if the results agree with our intuition. The computations are shown in table 6.3. The notion of entropy applies to continuous and multidimensional random variables equally well.

Table 6.3 Entropy computation for the pair of images in figure 6.1. The right-hand image has lower entropy and can be compressed more.

Left image	Right image
$x_1 = G, p(x_1) = \frac{4}{16} = 0.25$	$x_1 = G, p(x_1) = \frac{12}{16} = 0.75$
$x_2 = R, p(x_2) = \frac{4}{16} = 0.25$	$x_2 = R, p(x_2) = \frac{2}{16} = 0.125$
$x_3 = B, p(x_3) = \frac{4}{16} = 0.25$	$x_3 = B, p(x_3) = \frac{1}{16} = 0.0625$
$x_4 = Y, p(x_4) = \frac{4}{16} = 0.25$	$x_4 = Y, p(x_4) = \frac{1}{16} = 0.0625$
$\mathbb{H} = -(0.25 \log(0.25) + 0.25 \log(0.25)$ $+ 0.25 \log(0.25) + 0.25 \log(0.25))$ $= 1.386294$	$\mathbb{H} = -(0.75 \log(0.75) + 0.125 \log(0.125)$ $+ 0.0625 \log(0.0625) + 0.0625 \log(0.0625))$ $= 0.822265$

For a univariate continuous random variable X that takes values $x \in \{-\infty, \infty\}$ with probabilities $p(x)$,

$$\mathbb{H}(X) = -\int_{x=-\infty}^{\infty} p(x) \log p(x)\, dx \tag{6.5}$$

For a continuous multidimensional random variable X that takes values $\vec{x}$ in the domain D, $(\vec{x} \in D)$ with probabilities $p(\vec{x})$,

$$\mathbb{H}(X) = -\int_{\vec{x} \in D} p(\vec{x}) \log p(\vec{x})\, d\vec{x} \tag{6.6}$$

6.2.1 Geometrical intuition for entropy

Geometrically speaking, entropy is a function of how lopsided the PDF is (see figure 6.2). If all inputs are more or less equally probable, the density function is more or less flat and uniform in height everywhere (see figure 6.2a). The corresponding sample

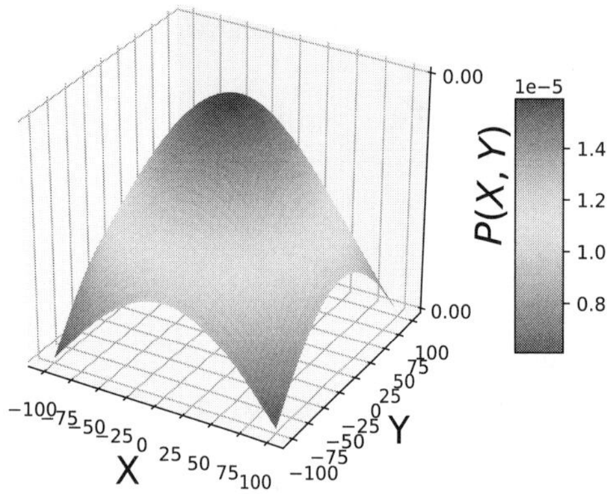

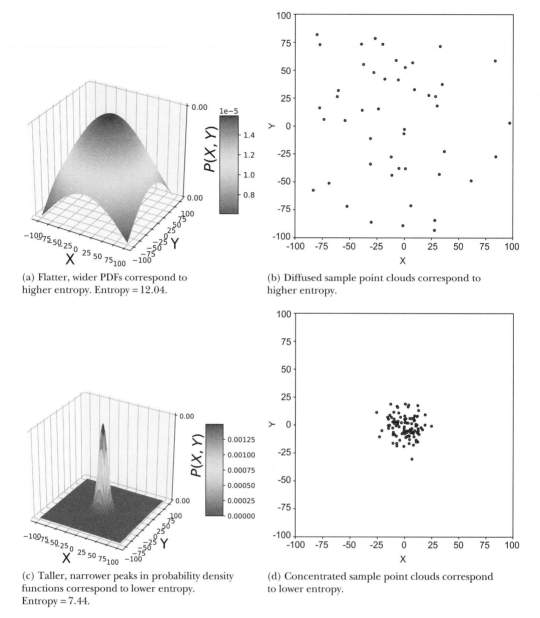

(a) Flatter, wider PDFs correspond to higher entropy. Entropy = 12.04.

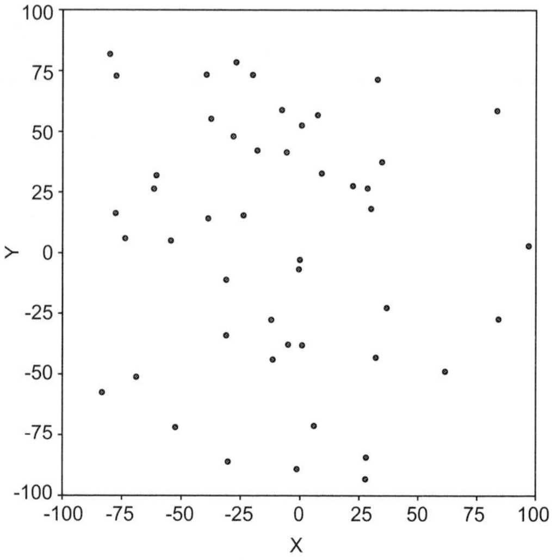

(b) Diffused sample point clouds correspond to higher entropy.

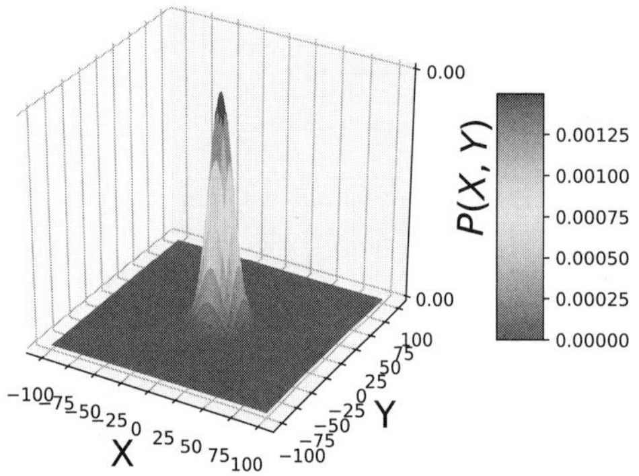

(c) Taller, narrower peaks in probability density functions correspond to lower entropy. Entropy = 7.44.

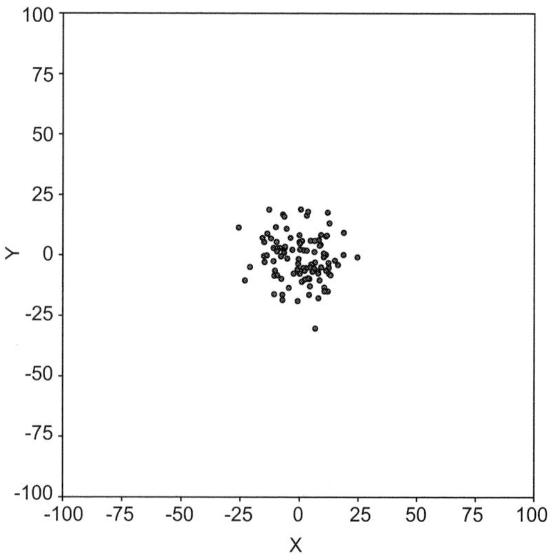

(d) Concentrated sample point clouds correspond to lower entropy.

Figure 6.2 Entropies of peaked and flat distributions

point cloud has a diffused mass: there are no regions with a high concentration of points. Such a system has high uncertainty or high entropy (see figure 6.2b). On the other hand, if a few of all the possible inputs have disproportionately high probabilities, the PDF has tall peaks in some regions and low heights elsewhere (see figure 6.2c). The corresponding sample point cloud has regions of high concentration matching the peaks in the density function and low concentration elsewhere (see figure 6.2d). Such a system has low uncertainty and low entropy.

NOTE Since the sum of all the probabilities is 1, if a few are high, the others have to be low. We cannot have all high or all low probabilities.

6.2.2 Entropy of Gaussians

The wider a Gaussian is, the less peaked it is, and the closer it is to being a uniform distribution. A univariate Gaussian's variance, σ, determines its fatness (see figure 5.10b). Consequently, we expect a Gaussian's entropy to be an increasing function of σ. Indeed, that is the case. In this section, we derive the entropy of a Gaussian in the univariate case and simply state the result for the multivariate case.

For a random variable x whose PDF is given by equation 5.22 (repeated here for convenience),

$$p(x) = \frac{1}{\sqrt{2\pi}\sigma} e^{\frac{-(x-\mu)^2}{2\sigma^2}}$$

From that, we get

$$log\, p(x) = -\frac{1}{2} log\ (2\pi) - log\ \sigma - \frac{(x-\mu)^2}{2\sigma^2}$$

Using equation 6.6, the entropy is

$$\begin{aligned}\mathbb{H}(X) &= -\int_{x=-\infty}^{\infty} p(x)\left(-\frac{1}{2} log\ (2\pi) - log\ \sigma - \frac{(x-\mu)^2}{2\sigma^2}\right) dx \\ &= \frac{1}{2} log\ (2\pi) \int_{x=-\infty}^{\infty} p(x)\, dx + log\ \sigma \int_{x=-\infty}^{\infty} p(x)\, dx + \frac{1}{2\sigma^2} \int_{x=-\infty}^{\infty} p(x)\,(x-\mu)^2\, dx\end{aligned}$$

Remembering the probability sum rule from equation 5.6, $\int_{x=-\infty}^{\infty} p(x)\, dx = 1$, we get

$$\mathbb{H}(X) = \frac{1}{2} log\ (2\pi) + log\ \sigma + \frac{1}{2\sigma^2} \int_{x=-\infty}^{\infty} p(x)\,(x-\mu)^2\, dx$$

Now, by definition (see section 5.7.2),

$$\int_{x=-\infty}^{\infty} p(x)\,(x-\mu)^2\, dx = \mathbb{E}\left((x-\mu)^2\right) = \sigma^2$$

Hence,

$$\mathbb{H}(X) = \frac{1}{2} log\ (2\pi) + log\ \sigma + \frac{\sigma^2}{2\sigma^2} = \frac{1}{2} log\ (2\pi) + log\ \sigma + \frac{1}{2} = \frac{1}{2} log\left(2\pi e \sigma^2\right) \quad (6.7)$$

Entropy for multivariate Gaussians is as follows:

$$\mathbb{H}(X) = \frac{1}{2} log\ (2\pi) + log\,(det\,(\boldsymbol{\Sigma})) + \frac{1}{2} = \frac{1}{2} log\,(2\pi\, e\, det\,(\boldsymbol{\Sigma})) \quad (6.8)$$

Listing 6.1 shows the Python PyTorch code to compute the entropy of a Gaussian.

NOTE Fully functional code to compute the entropy of a Gaussian distribution, executable via Jupyter Notebook, can be found at http://mng.bz/zx7B.

Listing 6.1 Computing the entropy of a Gaussian distribution

```
def entropy_gaussian_formula(sigma):
    return 0.5 * torch.log(2 * math.pi * math.e * sigma * sigma)    # Equation 6.7

p = Normal(0, 10)    # Instantiates a Gaussian distribution

H_formula = entropy_gaussian_formula(p.stddev)    # Computes the entropy using the direct formula

H = p.entropy()    # Computes the entropy using the PyTorch interface

assert torch.isclose(H_formula, H)    # Asserts that the entropies computed two different ways match
```

6.3 Cross-entropy

Consider a *supervised* classification problem where we have to analyze an image and identify which of the following objects is present: *cat*, *dog*, *airplane*, or *automobile*. We assume that one of these will always be present in our universe of images. Given an input image, our machine emits four probabilities: $p\,(cat)$, $p\,(dog)$, $p\,(airplane)$, and $p\,(automobile)$. During training, for each training data instance, we have a ground truth (GT): a known class to which that training data instance belongs. We have to estimate how different the network output is from the GT—this is the loss for that data instance. We adjust the machine parameters to minimize the loss and continue doing so until the loss stops decreasing.

How do we quantitatively estimate the loss—the difference between the known GT and the probabilities of various classes emitted by the network? One principled approach is to use the cross-entropy loss. Here is how it works.

Consider a random variable X that can take four possible values: $X = 1$ signifying *cat*, $X = 2$ signifying *dog*, $X = 3$ signifying *airplane*, and $X = 4$ signifying *automobile*. The random variable has the PDF $p\,(X = 1) \equiv p\,(cat)$, $p\,(X = 2) \equiv p\,(dog)$, $p\,(X = 3) \equiv p\,(airplane)$, $p\,(X = 4) \equiv p\,(automobile)$. The PDF for a GT, which selects one from the set of four possible classes, is a one-hot vector (one of the elements is 1, and the others are 0). Such random variables and corresponding PDFs can be associated with every GT and machine output. Here are some examples, which are also shown graphically in figure 6.3. A PDF for GT *cat* (one-hot vector) is shown figure 6.3a:

$$p_{gt\_cat} = \begin{bmatrix} \overbrace{1}^{p(cat)}, & \overbrace{0}^{p(dog)}, & \overbrace{0}^{p(airplane)}, & \overbrace{0}^{(automobile)} \end{bmatrix}$$

A PDF for a good prediction is shown figure 6.3b:

$$p_{good\_pred} = \begin{bmatrix} \overbrace{0.8}^{p(cat)}, & \overbrace{0.15}^{p(dog)}, & \overbrace{0.04}^{p(airplane)}, & \overbrace{0.01}^{(automobile)} \end{bmatrix}$$

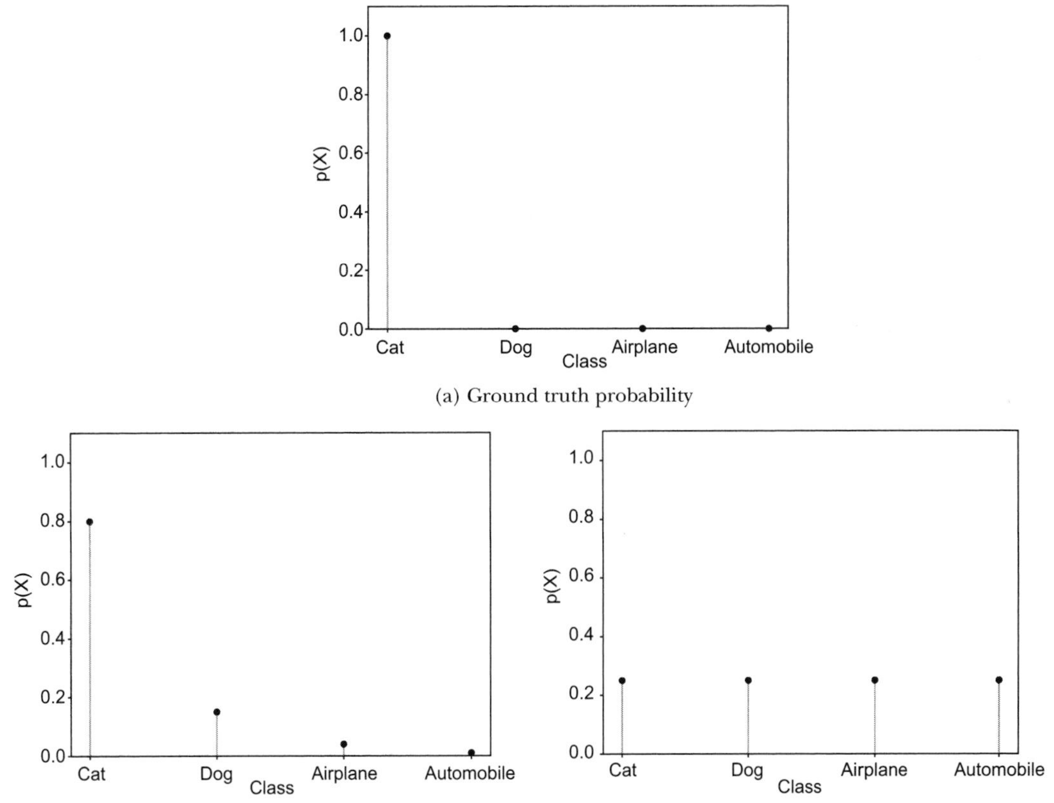

(a) Ground truth probability

(b) Good prediction: probabilities similar to ground truth. Cross-entropy loss = 0.22.

(c) Bad prediction: probabilities dissimilar to ground truth. Cross-entropy loss = 1.38.

Figure 6.3 Cross-entropy loss

A PDF for a bad prediction is shown figure 6.3c:

$$p_{bad\_pred} = \begin{bmatrix} \overbrace{0.25}^{p(cat)}, & \overbrace{0.25}^{p(dog)}, & \overbrace{0.25}^{p(airplane)}, & \overbrace{0.25}^{(automobile)} \end{bmatrix}$$

Let X_{gt} denote such a random variable for a specific GT and p_{gt} denote the corresponding PDF. Similarly, let X_{pred} and p_{pred} denote the random variable and PDF for the machine prediction. Consider the following expression:

$$\mathbb{H}_c\left(X_{gt}, X_{pred}\right) = -\sum_{i=1}^{4} p_{gt}(i) \log\left(p_{pred}(i)\right) \tag{6.9}$$

This is the expression for *cross-entropy*. It is a quantitative measure for how dissimilar the two PDFs p_{gt} and p_{pred} are: that is, how much error will be caused by approximating the PDF p_{gt} with p_{pred}. Equivalently, cross-entropy measures how well the machine is doing that output the prediction p_{pred} when the correct PDF is p_{gt}.

To gain insight into how $\mathbb{H}_c\left(X_{gt}, X_{pred}\right)$ measures dissimilarity between PDFs, examine the expression carefully. Remember that $\sum_{i=1}^{4} p_{gt}(i) = \sum_{i=1}^{4} p_{pred}(i) = 1$ (using the probability sum rule from equation 5.3):

Case 1: The i values where $p_{gt}(i)$ is high (close to 1).

Case 1a: If $p_{pred}(i)$ is also close to 1, then $\log\left(p_{pred}(i)\right)$ will be close to zero (since $\log 1 = 0$). Hence the term $p_{gt}(i)\log\left(p_{pred}(i)\right)$ will be close to zero since the product of anything with a near-zero number is near zero. These terms will contribute little to $\mathbb{H}_c\left(X_{gt}, X_{pred}\right)$.

Case 1b: On the other hand, at the i values where $p_{gt}(i)$ is high, if $p_{pred}(i)$ is low (close to zero), then $-\log\left(p_{pred}(i)\right)$ will be very high (since $\log 0 \to -\infty$).

Case 2: The i values where $p_{gt}(i)$ is low (close to 0). These will have low values and will contribute little to $\mathbb{H}_c\left(X_{gt}, X_{pred}\right)$ since the product of anything with a near zero number is near zero.

Thus, overall, large contributions can happen only in case 1b, where $p_{gt}(i)$ is high and $p_{pred}(i)$ is low—that is, p_{gt} and p_{pred} are very dissimilar. What if $p_{gt}(i)$ is low and $p_{pred}(i)$ is high? They are also dissimilar, so those terms will not contribute much! True, but if such terms exist, there must be other terms where $p_{gt}(i)$ is high and $p_{pred}(i)$ is low. This is because the sums of all $p_{gt}(i)$ and $p_{pred}(i)$ must be both 1. Either way, if there is dissimilarity, the cross-entropy is high.

For instance, consider the case where $X_{gt} = X_{gt\_cat}$ and $X_{pred} = X_{good\_pred}$ or $X_{pred} = X_{bad\_pred}$. We know p_{gt_cat} is a one-hot selector vector, meaning it has 1 as one element and 0s elsewhere. Only a single term survives, corresponding to $i = 0$, and

$$\mathbb{H}_c\left(X_{gt\_cat}, X_{pred}\right) = \begin{cases} -\sum_{i=1}^{4} p_{gt\_cat}(i)\ \log\left(p_{good\_pred}(i)\right) = -\log(0.8) = 0.22 \\ -\sum_{i=1}^{4} p_{gt\_cat}(i)\ \log\left(p_{bad\_pred}(i)\right) = -\log(0.25) = 1.38 \end{cases}$$

We see that cross-entropy is higher where similarity is lower (the prediction is bad).

Finally, we are ready to formally define the cross-entropy of two arbitrary random variables. Let X_1, X_2 be a pair of random variables that take values x from the same input domain D (that is, $x \in D$), with probabilities $p_1(x)$, $p_2(x)$, respectively:

$$\mathbb{H}_c\left(X_1, X_2\right) = \begin{cases} -\sum_{x \in D} p_1(x)\log\left(p_2(x)\right) & \text{discrete} \\ -\int_{x \in D} p_1(x)\log\left(p_2(x)\right)dx & \text{continuous univariate} \\ -\int_{\vec{x} \in D} p_1(\vec{x})\log\left(p_2(\vec{x})\right)d\vec{x} & \text{continuous multivariate} \end{cases} \tag{6.10}$$

Note that cross-entropy in equation 6.10 reduces to entropy (equations 6.5, 6.6) if $Y = X$. Listing 6.2 shows the Python PyTorch code to compute the entropy of a Gaussian.

NOTE Fully functional code to compute cross-entropy, executable via Jupyter Notebook, can be found at http://mng.bz/0mjN.

Listing 6.2 Computing cross-entropy

```
def cross_entropy(X_gt, X_pred):
    H_c = 0
    for x_gt, x_pred in zip(X_gt, X_pred):
        H_c += -1 * (x_gt * torch.log (x_pred))    # Direct computation of cross-entropy from equation 6.9
    return H_c

X_gt = torch.Tensor([1., 0., 0., 0.])    # Probability density function for the ground truth (one-hot vector)

X_good_pred = torch.Tensor([0.8, 0.15, 0.04, 0.01])    # Probability density function for a good prediction

X_bad_pred = torch.Tensor([0.25, 0.25, 0.25, 0.25])    # Probability density function for a bad prediction

H_c_good = cross_entropy(X_gt, X_good_pred)    # Cross-entropy between X_gt and X_good_pred (a low value)

H_c_bad = cross_entropy(X_gt, X_bad_pred)    # Cross-entropy between X_gt and X_bad_pred (a high value)
```

6.4 KL divergence

In section 6.3, we saw that cross-entropy, $\mathbb{H}_c\left(X_1, X_2\right)$, measures the dissimilarity between the distributions of two random variables X_1 and X_2 with probabilities $p_1(x)$ and $p_2(x)$. But cross-entropy has a curious property for a dissimilarity measure. If $X_1 = X_2$, the cross-entropy $\mathbb{H}_c\left(X_1, X_2\right)$ reduces to the entropy $\mathbb{H}\left(X_1\right)$. This is somewhat counterintuitive: we expect the dissimilarity between two copies of the same thing to be zero.

We should look at cross-entropy as a dissimilarity with an offset. Let's denote the pure dissimilarity measure as $D\left(X_1, X_2\right)$. Then

$$\mathbb{H}_c\left(X_1, X_2\right) = \overbrace{\mathbb{H}\left(X_1\right)}^{offset} + \overbrace{D\left(X_1, X_2\right)}^{\text{pure dissimilarity}}$$

This means the pure dissimilarity measure

$$\begin{aligned} D\left(X_1, X_2\right) = \mathbb{H}_c\left(X_1, X_2\right) - \mathbb{H}\left(X_1\right) &= -\sum_{x \in D} p_1(x) \log\left(p_2(x)\right) + \sum_{x \in D} p_1(x) \log\left(p_1(x)\right) \\ &= \sum_{x \in D} p_1(x) \log\left(p_1(x) - p_2(x)\right) = \sum_{x \in D} p_1(x) \log\left(\frac{p_1(x)}{p_2(x)}\right) \end{aligned}$$

This pure dissimilarity measure, $D\left(X_1, X_2\right)$, is called *Kullback–Leibler divergence* (KL divergence or KLD). As expected, it is 0 when the two random variables are identical.

Formally, KLD is as follows:

$$D\left(X_1, X_2\right) = \sum_{x \in D} p_1(x) \log\left(\frac{p_1(x)}{p_2(x)}\right) \tag{6.11}$$

For continuous univariate randoms,

$$D\left(X_1, X_2\right) = \int_{x \in D} p_1(x) \log\left(\frac{p_1(x)}{p_2(x)}\right) dx \tag{6.12}$$

For continuous multivariate randoms,

$$D\left(X_1, X_2\right) = \int_{\vec{x} \in D} p_1(\vec{x}) \log\left(\frac{p_1(\vec{x})}{p_2(\vec{x})}\right) d\vec{x} \tag{6.13}$$

Let's examine some properties of KLD:

- The KLD between identical random variables is zero. If $X_1 = X_2$, $p_1(x) = p_2(x)\ \forall x \in D$. Then the log term vanishes at every x, and KLD is zero.
- The KLD between non-identical probability distributions is always positive. We can see this by examining equation 6.11. At all values of x where $p_1(x) > p_2(x)$, the log term is positive (since the logarithm of a number greater than 1 is positive). On the other hand, at all values of x where $p_1(x) < p_2(x)$, the log term is negative (since the logarithm of a number less than 1 is negative). But the positive terms get higher weights because $p_1(x)$ are higher at these points. In this context, it is worth noting that given any pair of PDFs, *one cannot be uniformly higher than the other at all points.* This is because both of them must sum to 1. If one PDF is higher somewhere, it must be lower somewhere else to compensate.
- Given a GT PDF p_{gt} for a classification problem and a machine prediction p_{pred}, minimizing the cross-entropy $\mathbb{H}(gt, pred)$ is logically equivalent to minimizing the KLD $D(gt, pred)$. This is because the entropy $\mathbb{H}(gt)$ is a constant, independent of the machine parameters.
- The KLD is *not* symmetric: $D(X_1, X_2) \neq D(X_2, X_1)$.

6.4.1 KLD between Gaussians

Since the Gaussian probability distribution is so important, in this subsection we look at the KLD between two Gaussian random variables X_1 and X_2 having PDFs $p_1(x) = \mathcal{N}(x;\ \mu_1, \sigma_1)$ and $p_2(x) = \mathcal{N}(x;\ \mu_2, \sigma_2)$. We derive the expression for the univariate case and simply state the expression for the multivariate case:

$$D\left(X_1, X_2\right) = \int_{-\infty}^{\infty} \overbrace{\frac{1}{\sqrt{2\pi}\sigma_1} e^{\frac{-(x-\mu_1)^2}{2\sigma_1^2}}}^{\mathcal{N}(x;\ \mu_1, \sigma_1)} \log\left(\frac{\frac{1}{\sqrt{2\pi}\sigma_1} e^{\frac{-(x-\mu_1)^2}{2\sigma_1^2}}}{\frac{1}{\sqrt{2\pi}\sigma_2} e^{\frac{-\left(x-\mu_2\right)^2}{2\sigma_2^2}}}\right) dx$$

$$= \int_{-\infty}^{\infty} \mathcal{N}(x;\ \mu_1, \sigma_1)\left(\log\frac{\sigma_2}{\sigma_1} + \frac{(x-\mu_2)^2}{2\sigma_2^2} - \frac{(x-\mu_1)^2}{2\sigma_1^2}\right) dx$$

Opening the parentheses, we get

$$\log\frac{\sigma_2}{\sigma_1}\overbrace{\int_{-\infty}^{\infty}\mathcal{N}(x;\,\mu_1,\sigma_1)\,dx}^{=1,\text{ by equation 5.6}}+\frac{1}{2\sigma_2^2}\int_{-\infty}^{\infty}(x-\mu_2)^2\,\mathcal{N}(x;\,\mu_1,\sigma_1)\,dx$$

$$-\frac{1}{2\sigma_1^2}\overbrace{\int_{-\infty}^{\infty}(x-\mu_1)^2\,\mathcal{N}(x;\,\mu_1,\sigma_1)\,dx}^{=\sigma_1^2,\text{ by equation 5.13}}$$

$$=\log\frac{\sigma_2}{\sigma_1}+\frac{1}{2\sigma_2^2}\int_{-\infty}^{\infty}(x-\mu_1+\mu_1-\mu_2)^2\,\mathcal{N}(x;\,\mu_1,\sigma_1)\,dx-\frac{1}{2}$$

Expanding the square term, we get

$$D(X_1,X_2)=\log\frac{\sigma_2}{\sigma_1}$$

$$+\frac{1}{2\sigma_2^2}\int_{-\infty}^{\infty}\left((x-\mu_1)^2+(\mu_1-\mu_2)^2+2(x-\mu_1)(\mu_1-\mu_2)\right)\mathcal{N}(x;\,\mu_1,\sigma_1)\,dx-\frac{1}{2}$$

Since

$$\int_{-\infty}^{\infty}(x-\mu_1)\,\mathcal{N}(x;\,\mu_1,\sigma_1)\,dx=\mu_1-\mu_1=0$$

the final equation for the KLD between two univariate Gaussian random variables X_1, X_2 with PDFs $\mathcal{N}(x;\,\mu_1,\sigma_1)$ and $\mathcal{N}(x;\,\mu_2,\sigma_2)$ becomes

$$D(X_1,X_2)=\log\frac{\sigma_2}{\sigma_1}+\frac{\sigma_1^2+(\mu_1-\mu_2)^2}{2\sigma_2^2}-\frac{1}{2} \tag{6.14}$$

The KLD between two d-dimensional Gaussian random variables X_1, X_2 with PDFs $\mathcal{N}(\vec{x};\,\mu_1,\mathbf{\Sigma}_1)$ and $\mathcal{N}(\vec{x};\,\mu_2,\mathbf{\Sigma}_2)$ is

$$D(X_1,X_2)=\frac{1}{2}\left(tr\left(\mathbf{\Sigma}_2^{-1}\mathbf{\Sigma}_1\right)+(\vec{\mu}_2-\vec{\mu}_1)^T\,\mathbf{\Sigma}_2^{-1}(\vec{\mu}_2-\vec{\mu}_1)-d+\log\left(\frac{\det\mathbf{\Sigma}_2}{\det\mathbf{\Sigma}_1}\right)\right) \tag{6.15}$$

where the operator *tr* denotes the *trace* of a matrix (sum of diagonal elements) and the operator *det* denotes the determinant.

Listing 6.3 shows the Python PyTorch code to compute the KLD.

NOTE Fully functional code to compute the KLD, executable via Jupyter Notebook, can be found at http://mng.bz/KMyj.

Listing 6.3 Computing the KLD

```
from torch.distributions import kl_divergence

p = Normal(0, 5)
q = Normal(0, 10)
r = Normal(0, 20)

kld_p_p = kl_divergence(p, p)
kld_p_q = kl_divergence(p, q)
kld_q_p = kl_divergence(q, p)
kld_p_r = kl_divergence(p, r)

assert kld_p_p == 0

assert kld_p_q != kld_q_p

assert kld_p_q < kld_p_r
```

- Instantiates three Gaussian distributions with the same means but different standard deviations (p, q, r)
- Computes the KLD between various pairs of distributions
- The KLD between a distribution and itself is 0.
- The KLD is not symmetric.
- KLD(p, q) < KLD(p, r). See figure 6.4a.

In figure 6.4a, we compare three Gaussian distributions p, q, and r with the same μs but different σs. $KLD(p, q) < KLD(p, r)$ because σ_p is closer to σ_q than σ_r.

In figure 6.4b, we compare a uniform distribution p with two Gaussian distributions q and r that have different μs but the same σs. $KLD(p, q) < KLD(p, r)$ because μ_p is closer to μ_q than μ_r.

6.5 Conditional entropy

In section 6.2, we learned that entropy measures the uncertainty in a system. Earlier, in section 6.1.2, we studied conditional probability, which measures the probability of occurrence of one set of random variables under the condition that another set has known fixed values. In this section, we combine the two concepts into a new concept called *conditional entropy*.

Consider the following question from table 6.2. What is the entropy of the weight variable W under the condition that the value of the height variable H is F_1? As observed in section 6.1.1, the condition effectively restricts our universe to a single row (in this case, the top row) of the table. We can compute the entropy of the elements of that row mathematically, using equation 6.5, as

$$\overbrace{\mathbb{H}\left(W|H=F_1\right)}^{\text{conditional entropy of W given } H=F_1} = -\sum_{j=1}^{3} p\left(E_j|F_1\right) log\left(p\left(E_j|F_1\right)\right)$$

$$= -\left(0.77 \times log\left(0.77\right) + 0.154 \times log\left(0.154\right) + 0.077 \times log\left(0.077\right)\right) = 0.6868$$

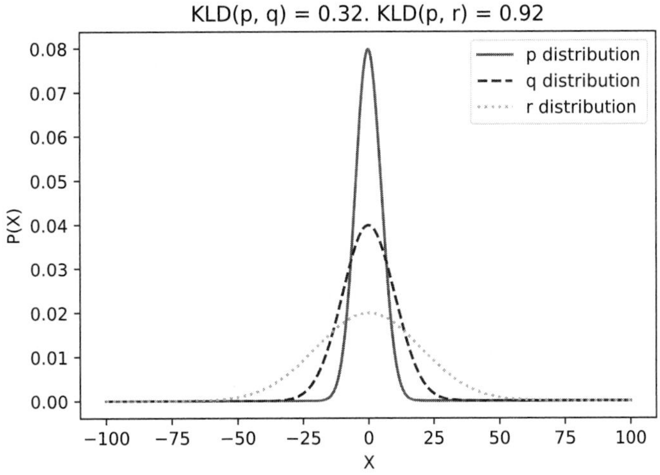

(a) $p \equiv \mathcal{N}(\mu = 0, \sigma = 5)$, $q \equiv \mathcal{N}(\mu = 0, \sigma = 10)$, $r \equiv \mathcal{N}(\mu = 0, \sigma = 20)$

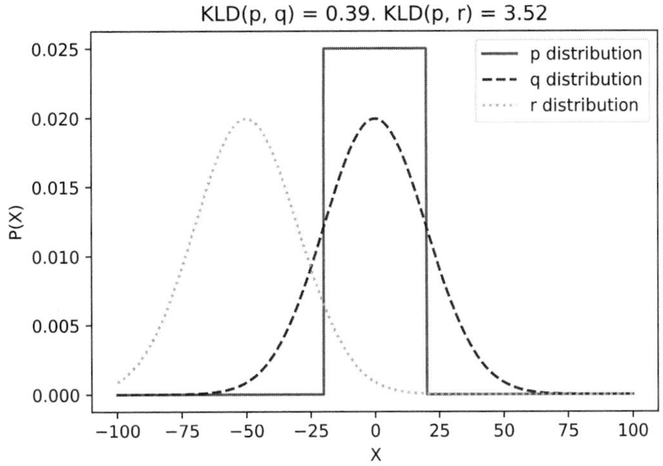

(b) $p \equiv U(a = -20, b = 20)$, $q \equiv \mathcal{N}(\mu = 0, \sigma = 20)$, $r \equiv \mathcal{N}(\mu = -50, \sigma = 20)$

Figure 6.4 KLD between example distributions

Similarly,

$$\begin{aligned}\mathbb{H}(W|H = F_2) &= -\sum_{j=1}^{3} p\left(E_j|F_2\right) log\left(p\left(E_j|F_2\right)\right)\\ &= -(0.083 \times log\,(0.083) + 0.83 \times log\,(0.83) + 0.083 \times log\,(0.083))\\ &= 0.5678\end{aligned}$$

$$\begin{aligned}\mathbb{H}(W|H = F_3) &= -\sum_{j=1}^{3} p\left(E_j|F_3\right) log\left(p\left(E_j|F_3\right)\right)\\ &= -(0.077 \times log\,(0.077) + 0.154 \times log\,(0.154) + 0.77 \times log\,(0.77))\\ &= 0.6868\end{aligned}$$

$\mathbb{H}(W|H=F_i)$ is the entropy of W given $H=F_i$ for $i=1$ or 2 or 3. What is the overall conditional entropy of W given H: that is, $\mathbb{H}(W|H)$? To compute this, we take the expected value (that is, the probability-weighted average; see equation 5.8) of the conditional entropy $\mathbb{H}(W|H=F_i)$ over all possible values of i:

$$\overbrace{\mathbb{H}(W|H)}^{\text{conditional entropy of W given } H} = \sum_{i=1}^{3} p(F_i)\left(-\sum_{j=1}^{3} p(E_j|F_i)\, log\,(p(E_j|F_i))\right)$$
$$= (0.6868*0.26+0.5678*0.48+0.6868*0.26) = 0.6297$$

This idea can be generalized. Formally, given two random variables X and Y that can take values $x \in D_x$, $y \in D_y$, respectively,

$$\mathbb{H}(X|Y) = \overbrace{\sum_{y\in D_y} p(y)\overbrace{\left(-\sum_{x\in D_x} p(x|y)\, log\,(p(x|y))\right)}^{\mathbb{H}(X|Y=y)}}^{\mathbb{E}_y\mathbb{H}(X|Y=y)} \Leftrightarrow \text{discrete} \tag{6.16}$$

$$\mathbb{H}(X|Y) = \int_{y\in D_y} p(y)\left(-\int_{x\in D_x} p(x|y)\, log\,(p(x|y))\, dx\right) dy \Leftrightarrow \text{continuous} \tag{6.17}$$

6.5.1 Chain rule of conditional entropy

This rule states:

$$\mathbb{H}(X|Y) = \mathbb{H}(X,Y) - \mathbb{H}(Y) \tag{6.18}$$

This can be derived from equation 6.17.

$$\mathbb{H}(X|Y) = \int_{y\in D_y} p(y)\left(-\int_{x\in D_x} p(x|y)\, log\,(p(x|y))\, dx\right) dy$$

Applying Bayes' theorem (equation 6.1),

$$\mathbb{H}(X|Y) = -\int_{y\in D_y}\int_{x\in D_x} \overbrace{p(y)\,p(x|y)}^{p(x,y)}\, log\,\overbrace{(p(x|y))}^{log\left(\frac{p(x,y)}{p(y)}\right)}\, dx\, dy$$

$$= \overbrace{-\int_{y\in D_y}\int_{x\in D_x} p(x,y)\, log\,(p(x,y))\, dx\, dy}^{\mathbb{H}(X,Y)} + \int_{y\in D_y} log\,(p(y)) \overbrace{\int_{x\in D_x} p(x,y)\, dx}^{\text{marginal probability } p(y)}\, dy$$
$$= \mathbb{H}(X,Y) - \mathbb{H}(Y) \tag{6.19}$$

6.6 Model parameter estimation

Suppose we have a set of sampled input data points $X = \{\vec{x}^{(1)}, \vec{x}^{(2)}, \cdots, \vec{x}^{(n)}\}$ from a distribution. We refer to the set collectively as *training data.* Note that we are *not* assuming it is *labeled* training data—we do not know the outputs corresponding to the inputs $\vec{x}^{(i)}$. Also, suppose that based on our knowledge of the problem, we have decided which model family to use. Of course, simply knowing the family is not enough; we need to know (or estimate) the model parameters before we can use the model. For instance, our model family might be Gaussian, $\mathcal{N}(x;\ \vec{\mu}, \mathbf{\Sigma})$. Until we know the actual value of the parameters $\vec{\mu}$ and $\mathbf{\Sigma}$, we do not fully know the model and cannot use it.

How do we estimate the model parameters from the unlabeled training data? This is what we cover in this section. At the moment, we are discussing it without referring to any specific model architecture, so let's denote model parameters with a generic symbol θ. For instance, when dealing with Gaussian models, $\theta = \{\vec{\mu}, \mathbf{\Sigma}\}$.

6.6.1 Likelihood, evidence, and posterior and prior probabilities

Before tackling the problem of parameter estimation, it is important to have a clear understanding of the terms *likelihood, evidence, posterior probability,* and *prior probability* in the current context. Equation 6.20 illustrates them. Using Bayes' theorem,

$$\overbrace{p(\theta|X)}^{\text{posterior probability}} = \frac{p(X,\theta)}{p(X)} = \frac{\overbrace{p(X|\theta)}^{\text{likelihood}}\ \overbrace{p(\theta)}^{\text{prior probability}}}{\underbrace{p(X)}_{\textit{evidence}}} \tag{6.20}$$

Let's first examine the likelihood term. Using the fact that data instances are independent of each other,

$$p(X|\theta) = p\left(\vec{x}^{(1)}, \vec{x}^{(2)}, \cdots, \vec{x}^{(n)}\middle|\theta\right) = \prod_{i=1}^{n} p\left(\vec{x}^{(i)}\middle|\theta\right)$$

Now, $p(\vec{x}^{(i)}|\theta)$ is essentially the probability density of the distribution family we have chosen. For instance, if the model in question in Gaussian, then given $\theta = \{\vec{\mu}, \mathbf{\Sigma}\}$, this will be

$$p\left(\vec{x}^{(i)}\middle|\theta\right) = \mathcal{N}\left(\vec{x}^{(i)};\ \vec{\mu}, \mathbf{\Sigma}\right) = \frac{1}{(2\pi \det \mathbf{\Sigma})^{\frac{1}{2}}} e^{-\frac{1}{2}\left(\vec{x}^{(i)} - \vec{\mu}\right)^T \mathbf{\Sigma}^{-1}\left(\vec{x}^{(i)} - \vec{\mu}\right)}$$

which is basically an expression for the Gaussian PDF: a restatement of equation 5.23 (but in equation 5.23, we dropped the "given θ," part in the notation and expressed $p\left(\vec{x}\middle|\theta\right)$ simply as $p(\vec{x})$). Thus, we can always express the likelihood from the PDF of the chosen model family using the independence of individual training data instances.

Now let's examine the prior probability, $p(\theta)$. It typically comes from some physical constraint—without referring to the input. A very popular approach is to say that, all other things being equal, we prefer parameters with smaller magnitudes. By this token, the larger the total magnitude $||\theta||^2$, the lower the prior probability. For instance, we may use

$$p(\theta) \propto e^{-||\theta||^2} \tag{6.21}$$

An indirect justification for favoring parameter vectors with the smallest length (magnitude) can be found in the principle of Occam's razor. It states, *Entia non sunt multiplicanda praeter necessitatem*, which roughly translates to "One should not multiply unnecessarily." This is often interpreted in machine learning and other disciplines as "favor the briefest representation."

As shown previously, we can always express the likelihood and prior terms. Using them, we can formulate different paradigms, each with a different quantity, to optimize in order to estimate the unknown probability distribution parameters from training data. These techniques can be broadly classified into the following categories:

- Maximum likelihood parameter estimation (MLE)
- Maximum a posteriori (MAP) parameter estimation

We provide an overview of them next. You will notice that, in all the methods, we typically preselect a distribution family as a model and then estimate the parameter values by maximizing one probability or another.

Later in the chapter, we look at MLE in the special case of the Gaussian family of distributions. Further down the line, we look at MLE with respect to Gaussian mixture models. Another technique outlined later is evidence maximization: we will visit it in the context of variational autoencoders.

The log-likelihood trick

If we choose a distribution family whose PDF is exponential (the most obvious example is Gaussian), instead of maximizing the likelihood, we usually maximize its logarithm, aka the *log-likelihood*. We can do this because whatever maximizes a quantity also maximizes its logarithm and vice versa. But the logarithm simplifies expressions in the case of exponential probability functions. This becomes obvious if we note that

$$log\,(e^x) = x$$

$$log\left(\prod e^{x^{(i)}}\right) = \sum x^{(i)}$$

6.6.2 *Maximum likelihood parameter estimation (MLE)*

In MLE of parameters, we ask, "What parameter values will maximize the joint likelihood of the training data instances?" In this context, remember that likelihood is the probability of a data instance occurring given specific parameter values (equation 6.20). Expressed mathematically,

> MLE estimates what value of θ maximizes $p\,(X|\theta)$. The geometric mental picture is as follows: we want to estimate the unknown parameters for our model probability distribution such that if we draw many samples from that distribution, the sample point cloud will largely overlap the training data.

Often we employ the log-likelihood trick and maximize the log-likelihood instead of the actual likelihood.

For some models, such as Gaussians, this maximization problem can be solved analytically, and a closed-form solution can be obtained (as shown in section 6.8).

For others, such as Gaussian mixture models (GMMs), the maximization problem yields no closed-form solution, and we go for an iterative solution (as shown in section 6.9.4).

6.6.3 Maximum a posteriori (MAP) parameter estimation and regularization

Instead of asking what parameter value maximizes the probability of occurrence of the training data instances, we can ask, "What are the most probable parameter values, given the training data?" Expressed mathematically, in MAP, we directly estimate the θ that maximizes $p(\theta|X)$. Using equation 6.20,

$$p(\theta|X) = \frac{p(X|\theta)\, p(\theta)}{p(X)} \tag{6.22}$$

Since the denominator is independent of θ, maximizing the numerator with respect to θ maximizes the fraction. Thus

In MAP parameter estimation, we look for parameters θ that maximize $p(X|\theta)\, p(\theta)$.

- The first factor, $p(X|\theta)$, is what we optimized in MLE and comes from the model definition (such as equation 5.23 for multivariate Gaussian models).
- The second factor, $p(\theta)$, is the prior term, which usually incentivizes the optimization system to choose a solution with predefined properties like smaller parameter magnitudes (equation 6.21).

Viewed this way, MAP estimation is equivalent to *MLE parameter estimation with regularization.* Regularization is a technique often used in optimization. In regularized optimization, we add a term to the expression being maximized or minimized. This term effectively incentivizes the system to choose the solution with the smallest magnitudes of the unknown from the set of possible solutions. It is easy to see that MAP estimation essentially imposes the prior probability term on top of MLE. This extra term acts as a regularizer, incentivizing the system to choose the lowest magnitude parameters while still trying to maximize the likelihood of the training data.

Equation 6.22 can be interpreted another way. When we have no training data, all we can do is estimate the parameters from our prior beliefs about the system: the prior term $p(\theta)$. When the training data set X arrives, it influences the system through the likelihood term $p(X|\theta)$. As more and more training data arrives, the prior term (whose magnitude does not change with training data) dominates less and less, and the posterior probability $p(\theta|X)$ is dominated more by the likelihood.

6.7 Latent variables and evidence maximization

Suppose we have the height and weight data for a population (say, for the adult residents of our favorite town, Statsville). A single data instance looks like this:

$$\vec{x} = \begin{bmatrix} \text{height} \\ \text{weight} \end{bmatrix}$$

Although the data is not explicitly labeled or classified, we know the data points can be clustered into two distinct classes, *male* and *female.* It is reasonable to expect that the distribution of each class is much simpler than the overall distribution. For instance, here, the distributions for males and females may be Gaussians individually (presumably, the means for females will occur at smaller height and weight values). The combined distribution does not fit any of the distributions we have discussed so far (later, we see it is a Gaussian mixture).

We look at such situations in more detail in connection to Gaussian mixture modeling and variational autoencoders. Here we only note that in these cases, it is often beneficial to introduce a variable for the class, say Z. In this example, Z is discrete: it can take one of two values, *male* or *female*. Then we can model the overall distribution as a combination of simple distributions, each corresponding to a specific value of Z.

Such variables Z that are *not* part of the observed data X but are introduced to facilitate modeling are called *latent* or *hidden* variables/parameters. Latent variables are connected to observed variables through the usual Bayesian expression:

$$p(\vec{x}, \vec{z}) = p\left(\vec{x}|\vec{z}\right) p\left(\vec{z}\right)$$

$$p\left(\vec{z}|\vec{x}\right) = \frac{p\left(\vec{x}|\vec{z}\right) p\left(\vec{z}\right)}{p\left(\vec{x}\right)}$$

How do we estimate the distribution of Z? One way is to ask, "What distribution of the hidden variables would maximize the probability of exactly these training data points being returned if we drew random samples from the distribution?" The philosophy behind this is as follows: we assume that the training data points are fairly typical and have a high probability of occurrence in the unknown data distribution. Hence, we try to find a distribution under which the training data points will have the highest probabilities.

Geometrically speaking, each data point (vector) can be viewed as a point in some d-dimensional space, where d is the number of elements in the vector $\vec{x}_i$. The training data points typically occupy a region within that space. We are looking for a distribution whose mass is largely aligned with the training data region. In other words, the probability associated with the training data points is as high as possible—the sample distribution cloud largely overlaps the training data cloud.

Expressed mathematically, we want to identify $p\left(\vec{x}|\vec{z}\right)$ and $p\left(\vec{z}\right)$ that maximize the quantity

$$p\left(X\right) = \int p\left(X, z\right) dz = \int \prod_{i=1}^{N} p\left(\vec{x}^{(i)}, \vec{z}\right) d\vec{z} = \int \prod_{i=1}^{N} p\left(\vec{x}^{(i)} \middle| \vec{z}\right) p\left(\vec{z}\right) d\vec{z} \tag{6.23}$$

As usual, we get $p\left(\vec{x}^{(i)} \middle| \vec{z}\right)$ from the PDF of our chosen model family and $p\left(\vec{z}\right)$ through some physical constraint.

6.8 Maximum likelihood parameter estimation for Gaussians

We look at this with a one-dimensional example, but the results derived apply to higher dimensions. Suppose we are trying to predict whether an adult Statsville resident is female, given that the resident's height lies in a specified range $[a, b]$. For this purpose, we have collected a set of height samples of adult *female* Statsville residents. These height samples constitute our training data. Let's denote them as $x^{(1)}, x^{(2)}, \cdots, x^{(n)}$. Based on physical considerations, we expect the distribution of heights of adult Statsville females to be a Gaussian distribution with unknown mean and variance. Our goal is to determine them from the training data via MLE, which effectively estimates a distribution whose sample cloud maximally matches the distribution of the training data points.

Let's denote the (as yet unknown) mean and variance of the distribution as μ and σ. Then, from equation 5.22, we get

$$p\left(x^{(i)} \middle| \mu, \sigma\right) = \frac{1}{\sqrt{2\pi}\sigma} e^{\frac{-\left(x^{(i)}-\mu\right)^2}{2\sigma^2}}$$

$$\prod_{i=1}^{n} p\left(x^{(1)}, x^{(2)}, \cdots, x^{(n)} \middle| \mu, \sigma\right) = \frac{1}{\left(\sqrt{2\pi}\sigma\right)^n} e^{\frac{-\sum_{i=1}^{n}\left(x^{(i)}-\mu\right)^2}{2\sigma^2}}$$

Employing the log-likelihood trick,

$$log \prod_{i=1}^{n} p\left(x^{(1)}, x^{(2)}, \cdots, x^{(n)} \middle| \mu, \sigma\right) = log\left(\frac{1}{\left(\sqrt{2\pi}\sigma\right)^n} e^{\frac{-\sum_{i=1}^{n}\left(x^{(i)}-\mu\right)^2}{2\sigma^2}}\right)$$

$$= -nlog\left(\sqrt{2\pi}\right) - nlog\sigma - \frac{\sum_{i=1}^{n}\left(x^{(i)}-\mu\right)^2}{2\sigma^2}$$

To maximize with respect to μ, we solve

$$\frac{\partial}{\partial\mu} log \prod_{i=1}^{n} p\left(x^{(1)}, x^{(2)}, \cdots, x^{(n)} \middle| \mu, \sigma\right) = 0$$

or

$$\frac{2\sum_{i=1}^{n}\left(x^{(i)}-\mu\right)}{2\sigma^2} = 0$$

or

$$\sum_{i=1}^{n}\left(x^{(i)}-\mu\right) = 0$$

Finally, we get a closed-form expression for the unknown μ in terms of the training data:

$$\mu = \frac{1}{n}\sum_{i=1}^{n} x^{(i)}$$

Similarly, to maximize with respect to σ, we solve

$$\frac{\partial}{\partial\sigma} log \prod_{i=1}^{n} p\left(x^{(1)}, x^{(2)}, \cdots, x^{(n)} \middle| \mu, \sigma\right) = 0$$

or

$$\frac{n}{\sigma} - \frac{2\sum_{i=1}^{n}\left(x^{(i)}-\mu\right)^2}{2\sigma^3} = 0$$

or

$$n\sigma^2 = \sum_{i=1}^{n} \left(x^{(i)} - \mu\right)^2$$

Finally, we get a closed-form expression for the unknown σ in terms of the training data:

$$\sigma^2 = \frac{1}{n} \sum_{i=1}^{n} \left(x^{(i)} - \mu\right)^2$$

Thus we see that for a Gaussian, the maximum-likelihood solutions coincide with the sample mean and variance of the training data. Once we have the mean and standard deviation, we can calculate the probability that a female resident's height belongs to a specified range $[a, b]$ by using the following equation:

$$prob(a < X <= b) = \int_a^b p(X)dX \tag{6.24}$$

In the multidimensional case:

Given a training dataset, $\left\{\vec{x}^{(1)}, \vec{x}^{(2)}, \cdots, \vec{x}^{(n)}\right\}$, the best fit Gaussian has the mean

$$\vec{\mu} = \frac{1}{n} \sum_{i=1}^{n} \vec{x}^{(i)} \implies \text{mean of the training data samples.} \tag{6.25}$$

and the covariance matrix

$$\mathbf{\Sigma} = \frac{1}{n} \sum_{i=1}^{n} \left(\vec{x}^{(i)} - \vec{\mu}\right) \left(\vec{x}^{(i)} - \vec{\mu}\right)^T \implies \text{covariance of the training data samples.} \tag{6.26}$$

We began this section by stating the problem of estimating the probability of an adult Statsville resident being female, given that their height lies in a specified range $[a, b]$, when we are provided a training dataset of n height values of adult Statsville female residents. Let's now revisit that problem. Using (scalar versions of) equations 6.25 and 6.26, we can estimate μ and σ and thereby define a Gaussian probability distribution

$$p\,(x) = \mathcal{N}\,(x;\; \mu, \sigma)$$

Using this, given any height x, we can compute the probability $p\,(x)$ that the resident is female. Let's see this using PyTorch.

6.8.1 Python PyTorch code for maximum likelihood estimation

Suppose we assume that the height values of adult female residents of Statsville follow a Gaussian distribution. If we know the parameters of this Gaussian (μ and σ), we know the Gaussian distribution fully. That allows us to estimate many interesting things: for instance, the expected height of an adult female resident of Statsville, or the probability that the height of an adult female Statsville resident lies in a certain range such as between 160 and 170 cm. The problem is, in a typical real-life situation, we do not know the parameters μ cm and σ. All we have is a large dataset X of height values of adult Statsville female residents—training data. We have to use this data to estimate the unknown parameters μ cm and σ. Once we have these, we have an estimated distribution (aka model) from which we can predict the probabilities of events of interest.

As we saw in section 6.6.2, MLE is a technique to estimate the parameters from given training data when the family to which the distribution belongs is known but the exact values of the parameters are not known. Listing 6.4 shows the PyTorch implementation of MLE for the Gaussian family.

NOTE Fully functional code for model parameter estimation using MLE and MAP, executable via Jupyter Notebook, can be found at http://mng.bz/9Mv7.

Listing 6.4 Maximum likelihood estimate for a Gaussian

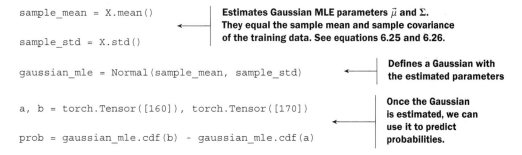

```
sample_mean = X.mean()

sample_std = X.std()

gaussian_mle = Normal(sample_mean, sample_std)

a, b = torch.Tensor([160]), torch.Tensor([170])

prob = gaussian_mle.cdf(b) - gaussian_mle.cdf(a)
```

- Estimates Gaussian MLE parameters $\vec{\mu}$ and Σ. They equal the sample mean and sample covariance of the training data. See equations 6.25 and 6.26.
- Defines a Gaussian with the estimated parameters
- Once the Gaussian is estimated, we can use it to predict probabilities.

6.8.2 Python PyTorch code for maximum likelihood estimation using gradient descent

In listing 6.4, we computed the MLE using the closed-form solution. Now, let's try to compute the MLE using a different method: gradient descent. In real-life scenarios, we do not use gradient descent to compute the MLE because the closed-form solution is available. However, we discuss this method here to highlight some of the challenges of using gradient descent and how MAP estimation addresses these challenges.

Our goal is to maximize the likelihood function using gradient descent. This can alternatively be viewed as minimizing the negative log-likelihood function. We choose to use the logarithm of the likelihood function since that leads to simpler computation without any loss of generalization. (If you want a quick refresher on gradient descent, see section 3.5.) Following is the equation for negative log-likelihood:

$$-\log p(X|\theta) = \frac{n}{2}\log 2\pi\sigma^2 + \frac{\sum_{i=1}^{n}(x^{(i)} - \mu)^2}{2\sigma^2} \tag{6.27}$$

Listings 6.5 and 6.6 show the PyTorch code for the minimization process.

Listing 6.5 Gaussian negative log-likelihood for training data

```
def neg_log_likelihood(X, mu, sigma):    <-- Equation 6.27
    N = X.shape[0]
    X_minus_mu = torch.sub(X, mu)
```

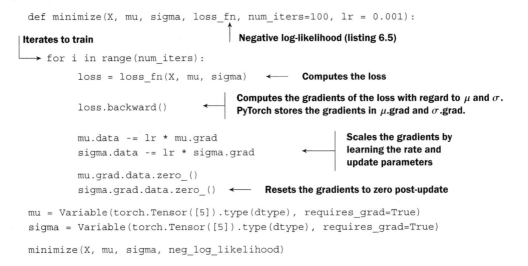

```
    t1 = torch.mul(0.5 * N,
             torch.log(2 * np.pi * torch.pow(sigma, 2)))
```
$\frac{n}{2}\log 2\pi\sigma^2$

```
    t2 = torch.div(torch.matmul(X_minus_mu.T, X_minus_mu),
              2 * torch.pow(sigma, 2))
```
$\frac{\sum_{i=1}^{n}(x_i-\mu)^2}{2\sigma^2}$

```
    return t1 + t2
```
Note how all the training data X is crunched in a single operation. Such vector operations are parallel and very efficient in PyTorch.

Listing 6.6 Minimizing MLE loss via gradient descent

```
def minimize(X, mu, sigma, loss_fn, num_iters=100, lr = 0.001):
    for i in range(num_iters):
        loss = loss_fn(X, mu, sigma)

        loss.backward()

        mu.data -= lr * mu.grad
        sigma.data -= lr * sigma.grad

        mu.grad.data.zero_()
        sigma.grad.data.zero_()

mu = Variable(torch.Tensor([5]).type(dtype), requires_grad=True)
sigma = Variable(torch.Tensor([5]).type(dtype), requires_grad=True)

minimize(X, mu, sigma, neg_log_likelihood)
```

- **Negative log-likelihood (listing 6.5)** (loss_fn)
- **Iterates to train** (for loop)
- **Computes the loss**
- **Computes the gradients of the loss with regard to μ and σ. PyTorch stores the gradients in μ.grad and σ.grad.**
- **Scales the gradients by learning the rate and update parameters**
- **Resets the gradients to zero post-update**

Figure 6.5 shows how μ and σ change with each iteration of gradient descent. We expect μ and σ to end up close to $\mu_{expected}$ and $\sigma_{expected}$, respectively. However, when μ and σ start off far from $\mu_{expected}$ and $\sigma_{expected}$ (as in figure 6.5a), they do not converge to the expected values and instead become very large numbers. On the other hand, when they are instantiated with values closer to $\mu_{expected}$ and $\sigma_{expected}$ (as in figure 6.5b), they converge to the expected values. MLE is very sensitive to the initial values and has no mechanism to prevent the parameters from exploding. This is why MAP estimation is preferred. The prior $p(\theta)$ acts as a regularizer and prevents the parameters from becoming too large. Figure 6.5c shows how μ and σ converge to the expected values using MAP even though they started far away.

The MAP loss function is as follows. Note that it is the same equation as the negative log-likelihood, but with two additional terms—μ^2 and σ^2—that act as regularizers:

$$-\log p(\theta|X) = \frac{N}{2}\log 2\pi\sigma^2 + \frac{1}{2\sigma^2}\sum_{i=1}^{n}(x^{(i)}-\mu)^2 + \underbrace{\mu^2+\sigma^2}_{Regularizer} \tag{6.28}$$

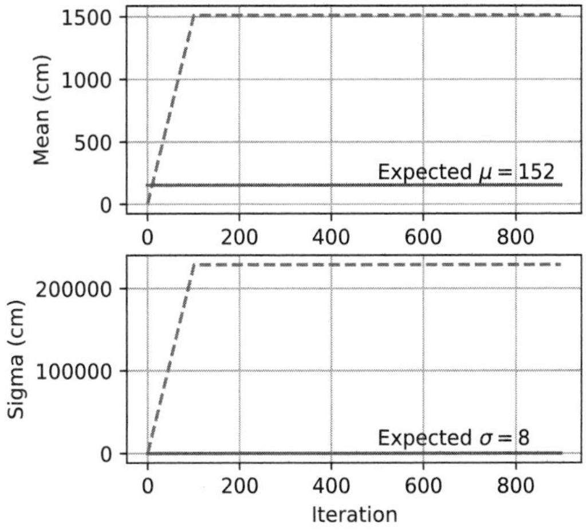

(a) MLE explodes: $\mu_{init} = 1$, $\sigma_{init} = 1$.

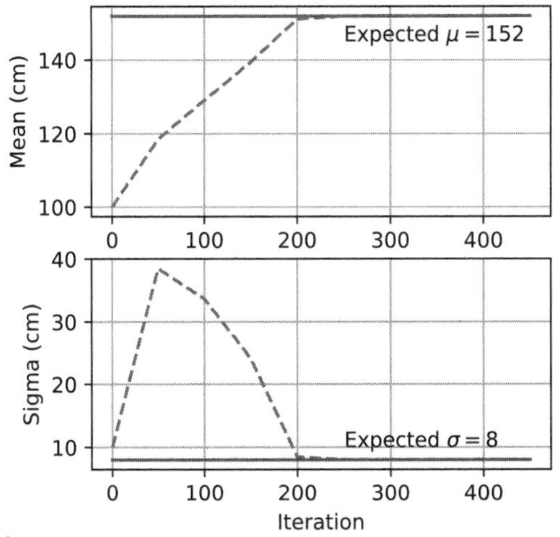

(b) MLE converges: $\mu_{init} = 100$, $\sigma_{init} = 10$.

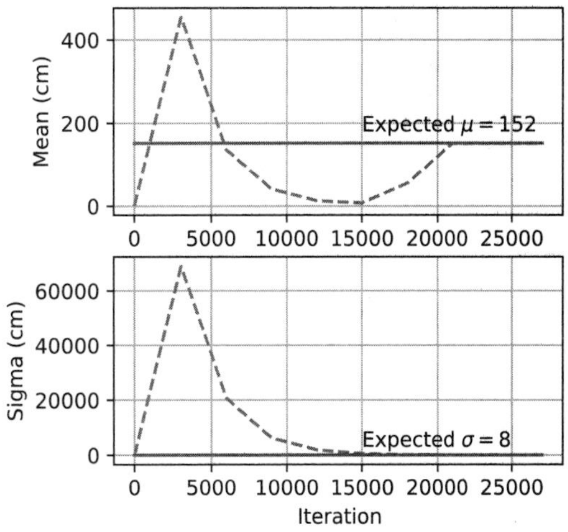

(c) MAP converges: $\mu_{init} = 1$, $\sigma_{init} = 1$.

Figure 6.5 Gaussian parameter estimation using maximum likelihood estimate and maximum a posteriori estimation. In figure 6.5a, the MLE explodes because μ and σ are initialized far from $\mu_{expected}$ and $\sigma_{expected}$. However, the MLE converges in figure 6.5b because μ and σ are initialized closed to $\mu_{expected}$ and $\sigma_{expected}$. Figure 6.5c shows how, for MAP, μ and σ are able to converge to $\mu._{expected}$ and $\sigma_{expected}$ even though they are initialized far away.

Listing 6.7 Gaussian negative log-likelihood with regularization

```
def neg_log_likelihood_reg(X, mu, sigma, k=0.2):
    N = X.shape[0]
    X_minus_mu = torch.sub(X, mu)
    t1 = torch.mul(0.5 * N,
                   torch.log(2 * np.pi * torch.pow(sigma, 2)))
```

Equation 6.28 (annotation on the `def` line)

$\frac{n}{2} \log 2\pi\sigma^2$ (annotation on `t1`)

```
t2 = torch.div(torch.matmul(X_minus_mu.T, X_minus_mu),
               2 * torch.pow(sigma, 2))
loss_likelihood = t1 + t2
loss_reg = k * (torch.pow(mu, 2) + torch.pow(sigma, 2))
return loss_likelihood + loss_reg
```

$\frac{\sum_{i=1}^{n}(x_i-\mu)^2}{2\sigma^2}$

Negative log-likelihood

Regularization

Note how all the training data X is crunched in a single operation. Such vector operations are parallel and very efficient in PyTorch.

6.9 Gaussian mixture models

In many real-life problems, the simple unimodal (single-peak) probability distributions we learned about in chapter 5 fail to model the true underlying distribution of the data. For instance, consider a situation where we are given the heights of many adult Statsville residents. Say there are two classes of adults in Statsville: male and female. The height data we have is *unlabeled*, meaning we do not know whether a given instance of height data is associated with a male or a female. Thus the data is one-dimensional, and there are two classes. Figure 6.6 depicts the situation. None of the simple probability distributions we discussed in chapter 5 can be fitted to figure 6.6. But the two partial bells in figure 6.6a suggest that we should be able to mix a pair of Gaussians (each of which looks like a bell) to mimic this distribution. This is also consistent with our knowledge that the distribution represents not one but two classes, each of which can be reasonably represented individually by Gaussians. The point cloud also indicates two separate clusters of points. While a single Gaussian will not work, a mixture of two separate 1D Gaussians can (and, as we shall shortly see, will) work.

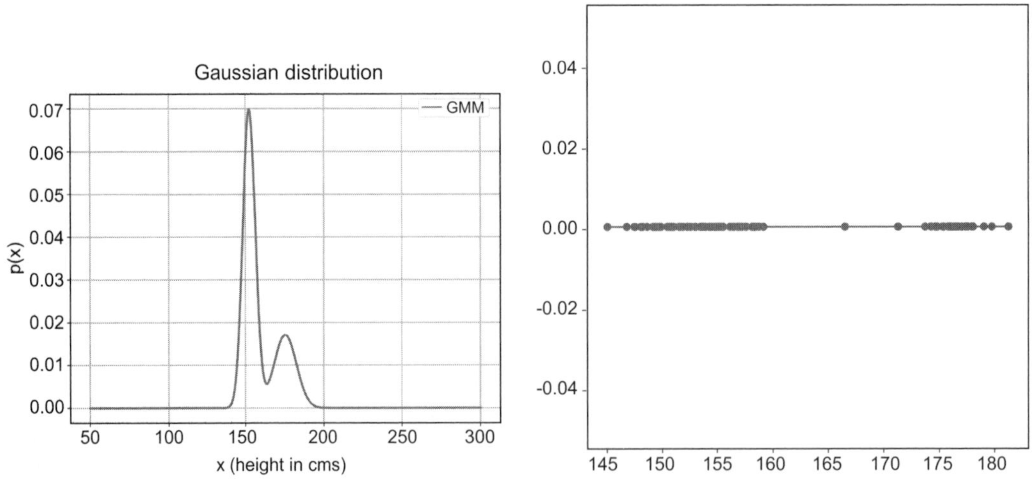

(a) PDF

(b) Sample point distribution

Figure 6.6 Probability density functions (PDFs) and sample point distributions for 1D height data of adult male and female residents of Statsville

Let's now discuss a slightly more complex problem in which the data is two-dimensional and has three classes. Here we are given the weights and heights of three classes of Statsville residents: adult females, adult males, and children. Again, the data is *unlabeled*, meaning we do not know whether a given instance of (height, weight) data is associated with a man, woman, or child. This is depicted in figure 6.7. Once again, none of the simple probability distributions we studied in chapter 5 can be fitted to this situation. But the PDF shows three bell-shaped peaks, the point cloud shows three clusters, and the physical nature of the problem indicates three separate classes, each of which can be reasonably represented by Gaussian. While a single Gaussian will not work, a mixture of three separate 2D Gaussians can (and, as we shall shortly see, will) work.

A Gaussian mixture model (GMM) is a weighted combination of a specific number of Gaussian components.

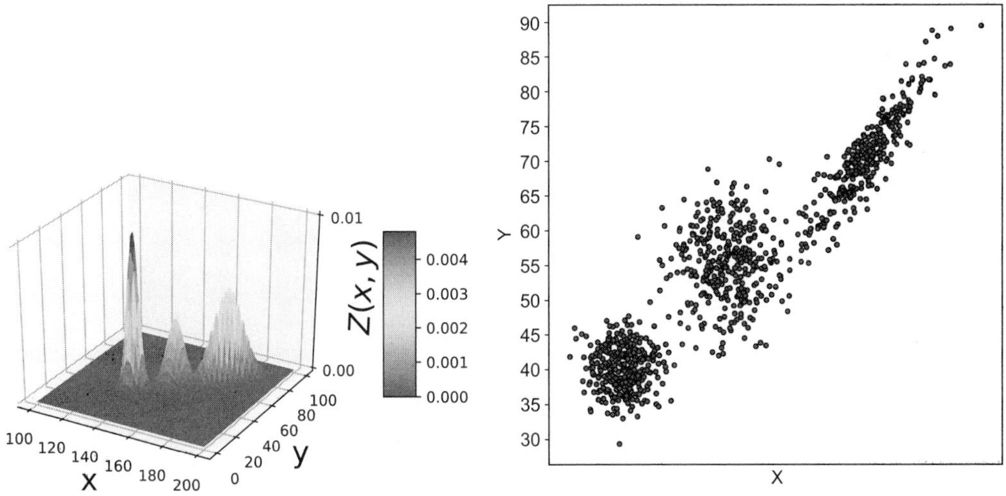

(a) PDF (b) Sample point distributions

Figure 6.7 Probability density functions (PDFs) and sample point distributions for 2D (height, weight) data of children, adult males, and adult females of Statsville

For instance, in our first problem with one dimension and two classes, we choose a mixture of two 1D Gaussians. For the second problem, we take a mixture of three 2D Gaussians. Each individual Gaussian component corresponds to a specific class.

6.9.1 Probability density function of the GMM

Formally,

The PDF for a GMM is

$$p\left(\vec{x}\right) = \sum_{k=1}^{K} \pi_k \, \mathcal{N}\left(\vec{x};\ \vec{\mu}_k, \boldsymbol{\Sigma}_k\right) \tag{6.29}$$

where π_k is the weight of the kth Gaussian component, satisfying

$$\sum_{k=1}^{k=K} \pi_k = 1$$

K is the number of classes or Gaussian components, and $\mathcal{N}(\vec{x};\ \vec{\mu}_k, \boldsymbol{\Sigma}_k)$ (defined in equation 5.23) is the PDF for the kth Gaussian component. Such a GMM models a K-peaked PDF or, equivalently, a K-clustered sample point cloud.

For instance, the PDF and sample point clouds shown in figure 6.6 correspond to the following Gaussian mixture:

$$p(x) = \overbrace{\pi_1}^{0.7} \mathcal{N}\left(x;\ \underbrace{\mu_1}_{152.0},\ \overbrace{\sigma_1}^{4.0}\right) + \overbrace{\pi_2}^{0.3} \mathcal{N}\left(x;\ \underbrace{\mu_2}_{175.0},\ \overbrace{\sigma_2}^{7.0}\right)$$

The 2D three-class problem, PDF, and sample point clouds shown in figure 6.7 correspond to the following Gaussian mixture:

$$p(x) = \overbrace{\pi_1}^{0.33} \mathcal{N}\left(\vec{x};\ \overbrace{\vec{\mu}_1}^{\begin{bmatrix}152\\55\end{bmatrix}}\ \overbrace{\boldsymbol{\Sigma}_1}^{\begin{bmatrix}20 & 0\\0 & 28\end{bmatrix}}\right) + \overbrace{\pi_2}^{0.33} \mathcal{N}\left(\vec{x};\ \overbrace{\vec{\mu}_2}^{\begin{bmatrix}175\\70\end{bmatrix}},\ \overbrace{\boldsymbol{\Sigma}_2}^{\begin{bmatrix}35 & 39\\39 & 51\end{bmatrix}}\right)$$

$$+ \overbrace{\pi_3}^{0.33} \mathcal{N}\left(\vec{x};\ \overbrace{\vec{\mu}_3}^{\begin{bmatrix}135\\40\end{bmatrix}},\ \overbrace{\boldsymbol{\Sigma}_3}^{\begin{bmatrix}10 & 0\\0 & 10\end{bmatrix}}\right)$$

The PDF and sample point distribution of the GMM depend on the values of π_ks, μ_ks, $\boldsymbol{\Sigma}_k$s, and K. In particular, K influences the number of peaks in the PDF (although if two peaks are very close, sometimes they merge). It also influences the number of clusters in the sample point cloud (again, if two clusters are too close, they may not be visually distinct). The π_ks regulate the relative heights of the hills. The μ_ks and $\boldsymbol{\Sigma}_k$s influence the individual hills in the PDF as well as the individual clusters in the sample point cloud. Specifically, μ_k regulates the locations of the kth peak in the PDF and the centroid of the kth cluster in the sample point cloud. The $\boldsymbol{\Sigma}_k$s regulate the shape of the kth individual hill and the kth cluster in the sample point cloud. Figures 6.8, 6.9, 6.10, and 6.11 show some example GMMs with various values of these parameters.

Figure 6.8 shows a pair of Gaussian distributions and various GMMs with those as components, with different values for the parameters. Figure 6.9 depicts 2D GMMs with various π_ks. Figure 6.10 shows GMMs with non-circular bases (non-symmetric Σs) and various μs).

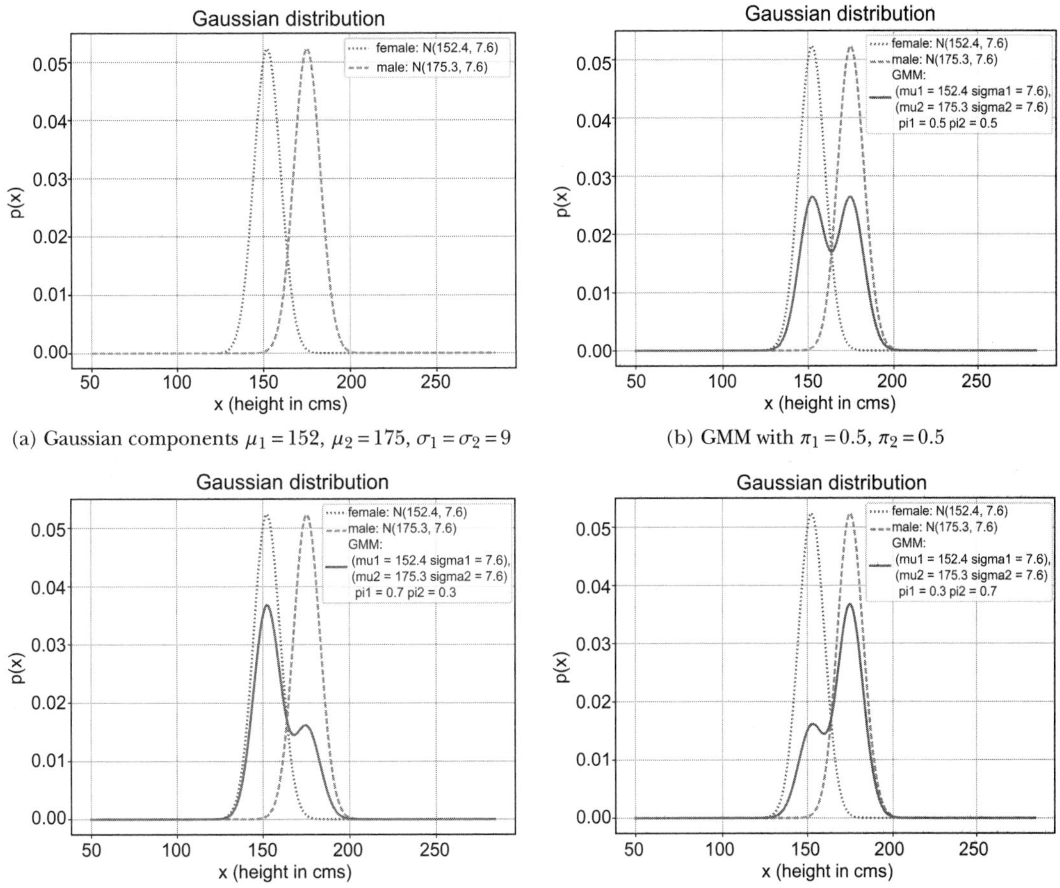

(a) Gaussian components $\mu_1 = 152$, $\mu_2 = 175$, $\sigma_1 = \sigma_2 = 9$

(b) GMM with $\pi_1 = 0.5$, $\pi_2 = 0.5$

(c) GMM with $\pi_1 = 0.7$, $\pi_2 = 0.3$

(d) GMM with $\pi_1 = 0.3$, $\pi_2 = 0.7$

Figure 6.8 Various GMMs (solid curves) with the same Gaussian components (dotted and dashed curves, respectively) but different π_1 and π_2 values

Another way to visualize GMMs is via sample point distributions. Figure 6.11 shows the sample points from a pair of 2D Gaussians and the points sampled from a GMM having those Gaussians as components and various mixture-selections probabilities.

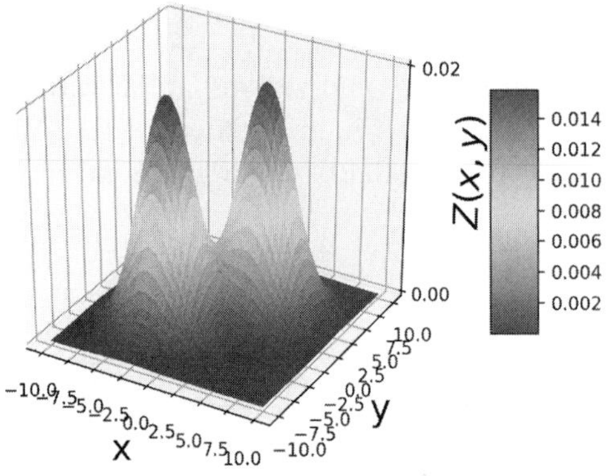

(a) $\pi_1 = 0.5$, $\pi_2 = 0.5$

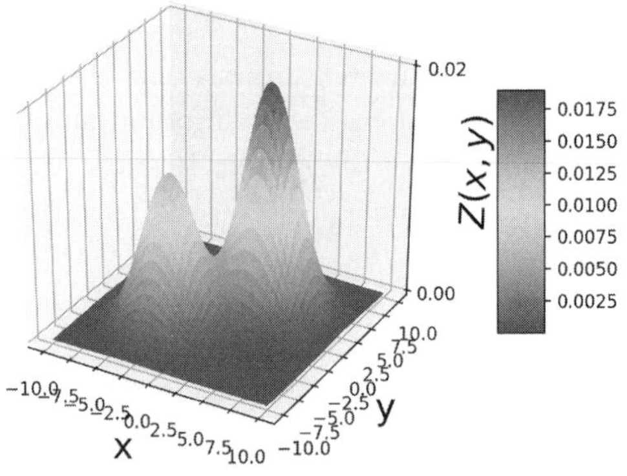

(b) $\pi_1 = 0.4$, $\pi_2 = 0.6$

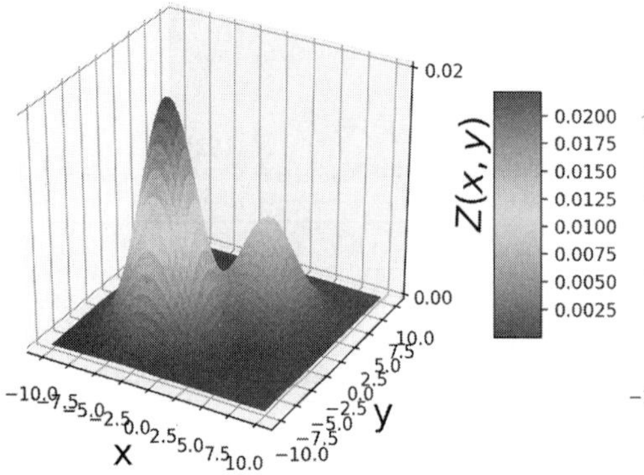

(c) $\pi_1 = 0.7$, $\pi_2 = 0.3$

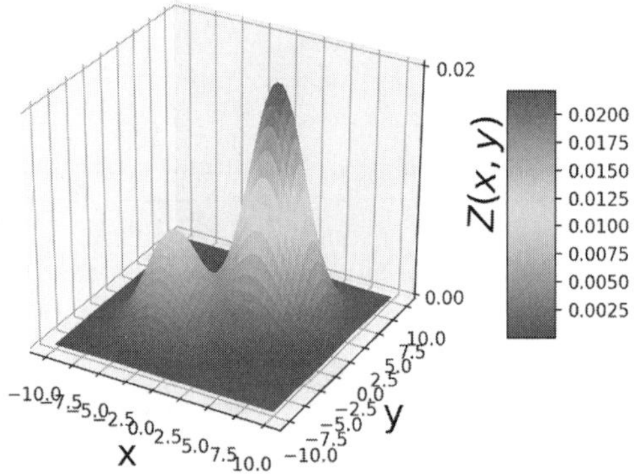

(d) $\pi_1 = 0.3$, $\pi_2 = 0.7$

Figure 6.9 Two-dimensional GMMs with circular bases, ($\Sigma_1 = \Sigma_2 = \begin{bmatrix} 5 & 0 \\ 0 & 5 \end{bmatrix}$), $\vec{\mu}_1 = \begin{bmatrix} -3 \\ -3 \end{bmatrix}$, $\vec{\mu}_2 = \begin{bmatrix} 3 \\ 3 \end{bmatrix}$. Note how the relative heights of the hills depend on πs.

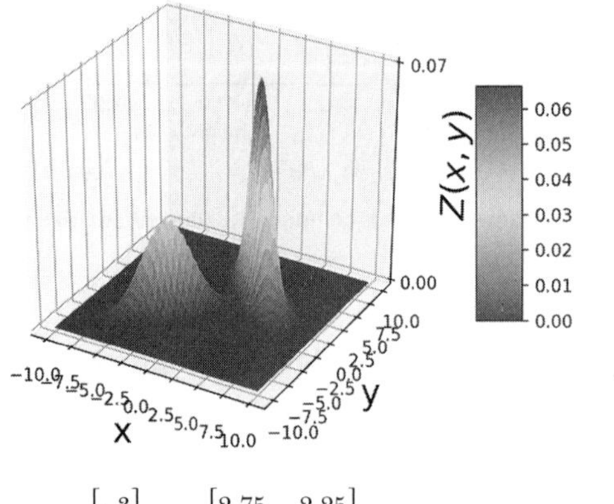

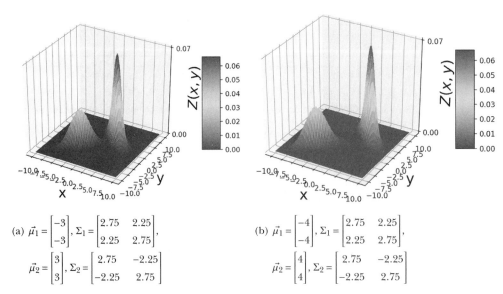

(a) $\vec{\mu}_1 = \begin{bmatrix} -3 \\ -3 \end{bmatrix}$, $\Sigma_1 = \begin{bmatrix} 2.75 & 2.25 \\ 2.25 & 2.75 \end{bmatrix}$,

$\vec{\mu}_2 = \begin{bmatrix} 3 \\ 3 \end{bmatrix}$, $\Sigma_2 = \begin{bmatrix} 2.75 & -2.25 \\ -2.25 & 2.75 \end{bmatrix}$

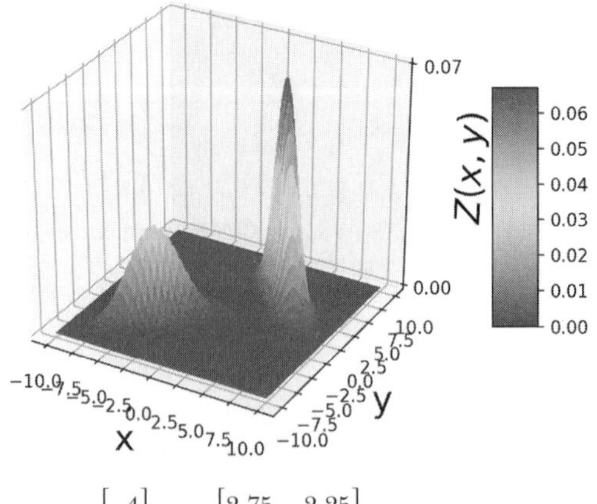

(b) $\vec{\mu}_1 = \begin{bmatrix} -4 \\ -4 \end{bmatrix}$, $\Sigma_1 = \begin{bmatrix} 2.75 & 2.25 \\ 2.25 & 2.75 \end{bmatrix}$,

$\vec{\mu}_2 = \begin{bmatrix} 4 \\ 4 \end{bmatrix}$, $\Sigma_2 = \begin{bmatrix} 2.75 & -2.25 \\ -2.25 & 2.75 \end{bmatrix}$

Figure 6.10 Two-dimensional GMMs with elliptical bases, $\pi_1 = 0.3$, $\pi_2 = 0.7$. Note how the shape of the hill base depends on Σ and how the hill positions depend on the $\vec{\mu}$s.

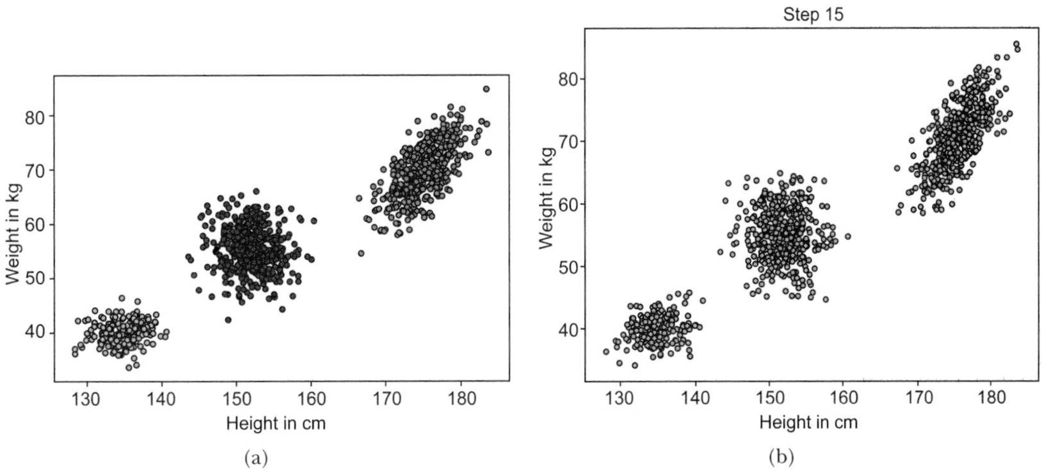

Figure 6.11 (a) $1,000$ random samples from three Gaussians with $\vec{\mu}_{woman} = \begin{bmatrix}152\\55\end{bmatrix}$, $\Sigma_{woman} = \begin{bmatrix}7 & 0\\0 & 15\end{bmatrix}$, $\vec{\mu}_{man} = \begin{bmatrix}175\\70\end{bmatrix}$, $\Sigma_{man} = \begin{bmatrix}9 & 10\\10 & 25\end{bmatrix}$, $\vec{\mu}_{child} = \begin{bmatrix}135\\40\end{bmatrix}$, $\Sigma_{child} = \begin{bmatrix}5 & 0\\0 & 5\end{bmatrix}$. (b) $1,000$ random samples from a GMM with the same three component Gaussians as in (a) and $\pi_1 = \pi_2 = 0.4$, $\pi_3 = 0.2$. Note how the GMM sample distribution shape mimics the combined sample distribution shape of the component Gaussians.

It can be proved that equation 6.29 is a proper probability: that is, it sums to 1 over the space of all possible inputs (all possible values of $\vec{x}$ in the d-dimensional space). Here is the proof outline:

$$\int_{\vec{x}\in\Re^d} p\left(\vec{x}\right) d\vec{x} = \int_{\vec{x}\in\Re^d} \left(\sum_{k=1}^{K} \pi_k \mathcal{N}\left(\vec{x};\ \vec{\mu}_k, \Sigma_k\right)\right) d\vec{x}$$

$$= \sum_{k=1}^{K} \pi_k \left(\overbrace{\int_{\vec{x}\in\Re^d} \mathcal{N}\left(\vec{x};\ \vec{\mu}_k, \Sigma_k\right) d\vec{x}}^{\text{equals 1, } \mathcal{N} \text{ being a PDF}}\right) = \sum_{i=1}^{K} \pi_k = 1$$

6.9.2 *Latent variables for class selection*

Let's discuss GMMs in more detail. In particular, we look at the physical meaning of the various terms in equation 6.29.

Before diving in, let's introduce an auxiliary random variable Z, which effectively is a *class selector*. In the context of equation 6.29, Z can take discrete values in the range $[1 \cdots K]$. It thus follows a categorical distribution (see section 5.9.6). Physically, $Z = k$ means the kth class—that is, the kth component of the Gaussian mixture—has been selected.

NOTE As usual, we are denoting the random variable with uppercase and the specific value it takes in a given instance with lowercase.

For instance, in the two-class problem shown in figure 6.6, Z can take one of two values: 1 (implying adult female) or 2 (implying adult male). For the three-class problem shown in figure 6.7, Z can take one of three values: 1 (adult female), 2 (adult male), or 3 (child). Z is called a *latent (hidden) random variable* because its values are not directly observed. Contrast this with the input random variable $\vec{x}$ whose values are explicitly observed. You may recognize Z as a latent variable in the GMM (latent variables were introduced in section 6.7).

Consider the joint probability $p\left(X=\vec{x}, Z=k\right)$, which we sometimes informally denote as $p\left(\vec{x}, k\right)$. This is the probability of the input variable $\vec{x}$ occurring together with the class k. Using Bayes' theorem,

$$p\left(\vec{x}, k\right) = p\left(\vec{x} \middle| k\right) p\left(k\right)$$

The conditional probability term $p\left(\vec{x} \middle| k\right)$ is the probability of $\vec{x}$ when the kth class has been selected. This means it is the PDF for the kth Gaussian component, which is a Gaussian distribution by assumption. As such, using equation 5.23,

$$p\left(\vec{x} \middle| k\right) = \mathcal{N}\left(\vec{x};\ \vec{\mu}_k, \Sigma_k\right) \quad k \in [1, K]$$

On the other hand, $p\left(Z=k\right)$, which we sometimes informally refer to as $p\left(k\right)$, is the *prior probability (that is, without reference to the input) of the input belonging to one of the classes.* Let's denote it as follows:

$$p\left(k\right) = \pi_k, \quad \forall k \in \{1, K\}$$

This is often modeled as the *fraction of training data points belonging to class k*:

$$\pi_k \approx \frac{N_k}{N} \quad k \in \{1, K\}$$

where N_k is the number of training data instances belonging to class k, and N is the total number of training data instances.

From this, we get

$$p\left(\vec{x}, k\right) = p\left(k\right) p\left(\vec{x} \middle| k\right) = \pi_k\ \mathcal{N}\left(\vec{x};\ \vec{\mu}_k, \Sigma_k\right) \quad k \in [1, K]$$

From equation 5.5, we get the marginal probability $p\left(x\right)$

$$p\left(x\right) = \sum_{k \in \{1,K\}} p\left(x, k\right) = \sum_{k=1}^{K} \pi_k\ \mathcal{N}\left(\vec{x};\ \vec{\mu}_k, \Sigma_k\right)$$

which is the same as equation 6.29.

This leads to the following physical interpretations:

- A GMM can be viewed as a weighted sum of K Gaussian components. Equation 6.29 depicts the PDF of the overall GMM.
- The *weights π_k are component selection probabilities.* Specifically, π_k can be interpreted as the prior probability $p(Z = k)$, aka $p(k)$, of selecting the kth subclass—modeled as the fraction of the population belonging to the kth subclass. The π_k are probabilities in a categorical distribution with K classes. The π_ks sum up to 1. Sampling from the GMM can be viewed as a two-step process:
  1. Randomly select a component. The probability of the kth component being selected is π_k. The sum of all π_ks is 1, which signifies that one or another component must be selected.
  2. Random sample from the selected Gaussian component. The probability of generating vector $\vec{x}$ is $\mathcal{N}(\vec{x};\ \vec{\mu}_k, \Sigma_k)$.
- Each of the K Gaussian components models an individual class. Geometrically speaking, the components correspond to the clusters in the sample point cloud or the peaks in the PDF of the GMM.
- The kth Gaussian component, $\mathcal{N}(\vec{x};\ \vec{\mu}_k, \Sigma_k)$, can be interpreted as the conditional probability, $p(\vec{x}|k)$. This is the likelihood—the probability of data value $\vec{x}$ occurring, *given* that the kth subclass has been selected.
- The product $\pi_k \mathcal{N}(\vec{x};\ \vec{\mu}_k, \Sigma_k)$ then represents the joint probability $p(\vec{x}, k) = p(\vec{x}|k)$ $p(k)$.
- The sum of all the joint subclass probabilities is the marginal probability $p(\vec{x})$ of the data value $\vec{x}$.

Listing 6.8 Gaussian mixture model distribution

```
from torch.distributions.mixture_same_family import MixtureSameFamily

pi = Categorical(torch.tensor([0.4, 0.4, 0.2]))

mu = torch.tensor([[175.0, 70.0], [152.0, 55.0], [135.0, 40.0]])

sigma = torch.tensor([[[30.0, 20.0], [20.0, 30.0]],
                      [[50.0, 0.0], [0.0, 10.0]],
                      [[20.0, 0.0], [0.0, 20.0]]])

gaussian_components = MultivariateNormal(mu, sigma)

gmm = MixtureSameFamily(pi, gaussian_components)
```

Annotations:
- **Pytorch supports distributions that are mixtures of the same family (here, Gaussian)** (import line)
- **Prior probabilities over the three classes (male, female, child): categorical distribution** (pi)
- **Mean height, weight for the three classes (male, female, child)** (mu)
- **Covariance matrices for the three classes (male, female, child)** (sigma)
- **Creates the component Gaussians** (gaussian_components)
- **Creates the GMM** (gmm)

6.9.3 *Classification via GMM*

A typical practical problem involving GMMs goes as follows. A set of unlabeled input data X (training data) is provided. It is important to note that this is unsupervised machine learning—the training data does not come with known output classes. The physical nature of the problem indicates the subclasses in the data (denoted by indices $[1 \cdots K]$). The goal is to classify any arbitrary input $\vec{x}$: that is, map it to one of the K classes. To do this, we have to fit a GMM (that is, derive the values of π_k, $\vec{\mu}_k$, $\mathbf{\Sigma}_k$ for all $k \in [1 \cdots K]$). Given an arbitrary $\vec{x}$, we compute $p\left(k|\vec{x}\right)$ for all the classes (all values of k). The value of k yielding the max value for $p\left(k|\vec{x}\right)$ is the class corresponding to $\vec{x}$. How do we compute $p\left(k|\vec{x}\right)$?

Using Bayes' theorem,

$$p\left(k|\vec{x}\right) = \frac{p\left(\vec{x}, k\right)}{p\left(\vec{x}\right)} = \frac{p\left(\vec{x}|k\right) p\left(k\right)}{\sum_{i=1}^{K} p\left(\vec{x}, k\right)} = \frac{\pi_k \mathcal{N}\left(\vec{x};\, \vec{\mu}_k, \mathbf{\Sigma}_k\right)}{\sum_{i=1}^{K} \pi_i \mathcal{N}\left(\vec{x};\, \vec{\mu}_i, \mathbf{\Sigma}_i\right)} \tag{6.30}$$

If we know all the GMM parameters, evaluating equation 6.30 is straightforward. We classify the input $\vec{x}$ by assigning it to the cluster k that yields the highest value of $p\left(Z=k|X=x\right)$. Geometrically, this assigns the input to the cluster with the "closest" mean—with distance normalized by the variance of the respective distribution. Basically, we are measuring the distance from the mean, but in clusters of high variance, we are more tolerant of distance from the mean. This makes intuitive sense: if the cluster is widely spread (has high variance), a point relatively far from the cluster mean can be said to belong to the cluster. On the other hand, a point the same distance from the mean of a tightly packed cluster may be deemed to be outside the cluster.

6.9.4 *Maximum likelihood estimation of GMM parameters (GMM fit)*

A GMM is fully described in terms of its parameter set $\theta = \left\{\pi_k, \vec{\mu}_k, \mathbf{\Sigma}_k \, \forall k \in [1 \cdots K]\right\}$. But how do we estimate these parameter values? In typical real-life situations, they are not given to us. We only have a set of observed unlabeled training data points $X = \left\{\vec{x}^{(i)}\right\}$, such as (weight, height) values for Statsville residents.

Geometrically speaking, each data instance in the training dataset corresponds to a single point in the multidimensional feature space. The training dataset is a point cloud that naturally clusters into Gaussian subclouds (otherwise, we should not be trying GMMs). Our GMM mimicking this dataset should have as many components as there are natural clusters in the data. The parameter values π_k, $\vec{\mu}_k$, $\mathbf{\Sigma}_k$ for $k \in [1 \cdots K]$ should be estimated such that the GMM's sample point cloud overlaps the training data point cloud as much as possible. That is the basic problem we try to solve in this section.

> **NOTE** We do not estimate K, the number of classes; rather, we use a fixed value of K, usually estimated from the physical conditions of the problem. For example, in the problem with men, women, and children, it is pretty obvious that $K=3$.

In section 6.8, we did MLE for a simple Gaussian. We computed an expression for the joint log-likelihood of all the training data given a Gaussian probability distribution. Then we took the gradient of that expression with respect to the parameters and equated it to zero. We were able to solve that equation to derive a *closed-form* solution for the parameters, $\vec{\mu}$ and Σ (equations 6.25 and 6.26). This means we simplified the equation into a form where the unknown (to be solved) appeared alone on the left-hand side and there were only known entities on the right-hand side.

Unfortunately, with GMMs, equating the gradient of the log-likelihood to zero leads to an equation that has no closed-form solution. So, we cannot reduce the equation to a form where the unknowns π_ks, μ_ks, and Σ_k appear alone on the left-hand sides and only known entities ($\vec{x}_i$s) appear on the right-hand side. Consequently, we have to go for an iterative approximation. We rewrite the equation we get by equating the gradient of the log-likelihood to zero such that the unknowns μs and σs appear alone on the right-hand side. It looks something like

$$\pi_k = f_1(X, \theta)$$

$$\vec{\mu}_k = f_2(X, \theta)$$

$$\Sigma_k = f_3(X, \theta)$$

where f_1, f_2, f_3 are some functions whose exact nature is unimportant at the moment. Note that the right-hand side also contains the unknowns: θ contains π_ks, μ_ks, and Σ_k. We cannot directly solve such equations, but we can use *iterative relaxation*, which works roughly as follows:

1. Start with random values of π_ks, $\vec{\mu}_k$s, and Σ_ks.
2. Evaluate the right-hand side by plugging current values of π_ks, $\vec{\mu}_k$s, and Σ_ks into functions f_1, f_2, and f_3.
3. Use the values estimated in step 2 to set new values of π_ks, $\vec{\mu}_k$s, and Σ_ks.
4. Repeat steps 1–3 until the parameter values stop changing appreciably.

The actual functions f_1, f_2, f_3 are worked out in (equations 6.36, 6.37, and 6.38). As iteration progresses, the values of π_ks, $\vec{\mu}_k$s, and Σ_ks start to converge to their true values. This is not a lucky coincidence. If we follow algorithm 6.1, it can be proved that every iteration improves the approximation, even if by a minuscule amount. Eventually, we reach a point when the approximation is no longer improving appreciably. This is called the *fixed point*, and we should stop iterating and declare the current values final.

Figure 6.12 shows the progression of an iterative GMM fit algorithm. Figure 6.12a shows the sampled training data distribution. Figure 6.12b shows the fitted GMM at the beginning: the parameters are essentially random, and the GMM looks nothing like the target training data distribution. It improves slowly until at iteration 15, it matches the target distribution snugly (figure 6.12d). Now let's discuss the details. We *already know* the dataset X that has been observed. What parameter set θ will maximize the conditional probability, $p(X|\theta)$, of exactly these data points, given the parameter set? In other words, what model parameters will maximize the overall likelihood of the training data? Those will be our best guesses for the unknown model parameters. This is MLE, which we encountered in section 6.6.2.

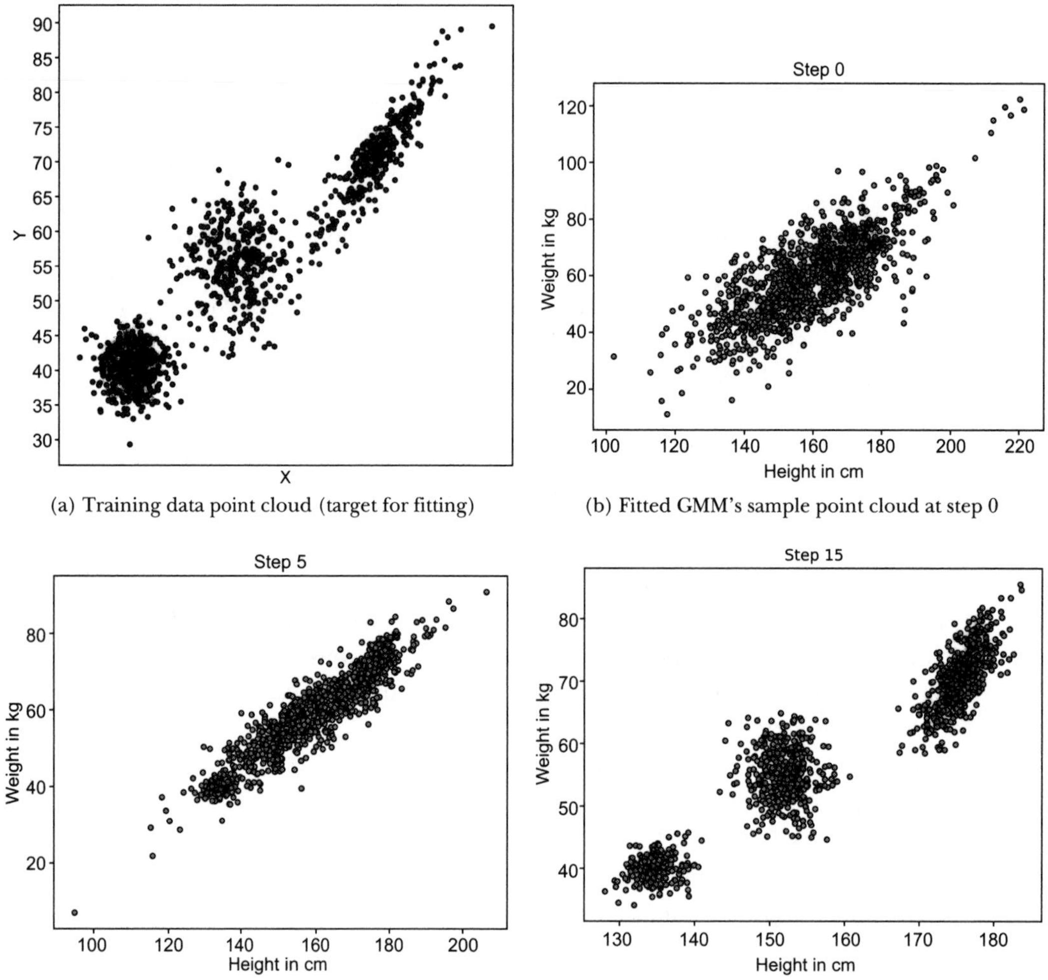

(a) Training data point cloud (target for fitting)

(b) Fitted GMM's sample point cloud at step 0

(c) Fitted GMM's sample point cloud at step 5

(d) Fitted GMM's sample point cloud at step 15. It almost matches the target.

Figure 6.12 Progression of maximum likelihood estimation for GMM parameters

Let $\left\{\vec{x}^{(1)}, \vec{x}^{(n)}, \cdots \vec{x}^{(n)}\right\}$ be the set of observed data points, aka training data. From equation 6.29,

$$\overbrace{p\left(\vec{x}^{(i)} \middle| \theta\right)}^{likelihood} = \sum_{k=1}^{K} \pi_k \, \mathcal{N}\left(\vec{x}^{(i)};\ \vec{\mu}_k, \boldsymbol{\Sigma}_k\right) \quad \forall i \in [1, n]$$

Henceforth, for simplicity, we drop the "given θ" part and refer to $p\left(\vec{x}^{(i)} \middle| \theta\right)$ simply as $p\left(\vec{x}^{(i)}\right)$. As usual, instead of maximizing the likelihood directly, we maximize its logarithm, the *log-likelihood*. This will yield the same parameters as maximizing the likelihood directly.

Since the $x^{(i)}$s are independent, their joint probability, as per equation 5.4, is

$$p\left(\vec{x}^{(1)}\right) p\left(\vec{x}^{(2)}\right) \cdots p\left(\vec{x}^{(n)}\right)$$

The corresponding log joint probability is

$$\overbrace{log\left(p\left(\vec{x}^{(1)}\right) p\left(\vec{x}^{(2)}\right) \cdots p\left(\vec{x}^{(n)}\right)\right)}^{\text{joint log-likelihood}} = \sum_{i=1}^{n} log\left(p\left(\vec{x}^{(i)}\right)\right)$$

$$= \sum_{i=1}^{n} log\left(\sum_{k=1}^{K} \pi_k \mathcal{N}\left(\vec{x}^{(i)};\ \vec{\mu}_k, \mathbf{\Sigma}_k\right)\right) \tag{6.31}$$

At this point, we begin to see a difficulty peculiar to GMMs. We have a logarithm of a sum, which is not a very friendly expression to handle; the logarithm of products is much nicer to deal with. But let's soldier on.

To identify the parameters $\vec{\mu}_1, \Sigma_1, \vec{\mu}_2, \Sigma_2, \cdots$ that will maximize the log joint probability, we take the gradient of the log joint probability with respect to these parameters, equate them to zero, and solve for the parameter value (as discussed in section 3.3.1). Here we demonstrate the process with respect to $\vec{\mu}_1$:

$$\nabla_{\vec{\mu}_1} log\left(p\left(\vec{x}^{(1)}\right) p\left(\vec{x}^{(2)}\right) \cdots p\left(\vec{x}^{(n)}\right)\right) = 0$$

Since the log of products is the sum of logs, we get

$$\nabla_{\vec{\mu}_1} \sum_{i=1}^{n} log\left(p\left(\vec{x}^{(i)}\right)\right) = 0$$

Applying equation 6.29, we get

$$\nabla_{\vec{\mu}_1} \sum_{i=1}^{n} log\left(\sum_{k=1}^{K} \pi_k \mathcal{N}\left(\vec{x}^{(i)};\ \vec{\mu}_k, \mathbf{\Sigma}_k\right)\right) = 0$$

Since the gradient is a linear operator, we can move it inside the summation:

$$\sum_{i=1}^{n} \nabla_{\vec{\mu}_1} log\left(\sum_{k=1}^{K} \pi_k \mathcal{N}\left(\vec{x}^{(i)};\ \vec{\mu}_k, \mathbf{\Sigma}_k\right)\right) = 0$$

Since $\frac{d}{dx} log\left(f\left(x\right)\right) = \frac{1}{f(x)} \frac{df}{dx}$, we get

$$\sum_{i=1}^{n} \frac{\nabla_{\vec{\mu}_1} \sum_{k=1}^{K} \pi_k \mathcal{N}\left(\vec{x}^{(i)};\ \vec{\mu}_k, \mathbf{\Sigma}_k\right)}{\left(\sum_{k=1}^{K} \pi_k \mathcal{N}\left(\vec{x}^{(i)};\ \vec{\mu}_k, \mathbf{\Sigma}_k\right)\right)} = 0$$

Now, if x_1 and x_2 are independent variables, $\frac{dx_2}{dx_1} = 0$. Consequently,

$$\nabla_{\vec{\mu}_1} \mathcal{N}\left(\vec{x}^{(i)};\ \vec{\mu}_k, \mathbf{\Sigma}_k\right) = 0 \quad \text{for } k \neq 1$$

Only a single term corresponding to $k = 1$ survives the differentiation (gradient) in the numerator. So,

$$\sum_{i=1}^{n} \frac{\pi_1 \nabla_{\vec{\mu}_1} \mathcal{N}\left(\vec{x}^{(i)};\ \vec{\mu}_1, \mathbf{\Sigma}_1\right)}{\left(\sum_{k=1}^{K} \pi_k\, \mathcal{N}\left(\vec{x}^{(i)};\ \vec{\mu}_k, \mathbf{\Sigma}_k\right)\right)} = 0$$

Now $\frac{d}{dx} e^{-(x-\mu)^2} = -2\,(x-\mu)\,e^{-(x-\mu)^2}$, and in multiple dimensions,

$$\nabla_{\vec{\mu}} e^{-\frac{1}{2}(\vec{x}-\vec{\mu})^T \Sigma^{-1} (\vec{x}-\vec{\mu})} = -\nabla_{\vec{\mu}} \left(\left(\vec{x}-\vec{\mu}\right)^T \Sigma^{-1} \left(\vec{x}-\vec{\mu}\right) \right) e^{-\frac{1}{2}(\vec{x}-\mu)^T \Sigma^{-1} (\vec{x}-\mu)}$$

Plugging equation 5.23 into our maximization problem, we get

$$\sum_{i=1}^{n} \frac{\nabla_{\vec{\mu}_1} \left(\left(\vec{x}^{(i)} - \vec{\mu}_1\right)^T \mathbf{\Sigma}_1^{-1} \left(\vec{x}^{(i)} - \vec{\mu}_1\right) \right) \pi_1\, \mathcal{N}\left(\vec{x}^{(i)};\ \vec{\mu}_1, \mathbf{\Sigma}_1\right)}{\left(\sum_{k=1}^{K} \pi_k\, \mathcal{N}\left(\vec{x}^{(i)};\ \vec{\mu}_k, \mathbf{\Sigma}_k\right)\right)} = 0$$

Furthermore, with a little effort, you can prove the following about the gradient of a quadratic form:

$$\nabla_{\vec{x}} \left(\vec{x}^T A \vec{x}\right) = A\vec{x} \tag{6.32}$$

Applying equation 6.32 to our problem, we get

$$\sum_{i=1}^{n} \frac{\mathbf{\Sigma}_1^{-1} \left(\vec{x}^{(i)} - \vec{\mu}_1\right) \pi_1\, \mathcal{N}\left(\vec{x}^{(i)};\ \vec{\mu}_1, \mathbf{\Sigma}_1\right)}{\left(\sum_{k=1}^{K} \pi_k\, \mathcal{N}\left(\vec{x}^{(i)};\ \vec{\mu}_k, \mathbf{\Sigma}_k\right)\right)} = 0$$

Multiplying both sides by the constant $\mathbf{\Sigma}_1$, we get

$$\sum_{i=1}^{n} \frac{\left(\vec{x}^{(i)} - \vec{\mu}_1\right) \pi_1\, \mathcal{N}\left(\vec{x}^{(i)};\ \vec{\mu}_1, \mathbf{\Sigma}_1\right)}{\left(\sum_{k=1}^{K} \pi_k\, \mathcal{N}\left(\vec{x}^{(i)};\ \vec{\mu}_k, \mathbf{\Sigma}_k\right)\right)} = 0$$

Substituting

$$\gamma_{i1} = \frac{\pi_1\, \mathcal{N}\left(\vec{x}^{(i)};\ \vec{\mu}_1, \mathbf{\Sigma}_1\right)}{\left(\sum_{k=1}^{K} \pi_k\, \mathcal{N}\left(\vec{x}^{(i)};\ \vec{\mu}_k, \mathbf{\Sigma}_k\right)\right)} \tag{6.33}$$

we get

$$\sum_{i=1}^{n} \left(\vec{x}^{(i)} - \vec{\mu}_1\right) \gamma_{i1} = 0$$

This expression has μ_1 inside γ_{i1} as well. It is impossible to extract μ_1 alone on the left side of the equation. In other words, we cannot create a *closed-form* solution for μ_1. Hence, we have to solve it iteratively.

We can rewrite the previous equation as

$$\vec{\mu}_1 = \frac{1}{N_1} \sum_{i=1}^{n} \gamma_{i1} \vec{x}^{(i)}$$

where

$$N_1 = \sum_{i=1}^{n} \gamma_{i1} \tag{6.34}$$

Proceeding similarly, we can derive the corresponding expressions for π_1 and $\mathbf{\Sigma}_1$. Let's collect all the equations for updating the GMM parameters:

$$N_1 = \sum_{i=1}^{n} \gamma_{i1} \tag{6.35}$$

$$\pi_1 = \frac{N_1}{n} \tag{6.36}$$

$$\vec{\mu}_1 = \frac{1}{N_1} \sum_{i=1}^{n} \gamma_{i1} \vec{x}^{(i)} \tag{6.37}$$

$$\mathbf{\Sigma}_1 = \frac{1}{N_1} \sum_{i=1}^{n} \gamma_{i1} \left(\vec{x}^{(i)} - \vec{\mu}_1\right) \left(\vec{x}^{(i)} - \vec{\mu}_1\right)^T \tag{6.38}$$

Equations 6.36, 6.37, and 6.38 provide the definitions for functions f_1, f_2, and f_3 that we saw at the beginning of this section in the context of iterative relaxation. We can deal similarly with $k = 2 \cdots K$.

Physical significance of γ_{ik}

We encountered the entity γ_{ik} while computing the gradient of the log-likelihood. It appeared as a multiplicative weight in the final iterative expression for computing μ_k and Σ_k in equations 6.37 and 6.38. It is not an arbitrary entity. By comparing equations 6.33 and 6.30, we can see that

$$\gamma_{ik} = p\left(k \middle| \vec{x}^{(i)}\right)$$

In other words, the quantity γ_{ik} is really the posterior probability: the conditional probability of the class k given the ith data point.

This gives us a new way to look at equations 6.35, 6.36, 6.37, and 6.38:

- Equation 6.35 essentially assigns to N_1 the probability mass concentrated in class 1 as per the current parameter values.
- Equation 6.36 assigns to π_1 the fractional mass in class 1 as per the current parameter values.
- Equation 6.37 assigns to μ_1 the centroid of all the training data points. Each data point's contribution is weighted by the posterior probability, as per the current parameter values, of that data point belonging to class 1.
- Equation 6.38 assigns to $\mathbf{\Sigma}_1$ the covariance of the training data points. Each data point's contribution is weighted by the posterior probability, as per the current parameter values, of that data point belonging to class 1.

Algorithm 6.1 ties together equations 6.33, 6.36, 6.37, and 6.38 into a complete approach for iterative MLE of GMM parameters. It is an example of a general class of algorithms called *expectation maximization.*

Algorithm 6.1 GMM fit (MLE of GMM parameters from unlabeled training data)

Input: $X = \vec{x}^{(i)}, \vec{x}^{(2)}, \cdots, \vec{x}^{(n)}$
Initialize parameters $\theta = \{\pi_k, \mu_k, \mathbf{\Sigma}_k \;\; k \in [1, K]\}$ with random values
▹ repeat E-step and M-step until likelihood stops increasing
while (likelihood is increasing) **do**
▹ E-step

$$\gamma_{ik} = \frac{\pi_k \mathcal{N}\left(\vec{x}^{(i)}; \; \vec{\mu}_k, \mathbf{\Sigma}_k\right)}{\sum_{k=1}^{K} \pi_k \mathcal{N}\left(\vec{x}^{(i)}; \; \vec{\mu}_k, \mathbf{\Sigma}_k\right)} \qquad \forall i, k \in [1, n] \times [1, K]$$

▹ M-step

$$\left.\begin{aligned} N_k &= \sum_{i=1}^{n} \gamma_{ik} \\ \pi_k &= \frac{N_k}{n} \\ \vec{\mu}_k &= \frac{1}{N_k} \sum_{i=1}^{n} \gamma_{ik} \vec{x}^{(i)} \\ \mathbf{\Sigma}_k &= \frac{1}{N_k} \sum_{i=1}^{n} \gamma_{ik} \left(\vec{x}^{(i)} - \vec{\mu}_k\right)\left(\vec{x}^{(i)} - \vec{\mu}_k\right)^T \end{aligned}\right\} \forall k \in [1, K]$$

end while
return $\{\pi_1, \mu_1, \mathbf{\Sigma_1}, \pi_2, \mu_2, \mathbf{\Sigma_2}, \cdots, \pi_K, \mu_K, \mathbf{\Sigma_K}\}$

NOTE Fully functional code for Gaussian mixture modeling, executable via Jupyter Notebook, can be found at http://mng.bz/j4er.

Listing 6.9 GMM fit

```
while (curr_likelihood - prev_likelihood) < 1e-4:   ◄── Repeats until the likelihood increase is negligible

    # E Step   ◄── Computes the posterior probabilities γ_{i,k} = p(Z = k|X = x_i) using current μ_k s and Σ_k s, equation 6.33

    pi = gmm.mixture_distribution.probs   ◄── Tensor of shape [K] holding π_k s for all k

    components = gmm.component_distribution   ◄── Gaussian objects N(x; μ_k, Σ_k) for all k
```

```
log_gamma_numerators = components.log_prob(
    X.unsqueeze(1)) + torch.log(pi).repeat(n, 1)
```

Vector computation of log of $\gamma_{i,k}$ numerators for all i, k, equation 6.33

In practice, the probability involving an exponential goes to 0. So we use the log probability.

```
log_gamma_denominators = torch.logsumexp(
    log_gamma_numerators, dim=1, keepdim=True).
```

Vector computation of the log of $\gamma_{i,k}$ denominators for all i, k, equation 6.33

```
log_gamma = log_gamma_numerators - log_gamma_denominators
self.gamma = torch.exp(log_gamma)
```

Vector computation of the $[n \times K]$ tensor $\gamma_{i,k}$, equation 6.33 for all i, k

```
# M Step

n = X.shape[0]

N = torch.sum(gamma, 0)

pi = N / n

mu = ((X.T @ gamma)/N).T
```

Updates $\vec{\mu}_k$ and Σ_k for all k using $\gamma_{i,k} = p(Z = k|X)$ from the E-step via equations 6.36, 6.37, and 6.38

Number of data points

Vector update of π_k for all k, equation 6.36

Vector update of $[K \times d]$ tensor, $\vec{\mu}_k$ for all k, equation 6.37

```
x_minus_mu = (X.repeat(K, 1, 1) - gmm.component_distribution.unsqueeze(1).
              repeat(1, n, 1))
x_minus_mu_squared = x_minus_mu.unsqueeze(3)  @ x_minus_mu.unsqueeze(2)
```

Vector computation of $(\vec{x}_i - \vec{\mu}_k)(\vec{x}_i - \vec{\mu}_k)^T$ for all i, k

```
sigma = torch.sum(gamma.T.unsqueeze(2).unsqueeze(3) * x_minus_mu_squared,
                  axis=1) / N.unsqueeze(1).unsqueeze(1).repeat(1, d, d)

prev_likelihood = curr_likelihood

curr_likelihood = torch.sum(gmm.log_prob(X))
```

Vector update of $K \times d \times d]$ tensor Σ_k for all k, equation 6.38

log likelihood, equation 6.31

Summary

In this chapter, we looked at the Bayesian tools for decision-making in uncertain systems. We discussed conditional probability and Bayes' theorem, which connects conditional probabilities to joint and marginal probabilities.

- Conditional probability is the probability of an event occurring subject to the condition that another event has already occurred. In machine learning, we are often interested in the conditional probability $p\left(\vec{x}|\theta\right)$ of an input $\vec{x}$ given that the parameters of the model predicting the input are θ. This conditional probability is known as the likelihood of the input. We are also interested in the conditional probability $p\left(\theta|\vec{x}\right)$, known as the posterior probability.

- Joint probability is the probability of a set of events occurring together. If the events are independent, the joint probability is the product of their individual probabilities. Whether events are independent or not, Bayes' theorem connects joint and conditional probabilities. Of particular interest in machine learning is the Bayes' theorem expression connecting the likelihood and joint and posterior probabilities of inputs and parameters: $p\left(\vec{x}, \theta\right) = p\left(\vec{x}\middle|\theta\right) p\left(\theta\right)$ and $p\left(\theta\middle|\vec{x}\right) = \frac{p(\vec{x}|\theta)p(\theta)}{p(\vec{x})}$. $p\left(\vec{x}\middle|\theta\right)$ is the probability distribution function of the chosen distribution family. $p\left(\theta\right)$ is the prior probability that codifies our belief, sans data, about the system. A popular choice is $p\left(\theta\right) \propto e^{-\|\theta\|^2}$, implying smaller probabilities for higher-magnitude parameters and vice versa.
- Entropy models the uncertainty in a system. Systems where all events have more or less similar probabilities tend to be high-entropy. Systems where a particular subset of possible events have significantly high probabilities and others have significantly low probabilities tend to be low-entropy. Equivalently, the probability density functions of low-entropy systems tend to have tall peaks, and their sample point clouds have a high concentration of points in some regions. High-entropy systems tend to have flat probability density functions and diffused sample point clouds.
- Cross-entropy allows us to quantify how good our modeling is against a known ground truth.
- Kullback–Leibler divergence gives us a measure of the dissimilarity between two probability distributions.
- Maximum likelihood estimation (MLE) and maximum a posteriori (MAP) estimation are two paradigms for estimating model parameters. MLE maximizes $p\left(X|\theta\right)$, and MAP maximizes $p\left(X|\theta\right) p\left(\theta\right)$. MLE essentially tries to estimate probability distribution parameters that maximize the overlap between the sample point cloud of the probability distribution and the training data point cloud.

  MAP is MLE with a regularization condition. The regularization condition is injected via the prior probability term $p\left(\theta\right)$, which favors solutions with a certain property (such as small parameter magnitudes) that we believe to be true from empirical knowledge without data.

  MLE for Gaussian distributions has a closed-form solution. The mean and variance (covariance in the multidimensional case) of the optimal probability distribution that best fits the training data are the sample mean and sample variance or covariance on the training dataset.
- Latent variables in a machine learning system are auxiliary variables that are not directly observed but can be derived from the input. They facilitate the expression of the goal of optimization or the loss to be minimized.
- Gaussian mixture models (GMM) are unsupervised probability models that fit multiclass data distributions having multiple clusters in the training dataset, each corresponding to a different class. Here, MLE does not yield a closed-form solution but instead yields an iterative solution to estimate the mixture weights, means, and variances of the individual Gaussians in the mixture.

7 Function approximation: How neural networks model the world

This chapter covers

- Expressing real-world problems as mathematical functions
- Understanding the building blocks of a neural network
- Approximating functions via neural networks

Computing to date has been dominated by the von Neumann architecture in which the processor and the program are separate. The program sits in memory and is fetched and executed by the processor. The advantage of this approach is that different programs solving unrelated problems can be loaded into memory, and the same processor can execute them. But neural networks have a fundamentally different architecture. There are no separate processors and programs; instead, there is a single entity called, well, the neural network, which can run on dedicated hardware or a Von Neumann computer. In this chapter, we discuss this paradigm in detail.

NOTE The complete PyTorch code for this chapter is available at http://mng.bz/K4zj in the form of fully functional and executable Jupyter notebooks.

7.1 Neural networks: A 10,000-foot view

In section 1.7, we provided an overview of neural networks. (You may want to do a quick refresher on chapter 1 at this point.) There we indicated that most intelligent tasks performed by humans can be expressed in terms of mathematical functions that we will refer to as *target functions*. So, to develop machines that perform intelligent tasks, we need to have machines that model target functions. While that gives us hope of developing automated solutions, we are hobbled by two serious difficulties:

- In addition to being arbitrarily complicated, the target functions underlying various real-life problems are completely different from one another. There is hardly any common pattern.
- For most problems, we do *not* know the underlying target function.

Despite all this, we want to come up with a mechanized repeatable solution for performing real-life intelligent tasks. And we do not want to start from scratch and design the underlying function for each such problem. This is where neural networks help:

> Neural networks provide a unified framework to model an extremely wide variety of arbitrarily complicated functions.

While the overall neural network models a complicated function, its building block is a fairly basic unit called a *neuron*. The neuron represents a relatively simple function. The full neural network is made up of many neurons with weighted connections between them. It can be made to approximate any arbitrary target function underlying a particular problem of interest by manipulating the number of neurons, the connectivity between them, and the connection weights.

The variety and complexity of the functions a neural network can represent are known as its *expressive power*. Expressive power increases with the number of neurons in the neural network and the number of connections between them. The more complex the target function, the more expressive power will be needed in the neural network modeling it. How can we make a neural network model/approximate/express a specific target function corresponding to a particular problem of interest? Answer: we can adjust the following two aspects of the neural network:

- *Architecture*—The number of neurons and the connections between them
- *Parameter values*—The weights of the connection between neurons

The architecture is typically chosen based on the nature of the problem. Some popular architectures are reused frequently, and a neural network engineer typically chooses an architecture that is historically known to be effective for a problem similar to the problem at hand. We look at several popular architectures later in this book—for instance, in chapter 11. Once the architecture is set, we determine the parameter values through a process called *training*.

Neural networks can be classified into two major classes: *supervised* and *unsupervised*. In supervised neural networks, we identify the desired output values corresponding to a set of sampled input values for the problem we are trying to solve. The desired output for these sampled inputs is typically chosen manually using a process called *labeling* (aka *manual annotation* or *manual curation*). The overall set of <sampled input, desired output> pairs constitutes the *supervised training data*. The set of desired outputs for training data inputs is sometimes collectively referred to as the *ground truth* or *target output*.

During training, the parameter values (aka weights) are adjusted such that the network's outputs on training inputs match the corresponding ground truth as closely as possible. If all goes well, at the end of training, we are left with a neural network whose outputs on training inputs are close to the ground truth. This *trained* neural network is then deployed to the real world, where it performs *inferencing*—it generates output on inputs it has never seen before. If we have chosen the architecture with enough expressive power and properly trained the network with adequate training data, it should emit accurate results during inferencing. Note that we cannot *guarantee* correct results during inferencing; we can only make a probabilistic statement that our output has a p probability of being correct.

Unsupervised neural networks do not need the manually labeled ground truth—they just work on the training inputs. The manual labor involved in labeling the training data is expensive and bothersome. Consequently, considerable research effort is going into neural networks that are unsupervised, semi-supervised (a fraction of the training data is labeled manually), or self-supervised (labeled training data is created programmatically rather than manually). However, unsupervised and semi-supervised neural network technology is less mature at the time of this writing, and it is harder to achieve desired accuracy levels with them. Later in this book, we examine unsupervised approaches, including *variational autoencoders* (chapter 14). But for now, we mostly talk about supervised approaches.

It is important to note that nowhere in the architecture selection or training process do we need a closed-form representation of either the function being approximated (the target function) or the approximator function (the modeling function). This is important. In most cases, it is impossible to know the target function—all we know are sample input and ground-truth pairs (training data). As for the modeling function, even when we know the architecture of the modeling neural network, the overall function it represents is so complicated that it is virtually intractable. Thus, the fact that we do not need to know the target or modeling function in closed form is what makes the technology practical.

7.2 Expressing real-world problems: Target functions

Consider the classic investor's problem: to sell or not sell a stock. The problem inputs could be the purchase price, current price, whether the investor's favorite expert is advising to sell or not, and so on. The problem can be solved by a function that takes these inputs and outputs as 0 (do not sell) or 1 (sell). If we could model this function, we would have a mechanical solution to this real-world problem.

Like this example, most real-world problems can be expressed as target functions. We collect all quantifiable variables that can have a bearing on the outcome: these constitute the *input variables*. The input variables are expressed as numeric entities: scalars, vectors, matrices, and so on. The outputs are also expressed as numeric variables called the *output variables*. Given a specific input (say, specific values for purchase price and current price), our model function emits an output (0 or 1 indicating do not sell or sell) that is a solution to the problem for that specific input.

We usually denote input variables with the symbol x; a sequence of input variables is often expressed as a vector $\vec{x}$. Output variables are denoted with the symbol y. The overall target function is usually expressed as $y = f\left(\vec{x}\right)$. We will often use subscripts to denote various elements of a vector $(x_0, x_1, \cdots, x_i)$ and superscripts to denote input instances, as in $y^{(0)} = f\left(\vec{x}^{(0)}\right), y^{(1)} = f\left(\vec{x}^{(1)}\right), \cdots, y^{(i)} = f\left(\vec{x}^{(i)}\right)$. But in some cases, we will use subscripts to denote different items of the training data. The usage should be obvious from the context.

Numeric quantities can occur in two distinct forms: continuous and categorical. *Continuous variables* can take any of the infinitely many real number values in a given range. For instance, the stock price in our "to sell or not sell a stock" problem can take any value greater than zero. *Categorical variables* can take one of a finite set of allowed values, where the value represents a category. A special categorical case is a binary variable, where there are only two categories. For instance, expert advice in our stock-selling problem can take only two values: 0 or 1, corresponding to the two categories of advice, "do not sell" and "sell," respectively.

In this section, we discuss three distinct families of target functions: logical functions, general functions, and classifiers.

7.2.1 Logical functions in real-world problems

These are functions whose inputs and outputs are binary variables: variables that can take only two values, 0 (aka "no" or "don't fire") and 1 (aka "yes" or "fire"). Machines emulating logical functions are often added on top of separate machines performing other tasks, as will be evident from the following examples:

- *Logical OR*—To look at logical OR functions, let's bring back the mythical cat whose brain we discussed in chapter 1. Say we are trying to build a machine that helps the poor creature make the binary decision whether to run away from the object in front of it or approach the object and purr. Being very timid, this cat runs away from anything that looks hard or sharp. The only time it will approach and purr is when the object in front of it looks neither hard nor sharp. Let's assume a separate machine outputs a binary decision 0 (not hard) or 1 (hard). Another machine outputs a binary decision 0 (not sharp) or 1 (sharp). The logical OR machine combines the binary decisions from the two separate machines, as shown in figure 7.1a.

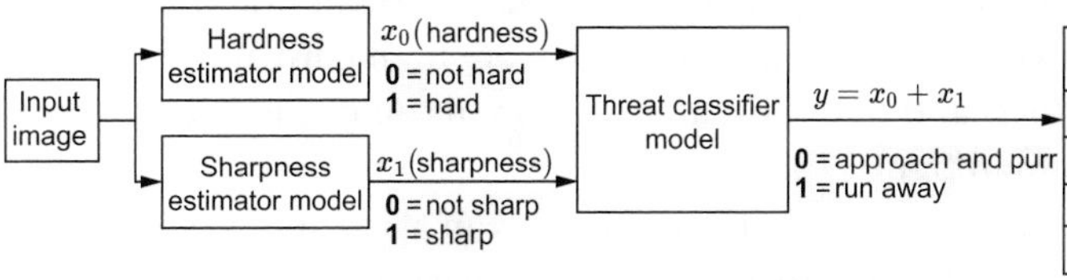

Truth table

x_0	x_1	$y = x_0 + x_1$
0	0	0
0	1	1
1	0	1
1	1	1

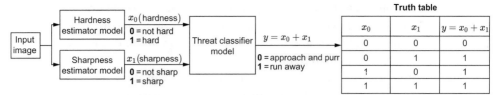

(a) Logical OR: a timid cat that runs away from things whose hardness exceeds threshold t_0 **OR** whose sharpness exceeds threshold t_1

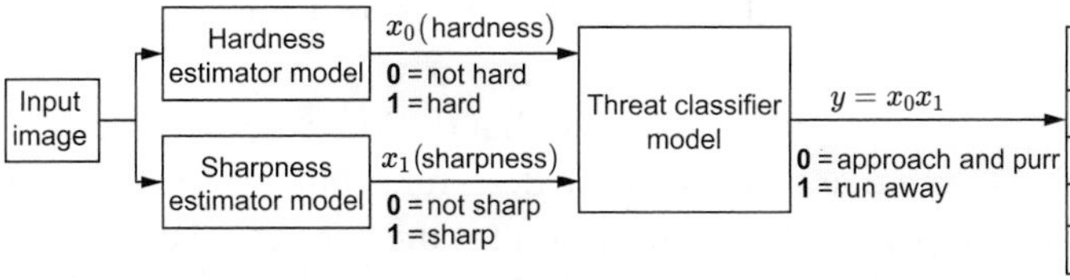

Truth table

x_0	x_1	$y = x_0 x_1$
0	0	0
0	1	0
1	0	0
1	1	1

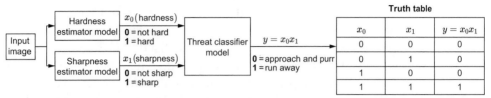

(b) Logical AND: a less timid cat that runs away from things whose hardness exceeds threshold t_0 **AND** whose sharpness exceeds threshold t_1

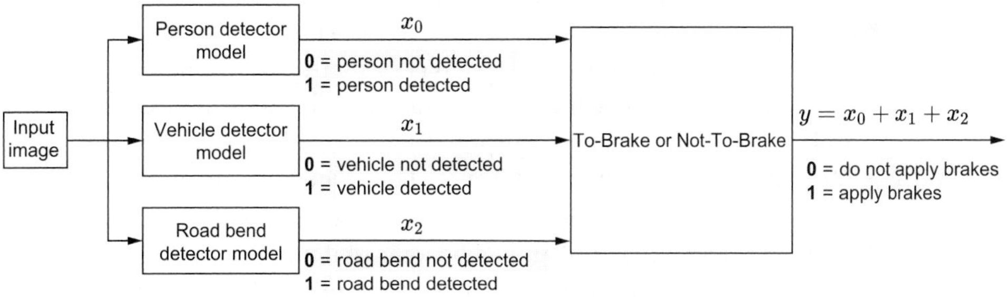

Truth table

x_0	x_1	x_2	$y = x_0 + x_1 + x_2$
0	0	0	0
0	0	1	1
0	1	0	1
0	1	1	1
1	0	0	1
1	0	1	1
1	1	0	1
1	1	1	1

(c) Multi-input logical OR: A self-driving car that applies the brake if it sees a person, vehicle, or bend in the road in front of it

Figure 7.1 Examples of logical operators (OR, AND) in real-life problems

- *Logical AND*—We also exemplify this in terms of the cat brain. Imagine a slightly less timid cat that runs away from things that are both hard and sharp. But it is not scared by hardness and sharpness alone. Its brain can be modeled by the system of machines shown in figure 7.1b.
- *Logical NOT*—Consider a machine that sounds an alarm if it sees any unauthorized person in a restricted access area. Let's assume that we also have a separate machine: a face detector that can recognize the faces of all authorized personnel. It emits a binary decision 1 (recognized face) or 0 (unrecognized face). The overall system takes the output of the face detector and performs a logical NOT operation on it.
- *Multi-input logical OR*—Imagine a machine that decides whether a self-driving car needs to brake. Assume that three separate detectors emit 1 if a person, vehicle, or bend in the road, respectively, is seen in front of the car. A brake must be applied if any of these separate detectors emits a 1. This is shown in figure 7.1c.
- *Multi-input logical AND*—Consider a machine that helps a venture capitalist decide whether to invest in a startup. Assume that three separate machines emit 1 when the following conditions are met: (1) the CEO has a track record of success, (2) the product elicits interest from targeted customers, and (3) the product is sufficiently novel, respectively. The machine will decide to invest if all three separate machines emit 1. Thus, the machine outputs 1 when condition (1) is met AND condition (2) is met AND condition (3) is met. This is an example of a three-input AND.
- *Logical XOR*—Suppose we are building a social media site. Assume we have a separate detector that, for any person, emits 1 if they like rock music and 0 otherwise. Using this information about two people, the problem is to decide whether they should be recommended as friends to each other. Friendship potential is high if they both like rock music or both dislike it. But if one person likes rock and the other dislikes it, they will probably not be good friends. Thus condition 1 is high rock-music affinity for person 1, and condition 2 is high rock-music affinity for person 2. The exclusive OR of the two conditions is 1 when one is true but the other is not. This machine outputs 1 if the NOT of the exclusive OR is true, meaning neither person likes rock music or both people like rock music. Figure 7.2 depicts this.
- *m-out-of-n trigger*—Imagine we are trying to create a face detector. We have already created separate part detectors for noses, eyes, lips, and ears. If we detect, say, any two of these together, we feel confident enough to declare a face. In computer vision, we often have a problem called *occlusion*, where an important object becomes invisible to the camera because another object blocks the camera's line of sight. Computer vision algorithms always try to be robust against occlusion, meaning they want to emit the right output even when occlusion occurs. This is why we do not want to mandate a positive signal from all the part detectors; we want to detect the face even when a few of the parts are occluded. Hence, our machine emits 1 when, say, two of the n parts (such as eyes and lips) are detected.

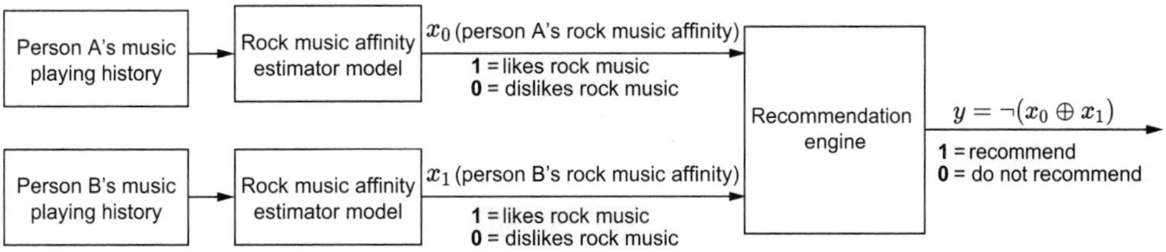

Truth table

x_0	x_1	$y = \neg(x_0 \oplus x_1)$
0	0	1
0	1	0
1	0	0
1	1	1

Figure 7.2 Example of logical NOT and XOR in a real-life problem. A social media system makes a friendship recommendation between persons A and B if and only if they both like or both dislike rock music. friendship = ¬ (rock-music-affinity-of-A ⊕ rock-music-affinity-of-B) where ¬ ⟹ logical NOT and ⊕ ⟹ logical XOR.

7.2.2 *Classifier functions in real-world problems*

A classifier is a function whose output is categorical. Inputs can be either continuous or categorical. Thus, given an input, the function chooses one category (aka class) or another. For instance, a face detector can be a classifier. Its input is an image, and its output is a categorical (binary) variable that takes one of two possible values: 1 (face) or 0 (not face). This is shown in figure 7.3a. As we saw in section 2.3, any image can be represented by a vector $\vec{x}$. Accordingly, the classifier function for the face detector

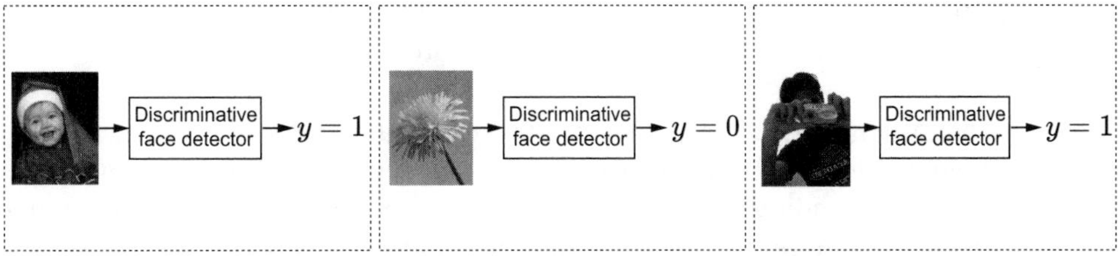

(a) Discriminative face detector (classifier). The output is categorical (face or not face).

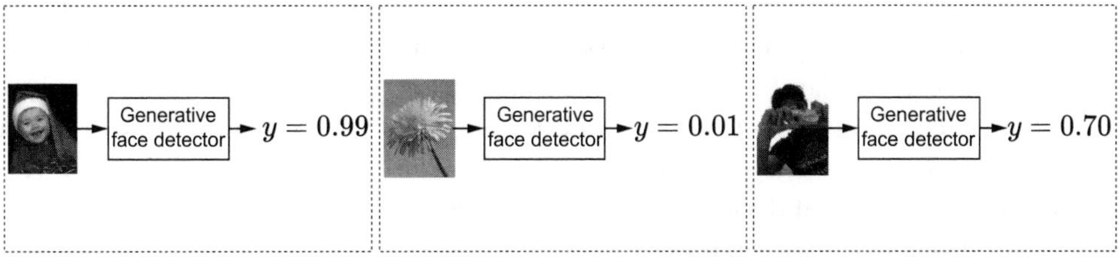

(b) Generative face detector. The output is continuous (the probability of an image containing a face).

Figure 7.3 The face detector takes an image as input and outputs a categorical or continuous variable.

can be written as the function

$$\phi(\vec{x}) = \begin{cases} 0 & \text{not a face} \\ 1 & \text{face} \end{cases}$$

How to design the function $\phi(\vec{x})$ is one of the primary topics of this chapter.

Geometrically, each scalar input variable forms a separate dimension in the input space. All possible combinations of these scalar input variables together form a multidimensional space called the *input space* (or feature space). Each specific combination of input values is a point (represented by the input vector $\vec{x}$) in this space.

For instance, in an image, each pixel can be taken as a separate input scalar variable that can take any 3-byte pixel color value between $RGB = \overline{00}\,\overline{00}\,\overline{00}$ (hex) (black) and $RGB = \overline{FF}\,\overline{FF}\,\overline{FF}$ (hex) (white), with successive bytes (demarcated by an overline) representing red, green, and blue components of the pixel, respectively. The input has as many dimensions as the number of pixels in the image. For instance, a 224×224 image forms a $50,176$-dimensional input space. Each specific image is a single point in this space. The face-classifier function $\phi(\vec{x})$ maps that point to either 0 (not face) or 1 (face).

For a simpler instance, consider our familiar cat brain example from section 1.4. There are two input variables: x_0, indicating *hardness*; and x_1, indicating *sharpness*. The overall input space is two-dimensional, in which a specific input combination is denoted by the 2D vector $\vec{x} = \begin{bmatrix} x_0 \\ x_1 \end{bmatrix}$. Our goal is to construct a machine that, given any input combination of hardness and sharpness, classifies it as either *threatening* or *nonthreatening*. This is equivalent to designing a function that maps arbitrary input vectors $\vec{x} \in \mathbb{R}^2$ to 0 or 1:

$$\phi(\vec{x}) = \begin{cases} 0 & \text{not a threat} \\ 1 & \text{threat} \end{cases}$$

GEOMETRICAL VIEW OF CLASSIFIERS: DECISION BOUNDARIES

Geometrically speaking, a classifier partitions the feature space into separate regions, each corresponding to a class. For instance, consider the simple cat-brain model from section 1.4. There are two input variables, hardness (x_0) and sharpness (x_1). Hence we have a two-dimensional input feature space that geometrically corresponds to a plane. Each combination of hardness and sharpness is represented by a specific vector $\vec{x} = [x_0, x_1]$ corresponding to a *point* on the plane. Note that unlike the machines shown in figures 7.1a and 7.1b, here we are talking about a machine that takes as input a *pair* of continuous values (hardness and sharpness)—that is, a point on the two-dimensional feature plane—and maps it to a discrete space corresponding to the *threat* versus *not a threat* categorical decision. This is illustrated in figure 7.4a.

The solid curve separates the *threat* and *not-threat* regions. Such curves that separate regions in input space belonging to different classes are known as *decision boundaries*. Estimating the decision boundary is effectively the same as building the classifier.

The dashed line represents an approximate linear decision boundary that does the job crudely but misclassifies the points between the solid and dashed curves. (Linear decision boundaries are easier to represent with neural networks, but they are inadequate for complex problems.)

Let's look briefly at the solid curve in figure 7.4a. At low hardness values, the sharpness threshold is high (if the object in front of the cat is not very hard, it must be very sharp to qualify as a threat). As hardness increases from $x_0 = 0$ to $x_0 = 20$, this threshold (the sharpness required to qualify as a threat) drops more or less linearly. Beyond $x_0 = 20$, the threshold drops at a much faster pace—if the object in front of the cat is sufficiently

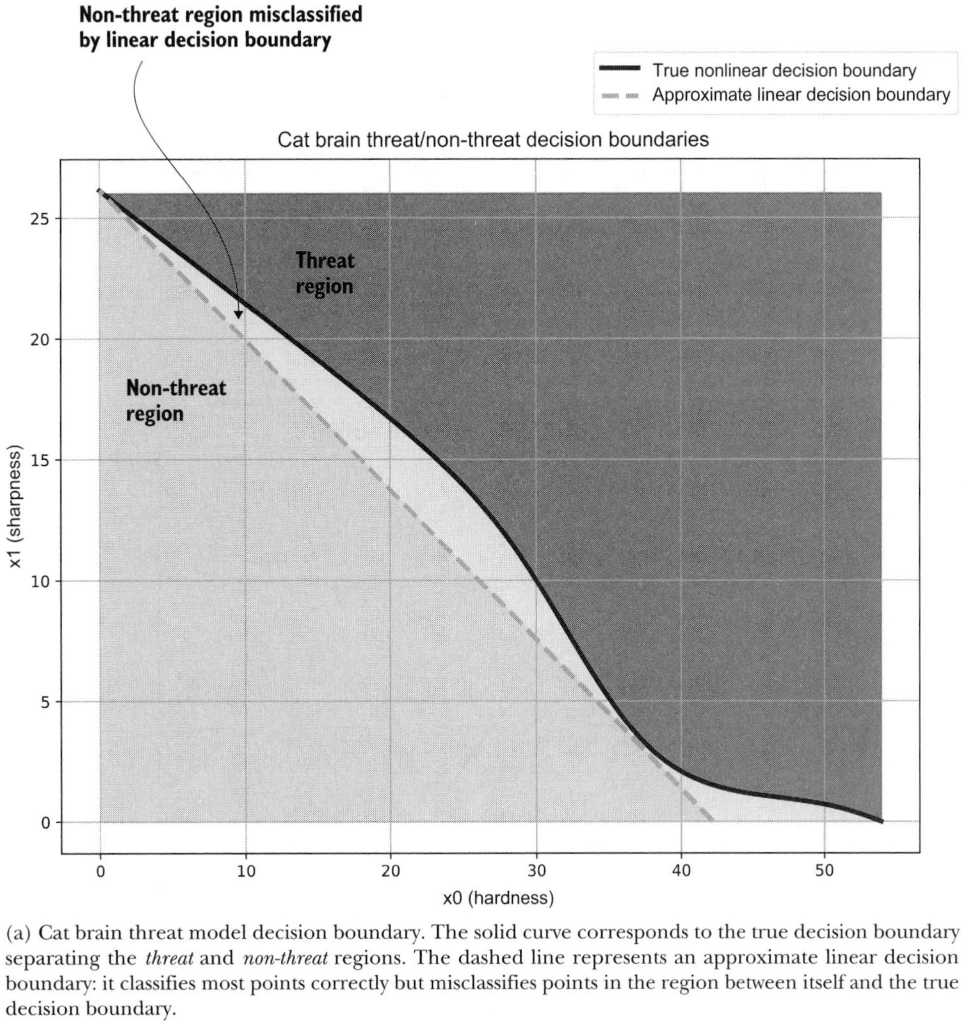

(a) Cat brain threat model decision boundary. The solid curve corresponds to the true decision boundary separating the *threat* and *non-threat* regions. The dashed line represents an approximate linear decision boundary: it classifies most points correctly but misclassifies points in the region between itself and the true decision boundary.

In practice, we get some sample points from each region through manual labeling.

Figure 7.4 Classifiers, decision boundaries, and training data. Data points from different classes are marked with different symbols (plus and dot). (*Figure continued on next page*)

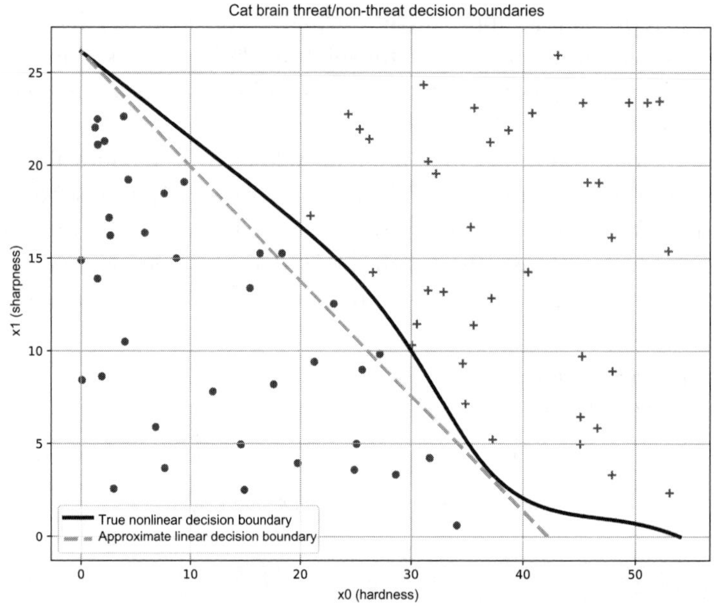

(b) Good training data. Sample points from each class roughly span the region of input space belonging to the class.

This yields a good decision boundary (solid line).

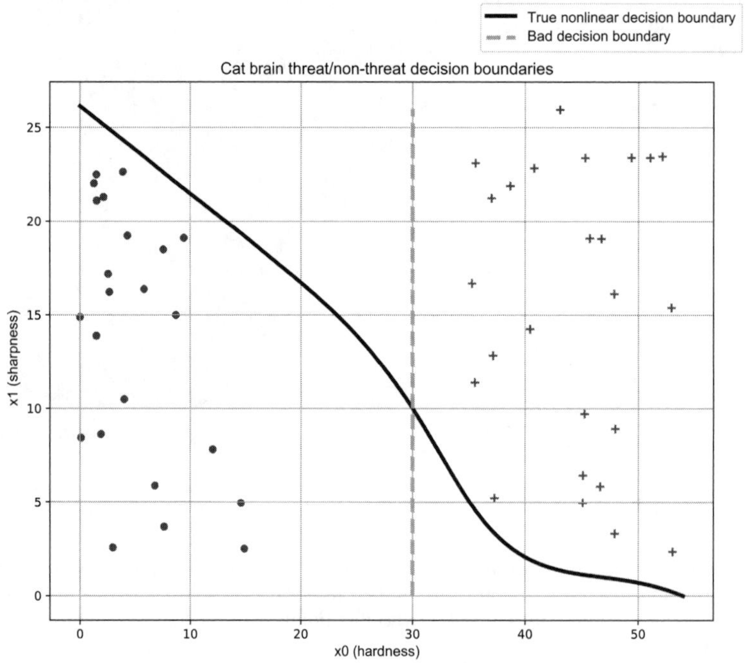

(c) Bad training data. Sample points from individual classes do not span the region of input space belonging to the class.

This yields a bad decision boundary (dashed line).

Figure 7.4 ***(Continued from previous page)***

hard, it need not be very sharp to pose a threat. Beyond $x_0 = 52$ or so, sharpness ceases to matter: sufficiently hard objects are threats even if they are not sharp. This is inherently a nonlinear situation.

To simplify neural network implementation, we might want to approximate the solid curve with a straight line—the dashed line is not too bad an approximation—but doing so entails errors. As shown in figure 7.4a, the region between the true and approximate curves will be wrongly classified.

Figure 7.4a is only a schematic. In reality, we do not know the exact regions in the input space that correspond to the classes of interest. We identify—via human labeling—some sample points on the input space, along with their correct class (the ground truth). Such a sampled set of <input point, correct output aka ground truth> pairs is called *training data*. An example training data set for the cat brain problem is shown in figure 7.4b (ground-truth training data points from different classes are marked with separate symbols: plus and dot, respectively). The decision boundary we create by training a neural network is optimized to classify the training data points (and nothing more) as nicely as possible. If the training data points' distribution is a reasonable reflection of the true distribution—that is, the sample points from each class more or less span the entire region in the input space corresponding to that class—the decision boundary obtained by training on that data set will be good. But if, as illustrated in figure 7.4c, the training data does not reflect the true distribution of the classes in the input space, the decision boundary learned by training on that data may be bad.

Unlike the cat brain example, most real-life input spaces have hundreds or even thousands of dimensions. The idea of a decision boundary as a hypersurface continues to hold in higher dimensions. For higher-dimensional input spaces, hyperplanes function as linear separators. In simpler problems with higher-dimensional input spaces, such linear separators suffice. In more complicated cases, we can have other curved hypersurfaces as nonlinear separators. We may not be able to visualize hyperspaces in our head, but we can form mental pictures with 3D analogs. Figure 7.5 shows some planar decision boundaries in 3D input space. Figure 7.5a shows a 3D space of input vectors along with a set of training data points. The task is to classify them into two classes. In this simple situation, the training points can be partitioned with a hyperplanar decision boundary. Figures 7.5b and 7.5c show some planes that partition the training data poorly, and figure 7.5d shows an optimal planar separator. The only differences between these planes are the values of $\vec{w}$ and b. This indicates that there are values of $\vec{w}$ and b that optimally partition the training data. These optimal values are determined by a process called *training*, which we discuss in detail in the next chapter.

SIGNIFICANCE OF SIGN: MATHEMATICAL EXPRESSIONS FOR DECISION BOUNDARIES

In a space with input vectors $\vec{x}$, the equation $\phi\left(\vec{x}\right) = 0$ represents a surface. If the space is 2D, the surface becomes a curve. For instance, the straight dashed line in figure 7.4b can be viewed as a special case of $\phi\left(\vec{x}\right) \equiv \vec{w}^T\vec{x} + b = 0$, which in this case becomes

$$0.62x_0 + x_1 - 26.14 = \begin{bmatrix} 0.62 \\ 1 \end{bmatrix}^T \begin{bmatrix} x_0 \\ x_1 \end{bmatrix} - 26.14 = 0$$

That is,

$$\vec{w} = \begin{bmatrix} 0.62 \\ 1 \end{bmatrix}$$
$$b = -26.14$$

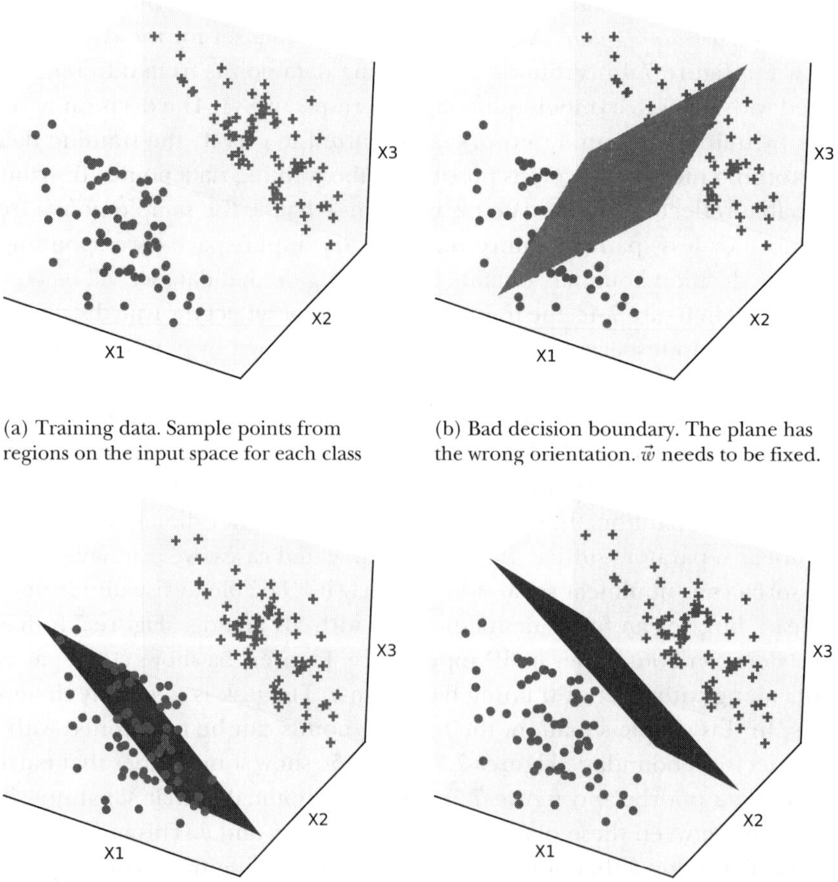

(a) Training data. Sample points from regions on the input space for each class

(b) Bad decision boundary. The plane has the wrong orientation. $\vec{w}$ needs to be fixed.

(c) Bad decision boundary. The plane has the correct orientation but the wrong position. b needs to be fixed.

(d) Optimal decision boundary. The plane has correct $\vec{w}$, b. Properly trained.

Figure 7.5 Classifiers with a linear decision boundary (hyperplane). Such decision boundaries are created by perceptrons (introduced in section 7.3.3). Data points from different classes are marked with different symbols (plus and dot).

In 3D, we have surfaces like planes and spheres. In more than three dimensions, we have hyperplanes, hyperspheres, and so on. For instance, the plane in figure 7.6 corresponds to

$$\phi(\vec{x}) \equiv x_0 + x_1 + x_2 = \begin{bmatrix} 1 \\ 1 \\ 1 \end{bmatrix}^T \begin{bmatrix} x_0 \\ x_1 \\ x_1 \end{bmatrix} + 0 = 0 \tag{7.1}$$

That is,

$$\vec{w} = \begin{bmatrix} 1 \\ 1 \\ 1 \end{bmatrix}$$

$$b = 0$$

In section 3.1.4, we saw that given any point $\vec{x}$ in the space, the sign of $\phi(\vec{x})$ tells us which side of the surface $\phi(\vec{x}) = 0$ the point $\vec{x}$ belongs to. Thus, if we estimate the surface corresponding to the decision boundary, given any point, we can determine the partition to which that point belongs. In other words, we can classify the point. Estimating the decision boundary is equivalent to building the classifier. For instance, the line in figure 7.4b corresponds to $0.62x_0 + x_1 - 26.14 = 0$. The points with $0.62x_0 + x_1 - 26.14 < 0$ are on one side and are indicated with dots. The points with $0.62x_0 + x_1 - 26.14 > 0$ are on the other side and indicated with plus signs (+).

The idea extends to higher dimensions. Figure 7.6 shows the same idea in a 3D input space. The plane corresponds to the equation $x_0 + x_1 + x_2 = 0$. The points with $x_0 + x_1 + x_2 < 0$ are on one side (indicated by – in figure 7.6), and points with $x_0 + x_1 + x_2 > 0$ are on the other side (indicated by + in figure 7.6).

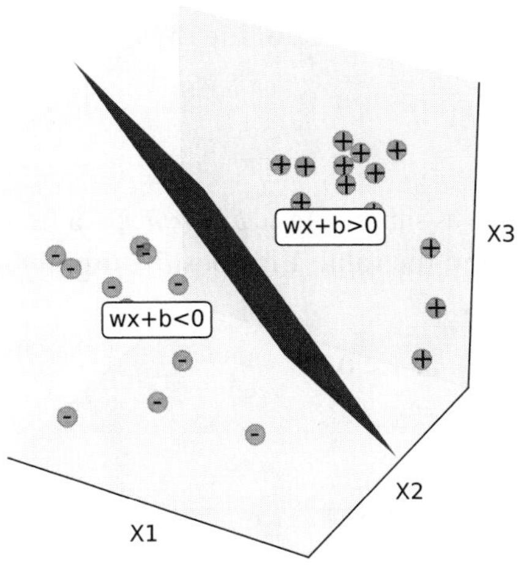

Figure 7.6 Significance of sign for $\phi(\vec{x}) \equiv \vec{w}^T \vec{x} + b$. Note that $\phi(\vec{x}) = 0$ implies that $\vec{x}$ lies on the plane, $\phi(\vec{x})$ negative implies one side of the plane, and $\phi(\vec{x})$ positive implies the other side of the plane.

7.2.3 General functions in real-world problems

There are problems where a categorical output variable will not do and a continuous output variable is called for: for instance, estimating the speed at which a self-driving vehicle should run. Using inputs like the speed limit for the road being traversed, speeds of neighboring vehicles, and so on, we need to estimate how fast the self-driving vehicle should go.

Another noteworthy situation where the output needs to be a continuous rather than a categorical variable is when we are modeling the *probability* of some event occurring. For instance, let's again consider the face detector. Given an image as input, the face classification function emits 0 to indicate *not a face* and 1 to indicate *face*. Such functions are called *discriminative*. We could also have a function that outputs the probability of the image containing a face. Such functions are called *generative*, and an example is shown in figure 7.3b.

7.3 The basic building block or neuron: The perceptron

In section 7.2, we saw that most real-world problems can be expressed as functions. This is good news, but the bad news is that these functions are usually unknown, and the functions underlying various problems are wildly different from each other. It may be possible to estimate them, but if we attack them individually without adopting a generic framework, there is little hope of developing a repeatable solution.

Neural networks provide an effective framework that can mechanically model an extremely wide variety of complicated functions. Furthermore, the target function need not be known in a closed form—sample input-output pairs are enough. They can represent (model) very complicated functions by connecting instances of a fairly simple building block, unsurprisingly called a *neuron*. In other words, the complete neural network can have huge *expressive power* even though a single neuron is very simple. Later, in sections 7.3.4, 7.4, 7.5, and so on, we discuss how neural networks model functions of increasing complexity. But first, in this section, we examine the building block: the neuron.

7.3.1 The Heaviside step function

The *Heaviside step function*, often referred to as simply the *step function*, is a function that takes the value 0 for negative arguments and the value 1 for positive arguments:

$$\phi\left(x\right) = \begin{cases} 0 & \text{if } x < 0 \\ 1 & \text{if } x >= 0 \end{cases} \tag{7.2}$$

Equation 7.2 is equivalent to the following algorithm. Figure 7.7 shows the graph of this equation.

Algorithm 7.1 Heaviside step function as an algorithm

if $x < 0$ **then**
  return 0
else
  return 1
end if

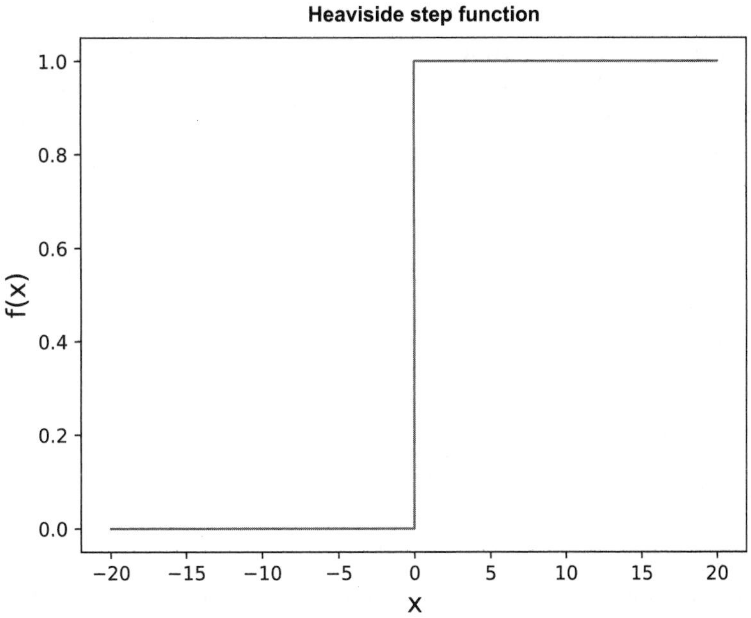

Figure 7.7 Heaviside step function graph

7.3.2 *Hyperplanes*

In section 2.8, we discussed hyperplanes. They are represented by equation 2.14. In figure 2.9, we saw the role that hyperplanes play in classifiers; we briefly revisit the idea here.

In section 2.1.1, we saw that d-element vectors are geometrical analogs of points in a d-dimensional space. Let $\vec{x}$ denote the vectors (or, equivalently, points) in the space of input vectors. For a fixed vector $\vec{w}$ and fixed scalar b, the equation for a hyperplane in that space is

$$\vec{w}^T\vec{x} + b = 0$$

(meaning all points $\vec{x}$ satisfying this equation lie on the plane). The vector $\vec{w}$ is the normal to the plane. This becomes intuitively obvious when we observe that if we take any two points on the plane, say $\vec{x_0}$ and $\vec{x_1}$, then

$$\vec{w}^T\vec{x_0} + b = 0$$

$$\vec{w}^T\vec{x_1} + b = 0$$

Subtracting, we get

$$\vec{w}^T(\vec{x_1} - \vec{x_0}) = 0$$

But $(\vec{x_1} - \vec{x_0})$ is the vector joining two arbitrary points on the plane. This means the *line joining any pair of points on the plane is perpendicular to* $\vec{w}$ (in section 2.5.2, we discussed dot products, and in section 2.6, we saw that if the dot product between two vectors is zero, the vectors are orthogonal—perpendicular to each other). Hence, $\vec{w}$ is orthogonal to all lines lying on the plane. In other words, $\vec{w}$ is normal to the plane.

The hyperplane $\vec{w}^T\vec{x} + b = 0$ partitions the space into two regions with distinct signs for the expression $\vec{w}^T\vec{x} + b$. That is to say, the hyperplane can serve as a decision boundary, as shown in figure 7.6. Not just a hyperplane but any hypersurface can partition space in this fashion. This is true for any dimensionality of $\vec{x}$:

- If the expression $\vec{w}^T\vec{x} + b$ evaluates to *zero*, the point $\vec{x}$ lies *on the hyperplane* $\vec{w}^T\vec{x} + b = 0$.
- If the sign of the expression $\vec{w}^T\vec{x} + b$ is *negative*, the point $\vec{x}$ lies on *one side of the hyperplane.*
- If the sign of the expression $\vec{w}^T\vec{x} + b$ is *positive*, the point $\vec{x}$ lies on the *other side of the hyperplane.*

7.3.3 Perceptrons and classification

The perceptron combines the step function and a hyperplane into a single function. It represents the function

$$P(\vec{x}) \equiv \phi\left(\vec{w}^T\vec{x} + b\right) \tag{7.3}$$

where ϕ is the Heaviside step function from equation 7.2. Combining our insights from sections 7.3.1 and 7.3.2, we can see that the perceptron function maps all points on one side of the $(\vec{w}, b)$ plane to zero and all points on the other side of the same plane to 1. In other words, it performs as a linear classifier, with the $(\vec{w}, b)$ plane as the decision boundary. Figure 7.8 graphs the perceptron function for a 2D input space (the graph itself is in 3D space: it maps points on one side of the decision boundary to the plane $Z = 0$ and points on the other side to the plane $Z = 1$).

Of course, in real life, we do not know the exact regions corresponding to classes. Rather, we have sampled input points with their manually labeled classes as training data. The decision surface must be constructed based on this training data only. In figure 7.4, we saw an example decision boundary in 2D along with some good and bad training data sets. To get a mental picture of sampled training data sets in higher dimensions, look at figure 7.5a again. In this simple situation, a single hyperplanar decision boundary is sufficient to partition the training points. This means a single perceptron-based neural network will suffice as a classifier. Figures 7.5b and 7.5c depict some planes (perceptrons with specific $(\vec{w}, b)$ values) that poorly partition the training data. Figure 7.5d shows an optimal perceptron (planar separator). This tells us that there are good values of $\vec{w}$ and b that optimally partition the training data, as well as

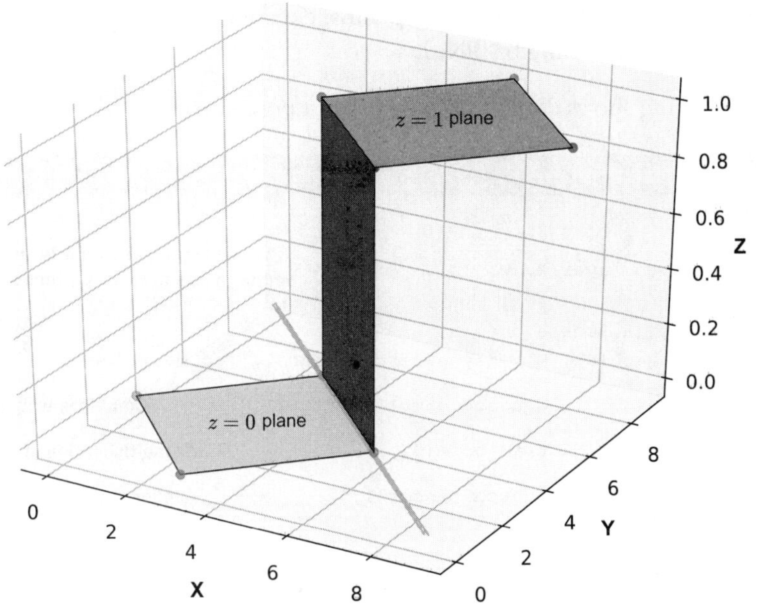

Figure 7.8 Graph of the perceptron function (equation 7.3) for a two-variable input space. Note that although the input space is 2D, the perceptron graph is 3D. The decision boundary is indicated by the long diagonal straight line. It maps points on one side of the decision boundary to the $Z = 0$ plane and the points on the other side to the $Z = 1$ plane.

bad values. As mentioned earlier, good values are determined through training, which we cover in chapter 8.

The perceptron effectively partitions with a *planar* decision surface. This works only in simple problems. For an instance of a situation where a planar decision surface will *not* work, see figure 7.9. It depicts a problem where one class maps to the set of points sandwiched between two planes and the other class to the rest of the points in the input space. It is impossible to achieve the required partitioning with a single plane, so such a decision boundary cannot be modeled with a single perceptron. Later we will see how to model such complex decision boundaries with multiple perceptrons.

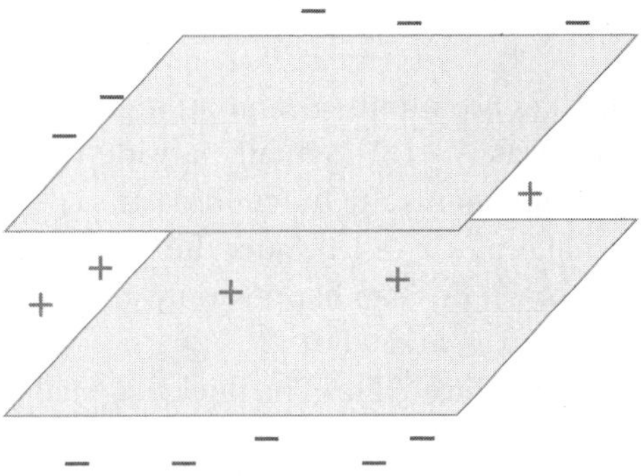

Figure 7.9 Multiplane decision boundary. One class corresponds to the points in the region sandwiched between the planes (marked +). The remaining points correspond to the other class (marked –). This decision boundary *cannot* be represented with a single plane.

NOTE Fully functional code for perceptrons, executable via Jupyter Notebook, can be found at http://mng.bz/9Ne7.

The following listing shows the PyTorch code for a perceptron.

Listing 7.1 Perceptron

```
def fully_connected_layer(X, w,  b):

    X = torch.cat((X, torch.ones(
            [X.shape[0], 1], dtype=torch.float32)), dim=1)

    W = torch.cat((W, b.unsqueeze(dim=1)), dim=1)

    y = torch.matmul(W, X.transpose(0, 1))

    y = torch.heaviside(y, torch.tensor(1.0))

    return y.transpose(0, 1)

def Perceptron(X, W, b):
    return fully_connected_layer(X, W, b)
```

- def fully_connected_layer: $X : n \times d$ tensor; each row is an input vector of size d. $w : m \times d$ tensor.
- X = torch.cat: Adds a column of 1s. $X \rightarrow n \times (d+1)$ tensor.
- W = torch.cat: Combines weights and biases
- y = torch.matmul: Matrix multiplication of X and W
- y = torch.heaviside: Applies the Heaviside step function
- def Perceptron: A single perceptron

7.3.4 Modeling common logic gates with perceptrons

Neural networks provide a structured way of modeling complex functions by connecting—via weighted edges—repeated instances of a simple building block called the perceptron. In this section, we explore the idea of function modeling via perceptrons. We start with modeling extremely simple logical functions (AND, OR, NOT, voting) that can be represented with single perceptrons. Then we look at the XOR function, one of the simplest functions that *cannot* be represented with a single perceptron; we see that it *can* be modeled with *multiple* perceptrons. Next we discuss Cybenko's theorem, which states that most functions of interest can be modeled with as much accuracy as we want via perceptrons, with a single hidden layer between inputs and outputs. Unfortunately, this is less practical than it sounds: the catch is that although any function can be modeled to any accuracy, there is no limit on how many perceptrons are required to do the modeling. The more complicated the target function is, the more perceptrons are required. In practice, we often use many layers instead of one.

A PERCEPTRON FOR LOGICAL AND

Figure 7.10a depicts this perceptron. It takes two inputs, x_0 and x_1, which are weighted with $w_0 = 1$ and $w_1 = 1$, respectively; the bias is -1.5 (actually, a wide range of bias values will do). Overall, the perceptron implements the function $\phi\,(x_0 + x_1 - 1.5)$. This function emits 1 when $x_0 + x_1 - 1.5 \geq 0$: that is, $x_0 + x_1 \geq 1.5$. Since the variables are binary (meaning they can only take the value 0 or 1), this can happen only when both inputs are 1. If either is zero, their sum is less than 1.5, and y is 0.

The situation is depicted geometrically in figure 7.11a. The thick diagonal line corresponds to $x_0 + x_1 \geq 1.5$. It partitions the plane into unshaded and shaded half-planes.

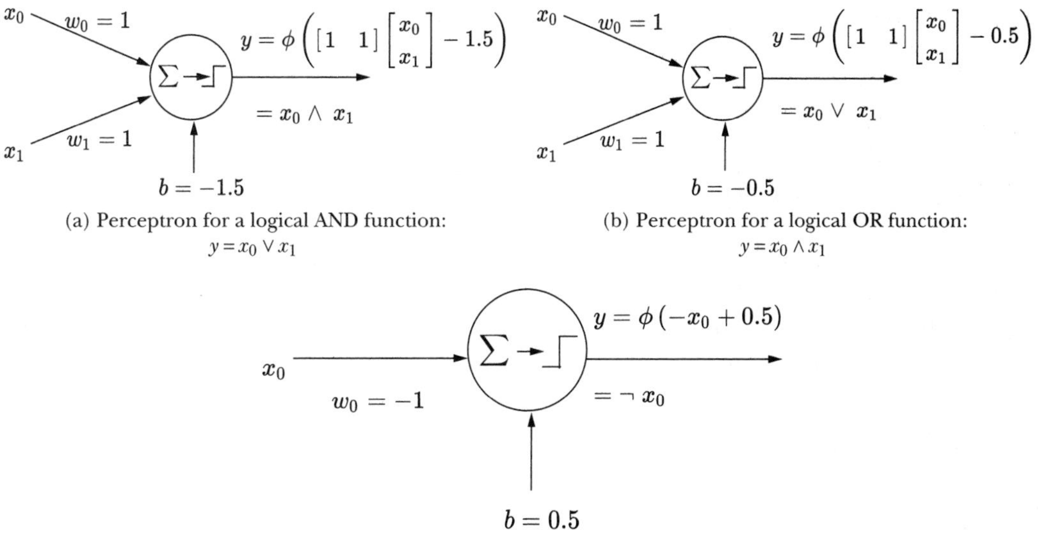

(a) Perceptron for a logical AND function: $y = x_0 \vee x_1$

(b) Perceptron for a logical OR function: $y = x_0 \wedge x_1$

(c) Perceptron for a logical NOT function: $y = \neg x_0$

Figure 7.10 Perceptrons for simple logical functions. A perceptron is depicted by a circle with summation followed by a step function to remind us of equation 7.3. Inputs and outputs for logical functions are binary, meaning they can be either 0 or 1.

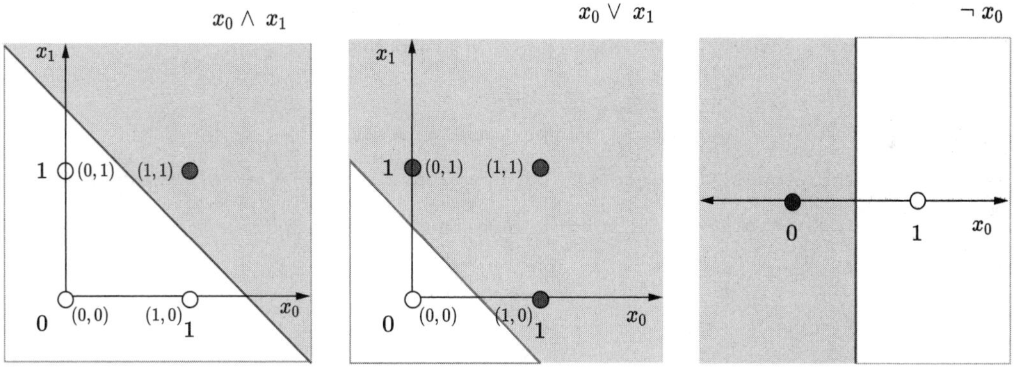

(a) Logical AND decision boundary: $x_0 + x_1 = 1.5$

(b) Logical OR decision boundary: $x_0 + x_1 = 0.5$

(c) Logical NOT decision boundary: $x_0 = 0.5$

Figure 7.11 Geometrical views for the perceptrons in figure 7.10. Each dot represents an input point (a $[x_0 \;\; x_1]$ vector). The shaded dots map to an output value of 1, and the unshaded dots map to an output value of 0. The thick line indicates the decision boundary.

All points on the unshaded half-plane have an output value $y = 0$, and all points on the shaded half-plane have the output value $y = 1$. There are only four possible input points: $(x_0 = 1, x_1 = 1)$, $(x_0 = 1, x_1 = 1)$, $(x_0 = 1, x_1 = 1)$, $(x_0 = 1, x_1 = 1)$. The point $(x_0 = 1, x_1 = 1)$ falls on the shaded side and the others on the unshaded side—which is exactly the logical AND function.

A PERCEPTRON FOR LOGICAL OR

Figure 7.10b depicts this perceptron. It takes two inputs, x_0 and x_1, which are weighted with $w_0 = 1$ and $w_1 = 1$, respectively; the bias is -0.5. Overall, the perceptron implements the function $\phi\,(x_0 + x_1 - 0.5)$. This function emits 1 when $x_0 + x_1 - 0.5 \geq 0$: that is, $x_0 + x_1 \geq 0.5$. Since the variables are binary (0 or 1), this can happen when either or both inputs are 1. If and only if both of them are zero, their sum is zero (less than 0.5), and y is 0.

The situation is shown geometrically in figure 7.11b. The thick line corresponds to $x_0 + x_1 \geq 0.5$, partitioning the input plane into an unshaded half-plane (all points on this half-plane have output $y = 0$) and a shaded half-plane (output $y = 1$). Of the four possible input points, (0, 0) falls on the unshaded side ($y = 1$) and the remaining three on the shaded side ($y = 1$)—which is exactly the logical OR function.

A PERCEPTRON FOR LOGICAL NOT

This perceptron is shown in figures 7.10c and 7.11c, which should be self-explanatory by now.

> **NOTE** Fully functional code for modeling various logical gates using perceptrons, executable via Jupyter Notebook, can be found at http://mng.bz/jBRr.

Listing 7.2 Modeling logical gates using perceptrons

```
# Logical AND
X = torch.tensor([[0., 0.],          ← Input data points
                  [0., 1.],
                  [1., 0.],
                  [1., 1.]], dtype=torch.float32)

W = torch.tensor([[1.0, 1.0]], dtype=torch.float32)     ← Instantiates the weights

b = torch.tensor([-1.5])     ← Instantiates the bias

Y = Perceptron(X=X, W=W, b=b, activation=torch.heaviside)     ← Output


# Logical OR
X = torch.tensor([[0., 0.],
                  [0., 1.],
                  [1., 0.],
                  [1., 1.]], dtype=torch.float32)
W = torch.tensor([[1.0, 1.0]], dtype=torch.float32)
b = torch.tensor([-1.5])
Y = Perceptron(X=X, W=W, b=b, activation=torch.heaviside)


# Logical NOT
X = torch.tensor([[0],
                  [1.]
                  ], dtype=torch.float32)
W = torch.tensor([[-1.0]], dtype=torch.float32)
b = torch.tensor([0.5])
Y = Perceptron(X=X, W=W, b=b, activation=torch.heaviside)
```

7.4 Toward more expressive power: Multilayer perceptrons (MLPs)

There is a remarkably simple logical function that, somewhat surprisingly, cannot be modeled with a single perceptron: XOR. We discuss it now.

7.4.1 MLP for logical XOR

Figure 7.12a shows the four possible input points on the plane and how the plane needs to be partitioned to model the XOR function. The points (0, 0), (1, 1) (unshaded) both map to output 0 and should be on the same side of the decision boundary, while the

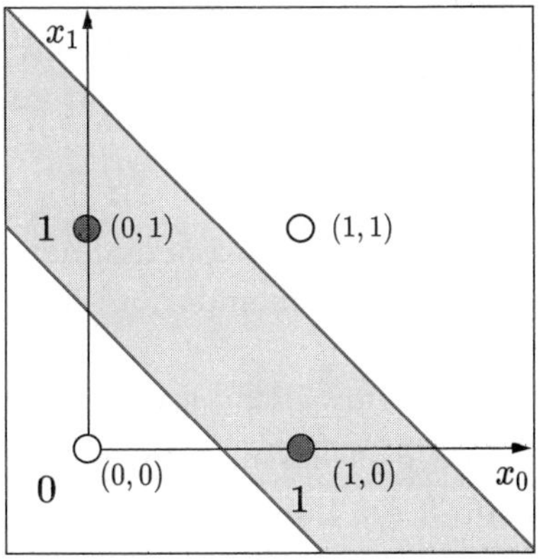

(a) Geometric view of the logical XOR perceptron. The decision boundary has *two* lines, so using a single perceptron is impossible.

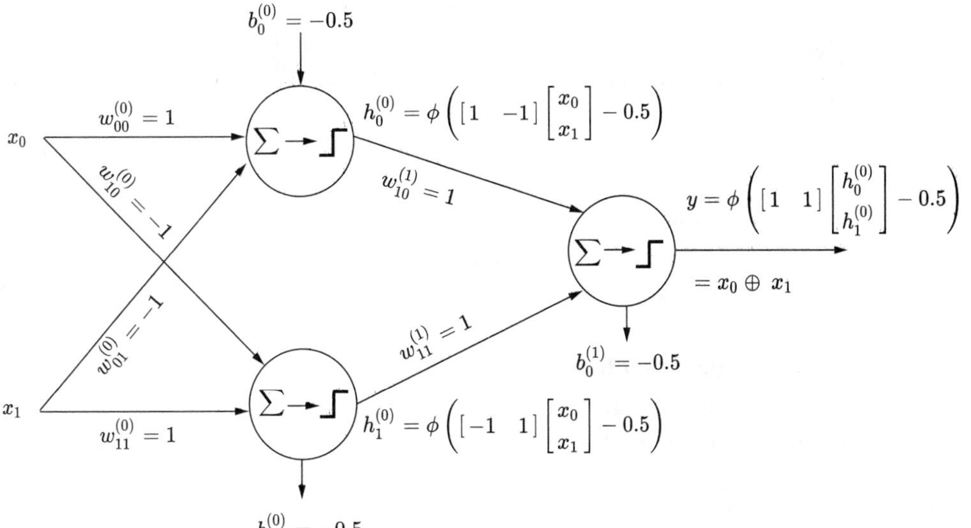

(b) MLP for the logical XOR function. Note that weights and biases have superscripts in parentheses indicating the layer index. This is a two-layered network. Layer 0 is hidden.

Figure 7.12 Logical XOR: Geometric and perceptron view

points (0, 1), (1, 0) (shaded) map to output value 1 and should be on the other side of the decision boundary.

It is easy to see that it is impossible to draw a single straight line in this plane such that the shaded points are on one side and the unshaded points are on the other. Remember, a perceptron essentially introduces a linear decision boundary. Hence it is impossible to have a single perceptron modeling this function.

However, it is possible to model the logical XOR function via multiple perceptrons. One such model is shown in figure 7.12b.

7.5 Layered networks of perceptrons: MLPs or neural networks

The XOR example tells us that we cannot do much with single perceptrons. We must connect more than one perceptron into a network to solve practical problems. This is a *neural network*. How do we organize such a network of connected perceptrons?

7.5.1 Layering

Layering is the most popular way to organize perceptrons into a neural network. Figure 7.12b is our first example of an MLP—most of the remainder of the book talks about MLPs.

Note how the perceptrons in the XOR network (figure 7.12b) are organized:

- The layers are numbered with increasing integers from input to output.
- The output of a perceptron in layer i is only fed as input to perceptrons in layer $i+1$. No other connections are allowed. This keeps the network manageable and facilitates updating the weights during training via a technique called *backpropagation*, which we discuss in the next chapter.
- Outputs of all layers but the last are invisible (do not directly contribute to the output). Such layers are called *hidden layers*. In figure 7.12b, layer 0 is hidden.
- Each weight and bias element belongs to one and only one layer. Throughout this book, we indicate the layer index for a weight or bias element as a superscript within parentheses.
- MLPs with two or more hidden layers can be called *deep neural networks*. This is the origin of the word *deep* in *deep learning*.

7.5.2 Modeling logical functions with MLPs

Any logical function can be expressed as a truth table. Hence, if we can prove that all truth tables can be implemented via MLPs, we are done. This is the approach we take here.

NOTE In the following discussion, no symbol (à la multiplication) between two variables indicates logical AND, and a + symbol indicates logical OR.

Table 7.1 Truth table for the logical function $y = \bar{x}_0 x_1 + x_0 \bar{x}_1$

x_0	x_1	y
0	0	0
0	1	1
1	0	1
1	1	0

Let's start with a simple two-variable logical functions $y = \bar{x}_0 x_1 + x_0 \bar{x}_1$. Table 7.1 shows the corresponding truth table. To create the equivalent MLP, we must pick the rows corresponding to $y = 1$. Each row can be expressed as an AND of the input variables or their complements. For instance, the row $x_0 = 0$ and $x_1 = 1, y = 1$ corresponds to $\bar{x}_0 x_1$—the first term of the function we are trying to implement—and can be implemented by the perceptron shown in figure 7.13a. The row $x_0 = 1$ and $x_1 = 0, y = 1$ corresponds to $x_0 \bar{x}_1$—the second term of the function we are trying to implement—and can be implemented by the perceptron shown in figure 7.13b. We have implemented the individual terms of the function; all that remains is to OR them together into a final MLP, as shown in figure 7.13c. This logical function is our old friend, logical XOR, and the overall function in figure 7.13 is the same as figure 7.12. In this fashion, arbitrary logical expressions in any number of variables can be modeled using MLPs.

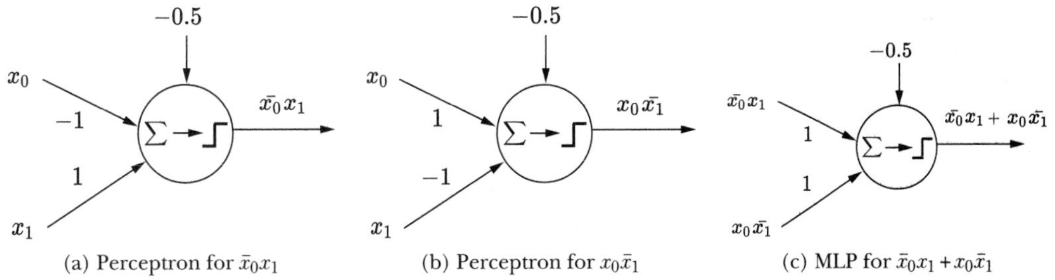

Figure 7.13 MLP for the logical function corresponding to table 7.1

Listing 7.3 Multilayered perceptron (MLP)

```
def MLP(X, W0, W1, b0, b1):        ← MLP
    y0 = fully_connected_layer(X=X, W=W0, b=b0)
    return fully_connected_layer(X=y0, W=W1, b=b1)
```

7.5.3 Cybenko's universal approximation theorem

Any function $y = f(x)$ that is continuous in an interval $x \in (a, b)$ can be approximated with a set of towers (vertical rectangles) in that interval. This is a direct consequence of the *mean value for integrals* theorem in calculus. The idea is depicted in figure 7.14, where a complicated function (depicted by the curve) is approximated by a sequence of towers of various heights. The thinner the towers, the greater the number of towers, and the more accurate the approximation.

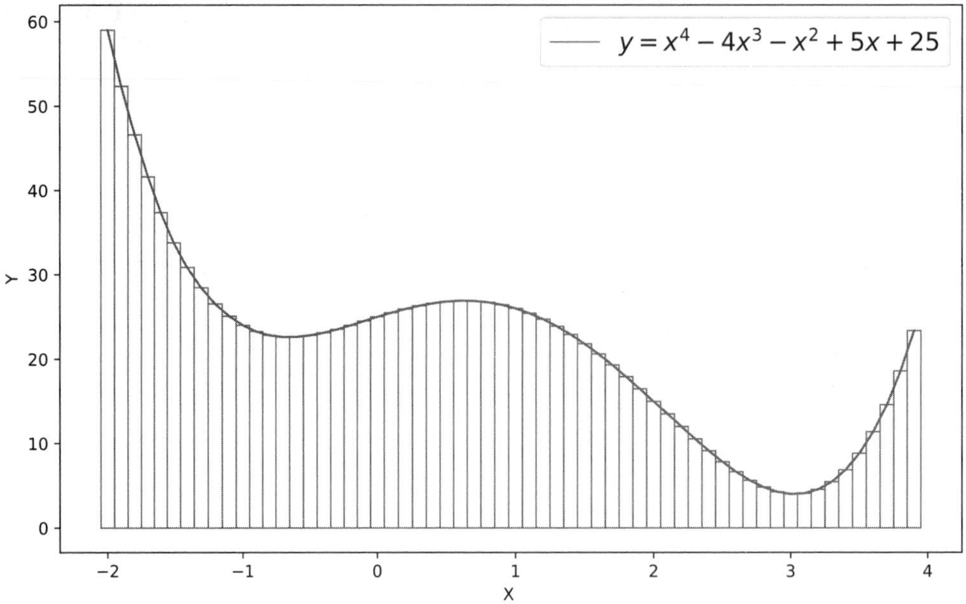

Figure 7.14 Approximating a complicated function with towers

In section 7.5.3, we show that any tower (with arbitrary height and location) can be constructed with MLPs. By summing these MLPs for individual towers, we can approximate the entire function. This is Cybenko's theorem in a nutshell.

> **NOTE** Although Cybenko's theorem guarantees that any continuous function can be modeled using an MLP with a single hidden layer, the number of perceptrons in that MLP can become arbitrarily impracticably large. This is why, in real life, we rarely try to approximate complicated functions with a single hidden layer. We see later that additional layers help us cut down the number of perceptrons required.

In particular, any decision boundary can be modeled in this fashion. Of course, the number of perceptrons needed may become impossibly large for many problems, making such a model practically unattainable.

GENERATING TOWERS WITH MLPS

The basic idea is depicted in figure 7.15. We can obviously generate a regular step with a perceptron implementing $y = \phi(x)$. The corresponding graph is shown in figure 7.15a. By imparting a bias of 5, we can shift this step leftwards. The corresponding function is $y = \phi(x + 5)$. Furthermore, using negative weight laterally flips the step. The corresponding function is $y = \phi(-x)$, whose graph is shown in figure 7.15c. By imparting a bias of 5, we can shift the flipped step rightwards. Figure 7.15e shows a flipped and right-shifted step corresponding to the function $y = \phi(-x + 5)$, whose perceptron is shown in figure 7.15f. Logically ANDing a left-shifted step with a flipped and right-shifted step yields a tower

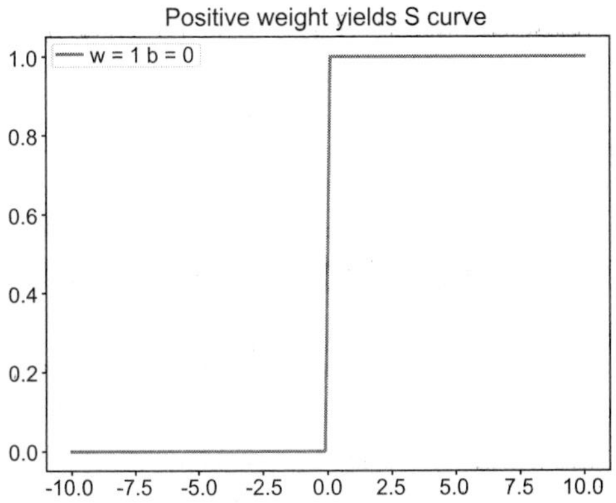

(a) $\phi(x)$: positive w yields a regular step

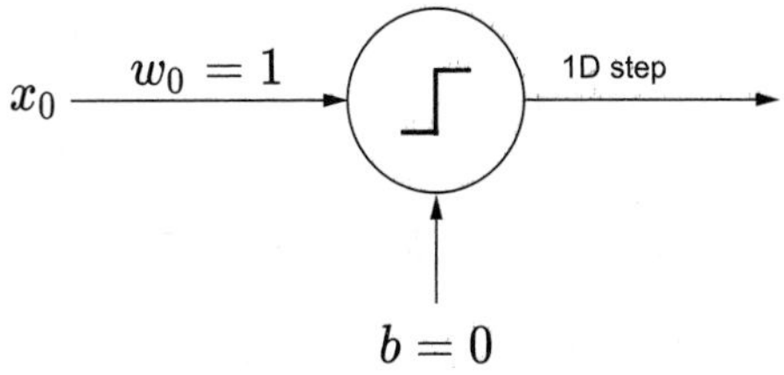

(b) Perceptron for a regular step

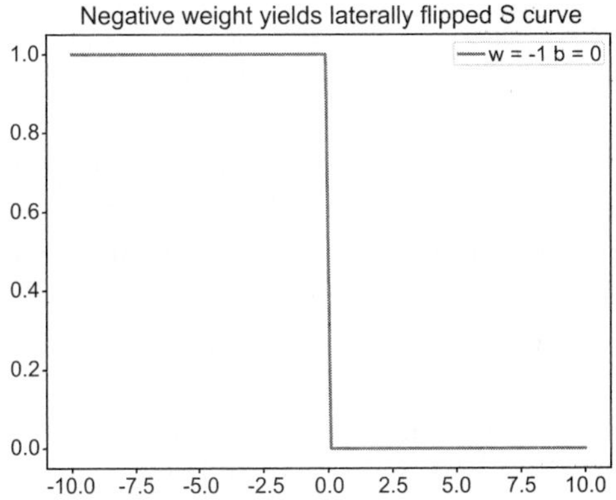

(c) $\phi(-x)$: negative w yields a laterally flipped step

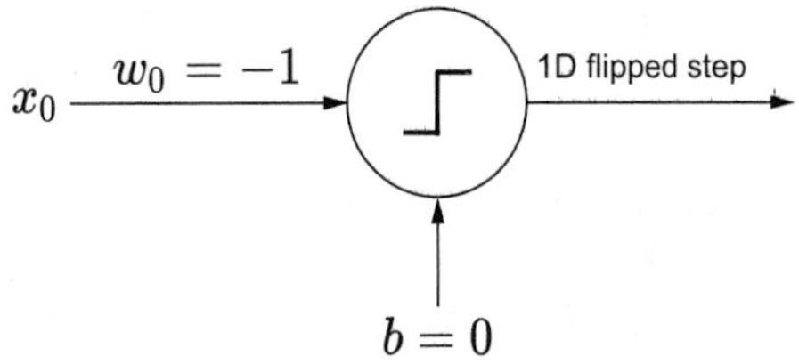

(d) Perceptron for a laterally flipped step

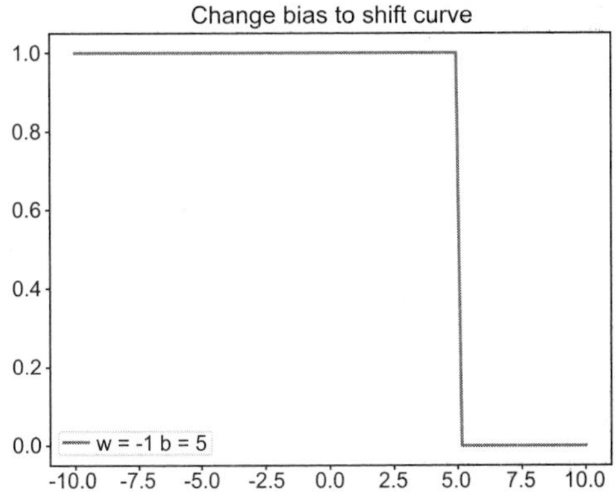

(e) $\phi(-x+5)$: changing the bias shifts the step left or right

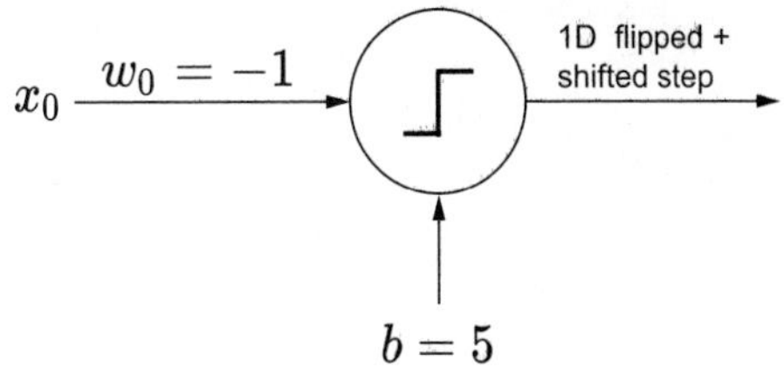

(f) Perceptron for a laterally shifted step

Figure 7.15 Generating a 1D tower with perceptrons. (*Figure continued on next page*)

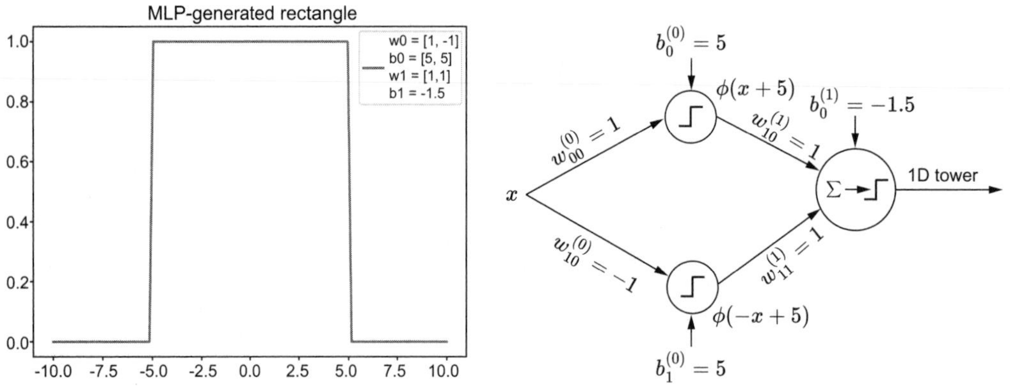

(g) $(\phi(x+5) + \phi(-x+5) - 1.5)$: ANDing a left-shifted step with a flipped, right-shifted step yields a tower

(h) MLP for a 1D tower

Figure 7.15 (*Continued from previous page*)

in 1D. This corresponds to the function $y = \phi(\phi(x+5) + \phi(-x+5) - 1.5)$, whose graph is shown in figure 7.15g.

The same idea also works for higher-dimensional inputs. We can generate a step in two variables (a 2D step) aligned to the x_0 direction using equation 7.4. This equation's graph is shown in figure 7.16a, and the perceptron implementing the equation is shown in figure 7.16b. The flipped version of the same step can be generated via equation 7.5. This equation's graph is shown in figure 7.16d, and the perceptron implementation is shown in figure 7.16e.

In the 1D case, we combine a regular step with its flipped and shifted version to generate a tower. The process is slightly more complicated in 2D. Here, combining a step along a specific coordinate axis with its flipped and shifted version generates a wave function along that axis. Thus, we have separate waves in each dimension. The

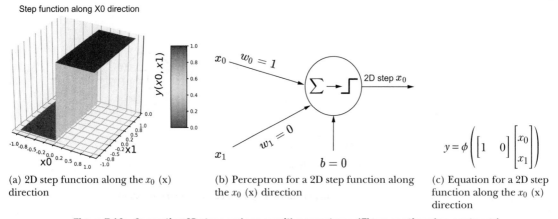

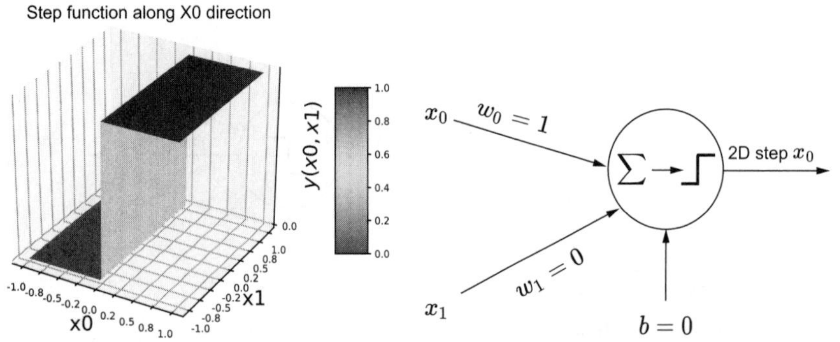

(a) 2D step function along the x_0 (x) direction

(b) Perceptron for a 2D step function along the x_0 (x) direction

$$y = \phi\left(\begin{bmatrix} 1 & 0 \end{bmatrix} \begin{bmatrix} x_0 \\ x_1 \end{bmatrix}\right)$$

(c) Equation for a 2D step function along the x_0 (x) direction

Figure 7.16 Generating 2D steps and waves with perceptrons. (*Figure continued on next page*)

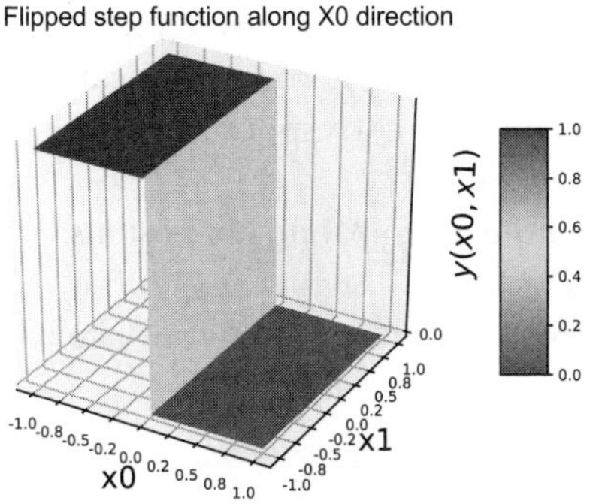

(d) Flipped 2D step along the x_0 (x) direction

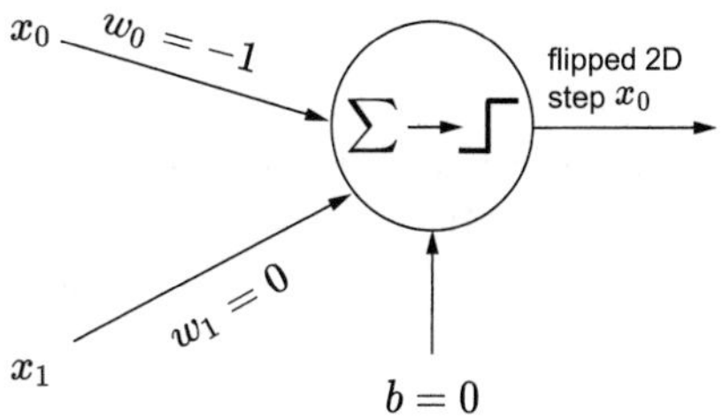

(e) Perceptron for a flipped 2D step along the x_0 (x) direction

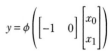

$$y = \phi\left(\begin{bmatrix}-1 & 0\end{bmatrix}\begin{bmatrix}x_0 \\ x_1\end{bmatrix}\right)$$

(f) Equation for a flipped 2D step along the x_0 (x) direction

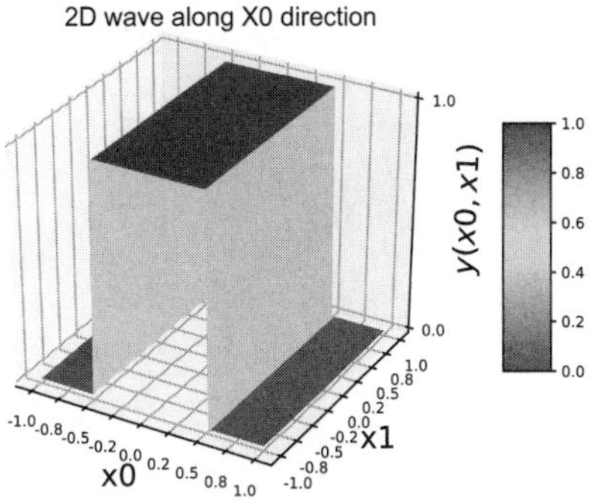

(g) 2D wave along the x_0 (x) direction

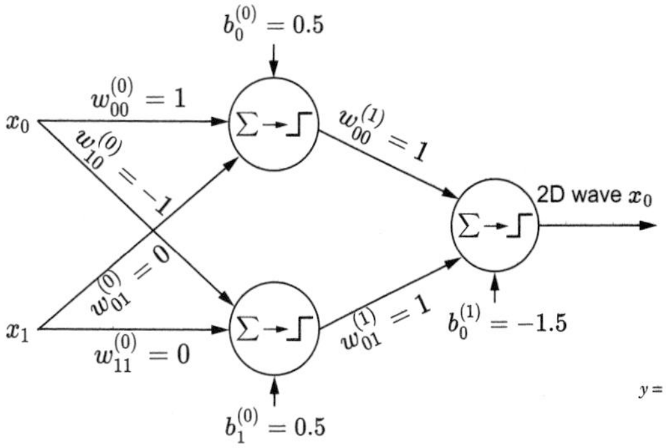

(h) MLP for a 2D wave along the x_0 (x) direction

$$y = \phi\left(\begin{bmatrix}1 & 1\end{bmatrix}\phi\left(\begin{bmatrix}1 & 0 \\ -1 & 0\end{bmatrix}\begin{bmatrix}x_0 \\ x_1\end{bmatrix} + \begin{bmatrix}0.5 \\ 0.5\end{bmatrix}\right) - 1.5\right)$$

(i) Equation for a 2D wave along the x_0 (x) direction

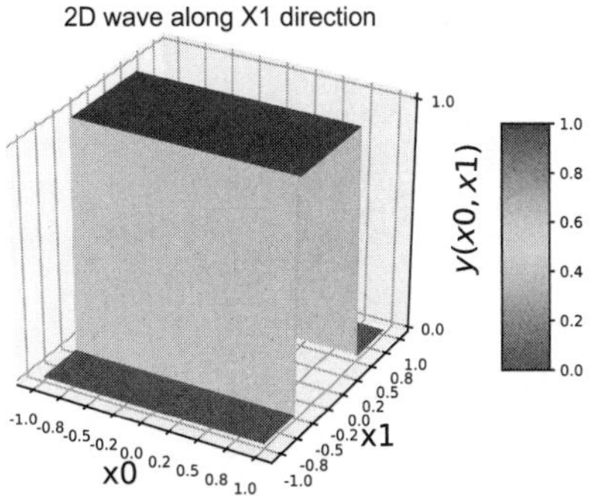

(j) 2D wave along the x_1 (y) direction

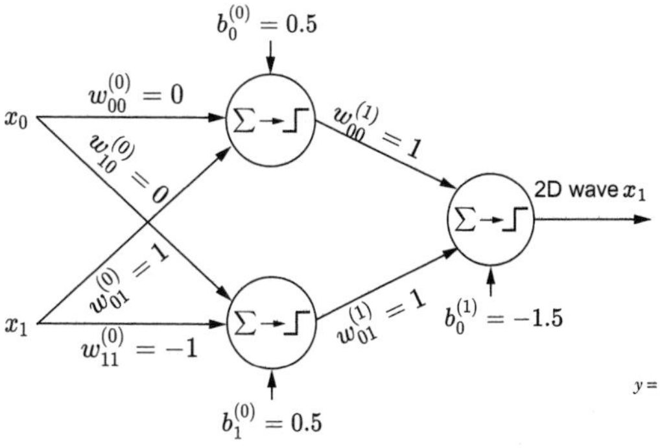

(k) MLP for a 2D wave along the x_1 (y) direction

$$y = \phi\left(\begin{bmatrix}1 & 1\end{bmatrix}\phi\left(\begin{bmatrix}0 & 1 \\ 0 & -1\end{bmatrix}\begin{bmatrix}x_0 \\ x_1\end{bmatrix} + \begin{bmatrix}0.5 \\ 0.5\end{bmatrix}\right) - 1.5\right)$$

(l) MLP for a 2D wave along the x_1 (y) direction

Figure 7.16 ***(Continued from previous page)***

wave along the x_0 axis corresponds to equation 7.6; its graph is shown in figure 7.16g. It is implemented by the MLP in figure 7.16h. Similarly, a 2D wave along the x_1 axis can be generated via equation 7.7 and is graphed in figure 7.16j. The corresponding MLP is shown in figure 7.16k.

To create a tower, we have to AND a pair of waves along the two separate dimensions. The final tower function is shown in equation 7.8; the corresponding tower graph is shown in figure 7.17a; the MLP is shown in figure 7.17b. Any continuous 2D surface can be approximated to arbitrary levels of accuracy by combining such 2D towers:

$$y = \phi\left(\begin{bmatrix}1 & 0\end{bmatrix}\begin{bmatrix}x_0 \\ x_1\end{bmatrix}\right) \Rightarrow \text{2D step along } x_0 \tag{7.4}$$

$$y = \phi\left(\begin{bmatrix}-1 & 0\end{bmatrix}\begin{bmatrix}x_0 \\ x_1\end{bmatrix}\right) \Rightarrow \text{Flipped 2D step along } x_0 \tag{7.5}$$

$$y = \phi\left(\begin{bmatrix}1 & 1\end{bmatrix}\phi\left(\begin{bmatrix}1 & 0 \\ -1 & 0\end{bmatrix}\begin{bmatrix}x_0 \\ x_1\end{bmatrix} + \begin{bmatrix}0.5 \\ 0.5\end{bmatrix}\right) - 1.5\right) \Rightarrow \text{2D wave along } x_0 \tag{7.6}$$

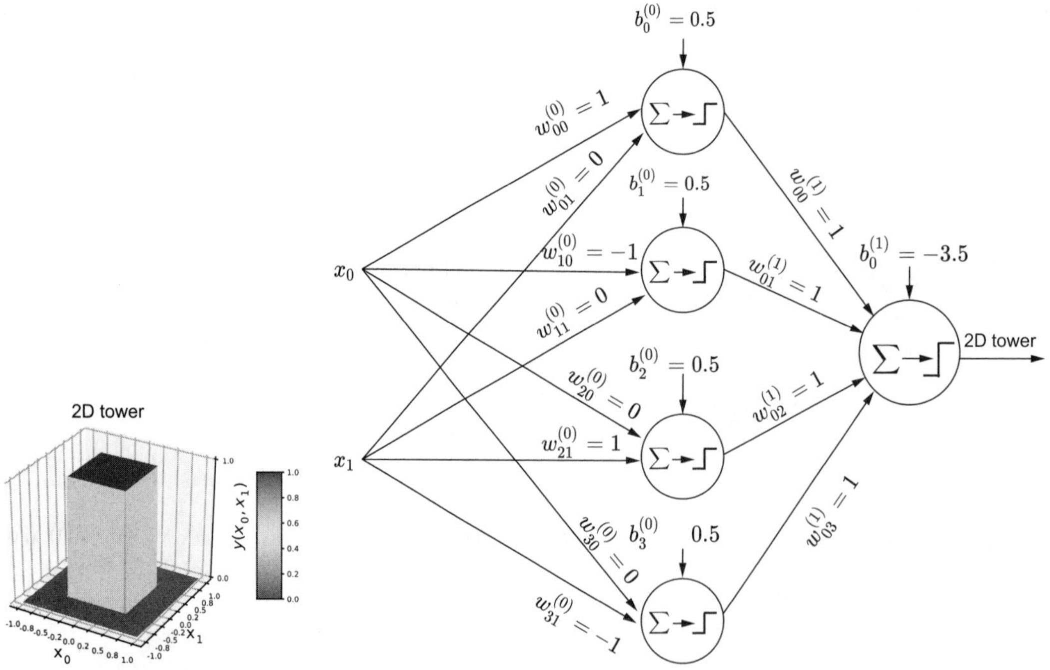

(a) 2D tower

(b) MLP for a 2D tower (equation 7.8)

Figure 7.17 Generating a 2D tower with perceptrons

$$y = \phi\left(\begin{bmatrix}1 & 1\end{bmatrix}\phi\left(\begin{bmatrix}0 & 1\\0 & -1\end{bmatrix}\begin{bmatrix}x_0\\x_1\end{bmatrix} + \begin{bmatrix}0.5\\0.5\end{bmatrix}\right) - 1.5\right) \Rightarrow \text{2D wave along } x_1 \tag{7.7}$$

$$y = \phi\left(\begin{bmatrix}1 & 1 & 1 & 1\end{bmatrix}\phi\left(\begin{bmatrix}1 & 0\\-1 & 0\\0 & 1\\0 & -1\end{bmatrix}\begin{bmatrix}x_0\\x_1\end{bmatrix} + \begin{bmatrix}0.5\\0.5\\0.5\\0.5\end{bmatrix}\right) - 3.5\right) \Rightarrow \text{2D tower} \tag{7.8}$$

NOTE Fully functional code for approximating surfaces using perceptrons, executable via Jupyter Notebook, can be found at http://mng.bz/WrKa.

Listing 7.4 Perceptrons and MLPs in 1D

```
x = torch.linspace(start=-10, end=10, steps=100)        ← 100D array

# 1D S curves - positive weight      ← See figures 7.15a and 7.15b.
w = torch.tensor([1.0], dtype=torch.float32)
b = torch.tensor([0.0])
y = Perceptron(X=x.unsqueeze(dim=1), W=w.unsqueeze(dim=1), b=b)

# 1D S curves - negative weight + shift      ← See figures 7.15e and 7.15f.
w = torch.tensor([-1.0], dtype=torch.float32)
b = torch.tensor([5.0])
y = Perceptron(X=x.unsqueeze(dim=1), W=w.unsqueeze(dim=1), b=b)

# 1D towers (Cybenko) - various W0      ← See figures 7.15g and 7.15h.
W0 = torch.tensor([[1.0], [-1.0]], dtype=torch.float32)
b0 = torch.tensor([5.0, 5.0])
W1 = torch.tensor([[1.0, 1.0]], dtype=torch.float32)
b1 = torch.tensor([0.0])
y = MLP(X=x.unsqueeze(dim=1), W0=W0, W1=W1, b0=b0, b1=b1)
```

Listing 7.5 Perceptrons and MLPs in 2D

```
X = torch.linspace(start=-1, end=1, steps=100)      ← 100D array
Y = torch.linspace(start=-1, end=1, steps=100)      ← 100D array

gridX, gridY = torch.meshgrid(X, Y)      ← 100 ×100 matrix
X = torch.tensor([(y, x) for y, x in
        zip(gridY.reshape(-1), gridX.reshape(-1))])      ← 10,000 ×1 matrix

# 2D Step function in X-direction      ← See equation 7.4 and figures 7.16a and 7.16b
W = torch.tensor([[1.0, 0.0]], dtype=torch.float32)
```

```
b = torch.tensor([0.0], dtype=torch.float32)
Z = Perceptron(X=X, W=W, b=b)

# 2D Flipped Step function along X-direction      ← See equation 7.5 and figures 7.16d and 7.16e
W = torch.tensor([[-1.0, 0.0]], dtype=torch.float32)
b = torch.tensor([0.0], dtype=torch.float32)
Z = Perceptron(X=X, W=W, b=b)

# 2D wave along X-direction      ← See equation 7.6 and figures 7.16g and 7.16h
W0 = torch.tensor([[1.0, 0.0],
                   [-1.0, 0.0]], dtype=torch.float32)
b0 = torch.tensor([0.5, 0.5], dtype=torch.float32)
W1 = torch.tensor([[1.0, 1.0]], dtype=torch.float32)
b1 = torch.tensor([-1.0])
Z = MLP(X=X, W0=W0, W1=W1, b0=b0, b1=b1)

# 2D wave along Y-direction      ← See equation 7.7 and figures 7.16j and 7.16k
W0 = torch.tensor([[0.0, 1.0],
                   [0.0, -1.0]], dtype=torch.float32)
b0 = torch.tensor([0.5, 0.5], dtype=torch.float32)
W1 = torch.tensor([[1.0, 1.0]], dtype=torch.float32)
b1 = torch.tensor([-1.0])
Z = MLP(X=X, W0=W0, W1=W1, b0=b0, b1=b1)

# 2D Tower      ← See equation 7.8 and figures 7.17a and 7.17b
W0 = torch.tensor([[1.0, 0.0],
                   [-1.0, 0.0],
                   [0.0, 1.0],
                   [0.0, -1.0]], dtype=torch.float32)
b0 = torch.tensor([0.5, 0.5, 0.5, 0.5], dtype=torch.float32)
W1 = torch.tensor([[1.0, 1.0, 1.0, 1.0]], dtype=torch.float32)
b1 = torch.tensor([-3.5])
Z = MLP(X=X, W0=W0, W1=W1, b0=b0, b1=b1)
```

7.5.4 MLPs for polygonal decision boundaries

We have seen that classifiers form an important use case for neural networks. In section 7.2.2, we also saw that classifiers essentially model decision boundaries in high-dimensional feature spaces. In this section, we model a simple class bounded with a fixed polygon to understand the process.

Figure 7.18a shows a feature space with the class to be identified corresponding to a rectangular region (shaded) bounded by the four straight lines:

$$x_0 = -5 \qquad x_0 = 5$$

$$x_1 = -2 \qquad x_1 = 2$$

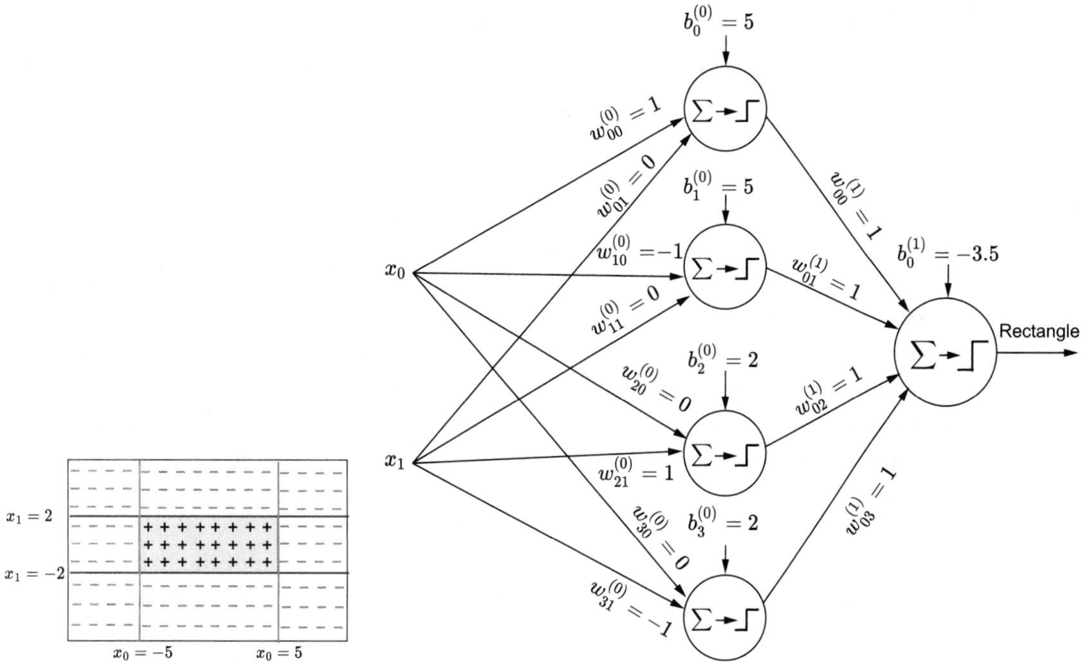

(a) Example feature space with decision boundaries enclosing the class of interest (shaded)

(b) MLP that fires only on points in the shaded region

Figure 7.18 Modeling a rectangular decision region with MLPs

Each of these lines partitions the feature space into two half-planes, indicated by minus and plus signs in figure 7.18a. The region containing the feature points for the class of interest is indicated by all + signs.

The shaded region corresponding to the class of interest is the region where $x_0 \geq -5$ AND $x_0 \leq 5$ AND $x_1 \geq -2$ AND $x_1 \leq 2$. Now consider the perceptron $\phi\,(x_0 + 5)$. It fires (outputs 1) on the region $x_0 \geq -5$. Similarly, the perceptrons $\phi\,(-x_0 + 5)$, $\phi\,(x_1 + 2)$, and $\phi\,(-x_1 + 2)$ fire on the regions $x_0 \leq 5$, $x_1 \geq -2$, and $x_1 \leq 2$, respectively. Hence, by logically ANDing the outputs of these perceptrons, we get an MLP that fires only on the shaded region of interest. Figure 7.18b shows this MLP. It implements the following function:

$$y = \phi\left(\begin{bmatrix}1 & 1 & 1 & 1\end{bmatrix}\phi\left(\begin{bmatrix}1 & 0\\ -1 & 0\\ 0 & 1\\ 0 & -1\end{bmatrix}\begin{bmatrix}x_0\\ x_1\end{bmatrix} + \begin{bmatrix}5\\ 5\\ 2\\ 2\end{bmatrix}\right) - 3.5\right)$$

All shapes on a plane can be approximated by polygons. Hence, given sufficient perceptrons, any shape on a plane can be depicted to an arbitrary level of accuracy.

Summary

In this chapter, we outlined how a large variety of real-world problems can be modeled as function evaluation:

- Any intelligent task can be modeled by a function. Of particular interest are classification tasks where, given an input, we estimate from a predetermined list of possible classes the class to which the input belongs. For instance, a binary classifier can group input images into two classes: those that contain a human face and those that do not. Classification tasks can be approximated by functions with categorical outputs.
- Neural networks provide a structured way to approximate arbitrary functions (including classifier functions). This is how they mimic intelligence.
- Neural networks are created by combining a basic building block called a perceptron. A perceptron is a simple function that returns a step function applied to the weighted sum of its inputs (plus a bias). A perceptron is effectively a linear classifier that divides space into two half-spaces with a hyperplane. The weights and bias of the perceptron correspond to the orientation and position of the hyperplane—they can be adjusted to separate the regions corresponding to individual classes as much as possible.
- A single perceptron can approximate only relatively simple functions, such as a classifier whose feature points are separable by a hyperplane. Perceptrons cannot approximate more complex functions, like classifiers whose input regions are to be separated with curved surfaces. Multilayer perceptrons (MLPs) are combinations of perceptrons where the outputs of one set (layer) of perceptrons are fed as input to the next set (layer). A neural network is essentially an MLP and can approximate such arbitrarily complex functions.
- Simple logical functions like AND, OR, and NOT can be emulated with a single perceptron. A logical XOR cannot be. For XORs and other complicated logical functions, we need MLPs. There is a mechanical way to construct an MLP for any logical function. A logical function can always be represented by a truth table. Each row of the truth table can be viewed as a logical AND function of the inputs, and the final output is a logical OR of the inputs. Since ANDs and ORs can be emulated with perceptrons, any truth table can be emulated as a combination of perceptrons (an MLP).
- The ability of an MLP to represent arbitrary functions is known as its expressive power. The larger the number of perceptrons and/or connections, the greater the expressive power of a neural network.
- Cybenko's theorem proves that a neural network is a universal approximator (meaning it can approximate any function). The basic idea is that any function can be approximated to an arbitrary degree of accuracy as a sum of rectangles (towers). The theorem demonstrates that a tower can be constructed in any dimensional space using MLPs.

- Neural networks can approximate any shape on a plane to arbitrary accuracy. This is because all shapes can be approximated by rectangles, and we can demonstrably approximate a rectangle on a plane with MLPs.
- In real-life problems, the regions corresponding to classes are unknown, but we manually label sample input points with desired outputs (ground truth) to create supervised training data. We tune the weights and biases to approximate the training data as closely as possible. This process of tuning is known as training. If the training data set is not a good representative of the real dataset, the neural network will be inaccurate even after training.

8 Training neural networks: Forward propagation and backpropagation

This chapter covers

- Sigmoid functions as differential surrogates for Heaviside step functions
- Layering in neural networks: expressing linear layers as matrix-vector multiplication
- Regression loss, forward and backward propagation, and their math

So far, we have seen that neural networks make complicated real-life decisions by modeling the decision-making process with mathematical functions. These functions can become arbitrarily involved, but fortunately, we have a simple building block called a *perceptron* that can be repeated systematically to model any arbitrary function. We need not even explicitly know the function being modeled in closed form. All we need is a reasonably sized set of sample inputs and corresponding correct outputs. This collection of input and output pairs is known as *training data*. Armed with this training data, we can *train* a multilayer perceptron (MLP, aka neural network) to emit reasonably correct outputs on inputs it has never seen before.

Such neural networks, where we need to know the output for each input in the training data set, are known as *supervised* neural networks. The correct output for the training inputs is typically generated via a manual process called *labeling*. Labeling is expensive and time-consuming. Much research is going on toward unsupervised, semi-supervised, and self-supervised networks, eliminating or minimizing the labeling process. But as of now, the accuracy of unsupervised and self-supervised networks in general does not match that of supervised networks. In this chapter, we focus on supervised neural networks. In chapter 14, we will study unsupervised networks.

What is this process of "training" a neural network? It essentially estimates the parameter values that would make the network emit output values as close as possible to the known correct outputs on the training inputs. In this chapter, we discuss how this is done. But before that, we have to learn a few other things.

NOTE The complete PyTorch code for this chapter is available at http://mng.bz/YAXa in the form of fully functional and executable Jupyter notebooks.

8.1 Differentiable step-like functions

In equation 7.3, we expressed the perceptron as a combination of a Heaviside step function ϕ and an affine transformation $\vec{w}^T \vec{x} + b$. This is the perceptron we used throughout chapter 7 and with which we were able to express (model) pretty much all functions of interest.

Despite its expressive power, the Heaviside step function has a drawback: it has a discontinuity at $x = 0$ and is *not differentiable*. Why is differentiability important? As we shall see in chapter 8 (and got a glimpse of in section 3.3), optimal training of a neural network requires evaluation of the gradient vector of a loss function with respect to weights. Since the gradient is nothing but a vector of partial derivatives, differentiability is needed for training.

In this section, we discuss a few functions that are differentiable and yet can mimic the Heaviside step function. The most significant among them is the sigmoid function.

8.1.1 Sigmoid function

The sigmoid function is named after its characteristic S-shaped curve (figure 8.1). The corresponding equation is

$$\sigma(x) = \frac{1}{1 + e^{-x}} \tag{8.1}$$

PARAMETERIZED SIGMOID FUNCTION

We can parametrize equation 8.1 as

$$\sigma(x) = \frac{1}{1 + e^{-(wx+b)}} \tag{8.2}$$

This allows us to

- Adjust the steepness of the linear portion of the S curve by changing w
- Adjust the position of the curve by changing b

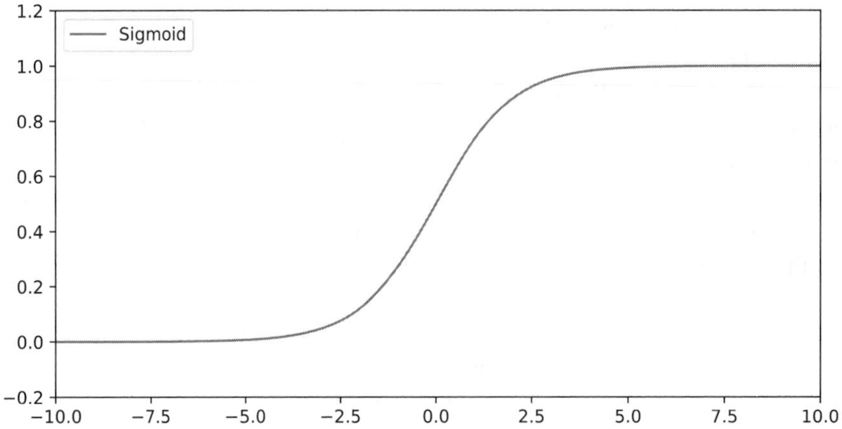

Figure 8.1 Graph of a 1D sigmoid function

Figure 8.2 shows how the parametrized sigmoid curve changes with different values for the parameters w and b. In particular, note that for large values of w, the parameterized sigmoid is virtually indistinguishable from the Heaviside step function (compare the dotted curve in figure 8.2a with figure 7.7), even though it remains differentiable. This is exactly what we desire in neural networks.

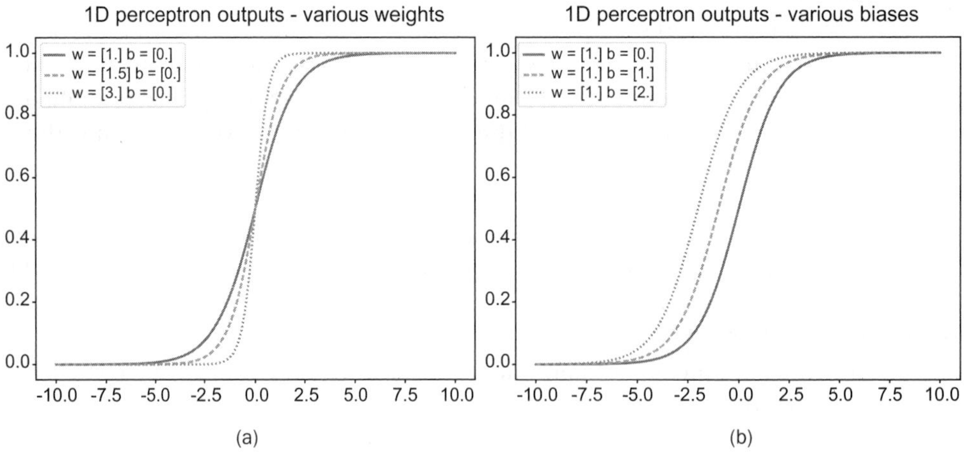

Figure 8.2 Sigmoid curves corresponding to various parameter values in equation 8.2

SOME PROPERTIES OF THE SIGMOID FUNCTION

The sigmoid function has several interesting properties, some of which are listed here with proof outlines.

- *Expression with positive x*:

$$\sigma\,(x) = \frac{e^x}{1 + e^x} \tag{8.3}$$

  This expression can be easily proved by multiplying both the numerator and denominator of equation 8.1 by e^x.

- *Sigmoid of negative x*:

$$\sigma(-x) = \frac{1}{1+e^{x}} = \frac{e^{-x}}{1+e^{-x}} = 1 - \frac{1}{1+e^{-x}} = 1 - \sigma(x) \tag{8.4}$$

- *Derivative of sigmoid*:

$$\begin{aligned}\frac{d\sigma(x)}{dx} &= \frac{d}{dx}\left((1+e^{-x})^{-1}\right) = \left(\frac{-1}{(1+e^{-x})^{2}}\right)\frac{d}{dx}\left((1+e^{-x})\right) \\ &= \left(\frac{-1}{(1+e^{-x})^{2}}\right)(-e^{-x}) = \left(\frac{1}{1+e^{-x}}\right)\left(\frac{e^{-x}}{1+e^{-x}}\right) = \sigma(x)\left(1-\sigma(x)\right)\end{aligned} \tag{8.5}$$

Figure 8.3 shows the graph of the derivative of the sigmoid superimposed on the sigmoid graph itself. As expected, the derivative has its maximum value at the middle of the sigmoid curve (where the sigmoid is climbing more or less linearly) and is near zero at both ends (where the sigmoid is saturated and flat, hardly changing).

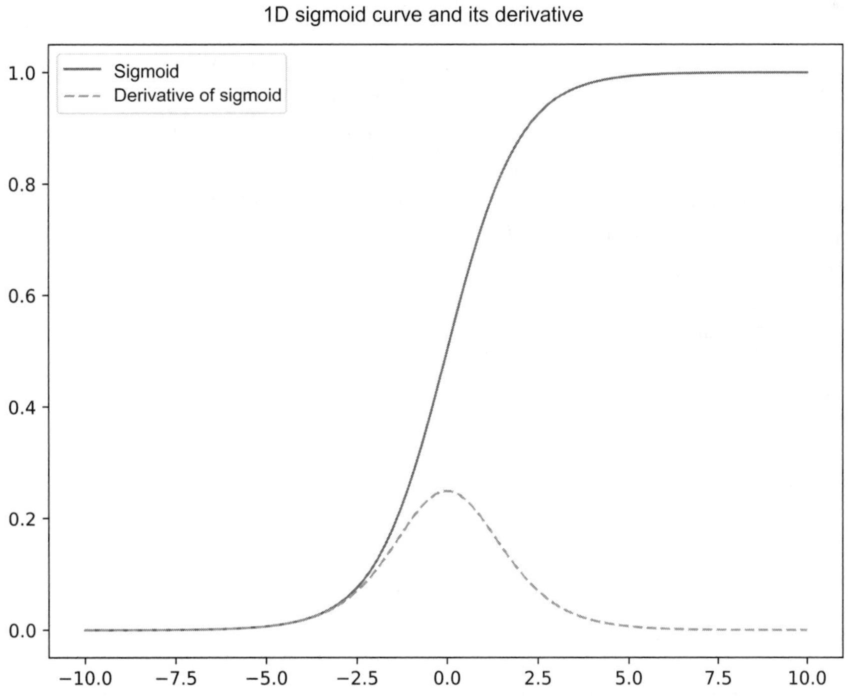

Figure 8.3 Graph of a 1D sigmoid function (solid curve) and its derivative (dashed curve)

8.1.2 Tanh function

An alternative to the sigmoid function is the *hyperbolic tangent* tanh function, shown in figure 8.4. It is very similar to the sigmoid function, but the range of output values is from [−1, 1] as opposed to [0, 1]. In essence, it is the sigmoid function stretched and

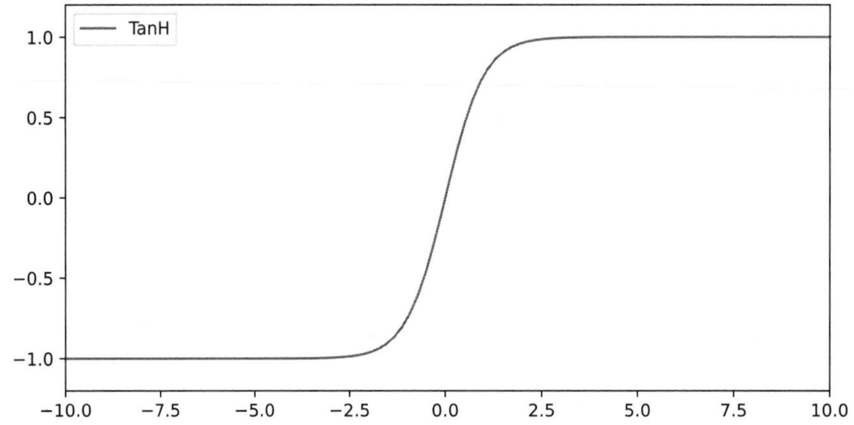

Figure 8.4 Graph of a 1D tanh function.

shifted so it is centered around 0. The equation of the tanh function is given by

$$tanh\,(x) = \frac{e^x - e^{-x}}{e^x + e^{-x}} \tag{8.6}$$

Why is tanh preferred over sigmoid? To understand this, consider figure 8.5. It compares the derivatives of the sigmoid and tanh functions. As the plot shows, the derivative (gradient) of the function near $x = 0$ is much higher for tanh than for sigmoid. Stronger gradients mean faster convergence, as the weight updates happen in larger steps. Note that this holds mainly when the data is centered around 0: in most preprocessing steps, we standardize the data (make it 0 mean) before feeding it into the neural network.

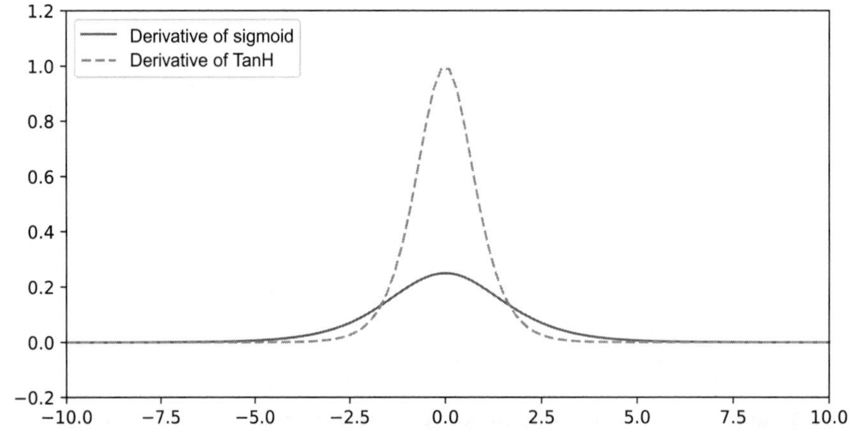

Figure 8.5 Graph of the derivatives of 1D sigmoid and tanh functions

8.2 Why layering?

In section 7.5, we encountered the idea of *layering* as the preferred way to organize multiple perceptrons. The main property of a layered network is that neurons in any layer take their input only from the outputs of the preceding layer. This means connections exist only between successive layers. No other connection exists in the MLP, which greatly simplifies the evaluation and training of the network, which will become apparent as we discuss forward propagation and backpropagation.

Why have layers at all? We have seen that multiple perceptrons allow us to model problems that cannot be solved by a single perceptron (such as the XOR problem discussed in section 7.4.1). In theory, it is possible to model all mathematical functions (and hence solve all quantifiable problems) with neurons organized in a single hidden layer (see Cybenko's theorem and proof in section 7.5.3). However, that does not mean a single hidden layer is the most *efficient* way of doing all modelings. We can often model complicated problems with *fewer* perceptrons if we organize them in more than one layer.

Why do extra layers help? The primary reason is the extra nonlinearity. Each layer brings in its own nonlinear (such as sigmoid) function. Nonlinear functions, with proper parametrization, can model more complicated functions. Hence, a larger count of nonlinear functions in the model typically implies greater expressive power.

8.3 Linear layers

Various types of layers are used in popular neural network architectures. In subsequent chapters, we shall look at different kinds of layers, such as convolution layers. But in this section, we examine the simplest and most basic type of layer: the *linear* layer. Here every perceptron from the previous layer is connected to every perceptron in the next layer. Such a layer is also known as *fully connected* layer. Thus if the previous layer has m neurons and the next layer has n neurons, there are mn connections, each with its own weight.

NOTE We use the words *neuron* and *perceptron* interchangeably.

Figure 8.6 shows a linear layer that is a slice of a bigger MLP. Figure 8.7 shows a bigger MLP with a linear layer. Consistent with previous chapters, we have used superscripts for layer IDs and subscripts for source and destination IDs.

The weight of the connection from the kth neuron in layer $(l-1)$ to the jth neuron in layer l is denoted $w_{jk}^{(l)}$. Here the subscript ordering is the destination (j) followed by the source (k). This is slightly counterintuitive but universally followed because it simplifies the matrix notation (described shortly). Note the following:

- We have split a single perceptron (weighted sum followed by sigmoid) into two separate layers, weighted sum and sigmoid.
- We have used sigmoid instead of Heaviside as the nonlinear function.

8.3.1 Linear layers expressed as matrix-vector multiplication

Let's revisit the perceptron in the context of the MLP. As we saw in equation 7.3, a single perceptron takes a weighted sum of its inputs and then performs a step function on the result. In an MLP, the inputs to any perceptron in the lth layer come from the previous layer: the $(l-1)$th layer.

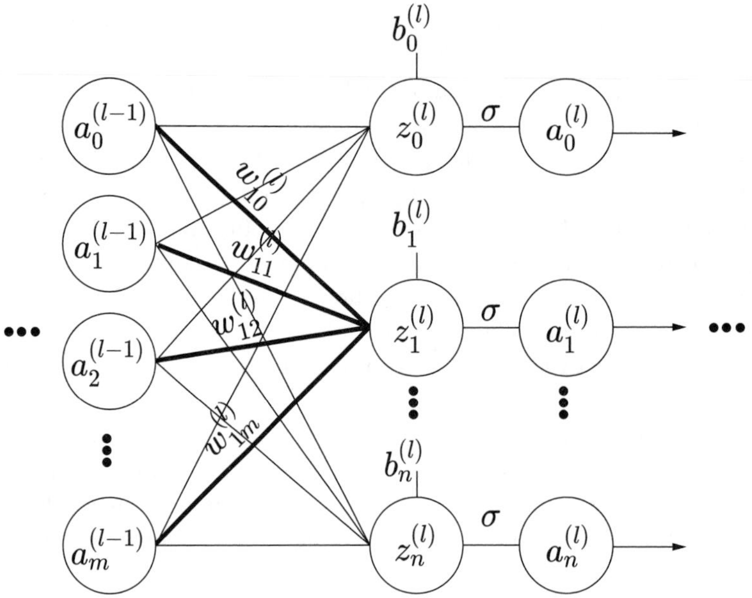

$$z_j^{(l)} = \sum_{k=0}^{m} w_{jk}^{(l)} a_k^{(l-1)} + b_j^{(l)} \qquad a_j^{(l)} = \sigma(z_j^{(l)})$$

Figure 8.6 Linear layer outputting layer l from layer $(l-1)$. The weights belonging to row 1 of the weight matrix (coming from all the input neurons, layer $(l-1)$, which sum together to form output neuron 1) are shown in bold.

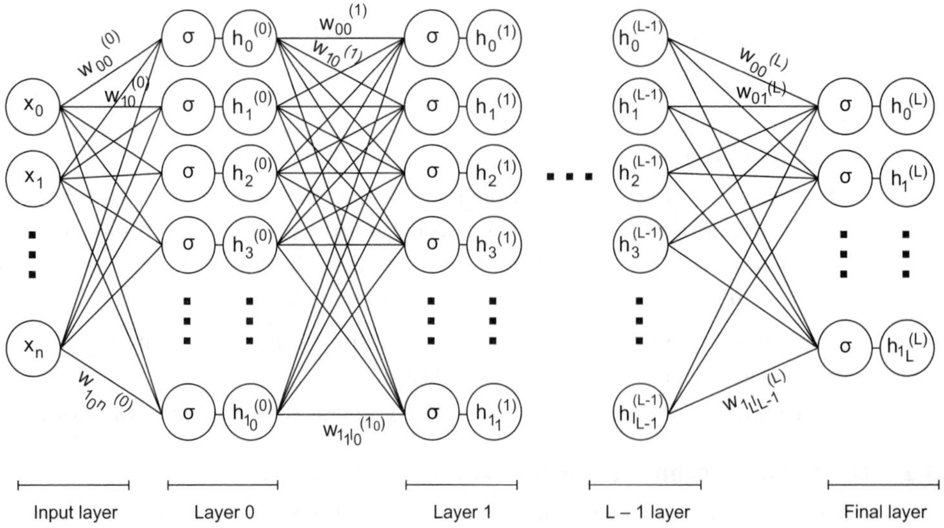

Figure 8.7 Multilayered neural networks: This is a complete deep neural network, a slice of which is shown in figure 8.6.

Let $a_0^{(l-1)}, a_1^{(l-1)}, \cdots, a_m^{(l-1)}$ denote the outputs of the m neurons in layer $(l-1)$ (the left-most input column of nodes in figure 8.6). And let $a_0^{(l)}, a_1^{(l)}, \cdots, a_n^{(l)}$ denote the outputs of the n neurons in layer l. Note that we typically use the symbol a, standing for activation, to denote the output of individual neurons. Now consider the jth neuron in layer l. For instance, check $z_1^{(l)}$ in figure 8.6: note the weights going into it and the activations at their source. Its output is $a_j^{(l)}$, where

$$\left.\begin{aligned} z_j^{(l)} &= \sum_{k=0}^{m} w_{jk}^{(l)} a_k^{(l-1)} + b_j^{(l)} \\ a_j^{(l)} &= \sigma\left(z_j^{(l)}\right) \end{aligned}\right\} \text{for } j = 0 \cdots n$$

We can rewrite the summation in these equations as a dot product between the weight and activation vectors:

$$\left.\begin{aligned} z_j^{(l)} &= \begin{bmatrix} w_{j0}^{(l)} & w_{j1}^{(l)} & \cdots & w_{jm}^{(l)} \end{bmatrix} \begin{bmatrix} a_0^{(l-1)} \\ a_1^{(l-1)} \\ \cdots \\ a_m^{(l-1)} \end{bmatrix} + b_j^{(l)} \\ a_j^{(l)} &= \sigma\left(z_j^{(l)}\right) \end{aligned}\right\} \text{for } j = 0 \cdots n$$

The complete set of equations for all js together can be written in a super-compact way using matrix-vector multiplication,

$$\begin{aligned} \vec{z}^{(l)} &= W^{(l)} \vec{a}^{(l-1)} + \vec{b}^{(l)} \\ \vec{a}^{(l)} &= \sigma\left(\vec{z}^{(l)}\right) \end{aligned} \tag{8.7}$$

where

- $W^{(l)}$ is an $n \times m$ matrix representing the weights of *all connections from layer $l-1$ to layer l*:

$$W^{(l)} = \begin{bmatrix} w_{00}^{(l)} & w_{01}^{(l)} & \cdots & w_{0m}^{(l)} \\ w_{10}^{(l)} & w_{11}^{(l)} & \cdots & w_{1m}^{(l)} \\ \vdots & & & \\ w_{j0}^{(l)} & w_{j1}^{(l)} & \cdots & w_{jm}^{(l)} \\ \vdots & & & \\ w_{n0}^{(l)} & w_{n1}^{(l)} & \cdots & w_{nm}^{(l)} \end{bmatrix} \tag{8.8}$$

- $\vec{a}^{(l)}$ represents the activations for the entire layer l. Applying the sigmoid function to a vector is equivalent to applying it individually to each element of the vector:

$$\vec{a}^{(l)} = \begin{bmatrix} a_0^{(l)} \\ a_1^{(l)} \\ \cdots \\ a_n^{(l)} \end{bmatrix} \qquad \vec{a}^{(l-1)} = \begin{bmatrix} a_0^{(l-1)} \\ a_1^{(l-1)} \\ \cdots \\ \cdots \\ a_m^{(l-1)} \end{bmatrix}$$

$$\vec{z}^{(l)} = \begin{bmatrix} z_0^{(l)} \\ z_1^{(l)} \\ \cdots \\ z_n^{(l)} \end{bmatrix} \qquad \sigma\left(\vec{z}^{(l)}\right) = \begin{bmatrix} \sigma\left(z_0^{(l)}\right) \\ \sigma\left(z_1^{(l)}\right) \\ \cdots \\ \sigma\left(z_n^{(l)}\right) \end{bmatrix}$$

The matrix-vector notation saves us from dealing with subscripts by working with all the weights, biases, activations, and so on in a *global fashion.*

8.3.2 Forward propagation and grand output functions for an MLP of linear layers

Equation 8.7 describes the forward propagation of a single linear layer. The final output of an MLP with fully connected (aka linear) layers $0 \cdots L$ on input $\vec{x}$ can be obtained by repeated application of this equation:

$$MLP\left(\vec{x}\right) = \vec{a}^{(L)} = \vec{y} = \sigma\left(W^{(L)} \ldots \sigma\left(W^{(1)} \sigma\left(W^{(0)}\vec{x} + \vec{b}^{(0)}\right) + \vec{b}^{(1)}\right) \cdots + \vec{b}^{(L)}\right) \tag{8.9}$$

In a computer implementation, this expression is evaluated step by step by repeated application of the linear layer:

$$\begin{aligned} \vec{a}^{0} &= \sigma\left(W^{(0)}\vec{x} + \vec{b}^{(0)}\right) \\ \vec{a}^{1} &= \sigma\left(W^{(1)}\vec{a}^{0} + \vec{b}^{(1)}\right) \\ &\ldots \\ \vec{a}^{L} &= \sigma\left(W^{(L)}\vec{a}^{L-1} + \vec{b}^{(L)}\right) \end{aligned} \tag{8.10}$$

It's easy to see that equation 8.10 is a restatement of equation 8.7.

Close examination of these equations reveals a beautiful property. The complicated equation 8.9 is *never explicitly evaluated.* Instead, we evaluate the outputs of successive layers, one layer at a time, as per equation 8.10. Every layer can be evaluated by taking the previous layer's output as input. No other input is necessary. That is to say, we can evaluate $\vec{a}^{(0)}$ directly from the input $\vec{x}$, then $\vec{a}^{(1)}$ from $\vec{a}^{(0)}$, $\vec{a}^{(2)}$ from $\vec{a}^{(1)}$, and so forth, all the way to $\vec{a}^{(L)}$ (which is the grand output of the MLP). During the evaluation, we need to keep only the previous and current layers in memory at any given time. This process greatly simplifies the implementation as well as the conceptualization and is known as *forward propagation.*

Listing 8.1 PyTorch code for forward propagation

```
def Z(x, W_l, b_l):
    return torch.matmul(W_l, x) + b_l

def A(z_l):
    return torch.sigmoid(z_l)

def forward(x, W, b):
    L = len(W) - 1
    a_l = x
    for l in range(0, L + 1):
        z_l = Z(a_l, W[l], b[l])
        a_l = A(z_l)
    return a_l
```

- `def Z(x, W_l, b_l):` — **x: activation of layer l-1 (1-d vector)**; **W_l: Weight matrix of layer l**; **b_l: Bias vector of layer l**
- `def A(z_l):` — **Sigmoid activation function (nonlinear layer)**
- `def forward(x, W, b):` — **x: 1-d input vector**; **W: list of matrices for layers 0 to L.**; **b: list of vectors for layers 0 to L**
- `for l in range(0, L + 1):` — **Loops through layers 0 to L**
- `z_l = Z(a_l, W[l], b[l])` — **Computes Z**
- `a_l = A(z_l)` — **Computes activation**

8.4 Training and backpropagation

Throughout the book, we have been discussing bits and pieces of this process. In sections 1.1 and 3.3 (specifically, algorithm 3.1), we saw an overview of the process for training a supervised model (you are encouraged to reread those if necessary). Training is an iterative process by which the parameters of the neural network are estimated. The goal is to estimate the parameters (weights and biases) such that on the training inputs, the neural network outputs are close as possible to the known ground-truth outputs.

In general, iterative processes improve (get closer to the goal) gradually. In each iteration, we make small adjustments to the parameters. Here, *parameter* refers to the weights and biases of the MLP, the $w_{jk}^{(l)}$s and $b_j^{(l)}$s from section 8.2. We keep adjusting the parameters so that in every iteration, the outputs on training data inputs come a little closer to the ground truth (GT). Eventually, after many iterations, we hopefully converge to optimal values. Note that there is no guarantee that the iterative process will converge to the best possible parameter values. The training might go completely astray or get stuck in a local minimum. (Local minima are explained in section 3.6; you are encouraged to reread it if necessary.) There is no good way to know whether we have reached optimal values (global minima) for the weights and biases. We typically run the neural network on test data, and if the results are satisfactory, we stop training. Test data should be *held back* during training, meaning we should never use test data to train. In the unfortunate event that the network has not reached the desired level of accuracy, we typically throw in more training data and/or try a modified loss function and/or a different architecture. Simply retraining the network from a different random start may also work. This is an experimental science with a lot of trial and error.

How do we know how to adjust the parameter values in each iteration? We define a loss (aka error) function. There are many popular formulations of loss functions, and we review many of them later, but their common property is that when the neural network output agrees more with the known output (GT), the loss becomes lower, and vice versa. Thus if y denotes the output of the neural network and $\bar{y}$ is the GT, a reasonable expression for the loss is the *mean squared error* (MSE) function $(y - \bar{y})^2$. For now, we use the MSE loss as our representative loss function. Later we discuss others.

Once the loss function is defined, we have a crisp, quantitative definition of the goal of neural network training. The goal is to minimize the total loss over the entire training data set. Note the clause *entire training data set*: we do not want to do well on one or two input instances at the cost of doing badly over the rest. If we have to choose between a solution that gives 10% error on all of, say, 100 training input instances versus one that yields 0% error on 50 training input instances but 40% on the remaining 50, we prefer the former.

Each weight in the MLP, $w_{jk}^{(l)}$, is adjusted by an amount proportional to $\delta w_{jk}^{(l)}$. Similarly, each bias $b_j^{(l)}$ is adjusted by an amount proportional to $\delta b_j^{(l)}$. We can denote all this compactly by saying we have a weight vector $\vec{w}$ and bias vector $\vec{b}$. In each iteration, we change $\vec{w}$ by amount $\delta\vec{w}$ and $\vec{b}$ by $\delta\vec{b}$ so that their new values are $\vec{w} - r\delta\vec{w}$ and $\vec{b} - r\delta\vec{b}$ (r is a constant known as the *learning rate* that needs to be set at the beginning of training). In this context, it is worthwhile to note that in section 8.3.1, we expressed the collection of weights in an MLP with a matrix, while here we are referring to the same thing as a vector. These are not incompatible because we can always rasterize the elements of a matrix (that is, walk over the elements of the matrix from top to bottom and from left to right) into a vector.

How do we estimate the adjustment amounts $\delta\vec{w}$ and $\delta\vec{b}$? This is where the notion of gradients comes in. These were discussed in detail in sections 3.3.1, 3.3.2, and 3.5 (again, you are encouraged to reread if necessary). In general, if a loss, denoted $\mathbb{L}$, is expressed as a function of the parameters, such as $\mathbb{L}\left(\vec{w}, \vec{b}\right)$, then the change in the parameters that optimally takes us toward lower loss is yielded by the gradient of the loss with respect to the parameters $\nabla_{\vec{w},b}\mathbb{L}\left(\vec{w}, b\right)$. The high-level process is described later in the chapter in algorithm 8.1. Here we look at the guts of it.

8.4.1 Loss and its minimization: Goal of training

Given a training data set $\mathbb{T}$ that is a set of <input, GT output> pairs $\mathbb{T} = \{\langle\vec{x}, \bar{y}\rangle\}$, the loss can be expressed as

$$\mathbb{L} = \frac{1}{2}\sum_{x\in\mathbb{T}}\left(\vec{y} - \bar{y}\right)^2 \tag{8.11}$$

where

$$\vec{y} = MLP\left(\vec{x}\right)$$

as per equation 8.9.

Now consider equation 8.7 again. We can rasterize each layer's weight matrix $W^{(l)}$ into a vector and then concatenate all these vectors from successive layers to form a giant weight vector $\vec{w}$, the vector of all weights in the MLP:

$$\vec{w} = \begin{bmatrix} w_{00}^{(0)} & w_{01}^{(0)} & \cdots & w_{00}^{(1)} & w_{01}^{(1)} & \cdots & w_{00}^{(L)} & w_{01}^{(L)} & \cdots \end{bmatrix}$$

Similarly, we can form a giant vector of all biases in the MLP:

$$\vec{b} = \begin{bmatrix} b_{0}^{(0)} & b_{1}^{(0)} & \cdots & b_{0}^{(1)} & b_{1}^{(1)} & \cdots & b_{0}^{(L)} & b_{1}^{(L)} & \cdots \end{bmatrix}$$

The ultimate goal of training is to find $\vec{w}$ and $\vec{b}$ that will minimize the loss $\mathbb{L}$. In chapter 3, we saw that we can solve for the minimum by setting the gradients $\nabla_{\vec{w}}\mathbb{L} = 0$ and $\nabla_{\vec{b}}\mathbb{L} = 0$. Computing the loss gradient from a combination of equations 8.9 and 8.11 is intractable. Instead, we go for an iterative solution: *gradient descent* on the loss surface, as described in the next section.

Listing 8.2 PyTorch code for MSE loss

```
def mse_loss(a_L, y):       # a: Activation of layer L (1D vector)
                            # y: Ground truth (1D vector)

    return 1./ 2 * torch.pow((a_L - y), 2)     # See equation 8.11.
```

8.4.2 Loss surface and gradient descent

Geometrically, the loss function $\mathbb{L}\left(\vec{w}, \vec{b}\right)$ can be viewed as a surface in a high-dimensional space. The domain of this space corresponds to all the dimensions in $\vec{w}$ plus all the dimensions in $\vec{b}$. This is shown in figure 8.8 with a 2D domain. In chapter 3, we also saw that given a function $\mathbb{L}\left(\vec{w}, \vec{b}\right)$, the best way to progress toward the minimum is to walk on the parameter space along the negative gradient. We adopt this approach to minimize the loss. We compute the gradients of the loss function with respect to weights and biases and update the weights and bias vectors by an amount proportional to the (negative) of these gradients. Doing this repeatedly takes us close to the minimum. In figure 8.8, the gradient descent path is shown with solid arrows, while an arbitrary non-optimal path to the minimum is shown with dashed arrows.

Thus the equations for updating weights and biases in gradient descent are

$$\begin{aligned} \vec{w} &= \vec{w} - r\nabla_{\vec{w}}\mathbb{L} \\ \vec{b} &= \vec{b} - r\nabla_{\vec{b}}\mathbb{L} \end{aligned} \tag{8.12}$$

where r is a constant. Here

$$\nabla_{\vec{w}}\mathbb{L} = \begin{bmatrix} \dfrac{\partial \mathbb{L}}{\partial w_{jk}^{(l)}} & \text{for all } l, j, k \end{bmatrix}$$

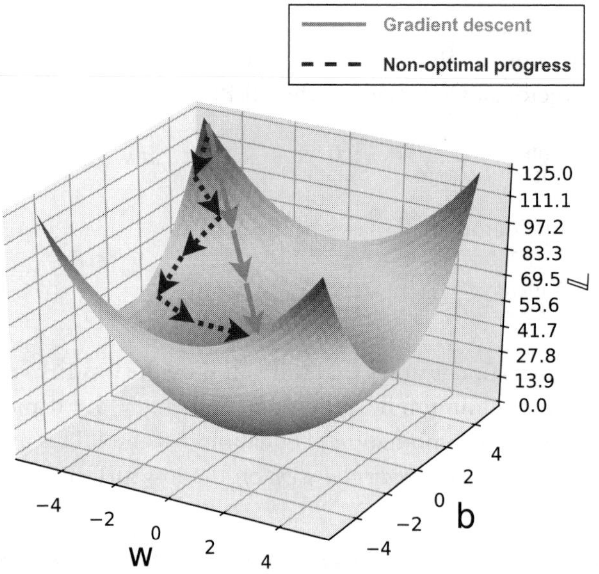

Figure 8.8 A representative loss surface $\mathbb{L}\,(w, b)$. Note that $\vec{w}$ and $\vec{b}$ have each been reduced to 1D for this figure.

$$\nabla_{\vec{b}}\mathbb{L} = \left[\frac{\partial \mathbb{L}}{\partial b_j^{(l)}} \quad \text{for all } l, j \right] \tag{8.13}$$

The vector update equation 8.12 can be expressed in terms of the scalar components as

$$w_{jk}^{(l)} = w_{jk}^{(l)} - r\frac{\partial \mathbb{L}}{\partial w_{jk}^{(l)}} \quad \text{for all } l, j, k$$
$$b_j^{(l)} = b_j^{(l)} - r\frac{\partial \mathbb{L}}{\partial b_j^{(l)}} \quad \text{for all } l, j \tag{8.14}$$

Note that we have to reevaluate these partial derivatives in each iteration since their values will change in every iteration.

8.4.3 Why a gradient provides the best direction for descent

Why does updating along the gradient reduce the function optimally? This is discussed in detail in chapter 3. Here we briefly recap the idea. Using multidimensional Taylor expansion, we can evaluate a function in the neighborhood of a known point. For instance, we can evaluate $\mathbb{L}\left(\vec{w} + \delta\vec{w}\right)$ for small offset $\delta\vec{w}$ from $\vec{w}$ as follows

$$\mathbb{L}\left(\vec{w} - \delta\vec{w}\right) = \mathbb{L}\left(\vec{w}\right) - \frac{1}{1!}\left(\delta\vec{w}\right)^T \nabla_{\vec{w}}\mathbb{L} + \frac{1}{2!}\left(\delta\vec{w}\right)^T H \left(\delta\vec{w}\right) + \cdots \tag{8.15}$$

where H, called the *Hessian matrix,* is defined as in equation 3.9. Since we are not going too far from $\vec{w}$, $||\delta\vec{w}||$ is small. This means the quadratic and higher-order terms are negligibly small, and we can drop them (the approximation is perfect in the limit when $||\delta\vec{w}|| \rightarrow 0$):

$$\mathbb{L}\left(\vec{w} - \vec{\delta w}\right) \approx \mathbb{L}\left(\vec{w}\right) - \frac{1}{1!}\left(\vec{\delta w}\right)^T \nabla_{\vec{w}}\mathbb{L}$$

But we know the dot product $\left(\vec{\delta w}\right)^T \nabla_{\vec{w}}\mathbb{L}$ will attain its maximum value when both the vectors point in the same direction: that is,

$$\vec{\delta w} = r\nabla_{\vec{w}}\mathbb{L}$$

for some constant of proportionality r.

In implementation, r is called the *learning rate*. A higher learning rate causes the optimization to progress more rapidly but also runs the risk of overshooting the minimum. We learn about these in more detail later. For now, simply note that r is a *tunable hyperparameter* of the system.

Thus, the largest decrease in value from $\mathbb{L}\left(\vec{w}\right)$ to $\mathbb{L}\left(\vec{w} - \vec{\delta w}\right)$ happens when $\delta\vec{w}$ is along the negative gradient. This is why we move toward the negative gradient in gradient descent: it is the fastest way to reach the minimum. The straight arrows in figure 8.8 illustrate the direction of the gradient. The dashed arrows show an arbitrary nongradient path for comparison.

We can deal with the bias vector $\vec{b}$ similarly.

8.4.4 Gradient descent and local minima

We should note that gradient descent can get stuck in a *local minimum*. Figure 8.9 shows this.

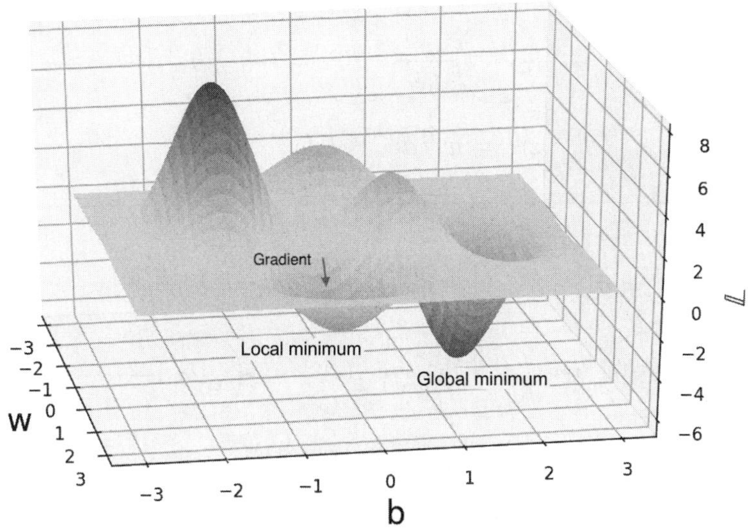

Figure 8.9 A nonconvex function with local and global minima. Depending on the starting point, gradient descent will take us to one or the other.

In earlier eras, optimization techniques tried hard to avoid local minima and converge to the global minimum. Techniques like simulated annealing and tunneling were carefully designed to avoid local minima. Modern-day neural networks have adopted a different attitude: they do not try very hard to avoid local minima. Sometimes a local minimum is an acceptable (accurate enough) solution. Otherwise, we can retrain the neural network: it will start from a random position, so this time it may go to a better minimum.

8.4.5 The backpropagation algorithm

We have seen that gradient descent progresses by repeatedly updating the weights and biases via equation 8.12. This is equivalent to repeatedly updating individual weights and biases using individual partial derivatives via equation 8.14.

Obtaining a closed-form solution for the gradients $\nabla_{\vec{w}}\mathbb{L}\left(\vec{w}, \vec{b}\right)$, $\nabla_{\vec{b}}\mathbb{L}\left(\vec{w}, \vec{b}\right)$ from equations 8.9 and 8.11—or, equivalently, obtaining a closed-form solution for the partial derivatives $\frac{\partial \mathbb{L}}{\partial w_{jk}^{(l)}}, \frac{\partial \mathbb{L}}{\partial b_j^{(l)}}$—is very difficult. Backpropagation is an algorithm that allows us to evaluate the gradients and update the weights and biases one layer at a time, like forward propagation (equation 8.10).

BACKPROPAGATION ALGORITHM ON A SIMPLE NETWORK

We first discuss backpropagation on a simple MLP with only a single neuron per layer. The main simplification resulting from this is that individual weights and biases no longer need subscripts, with only one weight and one bias between two successive layers. They still need superscripts to indicate layer IDs, however. Figure 8.10 shows this MLP. We use MSE loss (equation 8.11), but we work on a single input-output pair x_i, y_i. The

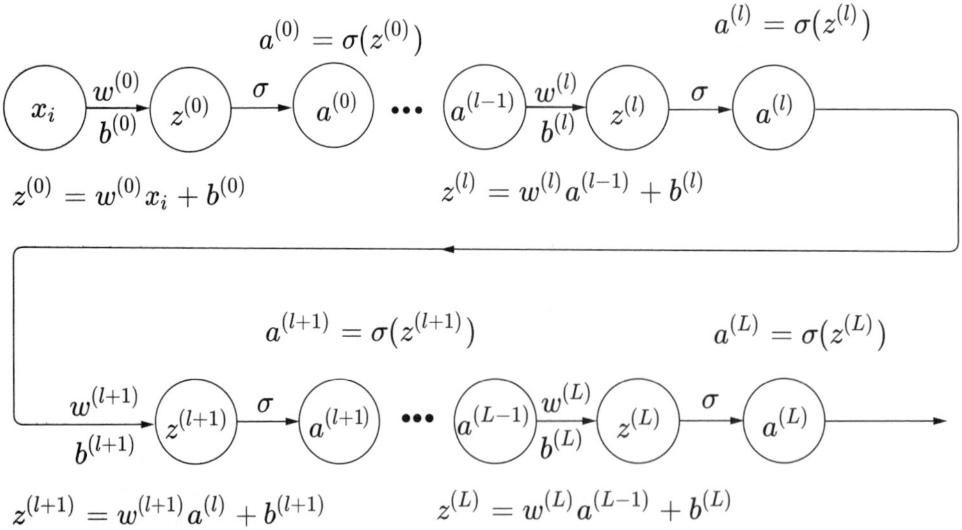

Figure 8.10 MLP with layers 0, . . ., L, one neuron per layer. Again, we have split every layer into a weighted sum and a sigmoid.

total loss (summation over all the training data instances) can easily be derived by repeating the same steps.

We first define an auxiliary variable:

$$\delta^{(l)} = \frac{\partial \mathbb{L}}{\partial z^{(l)}} \quad \text{for } l \in \{0, L\}$$

The physical significance of $\delta^{(l)}$ is that it is the rate of change of the loss with the (pre-activation) output of layer l (remember, in this network, layer l has a single neuron).

Let's establish a few important equations for the MLP in figure 8.10:

- *Forward propagation for an arbitrary layer* $l \in \{0, L\}$

$$z^{(l)} = w^{(l)} a^{(l-1)} + b^{(l)} \tag{8.16}$$

$$a^{(l)} = \sigma\left(z^{(l)}\right) \tag{8.17}$$

- *Loss*—Here we are working with a single training data instance, x_i, whose GT output is $\bar{y}_i$:

$$\mathbb{L} = \frac{1}{2}\left(a^{(L)} - \bar{y}_i\right)^2$$

- *Partial derivative of loss with respect to the weight and bias in terms of an auxiliary variable for the last layer, L*—Using the chain rule for partial derivatives,

$$\frac{\partial \mathbb{L}}{\partial w^{(L)}} = \frac{\partial \mathbb{L}}{\partial z^{(L)}} \frac{\partial z^{(L)}}{\partial w^{(L)}}$$

  Examining the terms on the right, we see

$$\frac{\partial \mathbb{L}}{\partial z^{(L)}} = \delta^{(L)}$$

  (auxiliary variable for layer L). And using the forward propagation equations,

$$\frac{\partial z^{(L)}}{\partial w^{(L)}} = a^{(L-1)}$$

  Together, they lead to

$$\frac{\partial \mathbb{L}}{\partial w^{(L)}} = \delta^{(L)} \cdot a^{(L-1)}$$

  Similarly,

$$\frac{\partial \mathbb{L}}{\partial b^{(L)}} = \frac{\partial \mathbb{L}}{\partial z^{(L)}} \frac{\partial z^{(L)}}{\partial b^{(L)}} = \delta^{(L)} \cdot 1$$

  Consequently, we have the following pair of equations expressing the partial derivative of loss with respect to weight and bias, respectively, in terms of the auxiliary variable for the last layer:

$$\frac{\partial \mathbb{L}}{\partial w^{(L)}} = \delta^{(L)} \cdot a^{(L-1)} \tag{8.18}$$

$$\frac{\partial \mathbb{L}}{\partial b^{(L)}} = \delta^{(L)} \tag{8.19}$$

- *Auxiliary variable for the last layer, L*—Using the chain rule for partial derivatives,

  $$\delta^{(L)} = \frac{\partial \mathbb{L}}{\partial z^{(L)}} = \frac{\partial \mathbb{L}}{\partial a^{(L)}} \frac{\partial a^{(L)}}{\partial z^{(L)}} = \left(a^{(L)} - \bar{y}_i\right) \frac{d\sigma\left(z^{(L)}\right)}{dz^{(L)}}$$

  Using equation 8.5 for the derivative of a sigmoid, we get

  $$\delta^{(L)} = \left(a^{(L)} - \bar{y}_i\right) \sigma\left(z^{(L)}\right)\left(1 - \sigma\left(z^{(L)}\right)\right)$$

  which, using equation 8.17, leads to

  $$\delta^{(L)} = \left(a^{(L)} - \bar{y}_i\right) a^{(L)}\left(1 - a^{(L)}\right) \tag{8.20}$$

- *Partial derivative of the loss with respect to the weight and bias in terms of an auxiliary variable for an arbitrary layer l*—Using the chain rule for partial derivatives,

  $$\frac{\partial \mathbb{L}}{\partial w^{(l)}} = \frac{\partial \mathbb{L}}{\partial z^{(l)}} \frac{\partial z^{(l)}}{\partial w^{(l)}}$$

  Using the definition of the auxiliary variable and the forward propagation equation 8.16, this leads to

  $$\frac{\partial \mathbb{L}}{\partial w^{(l)}} = \delta^{(l)} a^{(l-1)} \tag{8.21}$$

  Similarly,

  $$\frac{\partial \mathbb{L}}{\partial b^{(l)}} = \frac{\partial \mathbb{L}}{\partial z^{(l)}} \frac{\partial z^{(l)}}{\partial b^{(l)}}$$

  Using the definition of the auxiliary variable and the forward propagation equation 8.16, this leads to

  $$\frac{\partial \mathbb{L}}{\partial b^{(l)}} = \delta^{(l)} \tag{8.22}$$

- *Auxiliary variable for an arbitrary layer, l*—Using the chain rule for partial derivatives,

  $$\delta^{(l)} = \frac{\partial \mathbb{L}}{\partial z^{(l)}} = \frac{\partial \mathbb{L}}{\partial z^{(l+1)}} \frac{\partial z^{(l+1)}}{\partial a^{(l)}} \frac{\partial a^{(l)}}{\partial z^{(l)}}$$

  Using the definition of the auxiliary variable and the forward propagation equation 8.16, this leads to

  $$\delta^{(l)} = \delta^{(l+1)} w^{(l+1)} \frac{d\sigma\left(z^{(l)}\right)}{dz^{(l)}} = \delta^{(l+1)} w^{(l+1)} \sigma\left(z^{(l)}\right)\left(1 - \sigma\left(z^{(l)}\right)\right)$$

  which yields

  $$\delta^{(l)} = \delta^{(l+1)} w^{(l+1)} a^{(l)}\left(1 - a^{(l)}\right) \tag{8.23}$$

We first encountered the one-layer-at-a-time property in section 8.3.2 in connection with the forward propagation equations. Let's recap that in the context of training our simple network. Consider equations 8.16 and 8.17. We initialize the system with some values of weights $w^{(l)}$ and biases $b^{(l)}$. Using those, we can evaluate the layer 0 outputs. For starters, we can evaluate $z^{(0)}$ and $a^{(0)}$ easily (since all the inputs are known):

$$z^{(0)} = w^{(0)}x + b^{(0)}$$
$$a^{(0)} = \sigma\left(z^{(0)}\right)$$

Once we have $z^{(0)}$ and $a^{(0)}$, we can use them to evaluate $z^{(1)}$ and $a^{(1)}$ via equations 8.16 and 8.17. But if we have $z^{(1)}$ and $a^{(1)}$, we can use them to evaluate $z^{(2)}$ and $a^{(2)}$ via equations 8.16 and 8.17 again. And we can proceed in this fashion up to layer L to obtain $a^{(L)}$, which is the grand output of the MLP. In other words, we can iteratively evaluate the outputs of successive layers using *only* the outputs from the previous layer. No other layers need to be known. At any given iteration, we only have to keep the previous layer in memory: we can build the current layer from that. A single sequence of applications of equations 8.16 and 8.17 for layers 0 to L is known as a *forward pass.*

A similar trick can be applied to evaluate the auxiliary variables, except we go *backward.* We can evaluate the auxiliary variable for the last layer, $\delta^{(L)}$, via equation 8.20. But once we have $\delta^{(L)}$, we can evaluate $\delta^{(L-1)}$ via equation 8.23. From that, we can evaluate $\delta^{(L-2)}$. We can proceed in this fashion all the way to layer 0, evaluating successively $\delta^{(L)}$, $\delta^{(L-1)}, \cdots, \delta^{(0)}$. Every time we evaluate a $\delta^{(l)}$, we can also evaluate the $\frac{\partial \mathbb{L}}{\partial w^{(l)}}$ and $\frac{\partial \mathbb{L}}{\partial b^{(l)}}$ for the same layer via equations 8.21 and 8.22, respectively. We can also update the weight and bias of that layer right there using the just estimated partial derivatives, since the current values will never be needed again during training. Thus, starting from the last layer, we can update the weights and biases of all layers until layer 0 in this fashion. This is *backpropagation.*

Of course, we have to proceed in tandem: one forward propagation (which sets the values of zs and as) for layers 0 to L, followed by a backpropagation layer for L to 0. Repeat these steps until convergence.

NOTE Fully functional code for forward propagation, MSE loss, and backpropagation, executable via Jupyter Notebook, can be found at http://mng.bz/pJrw.

Listing 8.3 PyTorch code for forward and backward propagation

```
def forward_backward(x, y, W, b):
    L = len(W) - 1
    a = []
    for l in range(0, L+1):
        a_prev = x if l == 0 else a[l-1]      ◄— Forward propagation
        z_l = Z(a_prev, W[l], b[l])
        a_l = A(z_l)
        a.append(a_l)

    loss = mse_loss(a[L], y)      ◄— Computes MSE loss
```

```
deltas = [None for _ in range(L + 1)]
W_grads = [None for _ in range(L + 1)]
b_grads = [None for _ in range(L + 1)]

a_L = a[L]

deltas[L] = (a_L - y) * a_L * (1 - a_L)
W_grads[L] = torch.matmul(deltas[L], a[L - 1].T)
b_grads[L] = deltas[L]

for l in range(L-1, -1, -1):
    a_l = a[l]
    deltas[l] = torch.matmul(W[l+1].T, deltas[l + 1]) * a_l * (1 - a_l)
    W_grads[l] = torch.matmul(deltas[l], a[l - 1].T)
    b_grads[l] = deltas[l]

return loss, W_grads, b_grads
```

Arrays to store $\delta^{(l)}$, $\frac{\partial \mathbb{L}}{\partial w^{(l)}}$, $\frac{\partial \mathbb{L}}{\partial b^{(l)}}$ for layers 0 to L

Activation of the last layer - $a^{(L)}$

Computes the δ and gradients for layer L

Computes the δ and gradients for layers 0 to $L-1$

BACKPROPAGATION ALGORITHM ON AN ARBITRARY NETWORK OF LINEAR LAYERS

In section 8.4.5, we saw a simple network with only one neuron per layer. There was only one connection and hence one weight, one activation, and one auxiliary variable per layer. Consequently, we could drop the subscripts (although we had to keep the superscript indicating the layer) of all these variables. Now we examine a more generic network consisting of linear layers $0, \cdots, L$. An arbitrary slice of this network is shown in figure 8.6.

The ultimate goal is to evaluate the partial derivatives of the loss with respect to the weights and biases. Using them, we can update the current weights and biases to optimally reduce the loss.

Our overall strategy is as follows. We use the auxiliary variables again. We first derive expressions that allow us to compute the auxiliary variable for the last layer. Then we derive an expression that allows us to compute auxiliary variables for an arbitrary layer, l, given the auxiliary variables for layer $l+1$. Since we can directly compute auxiliary variables for the last layer, L, we can use this expression to compute auxiliary variables for the second-to-last layer $L-1$. But once we have them, we can compute auxiliary variables for layer $L-2$. We proceed like this until we reach layer 0. Thus we can compute all the auxiliary variables. We also derive expressions that allow us to compute, from the auxiliary variables, the partial derivatives of loss with respect to weights and biases. This gives us everything we need. Since we start by computing things pertaining to the last layer and proceed iteratively toward the initial layer, the process is called *backpropagation.*

You will notice the similarity between the expressions derived next and those derived for the one-neuron-per-layer network. The differences are explained:

- *Forward propagation (arbitrary layer l)*—Forward propagation through this network has already been described in section 8.3.1 and can be succinctly represented by equation 8.7 (repeated here for handy reference). On the left are the scalar equations, for one neuron at a time; and on the right are the vector equations, for the entire layer. They are equivalent:

$$z_j^{(l)} = \sum_{k=0}^{m} w_{jk}^{(l)} a_k^{(l-1)} + b_j^{(l)} \qquad \vec{z}^{(l)} = W^{(l)} \vec{a}^{(l-1)} + \vec{b}^{(l)}$$

$$a_j^{(l)} = \sigma\left(z_j^{(l)}\right) \qquad \vec{a}^{(l)} = \sigma\left(\vec{z}^{(l)}\right) \tag{8.24}$$

Indices j and k iterate over all the neurons in the relevant layer. By convention, we always use these variables for arbitrary neurons in a layer. The variable l is used to index the layers. When indexing weights, we typically use j to indicate the destination and k to indicate the source—remember that weights are indexed (destination, source) somewhat unexpectedly to simplify the math. Typically, vectors correspond to entire layers. Individual vector elements correspond to specific neurons and are indexed by j or k.

- *Loss*—Unlike the simple network, here, the final Lth layer can have multiple neurons. Hence the loss function becomes

$$\mathbb{L} = \frac{1}{2}\|\vec{a}^{(L)} - \bar{y}\|^2 = \frac{1}{2}\sum_j \left(a_j^{(L)} - \bar{y}_j\right)^2 \tag{8.25}$$

where the summation happens over all neurons in the last layer. Note that $\vec{a}^{(L)}$ is the output of the MLP: that is, $\vec{a}^{(L)} = \vec{y} = MLP\left(\vec{x}\right)$ for the training input $\vec{x}$ (see equation 8.10). The GT output corresponding to $\vec{x}$ is the constant vector $\bar{y}$. The closer $\vec{y}$ is to $\bar{y}$, the smaller the loss.

Note that we need to average the loss over the entire training data set. Here we are showing the loss computation for a single training data instance. The computation simply needs to be replicated for each training data instance, and the results averaged.

- *Auxiliary variables*—Now that a layer has multiple neurons, we have one auxiliary variable per neuron. Thus the auxiliary variable has a subscript identifying the specific neuron in that layer. It continues to have a superscript indicating its layer. We define

$$\delta_j^{(l)} = \frac{\partial \mathbb{L}}{\partial z_j^{(l)}} \quad \forall j \in \{0 \cdots \text{ number of neurons in layer } l\}, \forall l \in \{0 \cdots L\}$$

  – *Auxiliary variable for the last layer*

$$\delta_j^{(L)} = \frac{\partial \mathbb{L}}{\partial z_j^{(L)}} = \frac{\partial \mathbb{L}}{\partial a_j^{(L)}} \frac{\partial a_j^{(L)}}{\partial z_j^{(L)}}$$

Using equation 8.25 and observing that only one of the terms in the summation—the jth term—will survive the differentiation with respect to $a_j^{(L)}$ (since the a_js are independent of each other), we get

$$\frac{\partial \mathbb{L}}{\partial a_j^{(L)}} = \left(a_j^{(L)} - \bar{y}_j\right)$$

Also, using the lower-left equation from 8.24 and equation 8.5, we get

$$\frac{\partial a_j^{(L)}}{\partial z_j^{(L)}} = \frac{d\sigma\left(z_j^{(L)}\right)}{dz_j^{(L)}} = a_j^{(L)}\left(1 - a_j^{(L)}\right)$$

Combining these, we get

$$\delta_j^{(L)} = \left(a_j^{(L)} - \bar{y}_j\right) a_j^{(L)} \left(1 - a_j^{(L)}\right) \quad (8.26)$$

$$\vec{\delta}^{(L)} = \left(\vec{a}^{(L)} - \vec{\bar{y}}\right) \circ \vec{a}^{(L)} \circ \left(\vec{1} - \vec{a}^{(L)}\right) \quad (8.27)$$

Here, $\circ$ denotes the Hadamard product between two vectors. It is basically a vector of elementwise products of corresponding vector elements. Thus,

$$\vec{a} = \begin{bmatrix} a_0 \\ a_1 \\ \vdots \\ a_n \end{bmatrix} \qquad \vec{b} = \begin{bmatrix} b_0 \\ b_1 \\ \vdots \\ b_n \end{bmatrix} \quad (8.28)$$

$$\vec{a} \circ \vec{b} = \begin{bmatrix} a_0 b_0 \\ a_1 b_1 \\ \vdots \\ a_n b_n \end{bmatrix} \quad (8.29)$$

Equations 8.26 and 8.27 are identical. The former is a scalar equation expressing individual auxiliary variables of the last layer. The latter is a vector equation expressing all the auxiliary variables of the last layer together. We can compute these directly if we have performed a forward pass and have its results, the $a_j^{(L)}$s available along with the training data GT.

– *Auxiliary variable for an arbitrary layer, l*—This is significantly different and harder to understand than the one-neuron-per-layer case. We are trying to evaluate $\delta_j^{(l)} = \frac{\partial \mathbb{L}}{\partial z_j^{(l)}}$ in the general case: that is, for an arbitrary layer l. The loss does not *directly* depend on the inner layer variable $z_j^{(l)}$. The loss directly depends only on the last layer activations, which depend on the previous layer, and so forth. The zs in any one layer form a *complete* dependency set for the loss $\mathbb{L}$, meaning the loss can be expressed in terms of only these and no other variables. In particular, we can express the loss as $\mathbb{L}\left(z_0^{(l+1)}, z_1^{(l+1)}, z_2^{(l+1)}, \cdots\right)$. You can form a mental picture that $z_j^{(l)}$ fans out to $\mathbb{L}$ *through* all the zs in the next layer, $z_0^{(l+1)}$, $z_1^{(l+1)}$, $z_2^{(l+1)}$, and so on. Then, using the chain rule of partial differentiation,

$$\delta_j^{(l)} = \frac{\partial \mathbb{L}\left(z_0^{(l+1)}, z_1^{(l+1)}, z_2^{(l+1)}, \dots\right)}{\partial z_j^{(l)}} = \sum_k \frac{\partial \mathbb{L}}{\partial z_k^{(l+1)}} \frac{\partial z_k^{(l+1)}}{\partial z_j^{(l)}}$$

$$= \sum_k \frac{\partial \mathbb{L}}{\partial z_k^{(l+1)}} \frac{\partial z_k^{(l+1)}}{\partial a_j^{(l)}} \frac{\partial a_j^{(l)}}{\partial z_j^{(l)}}$$

Now, by definition,

$$\frac{\partial \mathbb{L}}{\partial z_k^{(l+1)}} = \delta_k^{(l+1)}$$

And using equation 8.24,

$$\frac{\partial z_k^{(l+1)}}{\partial a_j^{(l)}} = w_{kj}^{(l+1)}$$

while

$$\frac{\partial a_j^{(l)}}{\partial z_j^{(l)}} = \frac{d\sigma\left(z_j^{(l)}\right)}{dz_j^{(l)}} = a_j^{(l)}\left(1 - a_j^{(l)}\right)$$

Combining all these, we get the scalar expression for a single auxiliary variable. It is presented here along with its equivalent vector equation for the entire layer:

$$\delta_j^{(l)} = \sum_k \delta_k^{(l+1)} w_{kj}^{(l+1)} a_j^{(l)}\left(1 - a_j^{(l)}\right) \tag{8.30}$$

$$\vec{\delta}^{(l)} = \left(\left(W^{(l+1)}\right)^T \vec{\delta}^{(l+1)}\right) \circ \vec{a}^{(l)} \circ \left(\vec{1} - \vec{a}^{(l)}\right) \tag{8.31}$$

Here, $\circ$ denotes the Hadamard multiplication explained earlier and $W^{(+1l)}$ is the matrix representing the weights of *all connections from layer l to layer* $(l + 1)$ (see equation 8.8).

Equations 8.30 and 8.31 allow us to evaluate $\delta^{(l)}$s from the $\delta^{(l+1)}$s if the results of forward propagation (as) are available. We have already shown that the auxiliary variables for the last layer are directly computable from the activations of that layer. Hence, we can evaluate all the layers' auxiliary variables.

- *Derivatives of loss with respect to weights and biases in terms of auxiliary variables*—We have already seen how to compute auxiliary variables. Now we will express the partial derivatives of loss with respect to weights and biases in terms of those. This will provide us with the gradients we need to update the weights and biases along the negative gradient, which is the optimal move to minimize loss:

$$\frac{\partial \mathbb{L}}{\partial w_{jk}^{(l)}} = \frac{\partial \mathbb{L}}{\partial z_j^{(l)}} \frac{\partial z_j^{(l)}}{\partial w_{jk}^{(l)}} = \delta_j^{(l)} a_k^{(l-1)} \tag{8.32}$$

$$\nabla_{w^{(l)}}\mathbb{L} = \vec{\delta}^{(l)} \left(\vec{a}^{(l-1)}\right)^T \tag{8.33}$$

Equations 8.32 and 8.33 are equivalent. The first is scalar and pertains to individual weights in layer l, and the second describes the entire layer. Similarly, equations 8.34 and 8.35 are equivalent:

$$\frac{\partial \mathbb{L}}{\partial b_j^{(l)}} = \frac{\partial \mathbb{L}}{\partial z_j^{(l)}} \frac{\partial z_j^{(l)}}{\partial b_j^{(l)}} = \delta_j^{(l)} \tag{8.34}$$

$$\nabla_{b^{(l)}}\mathbb{L} = \vec{\delta}^{(l)} \tag{8.35}$$

The first is scalar and pertains to individual biases in layer l, and the second describes the entire layer.

8.4.6 Putting it all together: Overall training algorithm

Previously, we discussed forward propagation: passing an input vector $\vec{x}$ through a sequence of linear layers and generating an output prediction. We learned about MSE loss, $\mathbb{L}$, which calculates the deviation of the output prediction from the GT, y. We also learned to compute the gradients of $\mathbb{L}$ with respect to parameters W and b using backpropagation. In the following algorithm, we describe how these components come together in the training process:

Algorithm 8.1 Training a neural network

Initialize $\vec{w}, b$ with random values
while $\mathbb{L} > \textit{threshold}$ **do**
▷ Forward pass
for $l \leftarrow 0$ to L **do**
$\vec{z}^{(l)} = W^{(l)}\vec{a}^{(l-1)} + \vec{b}^{(l)}$
$\vec{a}^{(l)} = \sigma\left(\vec{z}^{(l)}\right)$
end for
▷ Loss
$\mathbb{L} = \frac{1}{2}\|\vec{a}^{(L)} - \vec{y}\|^2$
▷ Gradients for the last layer
$\vec{\delta}^{(L)} = \left(\vec{a}^{(L)} - \vec{y}\right) \circ \vec{a}^{(L)} \circ \left(\vec{1} - \vec{a}^{(L)}\right)$
$\nabla_{W^{(L)}}\mathbb{L} = \vec{\delta}^{(L)} \left(\vec{a}^{(L-1)}\right)^T$
$\nabla_{b^{(L)}}\mathbb{L} = \vec{\delta}^{(L)}$
▷ Gradients for the remaining layers
for $l \leftarrow L-1$ to 0 **do**
$\vec{\delta}^{(l)} = \left(\left(W^{(l+1)}\right)^T \vec{\delta}^{(l+1)}\right) \circ \vec{a}^{(l)} \circ \left(\vec{1} - \vec{a}^{(l)}\right)$
$\nabla_{W^{(l)}}\mathbb{L} = \vec{\delta}^{(l)} \left(\vec{a}^{(l-1)}\right)^T$
$\nabla_{b^{(l)}}\mathbb{L} = \vec{\delta}^{(l)}$
end for

▷ Parameter update

$W = W - r\nabla_W \mathbb{L}$

$b = b - r\nabla_b \mathbb{L}$

end while

8.5 Training a neural network in PyTorch

Now that we've seen how the training process works, let's look at how this can be implemented in PyTorch. For this purpose, let's take the following example. Consider an e-commerce company that's trying to solve the problem of demand prediction: the company would like to estimate the number of mobile phones that will be sold in the upcoming week so that it can manage its inventory accordingly. Our goal is to develop a model that can make such a prediction. Let's assume that the demand for a given week is a function of three variables: (a) the number of mobile phones sold in the previous week, (b) discounts offered, and (c) the number of weeks to the next holiday. Let's call these variables `prev_week_sales`, `discount_fraction`, and `weeks_to_next_holidays`, respectively. This example can be modeled as a regression problem wherein we predict the number of mobile phones sold in the upcoming week from an input vector of the form `[prev_week_sales, discount_fraction, weeks_to_next_holidays]`.

NOTE Fully functional code for this section, executable via Jupyter Notebook, can be found at http://mng.bz/O1Ra.

From historical data, we generate a large data set, `X`, that contains the values of the three variables for the last N weeks. `X` is represented as an N x 3 matrix, with each row representing an individual training data instance and N being the total number of data points available. We also have a GT vector $\bar{y}$ of length N, containing the actual sales of mobile phones for each of the weeks in the training data set. Table 8.1 shows sample data points from our training set.

Table 8.1 Sample training data for demand prediction

Previous week sales	Discount fraction (%)	Weeks to next holidays	Number of units sold
76,440	63	2	94,182
41,512	50	3	51,531
77,395	77	9	95,938
...	...	...	...
21,532	70	4	28,559

NOTE In this section, `X` and $\bar{y}$ refer to the entire batch of training data instances. This may be infeasible in practical settings because of large data sets. To address this, we typically use mini-batches of `X` and $\bar{y}$. We introduce the concept of mini-batches formally in the next chapter.

One important point about the data set is that the range of values for each feature is completely different. For example, the previous week's sales are expressed as a number on the order of tens of thousands of units, whereas the discount fraction is a percentage number between 0 and 100. In machine learning, it is a good practice to bring all the values to a common scale, because doing so can help improve the speed of training and reduce the chance of getting stuck at a local minimum. For our example, let's use min-max normalization to scale all the features to 0–1. The following code snippet shows how to perform min-max normalization in PyTorch. For the rest of the discussion, we assume that we are operating on the normalized data:

```
def min_max_norm(X, y):
    X, y = X.clone(), y.clone()          # Clones the data so as not to mutilate the original data

    X_min, X_max = torch.min(X, dim=0)[0],
            torch.max(X, dim=0)[0]       # Calculates the min and max values of each column of X

    X = (X - X_min) / (X_max - X_min)    # Normalizes X

    y_min, y_max = torch.min(y, dim=0)[0],
            torch.max(y, dim=0)[0]       # Calculates the min and max values of y

    y = (y - y_min) / (y_max - y_min)    # Normalizes y
    return X, y
```

To solve the regression problem, let's first define a two-layer neural network model that can take in 3D input vectors of the form [`prev_week_sales`, `discount_fraction`, `is_holidays_ongoing`] and generate output predictions. The following code snippet gives the PyTorch implementation:

```
class TwoLayeredNN(torch.nn.Module):
    def __init__(self, input_size, hidden1_size, hidden2_size, output_size):
        super(TwoLayeredNN, self).__init__()

        self.model = torch.nn.Sequential(    # Defines the network as a sequence of linear and sigmoid layers

            torch.nn.Linear(input_size, hidden1_size),    # First hidden layer with a weight matrix of size (input_size × hidden1_size)
            torch.nn.Sigmoid(),

            torch.nn.Linear(hidden1_size, hidden2_size),  # Second hidden layer with a weight matrix of size (hidden1_size × hidden2_size)
            torch.nn.Sigmoid(),

            torch.nn.Linear(hidden2_size, output_size)    # Output layer with a weight matrix of size (hidden2_size × output_size)
        )

    def forward(self, X):    # X is an N × 3 matrix. Each row is a (3D vector) representing a single data point.
        return self.model(X)

nn = TwoLayeredNN(input_size=X.shape[-1], hidden1_size=10,
                                  hidden2_size=5, output_size=1)
```

Neural network models in PyTorch should subclass `torch.nn.Module` and implement the `forward` method. Our two-layer neural network contains two linear layers, each followed by a sigmoid (nonlinear) activation layer. Finally, we have a linear layer that converts the final activation into the output prediction. These layers are chained together using the `torch.nn.Sequential` class to form the two-layer neural network. Whenever our model is called using `nn(X)`, the `forward` method is invoked, and the input `X` is passed through the individual layers to obtain the final output.

Now that we have defined the neural network and its forward pass, we need to define the loss function. We can use the MSE loss defined in equation 8.11. The loss function essentially compares the demand predicted by the neural network model with the actual demand from the GT and returns larger values when the difference is higher and smaller values when the difference is lower. MSE loss is readily available in PyTorch through the `torch.nn.MSELoss` class. The following code snippet shows a sample invocation:

```
loss = torch.nn.MSELoss()     ← Instantiates the loss function

loss(y_pred, y_gt)            ← compute loss
                                y_pred: Output of the neural network
                                y_gt: ground truth
```

Finally, we need a way to compute the gradients of the loss with respect to the parameters of our model so we can start the training process. Luckily, we don't have to explicitly compute the gradients ourselves because PyTorch automatically does this for us using automatic differentiation, aka autograd. (Refer to section 3.1 for more details about autograd.) For our current example, we can instruct PyTorch to run backpropagation and compute gradients by calling `loss.backward()`. With this, we're ready to start training. PyTorch code for training the neural network is shown next.

Listing 8.4 Training a neural network

```
nn = TwoLayeredNN(input_size=X.shape[-1],      ← Instantiates the neural network
                  hidden1_size=10,
                  hidden2_size=5,
                  output_size=1)

loss = torch.nn.MSELoss()      ← Instantiates the loss function

optimizer = torch.optim.SGD(nn.parameters(), lr=0.2,      ← Instantiates the optimizer
                            momentum=0.9)

num_iters = 1000

for i in range(num_iters):     ← Training loop
    y_out = nn(X)      ← Forward pass

    mse_loss = loss(y_out, y)      ← Computes the loss

    optimizer.zero_grad()      ← Clears the gradients and prevents accumulation of
                                 gradients from the previous step

    mse_loss.backward()      ← Runs backpropagation (computes gradients)

    optimizer.step()      ← Updates the weights
```

In the training loop, we iteratively run the forward pass, compute the loss, calculate the gradients, and update the weights. The neural network is initialized with random weights and hence makes arbitrary predictions for the demand in the early iterations of the training loop. This translates to a high initial loss value. However, as training proceeds, the weights are updated to minimize the loss value, and the predicted demand comes closer to the actual GT. To update the weights, we use what is known as an *optimizer*. During training, the gradients are computed by calling the `backward()` function on the `loss` object. Following that, the `optimizer.step` call updates the weights and biases. In this example, we used the stochastic gradient descent–based optimizer, which can be invoked using `torch.optim.SGD`. PyTorch offers various optimizers, such as Adam, AdaGrad, and so on, which will be discussed in detail in the next chapter. We typically run the training loop until the loss reaches a value low enough to be acceptable. Once the training loop completes, we have a model that can readily take in new data points and generate output predictions.

Summary

- The sigmoid function $\sigma\left(x\right) = \frac{1}{1+e^{-x}}$ has an S-shaped graph, is a differential version of the Heaviside step function, and, as such, is used in perceptrons. Thus the overall perceptron function becomes $P\left(\vec{x}\right) \equiv \sigma\left(\vec{w}^T\vec{x} + b\right)$. It is parametrized by $\vec{w}$ and b, which control the slope and position, respectively, of the S-shaped curve.
- Neural networks solve real-life problems that require intelligence by approximating the function that solves the problem in question. They are built of multiple perceptrons interconnected by weighted edges. Instead of connecting perceptrons haphazardly, we connect them as layers. In a layered network, a perceptron is only connected to perceptrons from the immediately preceding layer. Intra-layer and other connections are not allowed.
- Supervised neural networks have manually generated outputs for a sample set of input values (ground truth). This entire data set consisting of inputs and known outputs is known as the training data set.
- Loss is defined as the mismatch between the ground truth and actual output generated by the neural network on training data inputs. The simplest way to compute loss is to take the Euclidean distance between the neural network-generated output and ground-truth vectors. This is called the MSE (mean squared error) loss. Mathematically, given a training data set $\mathbb{T}$ that is a set of <input, GT output> pairs $\mathbb{T} = \{\langle\vec{x}, \bar{y}\rangle\}$, the loss can be expressed as

  $$\mathbb{L} = \frac{1}{2}\sum_{x_i \in \mathbb{T}} \left(\vec{y} - \bar{y}\right)^2$$

  where the output is $\vec{y}_i = MLP\left(\vec{x}_i\right)$.
- Training is the process of optimizing the connection weights and biases of a specific neural network so that the loss is minimal. Note that during inferencing, the neural network typically sees data it has never seen during training. Inferencing outputs

are good only if the distribution of training inputs roughly matches the overall input distribution.

- We minimize the loss by iteratively adjusting the weights and biases. The quickest way to reach the closest minimum of a multivariate function is to follow the gradient. Hence, we adjust the weights and biases following the gradient of the loss function. Mathematically,

$$W = W - r\nabla_W \mathbb{L}$$
$$b = b - r\nabla_b \mathbb{L}$$

- A forward pass is the process of generating outputs from inputs with a neural network: more specifically, a multilayer perceptron (MLP). Thus an MLP does inferencing via a forward pass. A beautiful property of a layered network is that we can do a forward pass dealing with one layer at a time, proceeding iteratively from layer 0 (closest to the input) to the output layer. Mathematically,

$$\vec{z}^{(l)} = W^{(l)}\vec{a}^{(l-1)} + \vec{b}^{(l)}$$
$$\vec{a}^{(l)} = \sigma\left(\vec{z}^{(l)}\right)$$

where $W^{(l)}$, $\vec{b}^{(l)}$ represent the weights and biases for layer l, and $\vec{a}^{(l)}$ represent the output for layer l (activation), which is also the input for layer $l+1$.

- A backward pass is the process by which the gradients of the loss with respect to all the weights and biases are generated. It relies on the result of the preceding forward pass and proceeds from the output layer toward the input layer. It uses auxiliary variables $\vec{\delta}^{(l)}$, which can be computed by iterating backward from the last (closest to output) layer to the first (closest to input) layer—hence the name *backward propagation*—and all the required gradients can be computed from those auxiliary variables. Mathematically,

$$\vec{\delta}^{(l)} = \left(\left(W^{(l+1)}\right)^T \vec{\delta}^{(l+1)}\right) \circ \vec{a}^{(l)} \circ \left(\vec{1} - \vec{a}^{(l)}\right)$$
$$\nabla_{W^{(l)}}\mathbb{L} = \vec{\delta}^{(l)} \left(\vec{a}^{(l-1)}\right)^T$$
$$\nabla_{b^{(l)}}\mathbb{L} = \vec{\delta}^{(l)}$$

- Training progresses by alternating forward and backward passes on the training data set.

Loss, optimization, and regularization

This chapter covers

- Geometrical and algebraic introductions to loss functions
- Geometrical intuitions for softmax
- Optimization techniques including momentum, Nesterov, AdaGrad, Adam, and SGD
- Regularization and its relationship to Bayesian approaches
- Overfitting while training, and dropout

By now, it should be etched in your mind that neural networks are essentially function approximators. In particular, neural network classifiers model the decision boundaries between the classes in the feature space (a space where every input feature combination is a specific point). Supervised classifiers mark sample training data inputs in this space with a—perhaps manually generated—class label (ground truth). The training process iteratively learns a function that essentially creates decision boundaries separating the sampled training data points into individual classes. If the training data set is a reasonable representative of the true distribution of possible inputs, the network (the learned function that models the class boundaries) will classify never-before-seen inputs with good accuracy.

When we select a specific neural network architecture (with a fixed set of layers, each with a fixed set of perceptrons with specific connections), we have essentially frozen the *family* of functions we use as a function approximator. We still have to "learn" the exact weights of the connectors between various *perceptrons* (aka *neurons*). The training process iteratively sets these weights so as to best classify the training data points. To do this, we design a loss function that measures the departure of the network output from the desired result. The network continually tries to minimize this loss. There are a variety of loss functions to choose from.

The iterative process through which loss is minimized is called *optimization*. We also have a multitude of optimization algorithms to choose from. In this chapter, we study loss functions, optimization algorithms, and associated topics like L1 and L2 regularization and dropout. We also learn about overfitting, a potential pitfall to avoid while training a neural network.

NOTE The complete PyTorch code for this chapter is available at http://mng.bz/aZv9 in the form of fully functional and executable Jupyter notebooks.

9.1 Loss functions

A loss function essentially measures the badness of the neural network output. In the case of a supervised network, the loss for an individual training data instance is the distance of the actual output of the neural network (aka prediction) from the desired ideal outputs (known or manually labeled ground truth [GT]) on that particular training input instance. Total training loss is obtained by summing the losses from all training data instances. Training is essentially an iterative optimization process that minimizes the total training loss.

9.1.1 Quantification and geometrical view of loss

Loss surfaces and their minimization are described in detail in section 8.4.2. Here we only do a quick review.

A full neural network can be described by the equation

$$\vec{y} = f\left(\vec{x}\middle|\vec{w}, \vec{b}\right) \tag{9.1}$$

Equation 9.1 says that given an input $\vec{x}$, the neural network with weights $\vec{w}$ and biases $\vec{b}$ emits the *output vector* or *prediction vector* $\vec{y}$. The weights and biases may be organized into layers; this equation does not care. The vectors $\vec{w}$, $\vec{b}$, respectively, denote the sets of *all* weights and biases from all layers aggregated. Evaluating the function $f(\cdot)$ is equivalent to performing one forward pass on the network. In particular, given a training input instance $\vec{x}^{(i)}$, the neural network emits $\vec{y}^{(i)} = f\left(\vec{x}^{(i)}\middle|\vec{w}, \vec{b}\right)$. We refer to $\vec{y}^{(i)}$ as the output of the ith training data instance.

During supervised training, for each training input instance $\vec{x}^{(i)}$, we have the GT (the known output), $\bar{y}^{(i)}$. We refer to $\bar{y}^{(i)}$ as the *GT vector* (as usual, we use superscript indices for training data instances).

Ideally, the output vector $\vec{y}^{(i)}$ should match the GT vector $\bar{y}^{(i)}$. The mismatch between them is the loss for that training data instance $\mathbb{L}^{(i)}\left(\vec{y}^{(i)}, \bar{y}^{(i)} \middle| \vec{w}, \vec{b}\right)$, which we sometimes denote as $\mathbb{L}^{(i)}\left(\vec{y}^{(i)}, \bar{y}^{(i)}\right)$. The overall training loss (to be minimized by the optimization process) is the sum of losses over all training data instances:

$$\mathbb{L}\left(\vec{w}, \vec{b}\right) = \sum_{i=0}^{n-1} \mathbb{L}^{(i)}\left(f\left(\vec{x}^{(i)} \middle| \vec{w}, \vec{b}\right), \bar{y}^{(i)}\right) = \sum_{i=0}^{n-1} \mathbb{L}^{(i)}\left(\vec{y}^{(i)}, \bar{y}^{(i)} \middle| \vec{w}, \vec{b}\right) \tag{9.2}$$

where the summation is over all training data instances, and n is the size of the training data set. Note that this summation over all training data points is needed to compute the loss for each training data instance. Thus an *epoch,* a single training loop over all training data instances, costs $O\left(n^2\right)$, where n is the number of training data points. Training usually requires many epochs. This makes the training process very expensive. In section 9.2.2, we study ways of mitigating this.

NOTE In this chapter, we use n to indicate the number of training data points and N to indicate the dimensionality of the output vector. For classifiers, the dimensionality of the output vector, N, matches the number of classes. We also use superscript (i) to index training data points and subscript j to index output vector dimensions. For classifiers, j indicates the class.

We can visualize $\mathbb{L}\left(\vec{w}, \vec{b}\right)$ as a hypersurface in high-dimensional space. Figures 8.8 and 8.9 show some low-dimensional examples of loss surfaces. These are illustrative examples. In reality, the loss surface is typically high dimensional and very complex. One good mental picture is that of a canyon (see figure 9.1). Traveling "downhill" at any point effectively follows the negative direction of the local gradient (the gradient of a loss surface was introduced in section 8.4.2). Traveling downhill along the gradient does not always lead to the global minimum. For instance, going downhill following the dashed

Figure 9.1 The loss surface can be viewed as a canyon.

arrow will take us to a local minimum, whereas the global minimum is where the water is going, indicated by the solid arrow. (See also section 8.4.4 and figure 8.9.)

Many loss formulations are possible, quantifying the mismatch $\mathbb{L}^{(i)}\left(\vec{y}^{(i)}, \bar{y}^{(i)}\right)$; some of them are described in the following subsections.

9.1.2 Regression loss

Regression loss is the simplest loss formulation. It is the L2 norm of the difference between the output and GT vectors. This loss was introduced in equation 8.11. We restate it here: the loss on the ith training data instance is

$$\mathbb{L}^{(i)}\left(\vec{y}^{(i)}, \bar{y}^{(i)}\right) = \|\vec{y}^{(i)} - \bar{y}^{(i)}\|^2 = \sum_{j=0}^{N-1}\left(y_j^{(i)} - \bar{y}_j^{(i)}\right)^2$$

where the summation is over the components of the output vector. N is the number of classes. The GT vector and output vector are both N-dimensional.

NOTE Fully functional code for regression loss, executable via Jupyter Notebook, can be found at http://mng.bz/g1a8.

Listing 9.1 PyTorch code for regression loss

```
from torch.nn.functional import mse_loss          # Imports the regression loss (mean squared error loss)

y_pred = torch.tensor([-0.10, -0.24,  1.43, -0.14, -0.59])   # N-d prediction vector

y_gt = torch.tensor([ 0.59, -1.92, -1.27, -0.40,  0.50])    # N-d ground truth vector

loss = mse_loss(y_pred, y_gt, reduction='sum')      # Computes the regression loss
```

9.1.3 Cross-entropy loss

Cross-entropy loss was discussed in the context of entropy in section 6.3. If necessary, this would be a great time to reread that. Here we review the idea quickly.

Cross-entropy loss is typically used to measure the mismatch between a classifier neural network output and the corresponding GT in a classification problem. Here, the GT is a one-hot vector whose length equals the number of classes. All but one of its elements are 0. The single nonzero element is 1, and it occurs at the index corresponding to the correct class for that training data instance.

Thus the GT vector looks like $\bar{y}^{(i)} = [0, \ldots, 0, 1, 0, \ldots, 0]$. The prediction vector should have elements with values between 0 and 1. Each element of the prediction vector $\vec{y}^{(i)}$ indicates the probability of a specific class. In other words, $\vec{y}^{(i)} = [p_0, p_1, \ldots, p_{N-1}]$, where p_j is the probability of the input i belonging to the jth class. In section 6.3, we illustrated with an example image classifier that predicts whether an image contains a cat (class 0), a dog (class 1), an airplane (class 2), or an automobile (class 3). One of the four is always assumed to be present in the image. If, for the ith training data instance, the GT vector is an image of cat, we have $\bar{y}^{(i)} = [1, 0, 0, 0]$. A prediction vector $\vec{y}^{(i)} = [0.8, 0.15, 0.04, 0.01]$ is good, while $\vec{y}^{(i)} = [0.25, 0.25, 0.25, 0.25]$ is bad. Note that sum of the elements of the GT as well as the prediction vector is always 1 since they are probabilities. Mathematically, given a training dataset X,

$$\sum_{j=0}^{N-1} \bar{y}_j^{(i)} = 1 \qquad \sum_{j=0}^{N-1} y_j^{(i)} = 1 \forall i \in X$$

Given such GT and prediction vectors, the cross-entropy loss (CE loss) is

$$\mathbb{L}^{(i)}\left(\vec{y}^{(i)}, \bar{y}^{(i)}\right) = -\sum_{j=0}^{N-1} \bar{y}_j^{(i)} \; log\left(y_j^{(i)}\right) \tag{9.3}$$

where the summation is over the elements of the prediction vector and N is the number of classes.

INTUITIONS BEHIND CROSS-ENTROPY LOSS

Note that only one element—the one corresponding to the GT class—survives in the summation of equation 9.3. The other elements vanish because they are multiplied by the 0 GT value. The (logarithm of) the predicted probability of the correct GT class is multiplied by 1. Hence, the CE loss always boils down to $-log\left(y_{j^*}^{(i)}\right)$, where j^* is the GT class. If this probability is 1, the CE loss becomes 0, rightly so, as the correct class is being predicted with a probability of 1. If the predicted probability of the correct class is 0, the CE loss is $-log\,(0) = \infty$, again rightly so, since this is the worst possible prediction. The closer the prediction for the correct class is to 1, the smaller the loss.

> **NOTE** Fully functional code for cross-entropy loss, executable via Jupyter Notebook, can be found at http://mng.bz/g1a8.

Listing 9.2 PyTorch code for cross-entropy loss

```
import torch

y_pred = torch.tensor([0.8, 0.15, 0.04, 0.01])      ← N-d prediction vector

y_gt = torch.tensor([1., 0., 0., 0.])      ← N-d one-hot ground truth vector

loss = -1 * torch.dot(y_gt, torch.log(y_pred))      ← Computes the cross-entropy loss
```

SPECIAL CASE OF TWO CLASSES

What happens if $N = 2$ (that is, we have only two classes)? Let's denote the predicted probability of class 0, for the ith training input, as $y^{(i)}$: that is, $\vec{y}_0^{(i)} = y^{(i)}$. Then, since these are probabilities, the prediction on the other class $\vec{y}_1^{(i)} = 1 - y^{(i)}$. Also, let $\bar{y}^{(i)}$ denote the GT probability for class 0 on this ith training input. Then $1 - \bar{y}^{(i)}$ is the GT probability for class 1. (We have slightly abused notations—up to this point, $\bar{y}$ has denoted a vector, but here it denotes a scalar.)

Then, following equation 9.3, the CE loss on the ith training data instance becomes

$$\mathbb{L}^{(i)}\left(y^{(i)}, \bar{y}^{(i)}\right) = -\bar{y}^{(i)} \; log\left(y^{(i)}\right) - \left(1 - \bar{y}^{(i)}\right) \; log\left(1 - y^{(i)}\right) \tag{9.4}$$

NOTE Fully functional code for binary cross-entropy loss, executable via Jupyter Notebook, can be found at http://mng.bz/g1a8.

Listing 9.3 PyTorch code for binary cross-entropy loss

```
from torch.nn.functional import binary_cross_entropy    # Imports the binary cross-entropy loss

y_pred = torch.tensor([0.8])    # Outputs the probability of class 0 - y0. A single value is sufficient because y1 = 1 - y0.

y_gt = torch.tensor([1.])    # The ground truth is either 0 or 1.

loss = binary_cross_entropy(y_pred, y_gt)    # Computes the cross-entropy loss
```

9.1.4 Binary cross-entropy loss for image and vector mismatches

Given a pair of normalized tensors (such as images or vectors) whose elements all have values between 0 and 1, a variant of the two-class CE loss can be used to estimate the mismatch between the tensors. Note that an image with pixel-intensity values between 0 and 255 can always be normalized by dividing each pixel-intensity value by 255, thereby converting it to the 0 to 1 range. Such a comparison of two images is used in image autoencoders, for example. We study autoencoders later; here, we provide a brief overview in the following sidebar.

> **Autoencoders**
>
> Autoencoders take an image as input, create a low-dimensional descriptor from the image—this descriptor is often referred to as an *embedding* of the image—and try to reconstruct the input image from the embedding. The image embedding is a compressed representation of the image. Reconstruction is a lossy process: the small, subtle variations in the signal are lost, and only the essential part is retained. The loss is the mismatch between the input image and the reconstructed image. By minimizing this loss, we incentivize the system to retain the essence of the input as much as possible within the embedding-size budget.

Let $\bar{y}$ denote the input image. Let $\vec{y}^{(i)}$ denote the reconstructed image outputted by the autoencoder. The binary cross-entropy loss is defined as

$$\mathbb{L}^{(i)}\left(\bar{y}^{(i)}, \vec{y}^{(i)}\right) = -\sum_{j=0}^{N-1}\left(\bar{y}_j^{(i)}\, log\left(y_j^{(i)}\right) + \left(1 - \bar{y}_j^{(i)}\right) log\left(1 - y_j^{(i)}\right)\right) \tag{9.5}$$

Note that here N is the number of pixels in the image, not the number of classes, as before. The summation is over the pixels in the image. Also, the GT vector $\bar{y}^{(i)}$ is not a one-hot vector; rather, it is the input image. These differences aside, equation 9.5 is based on the same idea as equation 9.4.

WHY DOES IT WORK?

Binary cross-entropy loss attains its minimum when the input matches the GT. We outline the proof next. (Note that we drop the superscripts and subscripts for simplicity.) We have

$$-\mathbb{L} = \bar{y} log\left(y\right) + \left(1-\bar{y}\right) log\left(1-y\right)$$

At the minimum, $\frac{\partial \mathbb{L}}{\partial y} = 0$. This implies

$$-\frac{\partial \mathbb{L}}{\partial y} = \bar{y}\frac{1}{y} - \left(1-\bar{y}\right)\frac{1}{1-y} = \frac{\bar{y}}{y} - \frac{1-\bar{y}}{1-y} = 0 \implies y = \bar{y}$$

Thus, the minimum of the binary cross-entropy loss occurs when the network output matches the GT. However, this does not mean this loss becomes zero when the output matches the GT.

> **NOTE** Binary cross-entropy loss is not necessarily zero even in the ideal case of the output matching the input (although the loss is indeed *minimal* in the ideal case, meaning the loss is higher for non-ideal cases with mismatched input and output).

Examining equation 9.5, when the two inputs match, we have $-\ \mathbb{L}\left(\bar{y}, \vec{y}\right)\Big|_{\vec{y}=\bar{y}}$. We intuitively expect this loss to be zero since the output is ideal. But it isn't. For example, if, for $\bar{y}_j^{(i)} = y_j^{(i)} = 0.25$

$$\mathbb{L}^{(i)}\left(\bar{y}_j^{(i)}, \vec{y}_j^{(i)}\right)\Big|_{\bar{y}_j=\vec{y}_j^{(i)}=0.25} = -\bar{y}_j^{(i)} log\left(y_j^{(i)}\right) - \left(1-\bar{y}_j^{(i)}\right) log\left(1-y_j^{(i)}\right)$$
$$= -0.25 log\left(0.25\right) - 0.75 log\left(0.75\right) = 0.56 \neq 0$$

In fact, the binary cross-entropy loss is zero only in special cases, like $y_j^{(i)} = \bar{y}_j^{(i)} = 1$.

9.1.5 Softmax

Suppose we are building a classifier: for instance, the image classifier we illustrated in section 6.3, which predicts whether an image contains a cat (class 0), a dog (class 1), and airplane (class 2), or an automobile (class 3). Our classifier can emit a score vector $\vec{s}$ corresponding to an input image. Element j of the score vector corresponds to the jth class. We take the max of the score vector and call that the neural network-predicted label for the image. For instance, in the example image classifier, a score vector may be $\begin{bmatrix} 9.99 & 10 & 0.01 & -10 \end{bmatrix}$. Since the highest score occurs at index 1, we conclude that the image contains a dog (class 1).

The scores are unbounded; they can be any real number in the range $[-\infty, \infty]$. In general, however, neural networks behave better when the loss function involves a bounded set of numbers in the same range. The training converges faster and to better minima, and the inferencing is more accurate. Consequently, it is desirable to convert the example scores to probabilities. These will be numbers in the range [0, 1] (and the elements of the vector will sum to 1).

The softmax function converts unbounded scores to probabilities. Given a score vector $\vec{s} = \begin{bmatrix} s_0 & s_1 & s_2 & \dots & s_{N-1} \end{bmatrix}$, the corresponding softmax vector is

$$softmax(\vec{s}) = \begin{bmatrix} \frac{e^{s_0}}{S} \\ \frac{e^{s_1}}{S} \\ \frac{e^{s_2}}{S} \\ \dots \\ \frac{e^{s_{N-1}}}{S} \end{bmatrix}$$

$$\text{where } S = \sum_{k=0}^{N-1} e^{s_k} \tag{9.6}$$

A few noteworthy points:

- The vector has as many elements as possible classes.
- The sum of the elements in the previous vector is 1.
- The jth element of the vector represents the predicted probability of class j.
- The formulation can handle arbitrary scores, including negative ones.

So in our example classification problem with the four classes (cat, dog, airplane, automobile), the score vector

$$\vec{s} = \begin{bmatrix} 9.99 & 10 & 0.01 & -10 \end{bmatrix}$$

will yield the softmax vector

$$softmax(\vec{s}) = \begin{bmatrix} 0.497 & 0.502 & 2.30e-5 & 1.04e-9 \end{bmatrix}.$$

The probability of cat is 0.497, and the probability of dog is slightly higher, 0.502. The probabilities of airplane and automobile are much lower: the neural network predicts that the image is that of a dog, but it is not very confident; it could also be a cat.

WHY THE NAME SOFTMAX?

The softmax function is a smooth (differentiable) approximation to the argmaxonehot function, which emits a one-hot vector corresponding to the index of the max score. The argmaxonehot function is *discontinuous*. To see this, consider a pair of two class score vectors:

$$\vec{p} = \begin{bmatrix} 9.99 & 10 \end{bmatrix}$$
$$\vec{q} = \begin{bmatrix} 10 & 9.99 \end{bmatrix}$$

Performing an argmaxonehot operation on them will yield the following one-hot vectors, respectively:

$$argmaxonehot(\vec{p}) = \begin{bmatrix} 0 & 1 \end{bmatrix}$$
$$argmaxonehot(\vec{q}) = \begin{bmatrix} 1 & 0 \end{bmatrix}$$

Thus we see that the vectors $argmaxonehot\left(\vec{p}\right)$ and $argmaxonehot\left(\vec{q}\right)$ are significantly far from each other, even though the points $\vec{p}$ and $\vec{q}$ are very close to each other. On the other hand, the corresponding softmax vectors are

$$softmax\left(\vec{p}\right) = \begin{bmatrix} 0.4975 & 0.5025 \end{bmatrix}$$

$$softmax\left(\vec{q}\right) = \begin{bmatrix} 0.5025 & 0.4975 \end{bmatrix}$$

Although the predicted classes still match those from the argmaxonehot vector, the softmax vectors are very close to each other. The closer the scores, the closer the softmax probabilities. In other words, the softmax is continuous.

Figure 9.2 depicts this geometrically. The argmaxonehot functions as a function of the score vector $[s0, s1]$ (for selecting classes 0 and 1, respectively) are shown in figures 9.2a and 9.2c. These are step functions on the $(s0, s1)$ plane, with $s0 = s1$ being the decision boundary. Their softmax approximations are shown in figures 9.2b and 9.2d. In section 8.1, we introduced the 1D sigmoid function (see figure 8.1), which approximates the 1D step function. Here we see the higher-dimensional analog of that.

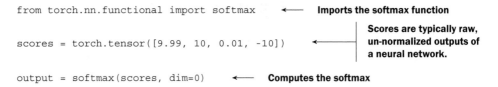

Listing 9.4 PyTorch code for softmax

```
from torch.nn.functional import softmax        ◄── Imports the softmax function

scores = torch.tensor([9.99, 10, 0.01, -10])   ◄── Scores are typically raw,
                                                   un-normalized outputs of
                                                   a neural network.

output = softmax(scores, dim=0)                ◄── Computes the softmax
```

9.1.6 *Softmax cross-entropy loss*

From the preceding discussion, it should be clear that it is desirable to make the last layer of a classifier neural network a softmax layer. Then, given an input, the network will emit probabilities for each class. During training, we can evaluate the loss on these probabilities with regard to the known GT probabilities. This can be done via the CE loss (see section 9.1.3). Thus the softmax is often followed by the CE loss during classifier training. Consequently, the combination (softmax CE loss) is available as a single operation in many deep learning packages, such as PyTorch. This is convenient because we do not need to call softmax and then CE loss. But the deeper reason for combining them is that the combination tends to be numerically better.

Let's look at an example to see how the softmax CE loss changes as the output prediction changes. Consider the image classification problem again, where we'd like to classify whether an image contains one of four categories: cat (class 0), dog (class 1), airplane (class 2), or automobile (class 3). Figure 9.3 represents this visually. Suppose the image we're classifying actually contains a dog (class 1). The GT is represented as a one-hot vector $\begin{bmatrix} 0 & 1 & 0 & 0 \end{bmatrix}$. If our classifier predicts the vector $\begin{bmatrix} 0.498 & 0.502 & 0 & 0 \end{bmatrix}$, it's predicting both cat and dog with almost equal probability. This is a bad prediction because

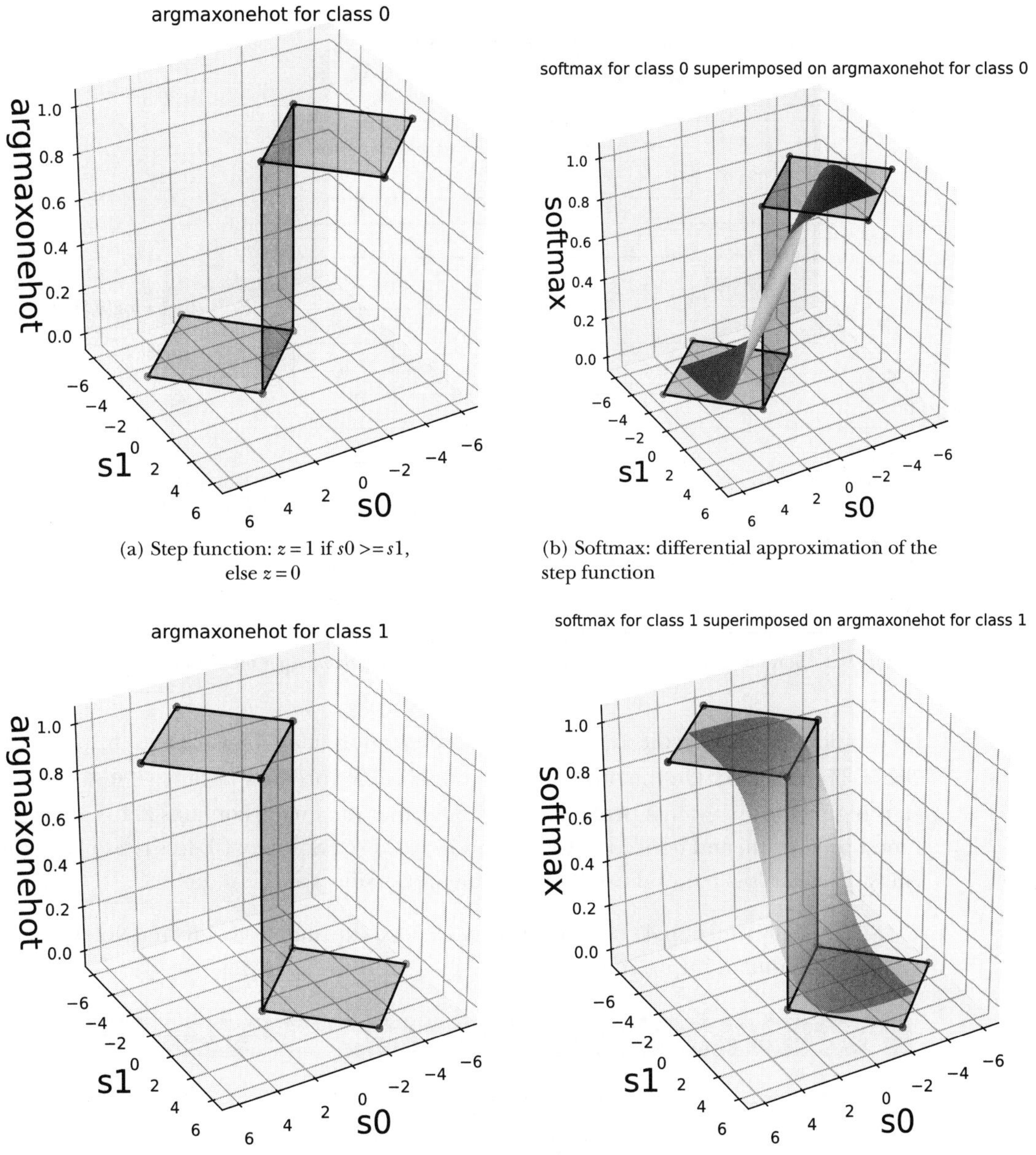

(a) Step function: $z = 1$ if $s0 >= s1$, else $z = 0$

(b) Softmax: differential approximation of the step function

(c) Step function: $z = 1$ if $s1 >= s0$, else $z = 0$

(d) Softmax: differential approximation of the step function

Figure 9.2 Two-class argmaxonehot and softmax (function of score vector $[s0, s1]$) on the $(s0, s1)$ plane. The decision boundary is the 45° line $s0 = s1$.

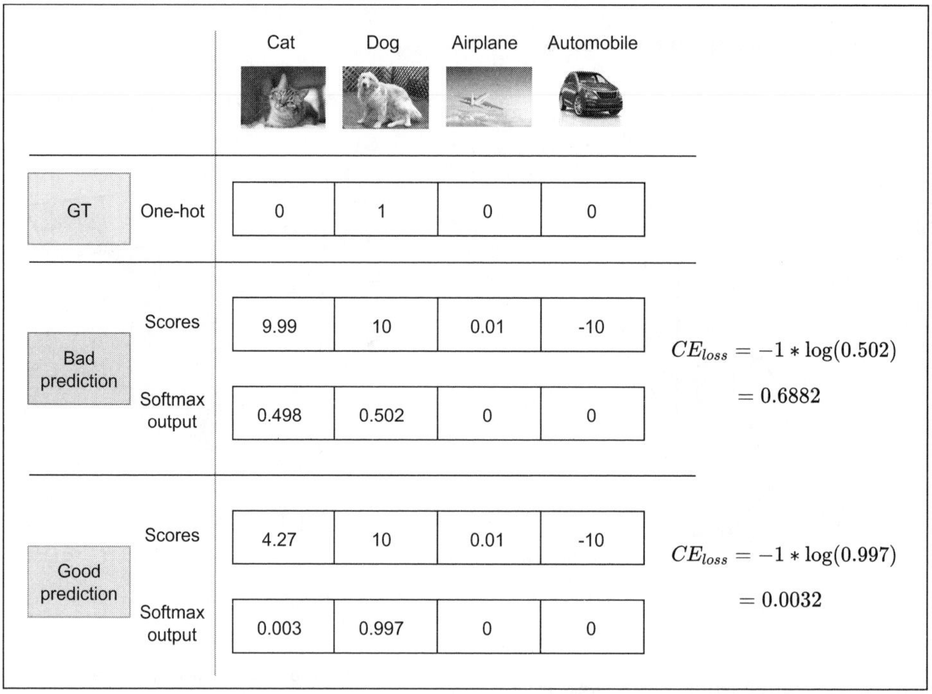

Figure 9.3 Softmax output and cross-entropy loss for good and bad output predictions

we would ideally expect it to confidently predict a dog (class 1). Consequently, the CE loss is high (0.688). On the other hand, if our classifier predicts $\begin{bmatrix} 0.003 & 0.997 & 0 & 0 \end{bmatrix}$, it is highly certain (with a probability of 0.997) that the image contains a dog. This is a good prediction, and hence the CE loss is low (0.0032). Softmax CE loss is probably the most popular loss method used for training in classifiers at the moment.

NOTE Fully functional code for softmax CE loss, executable via Jupyter Notebook, can be found at http://mng.bz/g1a8.

Listing 9.5 PyTorch code for softmax cross-entropy loss

```
from torch.nn.functional import cross_entropy

scores = torch.tensor([[9.99, 10, 0.01, -10]])

y_gt = torch.tensor([1])          # Ground truth class index
                                  # Ranges from 0 to num_classes 1

loss = cross_entropy(scores, y_gt)   # Computes the softmax cross-entropy loss
```

9.1.7 Focal loss

As training progresses, where should we focus our attention? This question becomes especially significant when there is *data imbalance*, meaning the number of training data instances available for some classes is significantly smaller than others. In such cases, not all training data is equally important. We have to use our training data instances wisely.

Intuitively, the greater bang for the buck is trying to improve the training data instances that are not doing well. In other words, instead of trying to squeeze out every bit of juice from the examples in which the network is doing well (the so-called "easy" examples), it is better to focus on the examples where the network is not doing as well ("hard" examples).

To stop focusing on easy examples and focus instead on hard examples, we can put more weight on the loss from training data instances that are far from the GT, and vice versa: that is, put less weight on the loss from training data instances that are close to GT. Consider the binary CE loss of equation 9.4 one more time. The loss for the ith training instance can be rewritten as follows:

$$\mathbb{L}^{(i)}\left(y^{(i)}, \bar{y}^{(i)}\right) = \begin{cases} -log\left(y^{(i)}\right) & \text{if GT is class 1: that is, } \bar{y}^{(i)} = 1 \\ -log\left(1 - y^{(i)}\right) & \text{if GT is class 0: that is, } \bar{y}^{(i)} = 0 \end{cases}$$

NOTE Going forward in this subsection, we drop the superscript (i) for the sake of notational simplification, although it remains implied.

Now, when the GT is class 1 (that is, $\bar{y} = 1$), the entity $(1 - y)$ measures the departure of the prediction from GT. We can multiply the loss by this to weigh down the losses from good predictions and weigh up the losses from bad predictions. In practice, we multiply by $(1 - y)^{\gamma}$ for some value of γ (such as $\gamma = 2$). Similarly, when the GT is class 0 (that is, $\bar{y} = 0$), the entity y measures the departure of the prediction from the GT. In this case, we multiply the loss by y^{γ}. The overall loss then becomes

$$\mathbb{L}\left(\vec{y}, \bar{y}\right) = \begin{cases} -\left(1 - y\right)^{\gamma} log\left(y\right) & \text{if the GT is class 1: } \bar{y} = 1 \\ -y^{\gamma} log\left(1 - y\right) & \text{if the GT is class 0: } \bar{y} = 0 \end{cases}$$

We can have a somewhat simplified expression

$$\mathbb{L}\left(\vec{y}, \bar{y}\right) = -\left(1 - y_t\right)^{\gamma} \; log\left(y_t\right) \tag{9.7}$$

where

$$y_t = \begin{cases} y & \text{if the GT is class 1: } \bar{y} = 1 \\ 1 - y & \text{if the GT is class 0: } \bar{y} = 0 \end{cases}$$

Equation 9.7 is the popular expression of focal loss. Its graph at various values of γ is shown in figure 9.4. Note how the loss becomes more and more subdued as the probability of the GT increases toward the right until it flattens out at the bottom.

NOTE Fully functional code for focal loss, executable via Jupyter Notebook, can be found at http://mng.bz/g1a8.

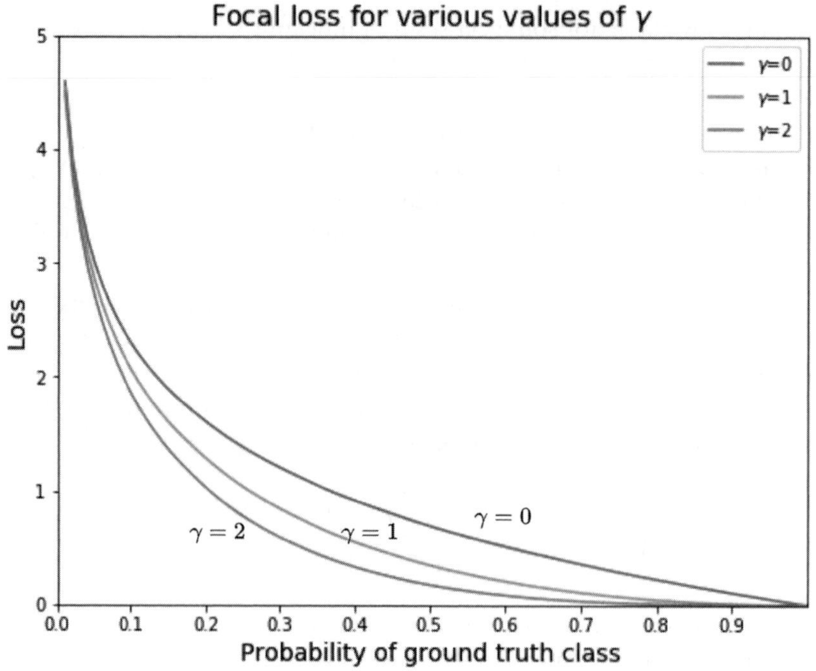

Figure 9.4 Focal loss graph (various γ values)

Listing 9.6 PyTorch code for focal loss

```
def focal_loss(y, y_gt, gamma):

    y_t = (y_gt * y) + ((1 - y_gt) * (1 - y))

    loss = -1 * torch.pow((1 - y_t), gamma) * torch.log(y_t)
    return loss
```

$y_t = y$ if y_{gt} is 1
$y_t = 1 - y$ if y_{gt} is 0

9.1.8 Hinge loss

The softmax CE loss becomes zero only under the ideal condition: the correct class has a finite score, and other classes have a score of negative infinity. Hence, that loss will continue to push the network toward improvement until the ideal is achieved (which never happens in practice). Sometimes we prefer to stop changing the network when the correct class has the maximum score, and we do not care about increasing the distance between correct and incorrect scores any further. This is where hinge loss comes in.

A hinged door opens in one direction but not in the other direction. Similarly, a hinge loss function increases if a certain goodness criterion is *not* satisfied but becomes zero (and does not reduce any further) if the criterion is satisfied. This is akin to saying, "If you are not my friend, the distance between us can vary from small to large (unboundedly), but I don't distinguish between friends. All my friends are at a distance of zero from me."

MULTICLASS SUPPORT VECTOR MACHINE LOSS: HINGE LOSS FOR CLASSIFICATION

Consider again our old friend, the classifier that predicts whether an image contains a cat (class 0), dog (class 1), airplane (class 2), or automobile (class 3). Our classifier emits an output vector $\vec{y}$ corresponding to an input image. Here, the outputs are scores: y_j is the score corresponding to the jth class. (In this subsection, we have dropped the superscripts indicating the training data index to simplify notations.)

Given a (training data instance, GT label) pair $(\vec{x}, c)$ (that is, the GT class corresponding to the input $\vec{x}$ is c), the multiclass support vector machine (SVM) loss is

$$\sum_{j=0, j \neq c}^{N-1} max\left(0, y_j - y_c + m\right) \tag{9.8}$$

where m is a margin (usually $m = 1$).

To understand this, consider the equation without the margin first:

$$\sum_{j=0, j \neq c}^{N-1} max\left(0, y_j - y_c\right)$$

In equation 9.8, we are summing over all the classes except the one that matches the GT. In other words, we are summing over only the incorrect classes. For these, we want the score y_j to be smaller than the score y_c for the correct class. There are two possibilities:

- *Good output*—Incorrect class score less than correct class score:

  $$y_j - y_c < 0 \implies max\left(0, y_j - y_c\right) = 0$$

  The contribution to the loss is zero (we do not distinguish between correct scores: all friends are at zero distance).
- *Bad output*—Incorrect class score more than correct class score:

  $$y_j > y_c \implies max\left(0, y_j - y_c\right) = y_j - y_c$$

  The contribution to the loss is positive (non-friends are at a positive distance that varies with the degree of non-friendness).

In practical settings, the margin is set to a positive number (usually 1) to penalize predictions where the score of the correct class is marginally greater than that of the incorrect classes. This forces the classifier to learn to predict the correct class with high confidence. Figure 9.5 shows how hinge loss differs for good and bad output predictions. One mental model to have about the multiclass SVM loss is that it is lazy. It stops changing as soon as the correct class score exceeds the incorrect scores by the margin m. The loss does not change if the correct class score goes still higher, which means it does not push the machine to improve beyond that point. This behavior is

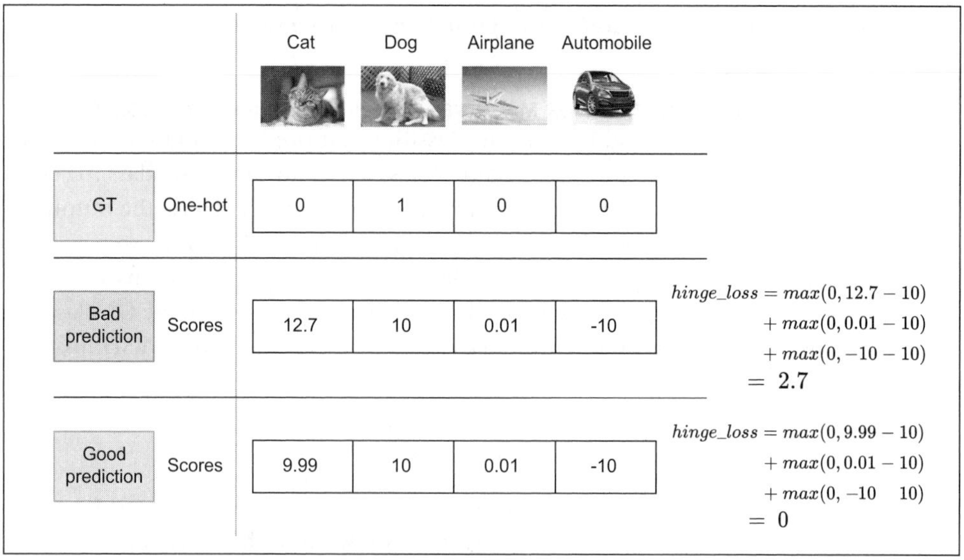

Figure 9.5 Hinge loss for good and bad output predictions

different from the softmax CE loss, which tries to push the machine to achieve an infinite score for the correct class.

9.2 Optimization

Neural network models define a loss function that estimates the badness of the network's output. During supervised training, the output on a particular training instance input is compared to a known output (GT) for that particular training instance. The difference between the GT and the network-generated output is called loss. We can sum up the losses from individual training data instances and compute the total loss over all the training data.

These losses are, of course, functions of the network parameters, $\vec{w}, \vec{b}$. We can imagine a space whose dimensionality is $dim\left(\vec{w}\right) + dim\left(\vec{b}\right)$. At each point in this space, we have a value for the total training loss. Thus, we can imagine a loss surface—a surface whose height represents the loss value—defined over the high-dimensional domain of network parameters (weights and biases).

Optimization is nothing but finding the lowest point on this surface. During training, we start with random values of network parameters: this is akin to starting at a random point on the surface. Then we constantly move locally downhill on the loss surface in the direction of the negative gradient. We hope this eventually takes us to the minimum or a sufficiently low point. Continuing our analogy of the loss surface as a ravine, the minimum is at sea level. This minimum provides us with the network parameter values (weights and biases) that will yield the least loss on the training data. If the training data set adequately represents the problem, the trained model will perform well on unseen data.

This process of traveling toward the minimum, the iterative updating of weights and biases to have minimal loss over the training dataset, is called *optimization*. The basic math was introduced in section 8.4.2 (equation 8.12). Here we study many practical nuances and variants.

At every iteration, we update the weights and biases, so if t denotes the iteration number, $\vec{w}_t$ denotes the weight values at iteration t, $\delta\vec{w}_t$ denotes the weight updates at iteration t, and so on:

$$\begin{aligned}\vec{w}_{t+1} &= \vec{w}_t - \delta\vec{w}_t \\ \vec{b}_{t+1} &= \vec{b}_t - \delta\vec{b}_t\end{aligned} \tag{9.9}$$

The basic update is along the direction of the negative gradient (see equation 8.12):

$$\begin{aligned}\delta\vec{w}_t &= \eta \nabla_{\vec{w}} \mathbb{L}\left(\vec{w}_t, \vec{b}_t\right) \\ \delta\vec{b}_t &= \eta \nabla_{\vec{b}} \mathbb{L}\left(\vec{w}_t, \vec{b}_t\right)\end{aligned} \tag{9.10}$$

Here, $\mathbb{L}\left(\vec{w}_t, \vec{b}_t\right)$ denotes the loss at iteration t. Ideally, we should evaluate the loss on every training data instance and average them. But that would imply that we must process every training data instance for every iteration, which is prohibitively expensive. Instead, we use sampling (see section 9.2.2):

- The constant η is called the *learning rate* (LR). A larger LR results in bigger steps (bigger adjustments to weights and biases per update) and vice versa. We use larger values of LR in the beginning: when the network is completely untrained, we want to take large steps toward the minimum. When we are close to the minimum, on the other hand, we want to take smaller steps, lest we overshoot it. The LR is typically a small number, like $\eta = 0.01$.
- In stochastic gradient descent (SGD; a popular approach), the LR η is typically held constant during an epoch (an *epoch* is a single pass over all the training data). Then the LR is decreased after one or more epochs. This process is called *learning rate decay*. So, the LR is not exactly a constant. We could have written it η_t to indicate the temporal nature, but we chose to keep it simple because (in SGD, at least) it changes infrequently.

We have to reevaluate the loss and its gradients in each iteration since their values will change in every iteration, because the weights and biases of the underlying neural network are changing.

How many iterations are necessary? Typically, this is a large number. We iterate *multiple times over the entire training dataset.* A typical training session has multiple epochs. In this context, note that for proper convergence, it is *extremely important* to randomly shuffle the order of occurrence of the training data after every epoch. In the following sections, we look at some practical nuances of the process.

9.2.1 Geometrical view of optimization

This topic is described in detail in section 8.4.2. You are encouraged to revisit that discussion if necessary.

Overall, neural network optimization is an iterative process. Ideally, in each iteration, we compute the gradient of the loss with respect to the current parameters (weights and biases) and obtain improved values for them by moving in the direction of the negative gradient.

9.2.2 Stochastic gradient descent and minibatches

How do we compute the gradient of the loss function? The loss is different for every training data instance. The sensible thing to do is to average them out. But as we mentioned earlier, that leads to a practical problem: we would have to process the entire training dataset on every iteration. If the size of the training dataset is n, an epoch is an $O\left(n^2\right)$ operation (every iteration, we have to process all of the n training data instances to compute the gradient, and an epoch has n iterations). Since n is a large number, often in the millions, $O\left(n^2\right)$ is prohibitively expensive.

In SGD, we do not average over the entire training data set to produce the gradient. Instead, we average over a random sampled subset of the training data. This randomly sampled subset of training data is called a *minibatch*. The gradient is computed by averaging the loss over the minibatch (as opposed to the entire training dataset). This gradient is used to update the weight and bias parameters.

9.2.3 PyTorch code for SGD

Now, let's implement SGD in PyTorch.

> **NOTE** Fully functional code for SGD, executable via Jupyter Notebook, can be found at http://mng.bz/ePyG.

Let's consider the example discussed in section 6.9. Our goal is to build a model that can predict whether a Statsville resident is a man, woman, or child using height and weight as input data. For this purpose, let's assume we have a large dataset X containing the heights and weights of various Statsville residents. X is of shape $(num\_samples, 2)$, where each row represents the $(height, weight)$ pair of a single resident. The corresponding labels are stored in y_{gt}, which contains $num\_samples$ elements. Each row of y_{gt} can be 0, 1, or 2, depending on whether the resident is a man, woman, or child. Figure 9.6 shows an example distribution of X.

Before training a model, we must first convert the data into a training-friendly format. We subclass `torch.utils.data.Dataset` to do so and implement the `__len__` and `__getitem__` methods. The ith training data instance can be accessed by calling `data_set[i]`. Remember that in SGD, we feed in minibatches that contain `batch_size` elements in every iteration. This can be achieved by calling the `__getitem__` method `batch_size` times. However, instead of doing this ourselves, we use PyTorch's `DataLoader`, which gives us a convenient wrapper. Using `DataLoader` is recommended in production settings because it provides a simple API through which we can (1) create minibatches,

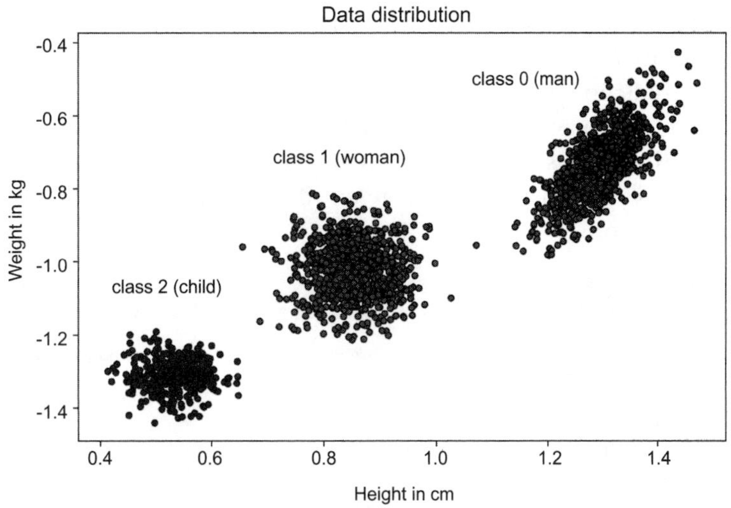

Figure 9.6 Height and weight of various Statsville residents. Class 0 (man) is represented by the right-most cluster, class 1 (woman) by the middle cluster, and class 2 (child) by the left-most cluster.

(2) speed up data-loading times via multiprocessing, and (3) randomly shuffle data in every epoch to prevent overfitting. The following code creates a custom PyTorch data set.

Listing 9.7 PyTorch code to create a custom dataset

```
from torch.utils.data import Dataset, DataLoader

class StatsvilleDataset(Dataset):        ← Subclasses torch.utils.data.Dataset
    def __init__(self, X, y_gt):
        self.X = X
        self.y_gt = y_gt

    def __len__(self):        ← Returns the size of the data set
        return len(self.X)

    def __getitem__(self, i):        ← Returns the ith training data element
        return self.X[i], self.y_gt[i]

dataset = StatsvilleDataset(X, y_gt)        ← Instantiates the data set

data_loader = DataLoader(dataset, batch_size=10,        ← Instantiates the data loader
                         shuffle=True)                    with a batch size of 10
                                                          and shuffle on
```

Our next step is to create a classifier model that can take the height and weight data (X) as input and predict the output class. Here, we create a simple neural network model that consists of two linear layers followed by a softmax layer. The output of the softmax layer has three values representing the probability of each of the three classes (man, woman, and child), respectively. Note that in the forward pass, we don't call the softmax layer because our loss function, PyTorch's CE loss, expects raw, un-normalized scores as input. Hence we pass the output of the second linear layer to the loss function. However, during prediction, we pass the scores to the softmax layer to get a probability vector and then take an argmax to get the predicted class. Notice that we have a function to initialize the weights of the linear layers: this is important because the starting value of the weights can often affect convergence. If the model starts too far from the minimum, it may never converge.

Listing 9.8 PyTorch code to create a custom neural network model

```
class Model(torch.nn.Module):        ← Subclasses torch.nn.Module

    def __init__(self, input_size, hidden_size, output_size):
        super(Model, self).__init__()
        self.linear1 = torch.nn.Linear(input_size, hidden_size)   ← Instantiates the
        self.linear2 = torch.nn.Linear(hidden_size, output_size)    linear layers and
        self.softmax = torch.nn.Softmax(dim=1)                      the softmax layer

    def forward(self, X):        ← Feeds forward the input through the two linear layers
        scores = self.linear2(self.linear1(X))
        return scores

    def predict(self, X):        ← Predicts the output class index
        scores = self.forward(X)
        y_pred = torch.argmax(self.softmax(scores), dim=1)
        return y_pred


def initialize_weights(m):
    if isinstance(m, torch.nn.Linear):                       Initializes the weights to help
        torch.nn.init.xavier_uniform_(m.weight.data)   ←     the model converge better
        torch.nn.init.constant_(m.bias.data, 0)

model = Model(input_size=2, hidden_size=100, output_size=3)
model.apply(initialize_weights)
```

Now that we have our data set and model, let's define our loss function and instantiate our SGD optimizer.

Listing 9.9 PyTorch code for a loss function and SGD optimizer

```
loss_fn = torch.nn.CrossEntropyLoss()                      Instantiates the SGD
optimizer = optim.SGD(model.parameters(), lr=0.02)   ←     optimizer with learning
                                                           rate = 0.02
```

Now we define the training loop, which is essentially one pass over the entire dataset. We iterate over the dataset in batches of size `batch_size`, run the forward pass, compute the gradients, and update the weights in the direction of the negative gradient. Note that we call `optimizer.zero_grad()` in every iteration to prevent the accumulation of gradients from the previous steps.

Listing 9.10 PyTorch code for one training loop

```
def train_loop(epoch, data_loader, model, loss_fn, optimizer):
    for X_batch, y_gt_batch in data_loader:      # Iterates through the data set in batches
        scores = model(X_batch)                  # Feeds forward the model to compute scores
        loss = loss_fn(scores, y_gt_batch)       # Computes the cross-entropy loss
        optimizer.zero_grad()                    # Clears the gradients accumulated from the previous step
        loss.backward()                          # Runs backpropagation and computes the gradients
        optimizer.step()                         # Updates the weights
```

With this, we are ready to train our model. The following code shows how to do so. Figure 9.7 shows the output predictions and loss at the end of every epoch.

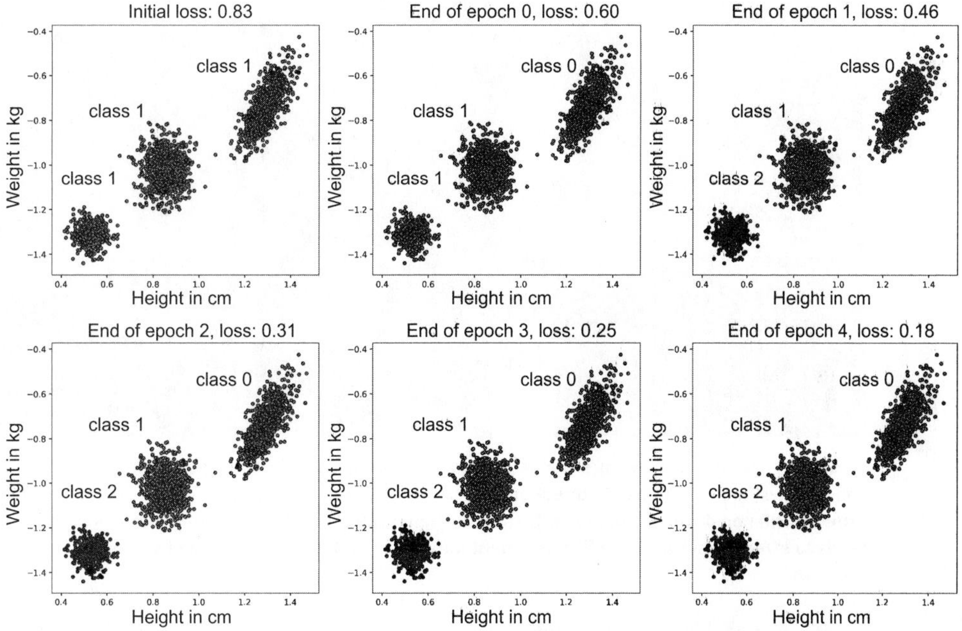

Figure 9.7 Model predictions at the end of every epoch. Notice how the loss is reduced with every epoch. In the beginning, all training data points are wrongly classified as class 1. After the end of epoch 1, most of the training data is classified correctly, and the distribution of the classifier's output has become close to the ground truth. The loss continues to decrease until epoch 4 (although the improvements are harder to see visually).

Listing 9.11 PyTorch code to run the training loop `num_epochs` times

```
num_epochs = 2
for epoch in range(num_epochs):
    train_loop(epoch, data_loader, model, loss_fn, optimizer)
```

9.2.4 Momentum

For real-life loss surfaces in high dimensions, the ravine analogy is quite appropriate. A loss surface is hardly like a porcelain cup with smooth walls; it is much more like the walls of the Grand Canyon (see figure 9.8). Furthermore, the gradient estimate (usually done over a minibatch) is noisy. Consequently, gradient estimates are never aligned in one direction—they tend to go hither and thither. Nonetheless, most of them tend to have a good downhill component. The other (non-downhill component) is somewhat random (see figure 9.8). So if we average them, the downhill components reinforce each other and are strengthened, while the non-downhill components cancel each other and are weakened.

Figure 9.8 Momentum. Noisy stochastic gradient estimates at different points on the loss surface (thick solid arrows) are not aligned in direction, but they all have a significant downhill component (thin solid arrows). The non-downhill components (thin dashed arrows) point in random directions. Hence, averaging tends to strengthen the downhill component and cancel out the non-downhill components.

Furthermore, if there is a small flat region with downhill areas preceding and following it, the vanilla gradient-based approach will get stuck in the small flat region (since the gradient there is zero). But averaging with the past allows us to have nonzero updates that take the optimization out of the local small flat region so that it can continue downhill.

A good mental picture in this context is that of a ball rolling downhill. The surface of the hill is rough, and the ball is not going directly downward. Rather, it takes a zigzag path. But as it travels, it gathers downward momentum, and its downward velocity becomes greater.

Following this theory, we take the weighted average of the gradient computed at this iteration with the update used in the previous iteration:

$$\overbrace{\delta\vec{w}_t}^{\text{current update}} = \gamma \overbrace{\delta\vec{w}_{t-1}}^{\text{last update}} + \eta \overbrace{\nabla_{\vec{w}}\mathbb{L}\left(\vec{w}_t, \vec{b}_t\right)}^{\text{current gradient}}$$

$$\overbrace{\delta\vec{b}_t}^{\text{current update}} = \gamma \overbrace{\delta\vec{b}_{t-1}}^{\text{last update}} + \eta \overbrace{\nabla_{\vec{b}}\mathbb{L}\left(\vec{w}_t, \vec{b}_t\right)}^{\text{current gradient}} \tag{9.11}$$

where γ, η are positive constants with values less than 1. The weights and bias parameters are updated in the usual fashion using equation 9.9.

UNROLLING THE RECURSION OF THE MOMENTUM EQUATION

Unraveling the recursive equation 9.11, we see

$$\begin{aligned}
\delta\vec{w}_t &= \eta\nabla_{\vec{w}}\mathbb{L}\left(\vec{w}_t, \vec{b}_t\right) + \gamma\delta\vec{w}_{t-1} \\
&= \eta\nabla_{\vec{w}}\mathbb{L}\left(\vec{w}_t, \vec{b}_t\right) + \eta\gamma\nabla_{\vec{w}}\mathbb{L}\left(\vec{w}_{t-1}, \vec{b}_{t-1}\right) + \gamma^2\delta\vec{w}_{t-2} \\
&= \eta\nabla_{\vec{w}}\mathbb{L}\left(\vec{w}_t, \vec{b}_t\right) + \eta\gamma\nabla_{\vec{w}}\mathbb{L}\left(\vec{w}_{t-1}, \vec{b}_{t-1}\right) + \eta\gamma^2\nabla_{\vec{w}}\mathbb{L}\left(\vec{w}_{t-2}, \vec{b}_{t-2}\right) + \gamma^3\delta\vec{w}_{t-3} \\
&\vdots \\
&= \eta\nabla_{\vec{w}}\mathbb{L}\left(\vec{w}_t, \vec{b}_t\right) + \eta\gamma\nabla_{\vec{w}}\mathbb{L}\left(\vec{w}_{t-1}, \vec{b}_{t-1}\right) + \cdots + \eta\gamma^t\nabla_{\vec{w}}\mathbb{L}\left(\vec{w}_0, \vec{b}_0\right) + \gamma^{t+1}\delta\vec{w}_{-1}
\end{aligned}$$

Assuming $\delta\vec{w}_{-1} = 0$, we get

$$\begin{aligned}
\delta\vec{w}_t = \eta\nabla_{\vec{w}}\mathbb{L}\left(\vec{w}_t, \vec{b}_t\right) &+ \eta\gamma\nabla_{\vec{w}}\mathbb{L}\left(\vec{w}_{t-1}, \vec{b}_{t-1}\right) + \eta\gamma^2\nabla_{\vec{w}}\mathbb{L}\left(\vec{w}_{t-2}, \vec{b}_{t-2}\right) \\
&+ \cdots \\
&+ \eta\gamma^t\nabla_{\vec{w}}\mathbb{L}\left(\vec{w}_0, \vec{b}_0\right)
\end{aligned} \tag{9.12}$$

Thus,

- We are taking a weighted sum of the gradients from past iterations. This is not quite a weighted average, though, as explained later.
- Older gradients are weighted by higher powers of γ. Since $\gamma < 1$, weights decrease with age (long-past iterations have less influence).
- The sum of the weights of the gradients, going backward from now to the beginning of time (the 0th iteration), is

  $$S_t = \eta\left(1 + \gamma + \gamma^2 + \gamma^3 \cdots \gamma^t\right)$$

  Now, using Taylor expansion,

  $$\lim_{t\to\infty}\left(1 + \gamma + \gamma^2 + \gamma^3 \cdots \gamma^{t-1}\right) = \frac{1}{1-\gamma}$$

  Thus the sum of the weights of the past gradients in momentum-based gradient descent is $\frac{\eta}{1-\gamma} \neq 1$. In other words, this is not quite a weighted average (where the weights should sum up to 1). This is a somewhat undesirable property and is rectified in the Adam algorithm discussed later.

A similar analysis can be done for the biases.

9.2.5 Geometric view: Constant loss contours, gradient descent, and momentum

Consider a network with a tiny two-element weight vector $\vec{w} = \begin{bmatrix} w_0 \\ w_1 \end{bmatrix}$ and no bias. Further, suppose that the loss function is $\mathbb{L} = ||\vec{w}||^2 = w_0^2 + w_1^2$. The constant loss contours are concentric circles with the origin as the center. The radius of the circle indicates the loss magnitude.

If we move along the circle's circumference, the loss does not change. The loss changes maximally along the orthogonal direction to that: the radius of the circle. This intuitive observation is confirmed by evaluating the gradient

$$\nabla_{\vec{w}} \mathbb{L} = 2 \begin{bmatrix} w_0 \\ w_1 \end{bmatrix}$$

Thus the gradient is along the radius, and the negative gradient direction is radially inward. So the loss decreases most rapidly if we move radially inward. If we move orthogonal to the radius (that is, along the circumference), the loss remains unchanged; of course, we are moving along the constant loss contour.

Optimization then takes us from outer, larger-radius circles to inner, smaller-radius circles. The minimum is at the origin; ideally, optimization should stop once we reach the origin.

Figure 9.9 shows optimization for a simple loss function $\mathbb{L} = ||\vec{w}||^2 = w_0^2 + w_1^2$. We start at an arbitrary pair of weight values and repeatedly update them via equation 9.9. For figure 9.9a, we use update without momentum (equation 9.10). For figure 9.9b, we use update with momentum (equation 9.11).

When the constant loss contours are concentric circles with the origin as the center, the loss surface is a cone with its apex on the origin. The cross sections are circles on planes parallel to the w_0, w_1 plane. Optimization takes us down the inner walls of the cone through smaller and smaller circular cross-sections as we approach the minimum. The global minimum is at the origin and corresponds to zero loss. The zero-loss contour is a circle with a zero radius, which is effectively a single point: the origin.

In both cases, progress slows down (step sizes become smaller) as we approach the minimum. This is because the magnitude of the gradient becomes smaller and smaller as we get closer to the minimum (imagine a bowl: it becomes flatter as we get closer to the bottom). However, this effect is countered to a certain extent if we have momentum. So, we can see that we need fewer steps to reach a circle with a smaller radius when we have momentum.

9.2.6 Nesterov accelerated gradients

One problem with momentum-based gradient descent is that it may overshoot the minimum. This can be seen in figure 9.10a where the loss decreases through a series of updates and then, when we are close to the minimum, an update (shown with a dotted arrow) overshoots the minimum and increases the loss (shown with a dotted circle).

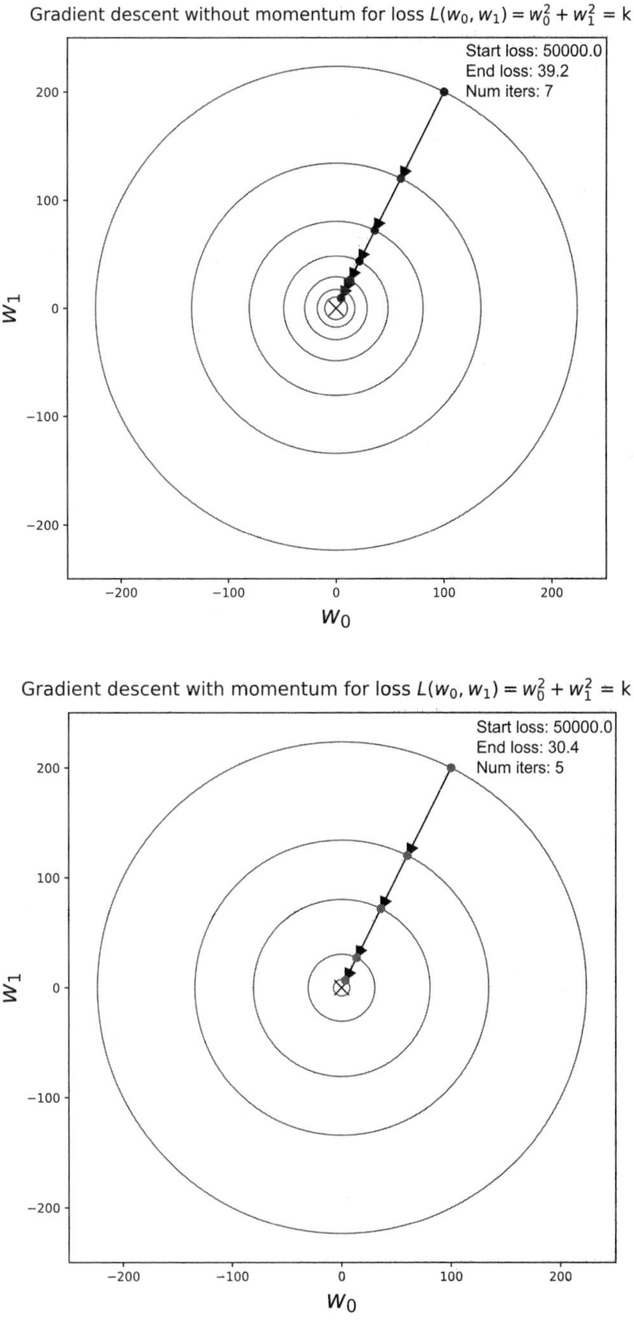

(a) A trajectory through constant loss contours for gradient descent *without* momentum

(b) A trajectory through constant loss contours for gradient descent *with* momentum

Figure 9.9 Constant loss contours and optimization trajectory for the loss function $\mathbb{L} = ||\vec{w}||^2 = w_0^2 + w_1^2$. The loss surface is a cone with its apex on the origin and its base a circle in a plane parallel to the w_0, w_1 plane. Optimization takes us down the cone toward smaller and smaller cross-sections as we approach the minimum at the origin. Updates are shown with arrows. Note how the momentum version arrives at a smaller circle in fewer steps.

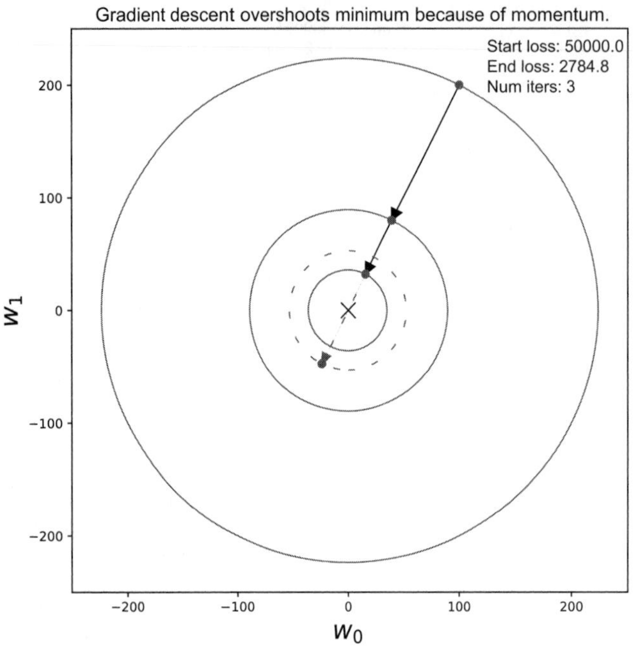

(a) Momentum gradient descent overshooting the minimum. Loss decreases for a while and then increases (dotted circle and arrow).

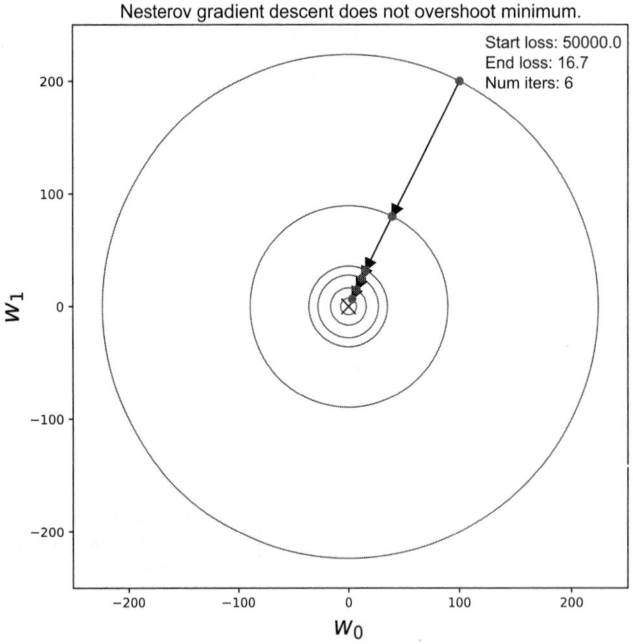

(b) Nesterov reduces the step size when we are about to overshoot the minimum.

Figure 9.10 Figure (a) shows momentum-based gradient descent overshooting the minimum. Overshooting the update is shown with a dotted arrow. A circle with a radius larger than the last step is shown with a dotted outline. Nesterov does better by taking smaller steps when overshooting is imminent.

This is the phenomenon that Nesterov's accelerated gradient-based optimization tries to tackle.

In Nesterov's technique, we do the following:

1. Estimate where this update will take us (that is, the destination point) by adding the previous step's update to the current point.
2. Compute the gradient at the estimated destination point. This is where the approach differs from the vanilla momentum-based approach, which takes the gradient at the current point.
3. Take a weighted average of the gradient (at the estimated destination point) with the previous step's update. That is the update for the current step.

Mathematically speaking,

$$\overbrace{\delta\vec{w}_t}^{\text{current update}} = \gamma \overbrace{\delta\vec{w}_{t-1}}^{\text{last update}} + \eta \overbrace{\nabla_{\vec{w}}\mathbb{L}\left(\overbrace{\vec{w}_t - \gamma\delta\vec{w}_{t-1}}^{\text{estimated destination}}, \overbrace{\vec{b}_t - \gamma\delta\vec{b}_{t-1}}^{\text{estimated destination}}\right)}^{\text{gradient at estimated destination}}$$

$$\overbrace{\delta\vec{b}_t}^{\text{current update}} = \gamma \overbrace{\delta\vec{b}_{t-1}}^{\text{last update}} + \eta \overbrace{\nabla_{\vec{b}}\mathbb{L}\left(\overbrace{\vec{w}_t - \gamma\delta\vec{w}_{t-1}}^{\text{estimated destination}}, \overbrace{\vec{b}_t - \gamma\delta\vec{b}_{t-1}}^{\text{estimated destination}}\right)}^{\text{gradient at estimated destination}} \quad (9.13)$$

where γ, η are constants with values less than 1. The weights and biases are updated in the usual fashion using equation 9.9.

Why does this help? Well, consider the following:

- When we are somewhat far away from the minimum (no possibility of overshooting), the gradient at the estimated destination is more or less the same as the gradient at the current point, so we progress toward the minimum in a fashion similar to momentum-based gradient descent.
- But when we are close to the minimum and the current update may potentially take us past it (see the dotted arrow in figure 9.10a), the gradient at the estimated destination will lie on the other side of the minimum. As before, imagine this loss surface as a cone with its apex at the origin and base above the apex. We have traveled down one of the cone's side walls and just started climbing back up. Thus the gradient at the estimated destination is in the opposite direction from the previous step. When we take their weighted average, they will cancel each other in some dimensions, resulting in a smaller magnitude. The resulting smaller step will mitigate the overshooting phenomenon.

NOTE Fully functional code for momentum and Nesterov accelerated gradients, executable via Jupyter notebook, can be found at http://mng.bz/p9KR.

9.2.7 AdaGrad

The momentum-based optimization approach (equation 9.11) and the Nesterov approach (equation 9.13) both suffer from a serious drawback: they treat all dimensions of the parameter vectors $\vec{w}$, $\vec{b}$ equally. But the loss surface is *not* symmetrical in all dimensions. The slope can be high along some dimensions and low along others. We cannot control everything with a single LR for all the dimensions. If we set the LR high, the high-slope dimensions will exhibit too much variance. If we set it low, the low-slope dimensions will barely progress toward the minimum.

What we need is *per-parameter LR*. Then each LR will adapt to the slope of its particular dimension. This is what AdaGrad tries to achieve. Dimensions with historically larger gradients have smaller LRs, while dimensions with historically smaller gradients have larger LRs.

How do we keep track of the historic magnitudes of gradients? To do this, AdaGrad maintains a state vector in which it accumulates the sum of the squared partial derivatives for each dimension of the gradient vector seen so far during training:

$$\vec{s}_t = \overbrace{\nabla_{\vec{w}} \mathbb{L}\left(\vec{w}_t, \vec{b}_t\right) \circ \nabla_{\vec{w}} \mathbb{L}\left(\vec{w}_t, \vec{b}_t\right)}^{\text{per-dimension gradient squared}} + \vec{s}_{t-1} = \begin{bmatrix} \left|\frac{\partial \mathbb{L}}{\partial w_0}\right|^2 \\ \left|\frac{\partial \mathbb{L}}{\partial w_1}\right|^2 \\ \vdots \\ \left|\frac{\partial \mathbb{L}}{\partial b_0}\right|^2 \\ \vdots \end{bmatrix} + \vec{s}_{t-1}$$

where $\circ$ denotes the Hadamard operator (elementwise multiplication of the two vectors). We can express the previous equation a bit more succinctly as

$$\vec{s}_t = |\nabla_{\vec{w}} \mathbb{L}\left(\vec{w}_t, \vec{b}_t\right)|^2 + \vec{s}_{t-1}$$

Unrolling the recursion, we get

$$\begin{aligned} \vec{s}_t &= |\nabla_{\vec{w}} \mathbb{L}\left(\vec{w}_t, \vec{b}_t\right)|^2 + \vec{s}_{t-1} \\ &= |\nabla_{\vec{w}} \mathbb{L}\left(\vec{w}_t, \vec{b}_t\right)|^2 + |\nabla_{\vec{w}} \mathbb{L}\left(\vec{w}_{t-1}, \vec{b}_{t-1}\right)|^2 + \vec{s}_{t-2} \\ &\vdots \\ &= |\nabla_{\vec{w}} \mathbb{L}\left(\vec{w}_t, \vec{b}_t\right)|^2 + |\nabla_{\vec{w}} \mathbb{L}\left(\vec{w}_{t-1}, \vec{b}_{t-1}\right)|^2 \cdots + |\nabla_{\vec{w}} \mathbb{L}\left(\vec{w}_0, \vec{b}_0\right)|^2 + \vec{s}_{-1} \end{aligned}$$

assuming $\vec{s}_{-1} = 0$, $\vec{s}_t$ is a vector that holds the cumulative sum over all training iterations of the squared slope for each dimension. For the dimensions with historically high slopes, the corresponding element of $\vec{s}_t$ is large, and vice versa. The overall update vector looks like this:

$$\vec{s}_t = |\nabla_{\vec{w}} \mathbb{L}\left(\vec{w}_t, \vec{b}_t\right)|^2 + \vec{s}_{t-1}$$
$$\delta\vec{w}_t = \frac{\eta}{\sqrt{\vec{s}_t + \epsilon}} \circ \nabla_{\vec{w}} \mathbb{L}\left(\vec{w}_t, \vec{b}_t\right) \tag{9.14}$$

Here ϵ is a very small constant added to prevent division by zero. Then we use equation 9.9 to update the weights as usual. A parallel set of equations exist for the bias.

Using AdaGrad, in the loss gradient, the dimensions that have seen big slopes in earlier iterations are given less importance during the update. We emphasize the dimensions that have not seen much progress in the past. This is a bit like saying, "I will pay less attention to a person who speaks all the time, and I will pay more attention to someone who speaks infrequently."

9.2.8 Root-mean-squared propagation

A significant drawback of the AdaGrad algorithm is that the magnitude of the vector $\vec{s}_t$ keeps increasing as iteration progresses. This causes the LR for all dimensions to become smaller and smaller. Eventually, when the number of iterations is high, the LR becomes close to zero, and the updates do hardly anything; progress toward the minimum slows to a virtual halt. Thus AdaGrad is an impractical algorithm to use in real life, although the idea of per-component LR is good.

Root mean squared propagation (RMSProp) addresses this drawback without sacrificing the dimension-adaptive nature of AdaGrad. Here again there is a state vector, but its equation is

$$\vec{s}_t = (1-\gamma)\ |\nabla_{\vec{w}} \mathbb{L}\left(\vec{w}_t, \vec{b}_t\right)|^2 + \gamma\, \vec{s}_{t-1}$$

Compare this with the state vector equation in AdaGrad:

$$\vec{s}_t = |\nabla_{\vec{w}} \mathbb{L}\left(\vec{w}_t, \vec{b}_t\right)|^2 + \vec{s}_{t-1}$$

They are almost the same, but the terms are weighted by $(1-\gamma)$ and γ, where $0 < \gamma < 1$ is a constant. This particular pair of weights in a recursive equation has a very interesting effect. To see it, we have to unroll the recursion:

$$\begin{aligned}
\vec{s}_t &= (1-\gamma)\ |\nabla_{\vec{w}} \mathbb{L}\left(\vec{w}_t, \vec{b}_t\right)|^2 + \gamma\, \vec{s}_{t-1} \\
&= (1-\gamma)\ |\nabla_{\vec{w}} \mathbb{L}\left(\vec{w}_t, \vec{b}_t\right)|^2 + (1-\gamma)\ \gamma\, |\nabla_{\vec{w}} \mathbb{L}\left(\vec{w}_{t-1}, \vec{b}_{t-1}\right)|^2 + \gamma^2\, \vec{s}_{t-2} \\
&= (1-\gamma)\ |\nabla_{\vec{w}} \mathbb{L}\left(\vec{w}_t, \vec{b}_t\right)|^2 + (1-\gamma)\ \gamma\, |\nabla_{\vec{w}} \mathbb{L}\left(\vec{w}_{t-1}, \vec{b}_{t-1}\right)|^2 \\
&\quad + (1-\gamma)\ \gamma^2\, |\nabla_{\vec{w}} \mathbb{L}\left(\vec{w}_{t-2}, \vec{b}_{t-2}\right)|^2 + \gamma^3\, \vec{s}_{t-3} \\
&\ \ \vdots \\
&= (1-\gamma)\ |\nabla_{\vec{w}} \mathbb{L}\left(\vec{w}_t, \vec{b}_t\right)|^2 + (1-\gamma)\ \gamma\, |\nabla_{\vec{w}} \mathbb{L}\left(\vec{w}_{t-1}, \vec{b}_{t-1}\right)|^2 \\
&\quad \cdots + (1-\gamma)\ \gamma^t\, |\nabla_{\vec{w}} \mathbb{L}\left(\vec{w}_0, \vec{b}_0\right)|^2
\end{aligned}$$

Thus $\vec{s}_t$ is a weighted sum of the past term-wise squared gradient magnitude vectors. Going back from now to the beginning of time (the 0th iteration), the weights are $(1-\gamma), (1-\gamma)\ \gamma, (1-\gamma)\ \gamma^2, \cdots, (1-\gamma)\ \gamma^t$. If we add these weights, we get

$$(1-\gamma)\ \left(1+\gamma+\gamma^2+\gamma^3\cdots\gamma^t\right)$$

As the number of iterations becomes high $(t \to \infty)$, this becomes

$$(1-\gamma)\ \lim_{t\to\infty}\left(1+\gamma+\gamma^2+\gamma^3\cdots\gamma^{t-1}\right) = \frac{1}{1-\gamma}\ (1-\gamma) = 1$$

where Taylor expansion has been used to evaluate the term in parentheses.

For a large number of iterations, the sum of the weights approaches 1. This implies that after many iterations, the RMSProp state vector effectively takes the *weighted average of the past term-wise squared gradient magnitude vectors.* With more iterations, the weights are redistributed and older terms become de-emphasized, but the overall magnitude does not increase. This eliminates the vanishing LR problem from AdaGrad. RMSProp continues de-emphasizing the dimensions with high cumulative partial derivatives with lower LRs, but it does so without making the LR vanishingly small.

The overall RMSProp update equations are

$$\begin{aligned}\vec{s}_t &= (1-\gamma)\ |\nabla_{\vec{w}}\mathbb{L}\left(\vec{w}_t, \vec{b}_t\right)|^2 + \gamma\, \vec{s}_{t-1} \\ \delta\vec{w}_t &= \frac{\eta}{\sqrt{\vec{s}_t + \epsilon}} \circ \nabla_{\vec{w}}\mathbb{L}\left(\vec{w}_t, \vec{b}_t\right)\end{aligned} \tag{9.15}$$

There is a parallel set of equations for the bias. The weights and bias parameters are updated in the usual fashion using equation 9.9.

9.2.9 Adam optimizer

Momentum-based gradient descent amplifies the downhill component more and more as iterations progress. On the other hand, RMSProp reduces the LR for dimensions that are seeing large gradients and vice versa to balance the progress rate along all dimensions.

Both of these are desirable properties. We want an optimization algorithm that combines them, and that algorithm is Adam. It is increasingly becoming the optimizer of choice for most deep learning researchers.

The Adam optimization algorithm maintains two state vectors:

$$\vec{v}_t = (1-\beta_1)\ \nabla_{\vec{w}}\mathbb{L}\left(\vec{w}_t, \vec{b}_t\right) + \beta_1\, \delta\vec{w}_{t-1} \tag{9.16}$$

$$\vec{s}_t = (1-\beta_2)\ |\nabla_{\vec{w}}\mathbb{L}\left(\vec{w}_t, \vec{b}_t\right)|^2 + \beta_2\, \vec{s}_{t-1} \tag{9.17}$$

where $0 < \beta_1 < 1$ and $0 < \beta_2 < 1$ are constants. Note the following:

- Equation 9.16 is essentially the momentum equation of equation 9.11 with one significant difference. We have changed the term weights to β_1 and $(1-\beta_1)$.

As we've seen, with $t \rightarrow \infty$, this results in the state vector being a weighted average of all the past gradients. This is an improvement over the original momentum scheme.

- The second state vector is basically the one from the RMSProp equation 9.15.

Using these two state vectors, Adam creates the update vector as follows:

$$\delta \vec{w}_t = \frac{\eta \, \vec{v}_t}{\sqrt{\vec{s}_t} + \epsilon} \circ \nabla_{\vec{w}} \mathbb{L}\left(\vec{w}_t, \vec{b}_t\right) \tag{9.18}$$

The $\vec{v}_t$ in the numerator pulls in the benefits of the momentum approach (with the enhancement of averaging). Otherwise, the equation is almost identical to the RMSProp; those benefits are also pulled in.

Finally, the weights and bias parameters are updated in the usual fashion using equation 9.9.

BIAS CORRECTION

The sum of weights of past values in the state vectors $\vec{v}_t$, $\vec{s}_t$ will approach ∞ only at large values of t. To improve the approximation at smaller values of t, Adam introduces a bias correction:

$$\hat{v}_t = \frac{\vec{v}_t}{\left(1 - \beta_1^t\right)} \tag{9.19}$$

$$\hat{s}_t = \frac{\vec{s}_t}{\left(1 - \beta_2^t\right)} \tag{9.20}$$

Instead of $\vec{v}_t$ and $\vec{s}_t$, we use the bias-corrected entities $\hat{v}_t$ and $\hat{s}_t$ in equation 9.18.

Listing 9.12 PyTorch code for various optimizers

```
from torch import optim

sgd_optimizer = optim.SGD([params], lr=0.01)        ← Sets the learning rate to 0.01

sgd_momentum_optimizer = optim.SGD([params], lr=0.01,
                                   momentum=0.9)     ← Sets the momentum to 0.9

sgd_nesterov_momentum_optimizer = optim.SGD([params], lr=0.01,
                                   momentum=0.9, nesterov=True)   ← Sets the Nesterov flag to True

adagrad_optimizer = optim.Adagrad([params], lr=0.001)

rms_prop_optimizer = RMSprop([params], lr=1e-2,
                             alpha=0.99)             ← Sets the smoothing constant to 0.99 (γ in 9.15)

adam_optimizer = optim.Adam([params], lr=0.001,
                             betas=(0.9, 0.999))
```

9.3 Regularization

Suppose we are teaching a baby to recognize cars. We show them red cars, blue cars, black cars, large cars, small cars, medium cars, cars with round tops, cars with rectangular tops, and so on. Soon the baby's brain realizes that there are too many varieties to remember them all by rote. So the brain starts forming *abstractions*: mysterious common features that occur together are stored in the baby's brain with the label *car*. The brain has learned to classify an abstract entity called a car. Even though it fails to *remember* every car it has seen, it can *recognize* cars. We can say it has developed *experience*. And so it is with neural networks. We do not want our network to *remember* every training instance. Rather, we want the network to form *abstractions* that will enable it to *recognize* an object during inferencing even though the exact likeness of the object instance encountered during inferencing was never seen during training.

Overfitting and underfitting

If the network has too much expressive power (too many perceptrons or, equivalently, too many weights) relative to the number of training instances, the network can and often will rote-remember the training instances. This phenomenon is called *overfitting*. Overfitting causes the network to perform very well over the training data but badly during testing or real-life inferencing. Stated another way, the network has adjusted itself to every nook, bend, and kink of the training data and thereby performs great on the training data—to the detriment of test data performance. This is illustrated in figure 9.11. *Regularization* refers to a bag of tricks that, in general, try to prevent overfitting. This is the topic of this section.

There is another phenomenon called *underfitting*, where the network simply does not have enough expressive power to model the training data. The symptom of underfitting is that the network performs badly on both training and testing data. If we see this, we should try a more complex network with more perceptrons.

9.3.1 Minimum descriptor length: An Occam's razor view of optimization

Is the set of weights and biases that minimizes a particular loss function unique? Let's examine a single perceptron (equation 7.3) with the output $\phi\left(\vec{w}^T\vec{x}+b\right)$. Let's say ϕ is the Heaviside step function (see section 7.3.1). Let $\vec{w}_*$, b_* be the weights and biases minimizing the loss function. It is easy to see that the perceptron output remains the same if we scale the weights, like $\alpha\vec{w}_*$ for all positive real values of α. Thus the weight vector $7\vec{w}_*$ will also minimize the loss function.

This is true in general for arbitrary neural networks (composed of many perceptrons): the set of weights and biases minimizing a loss function is non-unique. How does the neural network choose one? Which of them is correct? We can use the principle of Occam's razor to answer that.

Occam's razor is a philosophical principle. Its literal translation from Latin states, "Entities should not be multiplied beyond necessity." This is roughly taken

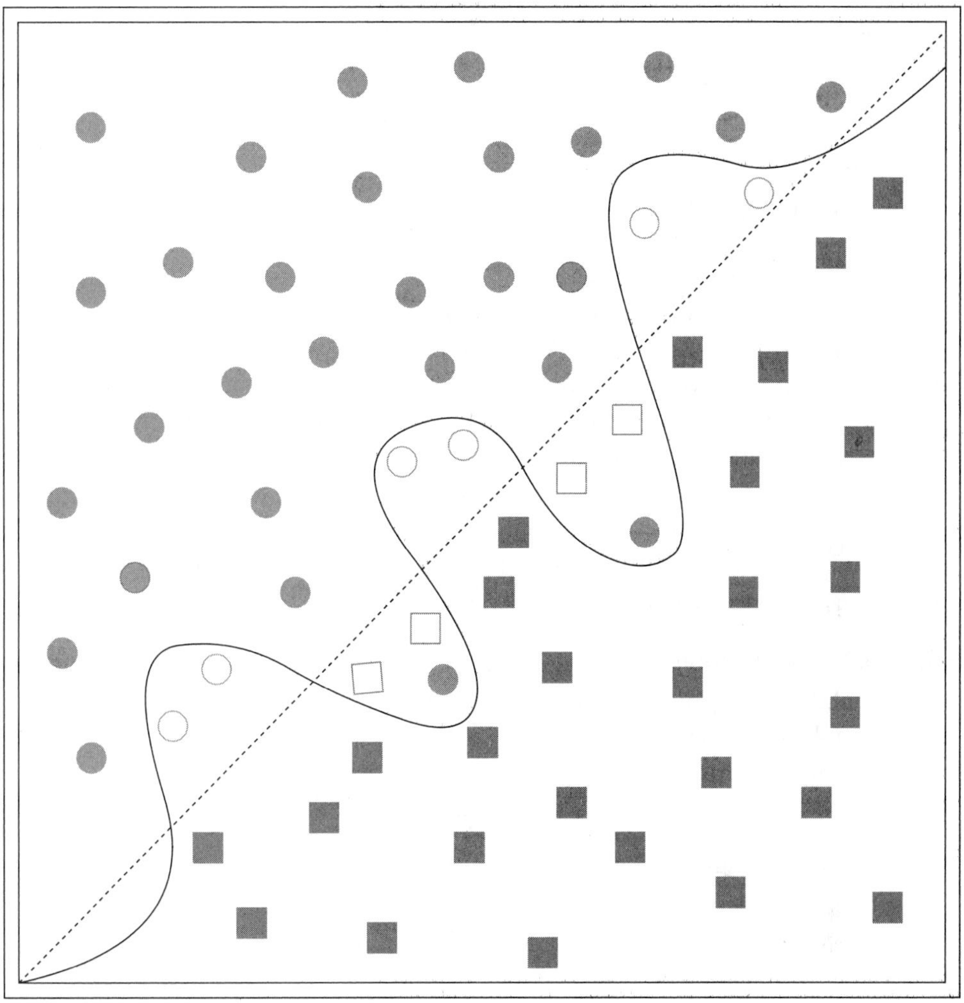

Figure 9.11 Overfitting: data points for a binary classifier. Points belonging to different classes are visually demarcated as squares and circles. Filled squares/circles indicate training data, and unfilled squares/circles indicate test data. There are some anomalous training data instances (filled circles in the square zone). The estimated decision boundary (solid line) has become wriggly to accommodate them, which is causing many test points (unfilled squares/circles) to be misclassified. The wiggly solid curve is an example of an overfitted decision boundary. If we had chosen a "simpler" decision boundary (dashed straight line), the two anomalous training points would have been misclassified, but the machine would have performed much better in tests.

to mean *among adequate explanations, the simplest one is the best.* In machine learning, this principle is typically interpreted as follows:

> Among the set of candidate neural network parameter values (weights and biases) that minimize the loss, the "simplest" one should be chosen.

The general idea is as follows. Suppose we are trying to minimize $\mathbb{L}(\theta)$ (here we have used θ to denote $\vec{w}$ and $\vec{b}$ together). We also want the solution to be as simple as possible. To achieve that, we add a penalty for departing from "simplicity" to the original loss term. Thus we minimize

$$\mathbb{L}(\theta) + \lambda R(\theta)$$

Here,

- The expression $R(\theta)$ indicates a measure for un-simplicity. It is sometimes called the *regularization penalty*. Adding a regularization penalty to the loss incentivizes the network to try to minimize un-simplicity $R(\theta)$ (or, equivalently, maximize simplicity) while trying to minimize the original loss term $\mathbb{L}(\theta)$.
- λ is a hyperparameter. Its value should be carefully chosen via trial and error. If λ is too low, this is akin to no regularization, and the network becomes prone to overfitting. If λ is too high, the regularization penalty will dominate, and the network will not adequately minimize the actual loss term.

There are two popular ways of estimating $R(\theta)$, outlined in sections 9.3.2 and 9.3.3, respectively. Both try to minimize some norm (length) of the parameter vector (which is basically a network descriptor). This is why regularization can be viewed as minimizing the descriptor length.

9.3.2 L2 regularization

In L2 regularization, we posit that shorter-length vectors are simpler. In other words, simplicity is inversely proportional to the square of the L2 norm (aka Euclidean norm). Thus,

$$R(\theta) = \left(||\vec{w}||^2 + ||\vec{b}||^2\right)$$

Overall, we minimize

$$\mathbb{L}\left(\vec{w}, \vec{b}\right) = \sum_{i=0}^{n-1} \mathbb{L}^{(i)}\left(\vec{y}^{(i)}, \bar{y}^{(i)}\right) + \lambda\left(||\vec{w}||^2 + ||\vec{b}||^2\right) \tag{9.21}$$

Compare this with equation 9.2.

L2 regularization is by far the most popular form of regularization. From this point on, we often use $\mathbb{L}\left(\vec{w}, \vec{b}\right)$ to mean the L2-regularized version (that is, equation 9.21). The hyperparameter λ is often called *weight decay* in PyTorch. Weight decay is usually set to a small number so that the second term of equation 9.21 (the norm of the weight vector) does not drown the actual loss term. The following code shows how to instantiate an optimizer with regularization enabled.

Listing 9.13 PyTorch code to enable L2 regularization

```
from torch import optim

optimizer = optim.SGD([params], lr=0.2, weight_decay=0.01)    ← Sets the weight decay to 0.01
```

9.3.3 *L1 regularization*

L1 regularization is similar in principle to L2 regularization, but it defines simplicity as the sum of the absolute values of the weights and biases:

$$R(\theta) = \left(|\vec{w}| + |\vec{b}|\right)$$

Thus, here we minimize

$$\mathbb{L}\left(\vec{w}, \vec{b}\right) = \sum_{i=0}^{n-1} \mathbb{L}^{(i)}\left(\vec{y}^{(i)}, \bar{y}^{(i)}\right) + \lambda\left(|\vec{w}| + |\vec{b}|\right) \tag{9.22}$$

9.3.4 *Sparsity: L1 vs. L2 regularization*

L1 regularization tends to create sparse models where many of the weights are 0. In comparison, L2 regularization tends to create models with low (but nonzero) weights.

To understand this, consider figure 9.12, which plots the loss function and its derivative for both L1 and L2 regularization. Let w be a single element of the weight vector $\vec{w}$.

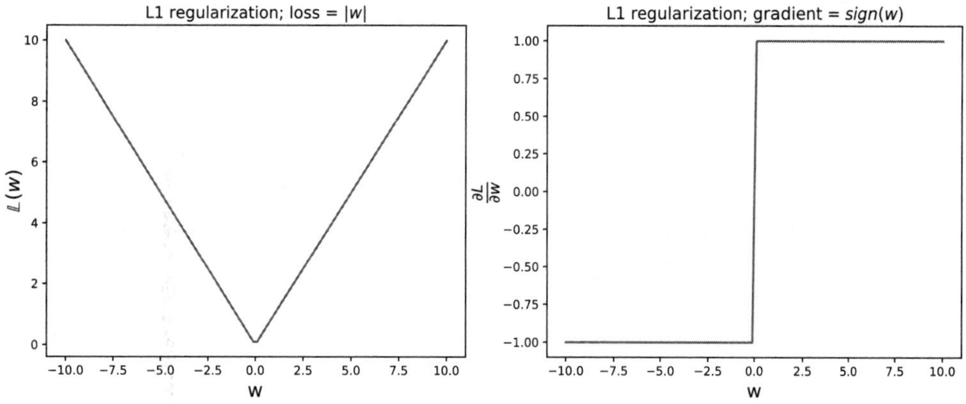

(a) L1 regularization

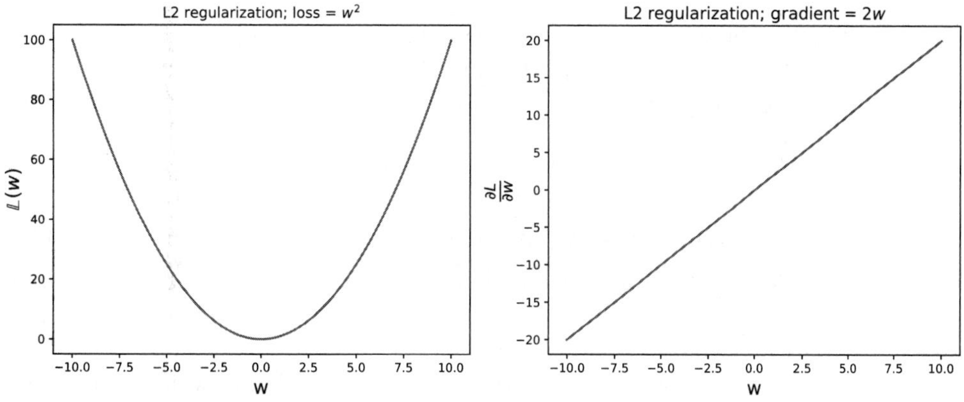

(b) L2 regularization

Figure 9.12 L1 and L2 regularization

In L1 regularization,

$$\mathbb{L}(w) = |w|$$

$$\frac{\partial \mathbb{L}(w)}{\partial w} = \begin{cases} -1 & \text{if } w < 0 \\ 0 & \text{if } w = 0 \\ 1 & \text{if } w > 0 \end{cases}$$

Since the gradient is constant for all values of w, L1 regularization pushes the weight toward 0 with the same step size at all values of w. In particular, the step toward 0 does not reduce in magnitude when close to 0. In L2 regularization,

$$\mathbb{L}(w) = w^2$$

$$\frac{\partial \mathbb{L}(w)}{\partial w} = 2w$$

Here, the gradient keeps decreasing in magnitude as w approaches 0. Hence, w comes closer to 0 but may never reach 0 since the updates take smaller and smaller steps as w approaches 0. Therefore, L2 regularization produces more dense weight vectors than L1 regularization, which produces sparse weight vectors with many 0s.

9.3.5 Bayes' theorem and the stochastic view of optimization

In sections 6.6.2 and 6.6.3, we discussed maximum likelihood estimation (MLE) and maximum a posteriori (MAP) in the context of unsupervised learning (you are encouraged to revisit those sections if necessary). Here, we study them in the context of supervised learning.

In the supervised optimization process, we have samples of the input and known output pairs (in the form of training data) $\langle \vec{x}^{(i)}, \bar{y}^{(i)} \rangle$. Of course, we can do the forward pass and generate the network output at each training data point

$$\vec{y}^{(i)} = f\left(\vec{x}^{(i)}, \theta\right)$$

where θ is the network's parameter set (representing weights and biases together).

Suppose we view the sample training data generation as a stochastic process. We can model the probability of a training instance $T^{(i)} = \langle \bar{y}^{(i)}, \vec{x}^{(i)} \rangle$ given the current network parameters θ as

$$p\left(T^{(i)} \middle| \theta\right) \propto e^{-\|\bar{y}^{(i)} - f\left(\vec{x}^{(i)}, \theta\right)\|^2} = e^{-\|\bar{y}^{(i)} - \vec{y}^{(i)}\|^2}$$

This makes intuitive sense. At an optimal value of θ, the network output $f\left(\vec{x}^{(i)}, \theta\right)$ would match the GT $\bar{y}^{(i)}$. We want our model distribution to have the highest probability density at the location where the network output matches the GT. The probability density should fall off with distance from that location.

A little thought reveals that this Gaussian-like formulation, which leads to a regression-loss-like numerator, is not the only one possible. We can use any loss function in the numerator since all of them have the property of being minimum when the network output matches the GT and gradually increase as the mismatch grows. In general,

$$p\left(T^{(i)} \middle| \theta\right) \propto e^{-\mathbb{L}^{(i)}\left(\bar{y}^{(i)}, f\left(\vec{x}^{(i)}, \theta\right)\right)} = e^{-\mathbb{L}^{(i)}\left(\bar{y}^{(i)}, \vec{y}^{(i)}\right)}$$

Assuming the training instances are mutually independent, the probability of the entire training dataset occurring jointly is the product of individual instance probabilities. If we denote the entire training dataset as T,

$$T = \left\{\left\langle \bar{y}^{(i)}, \vec{x}^{(i)} \right\rangle\right\}$$

Then

$$p\left(T|\theta\right) = \prod_{i=0}^{N} p\left(T^{(i)} \middle| \theta\right) \propto \prod_{i=0}^{N} e^{-\mathbb{L}^{(i)}\left(\bar{y}^{(i)}, \vec{y}^{(i)}\right)} = e^{-\sum_{i=0}^{N} \mathbb{L}^{(i)}\left(\bar{y}^{(i)}, \vec{y}^{(i)}\right)} = e^{-\mathbb{L}(\theta)}$$

At this point, we can take one of two possible approaches described in the next two subsections.

MLE-BASED OPTIMIZATION

In this approach, we choose the optimal value for the parameter set θ by maximizing the likelihood

$$p\left(T|\theta\right) \propto e^{-\mathbb{L}(\theta)}$$

This is equivalent to saying we will choose the optimal parameters θ such that the probability of occurrence of the training data is maximized. Thus the optimal parameter set θ_* is yielded by

$$\theta_* = \underset{\theta}{argmax}\ p\left(T|\theta\right) = \underset{\theta}{argmax}\ e^{-\mathbb{L}(\theta)}$$

Obviously, the optimal θ that maximizes the likelihood is the one that minimizes $\mathbb{L}\left(\theta\right)$. So, the maximum likelihood formulation is nothing but minimizing the total mismatch between predicted and GT output over the entire training dataset.

MAP OPTIMIZATION

By Bayes' theorem (equation 6.1),

$$p\left(\theta|T\right) = \frac{p\left(T|\theta\right)\ p\left(\theta\right)}{p\left(T\right)}$$

To estimate the optimal θ, we can also maximize the posterior probability on the left side of this equation. This is equivalent to saying we will choose the optimal parameters θ such that θ has the maximal conditional probability given the training dataset. Thus the optimal value for the parameter set θ is yielded by

$$\theta_* = \underset{\theta}{argmax}\ p\left(\theta|T\right) = \underset{\theta}{argmax}\ \frac{p\left(T|\theta\right)\ p\left(\theta\right)}{p\left(T\right)}$$

where the last equality is derived via Bayes' theorem.

Observing the previous equation, we see that the denominator $p\left(T\right)$ in the rightmost term does not involve θ and hence can be dropped from the optimization. So,

$$\theta_* = \underset{\theta}{argmax}\ p\left(\theta | T\right) = \underset{\theta}{argmax}\ p\left(T | \theta\right)\ p\left(\theta\right)$$

How do we model the *a priori* probability $p\left(\theta\right)$? We can use Occam's razor and say that we assign a higher *a priori* probability to smaller parameter values. Thus, we can say

$$p\left(\theta\right) \propto e^{-\lambda R(\theta)}$$

Then the overall posterior probability maximization becomes

$$\theta_* = \underset{\theta}{argmax}\ p\left(\theta | T\right) = \underset{\theta}{argmax}\ p\left(T | \theta\right)\ p\left(\theta\right) = e^{-(\mathbb{L}(\theta) + \lambda R(\theta))}$$

NOTE Maximizing this posterior probability is equivalent to minimizing the regularized loss. Maximizing the likelihood is equivalent to minimizing the un-regularized loss.

9.3.6 *Dropout*

In the introduction for section 9.3, we saw that too much expressive power (too many perceptron nodes) sometimes prevents the machine from developing general *abstractions* (aka *experience*). Instead, the machine may remember the training data instances (see figure 9.11). This phenomenon is called overfitting. We have already seen that one way to mitigate this problem is to add a regularization penalty—such as adding the L2 norm of the weights—to the loss to discourage the network from learning large weight values.

Dropout is another method of regularization. Here, somewhat crazily, we turn off random perceptrons in the network (set their value to 0) during training. To be precise, we attach a probability p_i^l with the ith node (perceptron) in layer l. In any training iteration, the node (perceptron) is off with a probability of $(1 - p)$. Typically, dropout is only enabled during training and is turned off during inferencing.

What good does it do? Well,

- Dropout prevents the network from relying too much on a small number of nodes. Instead, the network is forced to use all the nodes.
- Equivalently, dropout encourages the training process to spread the weights to multiple nodes instead of putting much weight on a few nodes. This makes the effect somewhat similar to L2 regularization.
- Dropout mitigates *co-adaptation*: a behavior whereby a group of nodes in the network behave in a highly correlated fashion, emitting similar outputs most of the time. This means the network could retain only one of them with no significant loss of accuracy.

DROPOUT SIMULATES AN ENSEMBLE OF SUBNETWORKS

Consider a small three-node intermediate layer of some neural network with dropout. The kth input to this layer can turn on with probability p_k. This means the probability of that input node turning off is $(1 - p_k)$. We can express this with a *binary* stochastic variable δ_k for $k = 0$ or $k = 1$ or $k = 2$. This variable δ_k takes one of two possible values:

0 or 1. The probability of it taking the value 1 is p_k. In other words, $p(\delta_k = 1) = p_k$, and $p(\delta_k = 0) = 1 - p_k$. The output of this small three-node layer with dropout can be expressed as

$$a^l = \sum_{k=0}^{2} \delta_k w_k a_k^{l-1}$$

We have three variables δ_0, δ_1, and δ_2, each of which can take two values. Altogether we have $2^3 = 8$ possible combinations. Each combination leads to a subnode shown in figure 9.13. Each of these combinations has a probability of occurrence P_i, also shown in the figure. These observations lead to a very important insight:

> The expected value of the output—that is, $\mathbb{E}(a_l)$—is the same as the expected value of the output if we deployed the subnetworks in figure 9.13 randomly, with probabilities P_i.

Why does this matter? Well, given a problem, none of us know the right number of perceptrons for the network to deploy. One thing to do under these circumstances is to deploy networks of various strengths randomly and take an average of their outputs. We have just established that dropout (turning inputs off randomly) achieves the same thing. But deploying a network where inputs get turned on or off randomly is much simpler than deploying a large number of subnetworks. All we have to do is deploy a *dropout* layer.

PYTORCH CODE FOR DROPOUT

In section 9.2.3, we created a simple two-layer neural network classifier to predict whether a Statsville resident is a man, woman, or child based on height and weight data. In this section, we show the same model with dropout layers added. Note that dropout should be enabled only during training, not during inferencing. To do this in PyTorch, you can call `model.eval()` before running inferencing. This way, your training and inferencing code remains the same, but PyTorch knows under the hood when to include the dropout layers and when not to.

Listing 9.14 Dropout

```
class ModelWithDropout(torch.nn.Module):
    def __init__(self, input_size, hidden_size, output_size):
        super(Model, self).__init__()
        self.net = torch.nn.Sequential(
            torch.nn.Linear(input_size, hidden_size),
            torch.nn.Dropout(p=0.2),        <-- Instantiates a dropout layer with
                                                a probability of dropout = 0.2

            torch.nn.Linear(hidden_size, output_size),
            torch.nn.Dropout(p=0.2)
        )

    def forward(self, X):
        return self.net(X)
```

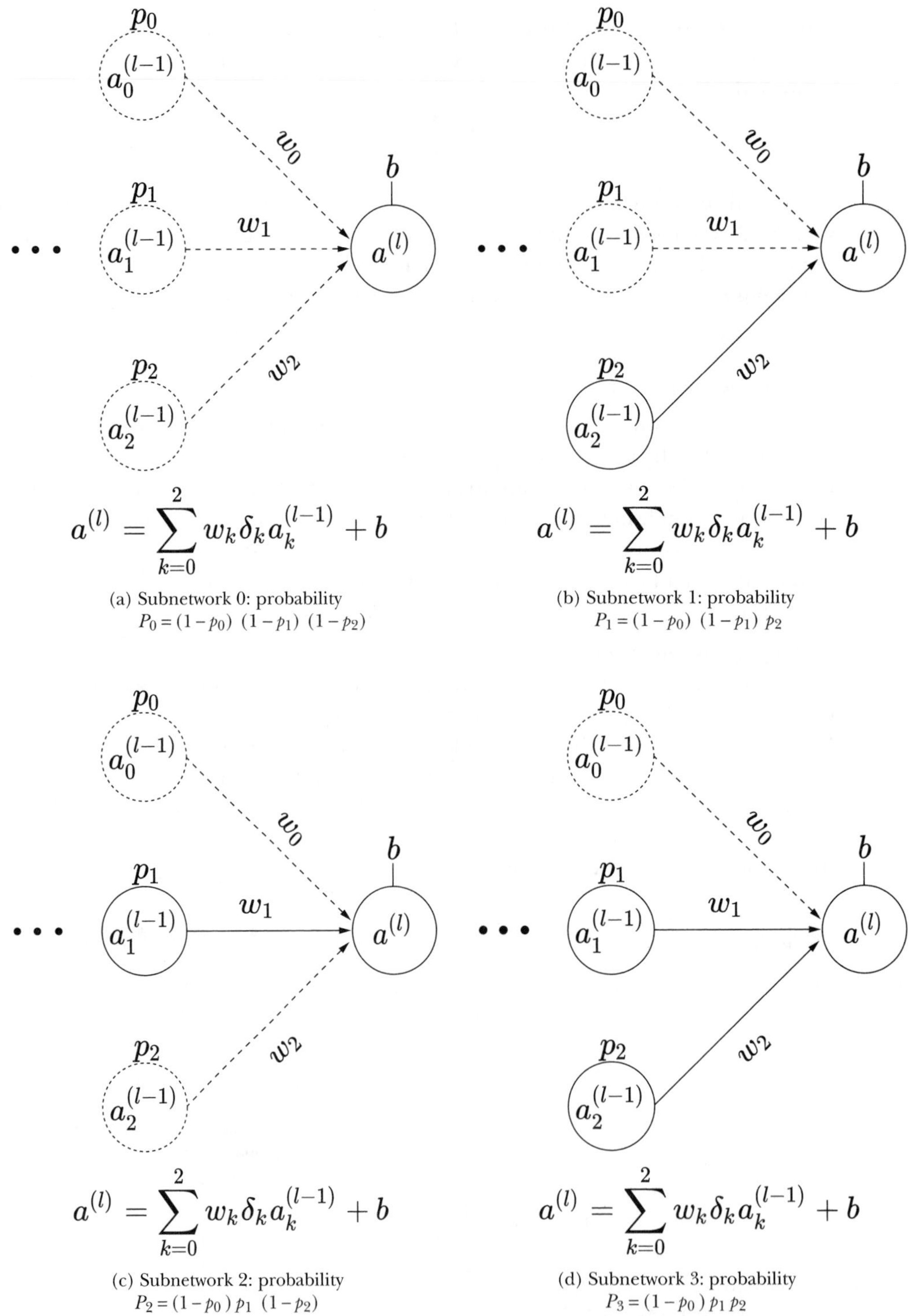

$$a^{(l)} = \sum_{k=0}^{2} w_k \delta_k a_k^{(l-1)} + b$$

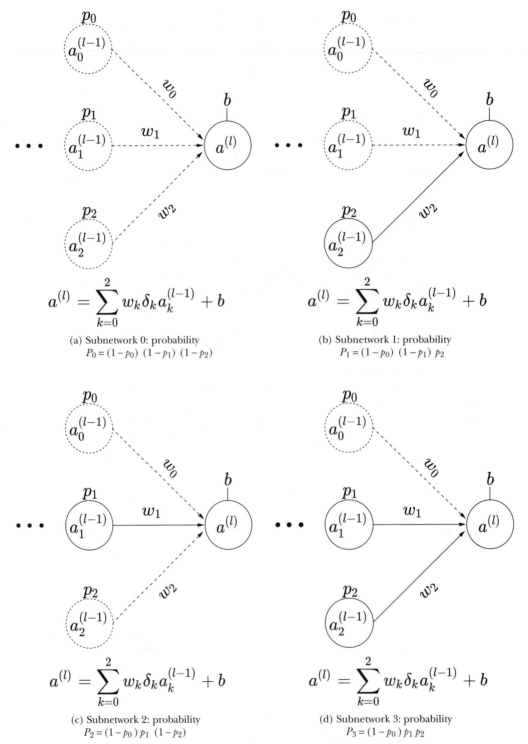

(a) Subnetwork 0: probability $P_0 = (1 - p_0)\ (1 - p_1)\ (1 - p_2)$

$$a^{(l)} = \sum_{k=0}^{2} w_k \delta_k a_k^{(l-1)} + b$$

(b) Subnetwork 1: probability $P_1 = (1 - p_0)\ (1 - p_1)\ p_2$

$$a^{(l)} = \sum_{k=0}^{2} w_k \delta_k a_k^{(l-1)} + b$$

(c) Subnetwork 2: probability $P_2 = (1 - p_0)\ p_1\ (1 - p_2)$

$$a^{(l)} = \sum_{k=0}^{2} w_k \delta_k a_k^{(l-1)} + b$$

(d) Subnetwork 3: probability $P_3 = (1 - p_0)\ p_1\ p_2$

Figure 9.13 Dropout simulates subnetworks: illustrated with a three-node intermediate layer of a neural network. The probability of input node $a_k^{(l-1)}$ being on is $p\ (\delta_k = 1) = p_k$.

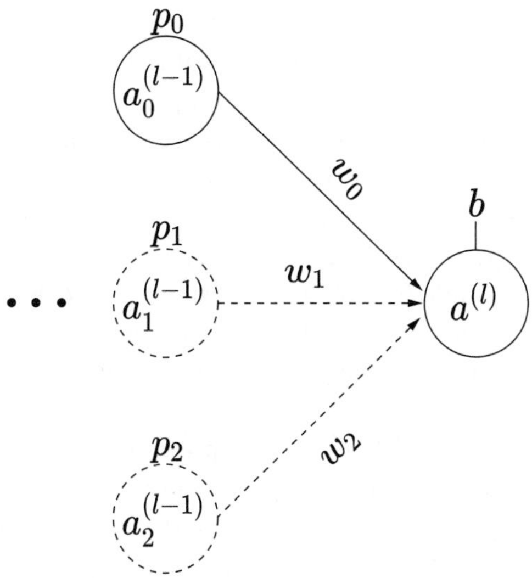

$$a^{(l)} = \sum_{k=0}^{2} w_k \delta_k a_k^{(l-1)} + b$$

(e) Subnetwork 4: probability
$P_4 = p_0\ (1 - p_1)\ (1 - p_2)$

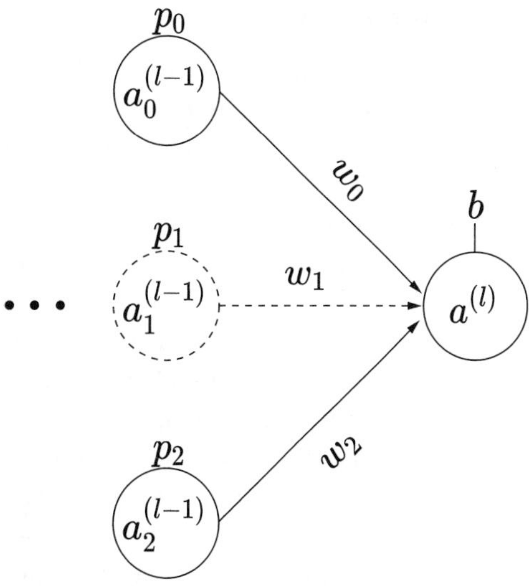

$$a^{(l)} = \sum_{k=0}^{2} w_k \delta_k a_k^{(l-1)} + b$$

(f) Subnetwork 5: probability
$P_5 = p_0\ (1 - p_1)\ p_2$

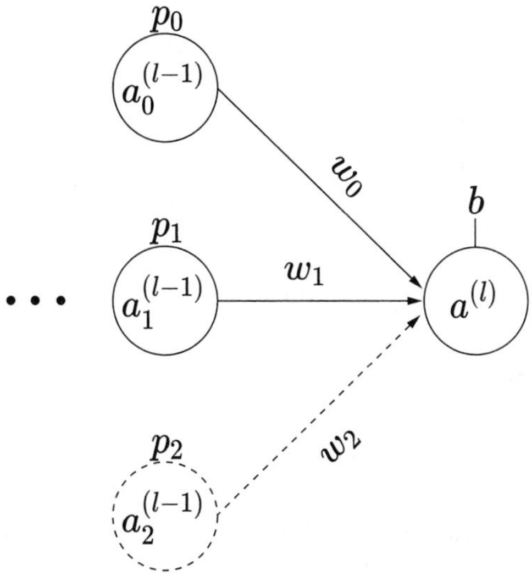

$$a^{(l)} = \sum_{k=0}^{2} w_k \delta_k a_k^{(l-1)} + b$$

(g) Subnetwork 6: probability
$P_6 = p_0\, p_1\ (1 - p_2)$

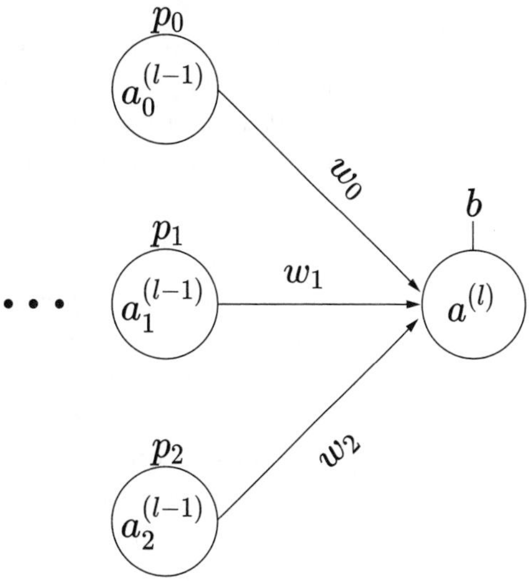

$$a^{(l)} = \sum_{k=0}^{2} w_k \delta_k a_k^{(l-1)} + b$$

(h) Subnetwork 7: probability
$P_7 = p_0\, p_1\, p_2$

Summary

- Training is the process by which a neural network identifies the optimal values for its parameters (weights and biases of the individual perceptrons). Training progresses iteratively: in each iteration, we estimate the loss and run an optimization step that updates the parameter values so as to decrease the loss. After doing this many times, we hope to arrive at optimal parameter values.
- In a supervised neural network, loss quantifies the mismatch between the desired output and the network output over sampled training data instances. The desired output (ground truth) is often estimated via manual effort. Training the neural network essentially identifies the weights and biases of the neural network that minimize the loss.
- The discrepancy between the ground truth and network output can be expressed in many different ways. Each corresponds to a different loss function. Denoting the ground truth probabilities of all the possible classes given the ith training input $\vec{x}^{(i)}$ as a vector $\bar{y}^{(i)}$ and the network output on the same as $y^{(i)}$,
  - Regression loss takes the L2 norm of the vector difference between the network output and ground-truth vectors and is mathematically expressed as $\|\vec{y}^{(i)} - \bar{y}^{(i)}\|^2 = \sum_{j=0}^{N-1} \left(y_j^{(i)} - \bar{y}_j^{(i)}\right)^2$.
  - If the neural network is a classifier, it typically outputs a vector of class probabilities. This means $\vec{y}^{(i)} = \left[p_0\left(\vec{x}^{(i)}\right) \quad p_1\left(\vec{x}^{(i)}\right) \quad p_j\left(\vec{x}^{(i)}\right) \quad \cdots \quad p_{N-1}\left(\vec{x}^{(i)}\right)\right]$ where $p_j\left(\vec{x}^{(i)}\right)$ is the network estimated probability of the input belonging to class j, and N is the number of possible classes. In general, given an input, a neural network computes per-class scores: the class with the highest score is the predicted class. The scores are unbounded numbers and can be arbitrarily large or small (even negative). The softmax operation converts them into probabilities. If $\vec{s} = \left[s_0 \quad s_1 \quad s_2 \quad \cdots \quad s_{N-1}\right]$ denotes the score vector, the corresponding softmax vector is $\vec{y}^{(i)} = \left[\frac{e^{s_0}}{S} \quad \frac{e^{s_1}}{S} \quad \frac{e^{s_2}}{S} \quad \cdots \quad \frac{e^{s_{N-1}}}{S}\right]$ where $S = \sum_{k=0}^{N-1} e^{s_k}$. The softmax output vector consists of probabilities, meaning they are numbers between 0 and 1 and they sum to 1.
  - Given the probability of each class, classifiers can employ the cross-entropy loss, which can be expressed as $-\sum_{j=0}^{N-1} \bar{y}_j^{(i)}\, log\left(y_j^{(i)}\right)$. Note that since the ground-truth vector is one-hot, only a single term in this expression survives: the one corresponding to the desired class, denoted j^*. The loss becomes the logarithm of the corresponding network output, $-log\left(y_{j^*}^{(i)}\right)$, and is zero if $y_{j^*}^{(i)} = 1$. This agrees with our expectation: if the network is predicting the GT class with probability 1, there is no loss.
  - Since during training, softmax is almost always followed by cross-entropy loss, PyTorch has a combined operator called softmax cross-entropy loss. It is preferred over doing these operations individually because it has better numerical properties.

  - Focal loss tries to tackle the data-imbalance problem by putting more weight on the "hard" examples with higher loss.
  - Hinge loss is another popular loss that becomes zero when the correct class is predicted with the maximum score. Once that criterion is achieved, it no longer tries to improve the relative values of scores.
- Total loss can be obtained by adding the losses from all the individual training data instances. However, this requires us to process all the training data points in every iteration, which is prohibitively expensive. Hence, we sample a subset of training data points to create a minibatch, estimate losses for each input data instance in the minibatch, and add them to obtain an estimate for the total loss. This process is known as stochastic gradient descent (SGD).
- Optimization is the process of updating the neural network parameters (weights and biases of perceptrons) so as to reduce the loss. We can plot the loss against weights and bias values and obtain a hypersurface defined over the domain of weights and bias values. Our ultimate goal is to reach the bottom (minimum point) of this loss hypersurface. Optimization is geometrically equivalent to moving down the hypersurface to reduce the loss. The steepest descent (toward the nearest minimum) happens along a negative gradient.
- We can combine several other criteria with the gradient to improve the convergence to the minimum loss value. Each of them results in a different optimization technique:
  - Due to noisy estimations, the local gradient may not always point toward the minimum, but it will have a strong component toward that minimum along with other noisy components. Instead of blindly following the current gradient, we can follow the direction corresponding to a weighted average of the current gradient estimate and the gradient estimate from the previous iteration. This is a recursive process, which effectively means the direction followed at any iteration is a weighted average of the current and all gradient estimates from the beginning of training. Recent gradients are weighted higher, and older gradients are weighed lower. All these gradients have strong components toward the minimum that reinforce each other, while the noisy components point in random directions and tend to cancel each other. Thus the overall weighted sum is a more reliable move toward the minimum. This is called momentum-based gradient descent.
  - A drawback of momentum is that it can result in overshooting the minimum. Nesterov accelerated gradients correct this drawback by calculating gradients via one-step lookahead. If the current update takes us to the other side of the minimum, the gradient will have an opposite direction there. We take a weighted average of the update suggested by momentum-based gradient descent and the gradient at the estimated destination point. If we are far from the minimum, it will be roughly equivalent to momentum-based gradient descent. But if we are about to overshoot the minimum, there will be cancelation, and the update will

be smaller than that of the pure momentum case. Thus we reduce the chances of overshooting the minimum.

  - AdaGrad is an optimization technique that imparts additional weight to infrequently changing axes of the loss hypersurface. The Adam optimizer combines many advantages of other optimizers and is often the modern optimizer of choice.

- The principle of Occam's razor essentially says that among adequate explanations, the simplest one should be preferred. In machine learning, this leads to regularization. There are typically many solutions to the loss-minimization problem. We want to choose the simplest one. Accordingly, we add a penalty for departing from simplicity (regularization loss) to whatever other losses we have. This incentivizes the system to go for the simplest solution. Regularization loss is often the total length of the parameter vector; thus, regularization pushes us toward solutions with smaller absolute values for parameters.
- Minimizing the loss function without the regularization term is equivalent to the Bayesian maximum likelihood estimation (MLE) technique. On the other hand, minimizing loss with the regularized term is equivalent to maximum a posteriori (MAP) estimation.
- Overfitting is a phenomenon where the neural network has learned all the nuances of the training data. Since anomalous nuances in training data points are often caused by noise, this leads to worse performance during inferencing. Overfitting is symptomized by great accuracy (low loss) on training data but bad accuracy on test data. It often happens because the network has more expressive power than necessary for the problem and is trying to memorize all nooks and bends of the training data. Regularization mitigates the problem. Another trick is dropout, where we deliberately turn off a random subset of neurons during training iterations. This forces all the neurons to learn to do the job with a reduced set of neurons.

10 Convolutions in neural networks

This chapter covers

- The graphical and algebraic view of neural networks
- Two-dimensional and three-dimensional convolution with custom weights
- Adding convolution layers to a neural network

Image analysis typically involves identifying *local* patterns. For instance, to do face recognition, we need to analyze local patterns of neighboring pixels corresponding to eyes, noses, and ears. The subject of the photograph may be standing on a beach in front of the ocean, but the big picture involving sand and water is irrelevant.

Convolution is a specialized operation that examines local patterns in an input signal. These operators are typically used to analyze images: that is, the input is a 2D array of pixels. To illustrate this, we examine a few examples of special-purpose convolution operations that detect the edges, corners, and average illumination in a small neighborhood of pixels from an image. Once we have detected such local properties, we can combine them and recognize higher-level patterns like ears, noses, and eyes. We can combine those in turn to detect still higher-level structures like faces. The system naturally lends itself to multilayer convolutional neural networks—the lowest layers(closest to the input) detect edges and corners, and the next layers detect ears, eyes, noses, and so forth.

In section 8.3, we discussed the *linear* neural network layer (aka *fully connected* layer). There, every output is connected to *all* inputs. This means an output is derived by taking a weighted linear combination of *all* input values. In other words, the output is derived from a *global* view of the input. Convolution layers are different. These are characterized by:

- *Local connections*—Only a small subset of neighboring input values are connected to one output value. Thus, each output is a weighted linear combination of only a small set of *adjacent* input values. As a consequence, only local patterns in the input are captured.
- *Shared weights*—The same weights are slid over the entire input. Consequently,
  - The number of weights is drastically reduced. Since convolution is typically used on images where the input size is large (number of pixels), fully connected layers are prohibitively expensive. Convolution repeats a (usually small) number of weights across the input, thereby keeping the number of weights manageable.
  - The nature of the local pattern extracted is fixed all over the input. If the convolution is an edge detector, it extracts edges all over the input. We cannot have an edge detector at one region of the input and a corner detector at another region, for instance. Of course, in a multilayered network, we can use different convolution layers to capture different local patterns. In particular, successive layers can capture local patterns in local patterns of the input, and so on, thereby capturing increasingly complex and increasingly global patterns at higher layers of the network.

The exact local pattern captured depends on the weights of the convolution operator. We don't know exactly what local patterns of the input to capture to recognize a specific higher-level structure of interest (such as a face). This means we do not want to *specify* the weights of the convolutions. The whole point of neural networks is to avoid such tailored feature engineering. Rather, we want to *learn*—through the process of *training* described in chapter 8—the weights of the convolution layers. Losses can be backpropagated through convolution just as they are through fully connected (FC) layers.

Just like FC layers, convolution layers can be expressed as matrix-vector multiplications. The structure of the weight matrix is a special case of equation 8.8, but it is a matrix all the same. Consequently, the forward propagation equation 8.7 and backpropagation equations 8.31 and 8.33 are still applicable. Forward propagation and backpropagation (training) through convolution proceed exactly as they do with FC layers.

Since the convolution is learned—as opposed to specified—in a neural network, there is no telling what local patterns such layers will learn to extract (although, in practice, the initial layers often learn to recognize edges and corners). All we know is that each output in a given layer is derived from only a *small subset of spatially adjoint* input values from previous layers. The final output is derived from a hierarchical local examination of the input.

NOTE Fully functional code for chapter 10, runnable via Jupyter Notebook, is available at our public GitHub repository at http://mng.bz/M2lW.

10.1 One-dimensional convolution: Graphical and algebraical view

As always, we examine the process of convolution with a set of examples. We examine convolutions in one, two, and three dimensions, but we start with one dimension for ease of understanding.

The best way to visualize 1D convolution is to imagine a stretched, straightened rope (the input array) over which a measuring ruler (the kernel) is sliding.

- In figures 10.1, 10.2, and 10.3, the ruler (kernel) is shown as shaded boxes, while the rope (input array) is shown as a sequence of white boxes. Successive steps in the figure represent successive positions (aka slide stops) of the sliding ruler. Notice that the shaded portion occupies a different position in each step.
- Rulers in successive positions during sliding can overlap. They overlap by varying amounts in figures 10.1, 10.2, and 10.3.
- The rope and the ruler are discrete 1D arrays in reality. At each slide stop, the ruler array elements rest on a subset of rope array elements.
- We multiply each input array element by the kernel element resting on it and sum the products. This is equivalent to taking a weighted sum of the input (rope) elements that fall under the current position of the kernel (ruler), with the kernel elements serving as weights. This weighted sum is emitted as a single output element. One output element results from each slide stop of the tile. As the ruler slides over the entire rope, left to right, a 1D output array is generated.

The following entities are defined for 1D convolution:

- *Input*—A one-dimensional array. We typically use the symbol n to represent input array length in 1D convolution. In figure 10.1, $n = 7$.
- *Output*—A one-dimensional array. We typically use the symbol o to represent the output array length in 1D convolution. In figure 10.1, $o = 5$. Section 10.2 shows how to calculate the output size from the independent parameters.
- *Kernel*—A small array of weights whose size is a parameter of the convolution. We typically use the symbol k to represent the kernel size in 1D convolution. In figure 10.1, $k = 3$; in figure 10.3, $k = 2$.
- *Stride*—The number of input elements over which the kernel slides after completing a single step. We typically use the symbol s to represent the stride in 1D convolution. This is a parameter of the convolution. In figure 10.1, $s = 1$; in figure 10.2, stride is 2. A stride of 1 means there is a slide stop at each successive element of the input. So, the output has roughly the same number of elements as the input (they may not be exactly equal because of padding, explained next). A stride of 2 means

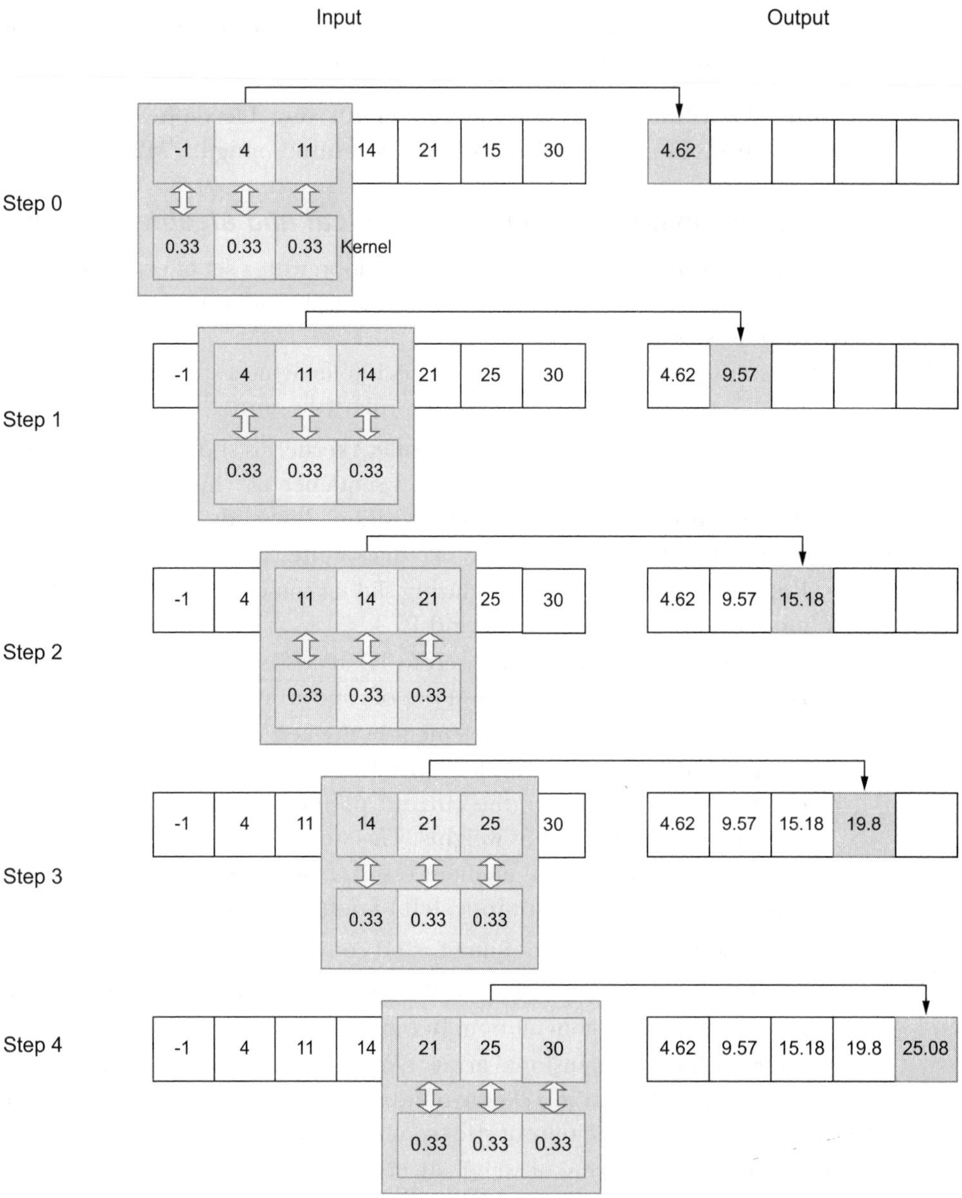

Figure 10.1 1D convolution with a local averaging kernel of size 3, stride 1, and valid padding on the input array of size 7

there is a slide stop at every *other* input element. So, the output size is roughly half of the input size. A stride of 3 means the output size is roughly one-third the input size.

- *Padding*—As the kernel slides toward the extremity of the input array, parts of it may fall outside the input array. In other words, part of the kernel falls over ghost

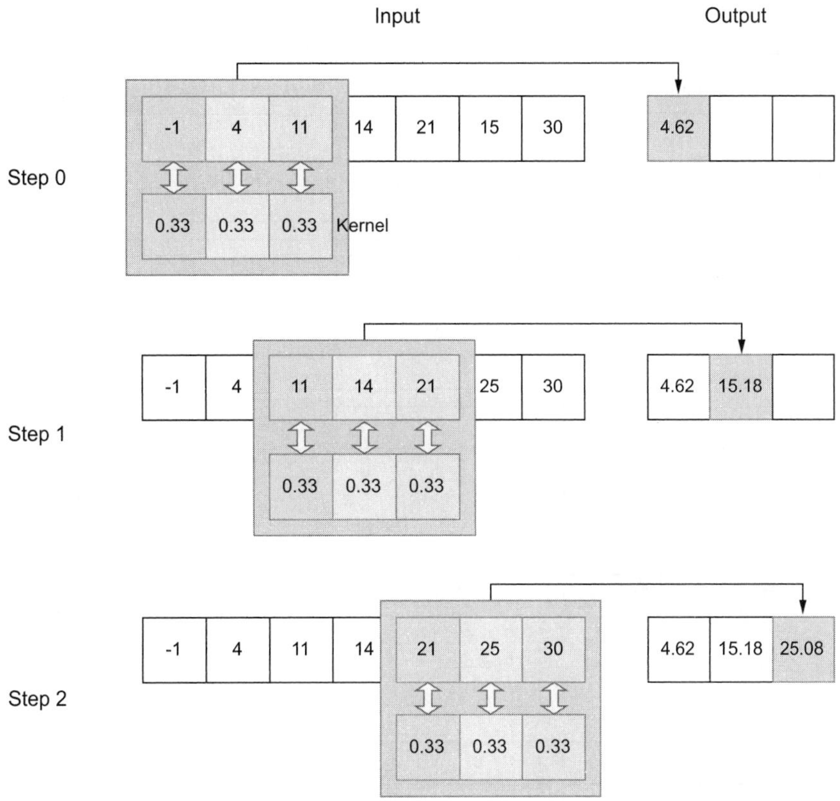

Figure 10.2 1D convolution with a local averaging kernel of size 3, stride 2, and valid padding

input elements. Figure 10.4 shows such a situation: the ghost input array elements are shown with dashed boxes. There are multiple strategies to deal with this:

- *Valid padding*—We stop sliding whenever any element of the kernel falls outside the input array. No ghost input elements are involved; the *entire* kernel always falls on valid input elements (hence the name *valid*). Note that this implies we will have fewer outputs than inputs. If we try to generate an output corresponding to, say, the last input element, all but the first kernel element will fall outside the input on ghost elements. So, we have to stop when the right-most kernel element falls on the right-most input element (see figures 10.1, 10.2, and 10.3). At this point, the left-most kernel element falls on the $(N - k)$th input element. We do not generate output for the last k inputs. Hence, even with a stride of 1 for valid padding, the output is slightly smaller than the input.
- *Same (zero) padding*—Here, we do not want to stop early. If the stride is 1, the output size matches the input size (hence the name *same*). We continue to slide the kernel until its left end falls on the right-most input. At this point, all but the left-most kernel element is falling on ghost input elements. We pretend these ghost input elements have a value of 0 (*zero padding*).

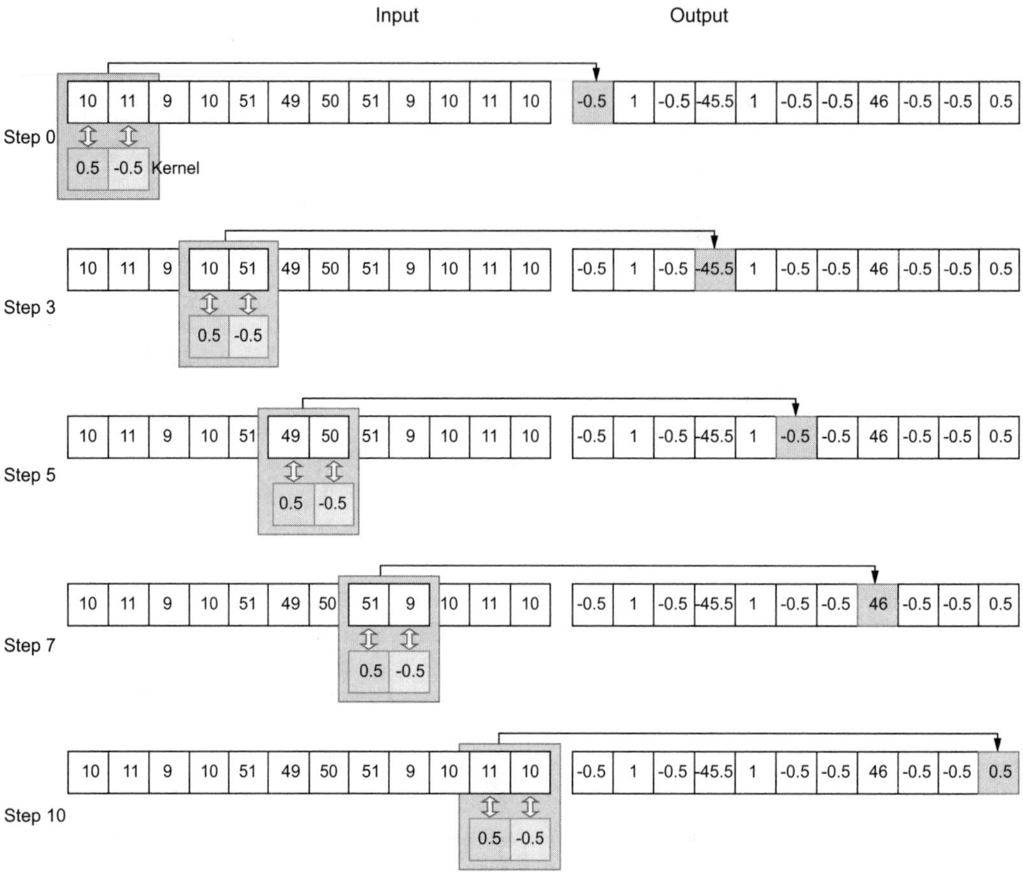

Figure 10.3 1D convolution with an edge-detection kernel of size 2, stride 1, valid padding. Not all slide stops (that is, steps) are shown.

Let's denote the input array's domain by S. It's a 1D grid:

$$S = [0, W - 1]$$

Every point in S is associated with a value X_x. Together, these values form the input X. On this grid of input points, we define a subgrid S_o of output points. S_o is obtained from S by applying stride-based stepping on the input. Assuming $s = [s_W]$ denotes the stride, the first slide stop has the top-left corner of the rope at $(x = 0)$. The next slide stop is at $(x = s_W)$, and the next is $(x = 2s_W)$, and so on. When we reach the right end, we stop. Overall, the output grid consists of the slide-stop points at which the top-left corner of the kernel (ruler) rests as it sweeps over the input volume: that is, $S_o = \{(x = 0)\,, (x = s_W) \cdots ,\}$. There is an output for each point in S_o.

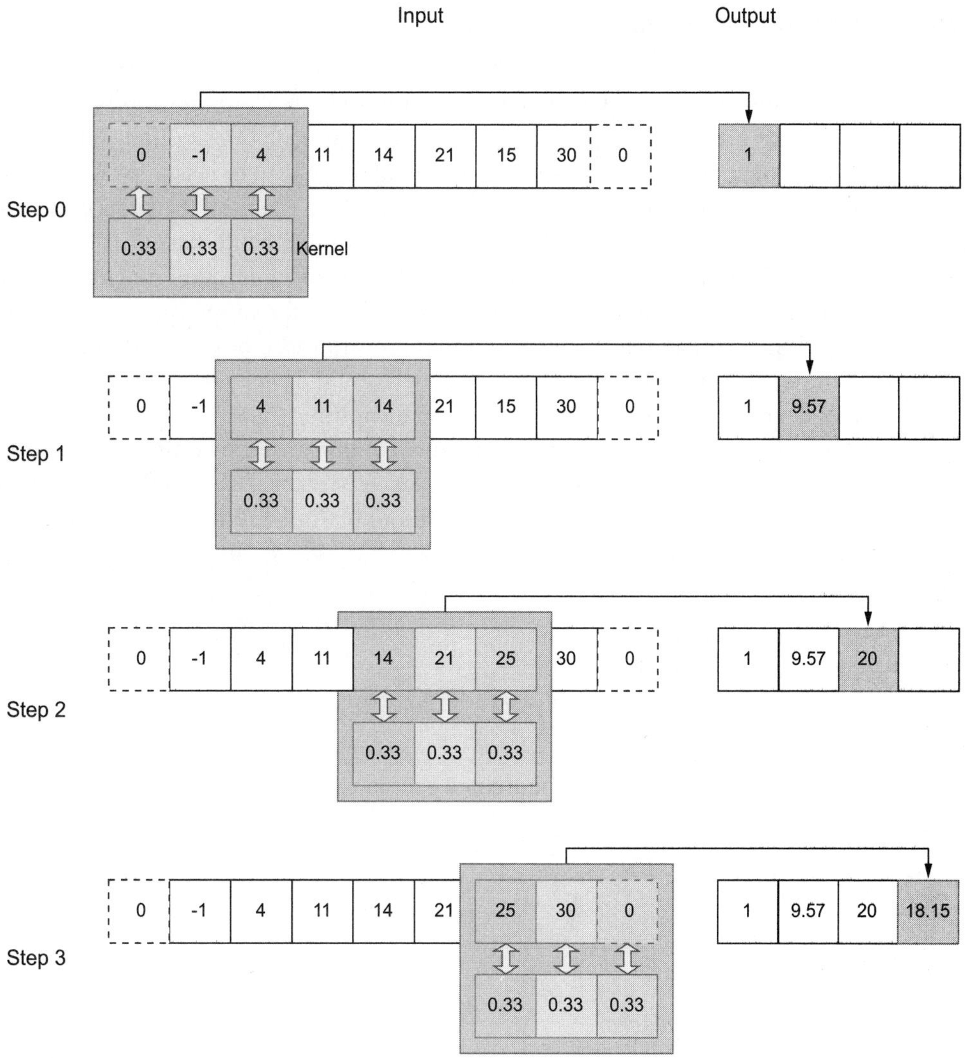

Figure 10.4 1D convolution with a local averaging kernel of size 3, stride 2, and zero padding

Equation 10.1 shows how a single output value is generated in 1D convolution. X denotes input, Y denotes output, and W denote kernel weights:

$$Y_x = \sum_{j=0}^{k_W} X_{x+j} W_j \quad \forall (x) \in S_o \tag{10.1}$$

Note that when the kernel of dimension k_W (ruler) has its origin on x, it covers all input pixels in the domain $[x..(x + k_W)]$. These are the pixels participating in equation 10.1. Each of these input pixels is multiplied by the kernel element covering it. Match equation 10.1 with figures 10.1, 10.2, and 10.3.

10.1.1 Curve smoothing via 1D convolution

In this section, we look at how to perform local averaging via convolution, from a physical and algebraic viewpoint, to get a comprehensive understanding. The 1D kernel with weight vector $\vec{w} = \begin{bmatrix} \frac{1}{3} & \frac{1}{3} & \frac{1}{3} \end{bmatrix}$ (shown in figure 10.1) essentially takes the moving average of successive sets of three input values. As such, it is a local averaging (aka smoothing) operator. This becomes apparent if we examine the plots of the raw input vector with regard to the input vector convolved with the kernel (figure 10.5). The input (solid line) weaves up and down, while the output is a smooth curve (dashed line) through the mean position of the input. In general, the output produced by convolving by a kernel with all equal weights (the weights must be normalized, meaning the sum of the weights is 1) is a smoothed (locally averaged) version of the input. Why do we want to smooth an input vector? Because it captures the broad trend in the input data while eliminating short-term fluctuations (often caused by noise). If you are familiar with Fourier transforms and frequency domains, you can see that this is essentially a low-pass filter, eliminating short-term, high-frequency noise and capturing the longer-term, low-frequency variation in the input data array.

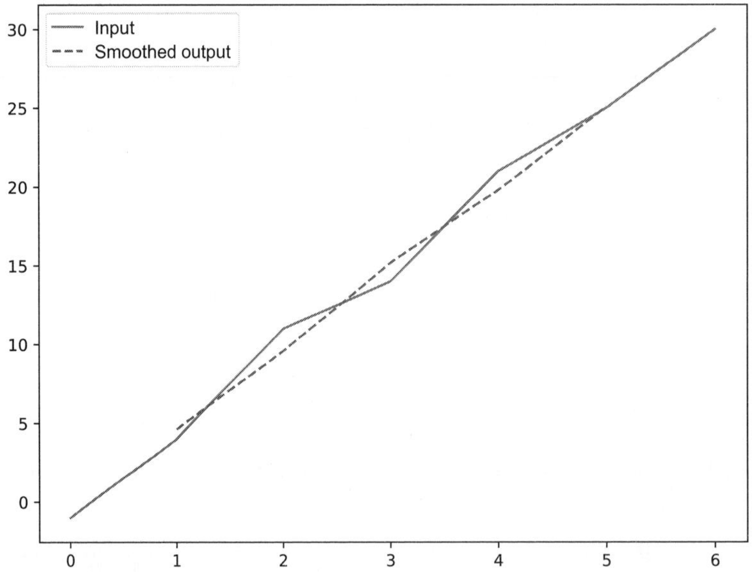

Figure 10.5 Graph of the input array (solid) and output array (dashed) from figure 10.1. Note that the output produced by convolving by the kernel with all equal normalized weights is a smoothed (locally averaged) version of the input. Such local soothing captures the low-frequency (long-term) broad trend of the function by eliminating high-frequency (short-term) noise.

10.1.2 Curve edge detection via 1D convolution

As mentioned earlier, a convolution's physical effect on an input array radically changes with the weights of the convolution kernel. Now let's examine a very different kernel that detects edges in the input data.

An *edge* is defined as a sharp change in the values in an input array. For instance, if two successive elements in the input array have a large absolute difference in values, that is an edge. If we graph the input array (that is, plot the input array values in the y axis against the array indices), an edge will appear in the graph. For instance, consider the input array in figure 10.3 (graphed in figure 10.6). At indices 0 to 3, we have values in the neighborhood of 10. At index 4, the value jumps to 51. We say there is an edge between indices 3 and 4. The values then remain in the neighborhood of 50 at indices 4 to 7. Then they jump back to the neighborhood of 10 in the remaining indices. We say there is another edge between indices 7 and 8. The convolution we examine here will emit a high response (output value) exactly at the indices of the jump—3 and 7—while emitting a low response at other indices. This is an edge-detection convolution (filter). Why do we want to detect edges? Because edges are important for understanding images. Locations at which the signal changes rapidly provide more semantic clues than flat uniform regions. Experiments on the human visual cortex have established that humans pay more attention to locations where color or shade changes rapidly than to flat regions.

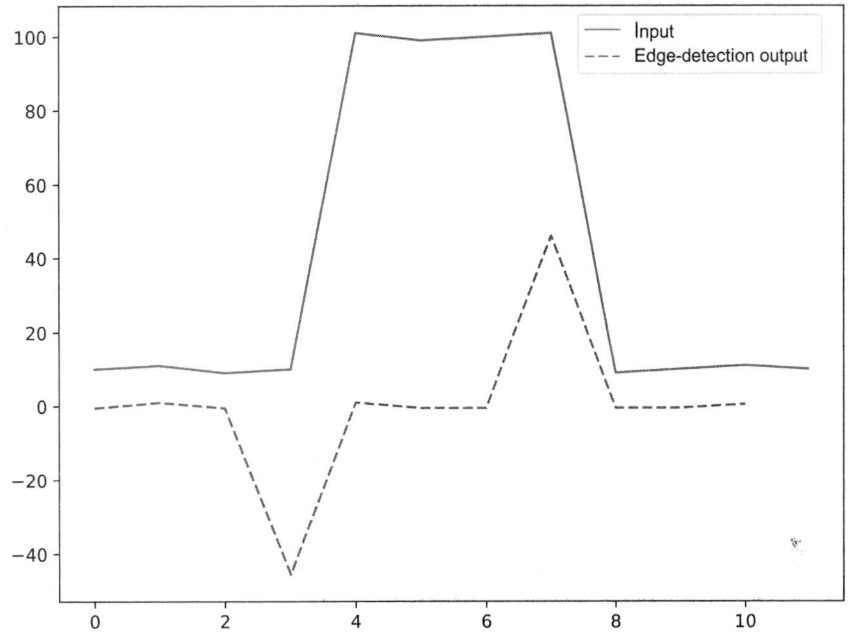

Figure 10.6 Graph of the input array (solid) and output array (dashed) from figure 10.3. The output produced by convolving the kernel with anti-symmetric normalized weights spikes at the edges of the input. Edges provide vital clues for understanding the signal.

10.1.3 One-dimensional convolution as matrix multiplication

Algebraically, the convolution with a kernel of size 3, stride 1, and valid padding can be shown as follows. Let the input array be

$$\vec{x} = \begin{bmatrix} x_0 & x_1 & x_2 & x_3 & x_4 & \cdots & x_{n-3} & x_{n-2} & x_{n-1} \end{bmatrix}$$

The convolving kernel is a matrix of weights of size 3; let's denote it as

$$\vec{w} = \begin{bmatrix} w_0 & w_1 & w_2 \end{bmatrix}$$

As shown in figure 10.1, in step 0 of the convolution, we place this kernel on the 0th element of the input x_0. Thus, w_0 falls on x_0,w_1 falls on x_1, and w_2 falls on x_2: $\begin{bmatrix} \mathbf{x_0} & \mathbf{x_1} & \mathbf{x_2} & x_3 & x_4 & \cdots & x_{n-3} & x_{n-2} & x_{n-1} \end{bmatrix}$, where the bold typeface identifies the input elements aligned with kernel weights. We multiply elements on corresponding positions and sum them, yielding the 0th element of the output $y_0 = w_0x_0 + w_1x_1 + w_2x_2$. Then we shift the kernel by one position (assuming the stride is 1; if the stride were 2, we would move the kernel two positions, and so on). So w_0 falls on x_1, w_1 falls on x_2, and w_2 falls on x_3:

$$\begin{bmatrix} x_0 & \mathbf{x_1} & \mathbf{x_2} & \mathbf{x_3} & x_4 & \cdots & x_{n-3} & x_{n-2} & x_{n-1} \end{bmatrix}$$

Again, we multiply elements at corresponding positions and sum them, yielding the first element of the output $y_1 = w_0x_1 + w_1x_2 + w_2x_2$. Similarly, in the next step, we right-shift the kernel one more time:

$$\begin{bmatrix} x_0 & x_1 & \mathbf{x_2} & \mathbf{x_3} & \mathbf{x_4} & \cdots & x_n \end{bmatrix}$$

The corresponding output is $y_2 = w_0x_2 + w_1x_3 + w_2x_4$. Overall, a stride 1, valid padding convolution of a vector $\vec{x}$ with a weight kernel $\vec{w}$ yields the output

$$\vec{y} = \vec{w} \circledast \vec{x} = \begin{bmatrix} w_0x_0 + w_1x_1 + w_2x_2 \\ w_0x_1 + w_1x_2 + w_2x_2 \\ \vdots \end{bmatrix}$$

Can you see what is happening? We are effectively taking linear combinations (see section 2.9) of successive sets of *kernel_size* (here, 3) input elements. In other words, the output is a *moving weighted local sum* of the input array elements. Depending on the actual weights, we are extracting local properties of the input.

For *valid* padding, the last output is yielded by

$$\begin{bmatrix} x_0 & x_1 & x_2 & x_3 & x_4 & \cdots & \mathbf{x_{n-3}} & \mathbf{x_{n-2}} & \mathbf{x_{n-1}} \end{bmatrix}$$

which generates the output

$$y_{n-3} = w_0x_{n-3} + w_1x_{n-2} + w_2x_{n-1}$$

For the *same* zero padding, the last output is yielded by

$$\begin{bmatrix} x_0 & x_1 & x_2 & x_3 & x_4 & \cdots & \mathbf{x_{n-1}} & \mathbf{0} & \mathbf{0} \end{bmatrix}$$

which generates the output

$$y_{n-1} = w_0 \cdot x_{n-1} + w_1 \cdot 0 + w_2 \cdot 0$$

In section 8.3.1, we saw that the FC (aka linear) layer can be expressed as a multiplication of the input vector by a weight matrix. Now, we will express convolution as matrix-vector multiplication. The weight matrix has a block-diagonal structure, as shown in equation 10.2. It is a special case of equation 8.8. As such, the forward propagation equation 8.7 and backpropagation equations 8.31 and 8.33 are still applicable. Thus, forward propagation and backpropagation (training) through convolution proceeds exactly as with FC layers.

Equation 10.2 expresses *kernel_size* 3, stride 1, valid padding convolution as a multiplication of a weight matrix W with input vector $\vec{x}$:

$$\vec{w} \circledast \vec{x} = W\vec{x} = \begin{bmatrix} w_0x_0 + w_1x_1 + w_2x_2 \\ w_0x_1 + w_1x_2 + w_2x_2 \\ \vdots \end{bmatrix} =$$

$$\overbrace{\begin{bmatrix} w_0 & w_1 & w_2 & 0 & 0 & 0 & \cdots & 0 & 0 & 0 \\ 0 & w_0 & w_1 & w_2 & 0 & 0 & \cdots & 0 & 0 & 0 \\ 0 & 0 & w_0 & w_1 & w_2 & 0 & \cdots & 0 & 0 & 0 \\ 0 & 0 & 0 & w_0 & w_1 & w_2 & \cdots & 0 & 0 & 0 \\ 0 & 0 & 0 & 0 & w_0 & w_1 & \cdots & 0 & 0 & 0 \\ \vdots & & & & & & & & & \\ 0 & 0 & 0 & 0 & 0 & 0 & \cdots & w_0 & w_1 & w_2 \end{bmatrix}}^{W\text{(conv weight matrix: kernel size 2, stride 1, valid pad. dim: }(n-2)\times n)} \overbrace{\begin{bmatrix} x_0 \\ x_1 \\ x_2 \\ x_3 \\ x_4 \\ \vdots \\ x_{n-1} \end{bmatrix}}^{\vec{x}\text{(input vector, size } n\times 1\text{)}} \tag{10.2}$$

Notice the *sparse, block-diagonal* nature of the weight matrix in equation 10.2. This is characteristic of convolution weight matrices. Each row contains all the kernel weights at contiguous positions. The size of the kernel is typically much less than the input vector size. Of course, for matrix multiplication to be possible, the number of columns in the weight matrix must match the size of the input vector. Thus, there are many vacant positions in the row besides those occupied by kernel weights. We fill these vacant elements with zeros. Each row of the weight matrix thus has all the kernel weights appearing somewhere contiguously, and the rest of the row is filled with zeros. *The position of kernel weights shifts rightward with each successive row.* This is what gives the block-diagonal appearance to the weight matrix. It also simulates the sliding of the kernel required for convolution. Each row represents a specific slide stop and generates one element of the output vector. Since the kernel is at a fixed position of the row and all other row elements are zero, only the input elements corresponding to the kernel positions are picked up. Other input elements are multiplied by zero: that is, they are ignored.

Equation 10.2 depicts a stride of 1. For instance, if the stride is 2, the kernel weights will shift by two positions in successive rows. This is shown in equation 10.3:

$$\vec{w} \circledast \vec{x} = W\vec{x} = \overbrace{\begin{bmatrix} w_0 & w_1 & w_2 & 0 & 0 & 0 & \cdots & 0 & 0 & 0 \\ 0 & 0 & w_0 & w_1 & w_2 & 0 & \cdots & 0 & 0 & 0 \\ 0 & 0 & 0 & 0 & w_0 & w_1 & \cdots & 0 & 0 & 0 \\ \vdots & & & & & & & & & \\ 0 & 0 & 0 & 0 & 0 & 0 & \cdots & w_0 & w_1 & w_2 \end{bmatrix}}^{W\left(\text{conv weight matrix: kernel size 2, stride 2, valid pad. dim: } \lfloor \frac{(n-2)}{2} + 1 \rfloor \times n\right)} \overbrace{\begin{bmatrix} x_0 \\ x_1 \\ x_2 \\ x_3 \\ x_4 \\ \vdots \\ x_{n-1} \end{bmatrix}}^{\vec{x}(\text{ input vector, size } n \times 1 \text{ })} \tag{10.3}$$

Note that while equation 10.3 provides a conceptual matrix-multiplication view of convolution, it is not the most efficient way of implementing convolution. PyTorch and other deep learning software have extremely efficient ways of implementing convolution.

10.1.4 PyTorch: One-dimensional convolution with custom weights

We have discussed the convolution of a 1D input vector with two specific 1D kernels. We have seen that a kernel with uniform weights, such as $\begin{bmatrix} \frac{1}{3} & \frac{1}{3} & \frac{1}{3} \end{bmatrix}$, results in local smoothing of the input vector, whereas a kernel with antisymmetric weights, such as $\begin{bmatrix} \frac{1}{2} & \frac{-1}{2} \end{bmatrix}$, results in an output vector that spikes at the edge locations in the input vector. Now we will see how to set the weights of a 1D kernel and perform 1D convolution with that kernel in PyTorch.

NOTE This is *not* a typical PyTorch operation. The more typical operation is to create a neural network with a convolution layer (where we specify the size, stride, and padding but not the weights) and then train the network so that the weights are learned. We usually don't care about the exact values of the learned weight. Then why are we discussing how to set the weights of a kernel in PyTorch? Mainly to show how convolution works in PyTorch, the various parameters of the convolution object, and so forth.

Listing 10.1 PyTorch code for 1D local averaging convolution

```
import torch

x = torch.tensor(              ← Instantiates a noisy input vector. Follows equation y = 5x
        [-1.,  4., 11., 14., 21., 25., 30.])
```

```
w = torch.tensor([0.33, 0.33, 0.33])          ← Instantiates the weights of the
                                                 convolutional kernel

x = x.unsqueeze(0).unsqueeze(0)
w = w.unsqueeze(0).unsqueeze(0)   ← PyTorch expects inputs and weights to be of the form
                                    N × C × L, where N is the batch size, C is the
                                    number of channels, and L is the sequence length.
                                    Here, N and C are 1. torch.unsqueeze converts
                                    our L-length vector into a 1 × 1 × L tensor.

conv1d = torch.nn.Conv1d(1, 1, kernel_size=3,    ← Instantiates the smoothing kernel
           stride=1, padding=[0], bias=False)

conv1d.weight = torch.nn.Parameter(w, requires_grad=False)   ← Sets the kernel weights

with torch.no_grad():       ← Instructs PyTorch to not compute gradients
                              since we currently don't require them

    y = conv1d(x)        ← Runs the convolution
```

Listing 10.2 PyTorch code for 1D edge detection

```
import torch

x = torch.tensor(                             ← Instantiates the input vector with edges
       [10.,  11., 9., 10., 101., 99.,
        100., 101., 9., 10., 11., 10.])

w = torch.tensor([0.5, -0.5])        ← Instantiates the weights of the edge-detection kernel

x = x.unsqueeze(0).unsqueeze(0)       ← Converts the inputs and weights to 1 × 1 × L
w = w.unsqueeze(0).unsqueeze(0)


conv1d = torch.nn.Conv1d(1, 1, kernel_size=3,   ← Instantiates the edge-detection kernel
           stride=1, padding=[0], bias=False)

conv1d.weight = torch.nn.Parameter(w, requires_grad=False)   ← Sets the kernel weights

with torch.no_grad():           ← Instructs PyTorch to not compute gradients
                                  since we currently don't require them

    y = conv1d(x)        ← Runs the convolution
```

These listings show how to perform 1D convolution in PyTorch using the `torch.nn.Conv1d` class. This is typically used in larger neural networks like those in subsequent chapters. We can alternatively use `torch.nn.functional.conv1d` to directly invoke the mathematical convolution operation. This takes input and weight tensors and returns the convolved output tensor, as shown in listing 10.3.

Listing 10.3 PyTorch code directly invoking the convolution function

```
import torch

x = torch.tensor(                              ← Instantiates the input tensor
        [10.,  11., 9., 10., 101., 99.,
         100., 101., 9., 10., 11., 10.])

w = torch.tensor([0.5, -0.5])                 ← Instantiates the weight tensor

x = x.unsqueeze(0).unsqueeze(0)                ← Converts the inputs and weights to 1 × 1 × L
w = w.unsqueeze(0).unsqueeze(0)

y = torch.nn.functional.conv1d(x, w, stride=1)      ← Runs the convolution
```

10.2 Convolution output size

Consider a kernel of size k sliding over an input of size n with stride s. Given a kernel of size k, if the left end is at index l, the right end is at index $l + (k - 1)$. Each shift advances the left (as well as the right) end of the kernel by s. If the initial position of the kernel was at index 0, then after m shifts, the left end is at ms. Correspondingly, the right end is at $ms + (k - 1)$. Assuming valid padding, this right-end position must be less than or equal to $(n - 1)$ (the last valid position of the input array).

How many times can we shift before the kernel spills out of the input? In other words, what is the maximum possible value of m, such that

$$ms + (k - 1) \leq (n - 1)$$

The answer is

$$m = \left\lfloor \frac{(n-1) - (k-1)}{s} \right\rfloor = \left\lfloor \frac{(n-k)}{s} \right\rfloor$$

But each shift produces one output value. The output size of the convolution, o, with valid padding, is $m + 1$ (the plus one is to account for the initial position). Hence,

$$o = \left\lfloor \frac{(n-k)}{s} \right\rfloor + 1$$

If we are zero-padding with p zeroes on each side of the input, the input size becomes $n + 2p$. The corresponding output size is

$$o = \left\lfloor \frac{(n+2p-k)}{s} \right\rfloor + 1 \qquad (10.4)$$

This can be extended to an arbitrary number of dimensions by repeating it for each dimension.

10.3 Two-dimensional convolution: Graphical and algebraic view

It is often said that an image is worth a thousand words. What is an image? As far as deep learning is concerned, it is a discrete two-dimensional entity—a 2D array of pixel values describing a scene at a fixed time. Each pixel represents a color intensity value. The color value can be a single element representing a gray level, or it can be three-dimensional, corresponding to R(ed), G(reen), B(lue) intensity values. (You may want to revisit section 2.3 before proceeding.)

At the time of this writing, image analysis is the most popular application of convolution. These applications use convolution to extract local patterns. How do we do this? In particular, can we rasterize the image (thus converting it into a vector) and use one-dimensional convolution?

The answer is *no*. To see why, examine figure 10.7. What is the spatial neighborhood of the pixel at location $(x = 0, y = 0)$? If we define the *neighborhood* of a pixel as the set

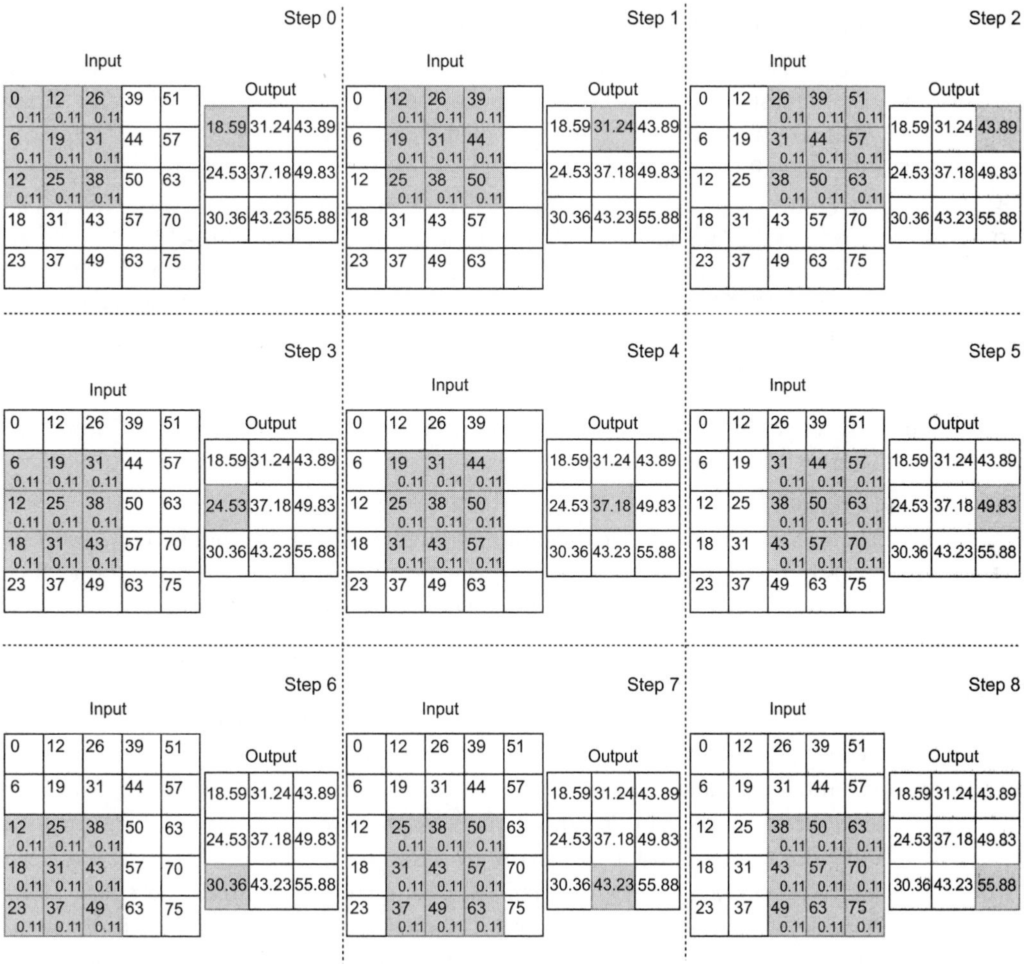

Figure 10.7 2D convolution with a local averaging kernel of size [3, 3], stride [1, 1], and valid padding. Each pixel is shown as a small rectangle, with the pixel's gray level written in the rectangle. The shaded rectangle identifies the current location of the kernel. The kernel is sliding over the input in raster order. Successive steps indicate slide stops. For each pixel that is overlapped by the kernel, the weight of the kernel element falling on it is written in small font.

of pixels within a Manhattan distance of [2, 2] with that pixel at the top-left corner, the neighborhood of $(x=0, y=0)$ consists of the set of pixels covered by the shaded rectangle in figure 10.7, step 0. But these pixels *will not be neighboring elements in a rasterized array representation of the image.* For instance, the pixel $(x=0, y=1)$, with value 6, is the fifth element in the rasterized array and, as such, will *not* be considered a neighbor of $(x=0, y=0)$, which is the 0th element in the rasterized array. Two-dimensional neighborhoods are *not* preserved by rasterization. So, two-dimensional convolution has to be a specialized operation beyond merely rasterizing 2D arrays into 1D and applying 1D convolution.

Euclidean distance and Manhattan distance

Euclidean distance measures the straight line distance between two points, whereas Manhattan distance measures the distance between two points with a constraint that you can only walk parallel to the axes (just like on the streets of Manhattan). Let's look at an example.

Consider two points A (3, 3) and B (6, 7). The Euclidean distance between A and B is the length of the line segment AB, which can be computed as $\sqrt{(6-3)^2+(7-3)^2}=5$. The Manhattan distance between A and B is $(6-3)+(7-3)=3+4=7$. In this chapter, we represent the Manhattan distance as [3, 4] to capture the distance along each axis separately.

The best way to visualize 2D convolution is to imagine a wall (the input image) over which a tile (the kernel) is sliding:

- In figures 10.7, 10.8 and 10.9, the shaded rectangle depicts the tile (kernel), while the larger white rectangle containing it depicts the wall (input image). Successive steps in the figure represent successive positions (aka slide stops) of the sliding tile. Notice that the shaded rectangle occupies a different position in each step.
- Tiles in successive positions during sliding can overlap. They overlap by varying amounts in figures 10.7, 10.8, and 10.9.
- The wall and the tile are discrete 2D arrays in reality. At each slide stop, the tile array elements rest on a subset of wall array elements.
- We multiply each input array element by the kernel element resting on it and sum the products. This is equivalent to taking a weighted sum of the input (wall) elements that fall under the current position of the kernel (tile), with the kernel elements serving as weights. This weighted sum is emitted as a single output element. One output element results from each slide stop of the tile. As the tile slides over the entire wall, left to right and top to bottom, a 2D output array is generated.

In 2D convolution, the input array, kernel size, and stride are all 2D vectors. Just as in 1D convolution, the following entities are defined for 2D convolution:

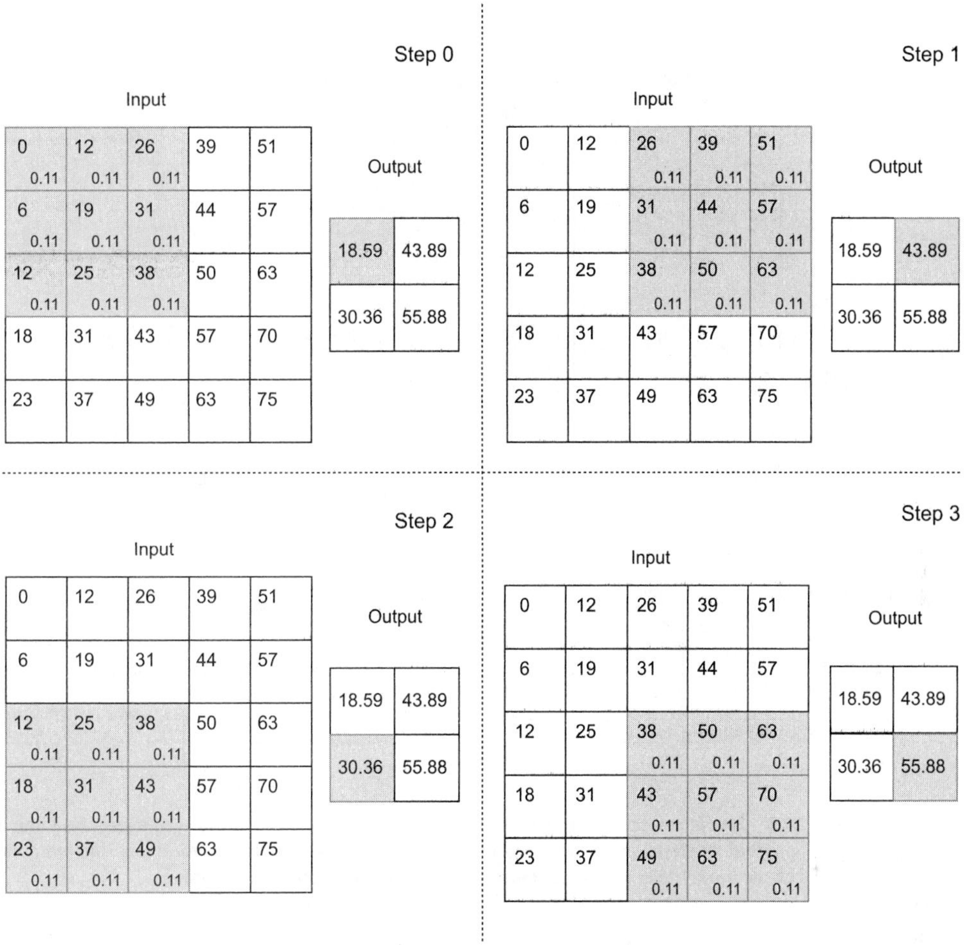

Figure 10.8 2D convolution with a local averaging kernel of size [3, 3], stride [2, 2], and valid padding

- *Input*—A two-dimensional array. We typically use the symbol $[H, W]$ (indicating the height and width of the array, respectively) to represent the input array size in 2D convolution. In figure 10.7, $H = 5, W = 5$.
- *Output*—A two-dimensional array. We typically use the symbol $\vec{o} = [o_H, o_W]$ to represent output array dimensions in 2D convolution. For instance, in figure 10.7, $\vec{o} = [3, 3]$. In section 10.2, we saw how to compute the output size for a single dimension. We have to repeat that computation once per dimension to obtain the output size in higher dimensions.
- *Kernel*—A small two-dimensional array of weights whose size is a parameter of the convolution. We typically use the symbol $\vec{k} = [k_H, k_W]$ to represent the kernel size (height, width) in 2D convolution. If (x, y) denotes the current position of the top-left corner of the 2D kernel, the bottom-right corner is at $(x + k_W - 1, y + k_H - 1)$. In figure 10.7, $\vec{k} = [3, 3]$; in figure 10.9, $\vec{k} = [2, 2]$.

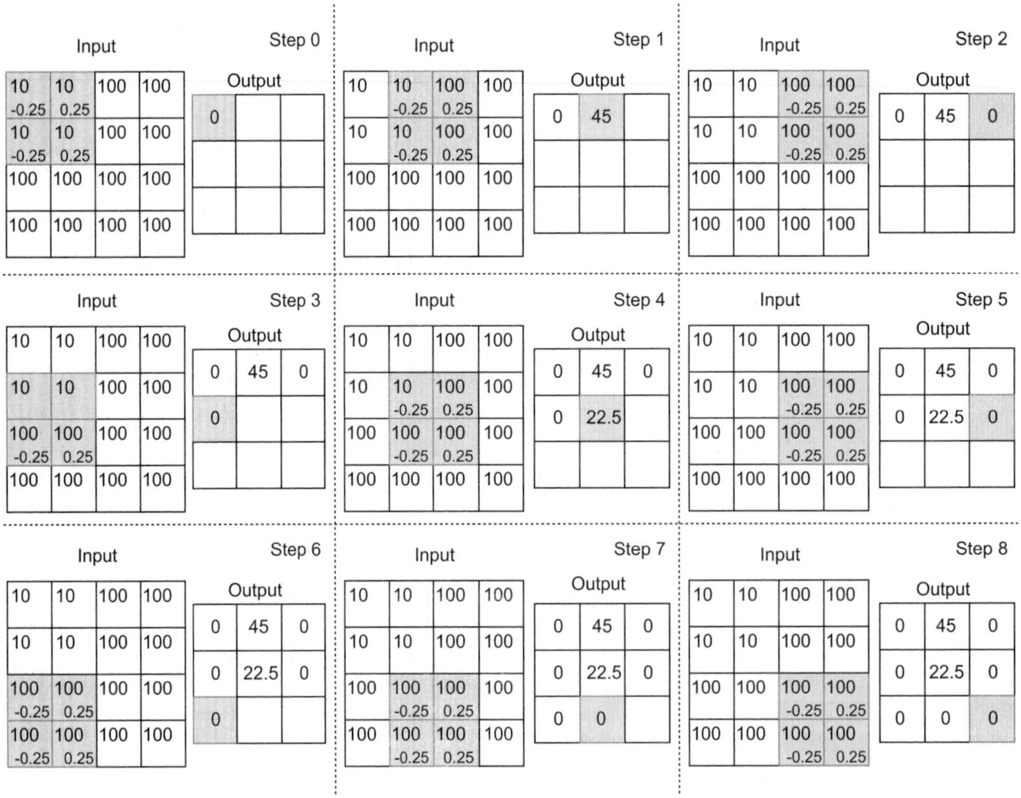

Figure 10.9 2D convolution with an edge-detection kernel of size 2, stride 1, and valid padding. Not all slide stops (that is, steps) are shown. Notice how the output is zero at a uniform location but spikes when one-half of the kernel falls on low values while the other half falls on high values.

- *Stride*—The number of input elements over which the kernel slides on completing a single step. We typically use the symbol $\vec{s} = [s_H, s_W]$ to represent the stride size (height, width) in 2D convolution. If (x, y) denotes the current position of the top-left corner of the 2D kernel, the next shift will put the top-left corner of the kernel at $(x + s_W, y)$ (see, for instance, the transition from step 0 to step 1 or step 1 to step 2 in figure 10.7). If this transition causes portions of the tile to fall outside the wall—that is, $x + s_W \geq W$—we set the next slide position such that the top-left corner of the kernel falls on $(0, y + 1)$ (see, for instance, the transition from step 2 to step 3 or step 5 to step 6 in figure 10.7). If $y + s_H \geq H$, we stop sliding. Stride size is a parameter of the convolution. In figure 10.7, $\vec{s} = [1, 1]$; in figure 10.8, stride is $\vec{s} = [2, 2]$. As in the 1D case, a stride of $\vec{s} = [1, 1]$ means there is a slide stop at each successive element of the input. So, the output has roughly the same number of elements as the input (they may not be exactly equal because of padding). A stride of $\vec{s} = [2, 2]$ means each row of the input will yield half the row size worth of output elements, and each column will generate half the column size worth of output elements. Hence, the output size is roughly a quarter of the input size. Overall, the reduction factor of the input-to-output size roughly matches the product of the elements in the stride vector.

- *Padding*—As the kernel slides toward the extremity of the input array along the width and/or height, parts of it may fall outside the input array. In other words, part of the kernel falls over ghost input elements. As in the 1D case, we deal with this via padding. Padding strategies in 2D convolution are straightforward extensions from 1D:
  - *Valid padding*—We stop sliding whenever any element of the kernel falls outside the input array, either in width and/or in height. No ghost input elements are involved; the *entire* kernel always falls on valid input elements (hence the name *valid*).
  - *Same (zero) padding*—Here, we do not want to stop early. We keep sliding as long as the top-left corner of the kernel falls on a valid input position. So, if the stride is 1, 1, the output size will match the input size (hence the name *same*). When we slide near the end of an input row (right extremity of the input), the right-most columns of the kernel will fall outside the input. Similarly, when we slide toward the bottom of the input, the bottom rows of the kernel will fall outside. If we slide near the bottom-right corner of the input, both the right-most columns and bottommost rows will fall outside the input. The rule is that all ghost input values outside the true boundaries of the input array are replaced by zeros.

Let's denote the input image domain by S. It is a 2D grid whose domain is

$$S = [0, H-1] \times [0, W-1]$$

Every point in S is a pixel with a color value (which can be a scalar—a gray-level value—or a vector of three values, R, G, B. On this grid of input points, we define a subgrid S_o of output points. S_o is obtained from S by applying stride-based stepping on the input. Assuming $\vec{s} = [s_H, s_W]$ denotes the 2D stride vector, the first slide stop has the top-left corner of the brick at $\vec{p}_0 \equiv (y = 0, x = 0)$. The next slide stop is at $\vec{p}_1 \equiv (y = 0, x = s_W)$, and the next is at $\vec{p}_2 \equiv (y = 0, x = 2s_W)$. When we reach the right end, we increment y. Overall, the output grid consists of the slide-stop points where the top-left corner of the kernel (brick) rests as it sweeps over the input volume: $S_o = \{\vec{p}_0, \vec{p}_1, \cdots, \}$. There is an output for each point in S_o.

The kernel also has two dimensions (in practice, it has two more dimensions corresponding to the input channels and batch—we are ignoring them now for simplicity—as discussed in section 10.3.3). Equation 10.5 shows how a single output value is generated in 2D convolution. X denotes input, Y denotes output, and W denote kernel weights:

$$Y_{y,x} = \sum_{i=0}^{k_H} \sum_{j=0}^{k_W} X_{y+i,x+j} W_{i,j} \quad \forall (y, x) \in S_o \tag{10.5}$$

Note that the kernel (tile) has its origin on $X_{y,x}$. Its dimensions are (k_H, k_W). So, it covers all input pixels in the domain $[y .. (y + k_H)] \times [x .. (x + k_W)]$. These are the pixels participating in equation 10.5. Each of these input pixels is multiplied by the kernel element covering it. Match equation 10.5 with figures 10.7, 10.8, and 10.9.

10.3.1 Image smoothing via 2D convolution

In section 10.1.1, we discussed one-dimensional local smoothing. We observed how it gets rid of local fluctuations so that longer-term patterns are discernible more cleanly. The same thing happens in two dimensions. Figure 10.10a shows an image with some text written on a background with salt-and-pepper noise. The noise has no semantic significance; it is the text that needs to be analyzed (perhaps via optical character recognition). We can eliminate the noise via 2D convolution using a kernel with uniform weights, such as

$$W = \begin{bmatrix} W_{0,0} = \frac{1}{9} & W_{0,1} = \frac{1}{9} & W_{0,2} = \frac{1}{9} \\ W_{1,0} = \frac{1}{9} & W_{1,1} = \frac{1}{9} & W_{1,2} = \frac{1}{9} \\ W_{2,0} = \frac{1}{9} & W_{2,1} = \frac{1}{9} & W_{2,2} = \frac{1}{9} \end{bmatrix}$$

The resulting denoised/smooth image is shown in figure 10.10b. What does the uniform kernel do? To see that, look at figure 10.8. It should be obvious that the kernel causes each output pixel to be a weighted local average of the neighboring 3×3 input pixels.

(a) Input image (b) Smoothed/denoised output image

Figure 10.10 Denoising/smoothing a noisy image by applying 2D convolution $\begin{bmatrix} \frac{1}{9} & \frac{1}{9} & \frac{1}{9} \\ \frac{1}{9} & \frac{1}{9} & \frac{1}{9} \\ \frac{1}{9} & \frac{1}{9} & \frac{1}{9} \end{bmatrix}$ **to figure 10.11a**

NOTE Fully functional code for image smoothing, executable via Jupyter Notebook, can be found at http://mng.bz/aDM7.

10.3.2 Image edge detection via 2D convolution

Not all pixels in an image have equal semantic importance. Imagine a photograph of a person standing in front of a white wall. The pixels belonging to the wall are uniform in color and uninteresting. The pixels that yield the most semantic clues are those belonging to the silhouette: the edge pixels. This agrees with the science of human vision, where, as we mentioned earlier, experiments indicate that the human brain pays more attention to regions with sharp changes in color. Humans treat sound in a very similar fashion, ignoring uniform buzz (such sounds often induce sleep) but becoming alert when the volume or frequency of the sound changes. Thus, identifying edges in an image is vital for image understanding.

Edges are local phenomena. As such, they can be identified by 2D convolution with specially chosen kernels. For instance, the vertical edges in figure 10.11b were produced by performing 2D convolution on the image in figure 10.11a using the kernel

$$W = \underbrace{\begin{bmatrix} W_{0,0} = -0.25 & W_{0,1} = 0.25 \\ W_{1,0} = -0.25 & W_{1,1} = 0.25 \end{bmatrix}}_{\text{2D kernel for vertical edge detection}}$$

Likewise, the vertical edges in figure 10.11c were produced by performing 2D convolution on the image in figure 10.11a using the kernel

$$W = \underbrace{\begin{bmatrix} W_{0,0} = -0.25 & W_{0,1} = -0.25 \\ W_{1,0} = 0.25 & W_{1,1} = 0.25 \end{bmatrix}}_{\text{2D kernel for horizontal edge detection}}$$

How do these kernels identify edges? To see this, look at figure 10.9. In a neighborhood with equal pixel values (for example, a flat wall), the kernel in figure 10.11b will yield zero (the positive and negative kernel elements fall on equal values, and their weighted sum is zero). Thus this kernel suppresses uniform regions. On the other hand, it has a high response if there is a sharp jump in color (the negative and positive halves of the kernel fall on very different values, and the weighted sum is a large negative or large positive).

NOTE Fully functional code for edge detection, executable via Jupyter Notebook, can be found at http://mng.bz/g4JV.

10.3.3 PyTorch: 2D convolution with custom weights

We have discussed the convolution of 2D input arrays with two specific 2D kernels. We have seen that a kernel with uniform weights, such as $\begin{bmatrix} \frac{1}{9} & \frac{1}{9} & \frac{1}{9} \\ \frac{1}{9} & \frac{1}{9} & \frac{1}{9} \\ \frac{1}{9} & \frac{1}{9} & \frac{1}{9} \end{bmatrix}$, results in local smoothing of the input array, whereas a kernel with antisymmetric weights, such as $\begin{bmatrix} \frac{1}{4} & \frac{-1}{4} \\ \frac{1}{4} & \frac{-1}{4} \end{bmatrix}$, results in an output array that spikes at the edge locations in the input array. Now we will see how to set the weights of a 2D kernel and perform 2D convolution with that kernel in PyTorch.

(a) Input image

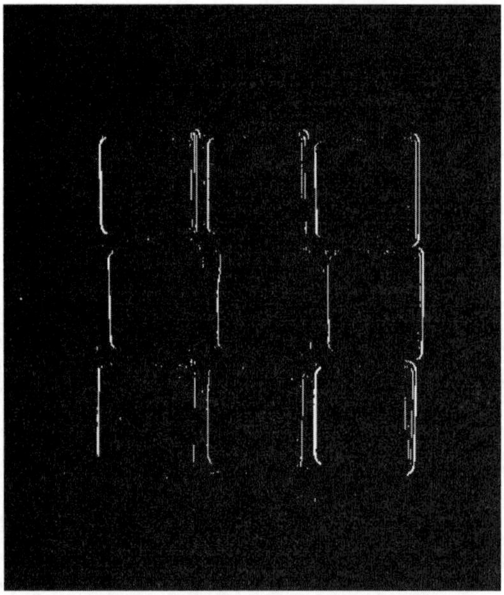

(b) Vertical edges detected by applying 2D convolution $\begin{bmatrix} -0.25 & 0.25 \\ -0.25 & 0.25 \end{bmatrix}$ to figure 10.11a

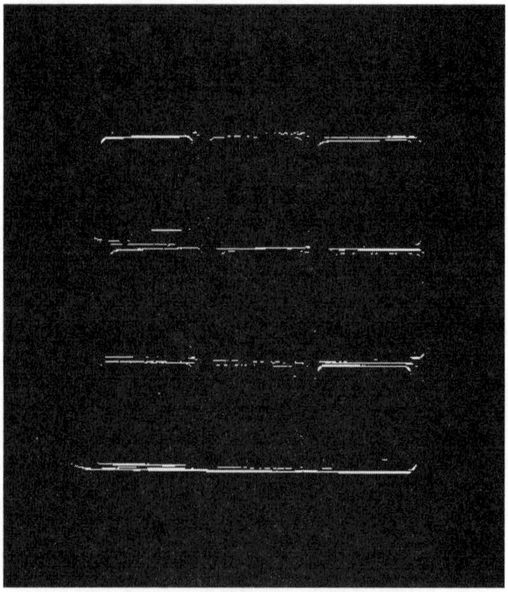

(c) Horizontal edges detected by applying 2D convolution $\begin{bmatrix} -0.25 & -0.25 \\ 0.25 & 0.25 \end{bmatrix}$ to figure 10.11a

Figure 10.11 Edge detection via 2D convolution. Identifying the vertical and horizontal edges in an image often helps us analyze the image.

NOTE This is *not* a typical PyTorch operation. The more typical operation is to create a neural network with a convolution layer (where we specify the size, stride, and padding but not the weights) and then train the network so that the weights are learned. We usually don't care about the exact values of the learned weight. A sample neural network with a 2D convolution layer can be seen in section 10.6.

Listing 10.4 shows local averaging convolution in two dimensions. While we saw in section that input arrays are 2D tensors of shape $H \times W$, the PyTorch interface to convolution expects 4D tensors of shape $N \times C \times H \times W$ as input:

- The first dimension, N, stands for the batch size. In a real neural network, inputs are fed in minibatches instead of one input instance at a time (this is for efficiency reasons, as discussed in section 9.2.2). N stands for the number of input images contained in the minibatch.
- The second dimension, C, stands for the number of channels. For the input to the entire neural network, in the case of RGB images, we have three channels R (red), G (green), and B (blue); in the case of grayscale images, we only have a single channel. For other layers, the number of channels can be anything, depending on the neural network's architecture. Typically, layers further from the input and closer to the output have more channels. Only channels at the grand input have fixed, clearly discernible physical significance (like R, G, B). Channels at the input to successive layers do not.
- The third dimension, H, stands for the height.
- The fourth dimension, W, stands for the width.

The weight tensor of a PyTorch `Conv2D` object has to be a 4D tensor. The listing shows a single grayscale image of size 5 × 5 as input. Hence $N = 1$, $C = 1$, $H = 5$, and $W = 5$. x is instantiated as a 2D tensor of size 5×5. To convert it to a 4D tensor, we use the `torch.unsqueeze()` function, which adds an extra dimension to the input.

Listing 10.4 PyTorch code for 2D local averaging convolution

```
import torch

x = load_img()          ← Loads a noisy grayscale input image

w = torch.tensor(       ← Instantiates the weights of the convolutional kernel
    [
        [0.11, 0.11, 0.11],
        [0.11, 0.11, 0.11],
        [0.11, 0.11, 0.11]
    ]
)

x = x.unsqueeze(0).unsqueeze(0)
w = w.unsqueeze(0).unsqueeze(0)
```

PyTorch expects inputs and weights to be of the form $N \times C \times H \times W$, where N is the batch size, C is the number of channels, H is the height, and W is the width. Here, $N = 1$ because we have a single image. $C = 1$ because we are considering a grayscale image. H and W are both 5 because the input is a 5×5 array. unsqueeze converts our 5×5 tensor into a $1 \times 1 \times 5 \times 5$ tensor.

```
conv2d = torch.nn.Conv2d(1, 1, kernel_size=2,
                    stride=1, bias=False)      ← Instantiates the 2D smoothing kernel

conv2d.weight = torch.nn.Parameter(w, requires_grad=False)  ← Sets the kernel weights

with torch.no_grad():           ← Instructs PyTorch to not compute gradients
                                  since we currently don't require them
    y = conv2d(x)         ← Runs the convolution
```

Listing 10.5 PyTorch code for 2D edge detection

```
import torch

x = load_img()        ← Loads a grayscale input image with edges

w = torch.tensor(       ← Instantiates the weights of the convolutional kernel
        [[-0.25, 0.25],
        [-0.25, 0.25]]
    )

x = x.unsqueeze(0).unsqueeze(0)      ← Converts the inputs to 1 × 1 × 4 × 4
w = w.unsqueeze(0).unsqueeze(0)

conv2d = torch.nn.Conv2d(1, 1, kernel_size=2,    ← Instantiates a 2D edge-detection kernel
                    stride=1, bias=False)

conv2d.weight = torch.nn.Parameter(w, requires_grad=False)  ← Sets the kernel weights

with torch.no_grad():           ← Instructs PyTorch to not compute gradients
                                  since we currently don't require them
    y = conv2d(x)         ← Runs the convolution
```

10.3.4 Two-dimensional convolution as matrix multiplication

In section 10.1.3, we saw how 1D convolution can be viewed as multiplying the input vector by a block-diagonal matrix (shown in equation 10.3). The idea can be extended to higher dimensions, although the matrix of weights becomes significantly more complex. Nonetheless, it is important to have a mental picture of this matrix. Among other things, it will help us better understand transposed convolution. In this matrix multiplication-oriented view of 2D convolution, the input image is represented as a rasterized 1D vector. Thus, an input matrix of size $m \times n$ becomes an mn-sized vector. The corresponding weight matrix has rows of length mn. Each row corresponds to a specific slide stop.

For ease of understanding, let's consider an input image with $[H, W] = [4, 4]$ (never mind that this image is unrealistically small). On this image, we are performing 2D convolution with a $[k_H, k_W] = [2, 2]$ kernel with stride $[s_H, s_W] = [1, 1]$. The situation is exactly as shown in figure 10.9. The input image X with size $H = 4, W = 4$

$$X = \begin{bmatrix} X_{0,0} & X_{0,1} & X_{0,2} & X_{0,3} \\ X_{1,0} & X_{1,1} & X_{1,2} & X_{1,3} \\ X_{2,0} & X_{2,1} & X_{2,2} & X_{2,3} \\ X_{3,0} & X_{3,1} & X_{3,2} & X_{3,3} \end{bmatrix} \triangleq \vec{x} = \begin{bmatrix} X_{0,0} \\ X_{0,1} \\ X_{0,2} \\ X_{0,3} \\ X_{2,0} \\ X_{2,1} \\ X_{2,2} \\ X_{2,3} \\ X_{3,0} \\ X_{3,1} \\ X_{3,2} \\ X_{3,3} \end{bmatrix}$$

rasterizes to the input vector $\vec{x}$ of length $4 * 4 = 16$. Let the kernel weights be denoted as $\begin{bmatrix} w_{0,0} & w_{0,1} \\ w_{1,0} & w_{1,1} \end{bmatrix}$ Consider the successive slide stops (steps in figure 10.9). The exact elements of the rasterized input vector that are multiplied by kernel weights for a specific step are shown below—these correspond to the shaded items for the same steps in figure 10.9: 2D convolution between an image X and a kernel W, denoted $Y = W \circledast X$, in the special case of an input image with $[H, W] = [4, 4]$. For this image, 2D convolution with a $[k_H, k_W] = [2, 2]$ kernel with stride $[s_H, s_W] = [1, 1]$ and valid padding can be expressed as the following matrix multiplication:

$$Y = W \circledast X = \begin{bmatrix} Y_{0,0} \\ Y_{0,1} \\ Y_{0,2} \\ Y_{1,0} \\ Y_{1,1} \\ Y_{1,2} \\ y_{2,0} \\ Y_{2,1} \\ y_{2,2} \end{bmatrix} = \begin{bmatrix} w_{0,0}X_{0,0} + w_{0,1}X_{0,1} + w_{1,0}X_{1,0} + w_{1,1}X_{1,1} \\ w_{0,0}X_{0,1} + w_{0,1}X_{0,2} + w_{1,0}X_{1,1} + w_{1,1}X_{1,2} \\ w_{0,0}X_{0,2} + w_{0,1}X_{0,3} + w_{1,0}X_{1,2} + w_{1,1}X_{1,3} \\ w_{0,0}X_{1,0} + w_{0,1}X_{1,1} + w_{1,0}X_{2,0} + w_{1,1}X_{2,1} \\ w_{0,0}X_{1,1} + w_{0,1}X_{1,2} + w_{1,0}X_{2,1} + w_{1,1}X_{2,2} \\ w_{0,0}X_{1,2} + w_{0,1}X_{1,3} + w_{1,0}X_{2,2} + w_{1,1}X_{2,3} \\ w_{0,0}X_{2,0} + w_{0,1}X_{2,1} + w_{1,0}X_{3,0} + w_{1,1}X_{3,1} \\ w_{0,0}X_{2,1} + w_{0,1}X_{2,2} + w_{1,0}X_{3,1} + w_{1,1}X_{3,2} \\ w_{0,0}X_{2,2} + w_{0,1}X_{2,3} + w_{1,0}X_{3,2} + w_{1,1}X_{3,3} \end{bmatrix}$$

This can be expressed as

$$
W \circledast X =
$$

$$
\begin{bmatrix}
w_{0,0} & w_{0,1} & 0 & 0 & w_{1,0} & w_{1,1} & 0 & 0 & 0 & 0 & 0 & 0 & 0 & 0 & 0 & 0 \\
0 & w_{0,0} & w_{0,1} & 0 & 0 & w_{1,0} & w_{1,1} & 0 & 0 & 0 & 0 & 0 & 0 & 0 & 0 & 0 \\
0 & 0 & w_{0,0} & w_{0,1} & 0 & 0 & w_{1,0} & w_{1,1} & 0 & 0 & 0 & 0 & 0 & 0 & 0 & 0 \\
0 & 0 & 0 & 0 & w_{0,0} & w_{0,1} & 0 & 0 & w_{1,0} & w_{1,1} & 0 & 0 & 0 & 0 & 0 & 0 \\
0 & 0 & 0 & 0 & 0 & w_{0,0} & w_{0,1} & 0 & 0 & w_{1,0} & w_{1,1} & 0 & 0 & 0 & 0 & 0 \\
0 & 0 & 0 & 0 & 0 & 0 & w_{0,0} & w_{0,1} & 0 & 0 & w_{1,0} & w_{1,1} & 0 & 0 & 0 & 0 \\
0 & 0 & 0 & 0 & 0 & 0 & 0 & 0 & w_{0,0} & w_{0,1} & 0 & 0 & w_{1,0} & w_{1,1} & 0 & 0 \\
0 & 0 & 0 & 0 & 0 & 0 & 0 & 0 & 0 & w_{0,0} & w_{0,1} & 0 & 0 & w_{1,0} & w_{1,1} & 0 \\
0 & 0 & 0 & 0 & 0 & 0 & 0 & 0 & 0 & 0 & w_{0,0} & w_{0,1} & 0 & 0 & w_{1,0} & w_{1,1}
\end{bmatrix}
\begin{bmatrix}
X_{0,0} \\ X_{0,1} \\ X_{0,2} \\ X_{0,3} \\ X_{2,0} \\ X_{2,1} \\ X_{2,2} \\ X_{2,3} \\ X_{3,0} \\ X_{3,1} \\ X_{3,2} \\ X_{3,3}
\end{bmatrix}
\tag{10.6}
$$

Note the following:

- The 2D convolution weight matrix shown in equation 10.6 is for the special case, but it illustrates the general principle.
- The 2D convolution weight matrix is block diagonal, just like the 1D version. The kernel weights are placed precisely to emulate figure 10.9.
- The convolution weight matrix has 9 rows and 16 columns. Thus it takes a 16-element input vector (rasterized from a 4×4 input image) and generates a 9-element output matrix (which can be folded into a 3×3 convolution output image.

10.4 Three-dimensional convolution

If a picture is worth a thousand words, a video is worth 10,000 words. Videos are a rich source of information about dynamic real-life scenes. As deep learning-based image analysis (2D convolution) is becoming more and more successful, at the time of this writing, video analysis is becoming the next research frontier to conquer.

Videos are essentially three-dimensional entities. The representation is *discrete* in all three dimensions. The three dimensions correspond to *space*, which is two-dimensional, having *height* and *width*, and *time*. A video consists of a *sequence of frames*. Each frame is an image: a discrete 2D array of pixels. A frame represents the entire video scene at a specific (sampled) point. A pixel in a frame represents the color of a sampled location in space belonging to the scene at the time corresponding to the frame. Thus a video is a sequence of frames representing the dynamic scene at a sampled set of discrete points (pixels) in space and time. The video extends over a *spatio-temporal volume* (aka *ST volume*), which can be imagined as a cuboid. Each cross-section is a rectangle representing a frame. This is shown in figure 10.12. To analyze the video, we need to extract local patterns from this 3D volume. Can we do it via repeated 2D convolutions?

The answer is *no*. There is extra information when we view the successive frames *together*, which is absent when we view the frames one at a time. For instance, imagine you are presented with an image of a half-open door. From that single image, can

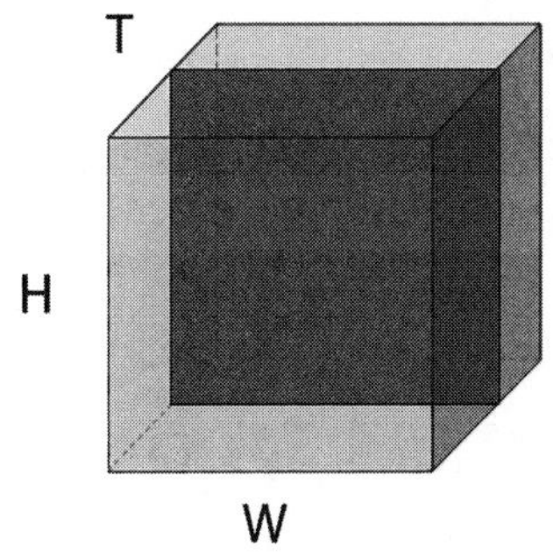

Figure 10.12 A spatio-temporal volume (light-shaded cuboid) representing a video. Individual frames of the video are cross-sectional rectangles in this ST volume. A single frame is also shown in darker shading.

you determine whether the door is *opening* or *closing*? No, you cannot. To make that determination, we need to see several successive frames. In other words, analyzing a video one frame at a time robs us of a vital modality of information: *motion*, which can be understood only if we analyze multiple successive frames together. This is why we need 3D convolution.

The best way to visualize a 3D convolution is to imagine a *brick* sliding over the entire volume of a *room*. The room corresponds to the ST volume of the video input to the convolution. The brick corresponds to the kernel. While sliding, the brick stops at successive positions; we call these slide stops. Figure 10.13 shows four slide stops at different positions. Each slide stop emits one output point. As the brick sweeps over the entire input ST volume, an output ST volume is generated. At each slide stop, we multiply each input pixel value by the kernel element covering it and take a sum of the products. This is effectively a weighted sum of all the input (room) elements covered by the kernel (brick), with the covering kernel elements serving as the weights.

Let's denote the input ST volume by S. It is a 3D grid whose domain is

$$S = [0, T-1] \times [0, H-1] \times [0, W-1]$$

Every point in S is a pixel with a color value (which can be a scalar—a gray-level value—or a vector of three values, R, G, B. On this grid of input points, we define a subgrid S_o of output points. S_o is obtained from S by applying stride-based stepping on the input. Assuming $\vec{s} = [s_T, s_K, s_W]$ denotes the 3D stride vector, the first slide stop has the top-left corner of the brick at $\vec{p}_0 \equiv (t=0, y=0, x=0)$. The next slide stop is at $\vec{p}_1 \equiv (t=0, y=0, x=s_W)$, and the next is at $\vec{p}_2 \equiv (t=0, y=0, x=2s_W)$. When we reach the right end, we increment y. When we reach the bottom, we increment t. When we reach the end of the room, we stop. $S_o = \{\vec{p}_0, \vec{p}_1, \cdots, \}$ are the points at which the top-left corner of the kernel (brick) rests as it sweeps over the input volume. There is an output for each point in S_o. The kernel also has three dimensions (in practice, it has two more dimensions corresponding to the input channels and batch—we are ignoring them now for simplicity—as discussed in section 10.6).

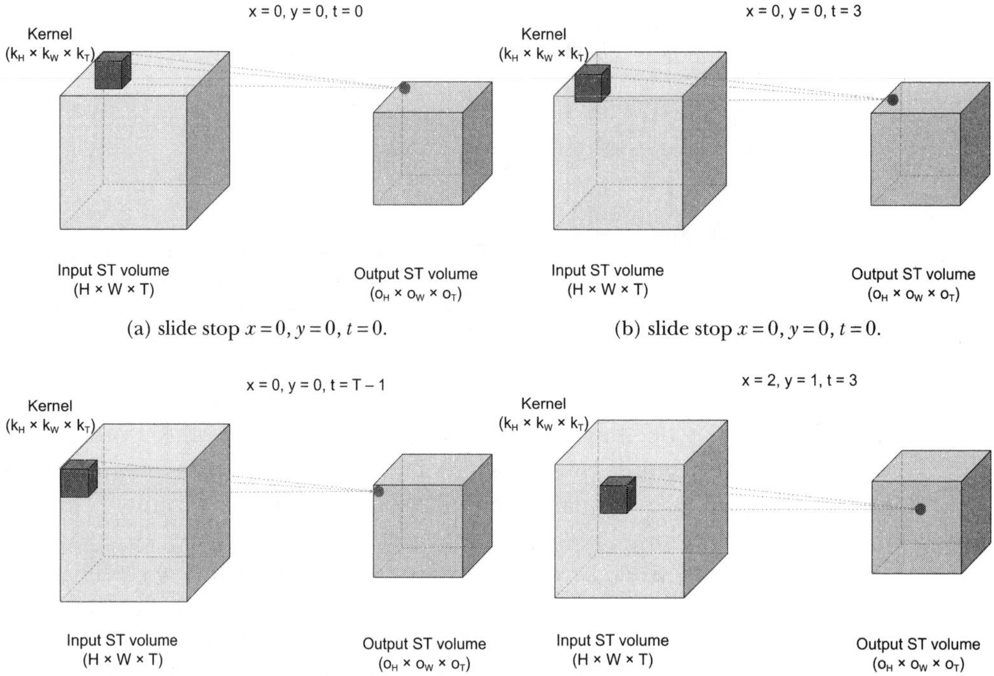

(a) slide stop $x = 0, y = 0, t = 0$. (b) slide stop $x = 0, y = 0, t = 0$.

(c) slide stop $x = 0, y = 0, t = 0$. (d) slide stop $x = 0, y = 0, t = 0$.

Figure 10.13 Spatio-temporal view of 3D convolution. The larger, light-shaded cuboid on the left of each figure represents the input ST volume (room). The small, dark-shaded cuboid inside the room represents the kernel (brick). The brick slides all over the room's internal volume. Neighboring positions of the brick may overlap in volume. Each position of the brick represents a slide stop; a weighted sum is taken of all points in the room (input points) covered by the brick. The brick point (kernel value) covering each input point serves as the weight. Four different slide stops are shown. Each slide stop generates a single output point. As the brick sweeps the input volume, an output ST volume (the smaller light-shaded cuboid) is generated.

Equation 10.7 shows how a single output value is generated in 3D convolution. X denotes the input, Y denotes the output, and W denote the kernel weights:

$$Y_{t,y,x} = \sum_{k=0}^{k_T} \sum_{i=0}^{k_H} \sum_{j=0}^{k_W} X_{t+k,y+i,x+j} W_{k,i,j} \quad \forall\,(t, y, x) \in S_o \tag{10.7}$$

Note that the kernel (brick) has its origin on $X_{t,y,x}$. Its dimensions are (k_T, k_H, k_W). So, it covers all input pixels in the domain $[t..\,(t + k_T)] \times [y..\,(y + k_H)] \times [x..\,(x + k_W)]$. These are the pixels participating in equation 10.7. Each of these input pixels is multiplied by the kernel element covering it. Match equation 10.7 with figure 10.13.

10.4.1 Video motion detection via 3D convolution

A moving object in a dynamic scene changes position from one video frame to another. Consequently, pixels are covered or uncovered at the boundary of motion. Pixels belonging to the background in one frame may be covered by the object in a subsequent frame and vice versa. If the background is a different color than the object, this will cause a color difference between pixels at identical spatial locations at different times, as illustrated in figure 10.14. The output of applying convolution to an ST volume is another ST volume. Figure 10.15 shows a few frames from the output resulting from applying our video motion detector to the input shown in figure 10.14.

Figure 10.14 Successive frames of a synthetic video of a moving ball, shown in a superimposed fashion with gradually increasing opacity for illustration purposes

How does a kernel extract motion information from a set of successive frames? As mentioned earlier, motion causes pixels at the same position in successive frames to have different colors. However, a single isolated pair of pixels may have different colors due to noise—we cannot draw any conclusions from that. If we average the pixel values in a small neighborhood in one frame and average the pixel values in the same neighborhood in the subsequent frames, and these two averages are different, that is a more reliable way to estimate motion. Following is a $2 \times 3 \times 3$ 3D kernel to do exactly that—average pixel values in a 3×3 spatial neighborhood in two successive frames and subtract one from the other:

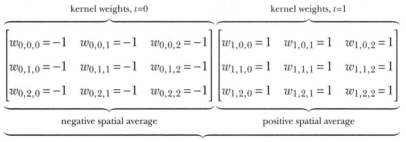

$$\underbrace{\underbrace{\overbrace{\begin{bmatrix} w_{0,0,0}=-1 & w_{0,0,1}=-1 & w_{0,0,2}=-1 \\ w_{0,1,0}=-1 & w_{0,1,1}=-1 & w_{0,1,2}=-1 \\ w_{0,2,0}=-1 & w_{0,2,1}=-1 & w_{0,2,2}=-1 \end{bmatrix}}^{\text{kernel weights, } t=0}}_{\text{negative spatial average}} \underbrace{\overbrace{\begin{bmatrix} w_{1,0,0}=1 & w_{1,0,1}=1 & w_{1,0,2}=1 \\ w_{1,1,0}=1 & w_{1,1,1}=1 & w_{1,1,2}=1 \\ w_{1,2,0}=1 & w_{1,2,1}=1 & w_{1,2,2}=1 \end{bmatrix}}^{\text{kernel weights, } t=1}}_{\text{positive spatial average}}}_{\text{temporal difference of spatial averages; motion detector kernel}}$$

The result of the subtraction is high in regions of motion and low in regions of no motion. In this context, it is worthwhile to note that since the object is of uniform color, pixels within the object are indistinguishable. Consequently, no motion is observed at the center of the object; motion is observed only at the boundary. A few individual frames of the result of this 3D convolution are shown in figure 10.15.

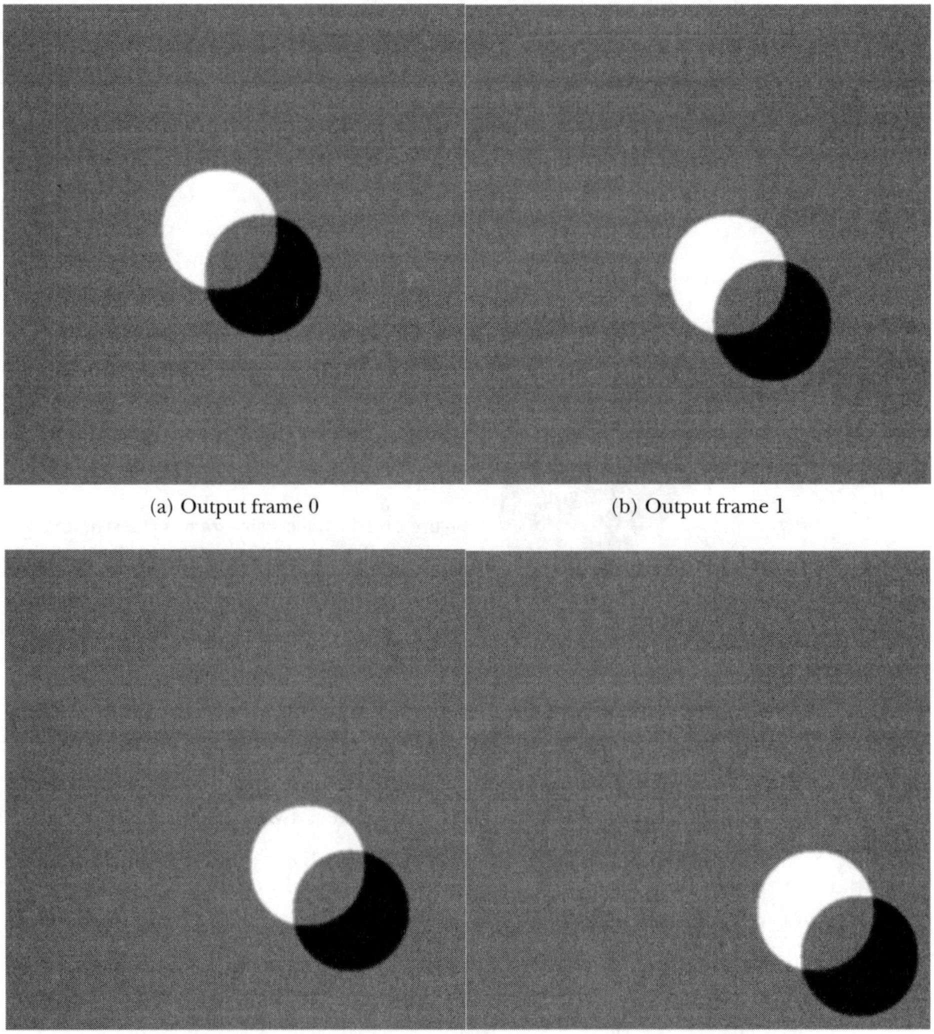

(a) Output frame 0 (b) Output frame 1

(c) Output frame 2 (d) Output frame 3

Figure 10.15 Result of applying a 3D convolution motion detector to the synthetic video of a moving ball. Gray signifies "no motion"; most of the output frames are gray. White and black signify motion.

NOTE Fully functional code for video motion detection, executable via Jupyter Notebook, can be found at http://mng.bz/enJQ.

10.4.2 PyTorch: Three-dimensional convolution with custom weights

In section 10.4.1, we saw how to detect motion in a sequence of input images using 3D convolutions. In this section, we see how to implement this in PyTorch. The PyTorch interface to 3D convolutions expects 5-dimensional input tensors of the form $N \times C \times D \times H \times W$. In addition to the dimensions discussed in section 10.4, there is an additional dimension for the input channels. Thus, there is a separate brick for each input channel. We are combining (taking the weighted sum of) them all:

- As discussed in the case of 2D convolutions (section 10.3.3), the first dimension N stands for the batch size (minibatches are fed to a real neural network instead of individual input instances for efficiency reasons), and C stands for the number of input channels.
- D stands for the sequence length. In our motion detector example, D represents the number of successive image frames fed to the 3D convolution layer.
- The third dimension, H, stands for height, and the fourth dimension, W, stands for width.

In our motion detector example, we have a sequence of five grayscale images as input, each with height = 320 and width = 320. Since we are considering only a single image sequence, $N = 1$. All images are grayscale, which implies that $C = 1$. The sequence length, D, is equal to 5. H and W are both 320.

PyTorch expects the 3D kernels to be of the form $C_{out} \times C_{in} \times k_T \times k_H \times k_W$:

- The first dimension, C_{out}, represents the number of output channels. You can think of the convolutional kernel as a bank of 3D filters, where each filter produces one output channel. C_{out} is the number of 3D filters in the bank.
- The second dimension, C_{in}, represents the number of input channels. This depends on the number of channels in the input tensor. When we are dealing with grayscale images, C_{in} is 1 at the grand input. For RGB images, C_{in} is 3 at the grand input. For layers further from the input, C_{in} equals the number of channels in the tensor fed to that layer.
- The third, fourth, and fifth dimensions, k_T, k_H, and k_W, represent the kernel sizes along the T, H, and W dimensions, respectively

In our motion detector example, we have a single kernel with k_T=2, k_H=3, and k_W = 3. Since we only have a single kernel, C_{out} = 1. And since we are dealing with grayscale images, C_{in} is also 1.

Listing 10.6 PyTorch code for 3D convolution

```
import torch

images = load_images()          ← Loads a sequence of five grayscale images with shape 320 x 320

x = torch.tensor(images)        ← Converts to a tensor of shape T x H x W = 5 x 320 x 320

w_2d_smoothing = torch.tensor(               ← Instantiates a 2D smoothing kernel of
        [[0.11, 0.11, 0.11],                   shape 3 x 3. Pads an extra dimension
         [0.11, 0.11, 0.11],                   so that two 2D kernels can be stacked
         [0.11, 0.11, 0.11]]).unsqueeze(0)     together to form a 3D kernel.
```

```
w = torch.cat(
        [-w_2d_smoothing, w_2d_smoothing])

x = x.unsqueeze(0).unsqueeze(0)

w = w.unsqueeze(0).unsqueeze(0)

conv3d = nn.Conv3d(1, 1, kernel_size=[2, 3, 3],
               stride=1, padding=0, bias=False)
conv3d.weight = torch.nn.Parameter(w, requires_grad=False)

with torch.no_grad():

    y = conv3d(x)
```

- `w = torch.cat(...)`: Concatenates the 2D smoothing kernel and its inverted version along the first dimension to form a 3D kernel of shape $2 \times 3 \times 3$
- `x = x.unsqueeze(0).unsqueeze(0)`: Converts the input tensor to $N \times C \times T \times H \times W = 1 \times 1 \times 5 \times 320 \times 320$
- `w = w.unsqueeze(0).unsqueeze(0)`: Converts the 3D kernel to $C_{out} \times C_{in} \times k_T \times k_H \times k_W = 1 \times 1 \times 2 \times 3 \times 3$
- `conv3d = nn.Conv3d(...)`: Instantiates and sets the weights of the Conv3d layer
- `with torch.no_grad():`: Instructs PyTorch to not compute gradients since we currently don't require them
- `y = conv3d(x)`: Runs the convolution

10.5 Transposed convolution or fractionally strided convolution

As usual, we examine this topic with an example. Consider a 1D convolution with kernel $\vec{w} = \begin{bmatrix} w_0 & w_1 & w_2 \end{bmatrix}$ of size 3, with valid padding. Let's consider a special case where the input size n is 5. Following equation 10.2, this convolution can be expressed as a multiplication of a block-diagonal matrix W constructed from the weights vector $\vec{w}$, with input vector $\vec{x}$ as follows:

$$\vec{y} = \vec{w} \circledast \vec{x} = W\vec{x}$$

$$= \begin{bmatrix} w_0x_0 + w_1x_1 + w_2x_2 \\ w_0x_1 + w_1x_2 + w_2x_2 \\ w_0x_2 + w_1x_{32} + w_2x_4 \end{bmatrix} = \begin{bmatrix} w_0 & w_1 & w_2 & 0 & 0 \\ 0 & w_0 & w_1 & w_2 & 0 \\ 0 & 0 & w_0 & w_1 & w_2 \end{bmatrix} \begin{bmatrix} x_0 \\ x_1 \\ x_2 \\ x_3 \\ x_4 \end{bmatrix}$$

What happens if we multiply the output vector $\vec{y}$ by the transposed matrix W^T?

$$\tilde{x} = W^T\vec{y}$$

$$= \begin{bmatrix} w_0 & 0 & 0 \\ w_1 & w_0 & 0 \\ w_2 & w_1 & w_0 \\ 0 & w_2 & w_1 \\ 0 & 0 & w_2 \end{bmatrix} \begin{bmatrix} y_0 \\ y_1 \\ y_2 \end{bmatrix} = \begin{bmatrix} w_0y_0 & & \\ w_1y_0+ & w_0y_1 & \\ w_2y_0+ & w_1y_1+ & w_0y_2 \\ & w_2y_1+ & w_1y_2 \\ & & w_2y_2 \end{bmatrix}$$

Following are some observations:

- We haven't quite recovered $\vec{x}$ from $\vec{y}$, but we have generated a vector, $\tilde{x}$, the same size as $\vec{x}$. Multiplying by the transpose of the weight matrix of the convolution performs a kind of upsampling, undoing the downsampling resulting from the forward convolution.
- It is impossible to recover $\vec{x}$ from $\vec{y}$. This is because when constructing $\vec{y}$ from $\vec{x}$, we multiplied by W and converted a vector with five independent elements to a vector with three independent elements—some information was irretrievably lost. This intuition is consistent with the fact that a 5×3 matrix W is *non-invertible*: there is no W^{-1}, so there is no way to get $\vec{x} = W^{-1}\vec{y}$.
- During transpose convolution, we are distributing elements of $\vec{y}$ back to the elements of $\tilde{x}$ in the same proportion as when we were doing the forward convolution (see figure 10.16). This should remind you of backpropagation from chapter 8. There, in equation 8.24 (right-hand side), we saw that for linear layers, forward propagation amounts to multiplying by an arbitrary weight matrix W (shown in equation 8.8). Backpropagation involves multiplying by the transpose of the same weight matrix (equation 8.31). The backpropagation does a *proportional blame distribution*—the loss is distributed back to the inputs in the same proportion as their contribution in creating the output. The same thing is happening here. Thus, multiplying by the transposed weight matrix in general distributes the output back in the same ratio in which it contributes to the output.

The idea extends to higher dimensions. Figure 10.17 illustrates a 2D transpose convolution operation.

10.5.1 Application of transposed convolution: Autoencoders and embeddings

Transposed convolution is typically required in autoencoders. We provide a very brief outline of autoencoders at this point to explain why they need transposed convolution. Most of the neural networks we have looked at so far are examples of supervised classifiers in that they take an input and directly output the class to which the input belongs. This is not the only paradigm possible. As hinted in section 6.9, we can also map an input to a vector (often called the *embedding*, aka *descriptor vector*) that captures the essential aspects of the class of interest and throws away the variable aspects. For instance, if the class of interest is a human, then given an image, the embedding will only capture the features that recognize the humans in the image and ignore the background (sky, sea, forest, building, and so on).

The mapping from input to embedding is done by a neural network called an *encoder*. If the input is an image, the encoder typically contains a sequence of convolution layers.

How do we train this neural network? How do we define its loss? Well, one possibility is that the embedding must maintain fidelity to the original input: that is, we should be able to reconstruct (at least approximately) the input from the embedding. Remember, the embedding is smaller in size (with fewer degrees of freedom) than the input, so perfect reconstruction is impossible. Still, we can define loss as the difference (for

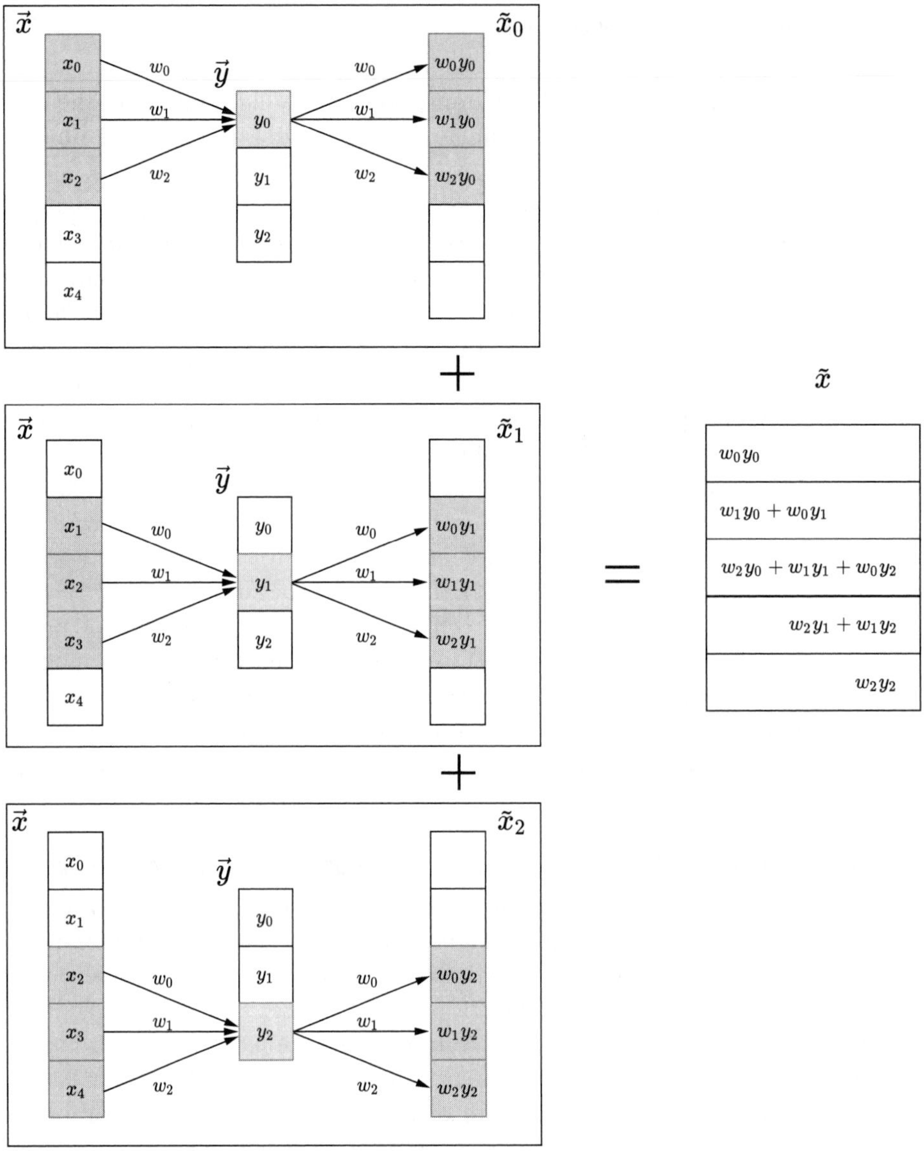

Figure 10.16 1D convolution and its transpose

example, Euclidean distance or binarized cross-entropy loss) between the original input and the reconstructed input.

How do we reconstruct the input from the embedding? This is where transposed convolution comes in. Remember, we did convolution (perhaps many times) in our encoder to generate the embedding. We can do a set of transposed convolutions on the embedding to generate a tensor of the same size as the input. The network to do this reconstruction is called the *decoder*. The decoder generates our reconstructed input.

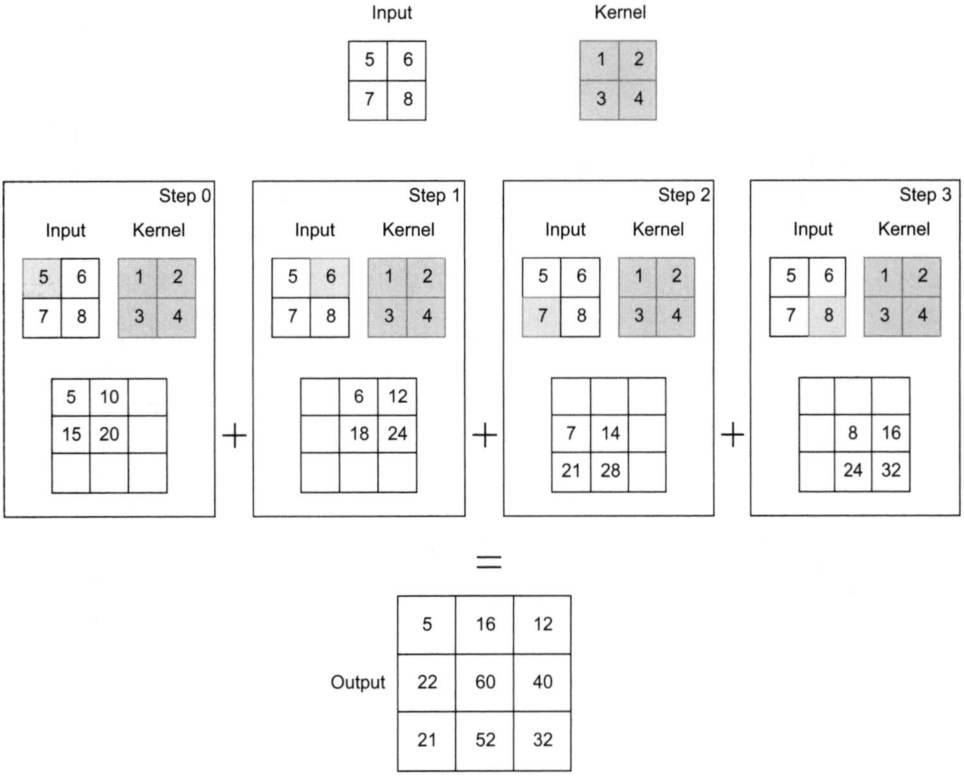

Figure 10.17 2D convolution and its transpose

We define a loss as the difference between the original and reconstructed input. We can train to minimize the loss and learn the weights of both the encoder and decoder. This is called *end-to-end learning*, and the encoder-decoder pair is called an *autoencoder*.

We train the autoencoder with many data instances, all belonging to the class of interest. Since it does not have the luxury of remembering the entire image (the embedding being smaller in size than the input), it is forced to learn how to retain the features common to all the training images: that is, the features that describe the class of interest. In our example, the autoencoder will learn to retain features that identify a human and drop the background. Note that this could also lead to a very effective *compression technique*—the embedding is a compact representation of the image in which only the objects of interest have been retained.

10.5.2 Transposed convolution output size

The output size of transposed convolution can be obtained by inverting equation 10.4:

$$o' = \left(n' - 1\right) s + k - 2p \tag{10.8}$$

For instance, transposed convolution with stride $s = 1$ on a $\vec{y}$ of size $n' = 3$ with valid padding ($p = 0$) and a kernel of size $k = 3$ creates an output $\tilde{x}$ of size $o' = 5$.

10.5.3 Upsampling via transpose convolution

In the previous section, we briefly discussed autoencoders, where an encoder network maps an input image into an embedding and a decoder network tries to reconstruct the input image from the embedding. The encoder network converts a higher-resolution input into a lower-resolution embedding by passing the input through a series of convolution and pooling layers (we discuss pooling layers in detail in the next chapter). The decoder network, which tries to reconstruct the original image from the embedding, has to upscale/upsample a lower-resolution input into a higher-resolution output.

Many interpolation techniques, such as nearest neighbor, bilinear, and bicubic interpolation, can be used to perform this upsampling operation. These techniques typically use predefined mathematical functions to map lower-resolution inputs to higher-resolution outputs. However, a more optimal way to perform upsampling is through transpose convolutions, where the mapping function is learned during the training process instead of being predefined. The neural network will learn the best way to distribute the input elements across a higher-resolution output map so that the final reconstruction error is minimized (that is, the final output is as close to the original input image as possible). We do not get into the details of training an autoencoder in this chapter; however, we show how input images can be upsampled using transpose convolutions:

- The input array is converted to a 4D tensor of shape $N \times C_{in} \times H \times W$, where N is the batch size, C_{in} is the number of input channels, H is the height, and W is the width.
- The kernel is a 4D tensor of shape $C_{in} \times C_{out} \times k_H \times k_W$, where C_{in} is the number of input channels, C_{out} is the number of output channels, k_H is the kernel height, and k_W is the kernel width. Note how this differs from the regular 2D convolutional kernel, which is expected to be of shape $C_{out} \times C_{in} \times k_H \times k_W$. Essentially, the input and output channel dimensions are interchanged.

Figure 10.18 shows an example with input of shape $1 \times 1 \times 2 \times 2$. The kernel is of shape $1 \times 1 \times 2 \times 2$. Transpose convolution with stride 2 results in an output of shape $1 \times 1 \times 4 \times 4$.

NOTE Fully functional code for transpose convolution, executable via Jupyter Notebook, can be found at http://mng.bz/radD.

Listing 10.7 PyTorch code for upsampling using transpose convolutions

```
import torch

x = torch.tensor([          ← Instantiates the input tensor
        [5., 6.],
        [7., 8.]
    ])
```

```
w = torch.tensor([                            ← Instantiates the weights of the kernel
        [1., 2.],
        [3., 4.]
    ])

x = x.unsqueeze(0).unsqueeze(0)               ← Converts the input tensor to N × C_in × H × W = 1 × 1 × 2 × 2

w = w.unsqueeze(0).unsqueeze(0)               ← Converts the kernel to C_in × C_out × k_H × k_W = 1 × 1 × 2 × 2

transpose_conv2d = torch.nn.ConvTranspose2d(  ← Instantiates the transpose convolution layer
    1, 1, kernel_size=2, stride=2, bias=False)

transpose_conv2d.weight = torch.nn.Parameter(w,    ← Sets the kernel weights
                requires_grad=False)

with torch.no_grad():                         ← Instructs PyTorch to not compute gradients
                                                since we currently don't require them
    y = transpose_conv2d(x)                   ← Runs the transpose convolution. y is of shape 4 × 4.
```

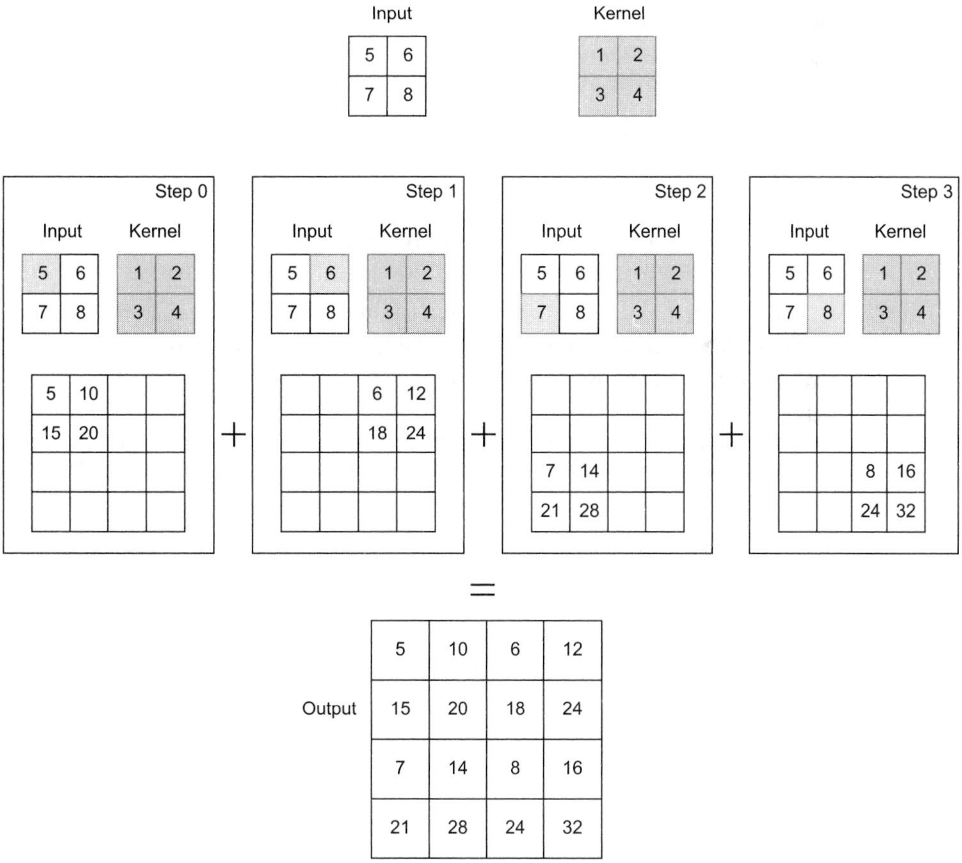

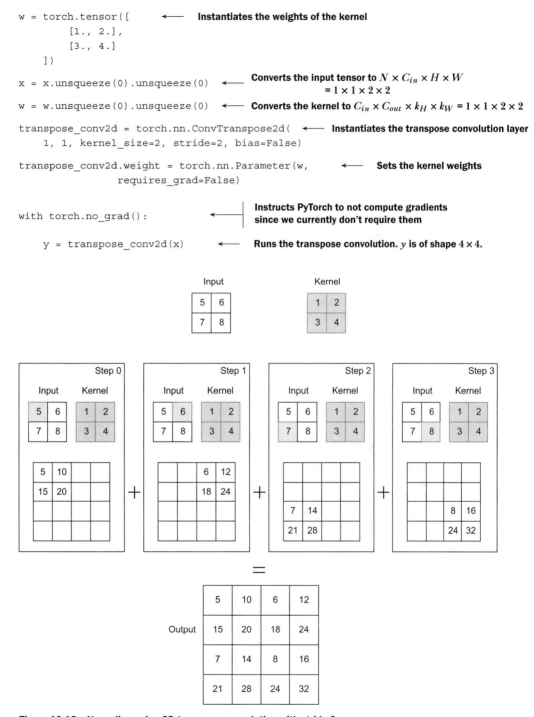

Figure 10.18 Upscaling using 2D transpose convolution with stride 2

10.6 Adding convolution layers to a neural network

Until now, we have been discussing convolution layers with custom weights that we set. While this gives us a conceptual understanding of how convolution works, in real neural networks, we do *not* set the convolution weights ourselves. Rather, we expect the weights to be learned from loss minimization via backpropagation, as described in chapters 8 and 9. We look at popular neural network architectures in the next chapter. But from a programming point of view, the most important thing to learn is how to add a convolution layer to a neural network. This is what we learn in the following section.

As part of setting up the neural network, we specify its dimensions but not the weights. We also initialize the weight values. The weight values are updated during the backpropagation (the `loss.backward()` call) somewhat behind the scene (although PyTorch allows us to view their values if we choose to).

10.6.1 PyTorch: Adding convolution layers to a neural network

Let's see how a convolutional layer is implemented as part of a larger neural network in PyTorch (the full neural network architecture is discussed in detail in the next chapter):

- A neural network typically subclasses the `torch.nn.Module` base class and implements the `forward()` method. The layers of the neural network are instantiated in the `__init__()` function.
- `torch.nn.Sequential` is used to chain multiple layers one after another. The output of the first layer is fed into the second layer, and so on.
- Each `torch.nn.Conv2d()` represents a single convolutional layer. Our code snippet instantiates three such convolutional layers with other layers in between (details are covered in the next chapter).

Listing 10.8 PyTorch code for a sample convolutional neural network

```
import torch

class SampleCNN(torch.nn.Module):
    def __init__(self, num_classes):
        super(LeNet, self).__init__()
        self.nn = torch.nn.Sequential(

            torch.nn.Conv2d(
                in_channels=1, out_channels=6,
                kernel_size=5, stride=1),

                          ...

            torch.nn.Conv2d(
                in_channels=6, out_channels=16,
                kernel_size=5, stride=1),

                          ...
```

- `self.nn = torch.nn.Sequential(`: **torch.nn.Sequential is used to chain a sequence of layers together.**
- `kernel_size=5, stride=1),` (first Conv2d): **Instantiates the convolutional layer**

```
        torch.nn.Conv2d(
            in_channels=16, out_channels=120,
            kernel_size=5, stride=1),        <-- Implements the forward pass

                    ...
    )

def forward(self, x):        <-- Runs the convolution
    out = self.nn(x)
    return out
```

10.7 Pooling

Until now, we have seen how a convolution layer slides over an input image and generates an output feature map that contains important features that describe the image. We looked at this in 1D, 2D, and 3D settings. In a typical deep neural network, multiple such convolution layers are stacked one after another to recognize more and more complex structures in the image. (We talk more about this in the next chapter.) A major drawback of the convolution layer is that it is very sensitive to the location of the features in the input. Minor variations in the position of input features can result in a different output feature map. Such variations can occur in the real world due to camera angle changes, rotations, crops, objects being present at varying distances from the camera, and so on. How do we handle such variations and make the neural network more robust?

One way to do so is via downsampling. A lower-resolution version of the feature map still contains the important features but at a lower precision/granularity. So even if important features are present at slightly varying locations in higher-resolution feature maps, they will be more or less at the same location in the lower-resolution feature maps. This is also known as *local translation invariance.*

In convolution neural networks, the downsampling operation is performed by *pooling* layers. Pooling layers essentially slide a small filter across the entire image. At each filter location, they capture a summary of the local patch using a pooling operation. The two most popular types of pooling operations are as follows:

- *Max pooling*—Calculates the maximum value for each patch
- *Average pooling*—Calculates the average value for each patch

Figure 10.19 illustrates this in detail. The size of the output feature map depends on the kernel size and the stride of the pooling layer. For example, if we use a 2×2 kernel with a stride of 2, as in figures 10.19 and 10.20, the output feature map becomes half the size of the input feature map. Similarly, using a 3×3 kernel with stride = 3 makes the output feature map one-third the size.

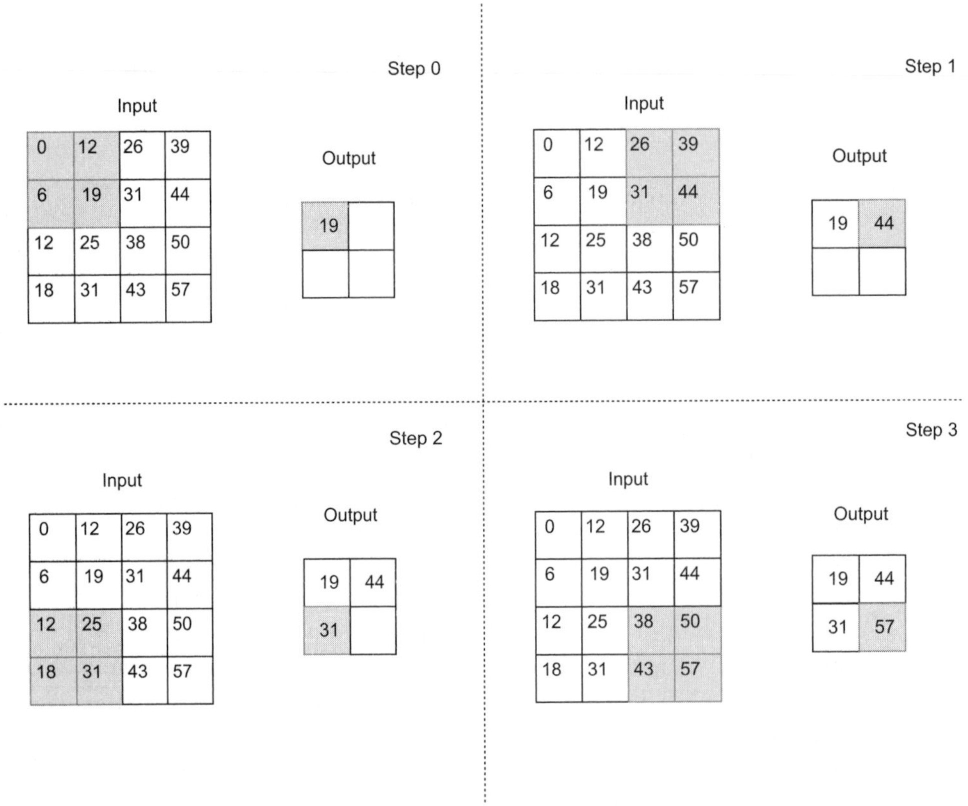

Figure 10.19 Max pooling using a 2×2 kernel with stride 2. The resulting output feature map is half the size of the input feature map. Each value of the output feature map is a max of the corresponding local patch in the input feature map.

Listing 10.9 PyTorch code for max and average pooling

```
import torch

X = torch.tensor([                       ← Instantiates a 4 × 4 input tensor
    [0, 12, 26, 39],
    [6, 19, 31, 44],
    [12, 25, 38, 50],
    [18, 31, 43, 57]
], dtype=torch.float32).unsqueeze(0).unsqueeze(0)

max_pool_2d = torch.nn.MaxPool2d(        ← Instantiates a 2 × 2 max pooling layer with stride 2
    kernel_size=2, stride=2)

out_max_pool = max_pool_2d(X)            ← Output feature map is of size 2 × 2

avg_pool_2d = torch.nn.AvgPool2d(        ← Instantiates a 2 × 2 average pooling layer with stride 2
    kernel_size=2, stride=2)

out_avg_pool = avg_pool_2d(X)            ← Output feature map is of size 2 × 2
```

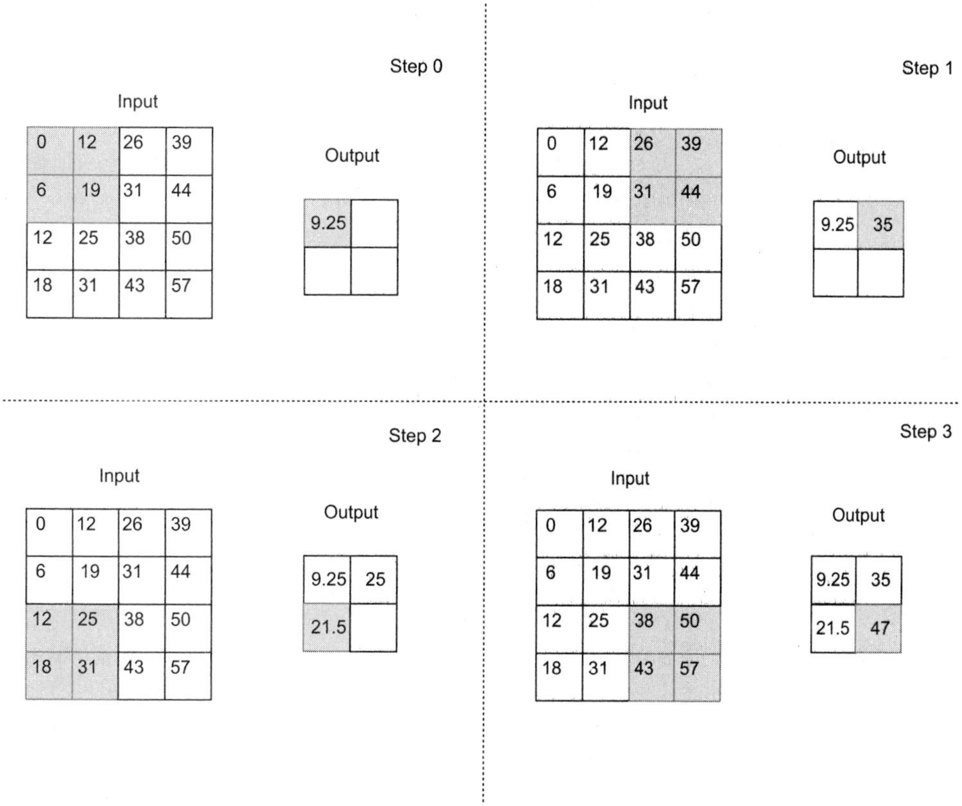

Figure 10.20 Average pooling using a 2 × 2 kernel with stride 2. The resulting output feature map is half the size of the input feature map. Each value of the output feature map is an average of the corresponding local patch in the input feature map.

Summary

In this chapter, we took an in-depth look at 1D, 2D, and 3D convolutions and their application to image and video analysis:

- Convolutional layers help capture local patterns in input data because they connect only a small set of adjacent input values to an output value. This is different from the fully connected layers (aka linear layers) discussed in the previous chapters, where all inputs are connected to every output value.
- A convolution operation involves sliding a kernel over an input array. It can conceptually be viewed as a matrix multiplication (though it is not implemented this way for efficiency reasons). The kernel size, stride, and padding affect the size of the output.
- The number of input elements over which the kernel slides upon completing a single step is known as *stride*.
- As the kernel reaches the extremities of the input array, parts of it may fall outside the array. To deal with such cases, multiple *padding* strategies can be applied. In

valid padding, the convolution operation stops when even a single kernel element falls outside the input array. In *same (zero) padding*, an input value of zero is assumed for all kernel elements that are outside the input array.

- 1D convolutions can conceptually be viewed as sliding a measuring ruler (1D kernel) across a stretched, straightened rope (1D input array). Real-world applications of 1D convolutions include smoothing and edge detection in curves.
- 2D convolutions can conceptually be viewed as sliding a tile (2D kernel) over the entire surface area of a wall (2D input array). Real-world applications of 2D convolutions include smoothing and edge detection in images.
- 3D convolutions can conceptually be viewed as sliding a brick (3D kernel) over the entire volume of a room (3D input array). Real-world applications of 3D convolutions include motion detection in an image sequence.
- In transpose convolutions, the input array elements are multiplied by the kernel weights and then distributed across the output array. Real-world applications of transpose convolutions include upsampling, where lower-resolution inputs are converted into higher-resolution outputs. Autoencoders use transpose convolutions to reconstruct images from embeddings.
- Pooling layers essentially slide a kernel across the input, capturing a summary of the local patch at each kernel location. They help improve the robustness of convolutional neural networks to minor variations in input features. The two most popular pooling operations are max pooling (calculates the maximum value of the local patch) and average pooling (calculates the average value of the local patch). Pooling layers result in downsampling of the input array. The output size depends on the size and stride of the pooling kernel.

11 Neural networks for image classification and object detection

This chapter covers

- Using deeper neural networks for image classification and object detection
- Understanding convolutional neural networks and other deep neural network architectures
- Correcting imbalances in neural networks

If a human is shown the image in figure 11.1, they can instantly recognize the objects in it, categorizing them as a bird, a plane, and Superman. In image classification, we want to impart this capability to computers—the ability to recognize objects in an image and classify them into one or more known and predetermined categories. Apart from identifying the object categories, we can also identify the location of the objects in the image. An object's location can be described by a *bounding box*: a rectangle whose sides are parallel to coordinate axes. A bounding box is typically specified by four parameters: $[(xtl, ytl), (xbr, ybr)]$, where (xtl, ytl) are the xy coordinates of the top-left corner and (xbr, ybr) are the xy coordinates of the bottom-right corner of the bounding

Figure 11.1 Is it a bird? Is it a plane? Is it Superman?

box. The problem of identifying and categorizing the objects present in the image is called *image classification.* If we also want to identify their location in the image, it is referred to as *object detection.* Image classification and object detection are some of the most fundamental problems in computer vision. While the human brain can both classify and localize objects in images almost intuitively, how do we train a machine to do this? Before deep learning, computer vision techniques involved hand-crafting image features (to encode color, edges, and shapes) and designing rules on top of these features to classify/localize objects. However, this is not a scalable approach because images are extremely complex and varied. Think of a simple object like an automobile. It can come in various sizes, shapes, and colors. It can be seen from afar or close (scales), from various viewpoints (perspectives), and on a cloudy day or a sunny day (lighting conditions). The car can be on a busy street or a mountain road (backgrounds). It is nearly impossible to engineer features and rules that can handle all such variations.

Over the last 10 years, a new class of algorithms has emerged: convolutional neural networks (CNNs). They do not rely on hand-engineered features but instead *learn* the relevant features from *data.* These models have shown tremendous success in several computer vision tasks, achieving (and sometimes even surpassing) human-level accuracy. They are increasingly used in the industry for applications ranging from medical diagnostics to e-commerce to manufacturing. In this chapter, we detail some of the most popular deep neural network architectures used for image classification and object detection. We look at some of their salient features, take a deep dive into the architectural details to understand how and why they work, and apply them to real-world problems.

NOTE Fully functional code for this chapter, executable via Jupyter Notebook, can be found at http://mng.bz/vojq

11.1 CNNs for image classification: LeNet

In chapter 10, we discussed the convolution operation in 1D, 2D, and 3D scenarios. We also saw how to implement a single convolutional layer as part of a larger neural network. This section shows how a neural network with multiple convolutional layers can be used for image classification. (If needed, you are encouraged to revisit chapter 10.) For this purpose, let's consider the MNIST data set, a large collection of handwritten digits (0 through 9). It contains a training set of 60,000 images and a test set of 10,000 images. Each image is 28 × 28 in size and contains a center crop of a single digit. Figure 11.2 shows sample images from the MNIST data set.

Figure 11.2 Sample images from the MNIST data set. (Source: "Gradient-based learning applied to document recognition"; http://mng.bz/Wz0a.)

We'd like to build a classifier that takes in a 28 × 28 image as input and emits a label from 0 to 9 based on the digit contained in the image. One of the most popular neural network architectures for this task is the LeNet, which was proposed by LeCun et al. in their 1998 paper, "Gradient-based learning applied to document recognition" (http://mng.bz/Wz0a). The LeNet architecture is illustrated in figure 11.3 (LeNet expects input images of size 32 × 32, so the 28 × 28 MNIST images are resized to 32 × 32 before being fed into the network):

- It consists of three convolutional layers with 5 × 5 kernels convolved with a stride of 1. The first convolution layer produces 6 feature maps of size 28 × 28, the

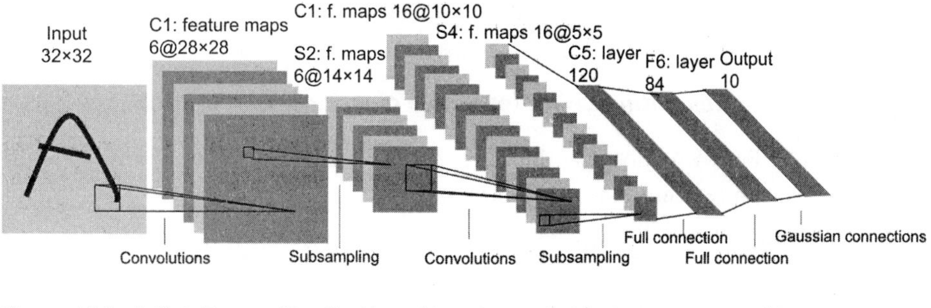

Figure 11.3 LeNet. (Source: "Gradient-based learning applied to document recognition"; http://mng.bz/Wz0a.)

second convolution layer produces 16 feature maps of size 10×10, and the third convolution layer produces 120 feature maps of size 1×1 (which are flattened into a 120-dimensional vector)

- The first two convolutional layers are followed by subsampling (aka pooling) layers, which perform a local averaging and subsampling of the feature map, thus reducing the resolution of the feature map and the sensitivity of the output to shifts and distortions in the input. A pooling kernel of size 2×2 is applied, reducing the feature map size to half its original size. Refer to section 10.7 for more about pooling.
- Every feature map is followed by a tanh activation layer. This introduces nonlinearity into the network, increasing its expressive power because it can now model the output as a nonlinear combination of the inputs. If we did not have a nonlinear activation function, no matter how many layers we had, the neural network would still behave as a single-linear-layer network because the combination of multiple linear layers is just another linear layer. While the original LeNet paper used tanh as the activation function, several activation functions such as ReLU and sigmoid can also be used. ReLU is discussed in detail in section 11.2.1. Detailed discussions of sigmoid and tanh can be found in sections 8.1 and 8.1.2.
- The output feature map is passed through two fully connected (FC, aka linear) layers, which finally produce a 10-dimensional *logits* vector that represents the score for every class. The logits scores are converted into probabilities using the softmax layer.
- `CrossEntropyLoss`, discussed in section 6.3, is used to compute the difference between the predicted probabilities and the ground truth.

NOTE A *feature map* is a 2D array of points (that is, a grid) with a fixed-size vector associated with every point. An image is an example of a feature map, with each point being a pixel and the associated vector representing the pixel's color. A convolution layer transforms an input feature map into an output feature map. The output feature map usually has smaller width and height but a longer per-point vector.

The LeNet performs very well on the MNIST data set, achieving test accuracies greater than 99%. A PyTorch implementation of LeNet is presented next.

11.1.1 PyTorch: Implementing LeNet for image classification on MNIST

NOTE Fully functional code for training the LeNet, executable via Jupyter Notebook, can be found at http://mng.bz/q2gz.

Listing 11.1 PyTorch code for the LeNet

```
import torch

class LeNet(torch.nn.Module):
    def __init__(self, num_classes):
        super(LeNet, self).__init__()
        self.conv1 = torch.nn.Sequential(
                        torch.nn.Conv2d(
                            in_channels=1, out_channels=6,       <--- 5 x 5 conv
                            kernel_size=5, stride=1),
                        torch.nn.Tanh(),        <--- Tanh activation
                        torch.nn.AvgPool2d(kernel_size=2))   <--- 2 x 2 average pooling
        self.conv2 = torch.nn.Sequential(
                        torch.nn.Conv2d(
                            in_channels=6, out_channels=16,
                            kernel_size=5, stride=1),
                        torch.nn.Tanh(),
                        torch.nn.AvgPool2d(kernel_size=2))
        self.conv3 = torch.nn.Sequential(
                        torch.nn.Conv2d(
                            in_channels=16, out_channels=120,
                            kernel_size=5, stride=1),
                        torch.nn.Tanh())
        self.fc1 = torch.nn.Sequential(
                        torch.nn.Linear(
                            in_features=120, out_features=84),   <--- First FC layer
                        torch.nn.Tanh())
        self.fc2 = torch.nn.Linear(
                in_features=84, out_features=num_classes)     <--- Second FC layer

    def forward(self, X):      <--- X.shape: N x 3 x 32 x 32. N is the batch size.
        conv_out = self.conv3(self.conv2(self.conv1(X)))
        batch_size = conv_out.shape[0]
        conv_out = conv_out.reshape(batch_size, -1)   <--- conv_out.shape: N x 120 x 1 x 1
        logits = self.fc2(self.fc1(conv_out))      <--- logits.shape: N x 10
        return logits

    def predict(self, X):
        logits = self.forward(X)
        probs = torch.softmax(logits, dim=1)       <--- Computes the probabilities using softmax
        return torch.argmax(probs, 1)
```

11.2 Toward deeper neural networks

The LeNet model is not a very deep network since it has only three convolutional layers. While this is sufficient to achieve accurate results on a simple data set like MNIST, it doesn't work well on real-world image classification problems since it does not have enough expressive power to model complex images. So, we typically go for much deeper neural networks with multiple convolutional layers. Adding more layers does the following:

- *Brings extra expressive power due to extra nonlinearity*—Since every layer brings with it a new set of learnable parameters and extra nonlinearity, a deeper network can model more complex relationships between input data elements. Lower layers typically learn simpler features of the object, like lines and edges, whereas higher layers learn more abstract features of the object, like shapes or sets of lines.
- *Achieves the same reach with fewer parameters*—Let's examine this via an example. Consider two output feature maps, one produced by a single 5×5 convolution on the input and another produced by two 3×3 convolutions applied one after another in sequence on the input. Assume a stride of 1 and the same (zero) padding. Figure 11.4 illustrates this scenario. Consider a single grid point in the output feature map. In both cases, the output value of the grid point is derived from a 5×5 patch in the input. We say the indicated 5×5 input patch is the *receptive field* of the output grid points. Thus, in both cases, the output grid point is a digest of the same input: that is, it expresses the same information. However, in the deeper network, there are fewer parameters. The number of parameters in a single 5×5 filter is 25, whereas that in two 3×3 filters is $2 \times 9 = 18$ (assuming a single channel input image). This is a 38% difference. Similarly, if we compare one 7×7 filter with three 3×3 filters, they have the same receptive field, but the 7×7 filter has 81% more parameters than the 3×3 filter.

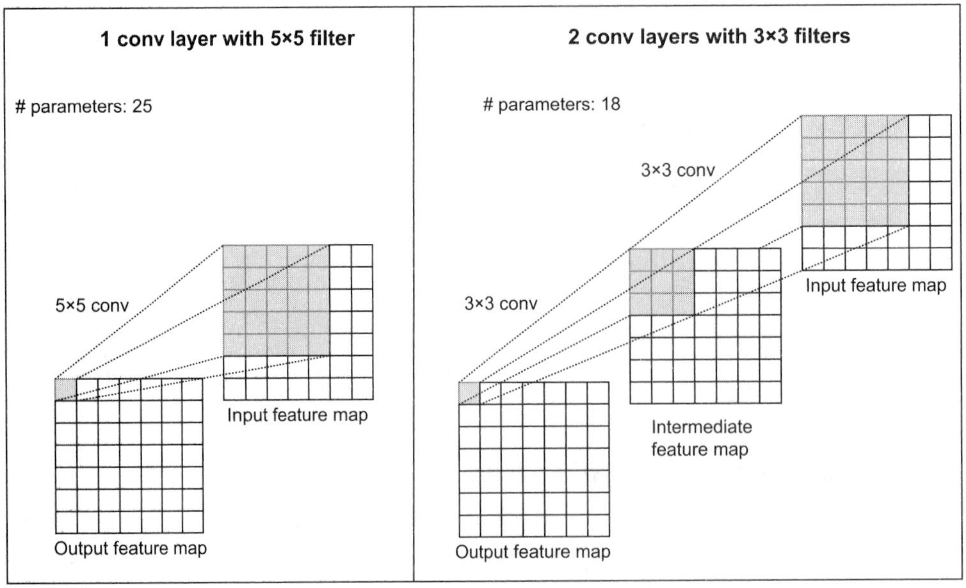

Figure 11.4 A single 5 × 5 convolution layer vs. two 3 × 3 convolution layers

Now, let's look at some of the most popular deep convolutional networks used for image classification. The first deep network that reignited the deep learning revolution was *AlexNet*, which was published by Krizhevsky et al. in 2012. It significantly outperformed all previous state-of-the-art algorithms on the ImageNet Large Scale Visual Recognition Challenge (ILSVRC), a complex data set with 1.3 million images across 1,000 classes. Since AlexNet, several deep networks have improved on the previous state of the art, such as GoogleNet, VGG, and ResNet. In this chapter, we discuss the key concepts that make each of these networks work. For a detailed review of their architectures, training methodologies, and final results, you are encouraged to read the original papers linked in each section.

11.2.1 VGG (Visual Geometry Group) Net

The VGG family of networks was created by the Visual Geometry Group from the University of Oxford (https://arxiv.org/pdf/1409.1556.pdf). Their main contribution was a thorough evaluation of networks of increasing depth using an architecture with very small (3×3) convolution filters. They demonstrated that by using 3×3 convolutions and networks with 16–19 weight layers, they could outperform previous state-of-the-art results on the ILSVRC-2014 challenge. The VGG network had two main differences compared to prior works:

- *Use of smaller (3×3) convolution filters*—Prior networks often relied on larger kernels of size 7×7 or 11×11 in the first convolution layers. VGG instead only used 3×3 kernels throughout the network. As discussed in section 11.2, three 3×3 filters have the same receptive field as a single 7×7 filter. So what does replacing the 7×7 filter with three smaller filters buy?
  - More nonlinearity and hence more expressive power because we have a ReLU activation function applied at the end of every convolution layer
  - Fewer parameters ($49C^2$ vs. $27C^2$), which means faster learning and more robustness to overfitting
- *Removal of the local response normalization (LRN) layers*—LRN was first introduced in the AlexNet architecture. Its purpose was twofold: to bound the output of the ReLU layer, which is an unbounded function and can produce outputs as large as the training permits; and to encourage *lateral inhibition* wherein a neuron can suppress the activity of its neighbors (this in effect acts as a regularization). The VGG paper demonstrated that adding LRN layers did not improve accuracy, so VGG chose to remove them from its architecture.

The VGG family of networks comes in five different configurations, which mainly differ in the number of layers (VGG-11, VGG-13, VGG-16, and VGG-19). Regardless of the exact configuration, the VGG family of networks follows a common structure. Here, we discuss these commonalities (a detailed description of the differences can be found in the original paper):

- All architectures work on 224×224 input images.

- All architectures have five convolutional blocks (conv blocks):
  - Each block can have multiple convolution layers followed by a max pool layer at the end.
  - All individual convolution layers use 3×3 kernels with a stride of 1 and same padding. Therefore, they don't change the spatial resolution of the output feature map.
  - All convolution layers within a single conv block have the same-sized output feature maps.
  - Each convolution layer is followed by a ReLU layer that adds nonlinearity.
  - The max pool layer at the end of every conv block reduces the spatial resolution to half.
- Since each conv block downsamples by 2, the input feature map is reduced 2^5 (32) times, resulting in an output feature map of size 7×7. Additionally, at each conv block, the number of feature maps is doubled.
- All architectures end with three FC layers:
  - The first takes a 51,277-sized input and converts it into a 4,096-dimensional output.
  - The second takes the resulting 4,096-dimensional output and converts it into another 4,096-dimensional output.
  - The final takes the resulting 4,096-dimensional output and converts it into a C-dimensional output, where C stands for the number of classes. In the case of ImageNet classification, C is 1,000.

The architecture diagram for VGG-11 is shown in figure 11.5. The column on the left represents the shape of the input tensor to each layer. The column on the right represents the shape of the output tensor from each layer.

RELU NONLINEARITY

As we've discussed previously, nonlinear layers give the deep neural network more expressive power to model complex mathematical functions. In chapter 8, we looked at two nonlinear functions: sigmoid and tanh. However, the VGG network (like AlexNet) consists of a different nonlinear layer called rectified linear unit (ReLU). To understand the rationale for this choice, let's revisit the sigmoid function and look at some of its drawbacks.

Figure 11.6 plots the sigmoid function along with its derivative. As the plot shows, the gradient (derivative) is maximum when the input is 0, and it quickly tapers down to 0 as the input increases/decreases. This is true for the tanh activation function as well. It means when the output of a neuron (before the sigmoid layer) is either high or low, the gradient becomes small. While this may not be an issue in shallow networks, it becomes a problem in larger networks because the gradients can become too small for training to work effectively. Gradients of neural networks are calculated using backpropagation. By the chain rule, the derivatives of each layer are multiplied down the network, starting from the final layer and moving toward the initial layers. If the gradients at each layer are

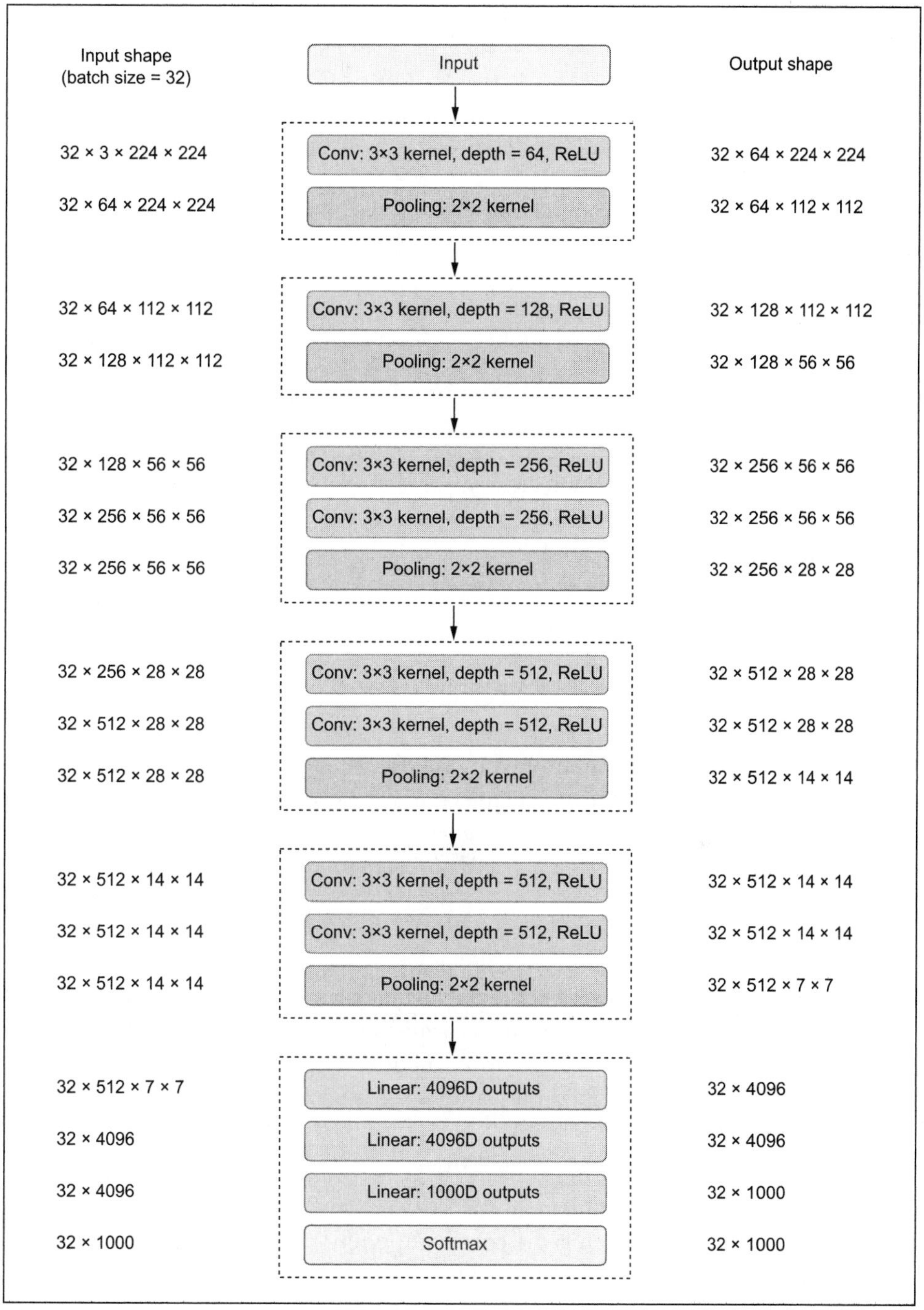

Figure 11.5 VGG-11 architecture diagram. All shapes are of the form N × C × H × W, where N is the batch size, C is the number of channels, H is the height, and W is the width.

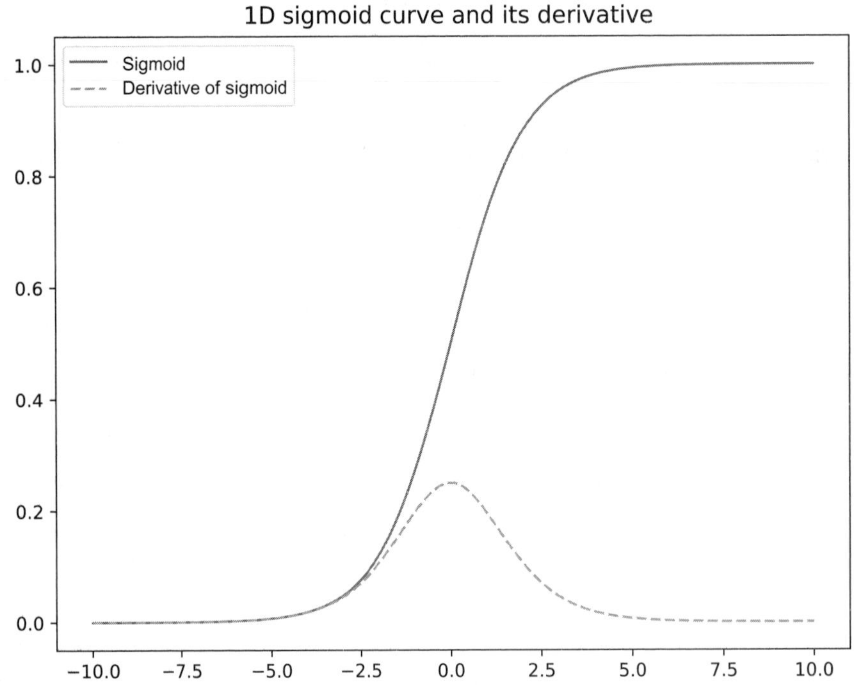

Figure 11.6 Graph of a 1D sigmoid function (dotted curve) and its derivative (solid curve)

small, a small number multiplied by another small number is an even smaller number. Thus the gradients at the initial layers are very close to 0, making the training ineffective. This is known as the *vanishing gradient* problem. The ReLU function addresses this problem. Figure 11.7 shows a graph of the ReLU function. Its equation is given by

$$ReLU\ (x) = max(0, x) \tag{11.1}$$

The derivative of ReLU is 1 (constant) when x is greater than 0, and 0 everywhere else. Therefore, it doesn't suffer from the vanishing gradient problem. Most deep networks today use ReLU as their activation function. The AlexNet paper demonstrated that using ReLU nonlinearity significantly speeds up training because it helps with faster convergence.

PYTORCH: VGG

Now let's see how to implement the VGG network in PyTorch. First, let's implement a single conv block, which is the core component of the VGG net. This conv block will later be repeated multiple times to form the entire VGG network.

> **NOTE** Fully functional code for the VGG network, executable via Jupyter Notebook, can be found at http://mng.bz/7WE4.

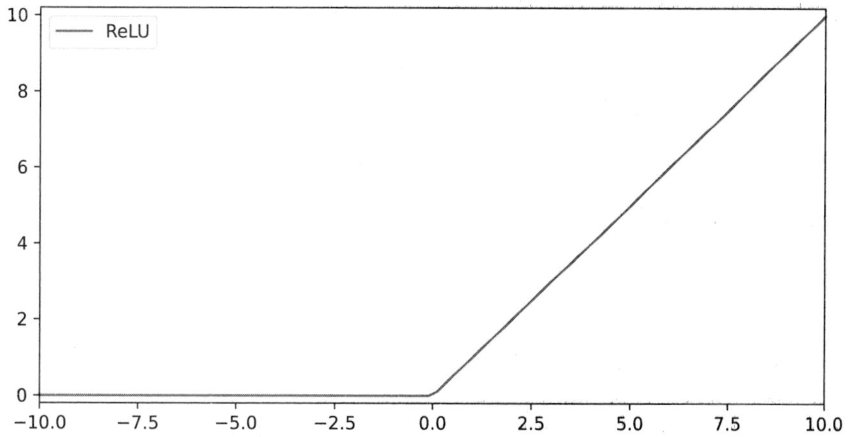

Figure 11.7 Graph of the ReLU function

Listing 11.2 PyTorch code for a convolutional block

```
class ConvBlock(nn.Module):
    def __init__(self, in_channels, num_conv_layers, num_features):
        super(ConvBlock, self).__init__()

        modules = []

        for i in range(num_conv_layers):
            modules.extend([
                nn.Conv2d(
                    in_channels, num_features,         ← 3 × 3 conv

                    kernel_size=3, padding=1),         ← ReLU nonlinearity
                nn.ReLU(inplace=True)
            ])

            in_channels = num_features
        modules.append(nn.MaxPool2d(kernel_size=2))    ← 2 × 2 max pooling
        self.conv_block = nn.Sequential(*modules)

    def forward(self, x):
        return self.conv_block(x)
```

Next, let's implement the convolutional backbone (conv backbone) builder, which allows us to create different VGG architectures via simple configuration changes.

Listing 11.3 PyTorch code for the conv backbone

```
class ConvBackbone(nn.Module):
    def __init__(self, cfg):     ← Cfg: [(in_channels, num_conv_layers, num_features),]
                                   The different VGG networks can be created without
                                   duplicating code by passing in the right cfg.

        super(ConvBackbone, self).__init__()

        self.cfg = cfg
```

```
        self.validate_config(cfg)

        modules = []
        for block_cfg in cfg:          ←  Iterates over conv block configurations
            in_channels, num_conv_layers, num_features = block_cfg
            modules.append(ConvBlock(      ←  Instantiates the conv block defined in listing 11.2
            in_channels, num_conv_layers, num_features))
        self.features = nn.Sequential(*modules)

    def validate_config(self, cfg):
        assert len(cfg) == 5 # 5  conv blocks
        for i, block_cfg in enumerate(cfg):
            assert type(block_cfg) == tuple and len(block_cfg) == 3
            if i == 0:
                assert block_cfg[0] == 3       ←  There must be three input channels.
            else:
                assert block_cfg[0] == cfg[i-1][-1]   ←  out_Features of the previous block should be equal to in_features of the current block.

    def forward(self, x):
        return self.features(x)
```

The conv backbone is instantiated with a config that contains the list of configurations for each of the conv blocks. The config for VGG-11 contains fewer layers, whereas that for VGG-19 contains more layers. The output of the conv backbone is fed into the classifier, which consists of three FC layers. Together, the conv backbone and the classifier form the VGG module.

Listing 11.4 PyTorch code for the VGG network

```
class VGG(nn.Module):
    def __init__(self, conv_backbone, num_classes):
        super(VGG, self).__init__()
        self.conv_backbone = conv_backbone    ←  Backbone network defined in listing 11.3
        self.classifier = nn.Sequential(
            nn.Linear(512 * 7 * 7, 4096),
            nn.ReLU(True),
            nn.Dropout(),
            nn.Linear(4096, 4096),      ←  The classifier is made up of three linear Layers. The first two are followed by ReLU nonlinearity.
            nn.ReLU(True),
            nn.Dropout(),
            nn.Linear(4096, num_classes)
        )

    def forward(self, x):
        conv_features = self.conv_backbone(x)

        logits = self.classifier(
            conv_features.view(
                conv_features.shape[0], -1))    ←  Flattens the conv features before passing it to the classifier
        return logits
```

A VGG-11 network can be instantiated as follows.

Listing 11.5 PyTorch code instantiating a VGG network from a specific config

```
vgg11_cfg = [          ← Creates the cfg for VGG-11
    (3, 1, 64),
    (64, 1, 128),
    (128, 2, 256),
    (256, 2, 512),
    (512, 2, 512)
]

vgg11_backbone = ConvBackbone(vgg11_cfg)          ← Instantiates the conv backbone
num_classes = 1000
vgg11 = VGG(vgg11_backbone, num_classes)          ← Instantiates the VGG network
```

While we have discussed how to implement VGG in PyTorch, we don't do this in practice because the `torchvision` package already implements the VGG network, along with several other popular deep networks. It is recommended that you use the `torchvision` implementation, as shown here:

```
import torchvision
vgg11 = torchvision.models.vgg11()
```

11.2.2 Inception: Network-in-network paradigm

Previously, we saw how increasing the depth of a neural network—that is, the number of layers—can improve accuracy because it increases the expressive power of the network. Alternatively, we could increase the width of the network—the number of units at each level—to improve accuracy. However, both these methods suffer from two main drawbacks. First, blindly increasing the size of the network can lead to overfitting, wherein the network memorizes certain patterns in the training data that don't extend well to test data. And second, increased computation resources are required during both training and inference times. The Inception architecture, introduced by Szegedy et al. in their paper "Going deeper with convolutions" (https://arxiv.org/pdf/1409.4842v1.pdf), aims to address both these drawbacks. The Inception architecture increases the network's depth and width while keeping the computational budget constant. In this section, we examine the main idea behind the Inception architecture. While there have been several improvements to it (Inception_v2, Inception_v3, Inception_ResNet, and so on), we discuss the original: Inception_v1.

Prior deep learning architectures typically stacked convolutional filters sequentially: each layer applied a set of convolutional filters of the same size and passed it to the subsequent layer. The kernel size of the filter at each layer depended on the architecture. But with such an architecture, how do we know we have chosen the right kernel size for each layer? If we are detecting a car, say, the fraction of the image area (that is, the number of pixels) occupied by the car is different in an image taken close up than in one taken from far away. We say the *scale* of the car object is different in the two images.

Consequently, the number of pixels that must be digested to recognize the car will differ at different scales. A larger kernel is preferred for information at a larger scale, and vice versa. An architecture that is forced to choose one kernel size may not be optimal. The Inception module tackles this problem by having multiple kernels of different sizes at each level and taking weighted combinations of the outputs. The network can learn to weigh the appropriate kernel more than others. The naive implementation of the Inception module performs convolutions on the input using three kernel sizes: 1×1, 3×3, and 5×5. Max pooling is also performed, using a 3×3 kernel with stride 1 and padding 1 (for output and input to be the same size). The outputs are concatenated and sent into the next Inception module. See figure 11.8 for details.

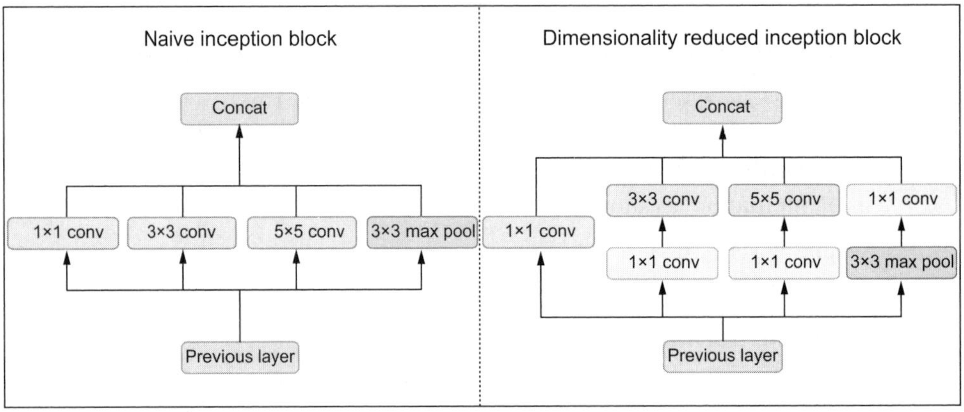

Figure 11.8 Inception_v1 architecture

This naive Inception block has a major flaw. Using even a small number of 5×5 filters can prohibitively increase the number of parameters. This becomes even more expensive when we add the pooling layer, where the number of output filters equals the number of filters in the previous stage. Thus, concatenating the output of the pooling layer with the outputs of convolutional layers would lead to an inevitable increase in the number of output features. To fix this, the Inception module uses 1×1 convolution layers before the 3×3 and 5×5 filters to reduce the number of input channels. This drastically reduces the number of parameters of the 3×3 and 5×5 convs. While it may seem counterintuitive, 1×1 convs are much cheaper than 3×3 and 5×5 convs. Additionally, 1×1 convolution is applied after pooling (see figure 11.8).

A neural network architecture was built using the dimension-reduced Inception module and was popularly known as GoogLeNet. GoogLeNet has nine such Inception modules stacked linearly. It is 22 layers deep (27, including the pooling layers). It uses global average pooling at the end of the last Inception module. With such a deep network, there is always the vanishing gradient problem; to prevent the middle part of the network from "dying out," the paper introduced two auxiliary classifiers. This is done by applying softmax to the output of two of the intermediate Inception modules and computing an auxiliary loss over the ground truth. The total loss function is a weighted sum of the auxiliary loss and the real loss. You are encouraged to read the original paper to understand the details.

PYTORCH: INCEPTION BLOCK

Let's see how to implement an Inception block in PyTorch. We typically don't do this in practice because end-to-end deep network architectures containing Inception blocks are already implemented in the `torchvision` package. However, we implement the Inception block from scratch to understand the details.

NOTE Fully functional code for the Inception block, executable via Jupyter Notebook, can be found at http://mng.bz/mxn0.

Listing 11.6 PyTorch code for a naive Inception block

```
class NaiveInceptionModule(nn.Module):
    def __init__(self, in_channels, num_features=64):
        super(NaiveInceptionModule, self).__init__()

        self.branch1x1 = torch.nn.Sequential(        <-- 1 × 1 branch
                        nn.Conv2d(
                            in_channels, num_features,
                            kernel_size=1, bias=False),
                        nn.BatchNorm2d(num_features, eps=0.001),
                        nn.ReLU(inplace=True))

        self.branch3x3 = torch.nn.Sequential(
                        nn.Conv2d(        <-- 3 × 3 branch
                            in_channels, num_features,
                            kernel_size=3, padding=1, bias=False),
                        nn.BatchNorm2d(num_features, eps=0.001),
                        nn.ReLU(inplace=True))

        self.branch5x5 = torch.nn.Sequential(        <-- 5 × 5 branch
                        nn.Conv2d(
                            in_channels, num_features,
                            kernel_size=5, padding=2, bias=False),
                        nn.BatchNorm2d(num_features, eps=0.001),
                        nn.ReLU(inplace=True))

        self.pool = torch.nn.MaxPool2d(        <-- 3 × 3 pooling
            kernel_size=3, stride=1, padding=1)

    def forward(self, x):
        conv1x1 = self.branch1x1(x)
        conv3x3 = self.branch3x3(x)
        conv5x5 = self.branch5x5(x)
        pool_out = self.pool(x)
        out = torch.cat(        <-- Concatenates the outputs of the parallel branches
            [conv1x1, conv3x3, conv5x5, pool_out], 1)
        return out
```

Listing 11.7 PyTorch code for a dimensionality reduced Inception block

```
class Inceptionv1Module(nn.Module):
    def __init__(self, in_channels, num_1x1=64,
                 reduce_3x3=96, num_3x3=128,
                 reduce_5x5=16, num_5x5=32,
                 pool_proj=32):
        super(Inceptionv1Module, self).__init__()

        self.branch1x1 = torch.nn.Sequential(
                    nn.Conv2d(          ← 1 × 1 branch
                        in_channels, num_1x1,
                        kernel_size=1, bias=False),
                    nn.BatchNorm2d(num_1x1, eps=0.001),
                    nn.ReLU(inplace=True))

        self.branch3x3_1 = torch.nn.Sequential(     ← 1 × 1 conv in the 3 × 3 branch
                    nn.Conv2d(
                        in_channels, reduce_3x3,
                        kernel_size=1, bias=False),
                    nn.BatchNorm2d(reduce_3x3, eps=0.001),
                    nn.ReLU(inplace=True))

        self.branch3x3_2 = torch.nn.Sequential(     ← 3 × 3 conv in the 3 × 3 branch
                    nn.Conv2d(
                        reduce_3x3, num_3x3,
                        kernel_size=3, padding=1, bias=False),
                    nn.BatchNorm2d(num_3x3, eps=0.001),
                    nn.ReLU(inplace=True))

        self.branch5x5_1 = torch.nn.Sequential(     ← 1 × 1 conv in the 5 × 5 branch
                    nn.Conv2d(
                        in_channels, reduce_5x5,
                        kernel_size=5, padding=2, bias=False),
                    nn.BatchNorm2d(reduce_5x5, eps=0.001),
                    nn.ReLU(inplace=True))
        self.branch5x5_2 = torch.nn.Sequential(     ← 5 × 5 conv in the 5 × 5 branch
                    nn.Conv2d(
                        reduce_5x5, num_5x5,
                        kernel_size=5, padding=2, bias=False),
                    nn.BatchNorm2d(num_5x5, eps=0.001),
                    nn.ReLU(inplace=True))

        self.pool = torch.nn.Sequential(     ← Max pooling followed by a 1 × 1 conv
                    torch.nn.MaxPool2d(
                        kernel_size=3, stride=1, padding=1),
                    nn.Conv2d(
                        in_channels, pool_proj,
                        kernel_size=1, bias=False),
                    nn.BatchNorm2d(pool_proj, eps=0.001),
                    nn.ReLU(inplace=True))
    def forward(self, x):
```

```
conv1x1 = self.branch1x1(x)
conv3x3 = self.branch3x3_2(self.branch3x3_1((x)))
conv5x5 = self.branch5x5_2(self.branch5x5_1((x)))
pool_out = self.pool(x)
out = torch.cat(          ← Concatenates the outputs of the parallel branches
    [conv1x1, conv3x3, conv5x5, pool_out], 1)
return out
```

11.2.3 ResNet: Why stacking layers to add depth does not scale

We start with a fundamental question: is learning better networks as easy as stacking multiple layers? Consider the graphs in figure 11.9.

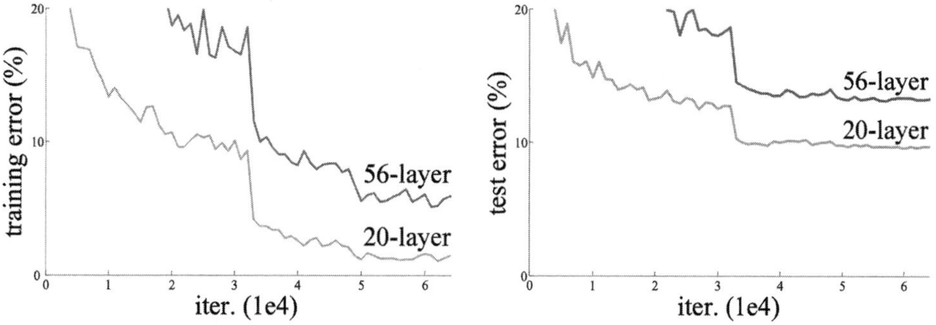

Figure 11.9 Training error (left) and test error (right) on the CIFAR-10 data set with 20-layer and 56-layer networks. (Source: "Deep residual learning for image recognition"; https://arxiv.org/pdf/1512.03385.pdf.)

This image from the ResNet paper "Deep residual learning for image recognition" (https://arxiv.org/pdf/1512.03385.pdf) shows the training and test error rates for two networks: a shallower network with 20 layers and a deeper network with 56 layers, on the CIFAR-10 data set. Surprisingly, the training and test errors are *higher* for the deeper (56-layer) network. This result is extremely counterintuitive because we expect deeper networks to have more expressive power and hence higher accuracies/lower error rates than their shallower counterparts. This phenomenon is referred to as the *degradation* problem: with the network depth increasing, the accuracy becomes saturated and degrades rapidly. We might attribute this to overfitting, but that is not the case because even the training errors are higher for the deeper network. Another cause could be vanishing/exploding gradients. However, the authors of the ResNet paper investigated the gradients at each layer and established that they are healthy (not vanishing/exploding). So, what causes the degradation problem, and how do we solve it?

Let's consider a shallower architecture with n layers and a deeper counterpart that adds more layers to it ($n + m$ layers). The deeper architecture should be able to achieve no higher loss than the shallow architecture. Intuitively, a trivial solution is to learn the exact

n layers of the shallow architecture and the identity function for the additional m layers. The fact that this doesn't happen in practice indicates that the neural network layers have a hard time learning the identity function. Thus the paper proposes "shortcut/skip connections" that enable the layers to potentially learn the identity function easily. This "identity shortcut connection" is the core idea of ResNet. Let's look at a mathematical analogy. Let $h(x)$ be the function we are trying to model (learn) via a stack of layers (not necessarily the entire network). It is reasonable to expect that the function $g(x) = h(x) - x$ is simpler than $h(x)$ and hence easier to learn. But we already have x at the input. So if we learn $g(x)$ and add x to it to obtain $h(x)$, we have effectively modeled $h(x)$ by learning the simpler $g(x)$ function. The name *residual* comes from $g(x) = h(x) - x$. Figure 11.10 shows this in detail.

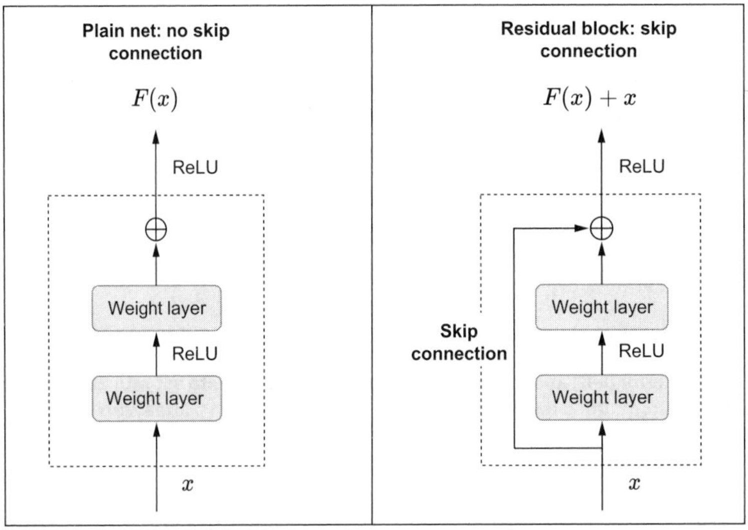

Figure 11.10 The left column shows a plain network block without skip connections, and the right column shows a residual block with skip connections.

Now let's revisit the earlier problem of degradation. We posited that normal neural network layers generally have difficulty learning the identity function. In the case of residual learning, to learn the identity function, $h(x) = x$, the layers need to learn $g(x)=0$. This can easily be done by driving all the layers' weights to 0. Here is another way to think about it: if we initialize a regular neural network's weights and biases to be 0 at the start, then every layer starts with the "zero" function: $g(x) = 0$. Thus, the output of every stack of layers with a shortcut connection, $h(x) = g(x) + x$, is already the identity function: $h(x) = x$ when $g(x) = 0$.

In real cases, it is important to note that identity mappings are unlikely to be optimal: the network layers will want to learn actual features. In such cases, this reformulation isn't preventing the network lawyers from doing so; the layers can still learn other functions like a regular stack of layers. We can think of this reformulation as preconditioning, which makes learning the identity function easier if needed. Additionally, by adding skip connections, we allow a direct path for the gradient to flow from layer to layer: the deeper layer has a direct path to x. This allows for better learning as information from the lower layers passes directly into the higher layers.

RESNET ARCHITECTURE

Now that we have seen the basic building block—a stack of convolutional (conv) layers with a skip connection—let's delve deeper into the architecture of ResNet. ResNet architectures are constructed by stacking multiple building blocks on top of each other. They follow the same idea as VGG:

- The convolutional layers mostly have 3×3 filters.
- The layers have the same number of filters for a given output feature-map size.
- If the feature-map size is halved, the number of filters is doubled to preserve the time complexity per layer.

ResNet uses conv layers with a stride of 2 to downsample, unlike VGG, which had multiple max pooling layers. The core architecture consists of the following components:

- *Five convolutional layer blocks*—The first convolutional block consists of a 7×7 kernel with `stride=2`, `padding=3`, and `num_features=64`, followed by a max pooling layer with a 3×3 kernel, `stride=2`, and `padding=1`. The feature map size is reduced from (224, 224) to (56, 56). The remaining convolutional blocks (`ResidualConvBlock`) are built by stacking multiple basic shortcut blocks together. Each basic block uses 3×3 filters, as described.
- *Classifier*—An average pooling block that runs on top of the conv block output, followed by a FC layer, which is used for classification.

You are encouraged to examine the diagrams in the original paper to understand the details. Now, let's see how to implement a ResNet in PyTorch.

PYTORCH: RESNET

In this section, we discuss how to implement a ResNet-34 from scratch. Note that this is seldom done in practice. The `torchvision` package provides ready-made implementations for all ResNet architectures. However, by building the network from scratch, we gain a deeper understanding of the architecture. First, let's implement a basic skip connection block (`BasicBlock`) to see how the shortcut connection works.

> **NOTE** Fully functional code for ResNet, executable via Jupyter Notebook, can be found at http://mng.bz/5K9q.

Listing 11.8 PyTorch code for `BasicBlock`

```
class BasicBlock(nn.Module):
    def __init__(self, in_channels, num_features, stride=1, downsample=None):
        super(BasicBlock, self).__init__()
        self.conv1 = nn.Sequential(        ←── Instantiates two conv layers of filter size 3 × 3
```

```
                    nn.Conv2d(
                        in_channels, num_features,
                        kernel_size=3, stride=stride, padding=1, bias=False),
                    nn.BatchNorm2d(num_features, eps=0.001),
                    nn.ReLU(inplace=True))
        self.conv2 = nn.Sequential(
                    nn.Conv2d(
                        num_features, num_features,
                        kernel_size=3, stride=1, padding=1, bias=False),
                    nn.BatchNorm2d(num_features, eps=0.001))

        self.downsample = downsample

        self.relu = nn.ReLU(inplace=True)

    def forward(self, x):
        conv_out = self.conv2(self.conv1(x))
        identity = x
        if self.downsample is not None:
            identity = self.downsample(x)
        assert identity.shape == conv_out.shape,
            f"Identity identity.shape and conv out conv_out.shape have different
shapes"

        out = self.relu(conv_out + identity)
        return out
```

When input and output feature maps are not the same size, the input feature map is downsampled using a 1 × 1 convolution layer. (annotates `self.downsample = downsample`)

Creates a skip connection (annotates `out = self.relu(conv_out + identity)`)

Notice how the output of the residual block is a function of both the input and the output of the convolutional layer: `ReLU(conv_out+x)`. This assumes that x and *conv_out* have the same shape. (Shortly, we discuss what to do when this isn't the case.) Also note that adding the skip connections does not increase the number of parameters. The shortcut connections are parameter-free. This makes the solution cheap from a computational point of view and is one of the charms of shortcut connections.

Next, let's implement a residual conv block consisting of a number of basic blocks stacked on top of each other. We have to handle two cases when it comes to basic blocks:

- *Case 1*—Output feature map spatial resolution = Input feature map spatial resolution AND Number of output features = Number of input features. This is the most common case. Since there is no change in the number of features or the spatial resolution of the feature map, we can easily add the input and output via shortcut connections.
- *Case 2*—Output feature map spatial resolution = 1/2 * Input feature map spatial resolution AND Number of output features = 2 * Number of input features. Remember that ResNet uses conv layers with a stride of 2 to downsample. The number of features is also doubled. This is done by the first basic block of every conv block (except the second conv block). In this case, the input and output are not the same size. So how do we add them together as part of the skip connection? 1 × 1

convs are the answer. The spatial resolution of the input feature map is halved, and the number of input features is doubled by using a 1×1 conv with `stride=2` and `num_features=2 * num_input_features`.

Listing 11.9 PyTorch code for `ResidualConvBlock`

```
class ResidualConvBlock(nn.Module):
    def __init__(self, in_channels, num_blocks, reduce_fm_size=True):
        super(ResidualConvBlock, self).__init__()

        num_features = in_channels * 2 if reduce_fm_size else in_channels
        modules = []

        for i in range(num_blocks):          ← The residual block is a stack of basic blocks.
            if i == 0 and reduce_fm_size:
                stride = 2
                downsample = nn.Sequential(
                    nn.Conv2d(         ← 1 × 1 convs to downsample the input feature map
                        in_channels, num_features,
                        kernel_size=1, stride=stride, bias=False),
                    nn.BatchNorm2d(num_features, eps=0.001),
                )
                basic_block = BasicBlock(
                    in_channels=in_channels, num_features=num_features,
                    stride=stride, downsample=downsample)
            else:
                basic_block = BasicBlock(
                    in_channels=num_features, num_features=num_features, stride=1)
            modules.append(basic_block)

        self.conv_block = nn.Sequential(*modules)

    def forward(self, x):
        return self.conv_block(x)
```

With this, we are ready to implement ResNet-34.

Listing 11.10 PyTorch code for ResNet-34

```
class ResNet34(nn.Module):
    def __init__(self, num_basic_blocks, num_classes):
        super(ResNet, self).__init__()
        conv1 = nn.Sequential(         ← Instantiates the first conv layer
            nn.Conv2d(3, 64, kernel_size=7,
                stride=2, padding=3, bias=False),
            nn.BatchNorm2d(64, eps=0.001),
            nn.ReLU(inplace=True),
            nn.MaxPool2d(
                kernel_size=3, stride=2, padding=1)
        )
```

```
        assert len(num_basic_blocks) == 4          <-- List of size 4, specifying the
                                                       number of basic blocks per
                                                       ResidualConvBlock

        conv2 = ResidualConvBlock(      <-- Instantiates four residual blocks
            in_channels=64, num_blocks=num_basic_blocks[0], reduce_fm_size=False)
        conv3 = ResidualConvBlock(
            in_channels=64, num_blocks=num_basic_blocks[1], reduce_fm_size=True)
        conv4 = ResidualConvBlock(
            in_channels=128, num_blocks=num_basic_blocks[2], reduce_fm_size=True)
        conv5 = ResidualConvBlock(
            in_channels=256, num_blocks=num_basic_blocks[3], reduce_fm_size=True)

        self.conv_backbone = nn.Sequential(*[conv1, conv2, conv3, conv4, conv5])

        self.avg_pool = nn.AdaptiveAvgPool2d((1, 1))
        self.classifier = nn.Linear(512, num_classes)

    def forward(self, x):
        conv_out = self.conv_backbone(x)
        conv_out = self.avg_pool(conv_out)      Flattens the conv feature before
        logits = self.classifier(          <-- passing it to the classifier

            conv_out.view(conv_out.shape[0], -1))
        return logits
```

As discussed earlier, we typically don't implement our own ResNet. Instead, we use the ready-made implementation from the *torchvision* package like this:

```
import torchvision

resnet34 = torchvision.models.resnet34()       <-- Instantiates resnet34 from
                                                   the torchvision package
```

While we looked at the ResNet-34, there are deeper ResNet architectures like ResNet-50, ResNet-101, and ResNet-151 that use a different version of `BasicBlock` called `BottleneckLayer`. Similarly, there are several other variants inspired by ResNet, like ResNext, Wide ResNet, and so on. We don't discuss these individual variants in this book because the core idea behind them remains the same. You are encouraged to read the original papers for a deeper understanding of the subject.

11.2.4 PyTorch Lightning

Let's revisit the problem of digit classification that we looked at earlier. We primarily discussed the LeNet architecture and implemented it in PyTorch. Now, let's implement the end-to-end code for training the LeNet model. Instead of doing it in vanilla PyTorch, we use the Lightning framework because it significantly simplifies the model development and training process.

Although PyTorch has all we need to train models, there's much more to deep learning than attaching layers. When it comes to the actual training, we need to write a lot of boilerplate code, as we have seen in previous examples. This includes transferring data from CPU to GPU, implementing the training driver, and so on. Additionally, if we need to scale training/inferencing on multiple devices/machines, another set of integrations often needs to be done.

PyTorch Lightning is a solution that provides the APIs required to build models, data sets, and so on. It provides clean interfaces with hooks to be implemented. The underlying Lightning framework calls these hooks at appropriate points in the training process. The idea is that Lightning leaves the research logic to us while automating the rest of the boilerplate code. Additionally, Lightning brings in features like multi-GPU training, floating-point 16, and training on TPU inherently without requiring any code changes. More details about PyTorch Lightning can be found at https://www.pytorch-lightning.ai/tutorials.

Training a model using PyTorch Lightning involves three main components: `DataModule`, `LightningModule`, and `Trainer`. Let's see what each of these does.

DATAMODULE

`DataModule` is a shareable, reusable class that encapsulates all the steps needed to process data. All data modules must inherit from `LightningDataModule`, which provides methods to be overridden. In this specific case, we will implement MNIST as a data module. This data module can now be used across multiple experiments spanning various models and architectures.

Listing 11.11 PyTorch code for an MNIST data module

```
class MNISTDataModule(LightningDataModule):
    DATASET_DIR = "datasets"

    def __init__(self, transform=None, batch_size=100):
        super(MNISTDataModule, self).__init__()
        if transform is None:
            transform = transforms.Compose(
                [transforms.Resize((32, 32)),
                transforms.ToTensor()])
        self.transform = transform
        self.batch_size = batch_size


    def prepare_data(self):        ◄── Download, tokenizes, and prepares the raw data

        datasets.MNIST(root = MNISTDataModule.DATASET_DIR,
            train=True, download=True)
        datasets.MNIST(root=MNISTDataModule.DATASET_DIR,
            train=False, download=True)

    def setup(self, stage=None):
        train_dataset = datasets.MNIST(
            root = MNISTDataModule.DATASET_DIR, train=True,
            download=False, transform=self.transform)
        self.train_dataset, self.val_dataset = random_split(   ◄── Splits the training data set into training and validation sets
            train_dataset, [55000, 5000])

        self.test_dataset = datasets.MNIST(
            root = MNISTDataModule.DATASET_DIR, train = False,
            download = False, transform=self.transform)
```

```
    def train_dataloader(self):        <-- Creates the train data loader, which
        return DataLoader(                 provides a clean interface for iterating
            self.train_dataset, batch_size=self.batch_size,   over the data set. It handles batching,
            shuffle=True, num_workers=0)   shuffling, and fetching data via
                                           multiprocessing, all under the hood.

    def val_dataloader(self):        <-- Creates the val data loader
        return DataLoader(
            self.val_dataset, batch_size=self.batch_size,
            shuffle=False, num_workers=0)

    def test_dataloader(self):        <-- Creates the test data loader
        return DataLoader(
            self.test_dataset, batch_size=self.batch_size,
            shuffle=False, num_workers=0)

    @property
    def num_classes(self):        <-- Number of object categories in the data set
        return 10
```

LIGHTNINGMODULE

`LightningModule` essentially groups all the research code into a single module, making it self-contained. Notice the clean separation between `DataModule` and `LightningModule`—this makes it easy to train/evaluate the same model on different data sets. Similarly, different models can be easily trained/evaluated on the same data set.

A Lightning module consists of the following:

- A model or system of models defined in the `init` method
- A training loop defined in `training_step`
- A validation loop defined in `validation_step`
- A testing loop defined in `testing_step`
- Optimizers and schedulers defined in `configure_optimizers`

Let's see how we can define the LeNet classifier as a Lightning module.

Listing 11.12 PyTorch code for LeNet as a Lightning module

```
class LeNetClassifier(LightningModule):

    def __init__(self, num_classes):        <-- In the init method, we typically define
                                                the model, the criterion, and any other
                                                setup steps required for training the
                                                model.
        super(LeNetClassifier, self).__init__()
        self.save_hyperparameters()

        self.conv1 = torch.nn.Sequential(
                        torch.nn.Conv2d(
                            in_channels=1, out_channels=6,
                            kernel_size=5, stride=1),
                        torch.nn.Tanh(),
```

```
                torch.nn.AvgPool2d(kernel_size=2))
    self.conv2 = torch.nn.Sequential(
                torch.nn.Conv2d(
                    in_channels=6, out_channels=16,
                    kernel_size=5, stride=1),
                torch.nn.Tanh(),
                torch.nn.AvgPool2d(kernel_size=2))
    self.conv3 = torch.nn.Sequential(
                torch.nn.Conv2d(
                    in_channels=16, out_channels=120,
                    kernel_size=5, stride=1),
                torch.nn.Tanh())
    self.fc1 = torch.nn.Sequential(
                torch.nn.Linear(in_features=120, out_features=84),
                torch.nn.Tanh())
    self.fc2 = torch.nn.Linear(in_features=84,
        out_features=num_classes)

    self.criterion = torch.nn.CrossEntropyLoss()    # Instantiates cross-entropy loss

    self.accuracy = torchmetrics.Accuracy()

def forward(self, X):    # Implements the model's forward pass. In this case, the input is a batch of images, and the output is the logits. X.shape: [batch_size, C, H, W].
    conv_out = self.conv3(
        self.conv2(self.conv1(X)))
    batch_size = conv_out.shape[0]
    conv_out = conv_out.reshape(
        batch_size, -1)
    logits = self.fc2(self.fc1(conv_out))
    return logits    # Logits.shape: [batch_size, num_classes]


def predict(self, X):    # Runs the forward pass, performs softmax to convert the resulting logits into probabilities, and returns the class with the highest probability
    logits = self.forward(X)
    probs = torch.softmax(logits, dim=1)
    return torch.argmax(probs, 1)

def core_step(self, batch):    # Abstracts out common functionality between the training and test loops, including the running forward pass, computing loss, and accuracy
    X, y_true = batch
    y_pred_logits = self.forward(X)
    loss = self.criterion(y_pred_logits, y_true)
    accuracy = self.accuracy(y_pred_logits, y_true)
    return loss, accuracy

def training_step(self, batch, batch_idx):    # Implements the basic training step: run forward pass, compute loss, accuracy. Logs any necessary values and returns the total loss.
    loss, accuracy = self.core_step(batch)
    if self.global_step % 100 == 0:
        self.log("train_loss", loss, on_step=True, on_epoch=True)
        self.log("train_accuracy", accuracy, on_step=True, on_epoch=True)
    return loss
```

```
def validation_step(self, batch,
    batch_idx, dataset_idx=None):          <-- Implements the basic validation step:
    return self.core_step(batch)               run forward pass, compute loss and
                                               accuracy, return them.

                                               Called at the end of all test steps
                                               for each epoch. The output of every
                                               test step is available via outputs.
                                               Here we compute the average test
                                               loss and accuracy by averaging
                                               across all test batches.
def validation_epoch_end(self, outputs):   <--
    avg_loss = torch.tensor([x[0] for x in outputs]).mean()
    avg_accuracy = torch.tensor([x[1] for x in outputs]).mean()
    self.log("val_loss", avg_loss)
    self.log("val_accuracy", avg_accuracy)
    print(f"Epoch self.current_epoch,
        Val loss: avg_loss:0.2f, Accuracy: avg_accuracy:0.2f")
    return avg_loss

def configure_optimizers(self):     <-- Configures the SGD optimizer

    return torch.optim.SGD(model.parameters(), lr=0.01,
                momentum=0.9)
                                        Implements logic to save the model.
                                        We save the model with the best
def checkpoint_callback(self):     <--  val accuracy.
    return ModelCheckpoint(monitor="val_accuracy", mode="max", save_top_k=1)
```

The model is independent of the data. This allows us to potentially run the `LeNet Classifier` model on other data modules without any code changes. Note that we are not doing the following steps:

1. Moving the data to a device
2. Calling `loss.backward`
3. Calling `optimizer.backward`
4. Setting `model.train()` or `eval()`
5. Resetting the gradients
6. Implementing the trainer loop

All of these are taken care of by PyTorch Lightning, thus eliminating a lot of boilerplate code.

TRAINER

We are ready to train our model, which can be done using the `Trainer` class. This abstraction achieves the following:

- We maintain control over all aspects via PyTorch code without an added abstraction.
- The trainer uses best practices embedded by contributors and users from top AI labs.
- The trainer allows us to override any key part that we don't want automated.

Listing 11.13 PyTorch code for Trainer

```
dm = MNISTDataModule()          ← Instantiates the data set
model = LeNetClassifier(num_classes=dm.num_classes)     ← Instantiates the model
exp_dir = "/tmp/mnist"
trainer = Trainer(      ← Instantiates the trainer
        default_root_dir=exp_dir,
        callbacks=[model.checkpoint_callback()],
        gpus=torch.cuda.device_count(), # Number of GPUs to run on
        max_epochs=10,
        num_sanity_val_steps=0
    )
trainer.fit(model, dm)          ← Trains the model
```

Note that we do not write the trainer loop: we just call `trainer.fit` to train the model. Additionally, the logging automatically enables us to look at the loss and accuracy curves via TensorBoard.

Listing 11.14 PyTorch code for inferencing a model

```
X, y_true = (iter(dm.test_dataloader())).next()
with torch.no_grad():
    y_pred = model.predict(X)        ← Runs model.predict()
```

To run inferencing using the trained model, we run `model.predict` on the input.

11.3 Object detection: A brief history

Until now, we have discussed the classification problem wherein we categorize an image as 1 of *N* object categories. But in many cases, this is not sufficient to truly describe an image. Consider figure 11.11—a very realistic image with four animals standing one on top of another, posing for the camera. It would be useful to know the object categories of each of the animals and their location (bounding-box coordinates) in the image. This is referred to as the object detection/localization problem. So, how do we localize objects in images?

Let's say we could extract regions in the image so that each region contained only one object. We could then run an image classifier deep neural network (which we looked at earlier) to classify each region and select the regions with the highest confidence. This was the approach adopted by one of the first deep learning-based object detectors, a region-based CNN (R-CNN; https://arxiv.org/pdf/1311.2524.pdf). Let's look at this in more detail.

11.3.1 R-CNN

The R-CNN approach to object detection consists of three main stages:

- *Selective search to identify regions of interest*—This step uses a computer vision-based algorithm capable of extracting candidate regions. We do not go into the details

Figure 11.11 An image with multiple objects of different shapes and sizes

of the selective search; you are encouraged to go through the original paper to understand the details. Selective search generates around 2,000 region proposals per image.

- *Feature extraction*—A deep convolution neural network extracts features from each region of interest. Since deep neural networks typically take in fixed-sized inputs, the regions (which could be arbitrarily sized) are warped into a fixed size before being fed into the deep neural network.
- *Classification/Localization*—A class-specific support vector machine (SVM) is trained on the extracted features to classify the region. Additionally, bounding-box regressors are added to fine-tune the object's location within the region. During training, each region is assigned a ground-truth (GT) class based on its overlap with GT boxes. It is assigned a positive label if there is a high overlap and a negative label otherwise.

11.3.2 Fast R-CNN

One of the biggest disadvantages of the R-CNN-based approach is that we have to extract features for every region proposal independently. So, if we generate 2,000 proposals for a single image, we have to run 2,000 forward passes to extract the region features. This is prohibitively expensive and extremely slow (during both training and inference). Additionally, training is a multistage pipeline—selective search, the deep network, the SVMs on top of the features, and the bounding-box regressors—that is cumbersome to train and inference. To solve these problems, the authors of the R-CNN introduced a new technique called a Fast R-CNN (https://arxiv.org/pdf/1504.08083.pdf). It significantly improved speeds: it is 9× faster than the R-CNN during training and 213× faster at test time. Additionally, it improves the quality of object detection.

Fast R-CNN makes two major contributions:

- *Region of interest (RoI) pooling*—As mentioned, one of the fundamental issues with R-CNN is the need for multiple forward passes to extract the features for the region proposals of a single image. Instead, can we extract the features in one go? This problem is solved using RoI pooling. The Fast R-CNN uses the entire image as the input to the CNN instead of a single region proposal. Then, the RoIs (region proposal bounding boxes) are used on top of the CNN output to extract the region features in one pass. We will go into the details of RoI pooling as part of our Faster R-CNN discussion.
- *Multitask loss*—The Fast R-CNN eliminates the need to use SVMs. Instead, the deep neural network does both classification and bounding-box regression. Unlike R-CNN, which only uses deep networks for feature extraction, the Fast R-CNN is more end-to-end. It is a single architecture for region proposal feature extraction, classification, and regression.

The high-level algorithm is as follows:

1. Use selective search to generate 2,000 region proposals/RoIs per image.
2. In a single pass of the Fast R-CNN, extract all the RoI features in a single pass using RoI pooling and then classify and localize objects using the classification and regression heads.

Since the feature extraction for all the region proposals happens in one pass, this approach is significantly faster than the R-CNN, where every proposal needs a separate forward pass. Additionally, since the neural network is trained end to end—that is, asked to do classification and regression—the accuracy of object detection is also improved.

11.3.3 Faster R-CNN

Why settle for fast when we can be faster? The Fast R-CNN was significantly faster than the R-CNN. However, it still needed selective search to be run to obtain region proposals. The selective-search algorithm can only be run on CPUs. Additionally, the algorithm is slow and time-consuming. Thus it became a bottleneck. Is there a way to get rid of selective search?

The obvious idea to consider is using deep networks to generate region proposals. This is the core idea of Faster R-CNN (FRCNN; https://arxiv.org/pdf/1506.01497.pdf): it eliminates the need for selective search and lets a deep network learn the region proposals. It was one of the first near-real-time object detectors. Since we are using a deep network to learn the region proposals, the region proposals are also better. Thus the resulting accuracy of the overall architecture is also much better.

We can view the FRCNN as consisting of two core modules:

- *Region proposal network (RPN)*—This is the module responsible for generating the region proposals. RPNs are designed to efficiently predict region proposals with a wide range of scales and aspect ratios.
- *R-CNN module*—This is the same as the Fast R-CNN. It receives a bunch of region proposals and performs RoI pooling followed by classification and regression.

Another important thing to note is that the RPN and the R-CNN module share the same convolutional layers: the weights are shared rather than learning two separate networks. In the next section, we discuss the Faster R-CNN in detail.

11.4 Faster R-CNN: A deep dive

Figure 11.12 shows the high-level architecture of the FRCNN. The convolutional layers (which we also call the convolutional backbone) extract feature maps from the input image. The RPN operates on these feature maps and emits candidate RoIs. The RoI pooling layer generates a fixed-sized feature vector for each region of interest and passes it on to a set of FC layers that emit softmax probability estimates over K object classes (plus a catch-all "background" class) and four numbers representing the bounding-box coordinates for each of the K classes. Let's look at each of the components in more detail.

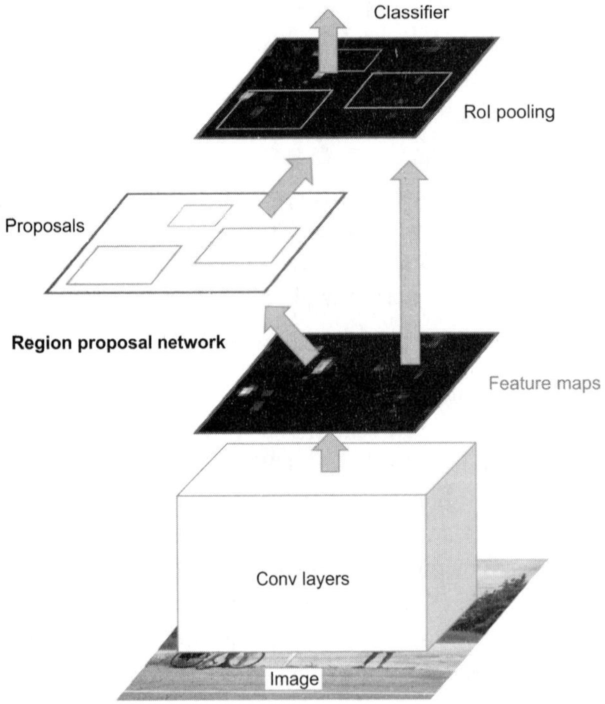

Figure 11.12 Faster R-CNN architecture. (Source: "Faster R-CNN: Toward real-time object detection with region proposal networks"; https://arxiv.org/abs/1506.01497.)

11.4.1 Convolutional backbone

In the original implementation, the FRCNN used the convolution layers of VGG-16 as the convolutional backbone for both the RPN and the R-CNN modules. There has been one minor modification: the last pooling layer after the fifth convolution layer (conv5) is removed. As we've discussed regarding VGG architectures earlier, VGG reduces the spatial size of the feature map by 2 in every conv block via max pooling. Since the last pooling layer is removed, the spatial size is reduced by a factor of $2^4 = 16$. So a 224×224 image is reduced to a 14×14 feature map at the output. Similarly, an 800×800 image would be reduced to a 50×50 feature map.

11.4.2 Region proposal network

The RPN takes in an image (of any arbitrary size) as input and emits a set of rectangular proposals that could potentially contain objects as output. The RPN operates on top of the convolutional feature map output by the last shared convolution layer. With the VGG backbone, an input image of size (h, w) is scaled down to (h/16, w/16). So each 16×16 spatial region in the input image is reduced to a single point on the convolutional feature map. Thus each point in the output convolutional feature map represents a 16×16 patch in the input image. The RPN operates on top of this feature map. Another subtle point to remember is that while each point in the convolutional feature map is chosen to correspond to a 16×16 patch, it has a significantly larger receptive field (the region in the input feature map that a particular output feature is affected by). The embedding at each point in the feature map is thus, in effect, the digest of a large receptive field.

ANCHORS

A key aspect of the object-detection problem is the variety of object sizes and shapes. Objects can range from very small (cats) to very large (elephants). Additionally, objects can have different aspect ratios. Some objects may be wide, some may be tall, and so on. A naive solution is to have a single neural network detector head capable of identifying and recognizing all these objects of varying sizes and shapes. As you can imagine, this would make the job of the neural network detector extremely complex. A simpler solution is to have a wide variety of neural network detector heads, each responsible for solving a much simpler problem. For example, one head will only focus on large, tall objects and will only fire when such objects are present in the image. The other heads will focus on other sizes and aspect ratios. We can think of each head as being responsible for doing a single simple job. This type of setup greatly aids and benefits learning.

This was the intuition behind the introduction of *anchors*. Anchors are like reference boxes of varying shapes and sizes. All proposals are made relative to anchors. Each anchor is uniquely characterized by its size and aspect ratio and is tasked with detecting similarly shaped objects in the image. At each sliding-window location, we have multiple anchors spanning different sizes and aspect ratios. The original FRCNN architecture supported nine anchor configurations spanning three sizes and three aspect ratios, thus supporting a wide variety of shapes. These correspond to anchor boxes of scales (8, 16, 32) and aspect ratios (0.5, 1.0, and 2.0), respectively (see figure 11.13). Anchors are now ubiquitous across object detectors.

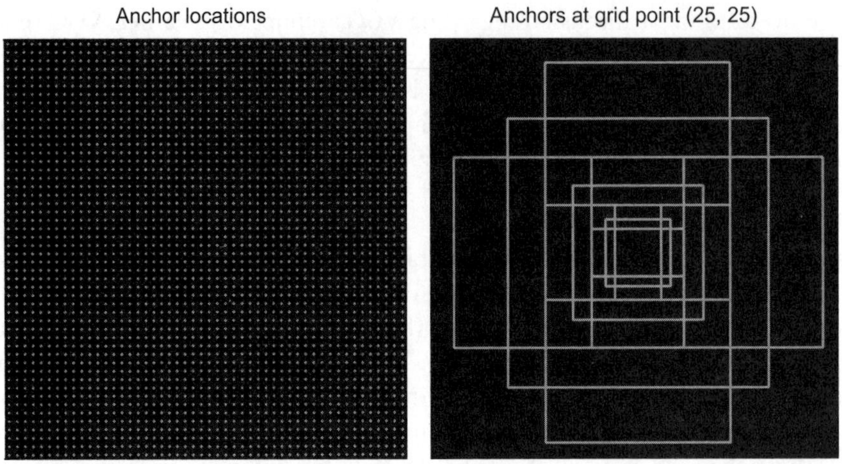

Figure 11.13 The left column shows the various grid-point locations on the output convolution feature map over which the small network is convolved. At each grid point location, we sample *k* (=9 in the original implementation) anchors across multiple sizes and aspect ratios. The right column shows the various anchors at a particular grid point.

NOTE Fully functional code for generating anchors, executable via Jupyter Notebook, can be found at http://mng.bz/nY48.

Listing 11.15 PyTorch code to generate anchors at a particular grid point

```
def generate_anchors_at_grid_point(
    ctr_x, ctr_y, subsample, scales, aspect_ratios):
    anchors = torch.zeros(
        (len(aspect_ratios) * len(scales), 4), dtype=torch.float)

    for i, scale in enumerate(scales):
        for j, aspect_ratio in enumerate(aspect_ratios):   ◄ Generates the height and width for different scales and aspect ratios

            w = subsample * scale * torch.sqrt(aspect_ratio)
            h = subsample * scale * torch.sqrt(1 / aspect_ratio)

            xtl = ctr_x - w / 2   ◄ Generates a bounding box centered around (ctr_x, ctr_y) with width w, and height h
            ytl = ctr_y - h / 2
            xbr = ctr_x + w / 2
            ybr = ctr_y + h / 2

            index = i * len(aspect_ratios) + j
            anchors[index] = torch.tensor([xtl, ytl, xbr, ybr])
    return anchors
```

Listing 11.16 PyTorch code to generate all anchors for a given image

```
def generate_all_anchors(
        input_img_size, subsample, scales, aspect_ratios):
    _, h, w = input_img_size
    conv_feature_map_size = (h//subsample, w//subsample)

    all_anchors = []

    ctr_x = torch.arange(
        subsample/2, conv_feature_map_size[1]*subsample+1, subsample)
    ctr_y = torch.arange(
        subsample/2, conv_feature_map_size[0]*subsample+1, subsample)

    for y in ctr_y:
        for x in ctr_x:
            all_anchors.append(
                generate_anchors_at_grid_point(
                    x, y, subsample, scales, aspect_ratios))

    all_anchors = torch.cat(all_anchors)
    return all_anchors

input_img_size = (3, 800, 800)
c, height, width = input_img_size
scales = torch.tensor([8, 16, 32], dtype=torch.float)
aspect_ratios = torch.tensor([0.5, 1, 2])
subsample = 16
anchors = generate_all_anchors(input_img_size, subsample, scales, aspect_ratios)
```

This isn't the most efficient way to generate anchors. We've written simple code to ease understanding.

Generates anchor boxes centered at every point in the conv feature map, which corresponds to a 16 × 16 (subsample, subsample) region in the input

Uses a function defined in listing 11.15

Defines config parameters and generates anchors

The RPN slides a small network over the output convolution feature map. The small network operates on an $n \times n$ spatial window of the convolution feature map. At each sliding-window location, it generates a lower-dimensional feature vector (512 dimensions for VGG) that is fed into a box-regression layer (reg) and a box-classification layer (cls). For each of the anchor boxes centered at that sliding window location, the classifier predicts *objectness*: a value from 0 to 1, where 1 indicates the presence of the object and the regressor predicts the region proposal relative to the anchor box. This architecture is naturally implemented with an $n \times n$ convolutional layer followed by two sibling 1×1 convolutional layers (for reg and cls), respectively. The original implementation in the FRCNN paper uses $n = 3$, which results in an effective receptive field of 228 pixels when using the VGG backbone. Figure 11.14 illustrates this in detail. Note that this network consists of only convolutional layers. Such an architecture is called a *fully convolutional network* (FCN). FCNs do not have an input size restriction. Because they

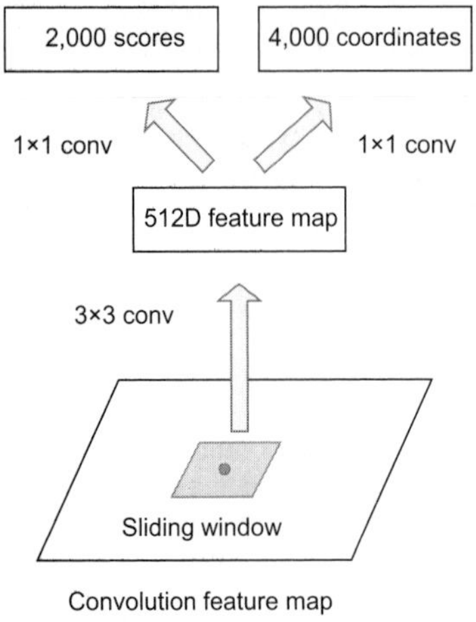

Figure 11.14 RPN architecture. From each sliding window, a 512-dimensional feature vector is generated using 3×3 convs. A 1×1 conv layer (classifier) takes the 512-dimensional feature vector as input and generates $2k$ scores (denoting the presence/absence of an object), where k is the number of anchors. Similarly, another 1×1 conv layer (regressor) generates $4k$ bounding-box coordinates from the 512-dimensional feature vector.

consist of only convolution layers, they can work with arbitrary-sized inputs. In the FCN, the combination of the $n \times n$ and 1×1 layers is equivalent to applying an FC layer over every embedding at each point in the convolutional feature map. Also, because we are convolving a convolutional network on top of the feature map to generate the regression and classification scores, the convolutional weights are common/shared across different positions on the feature map. This makes the approach translation invariant. A cat at the top of the image and a cat at the bottom of the image are picked up by the same anchor configuration (scale, aspect ratio) if they are similarly sized.

NOTE Fully functional code for the fully convolutional network of the RPN, executable via Jupyter Notebook, can be found at http://mng.bz/nY48.

Listing 11.17 PyTorch code for the FCN of the RPN

```
class RPN_FCN(nn.Module):

    def __init__(self, k, in_channels=512):
        super(RPN_FCN, self).__init__()
        self.conv = nn.Sequential(
            nn.Conv2d(
                in_channels, 512, kernel_size=3,
                stride=1, padding=1),
            nn.ReLU(True))
        self.cls = nn.Conv2d(512, 2*k, kernel_size=1)
        self.reg = nn.Conv2d(512, 4*k, kernel_size=1)

    def forward(self, x):
        out = self.conv(x)
```

Instantiates the small network that is convolved over the output conv feature map. It consists of a 3×3 conv layer followed by a 1×1 conv layer for classification and another 1×1 conv layer for regression.

Output of the backbone: a convolutional feature map of size (batch_size, in_channels, h, w)

```
        rpn_cls_scores = self.cls(out).view(
            x.shape[0], -1, 2)
        rpn_loc = self.reg(out).view(
            x.shape[0], -1, 4)
        return rpn_cls_scores          ,rpn_loc
```

Converts (batch_size, h, w, 2k) to (batch_size, h*w*k, 2)

Converts (batch_size, h, w, 4k) to (batch_size, h*w*k, 4)

(batch_size, num_anchors, 4) tensor representing the box coordinates relative to the anchor box

(batch_size, num_anchors, 2) tensor representing the classification score for each anchor box

GENERATING GT FOR AN RPN

So far, we have generated many anchor bounding boxes and a neural network capable of generating the classification and regression offsets for every anchor. While training the RPN, we need to provide a target (GT) that both the classifier and regressor should predict for each anchor box. To do so, we need to look at the objects in the image and assign them to relevant anchors that contain the object. The idea is as follows: out of the thousands of anchors,*the anchors that contain most of the object should try predicting and localizing the object.* We saw earlier that the intuition behind creating anchors was to ensure that each anchor is responsible for one particular type of object (shape, aspect ratio). Thus it makes sense that only anchors that contain the object are responsible for classifying it.

To measure whether the object lies within the anchor, we rely on intersection over union (IoU) scores. The IoU between two bounding boxes is defined as $\frac{area\ of\ overlap}{area\ of\ union}$. So, if the two bounding boxes are very similar, their overlap is high, and their union is close to the overlap, resulting in a high IoU. If the two bounding boxes are varied, then their area of overlap is minimal, resulting in a low IoU (see figure 11.15).

$$IoU = \frac{area\ of\ hatched\ shaded\ region}{total\ area\ of\ shaded\ region}$$

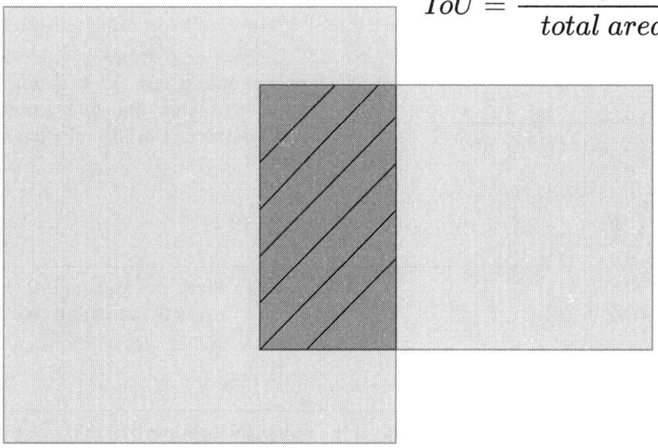

Figure 11.15 Intersection over the union between two bounding boxes. It is equivalent to the intersection of the two areas divided by the union of the two areas.

FRCNN provides some guidelines for assigning labels to the anchor boxes:

- We assign a positive label 1 (which represents an object being present in the anchor box) to two kinds of anchors:
  - The anchor(s) with the greatest IoU overlap with a GT box
  - An anchor that has an IoU overlap greater than 0.7 with the GT box
- We assign a negative label 0 (which represents no object being present in the anchor box, implying that it contains only background) to a non-positive anchor if its IoU ratio is less than 0.3 for all GT boxes.
- Anchors that are neither positive nor negative do not contribute to the training objective.

Note that a single GT object may assign positive labels to multiple anchors. These outputs must be suppressed later to prevent duplicate detections (we discuss this in the subsequent sections). Also, any anchor box that lies partially outside the image is ignored.

> **NOTE** Fully functional code for assigning GT labels to anchor boxes, executable via Jupyter Notebook, can be found at http://mng.bz/nY48.

Listing 11.18 PyTorch code to assign GT labels for each anchor box

```
valid_indices = torch.where(
    (anchors[:, 0] >=0) &
    (anchors[:, 1] >=0) &
    (anchors[:, 2] <=width) &
    (anchors[:, 3] <=height))[0]

rpn_valid_labels = -1 * torch.ones_like(
    valid_indices, dtype=torch.int)

valid_anchor_bboxes = anchors[valid_indices]

ious = torchvision.ops.box_iou(
    gt_bboxes, valid_anchor_bboxes)

assert ious.shape == torch.Size(
    [gt_bboxes.shape[0], valid_anchor_bboxes.shape[0]])

gt_ious_max = torch.max(ious, dim=1)[0]

# Find all the indices where the IOU = highest GT IOU

gt_ious_argmax = torch.where(

    gt_ious_max.unsqueeze(1).repeat(1, gt_ious_max.shape[1]) == ious)[1]
```

Code annotations:

- Finds valid anchors that lie completely inside the image
- Assigns s label of -1 (not any class) for each valid anchor
- Obtains the valid anchor boxes
- Tensor of shape (num_gt_bboxes, num_valid_anchor_bboxes), representing the IoU between the GT and anchors
- Finds the highest IoU for every GT bounding box
- Finds all the indices where the IOU = highest GT IOU

```
anchor_ious_argmax = torch.argmax(ious, dim=0)

anchor_ious = ious[anchor_ious_argmax, torch.arange(len(anchor_ious_argmax))]

pos_iou_threshold  = 0.7
neg_iou_threshold = 0.3

rpn_valid_labels[anchor_ious < neg_iou_threshold] = 0

rpn_valid_labels[anchor_ious > pos_iou_threshold] = 1

rpn_valid_labels[gt_ious_argmax] = 1
```

Finds the highest IoU for every anchor box

Assigns 0 (background) for negative anchors where IoU < 0.3

Assigns 1 (objectness) for positive anchor where IoU > 0.7

For every GT bounding box, assigns the anchor with the highest IoU as a positive anchor

DEALING WITH IMBALANCE

Given our strategy of assigning labels to anchors, notice that the number of negative anchors is significantly greater than the number of positive anchors. For example, for the example image, we obtained only 24 positive anchors as opposed to 7,439 negative anchors. If we train directly on such an imbalanced data set, neural networks can typically learn a local minimum by classifying every anchor as a negative anchor. In our example, if we predicted every anchor to be a negative anchor, our resulting accuracy would be 7439/(7439 + 22): 99.7%. However, the resulting neural network is practically useless because it has not learned anything. In other words, the imbalance will lead to bias toward the dominant class. To deal with this imbalance, there are typically three strategies:

- *Undersampling*—Sample less of the dominant class.
- *Oversampling*—Sample more of the less-dominant class.
- *Weighted loss*—Set the cost for misclassifying less-dominant classes much higher than the dominant class.

FRCNN utilizes the idea of undersampling. For a single image, there are multiple positive and negative anchors. From these thousands of anchors, we randomly sample 256 anchors in an image to compute the loss function, where the sampled positive and negative anchors have a ratio of up to 1:1. If there are fewer than 128 positive samples in an image, we pad the minibatch with negative ones.

ASSIGNING TARGETS TO ANCHOR BOXES

We have seen how to sample and assign labels to anchors. The next question is how to come up with the regression targets:

- *Case 1: label* = −1—Unsampled/invalid anchor. These do not contribute to the training objective, so regression targets do not matter.
- *Case 2: label* = 0—Background anchor. These anchors do not contain any objects, so they also should not contribute to regression.
- *Case 3: label* = 1—Positive anchor. These anchors contain objects. We need to generate regression targets for these anchors.

Let's consider only the case of positive anchors. The key intuition here is that *the anchors already contain a majority of the object.* Otherwise, they wouldn't have become positive anchors. So there is already significant overlap between the anchor and the object in question. Therefore it makes sense to learn the offset from the anchor bounding box to the object bounding box. The regressor is tasked with learning this offset: that is, what delta we must make to the anchor bounding box for it to become the object bounding box. the FRCNN adopts the following parameterization:

$$
\begin{aligned}
t_x &= (x - x_a)/w_a \\
t_y &= (y - y_a)/h_a \\
t_w &= log(w/w_a) \\
t_h &= log(h/h_a)
\end{aligned}
\tag{11.2}
$$

where x, y, w, and h denote the GT bounding box's center coordinates and its width and height, and x_a, y_a, w_a, and h_a denote the anchor bounding box's center coordinates and its width and height. t_x, t_y, t_w, and t_h are the regression targets. The regressor is, in effect, learning to predict the delta between the anchor bounding box and the GT bounding box.

NOTE Fully functional code for assigning regression targets to anchor boxes, executable via Jupyter Notebook, can be found at http://mng.bz/nY48.

Listing 11.19 PyTorch code to assign regression targets for each anchor box

```
def transform_bboxes(bboxes):          ← (n, 4) tensor in (xtl, ytl, xbr, ybr) format
    height = bboxes[:, 3] - bboxes[:, 1]
    width = bboxes[:, 2] - bboxes[:, 0]
    x_ctr = bboxes[:, 0] + width / 2
    y_ctr = bboxes[:, 1] +  height /2

    return torch.stack(          ← (n, 4 tensor) in (x, y, w, h) format

        [x_ctr, y_ctr, width, height], dim=1)


def get_regression_targets(roi_bboxes, gt_bboxes):     ← (n, 4) tensors representing the bounding boxes for the region of interest and GT, respectively

    assert roi_bboxes.shape == gt_bboxes.shape
    roi_bboxes_t = transform_bboxes(roi_bboxes)
    gt_bboxes_t = transform_bboxes(gt_bboxes)
    tx = (gt_bboxes_t[:, 0] - roi_bboxes_t[:, 0]) / roi_bboxes_t[:, 2]
    ty = (gt_bboxes_t[:, 1] - roi_bboxes_t[:, 1]) / roi_bboxes_t[:, 3]
    tw = torch.log(gt_bboxes_t[:, 2] / roi_bboxes_t[:, 2])
    th = torch.log(gt_bboxes_t[:, 3] / roi_bboxes_t[:, 3])


    return  torch.stack([tx, ty, tw, th], dim=1)     ← (n, 4) tensor containing the regression targets
```

RPN LOSS FUNCTION

We have defined the RPN fully convolutional network and how we can generate labels and regression targets for the outputs of the RPN FCN. Now we need to discuss the loss function that enables us to train the RPN. As you would expect, there are two loss terms:

- *Classification loss*—Applies to both the positive and negative anchors. We use the standard cross-entropy loss used in any standard classifier.
- *Regression loss*—Applies *only* to the positive anchors. Here we use smooth L1 loss, which is defined as

$$L_{1;smooth} = \begin{cases} 0.5(x_n - y_n)^2/beta, & \text{if } |x_n - y_n| < beta \\ |x_n - y_n| - 0.5 * beta, & \text{otherwise} \end{cases} \tag{11.3}$$

We can think of smooth L1 loss as a combination of L1 and L2 loss. If the value is < beta, it behaves like an L2 loss (mean squared error [MSE]). Otherwise, it behaves like an L1 loss. In the case of the FRCNN, beta is set to 1. The intuition behind this is simple. If we use pure L2 loss (MSE), then higher loss terms contribute to exponential loss because of the quadratic nature of the loss. This can lead to a bias where loss can be reduced by focusing on high-value items. Instead, if we use pure L1 loss, the higher loss terms still contribute more loss, but the effect is linear instead of quadratic. This still has a slightly worse bias toward higher loss terms. We get the best of both worlds by using L2 loss when the loss values are small and L1 loss when the loss values are large. When the loss value is small, because we are using L2 loss, its contribution is exponential/quadratic. And when the loss value is high, it still contributes linearly via L1 loss. Thus the network is incentivized to pay attention to low- and high-loss items.

Overall loss for an image can be defined as follows:

$$\begin{aligned} L_{cls} &= \frac{\sum_i CrossEntropy(p_i, p_i^*)}{N_{cls}} \\ L_{reg} &= \frac{\sum_i p_i^* L_{1;smooth}(t_i, t_i^*)}{N_{pos}} \\ L_{RPN} &= L_{cls} + \lambda L_{reg} \end{aligned} \tag{11.4}$$

where, p_i is the predicted objectness probability for the anchor i. p_i^* is the true objectness label for anchor i. It is 1 if the anchor is positive and 0 if the anchor is negative. $t_i = (t_x, t_y, t_w, t_h)$ are the regression predictions for anchor i, $t_i^* = (t_x^*, t_y^*, t_w^*, t_h^*)$ are the regression targets for anchor i, N_{cls} is the number of anchors, and N_{pos} is the number of positive anchors.

NOTE Fully functional code for the RPN loss function, executable via Jupyter Notebook, can be found at http://mng.bz/nY48.

Listing 11.20 PyTorch code for the RPN loss function

```
def rpn_loss(
    rpn_cls_scores, rpn_loc, rpn_labels,
    rpn_loc_targets, lambda_ = 10):          <-- rpn_cls_scores: (num_anchors, 2) tensor representing RPN classifier scores for each anchor. rpn_loc: (num_anchors, 4) tensor representing RPN regressor predictions for each anchor. rpn_labels: (num_anchors) representing the class for each anchor (-1, 0, 1). rpn_loc_targets: (num_anchors, 4) tensor representing RPN regressor targets for each anchor.

    classification_criterion = nn.CrossEntropyLoss(

        ignore_index=-1)        <-- Ignores -1 as they are not sampled

    reg_criterion = nn.SmoothL1Loss(reduction="sum")

    cls_loss = classification_criterion(rpn_cls_scores, rpn_labels)

    positive_indices = torch.where(rpn_labels==1)[0]     <-- Finds the positive anchors
    pred_positive_anchor_offsets = rpn_loc[positive_indices]
    gt_positive_loc_targets = rpn_loc_targets[positive_indices]
    reg_loss = reg_criterion(
        pred_positive_anchor_offsets,
        gt_positive_loc_targets) / len(positive_indices)
    return {
        "rpn_cls_loss": cls_loss,
        "rpn_reg_loss": reg_loss,
        "rpn_total_loss": cls_loss + lambda_* reg_loss

    }
```

GENERATING REGION PROPOSALS

We have so far discussed how the RPN works. The RPN predicts objectness and the regression offsets for every anchor. The next task is to generate good region proposals/RoIs and use them for training the R-CNN module. Since we are emitting objectness and regression offsets for every anchor, we have thousands of predictions. We cannot use all of them as RoIs. We need to generate the best RoIs from these scores and offsets to train our R-CNN. An obvious way to do this is to rely on the objectness scores: the higher the objectness score, the greater the likelihood that it contains an object and thus is a good RoI. Before we get there, we must do some basic processing steps:

1 Convert the predicted offsets to bounding boxes. This is done by reversing the sequence of transformations

$$
\begin{aligned}
x^* &= t_x^* * w_a + x_a \\
y^* &= t_y^* * h_a + y_a \\
w^* &= e^{t_w^*} * w_a \\
h^* &= e^{t_h^*} * h_a
\end{aligned}
\tag{11.5}
$$

where x^*, y^*, w^*, and h^* denote the predicted bounding box's center coordinates and its width and height, and t_x^*, t_y^*, t_w^*, and t_h^* are the RPN loc predictions. The bounding boxes are then converted back into `xtl`, `ytl`, `xbr`, `ybr` format.

2. The predicted bounding boxes can lie partially outside the image. We clip all the predicted bounding boxes to within the image.
3. Remove any predicted bounding boxes with height or width less than `min_roi_threshold`.

Once these processing steps are done, we sort the predicted bounding boxes by objectness score and select N candidates. $N = 12000$ during training and $N = 6000$ while testing.

NOTE Fully functional generating region proposals from the RPN output, executable via Jupyter Notebook, can be found at http://mng.bz/nY48.

Listing 11.21 PyTorch code to generate region proposals from RPN output

```
rois = generate_bboxes_from_offset(rpn_loc, anchors)

rois = rois.clamp(min=0, max=width)        ← Clips the ROIs

roi_heights = rois[:, 3] - rois[:, 1]      ← Threshold based on min_roi_threshold
roi_widths = rois[:, 2] - rois[:, 0]
min_roi_threshold = 16

valid_idxes = torch.where((roi_heights > min_roi_threshold) &
    (roi_widths > min_roi_threshold))[0]
rois = rois[valid_idxes]
valid_cls_scores = rpn_loc[valid_idxes]

objectness_scores = valid_cls_scores[:, 1]

sorted_idx = torch.argsort(      ← Sorts based on objectness
    objectness_scores, descending=True)
n_train_pre_nms = 12000
n_val_pre_nms = 300

rois = rois[sorted_idx][:n_train_pre_nms]
    ← Selects the top regions of interest. Shape: (n_train_pre_nms, 4).

objectness_scores = objectness_scores[
    sorted_idx][:n_train_pre_nms]
    ← Selects the top objectness scores. Shape: (n_train_pre_nms,).
```

NON-MAXIMAL SUPPRESSION (NMS)

Many of the proposals will overlap. We are effectively selecting anchors at a stride of 16 pixels. Therefore even a reasonably sized object is picked up by multiple anchors, each of which will try to predict the object independently. We can see this overlapping nature when we look at the positive anchors in figure 11.16. We want to choose the most effective set of RoIs. But it is evident that choosing all the similar proposals does

Figure 11.16 For the image under consideration, we have 24 positive anchors and 7,439 negative anchors. Training directly on such an imbalanced data set can lead to the network learning a local minimum where every anchor is classified as negative. To prevent this, the FRCNN under-samples the negative anchors before training.

not make a good set of RoIs because they carry redundant information. To address this problem, we use a technique called *non-maximal suppression* (NMS). NMS is an algorithm that suppresses highly overlapping bounding boxes. The algorithm takes in bounding boxes and scores and works as follows.

Algorithm 11.1 Non-maximal suppression

Input: A list of bounding boxes B, corresponding scores S, and overlap threshold N
Output: A list of filtered bounding boxes D
while likelihood is increasing **do**
  Select bounding box with highest confidence score
  Remove it from B and add it to the final list D
  Compare selected bounding box with remaining boxes in B using IoU
  Remove all bounding boxes from B with IoU > threshold
end while
return D

We use NMS with a 0.7 threshold to suppress the highly overlapping RoIs and choose the top N RoIs post-NMS to train the R-CNN. $N = 2000$ during training, and $N = 300$ while testing. Figure 11.17 shows bounding boxes on a sample image before and after NMS.

NOTE Fully functional code for NMS, executable via Jupyter Notebook, can be found at http://mng.bz/nY48.

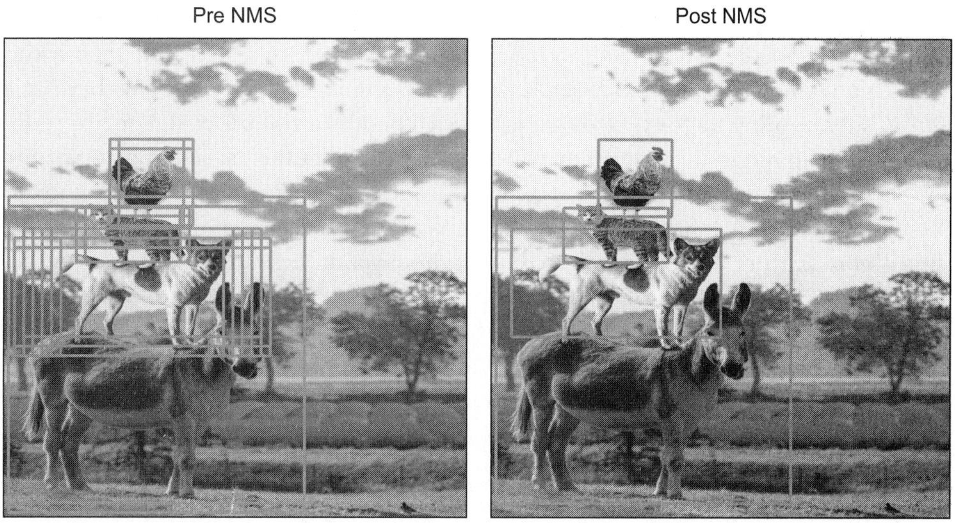

Figure 11.17 The left column shows the bounding boxes (24) before NMS. The right column shows the bounding boxes (4) that remain after NMS.

Listing 11.22 PyTorch code for NMS of RoIs

```
n_train_post_nms = 2000
n_val_post_nms = 300
nms_threshold = 0.7

post_nms_indices = torchvision.ops.nms(        ← Calls NMS implemented by torchvision
    rois, objectness_scores, nms_threshold)

post_nms_rois = rois[post_nms_indices[:n_train_post_nms]]
```

11.4.3 Fast R-CNN

In the previous section, we saw how the RPN network takes an input image and emits a set of regions of interest that are likely to contain objects. Now let's discuss the second leg of the FRCNN architecture, which takes in the RoIs and generates class probabilities and bounding-box coordinates for each object in the image. We briefly discussed this earlier. Here we revisit it in greater detail.

We are given a set of RoIs (some of which contain the object). Our task is to train an object detector capable of localizing the objects. To do this, we need to extract the features corresponding to each RoI and pass them through a neural network (classifier and regressor) that learns to predict the class and the regression targets. The R-CNN solved this in a naive way: it extracted each RoI one at a time, warped it to make it a fixed size, and passed it through a deep CNN to extract the features corresponding to the RoI. Each RoI required a separate forward pass, making the approach very slow. The question, as always, is: can we do better?

ROI POOLING

Let's consider the convolutional backbone. It processes the whole image with several conv and max pooling layers to produce a conv feature map. We have also seen a subsampling factor of 16: that is, 16×16 pixels in the input image are reduced to a single point in the feature map. Also remember that the embedding at every grid point on the feature map is the representation/digest of a region in the input image.

Key idea 1 is that the features corresponding to each RoI are already present in the conv feature map, and we can extract them via the feature map. For example, say our RoI is (0, 0, 256, 256). We know that the (0, 0, 256, 256) region in the input image is represented by (0, 0, 256/16, 256/16): that is, the (0, 0, 16, 16) region in the conv feature map. Since the embedding for a point in the conv feature map is a digest of the receptive field, we can use these features directly as the features of the RoI. So to obtain the features for an RoI of (0, 0, 256, 256), we take all the embeddings corresponding to the region (0, 0, 16, 16) in the conv feature map. Since we are performing this feature extraction directly on the convolutional feature map, which is obtained for the entire image, we can obtain the RoI features for all the RoIs in a single forward pass. This eliminates the need for multiple forward passes.

Key idea 2 is as follows. We discussed a clever way of extracting the features corresponding to each RoI, and we want to use these features to train our classifier and regressor. However, there is a problem. As we know, RoIs are different sizes. And different-sized RoIs will lead to different feature embedding sizes. For example, if our RoI is (0, 0, 256, 256), our RoI feature embeddings are (16, 16, 512): that is, all the embeddings (of size 512) in the (0, 0, 16, 16) region of the conv feature map. If our RoI is (0, 0, 128, 128), then our RoI feature embeddings are (8, 8, 512): all the embeddings in the (0, 0, 8, 8) region of the conv feature map. And we know that neural networks typically need same-sized input. So how do we deal with input embeddings of different sizes? The answer is *RoI pooling*.

Let's fix the size of the input ROI feature map that goes into the neural network. Our task is to reduce variable-sized RoI feature maps to a fixed size. If the fixed feature map size is set to be H, W, and our RoI corresponds to (r, c, h, w) in the conv feature map, we divide h and w into equal-sized blocks of size h/H and w/W, respectively, and apply max pooling on these blocks to obtain a H, W feature map. Going back to our example, let's fix $H = W = 4$. Our expected fixed feature map size is (4, 4, 512). So when our RoI is (0, 0, 256, 256), our RoI feature embeddings are (16, 16, 512): $h = w = 16$. We divide the 16×16 region into four (16/4, 16/4) regions and perform max pooling on each region to obtain a fixed-size (4, 4, 512) feature. Similarly, when our RoI is (0, 0, 128, 128), $h = w = 8$. We divide the 8×8 region into four (8/4, 8/4) regions and perform max pooling to obtain the fixed-size (4, 4, 512) feature.

Astute readers will notice that we have carefully chosen our RoIs so that they are multiples of H and W, resulting in integer values for h/H and w/W, respectively. But in reality, this rarely happens. h/H and w/W are often floating-point numbers. What do we do in this case? The answer is *quantization*: that is, we choose the integer closest to h/H and w/W, respectively (floor operation, in the original implementation). This has been improved on by RoIAlign, which uses bilinear interpolation instead of quantization. We do not get into the details of RoIAlign here.

In effect, if we have a large RoI, we divide the feature map into a fixed number of large regions and perform max pooling. And when we have a small RoI, we divide the feature map into a fixed number of small regions and perform max pooling. The size of the region used for pooling can change, but the output size remains fixed. The dimension of the RoI pooling output doesn't depend on the size of the input feature map or the size of the RoIs: it's determined solely by the number of sections we divide the RoI into—H and W (see figure 11.18).

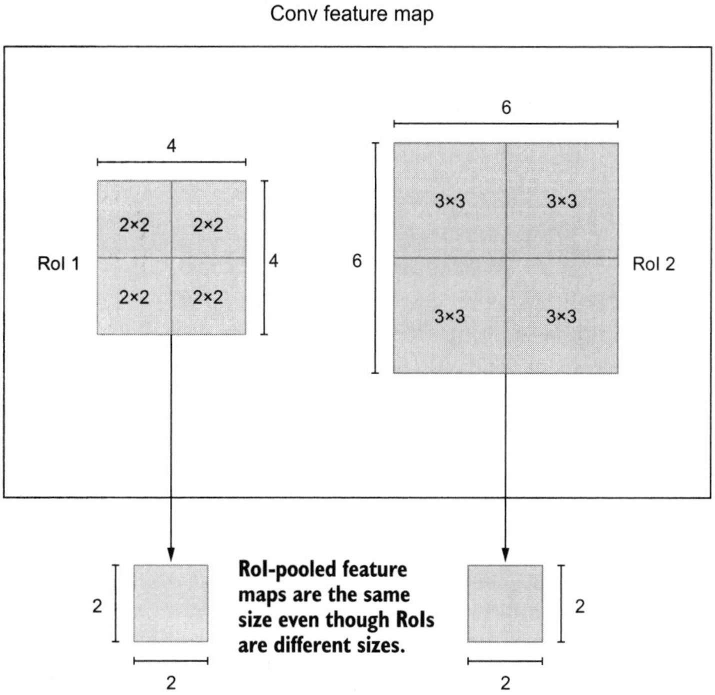

Figure 11.18 A conv feature map with two regions of interest of different sizes. RoI pooling extracts a fixed-sized output feature map (2 × 2 in this image) from each of the RoIs in a single pass via max pooling. This enables us to extract fixed-sized representative feature vectors for each RoI, which are then fed into further classifier and regressor layers for classification and localization.

Thus, the purpose of RoI pooling is to perform max pooling on inputs of non-uniform sizes to obtain fixed-size feature maps. The Fast R-CNN and Faster R-CNN use 7×7 as the fixed feature map size.

FAST R-CNN ARCHITECTURE

Given the conv feature map and a set of RoIs, we have seen how the RoI pooling layer extracts a fixed-length feature vector from the feature map. Each feature vector is fed into a sequence of FC layers that finally branch into two sibling output layers: a classifier that produces softmax probability estimates over K object classes plus a catch-all "background" class, and a regressor that produces four real-valued numbers for each of the K object classes.

GENERATING GT FOR THE FAST R-CNN

For every image, we have a list of RoIs generated by the RPN and a list of GT bounding boxes. How do we generate the GT and regression targets for each RoI? The idea remains the same as for our RPN: we use IoU scores. The algorithm is as follows:

1. Compute the IoU between all RoIs and GT boxes.
2. For each RoI, determine the GT bounding box with the highest IoU.
3. If the highest IoU is greater than a threshold (0.5), assign the corresponding GT label as the label for the RoI.
4. If the IoU is between [0.1, 0.5], assign the background label. Using a lower bound of 0.1 ensures that certain RoIs with small intersections with the GT are selected as background. This is helpful as it chooses hard examples for background; it is a form of hard negative mining.

NOTE Fully functional code for the Fast R-CNN RoI head, executable via Jupyter Notebook, can be found at http://mng.bz/nY48.

Listing 11.23 PyTorch code for the Fast R-CNN RoI head

```
class Fast_RCNN_ROI_Head(nn.Module):
    def __init__(self, num_classes, H, W, subsample=16, embedding_size=512):

        super(Fast_RCNN_ROI_Head, self).__init__()

        self.num_classes = num_classes
        self.H = H
        self.W = W
        self.embedding_size = embedding_size
        self.subsample = 16

        self.roi_head_classifier = nn.Sequential(
            nn.Linear(H*W*embedding_size, 4096),
            nn.ReLU(True),
            nn.Linear(4096, 4096),
            nn.ReLU(True),
        )
        self.cls = torch.nn.Linear(4096, num_classes+1)    # num_classes + background

        self.reg = torch.nn.Linear(4096, (num_classes+1)*4)


    def forward(self, x, rois):    # x : (1, c, h, w) tensor representing the conv feature map. rois: (n, 4) tensor representing bounding boxes of RoIs

        assert x.shape[0] == 1 # This code only supports batch size of 1
        roi_pooled_features = torchvision.ops.roi_pool(
            x, [rois], output_size=(self.H, self.W), spatial_scale=1/subsample)
        roi_pooled_features = roi_pooled_features.view(
            -1, self.H*self.W*self.embedding_size)
```

```
        fc_out = self.roi_head_classifier(roi_pooled_features)
        roi_cls_scores = self.cls(fc_out)
        roi_loc = self.reg(fc_out)

        return roi_cls_scores, roi_loc
```

roi_cls_scores: (n, num_classes+1) tensor representing classification scores for each RoI. roi_loc: (n, (num_classes + 1) * 4) tensor representing the regression scores for each RoI

TRAINING THE FAST R-CNN

The RPN generates about 2,000 RoIs per image. Due to computational constraints, we cannot use all N RoIs. Instead, we sample a subset of them. The training minibatches are sampled hierarchically, first by sampling K images and then by sampling R/K RoIs from each image. R is set to 128 in the FRCNN. For this discussion, we assume that $K = 1$: that is, we have a single image per minibatch. So, given the RoIs for a single image, how do we sample 128 RoIs from it?

A simple solution is to randomly sample 128 RoIs. However, this runs into the same data-imbalance issue that we discussed earlier: we end up sampling backgrounds a lot more frequently than the classes. To solve this problem, we adopt a sampling strategy similar to before. In particular, for a single image, we sample 128 RoIs such that the ratio of background to object is 0.75:0.25. If fewer than 32 RoIs contain the objects, we pad the minibatch with more background RoIs.

ASSIGNING TARGETS TO ROI BOXES

Just as in the case of the RPN, we generate regression targets as offsets of the GT box from the region of interest for all RoIs that contain objects. For all background RoIs, the regression targets are not applicable.

FAST R-CNN LOSS FUNCTION

We have defined the Fast R-CNN network and how we can generate labels and regression targets for its outputs. We need to discuss the loss function that enables us to train the Fast R-CNN. As you would expect, there are two loss terms:

- *Classification loss*— We use the standard cross-entropy loss used in any standard classifier.
- *Regression loss*—The regression loss applies *only* to the object RoIs: background RoIs do not contribute to regression. Here we use the smooth L1 loss as we did in the RPN.

Thus the overall loss for a single RoI can be defined as follows:

$$
\begin{aligned}
L_{cls} &= CrossEntropy(p, u) \\
L_{reg} &= L_{1;smooth}(t^u, v) \\
L_{RCNN} &= L_{cls} + \lambda\,[u > 0] L_{reg}
\end{aligned}
\tag{11.6}
$$

where p is the predicted label for the RoI, u is the true label for the RoI, $t^u = (t_x, t_y, t_w, t_h)$ are the regression predictions for class u, and $v = (v_x, v_y, v_w, v_h)$ are the regression targets.

The overall loss can therefore be defined as

$$L_{cls} = \frac{\sum_i CrossEntropy(p_i, p_i^*)}{N_{roi}}$$
$$L_{reg} = \frac{\sum_{\{\forall i | p_i^* != 0\}} L_{1;smooth}(t_i, t_i^*)}{N_{pos}}$$
$$L_{RCNN} = L_{cls} + \lambda L_{reg} \tag{11.7}$$

where p_i are the prediction probabilities for the RoI i, p_i^* is the true label for RoI i; $t_i = (t_x, t_y, t_w, t_h)$ are the regression predictions for RoI i corresponding to class p_i^*, $t_i^* = (t_x^*, t_y^*, t_w^*, t_h^*)$ are the regression targets for RoI i, $t_i^* = (t_x^*, t_y^*, t_w^*, t_h^*)$ are the regression targets for RoI i, and N_{pos} is the number of object RoIs (non-background RoIs).

NOTE Fully functional code for the Fast R-CNN loss function, executable via Jupyter Notebook, can be found at http://mng.bz/nY48.

Listing 11.24 PyTorch code for the Fast R-CNN loss function

```
def rcnn_loss(
    roi_cls_scores,        ← (128, num_classes) tensor: RCNN classifier scores for each RoI
    roi_loc,    ← (128, num_classes*4) tensor: RCNN regressor predictions for each class, RoI
    roi_labels,      ← (128,) tensor: true class for each RoI
    rcnn_loc_targets,      ← (128, 4) tensor: RoI regressor targets for each RoI
    lambda_ = 1):

    classification_criterion = nn.CrossEntropyLoss()
    reg_criterion = nn.SmoothL1Loss(reduction="sum")

    cls_loss = classification_criterion(roi_cls_scores, roi_labels)

    pos_roi_idxes = torch.where(roi_labels>0)[0]      ← Finds the positive RoIs
    pred_all_offsets = roi_loc[pos_roi_idxes]

    num_pos_rois = len(pos_roi_idxes)
    pred_all_offsets = pred_all_offsets.view(      ← (n, num_classes*4) to
        num_pos_rois, -1, 4)                          (n, num_classes, 4)

    pred_cls_offsets = pred_all_offsets[
        torch.arange(num_pos_rois) , roi_labels[pos_roi_idxes]]

    gt_offsets = rcnn_loc_targets[pos_roi_idxes]

    reg_loss = reg_criterion(pred_cls_offsets, gt_offsets) / num_pos_rois
    return {
        "rcnn_cls_loss": cls_loss,
        "rcnn_reg_loss": reg_loss,
        "rcnn_total_loss": cls_loss + lambda_* reg_loss

    }
```

FAST R-CNN INFERENCE

We have looked at how to train the Fast R-CNN module. Once the model is trained, the next question is how to use the model to generate output classes and bounding boxes.

The Fast R-CNN model outputs a classification score and regression offsets for every RoI. We can safely ignore the background RoIs. For the rest of the RoIs, the class with the highest probability is chosen as the output label, and the offsets corresponding to that class are chosen. We apply post-processing steps similar to that of the RPN:

1. We translate the offsets back to (`xtl`, `ytl`, `xbr`, `ybr`) format using the RoI.
2. We clip the output bounding box to within the image boundaries

We face a problem similar to before: the output probably has multiple bounding boxes corresponding to the same object. We deal with it in the same way as earlier: using NMS. There is one difference, however. In the case of the RPN, we applied a global NMS across all bounding boxes predicted by the RPN. Here, NMS is applied only across the bounding boxes belonging to the same class. This is done for all classes, which should intuitively make sense: there is no point in suppressing highly overlapping bounding boxes if the bounding boxes represent different classes.

NOTE Fully functional code for the Fast R-CNN inference, executable via Jupyter Notebook, can be found at http://mng.bz/nY48.

Listing 11.25 PyTorch code for the Fast R-CNN inference

```
def fast_rcnn_inference(
    frcnn_roi_head,          # Trained instance of Fast_RCNN_ROI_Head
    rois,                    # RoIs to inference
    conv_feature_map,        # (n, c, h, w) convolutional feature map
    nms_threshold=0.7):

    frcnn_roi_head.eval()    # Sets eval mode
    roi_cls_scores, roi_loc = frcnn_roi_head(conv_feature_map, rois)

    output_labels = torch.argmax(    # The predicted class is the class with the highest score.
        roi_cls_scores, dim=1)

    output_probs = nn.functional.softmax(
        roi_cls_scores, dim=1)[torch.arange(
            rois.shape[0]), output_labels]
    # The predicted probabilities are obtained via softmax. The highest
    # probability is chosen as the probability score for this prediction.

    output_offsets = roi_loc.view(
        rois.shape[0], -1, 4)
    # Converts locs from (n, num_classes*4) to (n, num_classes, 4)

    output_offsets = output_offsets[
        torch.arange(rois.shape[0]), output_labels]
    # Selects offsets corresponding to the predicted label

    assert output_offsets.shape == torch.Size(
        [rois.shape[0], 4])
    # Asserts that we have outputs for each RoI
```

```
output_bboxes = generate_bboxes_from_offset(      ← Converts offsets to (xtl, ytl, xbr, ybr)
    output_offsets, rois)

rois = output_bboxes.clamp(min=0, max=width)      ← Clips bounding boxes to within images

post_nms_labels, post_nms_probs, post_nms_boxes = [], [], []


for cls in range(1, frcnn_roi_head.num_classes+1):     ← 0 is background, thus ignored


    cls_idxes = torch.where(output_labels == cls)[0]    ← Performs NMS for each class
    cls_labels = output_labels[cls_idxes]
    cls_bboxes = output_bboxes[cls_idxes]
    cls_probs = output_probs[cls_idxes]
    keep_indices = torchvision.ops.nms(
        cls_bboxes, cls_probs, nms_threshold)

    post_nms_labels.append(cls_labels[keep_indices])
    post_nms_probs.append(cls_probs[keep_indices])
    post_nms_boxes.append(cls_bboxes[keep_indices])

return {
    "labels": torch.cat(post_nms_labels),
    "probs": torch.cat(post_nms_probs),
    "bboxes": torch.cat(post_nms_boxes)
}
```

11.4.4 Training the Faster R-CNN

As we have seen, the FRCNN consists of two subnetworks:

- An RPN responsible for generating good region proposals that contain objects
- A Fast R-CNN responsible for object classification and detection from a list of RoIs

Thus the FRCNN is a two-stage object detector. We have one stage that generates good region proposals and another that takes the region proposals and detects objects in the image. So how do we train the FRCNN?

A simple idea would be to train two independent networks (RPN and Fast R-CNN). However, we do not want to do this because it is expensive. Additionally, if we do so, each network will modify the convolutional layers in its own way. As discussed earlier, we want to share the convolutional layers across the RPN and the Fast R-CNN modules. This ensures efficiency (only one conv backbone as opposed to two independent backbones). Additionally, both the RPN and FRCNN are performing similar tasks, so it intuitively makes sense to share the same set of convolutional features. Therefore, we need to develop a technique that allows for sharing convolutional layers between the two networks rather than learning two separate networks. The original FRCNN paper proposed two techniques to train the model:

- *Alternate optimization (AltOpt)*—We first train RPN and use the proposals to train the Fast R-CNN. The network tuned by the Fast R-CNN is then used to initialize the RPN, and this process is iterated. This involves multiple rounds of training alternating between training the RPN and Fast R-CNN.

- *Approximate joint training*—The RPN and Fast R-CNN networks are merged into one network during training. In each SGD iteration, the forward pass generates region proposals that are treated just like fixed, precomputed proposals when training a Fast R-CNN detector. We combine the RPN and Fast R-CNN losses and perform backpropagation as usual. This training is significantly faster as we are training both networks together end to end. However, the optimization is approximate because we treat the RPN-generated proposals as fixed, whereas in reality, they are a function of the RPN. So, we're ignoring one derivative.

Both techniques give similar accuracy. So joint training, which is significantly faster, is preferred.

11.4.5 Other object-detection paradigms

So far, we have looked at the FRCNN in detail and discussed several key ideas that contribute to its success. Several other object-detection paradigms have also been developed. Some are inspired by the FRCNN, borrowing and/or improving on the ideas established by the FRCNN. In this section, we briefly look at a few of them.

YOU ONLY LOOK ONCE (YOLO)

The FRCNN is a two-stage detector: an RPN followed by the Fast R-CNN, which runs on the region proposals generated by the RPN. YOLO (https://arxiv.org/pdf/1506.02640.pdf), as the name implies, is a single-stage object detector. A single convolutional network simultaneously predicts multiple bounding boxes and class probabilities for those boxes directly from full images in one go. Some of the salient features of YOLO are as follows:

- YOLO is significantly faster (10× faster than the FRCNN) due to its much simpler architecture. YOLO can even be used for real-time object detection.
- Unlike the FRCNN, where the R-CNN module looks only at the region proposals, YOLO looks directly at the full image during training and testing.
- The speed of YOLO comes at the cost of accuracy. While YOLO is significantly faster, it is less accurate than the FRCNN.

Several other improvements have been made on top of YOLO to improve accuracy while trying to maintain the simple, fast architecture. These include YOLO v2, YOLO v3, and so on.

MULTIBOX SINGLE-SHOT DETECTOR (SSD)

SSD (https://arxiv.org/pdf/1512.02325.pdf) tries to achieve a good balance between speed and accuracy. It is a single-stage network like YOLO: that is, it eliminates the proposal-generation (RPN) and subsequent feature-resampling stages. It also borrows the ideas of anchors from the FRCNN: applying a conv net on top of feature maps to make predictions relative to a fixed set of bounding boxes.

Thus, a single deep network predicts class scores and box offsets for a fixed set of default bounding boxes using small convolutional filters applied to feature maps. To achieve high detection accuracy, feature maps at different scales are used to make predictions at different scales.

SSD is much more accurate than YOLO; however, it is still not as accurate as the FRCNN (especially for small objects).

FEATURE PYRAMID NETWORK (FPN)

The feature maps generated by conv nets are pyramidal: as we go deeper, the spatial resolution of the feature map keeps decreasing, and we expect the semantic information represented by the feature map to be more meaningful. High-resolution maps have low-level features, whereas low-resolution maps have more semantic features.

In the case of the FRCNN, we applied object detection on only the last convolution map. SSD shows that there is useful information by using other feature maps for prediction. But SSD builds this pyramid high up the network (past the fourth convolution layer [conv4] of VGG). It specifically avoids the use of lower-layer features. Thus it misses the opportunity to reuse the higher-resolution maps of the feature hierarchy. FPN shows that these features are important, especially for detecting small objects.

The FPN (https://arxiv.org/pdf/1612.03144.pdf) relies on an architecture that combines low-resolution, semantically strong features with high-resolution, semantically weak features via a top-down pathway and lateral connections. The bottom-up pathway is the forward pass of the convolutional layers. In the top-down path, there is a back connection from lower resolution to higher resolution via simple upsampling (it is merged with the bottom-up feature map using 1×1 convolutions). This merged feature map is used at every level to learn and make predictions.

The FPN was originally implemented on top of the FRCNN. It is much more accurate, but it is much slower than YOLO/SSD-style approaches.

We have only briefly mentioned the other prominent detection paradigms. The fundamental principles behind them remain the same. You are encouraged to read the papers to get a deeper and better understanding.

Summary

In this chapter, we took an in-depth look at various deep-learning techniques for object classification and localization:

- LeNet is a simple neural network that can classify handwritten digits from the MNIST data set.
- Simple networks like LeNet don't extend well to more real-world image classification problems. Hence deeper neural networks that have more expressive power are needed.
- The VGG network is one of the most popular deep convolutional neural networks. It improves on prior state-of-the-art deep neural networks by using more convolution layers with smaller (3×3) filters. Such an architecture has two advantages: (1) more expressive power because of the added nonlinearity that comes from stacking more layers, and (2) a reduced number of parameters. Three 3×3 filters

have $27C^2$ parameters, whereas a single 7×7 filter (which cover the same receptive field) has $49C^2$ parameters (81% more).

- VGG (and AlexNet) use ReLU nonlinear layers instead of sigmoid layers because they do not suffer from the vanishing gradient problem. Using ReLUs speeds up training, resulting in faster convergence.
- Inception blocks provide an efficient way to increase the depth and width of a neural network while keeping the computational budget constant. Multiscale filters are used at each convolution layer to learn patterns of different sizes, and 1×1 convolutions are used for dimensionality reduction (which reduces the number of parameters needed, thereby improving computational efficiency).
- ResNet is another popular convolutional neural network. The ResNet architecture was motivated by the fact that simply stacking layers beyond a certain point does not help and causes degradation even in training accuracies. This is a counterintuitive result because we expect that deeper networks can, at the very least, learn as much as their shallower counterparts. The authors of the ResNet papers showed that this may happen because the identity function is hard for neural networks to learn. To tackle this, they proposed shortcut/skip connections to simplify the neural network's learning objective. This is the key idea behind ResNet and enables training of much deeper neural networks.
- Faster R-CNN is one of the most popular object detectors. It is a two-stage network consisting of (1) a region proposal network (RPN), which is responsible for predicting regions of interest that could potentially contain objects; and (2) an R-CNN module, which takes the region proposals as input and emits class scores and bounding boxes efficiently.
- The RPN module uses multiple anchor boxes (at each point on the conv feature map) to handle objects of different sizes and aspect ratios. It convolves a small network over the conv feature map to make predictions about objectness and bounding boxes at each sliding window location. Remember that the small network is a fully convolutional network (FCN) comprising 3×3 convs followed by 1×1 convs, enabling this approach to work with arbitrary-sized inputs and making it translation invariant.
- RoI pooling provides an efficient way to extract a fixed-sized feature vector from region proposals of varying sizes, all in one pass. These feature vectors are fed to a classifier and regressor for classification and localization, respectively.
- Non-maxima suppression (NMS) is a technique to de-duplicate overlapping bounding boxes.
- FRCNN can be trained using two methods: alternative optimization (AltOpt) and approximate joint training. Both approaches lead to similar accuracy numbers, but approximate joint training is significantly faster.
- You Only Look Once (YOLO), MultiBox Single-Shot Detector (SSD), and feature pyramid networks (FPN) are some other popular object detectors.

12 Manifolds, homeomorphism, and neural networks

This chapter covers

- Introduction to manifolds
- Introduction to homeomorphism
- Role of manifolds and homeomorphism in neural networks

This is a short chapter that briefly introduces (barely scratching the surface of) a topic that could fill an entire mathematics textbook. A rigorous or even comprehensive treatment of manifolds is beyond the scope of this book. Instead, this chapter primarily focuses on geometric intuitions required for deep learning.

12.1 Manifolds

A *manifold* is a generalization of the notions of curve, surface, and volume into a unified concept that works in arbitrary dimensions. In machine learning, the input space can be viewed as a manifold. Usually, the input manifold is not very conducive to classification. We need to transform (map) that manifold to a different manifold that is friendlier to the classification problem at hand. This is what a neural network does.

In a multilayered neural network, each layer transforms (maps) from one manifold to another. For the classification problem, the end manifold is expected to be one where the classes can be separated by a linear surface (hyperplane). The last layer provides this linear separator. Figure 12.1 provides an example of a transformation to a space where classification is easier.

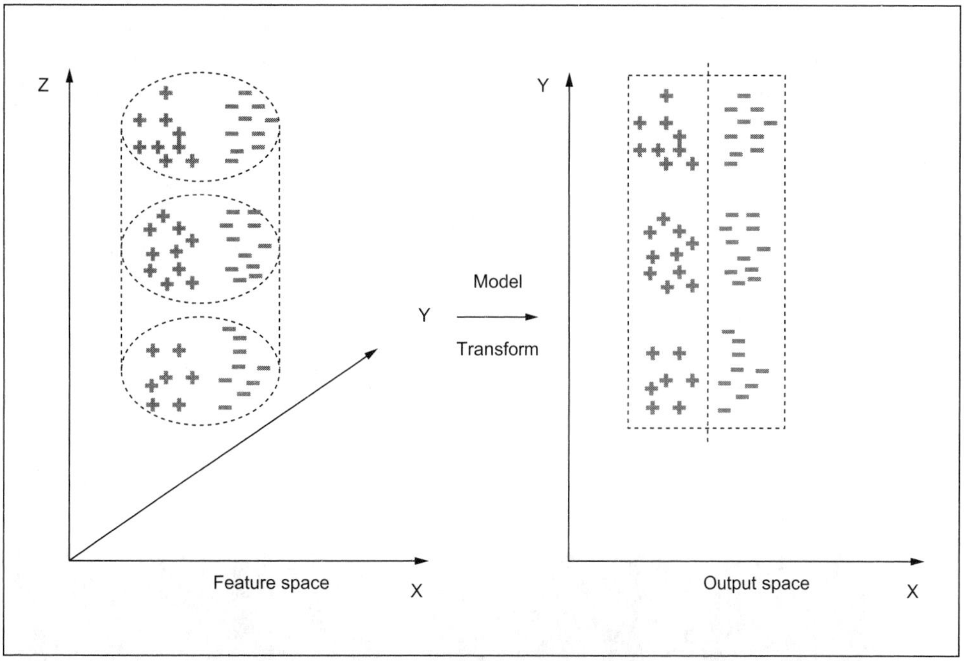

Figure 12.1 The input points lie on a cylindrical manifold (surface). Here, the two input classes (indicated by + and -, respectively) cannot be separated linearly. If we unroll (map) the cylinder surface into a plane, the two classes can be separated linearly.

Unlike physical surfaces we see and touch in everyday life, manifolds are not limited to three dimensions. Human imagination may fail in visualizing higher-dimension manifolds, but we can typically use three-dimensional analogies as surrogates—they often work, although not always. A neural network layer or sequence of layers can be viewed as mapping points from one manifold to another.

Manifolds are locally Euclidean. To get an intuitive understanding of this, imagine a circle with a very thin string wrapped around it. Now, take any point on the circle and take a small arc of the circle containing that point. If we cut off the portion of the string corresponding to that segment, we can straighten that little piece of string into a straight line without twisting or tearing it. In other words, the small neighborhood on the circle around the chosen point has 1:1 mapping with a line segment. All points on the circle satisfy this property. Such a curve is said to be *locally Euclidean*. The concept can be extended to higher dimensions. Consider the surface of a sphere (this is an example of a 2-manifold). Imagine a rubber sheet tightly fitted around the sphere. Take an arbitrary point and a small patch of the spherical surface containing the point (see figure 12.2c). If we cut off the rubber sheet corresponding to the patch, it can be flattened into a plane without twisting or tearing. So, the sphere surface is locally Euclidean. The torus surface (donut-shaped object) is another example of a 2-manifold. In general, d-manifold is a space (set of points) on which every point has a small neighborhood of points in the space that contains the point and can be mapped 1:1 to $\mathbb{R}^d$ without twisting or tearing. For instance, a circle is a 1D manifold, and every point on it has a container arc that can be mapped to a line ($\mathbb{R}^1$). A sphere surface is 2D manifold, and every point of it has a containing patch that maps 1:1 to a plane ($\mathbb{R}^2$). We say manifolds are locally Euclidean. Figure 12.2 illustrates the concept.

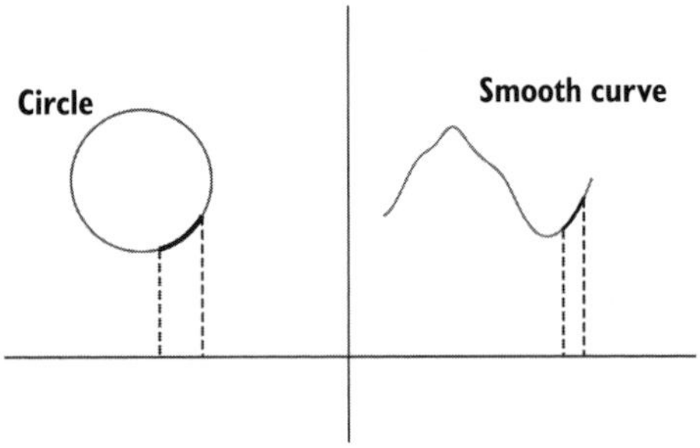

(a) Any arbitrary continuous curve (for example, a circle) is a 1D manifold.

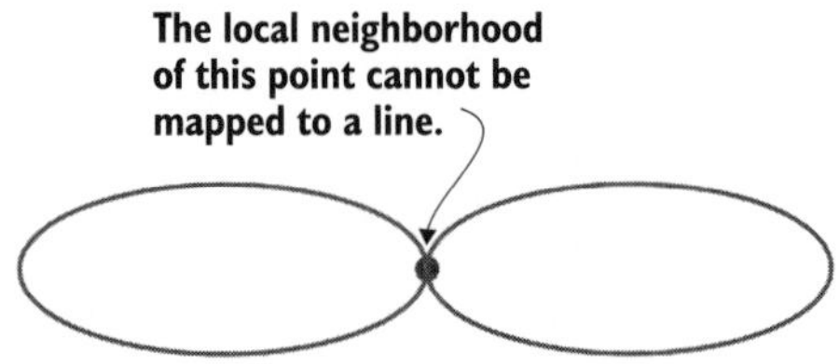

(b) The 8-curve is a non-manifold. The χ-shaped neighborhood of the marked point cannot be mapped $1:1$ to a straight-line segment.

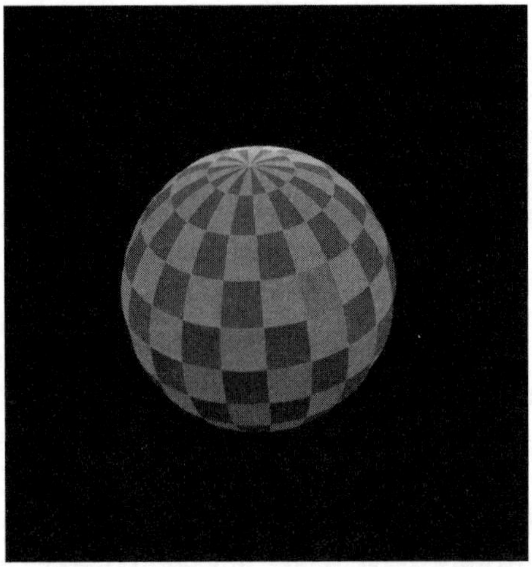

(c) A sphere is an example of a 2-manifold.

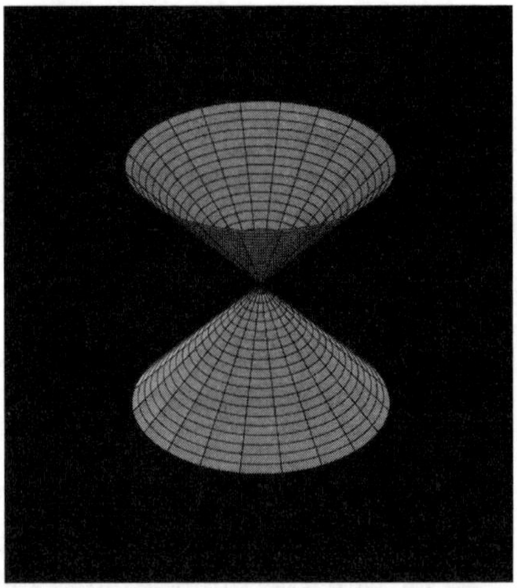

(d) An hourglass is an example of 2D non-manifold surface.

Figure 12.2 Manifolds and non-manifolds in 1D and 2D

A little thought will reveal that the locally Euclidean property makes calculus possible. For instance, how do we compute the area under a curve, $f(x)$ in the interval

$x = a$ and $x = b$? The formula is $\int_{x=a}^{x=b} f(x)\,dx$. We take infinitesimally small segments of the curve and pretend they are straight lines, which can be projected onto a tiny line segment on the X axis. The resulting narrow quadrilateral can be approximated by a rectangle whose sides are parallel to the X and Y axes. We sum (integrate) the areas of all the tiny rectangles that cover the same area as the one we are computing (see figure 12.3). This scheme depends on the ability to represent tiny segments of the curve as straight lines. A similar case can be made about computing the length of the curve segment. In higher dimensions, the same idea applies: calculus is dependent on the ability to pretend that a curve or surface can be locally approximated by something flat. The graph of any *continuous* vector function $\vec{y} = f(\vec{x})$, where $\vec{x}$ is any open subset of $\mathbb{R}^n$—that is, $\vec{x} \in \mathbb{U} \subset \mathbb{R}^n$ and $f(\vec{y}) \in \mathbb{R}^m$—yields a manifold in $(\vec{x}, \vec{y})$ in $\mathbb{R}^m \times \mathbb{R}^n$.

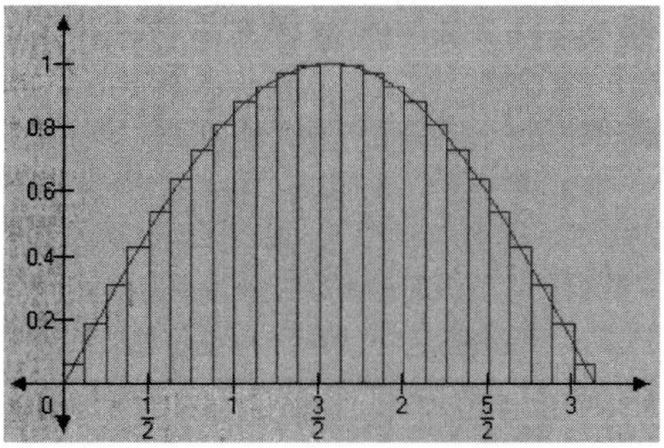

Figure 12.3 Area under a curve is computed by locally approximating curve segment with tiny straight lines—needs locally Euclidean property

In this context, note that the entire sphere *cannot* be mapped to a plane (try opening the sphere onto a plane). This is why it is impossible to draw a perfect map of the globe on a piece of paper with all regions drawn to scale. Typically, the polar regions occupy areas disproportionately large on the paper map. But small patches on the spherical surface can be mapped onto planes, which is enough to call this surface a manifold. Hence the word *local* in locally Euclidean.

12.1.1 Hausdorff property

Manifolds usually have another property, known as the Hausdorff property. If we take any pair of points on a manifold—no matter how close they are—we can find a pair of *disjoint* neighborhoods around the respective points consisting entirely of points on the manifold. Loosely speaking, this means if we take any pair of points on the manifold, we can find an infinite number of points between them, all belonging to the manifold. This is illustrated in figure 12.4. It's easy to see that this is true for the real line ($\mathbb{R}^1$): take any pair of points, and there are enough points between them to create a disjoint pair of neighborhoods centered on each.

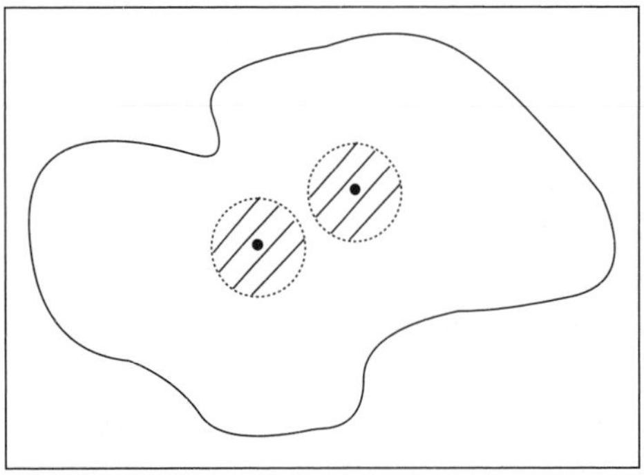

Figure 12.4 Hausdorff property: on a manifold, for any pair of points, we can find a disjoint neighborhood pair containing the respective points and consisting of points from the manifold.

12.1.2 Second countable property

Manifolds are second-countable. To explain this, we will first briefly outline a few concepts. (Disclaimer: the following explanations err toward ease of understanding as opposed to mathematical rigor.)

OPEN SETS, CLOSED SETS, AND BOUNDARIES

Consider the set of points belonging to the interval $A \equiv 0 < x < 1$ (you can imagine it to be a segment of the real line). Take any point in this set A, say $x = 0.93$. You can find a point on its left (say, 0.92) and on its right (say, 0.94), both of which are in the same set A. In some sense, the point is surrounded by points belonging to the same set. Hence it is an *internal* point. The funny thing is, in this set, *all points are internal.* In comparison, consider the set $A_c \equiv 0 \leq x \leq 1$. This includes the previous set A as well as the *boundary* points $x = 0$ and $x = 1$. Note that the boundary points can be approached from both inside and outside the set A. If we take a small neighborhood of any point in the boundary, consisting of all points within a small distance ϵ, there are points inside and outside A. A is an open set. If we add its boundary to itself, it becomes a closed set A_c.

The concept extends to higher dimensions. For instance, the set of 2D points belonging to the unit disc $S \equiv x^2 + y^2 < 1$ is an open set. If we add the boundary—the circle $S_c \equiv x^2 + y^2 = 1$—we get a closed set. All this is illustrated in figure 12.5.

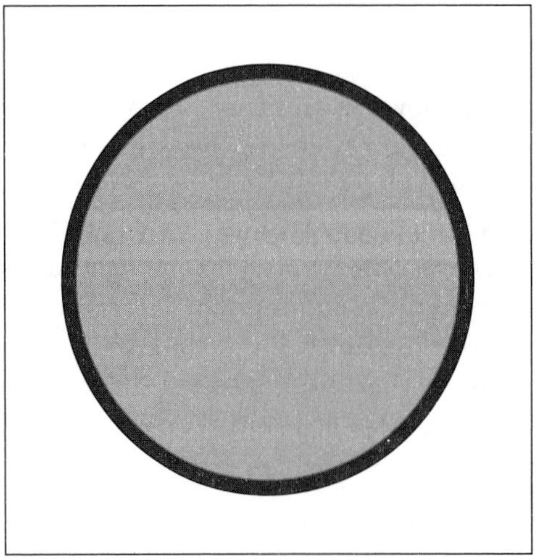

Figure 12.5 The open set, disk without a boundary is shown in gray. The boundary is shown in black. Gray+black is the closed set.

BOUNDED, COMPACT, AND PRECOMPACT SETS

A set is said to be bounded if all its points lie within a fixed distance of each other. The sets A, A_c, and S, S_c discussed previously are bounded. A *compact* set is *bounded as well as closed.* The sets A_c and S_c are compact. And a set is *precompact* if it can be converted into a compact set by just adding its boundary (for example, A and S). Note that not all open sets are precompact: for example, $-\infty < x < \infty$ is open but not precompact. All precompact sets are open, however.

Manifolds may or may not include a boundary. A disc is a 2-manifold with a boundary. Its boundary is the circle's circumference, which is a 1-manifold. A three-dimensional ball is a 3-manifold with a boundary. The boundary is the surface of the sphere, which is a 2-manifold. The open set of points on the disc sans the boundary is also a 2-manifold. A square area is a 2-manifold with a boundary whose boundary is the square, which is a 1-manifold. A three-dimensional cube is a 3-manifold with a boundary whose boundary is a 2-manifold corresponding to the surface of the cube. In general, the boundary of a d-manifold with boundary is a $d-1$-manifold.

Now, let's go back to the second countable property of manifolds. The second countable property of a manifold implies that every manifold has a basis of open sets. This means for every manifold M, there exists a countable collection $U \equiv \{U_i\}$, where U_i are precompact subsets of M and any open subsets of M can be expressed as a union of elements of U. This is illustrated in figure 12.6.

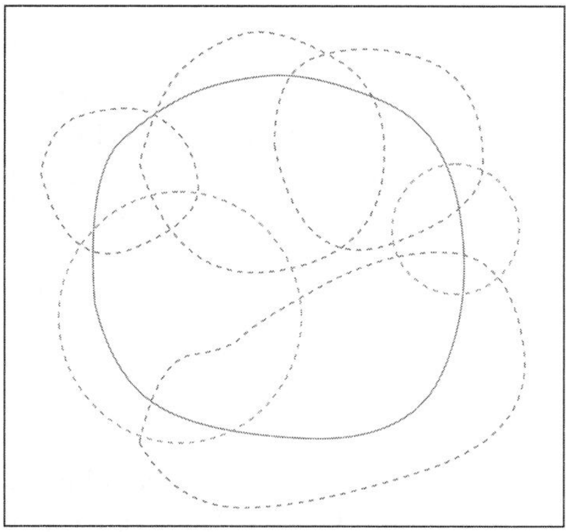

Figure 12.6 Second countable property for manifolds. The solid curve indicates the (missing) boundary of an arbitrary open subset of the manifold. The dashed balls indicate the (missing) boundaries of elements of the basis set U_i. The area within the solid curve is shown to be covered by a union of dashed ball-bounded areas.

12.2 Homeomorphism

We have been speaking about 1:1 mappings between an arc of a circle and a line segment. If we have a piece of string tightly fitted on the arc, all we have to do is to grab the string's two ends and pull it out to get the corresponding straight line—we do not have to do any twisting or tearing (see the black arc in figure 12.2a). Similarly, the mapping between a patch on the surface of a sphere can be mapped 1:1 to a plane by simply pulling an imaginary rubber sheet fitted on the patch (see the patch in figure 12.2c).

These are examples of a general class of mappings called *homeomorphism.* Formally, a homeomorphic mapping comprises a pair of functions f and f^{-1} between two sets of points X and Y such that

$$\vec{y} \in Y = f\left(\vec{x} \in X\right) \quad f : X \mapsto Y$$
$$\vec{x} \in X = f^{-1}\left(\vec{y} \in Y\right) \quad f^{-1} : Y \mapsto X$$

where

- f is 1:1: it maps each $\vec{x}$ to a *unique* $\vec{y}$, and distinct $\vec{x}$s are mapped to distinct $\vec{y}$s.
- f^{-1} is 1:1: it maps each $\vec{y}$ to an *unique* $\vec{x}$, and distinct $\vec{y}$s are mapped to distinct $\vec{x}$s.
- f is a continuous function: it maps nearby values of $\vec{x}$ to nearby values of $\vec{y}$.
- f^{-1} is continuous function: it maps nearby values of $\vec{y}$ to nearby values of $\vec{x}$.

An intuitive way to visualize homeomorphism is that it transforms one manifold to another by stretching or squishing but never by cutting, breaking, or folding. Homeomorphism preserves path-connectedness. A set of points is said to be path-connected if a path between any pair of them exists, comprising points belonging to the set.

12.3 Neural networks and homeomorphism between manifolds

Consider two classes A and B defined on the real line:

$$A \equiv \{-1 \leq x \leq 1\}$$
$$B \equiv \{-3 \leq x \leq -2 \text{ or } 2 \leq x \leq 3\}$$

The 1-manifolds corresponding to these classes are not clearly separable in their original space (see figure 12.7a) because class A is "surrounded" by class B. But if we pinch the origin and pull it up—in other words, perform a specific homeomorphism—to transform it, as shown in figure 12.7c, it is possible to separate the transformed manifolds with a straight line. Similarly, figure 12.7b shows two classes A and B:

$$A \equiv \left\{\|\vec{x}\|^2 \leq 1\right\}$$
$$B \equiv \left\{\|\vec{x}\|^2 \geq 4 \text{ and } \|\vec{x}\|^2 \leq 9\right\}$$

These are 2-manifolds that are hard to separate in their original space because, again, class B surrounds class A. But if we pinch and pull the origin to create the manifolds shown in figure 12.7d, they become separable by a plane (see figure 12.7d).

A linear layer of a neural network does the following transformation (discussed in detail in equation 8.7):

$$\vec{z} = \sigma\left(W\vec{x} + \vec{b}\right)$$

Note that all of these operations, multiplication with the weight matrix W, translation by $\vec{b}$, and the sigmoid nonlinearity are continuous invertible functions. Hence, they are homeomorphisms. The composite operation where these are applied in sequence is another homeomorphism. (Strictly speaking, *multiplication by a weight matrix is invertible*

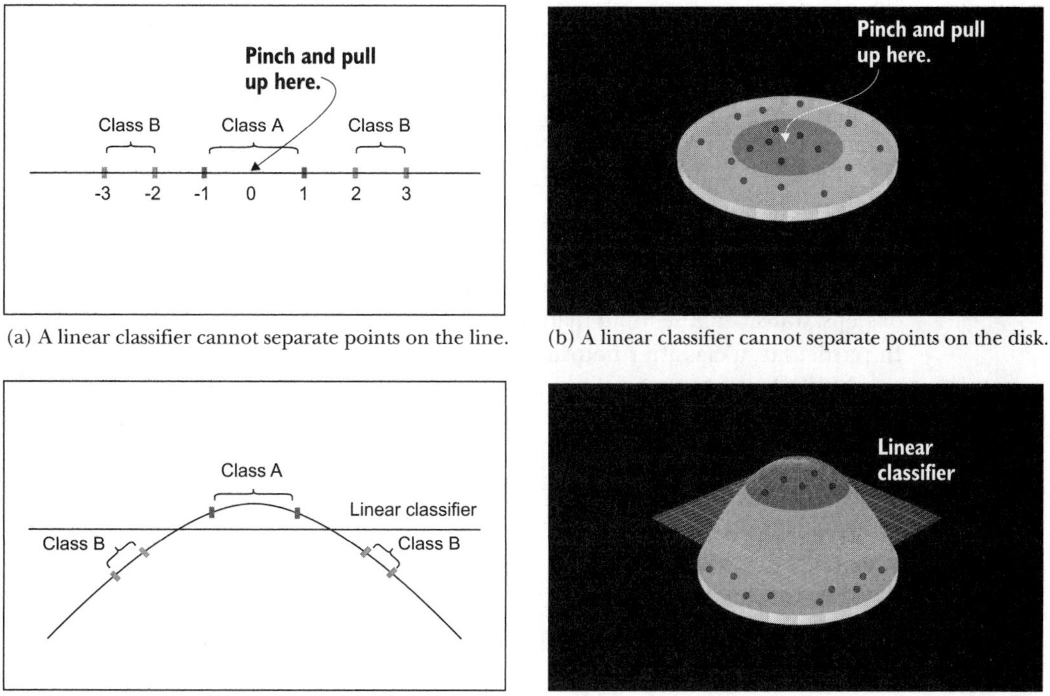

(a) A linear classifier cannot separate points on the line.

(b) A linear classifier cannot separate points on the disk.

(c) Lines transformed to a curved shape allow classification with a linear classifier (line).

(d) Disks transformed to a 3D bell-like shape allow classification with a linear classifier (plane).

Figure 12.7 Homeomorphism to a friendlier manifold can help the classification.

only when the weight matrix W is square with a nonzero determinant. And if the weight matrix has a zero determinant, the layer effectively does a dimensionality reduction.)

One way to view a multilayered neural network is that the successive layers homeomorphically transform the input manifold so that it becomes easier and easier to separate the classes. The final layer may be a simple linear separator (as in figure 12.7).

Summary

- A manifold is a hyperdimensional collection of points (space) that satisfies three properties: locally Euclidean, Hausdorff, and second countable.
- A d-manifold is a space in which every point has a small neighborhood that contains the point and can be mapped 1:1 to a subregion of $\mathbb{R}^d$ without folding, twisting, or tearing. In other words, the local neighborhood around any point on a manifold can be approximated by something flat. For instance, a continuous curve in 3D space is a 1-manifold: if we imagine the curve as a string, any local neighborhood is a substring that can be pulled and straightened into a straight line. Any continuous surface in 3D is a 2-manifold: if we imagine the surface as a rubber membrane, any local neighborhood can be pulled and stretched into a flat planar patch. This property (the ability to pretend that a curve or a surface can be locally replaced by a linear piece) is what enables us to perform calculus.

- Homeomorphism is a special class of transformation (mapping) that transforms one manifold to another via stretching/squishing without tearing, breaking, or folding.
- Homeomorphism preserves path-connectedness.
- Roughly speaking, a neural network layer can be viewed as a homeomorphic transform that maps points from its input manifold to an output manifold that is (hopefully) more suitable for the end goal. The entire multilayered perceptron (neural network) can be viewed as a sequence of homeomorphisms that, in a series of steps, transform the input manifold to a manifold that makes the end goal easier. In particular, a classifier neural network maps the input manifold to an output manifold where the points belonging to different classes are well-separated.

13 Fully Bayes model parameter estimation

This chapter covers

- Fully Bayes parameter estimation for unsupervised modeling
- Injecting prior belief into parameter estimation
- Estimating Gaussian likelihood parameters with known or unknown mean and precision
- Normal-gamma and Wishart distributions

Suppose we have a data set of interest: say, all images containing a cat. If we represent images as points in a high-dimensional feature space, our data set of interest forms a subspace of that feature space. Now we want to create an *unsupervised* model for our data set of interest. This means we want to identify a probability density function $p(\vec{x})$ whose sample cloud (the set of points obtained by repeatedly sampling the probability distribution many times) largely overlaps our subspace of interest. Of course, we do not know the exact subspace of interest, but we have collected a set of samples X from the data set of interest: that is, the training data. We can use the point cloud for X as a surrogate for the unknown subspace of interest. Thus, we are essentially trying to identify a probability density function $p(\vec{x})$ whose sample cloud, by and large, overlaps X.

Once we have the model $p\left(\vec{x}\right)$, we can use it to generate more data samples; these will be computer-generated cat images. This is generative modeling. Also, given a new image $\vec{a}$, we can estimate the probability of it being an image of a cat by evaluating $p\left(\vec{a}\right)$.

13.1 Fully Bayes estimation: An informal introduction

Let's recap Bayes' theorem:

$$\overbrace{p\left(\theta|X\right)}^{\text{posterior probability}} = \frac{p\left(X,\theta\right)}{p\left(X\right)} = \frac{\overbrace{p\left(X|\theta\right)}^{\text{likelihood}}\quad\overbrace{p\left(\theta\right)}^{\text{prior probability}}}{\underbrace{p\left(X\right)}_{\textit{evidence}}} \tag{13.1}$$

Here, $X=\left\{\vec{x}_1,\vec{x}_2,\cdots\right\}$ denotes the training data set. Our ultimate goal is to identify the likelihood function $p\left(\vec{x}|\theta\right)$. Estimating the likelihood function has two aspects: selecting the function family and estimating the parameters. We usually preselect the family from our knowledge of the problem and then estimate the model parameters. For instance, the family for our model likelihood function might be Gaussian: $p\left(\vec{x}|\theta\right)=\mathcal{N}\left(\vec{x};\,\vec{\mu},\boldsymbol{\Sigma}\right)$ (as before, the semicolon separates the model variables from model parameters). Then $\theta=\left\{\vec{\mu},\boldsymbol{\Sigma}\right\}$ are the model parameters to estimate. We estimate θ such that the overall likelihood $p\left(X|\theta\right)=\prod_i p\left(\vec{x}_i|\theta\right)$ best fits the training data X.

We want to re-emphasize the mental picture that *best fit* implies that the sample cloud of the likelihood function (repeated samples from $p\left(\vec{x}|\theta\right)$) largely overlaps the training data set X. For the Gaussian case, this implies that the mean $\vec{\mu}$ should fall at a place where there is a very high concentration of training data points, and the covariance matrix $\boldsymbol{\Sigma}$ should be such that the elliptical base of the likelihood function tightly contains as many training data points as possible.

13.1.1 Parameter estimation and belief injection

There are various possible approaches to parameter estimation. The simplest approach is *maximum likelihood parameter estimation* (MLE), introduced in section 6.6.2. In MLE, we choose the parameter values that maximize $p\left(X|\theta\right)$, the likelihood of observing the training data set. This makes some sense. After all, the only thing we know to be true is that the input data set X *has been observed*—this being unsupervised data, we do not know anything else. It is reasonable to choose the parameters that maximize the probability of that known truth. If the training data set is large, MLE estimation works well.

However, in the absence of a sufficiently large amount of training data, it often helps to inject our prior knowledge about the system into the estimation—prior knowledge can cover for the lack of data. This injection of guess/belief into the system is done via the prior probability density. To do this, we can no longer maximize the likelihood, as likelihood ignores the prior. We have to do maximum a posteriori (MAP) estimation, which maximizes the posterior probability. The posterior probability is the product of likelihood (which depends on the data) and the prior (which does not depend on data; we will make it reflect our prior belief).

There are two possible MAP paradigms. We saw one of them in section 6.6.3, where we injected our belief that the unknown parameters must be *small* in magnitude and set $p(\theta) \propto e^{-\|\theta\|^2}$ as a *regularizer*. The system was incentivized to select parameter values that are relatively smaller in magnitude. In this chapter, we study a different paradigm; let's illustrate it with an example.

Suppose we model the likelihood as a Gaussian: $p(\vec{x}|\theta) = \mathcal{N}(\vec{x};\ \vec{\mu}, \boldsymbol{\Sigma})$. We have to estimate the parameters $\theta = \{\vec{\mu}, \boldsymbol{\Sigma}\}$ from the training data X, for which we must maximize the posterior probability. To compute the posterior probability, we need the prior probability. In addition, we must somehow inject constant values as our belief (lacking observed data) about the parameter values. How about modeling the prior probability as a Gaussian probability density function in the parameter space? Ignoring the covariance matrix parameter for the sake of simplicity, we can model the probability density of the mean parameter as $p(\vec{\mu}) = \mathcal{N}(\vec{\mu};\ \vec{\mu}_0, \boldsymbol{\Sigma}_0)$. We are essentially saying that we believe the parameter $\vec{\mu}$ is likely to have a value near $\vec{\mu}_0$ with a confidence $\boldsymbol{\Sigma}_0$. In other words, we are injecting a constant value as our belief in the parameter $\vec{\mu}$. We can treat the covariance similarly. Later, we prove that in this paradigm, with a low volume of training data, the prior dominates. Once sufficient training data is digested, the effect of the prior fades, and the solution gets closer and closer to the MLE. This is the fully Bayes parameter estimation technique in a nutshell.

In this chapter, we discuss Bayes estimation of parameters for a Gaussian likelihood function for a series of increasingly complex scenarios. In section 13.3, we deal with the case where the variance of the parameters to be estimated is known (constant) but the mean is unknown, so the mean is expressed as a (Gaussian) random variable. Then, in section 13.6, we examine the case where the mean is known (constant) but the variance is unknown. Finally, in section 13.7, we examine the case where both are unknown. Both the univariate and multivariate cases are dealt with for each scenario.

NOTE Fully functional code for this chapter, executable via Jupyter Notebook, can be found at http://mng.bz/woYW.

13.2 MLE for Gaussian parameter values (recap)

We have discussed the details of this in section 6.8. Here we recap the main results. Suppose we have a data set $X = \{x^{(1)}, x^{(2)}, \cdots, x^{(n)}\}$. We have decided to model the data distribution as a Gaussian $\mathcal{N}(x;\ \mu, \sigma)$—we want to estimate the parameters μ, σ that best "explain" or "fit" the observed data set X. MLE is one of the simplest approaches to solving this problem. Here we estimate the parameters such that *the likelihood of the data observed during training is maximized.* This can be loosely visualized as estimating a probability density function whose peak coincides with the region in the input space with the densest population of training data. We looked at MLE in section 6.8. Here we simply restate the expressions.

Let's denote the (as yet unknown) mean and variance of the data distribution as μ and σ. Then from equation 5.22, we get

$$p\left(x^{(i)} \middle| \mu, \sigma\right) = \frac{1}{\sqrt{2\pi}\sigma} e^{\frac{-\left(x^{(i)}-\mu\right)^2}{2\sigma^2}}$$

$$p\left(X|\mu, \sigma\right) = p\left(x^{(1)}, \cdots, x^{(n)} \middle| \mu, \sigma\right) = \prod_{i=1}^{n} p\left(x^{(i)} \middle| \mu, \sigma\right) = \frac{1}{\left(\sqrt{2\pi}\sigma\right)^n} e^{\frac{-\sum_{i=1}^{n}\left(x^{(i)}-\mu\right)^2}{2\sigma^2}}$$

Maximizing the log-likelihood $p\left(X|\mu, \sigma\right)$ has a closed-form solution:

$$\mu = \bar{x} = \frac{1}{n}\sum_{i=1}^{n} x^{(i)}$$

$$\sigma^2 = s = \frac{1}{n}\sum_{i=1}^{n}\left(x^{(i)} - \bar{x}\right)^2 \tag{13.2}$$

Thus the MLE mean and variance are essentially the mean and variance of the training data samples (see section 6.6 for the derivation of these expressions).

The corresponding expressions for multivariate Gaussian MLE are

$$\vec{\mu} = \bar{\vec{x}} = \frac{1}{n}\sum_{i=1}^{n} \vec{x}^{(i)}$$

$$\mathbf{\Sigma} = S = \frac{1}{n}\sum_{i=1}^{n}\left(\vec{x}^{(i)} - \bar{\vec{x}}\right)\left(\vec{x}^{(i)} - \bar{\vec{x}}\right)^T \tag{13.3}$$

These MLE parameter values are to be used to evaluate $p\left(x\right) = \mathcal{N}\left(x; \mu, \sigma\right)$—the probability of an unknown data point x coming from the distribution represented by the training data set X.

13.3 Fully Bayes parameter estimation: Gaussian, unknown mean, known precision

MLE may not be that accurate when the available data set is small (that is, n, size of the data set X, is small). In many problems, we have a prior idea of the mean and sigma of the data set. Unfortunately, MLE provides no way to bake such a prior belief into the estimation. Fully Bayes parameter estimation techniques try to fix this drawback: here we are not simply maximizing the likelihood of the observed data. Instead, we maximize the posterior probability of the estimated parameter(s). This posterior probability involves the product of the likelihood and a prior probability (see equation 13.1). The likelihood term captures the effect of the training data—maximizing it alone is MLE—but does not capture the effect of a prior belief. On the other hand, the prior term does not depend on the data. This is where we bake in our belief or guess or prior knowledge about the data distribution. Thus, our estimate for the data distribution parameters will consider the data and the prior guess. We will soon see that the estimation is such that as the size of the data set (n, length of X) increases, the effect of the prior term decreases, and the effect of the likelihood term increases. In the limit, at infinite data availability, the Bayesian inference yields the MLE. At the other extreme, when no data is available ($n = 0$), the Fully Bayes estimates for the parameters are the same as the prior estimates.

Let's we examine Bayesian parameter estimation. For starters, we deal with a relatively simple case where we have a Gaussian data distribution with a known (constant) variance but unknown and modeled mean. The data distribution is Gaussian (as usual, the semicolon in $\mathcal{N}(x; \mu_n, \sigma)$ separates the variables from parameters):

$$p(x|\mu, \sigma) = p(x|\mu) = \mathcal{N}(x; \mu, \sigma) \propto e^{\frac{-(x-\mu)^2}{2\sigma^2}}$$

The training data set is denoted $X = \{x^{(1)}, x^{(2)}, \cdots, x^{(n)}\}$, and its overall likelihood is

$$p(X|\mu) = p\left(x^{(1)}, \cdots, x^{(n)}\middle|\mu\right) = \prod_{i=1}^{n} p\left(x^{(i)}\middle|\mu\right) \propto e^{-\frac{\sum_{i=1}^{n}\left(x^{(i)}-\mu\right)^2}{2\sigma^2}}$$

The variance is known by assumption—hence it is treated as a constant instead of a random variable. The mean μ is unknown and is treated as a Gaussian random variable, with mean μ_0 and variance σ_0 (not to be confused with μ and σ, the mean and variance of the data itself). So, the prior is

$$p(\mu) = \mathcal{N}(\mu; \mu_0, \sigma_0) \propto e^{\frac{-(\mu-\mu_0)^2}{2\sigma_0^2}}$$

The posterior probability of the unknown μ parameter is a product of two Gaussians, which is a Gaussian itself. Let's denote the (as-yet-unknown) mean and variance of this product Gaussian as μ_n and σ_n. Here the subscript n is to remind us that the posterior has been obtained by digesting n data instances from $X = \{x^{(1)}, x^{(2)}, \cdots, x^{(n)}\}$. Thus, the Gaussian posterior can be denoted as

$$p(\mu|X) = \mathcal{N}(\mu; \mu_n, \sigma_n) \propto e^{\frac{-(\mu-\mu_n)^2}{2\sigma_n^2}}$$

Using Bayes' theorem,

$$p(\mu|X) \propto p(X|\mu)\, p(\mu)$$

$$\text{or} \quad \overbrace{e^{\frac{-(\mu-\mu_n)^2}{2\sigma_n^2}}}^{posterior} \propto \overbrace{e^{-\frac{\sum_{i=1}^{n}\left(x^{(i)}-\mu\right)^2}{2\sigma^2}}}^{likelihood} \overbrace{e^{-\frac{(\mu-\mu_0)^2}{2\sigma_0^2}}}^{prior}$$

By comparing the coefficients of μ^2 and μ on the exponents of the left and right sides, we determine the unknown parameters of the posterior distribution:

$$\frac{1}{\sigma_n^2} = \frac{1}{\sigma_0^2} + \frac{n}{\sigma^2} \quad \text{or } \sigma_n^2 = \frac{\sigma_0^2 \sigma^2}{n\sigma_0^2 + \sigma^2}$$

$$\mu_n = \sigma_n^2 \left(\frac{\sum_{i=1}^n x^{(i)}}{\sigma^2} + \frac{\mu_0}{\sigma_0^2} \right) = \frac{\sigma_0^2 \sigma^2}{n\sigma_0^2 + \sigma^2} \left(\frac{n\bar{x}}{\sigma^2} + \frac{\mu_0}{\sigma_0^2} \right)$$

$$= \frac{\bar{x}}{1 + \frac{\sigma^2}{n\sigma_0^2}} + \frac{\mu_0}{1 + \frac{n\sigma_0^2}{\sigma^2}} \tag{13.4}$$

The significance of various closely named variables should be clearly understood:

- μ, σ are the mean and variance of the *data* distribution $p(x)$—assumed to be Gaussian. The final goal is to estimate μ, σ that best fits the data set X. On the other hand, μ_0, σ_0 are the mean and variance of the *parameter* distribution $p(\mu)$, which captures our prior belief about the value of the data mean μ (remember, by assumption, the data mean is also a Gaussian random variable). μ_n, σ_n are the mean and variance of the posterior distribution $p(\mu|X)$ for the data mean μ as computed from n data point samples. This is a Gaussian random variable because it is a product of two Gaussians.
- The posterior distribution of the unknown mean parameter, $p(\mu|X)$, is a Gaussian with mean μ_n. So, it will attain a maximum when $\mu = \mu_n$. In other words, the MAP estimate for the unknown mean μ is $\mu_{\text{MAP}} = \mu_n$.
- Even though μ_n is the best estimate of μ, σ_n is not approximating the σ of the data, σ is known in this case by assumption. Here, σ_n is the variance of the posterior distribution, reflecting our *uncertainty* about the estimate of μ. That is why, as the number of data instances becomes very large, σ_n approaches 0 (indicating we have zero uncertainty or full confidence in the estimate of the mean.)

The estimate for our data distribution is $p(x) = \mathcal{N}(x; \mu_n, \sigma)$, where μ_n is given by equation 13.4. Note that it is a combination of the MLE $\bar{x}$ and prior guess μ_0. Using this, given any arbitrary data instance x, we can infer the probability of x belonging to the class of the training data set X.

NOTE Fully functional code for Bayesian estimation with unknown mean and known variance, executable via Jupyter Notebook, can be found at http://mng.bz/ZA75.

Listing 13.1 PyTorch: Bayesian estimation with unknown mean, known variance

```
import torch

def inference_unknown_mean(X, prior_dist, sigma_known):
    mu_mle = X.mean()
    n = X.shape[0]

    mu_0 = prior_dist.mean
    sigma_0 = prior_dist.scale
```

Parameters of the prior

```
mu_n = mu_mle / (1 + sigma_known**2 / (n * sigma_0**2)) +
        mu_0 / (1 + n * sigma_0**2 / sigma_known**2)
```

Mean of the posterior, following equation 13.4

```
sigma_n = math.sqrt(
    (sigma_0**2 * sigma_known**2) /
    (n*sigma_0**2+sigma_known**2))
```

Standard deviation of the posterior, following equation 13.4

```
posterior_dist = torch.Normal(mu_n, sigma_n)
return posterior_dist
```

13.4 Small and large volumes of training data, and strong and weak priors

Let's examine the behavior of equation 13.4 when $n = 0$ (no data) and when $n \longrightarrow \infty$ (lots of data):

$$\lim_{n \longrightarrow 0} \begin{cases} \mu_n = \mu_0 \\ \sigma_n = \sigma_0 \end{cases}$$

$$\lim_{n \longrightarrow \infty} \begin{cases} \mu_n = \bar{x} = \mu_{MLE} \\ \sigma_n = 0 \end{cases}$$

This agrees with our notion that with little data, the posterior is dominated by the prior, while with lots of data, the posterior is dominated by the likelihood. With lots of data, the variance of the parameter is zero (we are saying with *full certainty* that the best value for the mean is the sample mean for the data, aka the MLE estimate for the mean). In general, with more training data (that is, larger values of n), the posterior shifts closer to the likelihood. This can be seen by analyzing equation 13.4. It agrees with our intuition that with little data, we try to compensate with our pre-existing (prior) belief as to the value of the parameters. As the number of training data instances increases, the effect of the prior is reduced, and the likelihood (which is a function of the data) begins to dominate.

A low variance for the prior (that is, small σ_0) essentially means we have low uncertainty in our prior belief (remember, the entropy/uncertainty of a Gaussian is proportional to its variance). Such high-confidence priors resist being overwhelmed by the data and are called *strong priors*. On the other hand, a large σ_0 implies low certainty/confidence in the prior mean value. This is a *weak prior* that is easily overwhelmed by the data. We can see this in the final expression for mean in equation 13.4: we have $\frac{n\sigma_0^2}{\sigma^2}$ in the denominator of the second term. In general, the second term vanishes with larger n, thereby removing the effect of the prior μ_0 and making the posterior mean coincide with the MLE mean. But the smaller the σ_0, the larger the n required to achieve this, and vice versa.

13.5 Conjugate priors

In section 13.3, given a Gaussian likelihood, choosing the Gaussian family for the prior made the posterior also belong to the Gaussian family. This simplified things considerably. If the prior was chosen from another family, the posterior—which is the product of the likelihood and prior—may not belong to a simple or even known distribution family.

Thus, a Gaussian likelihood with a Gaussian prior results in a Gaussian posterior for the mean. Such priors are said to be *conjugate*. Formally, for a specific family of likelihood, the choice of the prior that results in the posterior belonging to the same family as the prior is called a conjugate prior. For instance, Gaussians for the mean (with known variance) are conjugate to a Gaussian likelihood. Soon we will see that for a Gaussian likelihood, a gamma distribution for the precision (inverse of the variance) results in a gamma posterior. In other words, a gamma prior to the precision is conjugate to a Gaussian likelihood. In the multivariate case, instead of gamma, we have the Wishart distribution as a conjugate prior.

13.6 Fully Bayes parameter estimation: Gaussian, unknown precision, known mean

In section 13.3, we discussed fully Bayes parameter estimation with the assumption that we somehow know the variance σ and only want to estimate the mean μ. Now we examine the case where the mean is known but the variance is unknown and expressed as a random variable. The computations become simpler if we use precision λ instead of variance σ. They are related by the expression $\lambda = \frac{1}{\sigma^2}$. Thus we have a data set X, which is assumed to be sampled from a Gaussian distribution with a constant mean μ, while the precision λ is a random variable with a gamma distribution. The probability density function for the data is thus $p\left(x|\mu, \lambda\right) = \mathcal{N}\left(x;\ \mu, \frac{1}{\sqrt{\lambda}}\right)$.

We model the prior random variable for precision with a gamma distribution. The likelihood is Gaussian, and since the product of a Gaussian and gamma is another gamma (due to the conjugate prior property of gamma), the resulting posterior is a gamma. The gamma function parameters for the posterior can be derived via coefficient comparison. The maximum of the posterior is our estimate for the parameter.

> **Gamma distribution**
>
> The gamma distribution is introduced in the appendix; if necessary, please read that first. Here we state the relevant properties. The probability density function for a random variable λ having a gamma distribution is a function with two parameters α, β:
>
> $$p\left(\lambda|\alpha, \beta\right) = \gamma\left(\lambda; \alpha, \beta\right) = \frac{\beta^{\alpha}}{\Gamma\left(\alpha\right)}\lambda^{(\alpha-1)}e^{-\beta\lambda} \quad \text{where } \alpha, \beta > 0, \lambda \geq 0 \tag{13.5}$$

Maximum of a gamma distribution

To maximize the gamma probability density function $p(\lambda|X) = \lambda^{(\alpha_n - 1)} e^{-\beta_n \lambda}$ for a random variable λ, we take the derivative and equate to zero:

$$\frac{d}{d\lambda}\left(\lambda^{\alpha-1} e^{-\beta\lambda}\right) = 0 \implies (\alpha - 1)\,\lambda^{\alpha-2} e^{-\beta\lambda} + \lambda^{\alpha-1}(-\beta)\, e^{-\beta\lambda} = 0$$

$$\lambda = \frac{\alpha - 1}{\beta}$$

13.6.1 Estimating the precision parameter

Let's return to the fully Bayes estimation of the precision parameter when the mean is known. We model the data distribution with a Gaussian: $p(x|\mu, \lambda) = \mathcal{N}\left(x; \mu, \frac{1}{\sqrt{\lambda}}\right)$ (we have expressed this Gaussian in terms of the precision, λ, which is related to the variance σ as $\lambda = \frac{1}{\sigma^2}$). The training data set is $X = \left\{x^{(1)}, x^{(2)}, \cdots, x^{(n)}\right\}$, and its overall likelihood is

$$p(X|\mu, \lambda) = p(X|\lambda) = \prod_{i=1}^{n}\left(\mathcal{N}\left(x^{(i)}; \mu, \frac{1}{\sqrt{\lambda}}\right)\right) \propto \lambda^{\frac{n}{2}} e^{-\frac{\lambda}{2}\sum_{i=1}^{n}\left(x^{(i)} - \mu\right)^2}$$

We model the prior for the precision with a gamma distribution with parameters α_0, β_0:

$$p(\lambda) = \gamma(\lambda; \alpha_0, \beta_0) \propto \lambda^{(\alpha_0 - 1)} e^{-\beta_0 \lambda}$$

We know the corresponding posterior—a product of a Gaussian and a gamma—is another gamma distribution (due to the conjugate prior property of gamma distribution). Let's denote the posterior as

$$p(\lambda|X) = \gamma(\lambda; \alpha_n, \beta_n)$$

From Bayes' theorem,

$$p(\lambda|X) \propto p(X|\lambda)\, p(\lambda)$$

$$\text{or} \quad \overbrace{\lambda^{(\alpha_n - 1)} e^{-\beta_n \lambda}}^{posterior} \propto \overbrace{\frac{\lambda^{\frac{n}{2}}}{\sqrt{2\pi}} e^{-\frac{\lambda}{2}\sum_{i=1}^{n}\left(x^{(i)} - \mu\right)^2}}^{likelihood} \; \overbrace{\lambda^{(\alpha_0 - 1)} e^{-\beta_0 \lambda}}^{prior}$$

Substituting

$$s = \frac{1}{n}\sum_{i=0}^{n}\left(x^{(i)} - \mu\right)^2$$

and comparing the powers of λ and e, we get

$$\alpha_n = \frac{n}{2} + \alpha_0$$

$$\beta_n = \frac{1}{2}\sum_{i=1}^{n}\left(x^{(i)} - \mu\right)^2 + \beta_0 = \frac{n}{2}s + \beta_0 \tag{13.6}$$

Notice that as before, at low values of n, the posterior is dominated by the prior but gets closer and closer to the likelihood estimate as n increases. In other words, in the absence of sufficient data, we let our belief take over the estimation; but if and when data is available, the estimation is dominated by the data-based entity likelihood.

The MAP point estimate for the parameter λ given data set X is obtained by maximizing this posterior distribution $p(\lambda|X) = \gamma(\lambda; \alpha_n, \beta_n)$, which yields $\lambda_{MAP} = \frac{1}{\sigma^2_{MAP}} = \left(\frac{\alpha_n - 1}{\beta_n}\right)$. (Section A.5 in the appendix shows how to obtain the maximum of a gamma distribution.) Thus our estimate for the training data distribution is $p(x) = \mathcal{N}(x;\ \mu, \sigma_{MAP})$, where $\frac{1}{\sigma^2_{MAP}} = \left(\frac{\alpha_n - 1}{\beta_n}\right)$.

Given a large volume of data, the MAP estimate for the unknown precision/variance becomes identical to the MLE estimate (proof outline shown):

$$\lim_{n\to\infty} \frac{1}{\sigma^2_{MAP}} = \lim_{n\to\infty}\left(\frac{\alpha_n - 1}{\beta_n}\right) = \lim_{n\to\infty} \frac{\frac{n}{2} + \alpha_0 - 1}{\frac{n}{2}s + \beta_0} = \lim_{n\to\infty} \frac{1 + \frac{\alpha_0 - 1}{\frac{n}{2}}}{s + \frac{\beta_0}{\frac{n}{2}}} = \frac{1}{s}$$

$$\text{or} \quad \lim_{n\to\infty} \sigma^2_{MAP} = s = \frac{1}{n}\sum_{i=0}^{n}\left(x^{(i)} - \mu\right)^2 = \sigma^2_{MLE}$$

On the other hand, given no data, the MAP estimate for the unknown precision/variance is completely determined by the prior (proof outline shown):

$$\lim_{n\to 0} \frac{1}{\sigma^2_{MAP}} = \lim_{n\to 0}\left(\frac{\alpha_n - 1}{\beta_n}\right) = \lim_{n\to 0} \frac{\frac{n}{2} + \alpha_0 - 1}{\frac{n}{2}s + \beta_0} = \frac{\alpha_0 - 1}{\beta_0}$$

$$\text{or} \quad \lim_{n\to 0} \sigma^2_{MAP} = \frac{\beta_0}{\alpha_0 - 1}$$

NOTE Fully functional code for Bayesian estimation with a known mean and unknown variance, executable via Jupyter Notebook, can be found at http://mng.bz/2nZ9.

Listing 13.2 PyTorch: Bayesian estimation with unknown variance, known mean

```
import torch

def inference_unknown_variance(X, prior_dist):
    sigma_mle = torch.std(X)
    n = X.shape[0]

    alpha_0 = prior_dist.concentration
    beta_0 = prior_dist.rate                  # Parameters of the prior

    alpha_n = n / 2 + alpha_0
    beta_n = n / 2 * sigma_mle ** 2 + beta_0      # Parameters of the posterior

    posterior_dist = torch.Gamma(alpha_n, beta_n)
    return posterior_dist
```

13.7 Fully Bayes parameter estimation: Gaussian, unknown mean, unknown precision

In section 13.3, we saw that if the variance is known, the conjugate prior to the mean is a Gaussian (aka normal) distribution. Likewise, when the mean is known, the conjugate prior to the precision is a gamma distribution. If both are unknown, we end up with a normal-gamma distribution.

13.7.1 Normal-gamma distribution

Normal-gamma is a probability distribution of two random variables, say, μ and λ, whose density is defined in terms of four parameters $\mu^{'}, \lambda^{'}, \alpha^{'}, and \beta^{'}$, as follows:

$$p\left(\mu, \lambda;\ \mu^{'}, \lambda^{'}, \alpha^{'}, \beta^{'}\right) = \mathcal{N}\gamma\left(\mu, \lambda;\ \mu^{'}, \lambda^{'}, \alpha^{'}, \beta^{'}\right)$$
$$= \frac{\beta'^{\alpha'}\sqrt{\lambda'}}{\Gamma(\alpha')\sqrt{2\pi}} e^{-\frac{\lambda}{2}\lambda'\left(\mu-\mu'\right)^2} \lambda^{\alpha'-\frac{1}{2}} e^{-\beta'\lambda}$$

Although it looks complicated, a simple way to remember it is a product of a normal and a gamma distribution.

The normal-gamma distribution attains a maximum at

$$\mu = \mu^{'}$$
$$\lambda = \frac{\alpha^{'} - \frac{1}{2}}{\beta'}$$

13.7.2 Estimating the mean and precision parameters

As before, we model the data distribution with a Gaussian: $p(x|\mu, \lambda) = \mathcal{N}\left(x; \mu, \frac{1}{\sqrt{\lambda}}\right)$ (we have expressed this Gaussian in terms of the precision, λ, which is related to the variance σ as $\lambda = \frac{1}{\sigma^2}$). The training data set is $X = \left\{x^{(1)}, x^{(2)}, \cdots, x^{(n)}\right\}$, and its overall likelihood is

$$p(X|\mu, \lambda) = \prod_{i=1}^{n}\left(\mathcal{N}\left(x^{(i)}; \mu, \frac{1}{\sqrt{\lambda}}\right)\right) \propto \lambda^{\frac{n}{2}} e^{-\frac{\lambda}{2}\sum_{i=1}^{n}\left(x^{(i)}-\mu\right)^2}$$

We model the prior for the mean as a Gaussian with mean μ_0 and precision $\lambda_0\lambda$:

$$p(\mu|\lambda) = \mathcal{N}(\mu; \mu_0, \lambda_0\lambda) \propto \lambda^{\frac{1}{2}} e^{-\frac{\lambda_0\lambda}{2}(\mu-\mu_0)^2}$$

We model the prior for the precision as a gamma distribution with parameters α_0, β_0:

$$p(\lambda) = \gamma(\lambda; \alpha_0, \beta_0) \propto \lambda^{(\alpha_0-1)} e^{-\beta_0\lambda}$$

The overall prior probability for the mean and precision parameters is the product of the two, a normal-gamma distribution with parameters $\mu^0, \lambda^0, \alpha^0, \beta^0$:

$$p(\mu, \lambda) = \mathcal{N}\gamma\left(\mu, \lambda|\mu^0, \lambda^0, \alpha^0, \beta^0\right) \propto \lambda^{\frac{1}{2}} e^{-\frac{\lambda_0\lambda}{2}(\mu-\mu_0)^2}\ \lambda^{(\alpha_0-1)} e^{-\beta_0\lambda}$$

The posterior probability for the mean and precision parameters is the joint (that is, product) of the likelihood and the prior. As such, we know it is another normal-gamma distribution (due to the conjugate prior property of normal-gamma):

$$p(\mu, \lambda | X) = \mathcal{N}\gamma(\mu, \lambda | \mu^n, \lambda^n, \alpha^n, \beta^n) \propto e^{-\frac{\lambda}{2}\lambda_n(\mu-\mu_n)^2} \lambda^{\alpha_n - \frac{1}{2}} e^{-\beta_n \lambda}$$

Using Bayes' theorem,

$$p(\mu, \lambda | X) \propto p(X | \mu, \lambda)\, p(\mu, \lambda)$$

or

$$\overbrace{e^{-\frac{\lambda}{2}\lambda_n(\mu-\mu_n)^2} \lambda^{\alpha_n - \frac{1}{2}} e^{-\beta_n \lambda}}^{\text{posterior}} \propto \overbrace{\lambda^{\frac{n}{2}} e^{-\frac{\lambda}{2}\sum_{i=1}^{n}\left(x^{(i)}-\mu\right)^2}}^{\text{likelihood}} \overbrace{\lambda^{\frac{1}{2}} e^{-\frac{\lambda_0 \lambda}{2}(\mu-\mu_0)^2}}^{\text{prior mean}} \overbrace{\lambda^{(\alpha_0 - 1)} e^{-\beta_0 \lambda}}^{\text{prior precision}}$$

Substituting

$$s = \frac{1}{n}\sum_{i=0}^{n}\left(x^{(i)} - \mu\right)^2$$

and comparing coefficients, the unknown parameters of the posterior distribution can be determined:

$$\mu_n = \frac{(n\bar{x} + \mu_0 \lambda_0)}{n + \lambda_0} \qquad \lambda_n = n + \lambda_0$$

$$\alpha_n = \frac{n}{2} + \alpha_0 \qquad \beta_n = \frac{ns}{2} + \beta_0 + \frac{n\lambda_0}{2(n + \lambda_0)}(\bar{x} - \mu_0)^2 \tag{13.7}$$

To obtain the fully Bayes parameter estimate, we take the maximum of the normal-gamma posterior probability density function:

$$\mu = \mu_n$$

$$\lambda = \frac{\alpha_n - \frac{1}{2}}{\beta_n}$$

Thus the final probability density function for the data is $p(x) = \mathcal{N}\left(x; \mu_n, \sqrt{\frac{\beta_n}{\alpha_n - \frac{1}{2}}}\right)$.

NOTE Fully functional code for Bayesian estimation with an unknown mean and unknown variance, executable via Jupyter Notebook, can be found at http://mng.bz/1oQy.

Listing 13.3 PyTorch code for a normal-gamma distribution

```
import torch

class NormalGamma():

    def __init__(self, mu_, lambda_, alpha_, beta_):
        self.mu_ = mu_
        self.lambda_ = lambda_
        self.alpha_ = alpha_
        self.beta_ = beta_
```

Since PyTorch doesn't implement normal-gamma distribution, we implement a bare-bones version.

```
    @property
    def mean(self):
        return self.mu_, self.alpha_/ self.beta_

    @property
    def mode(self):
        return self.mu_, (self.alpha_-0.5)/ self.beta_
```

Listing 13.4 PyTorch: Bayesian estimation with unknown mean, unknown variance

```
import torch

def inference_unknown_mean_variance(X, prior_dist):
    mu_mle = X.mean()
    sigma_mle = X.std()
    n = X.shape[0]

    mu_0 = prior_dist.mu_                  # Parameters of the prior
    lambda_0 = prior_dist.lambda_
    alpha_0 = prior_dist.alpha_
    beta_0 = prior_dist.beta_

    mu_n = (n * mu_mle + mu_0 * lambda_0) / (lambda_0 + n)
    lambda_n = n + lambda_0
    alpha_n = n / 2 + alpha_0              # Parameters of the posterior
    beta_n = n / 2 * sigma_mle ** 2 + beta_0 +
             0.5* n * lambda_0/ (n + lambda_0) *
             (mu_mle - mu_0) ** 2

    posterior_dist = NormalGamma(mu_n, lambda_n, alpha_n, beta_n)

    return posterior_dist
```

13.8 Example: Fully Bayesian inferencing

Let's revisit the problem discussed in section 6.8 of predicting whether a resident of Statsville is female based on height. For this purpose, we have collected height samples from adult female residents of Statsville. Unfortunately, due to unforeseen circumstances, we collected a very small sample. Armed with our knowledge of Bayesian inference, we do not want to let this deter us from trying to build a model. Based on physical considerations, we can assume that the distribution of heights is Gaussian. Our goal is to estimate the parameters (μ, σ) of this Gaussian.

NOTE Fully functional code for this example, executable via Jupyter Notebook, can be found at http://mng.bz/Pn4g.

Let's first create the data set by sampling five points from a Gaussian distribution with $\mu = 152$ and $\sigma = 8$. In real-life scenarios, we do not know the mean and standard deviation of the true distribution. But for the sake of this example, let's assume that the mean height is 152 cm and the standard deviation is 8 cm. Our data matrix, X, is as follows:

$$X = \begin{bmatrix} 164.32 \\ 149.65 \\ 134.56 \\ 156.54 \\ 143.32 \end{bmatrix}$$

13.8.1 Maximum likelihood estimation

If we relied on MLE, our approach would be to compute the mean and standard deviation of the data set and use this normal distribution as our model. We use the following equations to compute the mean and standard deviation of our normal distribution:

$$\mu_{MLE} = \frac{1}{N} \sum_{i=1}^{n} x_i$$

$$\sigma_{MLE} = \frac{1}{N} \sum_{i=1}^{n} (x_i - \mu)^2$$

The mean, μ, comes out to be 149.68, and the standard deviation, σ, is 11.52. This differs significantly from the true mean (152) and standard deviation (8) because the number of data points is low. In such low-data scenarios, the maximum likelihood estimates are not very reliable.

13.8.2 Bayesian inference

Can we do better than MLE? One potential method is to use Bayesian inference with a good prior. How do we select a good prior? Well, let's say that we know from an old survey that the average and standard deviation of the height of adult female residents of Neighborville, the neighboring town, are 150 cm and 9 cm, respectively. Additionally, we have no reason to believe that the distribution of heights at Statsville is significantly different. So we can use this information to "initialize" our prior. The prior distribution encodes our beliefs about the parameter values.

Given that we are dealing with an unknown mean and unknown variance, we model the prior as a normal-gamma distribution:

$$p(\theta) = N\gamma(\mu_0, \lambda_0, \alpha_0, \beta_0)$$

We choose $p(\theta)$ such that $\mu_0 = 150$, $\lambda_0 = 100$, $\alpha_0 = 10.5$, and $\beta_0 = 810$. This implies that

$$p(\theta) = N\gamma(150, 100, 10.5, 810)$$

$p(\theta|X)$ is a normal-gamma distribution whose parameters can be computed using equations described in section 13.7. The PyTorch code for computing the posterior is shown next.

Listing 13.5 PyTorch: Computing posterior probability using Bayesian inference

```
prior_dist = NormalGamma(150, 100, 10.5, 810)            # Initializes the normal-gamma distribution

posterior_dist = inference_unknown_mean_variance(X, prior_dist)   # Computes the posterior

map_mu, map_precision =  posterior_dist.mode             # The mode of the distribution refers to parameter values with the highest probability density.

map_std = math.sqrt(1 / map_precision)                   # Computes the standard deviation using precision

map_dist = Normal(map_mu, map_std)                       # map_mu and map_std refer to the parameter values that maximize the posterior distribution.
```

The MAP estimates for μ and σ obtained using Bayesian inference are 149.98 and 9.56, respectively, which are better than the MLE estimates of 149.68 and 11.52 (the true μ and σ are 152 and 9, respectively).

Now that we've estimated the parameters, we can find out the probability that a sample lies in the range using the formula

$$p(a < X <= b) = \int_a^b p(X)dX$$

The details of this can be found in section 6.8.

13.9 Fully Bayes parameter estimation: Multivariate Gaussian, unknown mean, known precision

This is the multivariate case; the univariate version is discussed in section 13.3. The computations follow along the same lines as the univariate ones.

We model the data distribution as a Gaussian $p\left(\vec{x}|\vec{\mu},\mathbf{\Lambda}\right) = \mathcal{N}\left(\vec{x};\ \vec{\mu},\mathbf{\Lambda}^{-1}\right)$, where we have expressed the Gaussian in terms of the *precision matrix* $\mathbf{\Lambda}$ instead of the covariance matrix $\mathbf{\Sigma}$, where $\mathbf{\Lambda} = \mathbf{\Sigma}^{-1}$. The training data set is $X \equiv \left\{\vec{x}^{(1)}, \vec{x}^{(2)}, \cdots, \vec{x}^{(i)}, \cdots, \vec{x}^{(n)}\right\}$, and its overall likelihood is

$$p\left(X|\vec{\mu}\right) = \propto e^{-\frac{1}{2}\sum_{i=1}^{n}\left(\vec{x}^{(i)}-\vec{\mu}\right)^T\mathbf{\Lambda}\left(\vec{x}^{(i)}-\vec{\mu}\right)}$$

We model the prior for the mean as a Gaussian:

$$p\left(\vec{\mu}\right) = \mathcal{N}\left(\vec{\mu};\ \vec{\mu}_0, \mathbf{\Lambda}_0^{-1}\right) \propto e^{-\frac{1}{2}\left(\vec{\mu}-\vec{\mu}_0\right)^T\mathbf{\Lambda}_0\left(\vec{\mu}-\vec{\mu}_0\right)}$$

The posterior probability density is a Gaussian (because it is the product of two Gaussians). Let's denote it as

$$p\left(\vec{\mu}|X\right) = \mathcal{N}\left(\vec{\mu};\ \vec{\mu}_n, \mathbf{\Lambda}_n^{-1}\right) \propto e^{-\frac{1}{2}\left(\vec{\mu}-\vec{\mu}_n\right)^T\mathbf{\Lambda}_n\left(\vec{\mu}-\vec{\mu}_n\right)}$$

Using Bayes' theorem,

$$p\left(\vec{\mu}|X\right) \propto p\left(X|\vec{\mu}\right) p\left(\vec{\mu}\right)$$

$$\text{or}\quad \overbrace{e^{-\frac{1}{2}(\vec{\mu}-\vec{\mu}_n)^T \mathbf{\Lambda}_n (\vec{\mu}-\vec{\mu}_n)}}^{posterior} \propto \overbrace{e^{-\frac{1}{2}\sum_{i=1}^{n}\left(\vec{x}^{(i)}-\vec{\mu}\right)^T \mathbf{\Lambda}\left(\vec{x}^{(i)}-\vec{\mu}\right)}}^{likelihood} \overbrace{e^{-\frac{1}{2}(\vec{\mu}-\vec{\mu}_0)^T \mathbf{\Lambda}_0 (\vec{\mu}-\vec{\mu}_0)}}^{prior}$$

$$\propto e^{-\frac{1}{2}\left(\sum_{i=1}^{n}\left(\vec{x}^{(i)}-\vec{\mu}\right)^T \mathbf{\Lambda}\left(\vec{x}^{(i)}-\vec{\mu}\right)+(\vec{\mu}-\vec{\mu}_0)^T \mathbf{\Lambda}_0 (\vec{\mu}-\vec{\mu}_0)\right)}$$

Let's examine the exponent of the rightmost expression.

$$\sum_{i=1}^{n}\left(\vec{x}^{(i)}-\vec{\mu}\right)^T \mathbf{\Lambda}\left(\vec{x}^{(i)}-\vec{\mu}\right) + \left(\vec{\mu}-\vec{\mu}_0\right)^T \mathbf{\Lambda_0}\left(\vec{\mu}-\vec{\mu}_0\right)$$

$$= \sum_{i=1}^{n} \vec{x}^{(i)^T} \mathbf{\Lambda} \vec{x}^{(i)} + \sum_{i=1}^{n} \vec{\mu}^T \mathbf{\Lambda} \vec{\mu} - 2\vec{\mu}^T \mathbf{\Lambda} \overbrace{\sum_{i=1}^{n} \vec{x}^{(i)}}^{n\bar{\vec{x}}} + \vec{\mu}^T \mathbf{\Lambda_0} \vec{\mu} - 2\vec{\mu}^T \mathbf{\Lambda_0} \vec{\mu}_0 + \vec{\mu}_0^T \mathbf{\Lambda_0} \vec{\mu}_0$$

$$= \sum_{i=1}^{n} \vec{x}^{(i)^T} \mathbf{\Lambda} \vec{x}^{(i)} + n\vec{\mu}^T \mathbf{\Lambda} \vec{\mu} - 2n\vec{\mu}^T \mathbf{\Lambda} \bar{\vec{x}} + \vec{\mu}^T \mathbf{\Lambda_0} \vec{\mu} - 2\vec{\mu}^T \mathbf{\Lambda_0} \vec{\mu}_0 + \vec{\mu}_0^T \mathbf{\Lambda_0} \vec{\mu}_0$$

$$= \vec{\mu}^T \left(n\mathbf{\Lambda} + \mathbf{\Lambda_0}\right) \vec{\mu} - 2\vec{\mu}^T \left(n\mathbf{\Lambda}\bar{\vec{x}} + \mathbf{\Lambda_0}\vec{\mu}_0\right) + \text{ constant terms without } \vec{\mu}$$

We ignored the last constant terms (because they will be rolled into the overall constant of proportionality). Thus

$$p\left(\vec{\mu}|X\right) \propto e^{-\frac{1}{2}(\vec{\mu}-\vec{\mu}_n)^T \mathbf{\Lambda}_n (\vec{\mu}-\vec{\mu}_n)}$$

$$\propto e^{-\frac{1}{2}\left(\vec{\mu}^T (n\mathbf{\Lambda}+\mathbf{\Lambda_0})\vec{\mu} - 2\vec{\mu}^T \left(n\mathbf{\Lambda}\bar{\vec{x}}+\mathbf{\Lambda_0}\vec{\mu}_0\right) + \text{ constant terms without } \vec{\mu}\right)}$$

Comparing coefficients:

$$\mathbf{\Lambda}_n = n\mathbf{\Lambda} + \mathbf{\Lambda}_0 \qquad \vec{\mu}_n = \mathbf{\Lambda}_n^{-1}\left(n\mathbf{\Lambda}\bar{\vec{x}} + \mathbf{\Lambda}_0\vec{\mu}_0\right) \text{ (remember } \mathbf{\Lambda} \text{ is known)}$$

The posterior probability maximizes at $\vec{\mu}_n$. Thus $\vec{\mu}_{\text{MAP}} = \vec{\mu}_n$ is the MAP estimate for the mean parameter of the multivariate Gaussian data distribution: $p\left(\vec{x}\right) = \mathcal{N}\left(\vec{x};\ \vec{\mu}_n, \mathbf{\Lambda}^{-1}\right)$.

Note the following:

$$\left.\begin{aligned} &\lim_{n\to\infty} n\mathbf{\Lambda}_n^{-1} = \lim_{n\to\infty} n\left(n\mathbf{\Lambda}+\mathbf{\Lambda}_0\right)^{-1} \\ &= \lim_{n\to\infty}\left(n^{-1}\right)^{-1}\left(n\mathbf{\Lambda}+\mathbf{\Lambda}_0\right)^{-1} = \lim_{n\to\infty}\left(n^{-1}n\mathbf{\Lambda}+n^{-1}\mathbf{\Lambda}_0\right)^{-1} = \mathbf{\Lambda}^{-1} \\ &\lim_{n\to\infty}\mathbf{\Lambda}_n^{-1} = \lim_{\to\infty} n^{-1}n\mathbf{\Lambda}_n^{-1} = \lim_{n\to\infty} n^{-1}\mathbf{\Lambda}^{-1} = 0 \end{aligned}\right\} \lim_{n\to\infty}\vec{\mu}_n = \bar{\vec{x}}$$

$$\lim_{n\to 0}\vec{\mu}_n = \vec{\mu}_0$$

With a large volume of data, the estimated mean parameter $\vec{\mu}_{\text{MAP}} = \vec{\mu}_n$ approaches the MLE $\vec{\mu}_{\text{MLE}} = \bar{\vec{x}}$. With a low volume of data, the estimated posterior mean parameter $\vec{\mu}_{\text{MAP}} = \vec{\mu}_n$ approaches the prior $\vec{\mu}_0$.

NOTE Fully functional code for multivariate Bayesian inferencing of the mean of a Gaussian likelihood with known precision, executable via Jupyter Notebook, can be found at http://mng.bz/J2AP.

Listing 13.6 PyTorch: Multivariate Bayesian inferencing, unknown mean

```
def inference_known_precision(X, prior_dist, precision_known):
    mu_mle = X.mean(dim=0)
    n = X.shape[0]

    mu_0 = prior_dist.mean
    precision_0 = prior_dist.precision_matrix    ← Parameters of the prior

    precision_n = n * precision_known + precision_0    ← Parameters of the posterior
    mu_n = torch.matmul(
        n * torch.matmul(
            mu_mle.unsqueeze(0), precision_known) + torch.matmul(
                mu_0.unsqueeze(0), precision_0),
        torch.inverse(precision_n)
    )

    posterior_dist = MultivariateNormal(
        mu_n, precision_matrix=precision_n)
    return posterior_dist
```

13.10 Fully Bayes parameter estimation: Multivariate, unknown precision, known mean

In section 13.6, we discussed the univariate case, and now we examine the multivariate case. For the univariate case, we had to look at the gamma distribution. For the multivariate case, we have to look at the Wishart distribution.

13.10.1 Wishart distribution

Suppose we have a Gaussian random data vector $\vec{x}$ with probability density function $\mathcal{N}\left(\vec{x};\ \vec{\mu}, \mathbf{\Sigma}\right)$. Once again, we use *precision matrix* $\mathbf{\Lambda}$ instead of the covariance matrix $\mathbf{\Sigma}$, where $\mathbf{\Lambda} = \mathbf{\Sigma}^{-1}$. Consider the case where we know the mean $\vec{\mu}$ but want to estimate the precision $\mathbf{\Lambda}$. How do we express the prior? Note that $p\left(\mathbf{\Lambda}\right)$ is the probability density function of a *matrix*. So far, we have encountered probability distributions of scalars and vectors, not a matrix. Also, this is not an arbitrary matrix. We are talking about a *symmetric, non-negative definite* matrix (all covariance and precision matrices belong to this category). Consequently, the distribution we are looking for is not a joint distribution of all the d^2 matrix elements (d denotes the dimensionality of the data: that is, all $\vec{x}$ and $\vec{\mu}$ vectors are $d \times 1$). Rather, it is a joint distribution of $\frac{d(d+1)}{2}$ elements in the matrix—the diagonal and those above or below (diagonal elements above and below are identical because the matrix is symmetric).

The space of such matrices is called a *Wishart ensemble*. The probability of a random-precision matrix $\mathbf{\Lambda}$ of size $d \times d$ can be expressed as a Wishart distribution. This distribution has two parameters:

- ν, a scalar, satisfying $\nu > d - 1$
- $\mathbf{W}$, a $d \times d$ symmetric non-negative definite matrix

The probability density function is

$$p\left(\mathbf{\Lambda}; \nu, \mathbf{W}\right) = \mathcal{W}\left(\mathbf{\Lambda}; \nu, \mathbf{W}\right) = \frac{|\mathbf{\Lambda}|^{\frac{\nu-d-1}{2}} e^{-\frac{1}{2}Tr\left(W^{-1}\mathbf{\Lambda}\right)}}{2^{\frac{\nu d}{2}} |\mathbf{W}|^{\frac{\nu}{2}} \Gamma_d\left(\frac{\nu}{2}\right)}$$

where

- $\mathcal{W}$ denotes Wishart.
- $|\mathbf{W}|$, $|\mathbf{\Lambda}|$ denote the determinants of the matrices $\mathbf{W}$ and $\mathbf{\Lambda}$, respectively.
- $Tr\left(A\right)$ denotes the trace of a matrix A (sum of the diagonal elements).
- Γ denotes the multivariate gamma function

$$\Gamma_d\left(\frac{n}{2}\right) = \pi^{\frac{d(d-1)}{4}} \prod_{j=1}^{d} \Gamma\left(\frac{n-j+1}{2}\right)$$

The Wishart is the multivariate version of the gamma distribution. Its expected value is

$$\mathbb{E}\left(\mathbf{\Lambda}\right) = \nu \mathbf{W}$$

Its maxima occur at

$$\mathbf{\Lambda} = \left(\nu - d - 1\right) \mathbf{W} \text{ for } \nu \geq d + 1$$

13.10.2 Estimating precision

As before, we model the data distribution as a Gaussian $p\left(\vec{x} \middle| \vec{\mu}, \mathbf{\Lambda}\right) = \mathcal{N}\left(\vec{x};\ \vec{\mu}, \mathbf{\Lambda}^{-1}\right)$, where we have expressed the Gaussian in terms of the *precision matrix* $\mathbf{\Lambda}$ instead of the covariance matrix $\mathbf{\Sigma}$, where $\mathbf{\Lambda} = \mathbf{\Sigma}^{-1}$.

The training data set is $X \equiv \left\{\vec{x}^{(1)}, \vec{x}^{(2)}, \cdots, \vec{x}^{(i)}, \cdots, \vec{x}^{(n)}\right\}$, and its overall likelihood is

$$p\left(X|\mathbf{\Lambda}\right) =\propto |\mathbf{\Lambda}|^{\frac{n}{2}} e^{-\frac{1}{2}\sum_{i=1}^{n}\left(\vec{x}^{(i)}-\vec{\mu}\right)^T \mathbf{\Lambda}\left(\vec{x}^{(i)}-\vec{\mu}\right)}$$

We model the prior probability of the precision matrix as a Wishart distribution. Hence,

$$p\left(\mathbf{\Lambda}\right) = \mathcal{W}\left(\mathbf{\Lambda}; \nu_0, \mathbf{W_0}\right) \propto |\mathbf{\Lambda}|^{\frac{\nu_0-d-1}{2}} e^{-\frac{1}{2}Tr\left(\mathbf{W_0}^{-1}\mathbf{\Lambda}\right)}$$

The posterior is another Wishart (owing to the Wishart conjugate prior property):

$$p\left(\mathbf{\Lambda}|X\right) = \mathcal{W}\left(\mathbf{\Lambda}; \nu_n, \mathbf{W_n}\right) \propto |\mathbf{\Lambda}|^{\frac{\nu_n-d-1}{2}} e^{-\frac{1}{2}Tr\left(\mathbf{W_n}^{-1}\mathbf{\Lambda}\right)}$$

Using Bayes' theorem for the training data set X,

$$\underbrace{p(\mathbf{\Lambda}|X)}_{posterior} \propto \underbrace{p(X|\mathbf{\Lambda})}_{likelihood} \; \underbrace{p(\mathbf{\Lambda})}_{prior}$$

$$\overbrace{|\mathbf{\Lambda}|^{\frac{\nu_n-d-1}{2}} e^{-\frac{1}{2}Tr\left(\mathbf{W}_n^{-1}\mathbf{\Lambda}\right)}}^{posterior} \propto \overbrace{|\mathbf{\Lambda}|^{\frac{n}{2}} e^{-\frac{1}{2}\sum_{i=1}^{n}\left(\vec{x}^{(i)}-\vec{\mu}\right)^T \mathbf{\Lambda}\left(\vec{x}^{(i)}-\vec{\mu}\right)}}^{likelihood} \; \overbrace{|\mathbf{\Lambda}|^{\frac{\nu_0-d-1}{2}} e^{-\frac{1}{2}Tr\left(\mathbf{W}_0^{-1}\mathbf{\Lambda}\right)}}^{prior}$$

Let's study a pair of simple lemmas that will come in handy.

$$\vec{x}^T A\vec{x} = Tr\left(\vec{x}^T A\vec{x}\right)$$
$$\vec{x}^T A\vec{x} = Tr\left(A\vec{x}\vec{x}^T\right)$$

where Tr refers to Trace of a matrix (sum of diagonal elements).

- The first lemma is almost trivial—the quadratic form $\vec{x}^T A\vec{x}$ is a scalar, so of course it is the same as its trace.
- The second lemma follows directly from the matrix property of a trace: $Tr(BC) = Tr(CB)$.

Using the lemmas, the exponent of the likelihood term is

$$\sum_{i=1}^{n}\left(\vec{x}^{(i)}-\vec{\mu}\right)^T \mathbf{\Lambda}\left(\vec{x}^{(i)}-\vec{\mu}\right) = \sum_{i=1}^{n} Tr\left(\left(\vec{x}^{(i)}-\vec{\mu}\right)\left(\vec{x}^{(i)}-\vec{\mu}\right)^T \mathbf{\Lambda}\right)$$

$$= Tr\left(\overbrace{\sum_{i=1}^{n}\left(\vec{x}^{(i)}-\vec{\mu}\right)\left(\vec{x}^{(i)}-\vec{\mu}\right)^T}^{nS} \mathbf{\Lambda}\right) = Tr(nS\mathbf{\Lambda})$$

where

$$S = \frac{1}{n}\sum_{i=1}^{n}\left(\vec{x}^{(i)}-\vec{\mu}\right)\left(\vec{x}^{(i)}-\vec{\mu}\right)^T \quad \text{(remember, } \vec{\mu} \text{ is known).}$$

Thus, the posterior density is

$$p(\mathbf{\Lambda}|X)\; p(\mathbf{\Lambda}) \propto |\mathbf{\Lambda}|^{\frac{n}{2}} e^{-\frac{1}{2}Tr(nS\mathbf{\Lambda})} |\mathbf{\Lambda}|^{\frac{\nu_0-d-1}{2}} e^{-\frac{1}{2}Tr\left(\mathbf{W}_0^{-1}\mathbf{\Lambda}\right)}$$
$$\propto |\mathbf{\Lambda}|^{\frac{n+\nu_0-d-1}{2}} e^{-\frac{1}{2}\left(Tr(nS\mathbf{\Lambda})+Tr\left(\mathbf{W}_0^{-1}\mathbf{\Lambda}\right)\right)}$$

Since $Tr(A) + Tr(B) = Tr(A+B)$,

$$p(X|\mathbf{\Lambda})\; p(\mathbf{\Lambda}) \propto |\mathbf{\Lambda}|^{\frac{\overbrace{n+\nu_0}^{\nu_n}-d-1}{2}} e^{-\frac{1}{2}Tr\left(\left(\overbrace{nS+\mathbf{W}_0^{-1}}\right)\mathbf{\Lambda}\right)} \propto |\mathbf{\Lambda}|^{\frac{\nu_n-d-1}{2}} e^{-\frac{1}{2}Tr\left(\mathbf{W}_n^{-1}\mathbf{\Lambda}\right)}$$

Comparing coefficients, we determine the unknown parameters of the posterior distribution:

$$\boldsymbol{W_n}^{-1} = \left(nS + \boldsymbol{W_0}^{-1}\right)$$

$$\nu_n = n + \nu_0$$

where

$$S = \frac{1}{n}\sum_{i=1}^{n}\left(\vec{x}^{(i)} - \vec{\mu}\right)\left(\vec{x}^{(i)} - \vec{\mu}\right)^T$$

The maximum of the posterior density function, $\mathcal{W}\left(\boldsymbol{\Lambda}; \nu_n, \boldsymbol{W_n}\right)$, yields an estimate for the precision parameter of the data distribution:

$$\boldsymbol{\Lambda} = (\nu_n - d - 1)\,\boldsymbol{W_n} \text{ for } \nu_n \geq d + 1$$

i.e., $p\left(\vec{x}\right) = \mathcal{N}\left(\vec{x};\ \vec{\mu},\ \frac{\left(nS + \boldsymbol{W_0}^{-1}\right)}{(\nu_n - d - 1)}\right)$.

Summary

- A generative model that models the underlying data distribution can be more powerful than a black box discriminative model. Once we choose a model family, we need to estimate the model parameters, θ. We can estimate the best values of θ from the training data X using Bayes' theorem.
- The posterior distribution $p\left(\theta|X\right)$ is a function of the product of likelihood $p\left(X|\theta\right)$ and the prior $p\left(\theta\right)$. The prior expresses our belief in the value of the parameters. The posterior is dominated by the prior for small data sets and the likelihood for large data sets. Injecting belief via a good prior distribution can be helpful in settings with very little training data.
- Maximum likelihood estimation only relies on the data, in contrast to maximum a posteriori (MAP) estimation, which relies on the data as well as the prior information.
- We can use Bayesian estimation for the mean of a Gaussian likelihood when the variance is known. When the likelihood is Gaussian $p(X) \sim N(\mu, \sigma)$, we model the prior as a normal distribution $p\left(\mu\right) \sim N\left(\mu_0, \sigma_0\right)$. The posterior distribution is also a normal distribution $p\left(\mu|X\right) \sim N\left(\mu_n, \sigma_n\right)$, where $\sigma_n^2 = \frac{\sigma_0^2\sigma^2}{n\sigma_0^2 + \sigma^2}$ and $\mu_n = \frac{\bar{x}}{1 + \frac{\sigma^2}{n\sigma_0^2}} + \frac{\mu_0}{1 + \frac{n\sigma_0^2}{\sigma^2}}$. We can also use the estimated parameter to make predictions about new instances of data.
- Weak priors imply a high degree of uncertainty/lower confidence in our prior belief and can easily be overwhelmed by the data. In contrast, strong priors imply a lower degree of uncertainty/higher confidence in our prior belief and will resist data overload.
- For a specific family of likelihood, the choice of the prior that results in the posterior belonging to the same family as the prior is called a conjugate prior.

- The gamma function is $(\Gamma(\alpha) = \int_{x=0}^{\infty} x^{(\alpha-1)} e^{-x} dx)$, and the gamma distribution is $p(\lambda|\alpha, \beta) = \gamma(\lambda; \alpha, \beta) = \frac{\beta^{\alpha}}{\Gamma(\alpha)} \lambda^{(\alpha-1)} e^{-\beta\lambda}$. The gamma distribution varies with different values of α and β.
- In the case of Bayesian estimation of the precision of the Gaussian likelihood for a known mean, the precision λ is the inverse of the variance. We can model the prior as a gamma distribution $p(\lambda) = \frac{\beta_0^{\alpha_0}}{\Gamma(\alpha_0)} \lambda^{(\alpha_0-1)} e^{-\beta_0\lambda}$. The posterior distribution is also a gamma distribution, $p(\lambda|X) = \frac{\beta_n^{\alpha_n}}{\Gamma(\alpha_n)} \lambda^{(\alpha_n-1)} e^{-\beta_n\lambda}$, where $\alpha_n = \frac{n}{2} + \alpha_0$ and $\beta_n = \frac{1}{2} \sum_{i=1}^{n} \left(x^{(i)} - \mu\right)^2 + \beta_0 = \frac{n}{2}s + \beta_0$.
- In Bayesian estimation of both the mean and precision of a Gaussian likelihood, we model the prior as a normal-gamma distribution. The posterior is another normal-gamma distribution. The posterior distribution can be used to predict new data instances.
- The multivariate setting of Bayesian inferencing of the mean of a Gaussian likelihood is known as precision. We can model the prior as a multivariate normal distribution; the posterior is also a multivariate normal distribution.
- The Wishart distribution is the multivariate version of the gamma distribution. With multivariate Bayesian inferencing of the precision of a Gaussian likelihood with a known mean, we can model the prior as a Wishart distribution. The corresponding posterior is also a Wishart distribution.

14 Latent space and generative modeling, autoencoders, and variational autoencoders

This chapter covers

- Representing inputs with latent vectors
- Geometrical view, smoothness, continuity, and regularization for latent spaces
- PCA and linear latent spaces
- Autoencoders and reconstruction loss
- Variational autoencoders (VAEs) and regularizing latent spaces

Mapping input vectors to a transformed space is often beneficial in machine learning. The transformed vector is called a *latent vector*—latent because it is not directly observable—while the input is the underlying *observed vector*. The latent vector (aka embedding) is a simpler representation of the input vector where only features that help accomplish the ultimate goal (such as estimating the probability of an input belonging to a specific class) are retained, and other features are forgotten. Typically, the latent representation has fewer dimensions than the input: that is, encoding an input into a latent vector results in *dimensionality reduction.*

The mapping from input to latent space (and vice versa) is usually learned—we train a machine, such as a neural network, to do it. The latent vector needs to be as faithful a representation as possible of the input within the dimensionality allocated to it. So, the neural network is incentivized to minimize the loss of information caused by the transformation. Later, we see that in autoencoders, this is achieved by reconstructing the input from the latent vector and trying to minimize the difference between the actual and reconstructed input. However, given the reduced number of dimensions, the network does not have the luxury of retaining everything in the input. It has to learn what is essential to the end goal and retain only that. Thus the embedding is a compact representation of the input that is streamlined to achieve the ultimate goal.

14.1 Geometric view of latent spaces

Consider the space of all digital images of height H, width W, with each pixel representing a 24-bit RGB color value. This is a gigantic space with $(2^{24})^{HW}$ points. Every possible RGB $\times H \times W$ image is a point in this space. But if an image is a natural image, neighboring points tend to have similar colors. This means points corresponding to natural images are correlated: they are not distributed uniformly over the space of possible images. Furthermore, if the images have a common property (say, they all contain giraffes), the corresponding points form clusters in the $(2^{24})^{HW}$-sized input space. In stochastic parlance, the probability distribution of natural images with a common property over the space of possible images is highly non-uniform (low entropy).

Figure 14.1a illustrates points with some common property clustered around a planar manifold. Similarly, figure 14.1b illustrates points with some common property clustered around a curved manifold. These points have a common property. At the moment, we are not interested in what that property is or whether the manifold is planar or curved. All we care about is that these points of interest are distributed around a manifold. The manifold captures the essence of that common property, whatever it is. If the common property is, say, the presence of a giraffe in the image, then the manifold captures *giraffeness*: the points on or near the manifold all correspond to images with giraffes. If we travel along the manifold, we encounter various flavors of giraffe photos. If we go far from the manifold—that is, travel a long distance in a direction orthogonal to the manifold—the probability of the point representing a photo with a giraffe is low.

Given training data consisting of sampled points of interest (such as many giraffe photos), we can train a neural network to learn this manifold—it is the optimal manifold that minimizes the average distance of all the training data points from the manifold. Then, at inference time, given an arbitrary input point, we can estimate its distance from the manifold, giving us the probability of that input satisfying the property represented by the manifold.

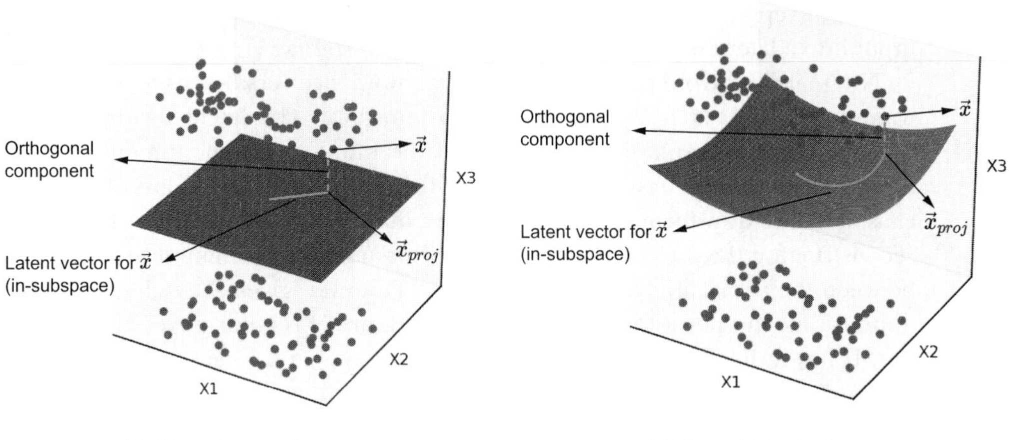

(a) Planar latent subspaces (b) Curved latent subspace

Figure 14.1 Two examples of latent subspaces, with planar and curved manifolds, respectively. The solid line shows the latent vector, and the dashed line represents the information lost by projecting onto the latent subspace.

Thus, the input vector can be decomposed into an in-manifold component (solid line in figure 14.1) and an orthogonal-to-manifold component (dashed line in figure 14.1). Latent space modeling effectively eliminates the orthogonal component and retains the in-manifold component as the latent vector (aka embedding). Equivalently, we are projecting the input vector onto the manifold. This is the core idea of latent space modeling—we learn a manifold that represents a property of interest and represents all inputs by a latent vector, which is the input point's projection onto this manifold. The latent vector is a more compact representation of the input where only information related to the property of interest is retained.

Latent space modeling in a nutshell

In latent space modeling, we train a neural network to represent a manifold around which the input points satisfying a property of interest are distributed. The property of interest could be membership in a specific class, such as images containing a giraffe. Thus, the learned manifold is a collection of points that satisfy the property. The input point is projected onto this manifold to obtain a latent vector representation of the input (aka embedding). This is equivalent to throwing away the input vector component that is orthogonal to the manifold. The eliminated component is orthogonal to the manifold and hence unrelated to the property of interest (may represent background pixels of the image), so the information loss caused by the projection does not hurt. We have created a less noisy, more compact representation of the input that focuses on the things we care about.

Training data consists of a set of sampled data inputs, all satisfying the property of interest. The system essentially learns the manifold, which is optimally located to minimize its average distance from all the training data points. During inferencing, given an arbitrary input point, its distance from the manifold is an indicator of the probability of that input satisfying the property of interest.

A subtle point is that the latent vector is the in-manifold component of the original point's position vector. By switching to the latent vector representation, we lose the location of the point in the original higher-dimensional input space. We can go back to the higher-dimensional space by providing the location of the manifold for the lost orthogonal component, but doing so does not recover the original point: it recovers only the projection of the original point onto the subspace. We are replacing the individual orthogonal components with an aggregate entity (the location of a manifold) but do not recover the exact original point. Some information is irretrievably lost during projection.

A special case of latent space representation is principal component analysis (PCA), introduced in section 4.4 (section 14.4 provides a contextual recap of PCAs). It projects input points to an optimal planar latent subspace (as in figure 14.1a). But except for some lucky special cases, the best latent subspace is not a hyperplane. It is a complex curved surface (see figure 14.1b). Neural networks, such as autoencoders, can learn such nonlinear projections.

14.2 Generative classifiers

During inferencing, the supervised classifiers we have encountered in previous chapters typically emit the class to which an input belongs, perhaps along with a bounding box. This is somewhat black-box-like behavior. We do not know how well the classifier has mastered the space except through the quantized end results. Such classifiers are called *discriminative* classifiers. On the other hand, latent space models map arbitrary input points to probabilities of belonging to the class of interest. Such models are called *generative* models, and they have some desirable properties:

- *Smoother, denser manifolds*—Discriminative models learn decision boundaries separating data points of interest from those not of interest in the input space. On the other hand, generative models try to model the distribution of the data points of interest in the input space using smooth probability density functions. As such, the generative model can't learn a very irregularly shaped function that overfits the training data. This is illustrated in figure 14.2, whereas the discriminative model may converge to a manifold that follows the nooks and bends of the training data too closely (overfits) as in figure 14.2b. This difference between discriminative and generative classifiers becomes especially significant when we have less training data. We can always create a discriminative classifier from a generative classifier by putting a threshold on the probability.

NOTE We can always create a discriminative classifier from a generative classifier by putting a threshold on the probability.

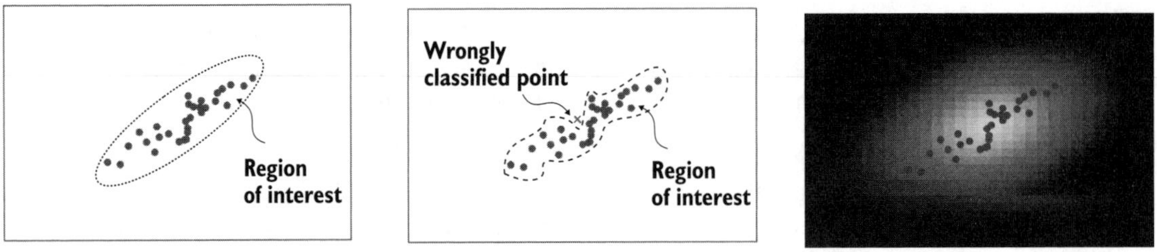

(a) A good discriminative classifier—smooth decision boundary

(b) A bad discriminative classifier—irregular decision boundary

(c) Generative model—no decision boundary (heat map indicates the probability density)

Figure 14.2 Solid circles indicate training data points (all belonging to the class of interest). The dashed curve indicates the decision boundary separating the class of interest from the class of non-interest. In a generative model, there is no decision boundary. Every point in the space is associated with a probability of belonging to the class of interest (indicated as a heat map in figure 14.2c).

- *Extra insight*—Generative models offer more insight into the inner workings of the model. Consider a model that recognizes horses. Suppose we feed some horse images to the model, and it calls them horses (good). Then we feed the model some zebra images, and it calls them horses, too (bad). Do we have a useless model that calls everything a horse? If it is a discriminative model, we must test it with totally different images (say, bird images) to get the answer. But if we have a generative model, it says the probabilities of the true horse images are, say, 0.9 and above, while the probabilities for the zebra images are around 0.7. We begin to see that the model is behaving reasonably and does realize that zebras are less "horsy" than real horses.
- *New class instances*— A generative model learns the *distribution* of input points belonging to the class. An advantage related to learning the distribution is that we can sample the distribution to generate new members of the class (for example, to generate artificial horse images). This leads to the name *generative* modes. If we train a generative model with writings of Shakespeare, it will emit Shakespeare-like text pieces. Believe it or not, this has been tried with some success.

14.3 Benefits and applications of latent-space modeling

Let's recap at a high level why we want to do latent-space modeling:

- *Generative models are often based on latent space models*—all the benefits of generative modeling as outlined in section 14.2 apply to latent space modeling too.
- *Attention to what matters*—Redundant information that does not contribute to the end goal is eliminated, and the system focuses on truly discriminative information. To visualize this, imagine an input data set of police mugshots consisting of people standing in front of the same background. Latent-space modeling trained to recognize people typically eliminates the common background from the representation and focuses on the photograph's subject matter (people).
- *Streamlined representation of data*—The latent vector is a more compact representation of the input vector (reduced dimensions and hence smaller) with no meaningful information lost.

- *Noise elimination*—Latent-space modeling eliminates the low-variance orthogonal-to-latent-subspace component of the data. This is mostly data that does not help in the problem of interest and hence is noise.
- *Transformation to a manifold that is friendlier toward the end goal*—We have seen this notion previously, but here let's look at an interesting simple example. Consider a set of 2D points in Cartesian coordinates (x, y). Suppose we want to classify the points into two sets: those that lie *inside* the circle $x^2 + y^2 = a^2$ and those that lie *outside* the circle. In the original Cartesian space, the decision boundary is not linear (it is circular). But if we transform the Cartesian input points to a latent space in polar coordinates—that is, each (x, y) is mapped to (r, θ) such that $x = rcos\,(\theta)\,, y = rsin\,(\theta)$—the circle transforms into a line $r = a$ in the latent space . A simple linear classifier $r = a$ in the latent space can achieve the desired classification.

Some applications of latent-space modeling are as follows:

- Generating artificial images or text (as explained in the context of generative modeling).
- *Similarity estimation between inputs*—If we map inputs to latent vectors, we can assess the similarity between inputs by computing the Euclidean distance between the latent vectors. Why is this better than taking the Euclidean distance between the input vectors?

  Suppose we are building a recommendation engine that suggests other clothing items "similar" to the one a potential buyer is currently browsing. We want to retrieve other clothing items that look similar but not identical to the one viewed. But similarity is a subjective concept, not quite measurable via the similarity of the inputs' pixel colors. Consider a shirt with black vertical stripes on a white base. If we switch the stripe color with the base color, we get a shirt with white vertical stripes on a black base. If we do pixel-to-pixel color matching, these are very different, yet they are considered similar by humans. For this problem, we have to train the latent space model, creating neural networks so that images perceived to be similar by humans map to points in latent space that are close to each other. For example, both white-on-black and black-on-white shirts should map to latent vectors that are close to each other in the latent space even though they are far apart in the input space.
- *Image or other data compression*—The latent vector approximates the data with a smaller-dimensional vector that mimics the original vector as faithfully as possible. Thus the latent vector is a lossy compressed representation of the input.
- *Denoising*—The latent vector eliminates the non-meaningful part of the input information, which is noise.

NOTE Fully functional code for this chapter, executable via Jupyter Notebook, can be found at http://mng.bz/6XG6.

14.4 Linear latent space manifolds and PCA

PCAs (which we discussed in section 4.4) project input data onto linear hyperplanar manifolds. Revisiting this topic will set up the correct context for the rest of this chapter. Consider a set of 3D input data points clustered closely around the $X_0 = X_2$ plane, as shown in figure 14.3.

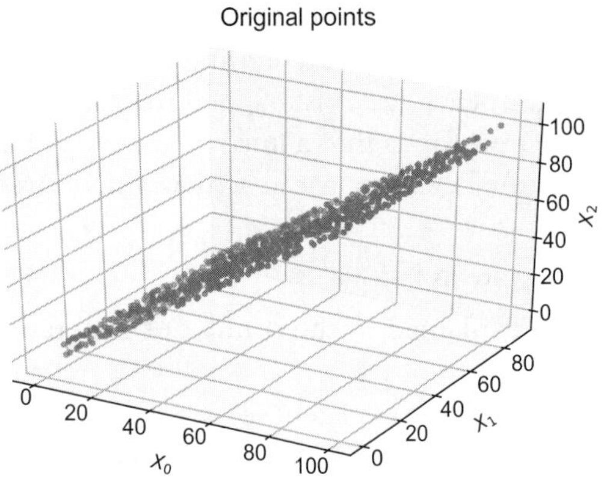

(a) Original 3D data

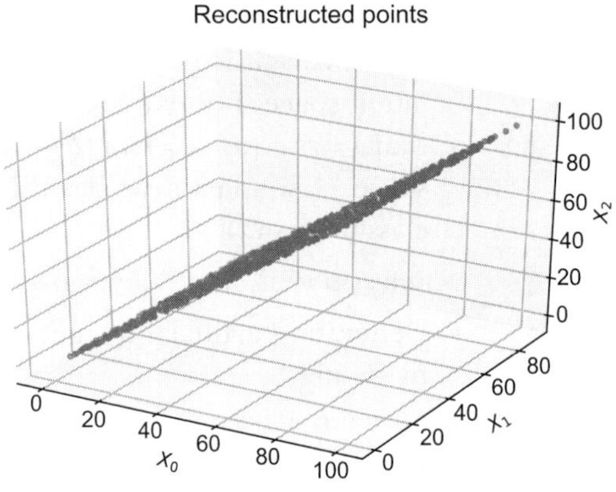

(b) Lower-dimensional 2D representation obtained by setting the third principal value to zero

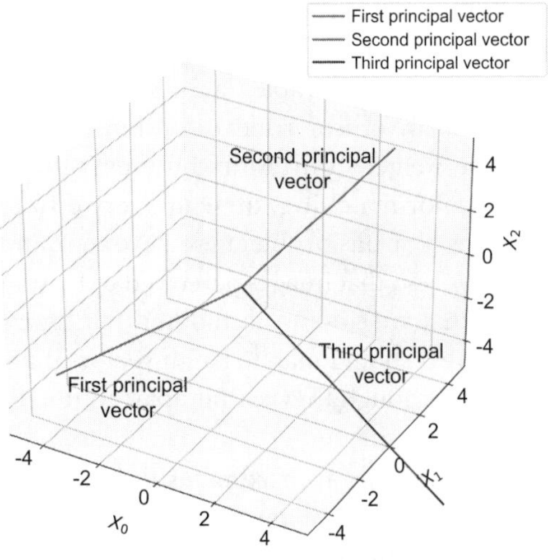

(c) The principal vectors of the original data. The third principal vector is normal to $X_0 = X_2$ plane; the other two are in-plane.

Figure 14.3 The original 3D data in figure 14.3a shows high correlation: points are clustered around the $X_0 = X_2$ plane. The first principal component corresponds to the direction of maximum variance. The last (third) principal component corresponds to the direction of lowest variance. Eliminating components of the input vector along the third principal vector effectively projects all points into the $X_0 = X_2$ plane (latent subspace). This is latent vector modeling with the 3D input reduced to a 2D latent vector.

NOTE We denote the successive axes (dimensions) as X_0, X_1, X_2 instead of the more traditional X, Y, Z for easy extension to higher dimensions.

Using PCA, we can recognize that the data has low variation along some dimensions. When we do PCA, we get the principal value and principal vector pairs. The largest principal value corresponds to the direction of maximum variance in the data. The corresponding principal vector yields that direction, and that principal value indicates the magnitude of the variance along that direction. The next principal value, the principal vector pair, is the orthogonal direction with the next-highest variance, and so on. For instance, in figure 14.3, the principal vectors corresponding to the larger two principal values lie in the $X_0 = X_2$ plane, while the smallest principal value corresponds to the normal-to-plane vector. The third principal value is significantly smaller than the others. This tells us that variance along that axis is low, and components along that axis can be dropped with relatively little loss of information: that is, low reconstruction loss. The variations along the small principal value axes are likely noise, so eliminating them cleans up the data. In figure 14.3, this effectively projects the data onto the $X_0 = X_2$ plane.

Dimensionality reduction

PCA essentially projects inputs to the *best-fit plane* for the training data. Assuming all the training data points are sampled with a common property, this plane represents that common property. By projecting, we eliminate that common property and retain only the discriminating aspects of the data. The eliminated information is remembered *approximately* in the parameters of the plane and supplied during reconstruction (aka decoding) to map us back to the same dimensionality as the input (but not exactly the same point). This is the essence of dimensionality reduction via PCA.

Following are the steps involved in PCA-based dimensionality reduction. This was described in detail with proofs in section 4.5; here we recap the main steps without proof.

NOTE This treatment is similar but not identical to that in section 4.5. Here we have switched the variables m and n to be consistent with our use of n to denote the data instance count. We have also switched to a slightly different flavor of the SVD.

1. Represent the data as a matrix X, where each row is an individual data instance. The number of rows n is the size of the data set. The number of columns d is the original (input) dimensionality of the data. Thus X is a $n \times d$ matrix.
2. Compute the mean data vector

$$\vec{\mu} = \frac{1}{n} \sum_{i=1}^{n} \vec{x}^{(i)}$$

   where $\vec{x}^{(i)}$ for $i = 1$ to $i = n$ denote the training data vector instances (which form rows of the matrix X).

3 Shift the origin of the coordinate system to the mean by subtracting the mean vector from each data vector:

$$\vec{x}^{(i)} = \vec{x}^{(i)} - \vec{\mu} \quad \text{for all } i$$

The data matrix X now has the mean-subtracted data instances as rows.

4 The matrix $X^T X$ (where X is the mean-subtracted data matrix) is the covariance matrix (as discussed in detail in section 5.7.2). The eigenvalue, eigenvector pairs of the matrix $X^T X$ are known as principal values and principal vectors (together referred to as principal components). Since $X^T X$ is a $d \times d$ matrix, there are d scalar eigenvalues and d eigenvectors, each of dimension $d \times 1$. Let's denote the principal components as $(\lambda_1, \vec{v}_1)$, $(\lambda_2, \vec{v}_2)$, $\cdots$, $(\lambda_{dm}, \vec{v}_d)$.

5 We can assume $\lambda_1 \geq \lambda_2 \geq \cdots \geq \lambda_d$ (if necessary, we can make this true by renumbering the principal components). Then the first principal component corresponds to the direction of maximum variance in the data (proof with geometrical intuition can be found in section 5.7.2). The corresponding principal value yields the actual variance. The next principal value corresponds to the second-highest variance (among directions orthogonal to the first principal direction), and so forth. For every component, the principal value yields the actual variance, and the principal vector yields the direction.

6 Consider the matrix of principal vectors:

$$V = \begin{bmatrix} \vec{v}_1 & \vec{v}_2 & \cdots \vec{v}_d \end{bmatrix}$$

If we want the data to be a space with m dimensions with minimal loss of information, we should drop the last m vectors of V. This eliminates the m least-variance dimensions. Dropping the last m vectors from V yields a matrix

$$V_{d-m} = \begin{bmatrix} \vec{v}_1 & \vec{v}_2 & \cdots \vec{v}_{d-m} \end{bmatrix}$$

Note that the best way to obtain the V matrix is to perform SVD on the mean-subtracted X (see section 4.5).

7 Premultiplying V_{d-m}, the truncated principal vectors matrix, with the original data matrix X projects the data onto a space corresponding to the first $d - m$ principal components. Thus, to create $d - m$-dimensional linearly encoded latent vectors from d-dimensional data,

$$X_{d-m} = X V_{d-m}$$

X_{d-m} is the reduced dimension data set. Its dimensionality is $n \times (d - m)$.

It can be shown that

$$X V_{d-m} = U \Sigma_{d-m}$$

where U is from SVD (see section 4.5) and Σ_{d-m} is a truncated version of the diagonal matrix Σ from SVD with its smallest m elements chopped off. This offers an alternative way to do PCA-based dimensionality reduction.

8 How do we reconstruct? In other words, what is the decoder? Well, to reconstruct, we need to save the original principal vectors: that is, the V matrix. If we have that, we can introduce m zeros at the right of every row in X_{d-m} to make it a $n \times d$ matrix again. Then we post-multiply by V^T, which rotates the coordinate system back from one with principal vectors as axes to one with the original input axes. Finally, we add the mean $\vec{\mu}$ to each row to shift the origin back to its original position, which yields the reconstructed data matrix $\tilde{X}$. The reconstruction loss is $||X - \tilde{X}||^2$. Note that, in effect, $\tilde{X}$ is $U\Sigma V^T$ with the last m diagonal elements of Σ set to zero.

9 The reconstructed data $\tilde{X}$ is *not* identical to the original data. The information we lost during dimensionality reduction (the normal-to-plane components) is lost permanently. Nonetheless, this principled way of dropping information ensures that the reconstruction loss is minimal in some sense, at least among all $\tilde{X}$ linearly related to X.

14.4.1 PyTorch code for dimensionality reduction using PCA

Now, let's implement dimensionality reduction in PyTorch. Let X be a data matrix representing points clustered around the $X_0 = X_2$ plane. X is of shape [1000, 3], with each row of X representing a three-dimensional data point. The following listing shows how to project X into a lower-dimensional space with minimal loss of information. It also shows how to reconstruct the original data points from the lower-dimensional representations. Note that the reconstructions are approximate because we have lost information (albeit minimal) in the dimensionality-reduction process.

NOTE Fully functional code for dimensionality reduction using PCA, executable via Jupyter Notebook, can be found at http://mng.bz/7yJg.

Listing 14.1 PyTorch: PCA revisited

```
import torch

X = get_data()          ← Data matrix of shape (1000, 3)

X_mean = X.mean(axis=0)     ← Stores the mean so we can reconstruct
                              the original data points later

X = X - X_mean          ← Subtracts the mean before performing SVD

U, S, Vh = torch.linalg.svd(X, full_matrices=False)     ← Runs SVD

V = Vh.T        ← Columns of V are the principal vectors.
```

```
V_trimmed =  V[:, 0: 2]    # Removes the last principal vector. This is along the direction of least variance (perpendicular to X0 = X2 plane).

X_proj = torch.matmul(X, V_trimmed)    # Projects the input data points into the lower-dimensional space

X_proj = torch.cat([X_proj,    # Pads with zeros to make an n x d matrix
             torch.zeros((X_proj.shape[0], 1))], axis=1)

X_recon = torch.matmul(X_proj, Vh)    # Post-multiplies with V^T to project back to the original space

X_recon = X_recon + X_mean    # Adds the mean
```

14.5 Autoencoders

Autoencoders are neural network systems trained to generate latent-space representations corresponding to specified inputs. They can do nonlinear projections and hence are more powerful than PCA systems (see figure 14.4). The neural network mapping the input vector to a latent vector is called an *encoder*. We also train a neural network called a *decoder* that maps the latent vector back to the input space. The decoder output is the reconstructed input from the latent vector. The reconstructed input (that is, the output of the decoder) will never match the original input exactly—information was lost during encoding and cannot be brought back—but we can try to ensure that they match as closely as possible within the constraints of the system. The reconstruction loss is a measure of the difference between the original input and the reconstructed input. The encoder-decoder pair is trained end to end to minimize reconstruction loss (along with, potentially, some other losses). This is an example of *representation learning*, whereby we learn to represent input vectors with smaller latent vectors representing the input as closely as possible in the stipulated size budget. The budgeted size of the latent space is a hyperparameter.

Figure 14.4 A 2D data distribution with a curved underlying pattern. It is impossible to find a straight line or vector such that all points are near it. PCA will not do well.

NOTE A hyperparameter is a neural network parameter that is *not* learned. Its value is set based on our knowledge of the system and held constant during training.

The desired output is implicitly known in autoencoders: it is the input. Consequently, no human labeling is needed to train autoencoders; they are *unsupervised*. An autoencoder is shown schematically in figure 14.5.

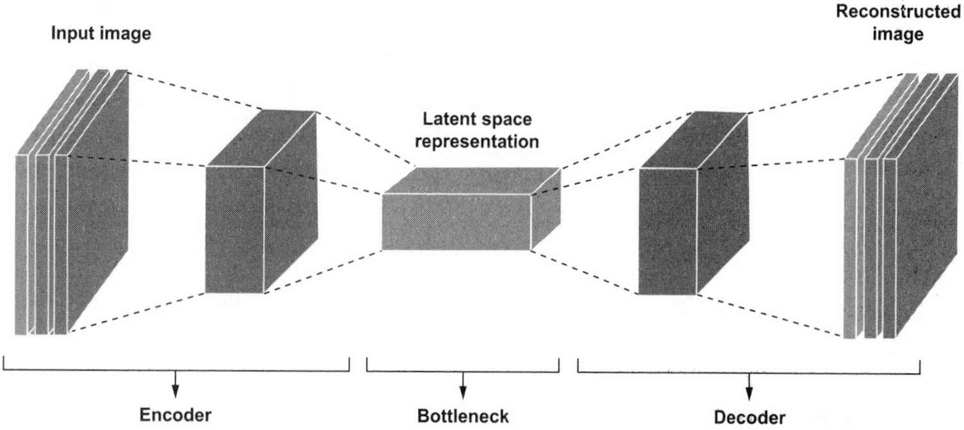

Figure 14.5 Schematic representation of an autoencoder. The encoder transforms input into a latent vector. The decoder transforms the latent vector into reconstructed input. We minimize the reconstruction loss—the distance between the reconstructed input and the original input.

- The encoder takes an input $\vec{x}$ and maps it to a lower-dimensional latent vector $\vec{z}$. An example of an encoding neural network for image inputs is shown in listing 14.2. Note how the image height and width keep decreasing with each successive sequence of convolution, ReLU, and max pool layers.
- The decoder is a neural network that generates reconstructed image $\tilde{\vec{x}}$ from the latent vector $\vec{z}$. Listing 14.3 shows an example of a decoder neural network. Note the transposed convolutions and how the height and width of the image keep increasing with each successive sequence of transposed convolution, batch normalization, and ReLU. (Transposed convolutions are discussed in section 10.5.) The decoder essentially remembers—not exactly, but in an average sense—the information discarded during encoding. Equivalently, it remembers the position of the latent space manifold in the overall input space. Adding that back to the latent space representation takes us back to the same dimensionality as the input vector but not to the same input point.
- The system minimizes the information loss from the encoding (the reconstruction loss). We are ensuring that for each input, the corresponding latent vector produced by the encoder can be mapped back to a reconstructed value by the decoder that is as close as possible to the input. Equivalently, each latent vector is a faithful representation of the input, and there is a 1 : 1 mapping between inputs and latent vectors.
- The encoder and decoder need not be symmetric.

Mathematically,

$$\text{Encoder:} \quad \overbrace{\vec{z}}^{\text{latent vector}} = E\left(\vec{x}\right)$$

$$\text{Decoder:} \quad \overbrace{\tilde{\vec{x}}}^{\text{reconstructed image}} = D\left(\vec{z}\right)$$

$$\text{Loss:}\mathcal{L} = \overbrace{\|\vec{x} - \tilde{\vec{x}}\|^2}^{\text{distance between input and reconstructed image}}$$

The end-to-end system is trained to minimize the loss $\mathcal{L}$.

NOTE Fully functional code for autoencoders, executable via Jupyter Notebook, can be found at http://mng.bz/mOzM.

Listing 14.2 PyTorch: Autoencoder encoder

```
from torch import nn
nz = 10
input_image_size = (1, 32, 32)          ← Input image size in (c, h, w) format
conv_encoder = nn.Sequential(
            nn.Conv2d(in_channels, 32, kernel_size=3, stride=1, padding=1),
            nn.BatchNorm2d(32),
            nn.ReLU(),
            nn.MaxPool2d(kernel_size=2),     ← Reduces to a (32, 16, 16)-sized tensor

            nn.Conv2d(32, 128, kernel_size=3, stride=1, padding=1),
            nn.BatchNorm2d(128),
            nn.ReLU(),
            nn.MaxPool2d(kernel_size=2),     ← Reduces to a (128, 8, 8)-sized tensor

            nn.Conv2d(128, 256, kernel_size=3, stride=1, padding=1),
            nn.BatchNorm2d(256),
            nn.ReLU(),
            nn.MaxPool2d(kernel_size=2),     ← Reduces to a (256, 4, 4)-sized tensor

            nn.Flatten()      ← Flattens to a 4096-sized tensor
        )
fc = nn.Linear(4096, nz)      ← Reduces the 4096-sized tensor to an nz-sized tensor
```

Listing 14.3 PyTorch: Autoencoder decoder

```
from torch import nn
decoder = nn.Sequential(
            nn.ConvTranspose2d(self.nz, out_channels=256,
             kernel_size=4, stride=1,
             padding=0, bias=False),     ← Converts (nz, 1, 1) to a
                                           (256, 4, 4)-sized tensor
```

```
        nn.BatchNorm2d(256),
        nn.ReLU(True),
        nn.ConvTranspose2d(256, 128, kernel_size=2,
          stride=2, padding=0, bias=False),            # Increases to a (128, 8, 8)-sized tensor
        nn.BatchNorm2d(128),
        nn.ReLU(True),
        nn.ConvTranspose2d(128, 32, kernel_size=2,
          stride=2, padding=0, bias=False),            # Increases to a (32, 16, 16)-sized tensor
        nn.BatchNorm2d(32),
        nn.ReLU(True),
        nn.ConvTranspose2d(32, in_channels, kernel_size=2,
          stride=2, padding=0, bias=False),            # Increases to a (1, 32, 32)-sized tensor
        nn.Sigmoid()
    )
```

Listing 14.4 PyTorch: Autoencoder training

```
from torch import nn
from torch.nn import functional as F

conv_out = conv_encoder(X)        # Passes the input image through the convolutional encoder

z =  fc(conv_out)                 # Reduces to nz dimensions

Xr = decoder(z)                   # Reconstructs the image using z via the decoder

recon_loss = F.mse_loss(Xr, X)    # Computes the reconstruction loss
```

14.5.1 Autoencoders and PCA

It is important to realize that autoencoders perform a much more powerful dimensionality reduction than PCA. PCA is a linear process; it can only project data points to best-fit hyperplanes. Autoencoders can fit arbitrary complex nonlinear hypersurfaces to the data, limited only by the expressive powers of the encoder-decoder pair. If the encoder and decoder have only a single linear layer (no ReLU or other nonlinearity), then the autoencoder projects the data points to a hyperplane like PCA (not necessarily the same hyperplane).

14.6 Smoothness, continuity, and regularization of latent spaces

Minimizing the reconstruction loss does not yield a unique solution. For instance, figure 14.6 shows two examples of transforming 2D inputs into 1D latent-space representations, linear and curved, respectively. Both the regularized (solid line) and the non-regularized zigzag manifold (dashed line) fit the training data well with low reconstruction error. But the former is smoother and more desirable.

Note the pair of points marked p_1, p_2 and p_3, p_4(square markers). The distance between them is more or less the same in the input space. But when projected on the dashed curve (unregularized latent space), their distances (measured along the curve)

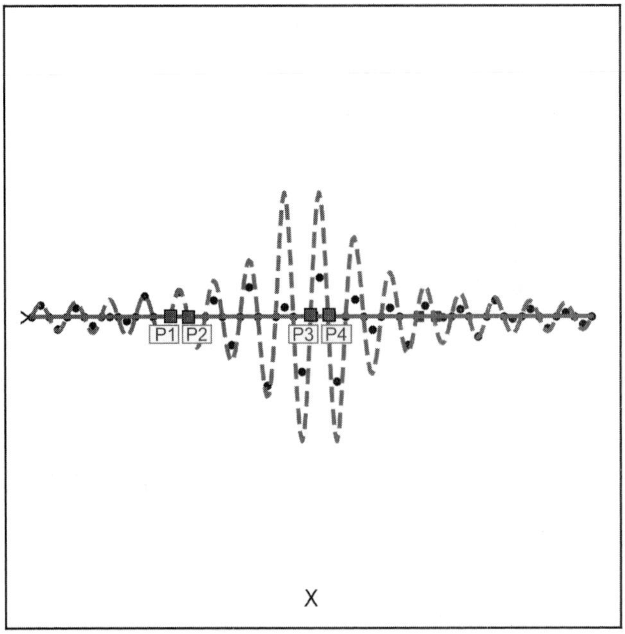

(a) Linear latent space

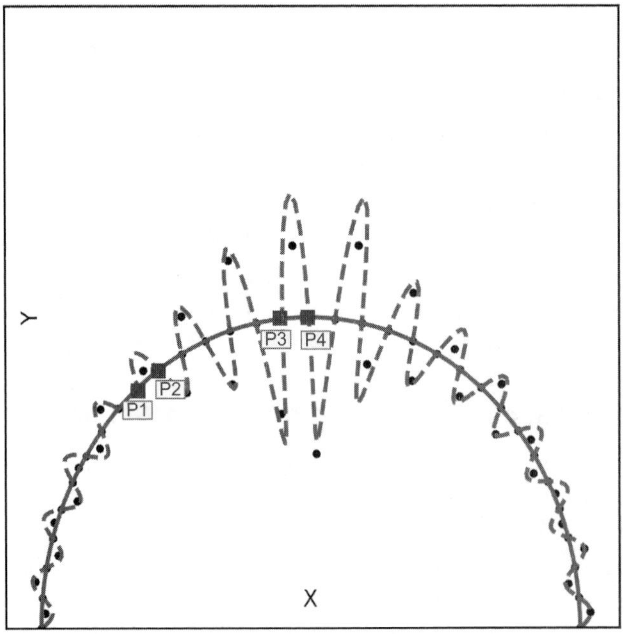

(b) Curved latent space

Figure 14.6 Two examples of mapping from a 2D input space to a 1D latent space. Both show regularized (solid) vs. unregularized (dashed) latent space manifolds. Solid little circles depict training data points.

become quite different. This is undesirable and does not happen in the regularized latent space (here, the distance is measured along a solid line). It becomes much more pronounced in high dimensions.

The zigzag curve segment containing the training data set is longer than the smooth one. A good latent manifold typically has fewer twists and turns (is smooth) and hence has a "length" that is minimal in a sense. This is reminiscent of the minimum descriptor length (MDL) principle, which we discussed in section 9.3.1.

How do we ensure that this smoothest latent space is chosen over others that also minimize the reconstruction loss? By putting additional constraints (losses) over and above the ubiquitous reconstruction loss. Recall the notion of regularization, which we looked at in sections 6.6.3 and 9.3. There we introduced an explicit loss that penalizes longer solutions (which was equivalent to maximizing the a posteriori probability of parameter values as opposed to the likelihood). A related approach that we explore in this chapter is to model the latent space as a probability distribution belonging to a known family (for example, Gaussian) and minimize the difference (KL divergence) of this estimated distribution from a zero-mean univariance Gaussian. The encoder-decoder neural network pair is trained end to end to minimize a loss that is a weighted sum of the reconstruction loss and this KL divergence. Trying to remain close to the zero-mean unit-variance Gaussian penalizes departure from compactness and smoothness. This is the basic idea of variational autoencoders (VAEs).

The overall effect of regularization is to create a latent space that is more compact. If we only minimize the reconstruction loss, the system can achieve that by mapping points very far from each other (space being infinite). Regularization combats that and incentivizes the system to not map the training points too far from one another. It tries to limit the total latent-space volume occupied by the points corresponding to the training inputs.

14.7 Variational autoencoders

VAEs are a special case of autoencoders. They have the same architecture: a pair of neural networks that encode and decode the input vector, respectively. They also have the reconstruction loss term. But they have an additional loss term called KL divergence loss that we explain shortly.

NOTE Throughout this chapter, we denote latent variables with $\vec{z}$ and input variables with $\vec{x}$.

14.7.1 Geometric overview of VAEs

Figure 14.7 attempts to provide a geometrical view of VAE latent-space modeling. During training, given an input $\vec{x}$, the encoder does not directly emit the corresponding latent-space representation $\vec{z}$. Instead, the encoder emits the parameters of a distribution from a prechosen family. For instance, if the prechosen family is Gaussian, the encoder emits a pair of parameter values $\vec{\mu}\left(\vec{x}\right)$, $\mathbf{\Sigma}\left(\vec{x}\right)$. These are the mean and covariance matrix of a specific Gaussian distribution $\mathcal{N}\left(\vec{z};\ \vec{\mu}\left(\vec{x}\right),\ \mathbf{\Sigma}\left(\vec{x}\right)\right)$ in the latent space. The latent-space

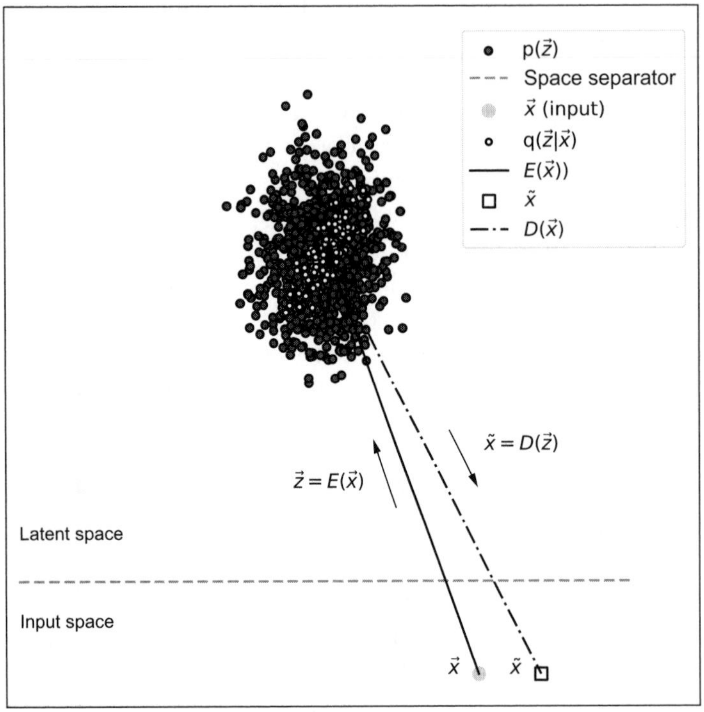

Figure 14.7 Geometric depiction of VAE latent-space modeling distributions

representation $\vec{z}$ corresponding to the input $\vec{x}$ is obtained by sampling this distribution emitted by the encoder. Thus in the Gaussian case, we have $\vec{z} \sim \mathcal{N}\left(\vec{z};\ \vec{\mu}\left(\vec{x}\right), \Sigma\left(\vec{x}\right)\right)$.

NOTE The symbol ~ indicates sampling from a distribution.

This distribution, which we call the *latent-space map* of the input $\vec{x}$, is shown by hollow circles with dark borders in figure 14.7. Such mapping is called *stochastic mapping*.

The latent-space map distribution should have a narrow, single-peaked probability density function (for example, a Gaussian with small variance: that is, small $\|\Sigma\|$). The narrow-peakedness of the probability density function implies that the cloud of sample points forms a tight, small cluster—any random sample from the distribution will likely be close to the mean. So, sampling $\vec{z}$ from such a distribution is not very different from a deterministic mapping from $\vec{x}$ to $\vec{z} = \vec{\mu}\left(\vec{x}\right)$. This sampling to obtain the latent vector is done only during training. During inferencing, we use the mean emitted by the encoder directly as the latent-space representation of the input: that is, $\vec{z} = \vec{\mu}\left(\vec{x}\right)$.

The decoder maps the latent vector representation $\vec{z}$ back to a point, say $\tilde{x}$, in the input space. This is the reconstructed version of the input vector (shown by a little white square with a black border in figure 14.7). The decoder is thus estimating (reconstructing) the input given the latent vector.

14.7.2 VAE training, losses, and inferencing

Training comprises the following steps:

1. Choose a simple distribution family for $q(\vec{z} \mid \vec{x})$. Gaussian is a popular choice.
2. Each input $\vec{x}$ maps to a separate distribution. The encoder neural network emits the parameters of this distribution. For the Gaussian case, the encoder emits $\mu(\vec{x}), \Sigma(\vec{x})$. The latent vector $\vec{z}$ is sampled from this emitted distribution.
3. The decoder neural network takes $\vec{z}$ as input and emits the reconstructed input $\tilde{x}$.

Given the input, reconstructed input, and latent vector we can compute the reconstruction loss and KL Divergence loss described below. The goal of the training process is to iteratively minimize these losses. Thus, the VAE is trained to minimize a weighted sum of the following two loss terms on each input batch:

- *Reconstruction Loss*—Just as in an autoencoder, in a properly trained VAE, the reconstruction $\tilde{x}$ should be close to the original input $\vec{x}$. So, reconstruction loss is

$$\mathcal{L}_{recon} = ||\vec{x} - \tilde{x}||^2$$

- *KL divergence loss*— In VAE, we also have a loss term proportional to the KL divergence between the distribution emitted by the encoder and the zero mean unit variance Gaussian. KL divergence measured the dissimilarity between two probability distributions and was discussed in detail in section 6.4. Here we state (following equation 6.13) that the KL divergence loss for VAE is

$$\mathcal{L}_{kld} = KLD\left(q\left(\vec{z}|\vec{x}\right), p\left(\vec{z}\right)\right) = \int_{\vec{z} \in D} q\left(\vec{z}|\vec{x}\right); \log\left(\frac{q\left(\vec{z}|\vec{x}\right)}{p\left(\vec{z}\right)}\right) d\vec{z}$$

where $q\left(\vec{z}|\vec{x}\right)$ denotes the latent-space map probability distribution and $p\left(\vec{z}\right)$ is a fixed target distribution. We want our global distribution of latent vectors to mimic the target distribution. The target is typically chosen to be a compact distribution so that the global latent vector distribution is also compact.

The popular choice for the prechosen distribution family is Gaussian and for the fixed distribution is the zero-mean unit covariance matrix Gaussian:

$$q\left(\vec{z}|\vec{x}\right) = \mathcal{N}\left(\vec{z};\ \vec{\mu}\left(\vec{x}\right), \boldsymbol{\Sigma}\left(\vec{x}\right)\right) \text{ and } p\left(\vec{z}\right) = \mathcal{N}\left(\vec{z};\ \vec{0}, \mathbf{I}\right)$$

It should be noted that for the above choice of prior, we can evaluate the KLD loss via a closed form formula as described in section 14.7.7.

Minimizing $\mathcal{L}_{kld}$ essentially demands that $q\left(\vec{z}|\vec{x}\right)$ is high—that is, close to one—at the $\vec{z}$ values where $p\left(\vec{z}\right)$ is high (see figure 14.8), because then their ratio is close to one and the logarithm is close to zero. The values of $p\left(\vec{z}\right)$ at the places where $q\left(\vec{z}|\vec{x}\right)$ is low (close to zero) do not matter because $q\left(\vec{z}|\vec{x}\right)$ appears as a factor in $\mathcal{L}_{kld}$—the contributions to the loss by these terms are close to zero anyway.

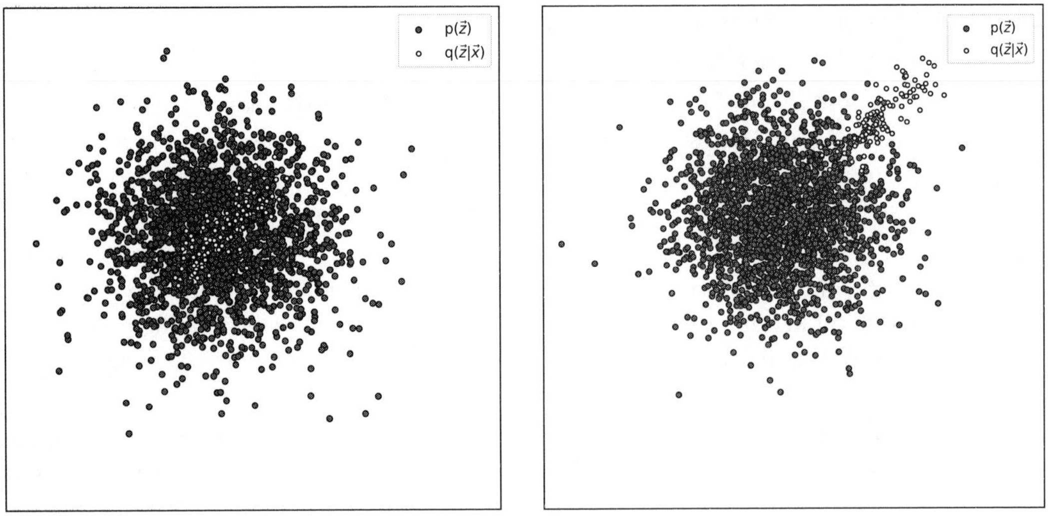

(a) Low KL divergence loss (high $q\left(\vec{z}|\vec{x}\right)$ coincides with high $p\left(\vec{z}\right)$

(b) High KL divergence loss (high $q\left(\vec{z}|\vec{x}\right)$ coincides with low $p\left(\vec{z}\right)$

Figure 14.8 KL divergence loss in VAEs is high when there is a large amount of overlap in mass between the encoder-generated distribution ($\mathcal{N}\left(\vec{z};\ \vec{\mu}\left(\vec{x}\right), \Sigma\left(\vec{x}\right)\right)$) and the target distribution $p\left(\vec{z}\right)$ (here $p\left(\vec{z}\right) \equiv \mathcal{N}\left(\vec{z};\ \vec{0}, \mathbf{I}\right)$) or, equivalently, low KL divergence between them.

Thus, KLD loss essentially tries to ensure that most of the sample point cloud of $q\left(\vec{z}|\vec{x}\right)$ falls on a densely populated region of the sample point cloud of $p\left(\vec{z}\right)$. Geometrically, this means the cloud of little hollow circles with black borders has a lot of overlapping mass with the target distribution. If every training data point is like that, the overall global cloud of latent vectors will also have significant overlap with the target distribution. Since the target distribution is typically chosen to be compact, this in turn ensures that the overall latent vector distribution (dark filled circles in figure 14.7) is compact. For instance, in the case when the target distribution is the zero-mean unit covariance matrix Gaussian $\mathcal{N}\left(\vec{z};\ \vec{0}, \mathbf{I}\right)$, most of the mass of the latent vectors is contained within the unit radius ball. Without the KL divergence term, the latent vectors will spread throughout the latent space. In short, the KLD loss *regularizes the latent space.*

The encoder-decoder pair of neural networks is trained end to end to minimize the weighted sum of reconstruction loss and KLD loss. In particular, the encoder learns to emit the parameters of the $q\left(\vec{z}|\vec{x}\right)$ distribution.

During inferencing, only the encoder is used. The encoder takes an input $\vec{x}$ and outputs $\vec{\mu}\left(\vec{x}\right)$ and $\boldsymbol{\Sigma}\left(\vec{x}\right)$. We do not sample here. Instead, we use the mean directly as the latent-space representation of the input.

Notice that each input point $\vec{x}$ maps to a separate Gaussian distribution $q(\vec{z}|\vec{x} = N(\vec{z};\ \vec{\mu}(\vec{x}),\ \Sigma(\vec{x}))$. The overall distribution $p(\vec{x})$ modeled by all of these together can be very complex. Yet that complexity does not affect our computation which involves only $q(z|x)$ and $p(z)$. This is what makes the approach powerful.

14.7.3 VAEs and Bayes' theorem

During training, the encoder neural network stochastically maps a specific input data instance, a point $\vec{x}$ in the input space, to a latent-space point $\vec{z} \sim \mathcal{N}\left(\vec{z};\ \vec{\mu}\left(\vec{x}\right), \mathbf{\Sigma}\left(\vec{x}\right)\right)$. Thus the latent-space map effectively models the posterior probability $p\left(\vec{z}|\vec{x}\right)$. Note that we are using the symbol $q\left(\vec{z}|\vec{x}\right)$ to denote the actual distribution emitted by the encoder, while we are using the symbol $p\left(\vec{z}|\vec{x}\right)$ to denote the true (unknown) posterior probability distribution. Of course, we want these two to be as close as possible to each other: that is, we want the KL divergence between them to be minimal. Later in this section, we see how minimizing the KL divergence between $q\left(\vec{z}|\vec{x}\right)$ and $p\left(\vec{z}|\vec{x}\right)$ leads to the entire VAE algorithm.

The decoder maps this point $\left(\vec{z}\right)$ in latent space back to the input space point $\tilde{x}$. As such, it models the probability distribution $p\left(\vec{x}|\vec{z}\right)$.

The global distributions of the latent vectors $\vec{z}$ effectively model $p\left(\vec{z}\right)$ (shown by dark-shaded filled little circles in figure 14.7). These probabilities are connected by our old friend, Bayes' theorem:

$$\overbrace{p\left(\vec{z}|\vec{x}\right)}^{\text{encoder / posterior}} = \frac{\overbrace{p\left(\vec{x}|\vec{z}\right)}^{\text{decoder / likelihood}} \quad \overbrace{p\left(\vec{z}\right)}^{\text{prior}}}{\underbrace{p\left(\vec{x}\right)}_{\text{evidence, constant wrt } \vec{z}}}$$

14.7.4 Stochastic mapping leads to latent-space smoothness

Sampling the encoder's output from a narrow distribution is similar, but not identical, to deterministic mapping. It has a rather unexpected advantage over direct encoding. A specific input point is mapped to a slightly different point in the latent space every time it is encountered during training—all these points have to decode back to the same region in the input space. This enforces an overall smoothness over the latent space: nearby $\vec{z}$ values all correspond to nearby $\vec{x}$ values.

14.7.5 Direct minimization of the posterior requires prohibitively expensive normalization

The Bayes' theorem expression of a VAE in section 14.7.3 gives us an idea. Why not train the neural network to directly maximize the posterior probability $p\left(\vec{z}\middle|\vec{X}\right)$, where X denotes the training data set? It certainly makes theoretical sense; we are choosing the latent space whose posterior probability is maximum given the training data. Of course, we must optimize one batch at a time, as we always do with neural networks.

How do we evaluate the posterior probability? The formula is as follows:

$$p\left(\vec{z}|\vec{x}\right) = \frac{p\left(\vec{x}|\vec{z}\right)\ p\left(\vec{z}\right)}{p\left(\vec{x}\right)} = \frac{p\left(\vec{x}|\vec{z}\right)\ p\left(\vec{z}\right)}{\int_{\vec{z}} p\left(\vec{x}|\vec{z}\right) p\left(\vec{z}\right) d\vec{z}}$$

The denominator contains a sum over all values of $\vec{z}$. Remember, with every iteration, the neural network weights change, and all previously computed latent vectors become invalid. This means we have to recompute all latent vectors every iteration, which is intractable. Each iteration is $O(n)$, and each epoch then is $O(n^2)$, where n is the number of training data instances (could be on the order of millions). We have to look for other methods. That takes us to *evidence lower bound* (ELBO) types of approaches.

14.7.6 ELBO and VAEs

We do not know the true probability distribution $p(\vec{z}|\vec{x})$. Let's try to learn an approximate probability distribution $q(\vec{z}|\vec{x})$ that is as close as possible to $p(\vec{z}|\vec{x})$. In other words, we want to minimize the KL divergence between the two (KL divergence was introduced in section 6.4). This KL divergence is

$$KLD(q, p) = \int_{\vec{z} \in D} q(\vec{z}|\vec{x}) \, ln\left(\frac{q(\vec{z}|\vec{x})}{p(\vec{z}|\vec{x})}\right) d\vec{z}$$

We can expand this as

$$\begin{aligned}
KLD(q, p) &= \int_{\vec{z} \in D} q(\vec{z}|\vec{x}) \, ln\left(\frac{q(\vec{z}|\vec{x})}{p(\vec{z}|\vec{x})}\right) d\vec{z} \\
&= \int_{\vec{z} \in D} q(\vec{z}|\vec{x}) \, ln\left(q(\vec{z}|\vec{x})\right) d\vec{z} - \int_{\vec{z} \in D} q(\vec{z}|\vec{x}) \, ln\left(p(\vec{z}|\vec{x})\right) d\vec{z} \\
&= \int_{\vec{z} \in D} q(\vec{z}|\vec{x}) \, ln\left(q(\vec{z}|\vec{x})\right) d\vec{z} - \int_{\vec{z} \in D} q(\vec{z}|\vec{x}) \, ln\left(p(\vec{z}, \vec{x})\right) d\vec{z} + \int_{\vec{z} \in D} q(\vec{z}|\vec{x}) \, ln\left(p(\vec{x})\right) d\vec{z} \\
&= \overbrace{\int_{\vec{z} \in D} q(\vec{z}|\vec{x}) \, ln\left(q(\vec{z}|\vec{x})\right) d\vec{z}}^{-H_q \text{ (negative of entropy)}} - \overbrace{\int_{\vec{z} \in D} q(\vec{z}|\vec{x}) \, ln\left(p(\vec{z}, \vec{x})\right) d\vec{z}}^{E_q(ln(p(\vec{x},\vec{z})))} + ln\left(p(\vec{x})\right) \overbrace{\int_{\vec{z} \in D} q(\vec{z}|\vec{x}) \, d\vec{z}}^{=1} \\
&= -H_q - E_q\left(ln\left(p(\vec{x}, \vec{z})\right)\right) + ln\left(p(\vec{x})\right)
\end{aligned}$$

where D is the domain of $\vec{z}$: that is, the latent space, H_q is the entropy of the probability distribution (entropy was introduced in section 6.2), and $E_q\left(ln\left(p(\vec{x}, \vec{z})\right)\right)$ is the expected value of $ln\left(p(\vec{x}, \vec{z})\right)$ under the probability density $q(\vec{z}|\vec{x})$. Rearranging terms, we get

$$KLD(q, p) + H_q + E_q\left(ln\left(p(\vec{x}, \vec{z})\right)\right) = \overbrace{ln\left(p(\vec{x})\right)}^{\text{constant}}$$

where the right-hand side is constant because it is a property of the data and cannot be adjusted during optimization. Defining the evidence lower bound (ELBO) as

$$ELBO = H_q + E_q\left(ln\left(p(\vec{x}, \vec{z})\right)\right)$$

we get

$$KLD(q, p) + ELBO = constant$$

So, *minimizing* the KL divergence between $p(\vec{z}|\vec{x})$ and its approximation $q(\vec{z}|\vec{x})$ is equivalent to *maximizing* the ELBO. We soon see that this leads to a technique for optimizing variational autoencoders.

SIGNIFICANCE OF THE NAME ELBO

Why do we call it *evidence lower bound*? Well, the answer is hidden in the relation $KLD(q, p) + ELBO = ln(p(\vec{x}))$. The right-hand side is the evidence log-likelihood. Remember, KL divergence is always non-negative. So, the lowest value of $ln(p(\vec{x}))$ happens when KL divergence is zero when $ln(p(\vec{x})) = ELBO$. This means the evidence log-likelihood cannot be lower than the ELBO value. Thus the ELBO is the lower bound of the evidence log-likelihood; in short, it is the evidence lower bound.

PHYSICAL SIGNIFICANCE OF THE ELBO

Let's look at the physical significance of ELBO maximization:

$$ELBO = H_q + E_q(ln(p(\vec{x}, \vec{z})))$$

The first term is entropy. As we saw in section 6.2, this is a measure of the diffuseness of the distribution. If the points are evenly spread out in the distribution—the probability density is flat with no high peak—the entropy is high. When the distribution has few tall peaks and low values elsewhere, entropy is low (remember, for a probability density, having tall peaks implies low values elsewhere since the total volume under the function is constant: one). Thus, maximizing the ELBO means we are looking for a diffuse distribution $q(\vec{z}|\vec{x})$. This, in turn, encourages smoothness in the latent space since we are effectively saying an input point $\vec{x}$ can map to any point around the mean $\vec{\mu}(\vec{x})$ (as emitted by the encoder) with almost equal high probability. Note that this fights a bit with the notion that each input should map to a unique point in the latent space. The solution tries to optimize between these conflicting requirements.

The other term—expectation of the log of joint density $p(\vec{x}, \vec{z})$ under the probability density $q(\vec{z}|\vec{x})$—effectively measures the overlap between the two. Maximizing it is equivalent to saying $q(\vec{z}|\vec{x})$ must be high where $p(\vec{x}, \vec{z})$ is high. This seems intuitively true. The joint density $p(\vec{x}, \vec{z}) = p(\vec{z}|\vec{x})\, p(\vec{z})$. It is high where *both* the posterior $p(\vec{z}|\vec{x})$ and prior $p(\vec{z})$ are high. If $q(\vec{z}|\vec{x})$ approximates the posterior, it should be high where the joint is high.

Let's continue to explore the ELBO. More physical significances will emerge along with an algorithm for VAE optimization:

$$\begin{aligned}
ELBO &= H_q + E_q(ln(p(\vec{x}, \vec{z}))) \\
&= -\int_{\vec{z} \in D} q(\vec{z}|\vec{x})\, ln(q(\vec{z}|\vec{x}))\, d\vec{z} + \int_{\vec{z} \in D} q(\vec{z}|\vec{x})\, ln(p(\vec{z}, \vec{x}))\, d\vec{z} \\
&= -\int_{\vec{z} \in D} q(\vec{z}|\vec{x})\, ln(q(\vec{z}|\vec{x}))\, d\vec{z} + \int_{\vec{z} \in D} q(\vec{z}|\vec{x})\, ln(p(\vec{x}|\vec{z})\, p(\vec{z}))\, d\vec{z} \\
&= -\int_{\vec{z} \in D} q(\vec{z}|\vec{x})\, ln(q(\vec{z}|\vec{x}))\, d\vec{z} + \int_{\vec{z} \in D} q(\vec{z}|\vec{x})\, ln(p(\vec{x}|\vec{z}))\, d\vec{z} + \int_{\vec{z} \in D} q(\vec{z}|\vec{x})\, ln(p(\vec{z}))\, d\vec{z}
\end{aligned}$$

Rearranging terms and simplifying

$$ELBO = \overbrace{\int_{\vec{z} \in D} q\left(\vec{z}|\vec{x}\right) ln\left(p\left(\vec{x}|\vec{z}\right)\right) d\vec{z}}^{E_q(ln(p(\vec{x}|\vec{z})))} - \overbrace{\int_{\vec{z} \in D} q\left(\vec{z}|\vec{x}\right) ln\left(\frac{q\left(\vec{z}|\vec{x}\right)}{p\left(\vec{z}\right)}\right) d\vec{z}}^{KLD(q(\vec{z}|\vec{x}),p(\vec{z}))}$$

$$ELBO = E_q\left(ln\left(p\left(\vec{x}|\vec{z}\right)\right)\right) - KLD\left(q\left(\vec{z}|\vec{x}\right), p\left(\vec{z}\right)\right)$$

This last expression yields more physical interpretation and leads to the VAE algorithm. Let's examine the two terms in the final ELBO expression in detail. The first term is $E_q\left(ln\left(p\left(\vec{x}|\vec{z}\right)\right)\right)$. This is high when $q\left(\vec{z}|\vec{x}\right)$ and $p\left(\vec{x}|\vec{z}\right)$ are both high at the same $\vec{z}$ values. For a given $\vec{x}$, $q\left(\vec{z}|\vec{x}\right)$ is high at those $\vec{z}$ values that are likely encoder outputs (that is, latent representations) of input $\vec{x}$. High $p\left(\vec{x}|\vec{z}\right)$ at these same $\vec{z}$ locations implies a high probability of decoding back to the same $\vec{x}$ value from those $\vec{z}$ locations. Thus, this term basically says if $\vec{x}$ *encodes* to $\vec{z}$ with a high probability, then $\vec{z}$ should *decode* back to $\vec{x}$ with a high probability, too. Stated differently, a round trip from input to latent space back to input space should not take us far from the original input. In figure 14.7, this means the input point marked $\vec{x}$ lies close to the output point marked $\tilde{\vec{x}}$. In other words, *minimizing reconstruction loss leads to ELBO maximization.*

Now consider the second term. It comes with a minus sign. Maximizing this is equivalent to minimizing the KL divergence between $q\left(\vec{z}|\vec{x}\right)$ and $p\left(\vec{z}\right)$. This is the regularizing term. Viewed in another way, this is the term through which we inject our belief about the basic organization of the latent space into the system. Remember that the KL divergence $KLD\left(q\left(\vec{z}|\vec{x}\right), p\left(\vec{z}\right)\right)$ sees very little contribution from the small values of $q\left(\vec{z}|\vec{x}\right)$. It is dominated by the large values of $q\left(\vec{z}|\vec{x}\right)$. In terms of figure 14.7, minimizing this KL divergence essentially ensures that most of the hollow circles fall on an area highly populated with filled circles.

Thus, overall, maximization of ELBO is equivalent to minimizing reconstruction loss with regularization in the form of minimizing KL divergence from a specific prior distribution. This is what we do in VAEs. In every iteration, we minimize the reconstruction loss (as in ordinary AEs) and also minimize divergence from a known (or guessed) prior. Note that this does not require us to encode all training inputs per iteration. The approach is *incremental*—one input or input batch at a time—like any other neural network optimization. Also, although we started from finding an approximation to $p\left(\vec{z}|\vec{x}\right)$, the final expression does not have that anywhere. There is only the prior $p\left(\vec{z}\right)$ for which we can use some suitable fixed distribution.

14.7.7 Choice of prior: Zero-mean, unit-covariance Gaussian

The popular choice for the known prior is a zero-mean, unit-covariance matrix Gaussian, $\mathcal{N}\left(\vec{0}, \mathbf{I}\right)$, where $\mathbf{I}$ is the $d \times d$ identity matrix (d is the dimensionality of the latent space), $\vec{0}$ is $d \times 1$ vector of all zeros. Note that minimizing the KL divergence from $\mathcal{N}\left(\vec{0}, \mathbf{I}\right)$ is equivalent to restricting most of the mass within the unit ball (a hypersphere with its center at the origin and radius 1). In other words, this KL divergence term restrains the latent vectors from spreading over the $\Re^d$ and remains mostly within the unit ball. Remember that a compact set of latent vectors translates in a sense to the simplest (minimum descriptor length) representations for the input vectors: that is, a regularized latent space (section 14.6).

KL divergence from a Gaussian has a closed-form expression that we derive in section 6.4.1. We first repeat equation 6.14 for KL divergence between two Gaussians and then obtain the expression for the special case where one of the Gaussians is a zero-mean, unit-covariance Gaussian:

$$D\left(q,p\right)=\frac{1}{2}\left(tr\left(\mathbf{\Sigma}_p^{-1}\mathbf{\Sigma}_q\right)+\left(\vec{\mu}_p-\vec{\mu}_q\right)^T\mathbf{\Sigma}_p^{-1}\left(\vec{\mu}_p-\vec{\mu}_q\right)-d+\log\left(\frac{\det\mathbf{\Sigma}_p}{\det\mathbf{\Sigma}_q}\right)\right) \tag{14.1}$$

where the operator *tr* denotes the *trace* of a matrix (sum of diagonal elements) and operator *det* denotes the determinant. By assumption, $p\left(\vec{z}\right)=\mathcal{N}\left(\vec{0},\mathbf{I}\right)$: that is, $\vec{\mu}_p=\vec{0}$ and $\mathbf{\Sigma}_p=\mathbf{I}$. Thus,

$$D\left(q,p\right)=\frac{1}{2}\left(tr\left(\mathbf{\Sigma}_q\right)+\vec{\mu}_q^T\mathbf{I}\vec{\mu}_q-d-\log\left(\det\mathbf{\Sigma}_q\right)\right)$$

At this point, we introduce another simplifying assumption: that *the covariance matrix* $\mathbf{\Sigma}_q$ *is a diagonal matrix.* This means the matrix can be expressed compactly as

$$\mathbf{\Sigma}_q=\vec{\sigma}_q$$

where $\vec{\sigma}_q$ contains the elements of the main diagonal and we are not redundantly expressing the zeros in the off-diagonal elements. Note that this is not an outlandish assumption to make. We are approximating $p\left(\vec{z}|\vec{x}\right)$ with a Gaussian $q\left(\vec{z}|\vec{x}\right)$ whose axes are uncorrelated.

Because of this assumption,

$$Tr\left(\mathbf{\Sigma}_q\right)=\sum_{i=1}^{d}\vec{\sigma}_q^2\left[i\right]$$

$$\log\left(\det\mathbf{\Sigma}_q\right)=\sum_{i=1}^{d}log\left(\vec{\sigma}_q^2\left[i\right]\right)$$

$$D\left(q,p\right)=\frac{1}{2}\left(\sum_{i=1}^{d}\vec{\sigma}_q^2\left[i\right]+\|\vec{\mu}_q\|^2-\sum_{i=1}^{d}log\left(\vec{\sigma}_q^2\left[i\right]\right)a-d\right)$$

$$=\frac{1}{2}\left(\|\vec{\mu}_q\|^2+\sum_{i=1}^{d}\left(\vec{\sigma}_q^2\left[i\right]-2log\left(\vec{\sigma}_q\left[i\right]\right)\right)-d\right)$$

$$=\frac{1}{2}\left(\sum_{i=1}^{d}\left(\vec{\mu}_q^2\left[i\right]+\vec{\sigma}_q^2\left[i\right]-2log\left(\vec{\sigma}_q\left[i\right]\right)-1\right)\right)$$

It is easy to see the expression $\left(\vec{\sigma}_q^2\,[i] - 2log\,(\vec{\sigma}_q\,[i])\right)$ reaches a minimum when $\vec{\sigma}_q\,[i] = 1$. Thus, overall, KL divergence with the zero-mean, unit-covariance Gaussian is minimized when the mean is at the origin and the variances are all ones. This is equivalent to minimizing the spread of the latent vectors outside the ball of unit radius centered on the origin.

An alternative choice for the prior is a Gaussian mixture with as many components as the known number of classes. We do not discuss that here.

14.7.8 *Reparameterization trick*

We have avoided talking about one nasty problem so far. We said that in VAEs, the encoder emits the mean and variance of the probability density function $p\,(\vec{z}|\vec{x})$ from which we *sample* the encoder output. There is a problem, however. The encoder-decoder pair are neural networks that learn via backpropagation. That is based on differentiation. Sampling is *not* differentiable. How do we deal with this?

We can use a neat trick: the so-called *reparameterization trick*. Let's first explain it in the univariate case. Sampling from a Gaussian $\mathcal{N}\,(\mu, \sigma)$ can be viewed as a combination of the following two steps:

1. Take a random sample from x from $\mathcal{N}\,(0, 1)$. Note that there is no learnable parameter here; it's a sample from a constant density function.
2. Translate the sample (add μ), and scale it (multiply by σ).

This essentially takes the sampling part out of the path for backpropagation. The encoder emits μ and σ, which are differentiable entities that we learn. Sampling is done separately from a constant density function.

The idea can be extended to a multivariate Gaussian. Sampling from $\mathcal{N}\,(\vec{\mu}, \boldsymbol{\Sigma})$ can be broken down into sampling from $\mathcal{N}\left(\vec{0}, \mathbf{I}\right)$ and scaling the vector by multiplying by the matrix $\boldsymbol{\Sigma}$ and translating by $\vec{\mu}$. Thus, we have a multivariate encoder that can learn via backpropagation.

NOTE Fully functional code for VAEs, executable via Jupyter Notebook, can be found at http://mng.bz/5QYD.

Listing 14.5 PyTorch: Reparameterization trick

```
def reparameterize(mu, log_var):
        std = torch.exp(0.5 * log_var)      # Converts the log variance to the standard deviation

        eps = torch.randn_like(std)         # Samples from N(0, I)

        return mu + eps * std               # Scales by multiplying by Σ and translates by μ
```

Listing 14.6 PyTorch: VAE

```
from torch import nn
nz = 10
input_image_size = (1, 32, 32)        <-- Input image size in (c, h, w) format
conv_encoder = nn.Sequential(
            nn.Conv2d(in_channels, 32, kernel_size=3, stride=1, padding=1),
            nn.BatchNorm2d(32),
            nn.ReLU(),
            nn.MaxPool2d(kernel_size=2),     <-- Reduces to a (32, 16, 16)-sized tensor
            nn.Conv2d(32, 128, kernel_size=3, stride=1, padding=1),
            nn.BatchNorm2d(128),
            nn.ReLU(),
            nn.MaxPool2d(kernel_size=2),     <-- Reduces to a (128, 8, 8)-sized tensor
            nn.Conv2d(128, 256, kernel_size=3, stride=1, padding=1),
            nn.BatchNorm2d(256),
            nn.ReLU(),
            nn.MaxPool2d(kernel_size=2),       <-- Reduces to a (256, 4, 4)-sized tensor

            nn.Flatten()       <-- Flattens to a 4096-sized tensor
        )
mu_fc = nn.Linear(4096, nz)      <-- Reduces a 4096-sized tensor to an nz-sized μ tensor
logvar_fc = nn.Linear(4096, nz)     <-- Reduces a 4096-sized tensor
                                        to an nz-sized log(σ^2) tensor
```

Listing 14.7 PyTorch: VAE decoder

```
from torch import nn
decoder = nn.Sequential(
            nn.ConvTranspose2d(self.nz, out_channels=256,
             kernel_size=4, stride=1,
             padding=0, bias=False),      <-- Converts (nz, 1, 1) to
            nn.BatchNorm2d(256),               a (256, 4, 4)-sized tensor
            nn.ReLU(True),
            nn.ConvTranspose2d(256, 128, kernel_size=2,
              stride=2, padding=0, bias=False),     <-- Increases to a
            nn.BatchNorm2d(128),                         (128, 8, 8)-sized tensor
            nn.ReLU(True),
            nn.ConvTranspose2d(128, 32, kernel_size=2,
              stride=2, padding=0, bias=False),     <-- Increases to a
            nn.BatchNorm2d(32),                          (32, 16, 16)-sized tensor
            nn.ReLU(True),
            nn.ConvTranspose2d(32, in_channels, kernel_size=2,
              stride=2, padding=0, bias=False),     <-- Increases to a
            nn.Sigmoid()                                 (1, 32, 32)-sized tensor
        )
```

Listing 14.8 PyTorch: VAE loss

```
recon_loss = F.binary_cross_entropy(Xr, X,
                 reduction="sum")

kld_loss = -0.5 * torch.sum(1 + log_var
                     - mu.pow(2) - log_var.exp())

total_loss = recon_loss + beta * kld_loss
```

- `recon_loss`: **Binary cross-entropy loss**
- `kld_loss`: $KLD\left(q\left(\vec{z}|\vec{x}\right), p\left(\vec{z}\right)\right)$ **where** $\vec{z} \sim \mathcal{N}\left(\vec{0}, \mathrm{I}\right)$
- `total_loss`: **Computes the total loss**

Listing 14.9 PyTorch: VAE training

```
conv_out = conv_encoder(X)

mu = mu_fc(conv_out)

log_var = logvar_fc(conv_out)

z = reparameterize(mu, log_var)

Xr = self.decoder(z)

total_loss = recon_loss + beta * kld_loss
```

- `conv_out`: **Passes the input image through the convolutional encoder**
- `mu`: **Computes μ, an nz-dimensional tensor**
- `log_var`: **Computes $log(\sigma^2)$, an nz-dimensional tensor**
- `z`: **Samples z via the reparameterization trick**
- `Xr`: **Reconstructs the image using z via the decoder**
- `total_loss`: **Computes the total loss**

AUTOENCODERS VS. VAES

Let's revisit the familiar MNIST digits data set. It contains a training set of 60,000 images and a test set of 10,000 images. Each image is 28 × 28 in size and contains a center crop of a single digit.

Earlier, we used this data set for classification. Here, we use it an unsupervised manner: we ignore the labels during training/testing. We train both the autoencoder and the VAE end to end on this data set and look at the results (see figures 14.9 and 14.10).

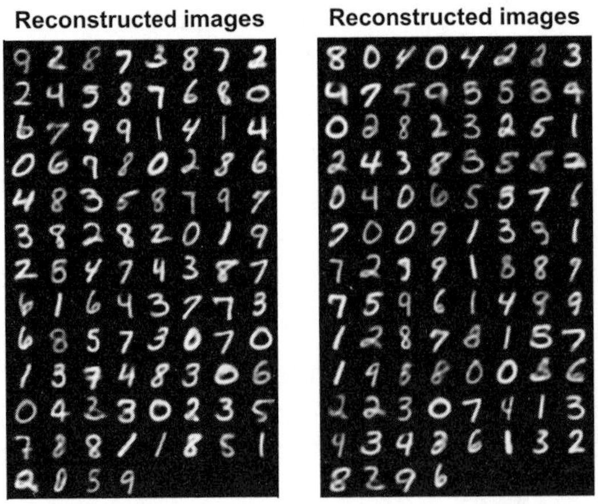

(a) Autoencoder-reconstructed images

(b) VAE-reconstructed images

Figure 14.9 Comparing the reconstructed images on the test set for the autoencoder and VAE trained end to end. On a simple data set like MNIST, both the autoencoder and VAE do a pretty good job of reconstructing images from the test set.

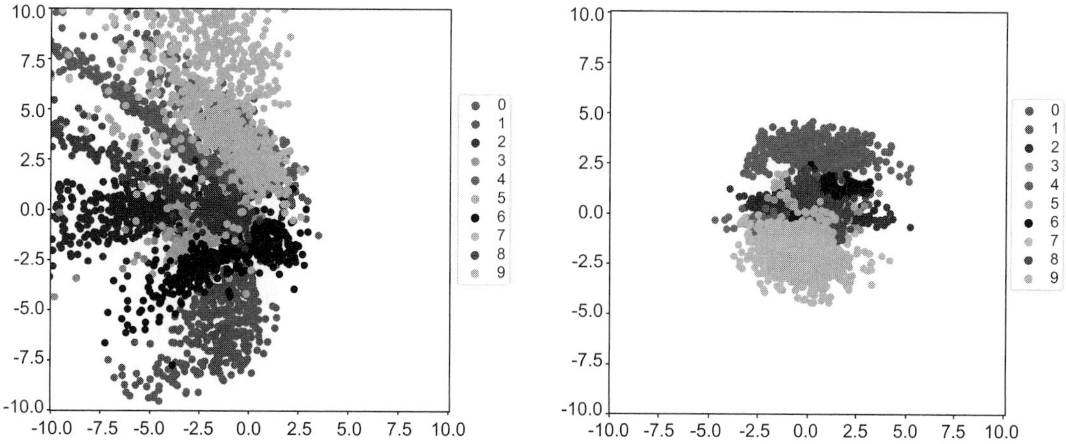

(a) Autoencoder latent space (nz=2) (b) VAE latent space (nz=2)

Figure 14.10 The difference between the learned latent spaces of the autoencoder and VAE. We train an autoencoder and a VAE with $nz = 2$ on MNIST and plot the latent space for the test set. Autoencoders only minimize the reconstruction loss, so any latent space is equally acceptable as long as the reconstruction loss is low. As expected, the learned latent space is sparse and has a very high spread. VAEs, in contrast, minimize reconstruction loss with regularization. This is done by minimizing the KL divergence between the learned latent space and a known prior distribution $\mathcal{N}\left(\vec{0}, \mathbf{I}\right)$. Adding this regularization term ensures that the latent space is constrained within a unit ball. This can be seen in figure 14.10b, where the learned latent space is much more compact.

The autoencoder is trained to minimize the MSE between the input image and the reconstructed image. There is no other restriction on the latent space.

The VAE is trained to maximize the ELBO. As we saw in the previous section, we can maximize the ELBO by minimizing the reconstruction loss with regularization in the form of minimizing KL divergence from a specific prior distribution: $\mathcal{N}\left(\vec{0}, \mathbf{I}\right)$ in the case of VAE. So the network is incentivized to ensure that the latent space learned is constrained within the unit ball.

One minor implementation detail to note is that we use binary cross-entropy instead of MSE when training VAEs. In practice, this leads to better convergence.

Summary

- In latent-space modeling, we map input data points onto a lower-dimensional latent space. The latent space is typically a manifold consisting of points that have a property of interest in common. The property of interest can be membership to a specific class, such as all paragraphs written by Shakespeare. The latent vectors are simpler, more compact representations of the input data in which only information related to the property of interest is retained and other information is eliminated.
- In latent space modeling, all training data input satisfies the property of interest. For instance, we can train a latent space model on paragraphs written by Shakespeare. Then the learned manifold contains points corresponding to various Shakespeare

like paragraphs. Points far away from the manifold are less Shakespeare-like. By inspecting this distance, we can estimate the probability of a paragraph being written by Shakespeare. By sampling the probability distribution, we may even be able to emit pseudo-Shakespeare paragraphs.

- Geometrically speaking, we project the input point onto the manifold. PCA performs a special form of latent space modeling where the manifold is a best-fit hyperplane for the training data.
- Autoencoders can perform a much more powerful dimensionality reduction than PCA. An autoencoder consists of an encoder (E), which maps the input data point into the lower-dimensional space, and a decoder (D), which maps the lower-dimensional representation back into the input space. It is trained to minimize the reconstruction loss: that is, the distance between the input and reconstructed (encoded, then decoded) vectors.
- Variational autoencoders (VAEs) model latent spaces as probability distributions to impose additional constraints (over and above reconstruction loss) so that we can generate more regularized latent spaces.
  - In VAEs, the encoder maps the input to a latent representation via a stochastic process (rather than a deterministic one). It emits $p\left(\vec{z}|\vec{x}\right)$ as opposed to directly emitting $\vec{z}$. $\vec{z}$ is obtained by sampling $p\left(\vec{z}|\vec{x}\right)$. The decoder maps a point in latent space $\vec{z}$ back to the input space. It is also modeled as a probability distribution $p\left(\vec{x}|\vec{z}\right)$.
  - The latent space learned by a VAE is much more compact and smoother (and hence more desirable) than that learned by an autoencoder.

appendix

A.1 Dot product and cosine of the angle between two vectors

In section 2.5.6, we stated that the component of a vector $\vec{a}$ along another vector $\vec{b}$ is $\vec{a} \cdot \vec{b} = \vec{a}^T\vec{b}$. This is equivalent to $||\vec{a}||\,||\vec{b}||cos\,(\theta)$, where θ is the angle between the vectors $\vec{a}$ and $\vec{b}$.

In this section, we offer a proof of this for the two-dimensional case to deepen your intuition about the geometry of dot products. From figure A.1b, we can see that

$$a_x = ||\vec{a}||cos\,(\theta + \phi) \qquad a_y = ||\vec{a}||sin\,(\theta + \phi)$$

$$b_x = ||\vec{b}||cos\,(\phi) \qquad b_y = ||\vec{b}||sin\,(\phi)$$

which can be rewritten as

$$cos\,(\theta + \phi) = \frac{a_x}{||\vec{a}||} \qquad sin\,(\theta + \phi) = \frac{a_y}{||\vec{a}||} \tag{A.1}$$

$$cos\,(\phi) = \frac{b_x}{||\vec{b}||} \qquad sin\,(\phi) = \frac{b_y}{||\vec{b}||} \tag{A.2}$$

Using well-known trigonometric identities in equation A.1, we get

$$cos\,(\theta + \phi) = cos\phi cos\theta - sin\phi sin\theta = \frac{a_x}{||\vec{a}||}$$

$$sin\,(\theta + \phi) = sin\phi cos\theta + cos\phi sin\theta = \frac{a_y}{||\vec{a}||}$$

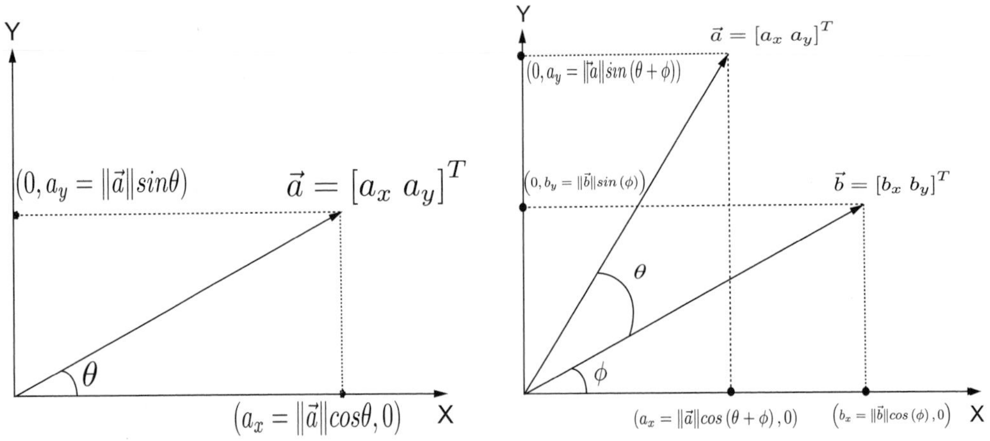

(a) Components of a 2D vector along coordinate axes. Note that $||\vec{a}||$ is the length of hypotenuse.

(b) Dot product as a component of one vector along another $\vec{a} \cdot \vec{b} = \vec{a}^T \vec{b} = a_x b_x + a_y b_y = ||\vec{a}|| \, ||\vec{b}|| cos\,(\theta)$.

Figure A.1 Vector components and dot product

Substituting for $cos\phi$ and $sin\phi$ from equation A.2, we have a system of simultaneous linear equations with $cos\theta$ and $sin\theta$ as unknowns:

$$\frac{b_x}{||\vec{b}||} cos\theta - \frac{b_y}{||\vec{b}||} sin\theta = \frac{a_x}{||\vec{a}||}$$

$$\frac{b_y}{||\vec{b}||} cos\theta + \frac{b_x}{||\vec{b}||} sin\theta = \frac{a_y}{||\vec{a}||}$$

This system of simultaneous linear equations can be compactly written in matrix-vector form

$$\begin{bmatrix} \frac{b_x}{||\vec{b}||} & -\frac{b_y}{||\vec{b}||} \\ \frac{b_y}{||\vec{b}||} & \frac{b_x}{||\vec{b}||} \end{bmatrix} \begin{bmatrix} cos\theta \\ sin\theta \end{bmatrix} = \begin{bmatrix} \frac{a_x}{||\vec{a}||} \\ \frac{a_y}{||\vec{a}||} \end{bmatrix}$$

which can be simplified to

$$\frac{1}{||\vec{b}||} \begin{bmatrix} b_x & -b_y \\ b_y & b_x \end{bmatrix} \begin{bmatrix} cos\theta \\ sin\theta \end{bmatrix} = \frac{1}{||\vec{a}||} \begin{bmatrix} a_x \\ a_y \end{bmatrix}$$

This equation can be solved to yield

$$cos\theta = \frac{a_x b_x + a_y b_y}{||\vec{a}|| \, ||\vec{b}||}$$

$$sin\theta = \frac{a_y b_x - a_x b_y}{||\vec{a}|| \, ||\vec{b}||}$$

So, $||\vec{a}|| \, ||\vec{b}|| cos\theta = a_x b_x + a_y b_y$, which was to be proved.

A.2 Determinants

Determinant computation is tedious and numerically unstable if done naively. You should never compute one by hand—all linear algebra software packages provide routines to do this. Hence we only describe the algorithm to compute the determinant of a 2×2 matrix. This determinant can be computed as

$$det(A) = a_{11}a_{22} - a_{12}a_{21}$$

The inverse is

$$A^{-1} = \frac{1}{det(A)} \begin{bmatrix} a_{22} & -a_{12} \\ -a_{21} & a_{11} \end{bmatrix}$$

A.3 Computing the variance of a Gaussian distribution

From the integral form of equation 5.13, we have

$$var_{gaussian}(x) = \int_{x=-\infty}^{\infty} (x-\mu)^2 p(x)\, dx$$

Substituting equation 5.22, $p(x) = \frac{1}{\sqrt{2\pi}\sigma} e^{\frac{-(x-\mu)^2}{2\sigma^2}}$ in that, we get

$$var_{gaussian}(x) = \int_{x=-\infty}^{\infty} (x-\mu)^2 \frac{1}{\sqrt{2\pi}\sigma} e^{\frac{-(x-\mu)^2}{2\sigma^2}} dx$$

Substituting $y = \frac{(x-\mu)}{\sqrt{2}\sigma}$, which implies $dy = \frac{dx}{\sqrt{2}\sigma}$ and $2\sigma^2 y^2 = (x-\mu)^2$, we get

$$var_{gaussian}(x) = \frac{2\sigma^2}{\sqrt{\pi}} \int_{-\infty}^{\infty} y^2 e^{-y^2} dy = \frac{2\sigma^2}{\sqrt{\pi}} \int_{-\infty}^{\infty} y\left(ye^{-y^2}\right) dy$$

Using integration by parts,

$$\int_{-\infty}^{\infty} y\left(ye^{-y^2}\right) dy = \left[y\left(\int ye^{-y^2} dy\right)\right]_{-\infty}^{\infty} - \int_{-\infty}^{\infty} \frac{dy}{dy}\left(\int ye^{-y^2}\right) dy$$

Now, substituting $v = y^2$, which implies $\frac{dv}{2} = ydy$,

$$\int ye^{-y^2} dy = \int e^{-y^2}(ydy) = \frac{1}{2}\int e^{-v} dv = -\frac{e^{-v}}{2} = -\frac{e^{-y^2}}{2}$$

Hence,

$$\left[y\left(\int ye^{-y^2} dy\right)\right]_{-\infty}^{\infty} = \left[y\left(\frac{e^{-y^2}}{2}\right)\right]_{-\infty}^{\infty} = \frac{1}{2}\left(\lim_{y\to\infty} \frac{y}{e^{y^2}} - \lim_{y\to-\infty} \frac{y}{e^{y^2}}\right)$$

Such limits can be evaluated using L'Hospital's rule:

$$\lim_{y\to\infty}\frac{y}{e^{y^2}}=\lim_{y\to\infty}\frac{\frac{dy}{dy}}{\frac{d\left(e^{y^2}\right)}{dy}}=\lim_{y\to\infty}\frac{1}{2ye^{y^2}}=0$$

$$\lim_{y\to-\infty}\frac{y}{e^{y^2}}=\lim_{y\to-\infty}\frac{\frac{dy}{dy}}{\frac{d\left(e^{y^2}\right)}{dy}}=\lim_{y\to-\infty}\frac{1}{2ye^{y^2}}=0$$

In both cases, the limit is zero because e^{y^2} goes to positive infinity regardless of whether y goes to positive or negative infinity. Hence the denominator goes to infinity in both cases, causing the fraction to go to zero.

Thus the first term in the computation of $var_{gaussian}(x)$ becomes $\left[y\left(\int ye^{-y^2}dy\right)\right]_{-\infty}^{\infty}=$ $0-0=0$. The second term

$$\int_{-\infty}^{\infty}\frac{dy}{dy}\left(\int ye^{-y^2}\right)dy=\frac{1}{2}\int_{-\infty}^{\infty}e^{-y^2}dy$$

This last integral is a special one. To evaluate it, we need to go from one to two dimensions—this may be one of the very few cases where making a problem more complex helps. It is worth examining, so let's look at it. Let

$$I=\int_{-\infty}^{\infty}e^{-x^2}dx$$

Since the variable of integration does not matter, we can also write

$$I=\int_{-\infty}^{\infty}e^{-y^2}dy$$

Let's multiply them together:

$$I^2=\int_{-\infty}^{\infty}e^{-x^2}dx\int_{-\infty}^{\infty}e^{-y^2}dy=\int_{-\infty}^{\infty}\int_{-\infty}^{\infty}e^{-x^2}e^{-y^2}dxdy=\int_{-\infty}^{\infty}\int_{-\infty}^{\infty}e^{-\left(x^2+y^2\right)}dxdy$$

This double integral's domain (aka region of integration) is the infinite XY plane, where x and y both range from $-\infty$ to ∞. This same plane can also be viewed as an infinite-radius circle (an infinite-radius circle is the same as a rectangle with infinite-length sides!). Consequently, we can switch to polar coordinates, using the transformation

$$x=r\cos(\theta)$$

$$y=r\cos(\theta)$$

which implies

$$x^2 + y^2 = r^2$$
$$dxdy = rdrd\theta$$

$$I^2 = \int_{r=0}^{r=\infty} \int_{\theta=0}^{\theta=2\pi} e^{-r^2} r\,dr\,d\theta = \int_{r=0}^{r=\infty} e^{-r^2} r\,dr \int_{\theta=0}^{\theta=2\pi} d\theta = 2\pi \int_{r=0}^{r=\infty} e^{-r^2} r\,dr$$

Substituting $v = r^2$, which implies $dv = 2rdr$, we get

$$I^2 = \pi \int_0^{\infty} e^{-v} dv = \pi \left[-e^{-v} \right]_{v=0}^{v=\infty} = \pi \Rightarrow I = \sqrt{\pi}$$

Thus, the second term of $var_{gaussian}(x)$ evaluates to $\frac{\sigma^2}{\sqrt{\pi}} \frac{\sqrt{\pi}}{2}$. We have already shown that the first term evaluates to zero. So, we get

$$var_{gaussian}(x) = \sigma^2$$

Thus the σ in the probability density function $p(x) = \frac{1}{\sqrt{2\pi}\sigma} e^{\frac{-(x-\mu)^2}{2\sigma^2}}$ is the standard deviation (square root of the variance), and the μ is the expected value.

A.4 Two theorems in statistics

In this section, we study two important inequalities in multivariate statistics: Jensen's inequality and the log-sum inequality.

A.4.1 Jensen's Inequality

Consider a random variable X. For now, let's think of these as discrete variables, although the results we will come up with apply equally well to continuous variables. Thus, let the random variable take the discrete values $\vec{x}_1, \vec{x}_2, \cdots, \vec{x}_n$, with probabilities $p(\vec{x}_1), p(\vec{x}_2), \cdots, p(\vec{x}_n)$.

Now suppose $g(\vec{x})$ is a convex function whose domain includes these random variables. From equation 3.11, section 3.7, we know that given any convex function $g(\vec{x})$, for an arbitrary set of its input values $\vec{x}_i$, $i = 1 \cdots n$ and a set of weights α_i $i = 1 \cdots n$ satisfying $\sum_{i=1}^{n} \alpha_i = 1$, the weighted sum of the function outputs is greater than or equal to the function's output on the weighted sum of inputs: that is, $\sum_{i=1}^{n} \alpha_i g(\vec{x}_i) \geq g\left(\sum_{i=1}^{n} \alpha_i \vec{x}_i\right)$.

In particular, let's choose the set of all random variables as input values and their probabilities as weights $(\alpha_i = p(\vec{x}_i))$. We can do this because probabilities sum to 1, exactly as weights are supposed to do. This leads to

$$\sum_{i=1}^{n} p(x_i)\, g(\vec{x}_i) \geq g\left(\sum_{i=1}^{n} p(x_i)\, \vec{x}_i\right) \implies \mathbb{E}(g(X)) \geq g(\mathbb{E}(X)) \tag{A.3}$$

Equation A.3 is Jensen's inequality. A good mnemonic for it is: *for a convex function, the expected value of the function is greater than or equal to the function of expected value.* It holds for continuous random variables, too.

A.4.2 Log sum inequality

Suppose we have two sets of positive numbers $a_1, a_2, \cdots, a_n$ and $b_1, b_2, \cdots, b_n$. Let $a = \sum_{i=1}^{n} a_i$ and $b = \sum_{i=1}^{n} b_i$. Given these, the log sum inequality theorem says,

$$\sum_{i=1}^{n} a_i log\left(\frac{a_i}{b_i}\right) \geq a log\left(\frac{a}{b}\right) \tag{A.4}$$

To see why this is true, let's carve out an informal proof. First let's define $g(x) = xlogx$. This is a convex function because

$$\frac{dg}{dx} = \frac{dx}{dx} logx + x\frac{d(logx)}{dx} = logx + x\frac{1}{x} = logx + 1 \implies \frac{d^2g}{dx^2} = \frac{1}{x} > 0 \quad \text{(for positive } x\text{)}$$

Now, with that definition of g,

$$\sum_{i=1}^{n} a_i log\frac{a_i}{b_i} = \sum_{i=1}^{n} b_i g\left(\frac{a_i}{b_i}\right) = b\sum_{i=1}^{n} \frac{b_i}{b} g\left(\frac{a_i}{b_i}\right)$$

This last expression is a weighted sum of convex function outputs with the weights summing to 1 (since $\sum_{i=1}^{n} \frac{b_i}{b} = 1$). So, we can use equation 3.11, section 3.7. Then we get

$$b\sum_{i=1}^{n} \frac{b_i}{b} g\left(\frac{a_i}{b_i}\right) \geq b\, g\left(\sum_{i=1}^{n} \frac{b_i}{b}\frac{a_i}{b_i}\right) = b\, g\left(\sum_{i=1}^{n} \frac{a_i}{b}\right) = b\, g\left(\frac{\sum_{i=1}^{n} a_i}{b}\right) = b\, g\left(\frac{a}{b}\right) = a\, log\left(\frac{a}{b}\right)$$

A.5 Gamma functions and distribution

To understand the gamma distribution, we need to understand the basic gamma function. First let's do an overview of the gamma function.

A.5.1 Gamma function

The gamma function is in some sense a generalization of the factorial. The factorial function is only defined for integers and is characterized by the basic equation

$$n! = n\,(n-1)!$$

The gamma function is defined by

$$\Gamma(\alpha) = \int_{x=0}^{\infty} x^{(\alpha-1)} e^{-x} dx \tag{A.5}$$

Applying integration by parts to equation A.5, we get

$$\begin{aligned}\Gamma(\alpha) &= \left[x^{(\alpha-1)}\left(-e^{-x}\right)\right]_0^{\infty} - \int_{x=0}^{\infty} (\alpha-1)\, x^{(\alpha-2)}\left(-e^{-x}\right) dx \\ &= \left[x^{(\alpha-1)}\left(-e^{-x}\right)\right]_0^{\infty} + \int_{x=0}^{\infty} (\alpha-1)\, x^{(\alpha-2)}\left(e^{-x}\right) dx\end{aligned}$$

The first term is zero. This is because

$$\lim_{x \longrightarrow 0} \frac{x^{(\alpha-1)}}{e^x} = 0$$

$$\lim_{x \longrightarrow \infty} \frac{x^{(\alpha-1)}}{e^x} = 0 \text{ by repeated application of L'Hospital's rule}$$

Hence,

$$\Gamma(\alpha) = \int_{x=0}^{\infty} (\alpha - 1) x^{(\alpha-2)} (e^{-x}) dx = (\alpha - 1) \Gamma(\alpha - 1)$$

Thus, for integer values $\alpha = n$, $\Gamma(n) = n!$. There are other equivalent definitions of the gamma function, but we will not discuss them here. Instead, let's talk about the gamma distribution.

A.5.2 Gamma distribution

The probability density function for a random variable having a gamma distribution is a function with two parameters α and β:

$$p(x|\alpha, \beta) = \gamma(x; \alpha, \beta) = \frac{\beta^\alpha}{\Gamma(\alpha)} x^{(\alpha-1)} e^{-\beta x} \quad \text{where } \alpha, \beta > 0, x \geq 0 \tag{A.6}$$

It is not hard to see that this is a proper probability density function:

$$\int_{x=0}^{\infty} p(x|\alpha, \beta) dx = 1$$

By substituting $y = \beta x$, we get

$$p(x|\alpha, \beta) = \frac{\beta^\alpha}{\Gamma(\alpha)} \int_{y=0}^{y=\infty} \left(\frac{y}{\beta}\right)^{(\alpha-1)} e^{-y} \frac{dy}{\beta} = \frac{\int_{y=0}^{\infty} y^{(\alpha-1)} e^{-y} dy}{\Gamma(\alpha)} = \frac{\Gamma(\alpha)}{\Gamma(\alpha)} = 1$$

If $\alpha = 1$, the gamma distribution reduces to

$$p(x) = \frac{\beta}{\Gamma(1)} e^{-\beta x} = \beta\, e^{-\beta x} \text{ (it can be shown that } \Gamma(1) = 1 \text{)}$$

which is graphed in figure A.2a at several values of β. The gamma distribution has two terms $x^{\alpha-1}$ and $e^{-\beta x}$ that have somewhat opposite effects: the former increases with x, while the latter deceases with x. At smaller values of x, the former wins, and the product increases with x. But eventually, the exponential starts winning and pulls the product downward asymptotically toward zero. Thus the gamma distribution has a peak. Larger β results in taller peaks and a sharper decline toward zero. Larger α moves the peak further to the right. The expected value is $\mathbb{E}(x) = \frac{\alpha}{\beta}$, as illustrated in figure A.2.

The expected value of the gamma distribution $\mathbb{E}(x) = \frac{\alpha}{\beta}$. This can be proved using a little trick so cool that it is worth discussing for that reason alone:

$$\mathbb{E}(x) = \int_{x=0}^{\infty} x p(x|\alpha, \beta) dx = \frac{\beta^\alpha}{\Gamma(\alpha)} \int_{x=0}^{\infty} x x^{(\alpha-1)} e^{-\beta x} dx = \frac{\beta^\alpha}{\Gamma(\alpha)} \int_{x=0}^{\infty} x^\alpha e^{-\beta x} dx$$

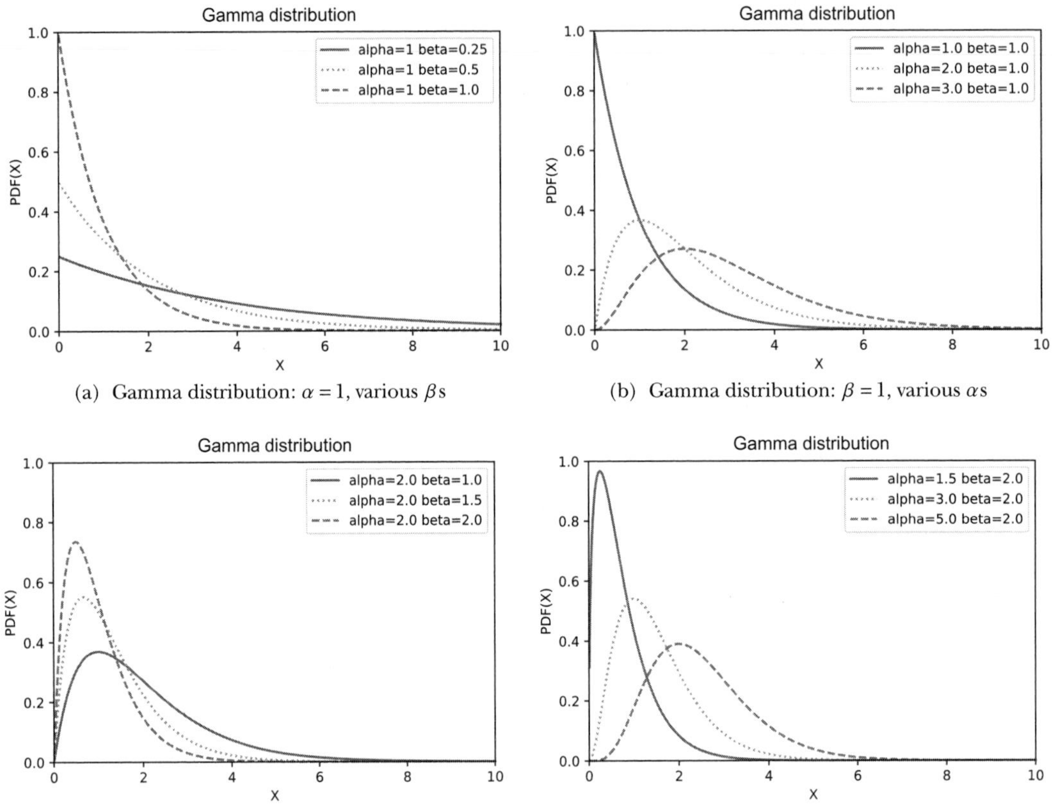

(a) Gamma distribution: $\alpha = 1$, various βs

(b) Gamma distribution: $\beta = 1$, various αs

(c) Gamma distribution: $\alpha = 2$, various βs

(d) Gamma distribution: $\beta = 2$, various αs

Figure A.2 Graph of a gamma distribution for various values of α and β. Larger β results in taller peaks and a sharper decline toward zero. Larger α moves the peak to the right. The expected value is $\mathbb{E}(x) = \frac{\alpha}{\beta}$.

But the gamma distribution

$$p(x|\alpha+1, \beta) = \frac{\beta^{\alpha+1}}{\Gamma(\alpha+1)} x^{(\alpha)} e^{-\beta x}$$

or

$$x^{(\alpha)} e^{-\beta x} = \frac{\Gamma(\alpha+1)}{\beta^{\alpha+1}} p(x|\alpha+1, \beta)$$

Using this,

$$\mathbb{E}(x) = \frac{\beta^{\alpha}}{\Gamma(\alpha)} \frac{\Gamma(\alpha+1)}{\beta^{\alpha+1}} \overbrace{\int_{x=0}^{\infty} p(x|\alpha+1, \beta)\, dx}^{=1} = \frac{\beta^{\alpha}}{\Gamma(\alpha)} \frac{\alpha\Gamma(\alpha)}{\beta\beta^{\alpha}} = \frac{\alpha}{\beta}$$

MAXIMUM OF A GAMMA DISTRIBUTION

To maximize the gamma probability density function $p(\lambda|X) = \lambda^{(\alpha_n - 1)} e^{-\beta_n \lambda}$ for a random variable λ, we take the derivative and equate to zero:

$$\frac{d}{d\lambda}\left(\lambda^{\alpha-1} e^{-\beta\lambda}\right) = 0 \Longrightarrow (\alpha - 1)\lambda^{\alpha-1} e^{-\beta\lambda} + \lambda^{\alpha-1}(-\beta) e^{-\beta\lambda} = 0$$

$$\lambda = \frac{\alpha - 1}{\beta}$$

notations

- The symbol $\mathbb{R}$ stands for the field (set) of real numbers.
- The symbol $\in$ should be read as "belongs to the set."
- Vectors are denoted via overhead arrows: for example, $\vec{x}$.
- $\vec{x} \in \mathbb{R}^n$ indicates that $\vec{x}$ is a vector with n elements, each of which is a real number.
- Matrices are denoted via uppercase symbols: for example, A. Sometimes $A_{m,n}$ is used to indicate a matrix with m rows and n columns.
- $A \in \mathbb{R}^{m \times n}$ indicates that A is a matrix with m rows and n columns, each of whose elements is a real number.
- Vector and matrix transformations are indicated via superscript T: for example, $\vec{x}^T$ or A^T.
- Individual elements of a vector or matrix are denoted via subscript: for example, A_{ij} or $\vec{x}_i$.
- $\langle \vec{x}, \vec{y} \rangle$ denotes the inner product of the two vectors $\vec{x}$ and $\vec{y}$. For finite-dimensional vectors, this is equivalent to $\vec{x}^T \vec{y}$.
- $\hat{l}$ denotes a unit vector: $||\hat{l}|| = 1$.
- The symbol $\exists$ should be read as "there exists."
- The symbol $\forall$ should be read as "for all."

index

A

B

C

D

E

M

N

O

W

RELATED MANNING TITLES

Inside Deep Learning
by Edward Raff
Foreword by Kirk Borne

ISBN 9781617298639
600 pages, $59.99
April 2022

Deep Learning with Python, Second Edition
by François Chollet

ISBN 9781617296864
504 pages, $59.99
October 2021

Grokking Artificial Intelligence Algorithms
by Rishal Hurbans

ISBN 9781617296185
392 pages, $59.99
July 2020

Machine Learning Algorithms in Depth
by Vadim Smolkyakov

ISBN 9781633439214
328 pages (estimated), $79.99
February 2024 (estimated)

For ordering information, go to www.manning.com